Only yesterday man was nearly colour-blind; Homer thought that the sea was the same colour as wine. If man's sensitivity has expanded so much within a mere tick of the cosmic clock, what will we be seeing tomorrow?

'Refreshingly optimistic about the future of man. *The Occult*, always stimulating, provocative'

Sunday Express

'I am very impressed by this book, not only by its erudition but by the marshalling of it, and above all by the good-natured, unaffected charm of the author whose reasoning is never too far-fetched, who is never carried away by preposterous theories. Mr Wilson's mental processes are akin to Aldous Huxley'

Cyril Connolly, *Sunday Times*

'A tour de force. An immensely powerful synthesis of all the relevant indications. An intensely felt, deeply impressive essay by a mind from which ideas spurt like exploding lava'

Evening News

'*The Occult* is the most interesting, informative and thought-provoking book on the subject I have read. Colin Wilson has mastered the literature and retails it with tremendous gusto. And if publishers have done their astrological homework correctly, occultism is in the ascendant'

Arthur Calder-Marshall, *Sunday Telegraph*

The power of the mind to establish direct union with Reality may be produced by the reaction of a chemical called Serotonin on the pineal gland. The Bo-tree under which the Buddha is said to have achieved enlightenment produces figs with an exceptionally high Serotonin content.

'Colin Wilson's new book on *The Occult* is by far and away his best work to date, and worthy to be placed on the same shelf alongside William James, F. W. H. Myers' monumental study of *Human Personality* and Frazer's *Golden Bough*. And it has something of the thoroughness and erudition of Havelock Ellis' celebrated *Studies*. For those with insight, this stupendous volume is the natural sequel to *The Outsider*. It is an essential volume for all readers interested in any way whatsoever in the wide spectrum of interrelated occult subjects which he discusses with such penetration and intelligence – a "must" for anyone with the remotest interest in the future of civilised man'

Alan Hull Walton, *Books and Bookmen*

'*The Occult*, a cheerful perambulation through the marshes, forests and badlands of magic and superstition, is a book which should encourage those who share Wilson's conviction that man must evolve in order to survive, and that his only path of evolution lies in the development of his neglected paranormal faculties ... Genial and open-hearted ... my final feeling for it is one of strong affection. Wilson is rather like the headmaster of some appalling school who contrives, in his innocence and benevolence, to find a good word on even the most outrageous of his pupils. It displays, more fully than any other Wilson book that I have read since *The Outsider*, the full array of his amiable virtues'

Philip Toynbee, *Observer*

By the same author

Non-Fiction

The Outsider cycle:

The Outsider

Religion and the Rebel

The Age of Defeat

The Strength to Dream

*Origins of the Sexual Impulse Beyond
the Outsider*

*Introduction to the New
Existentialism*

Books on the occult and
paranormal:

Beyond the Occult

Mysteries

Poltergeist

Psychic Detectives

Strange Powers

The Geller Phenomenon

A Dictionary of Possibilities
(with John Grant)

Other Non-Fiction:

An Encyclopedia of Murder
(with Pat Pitman)

*An Encyclopedia of Modern
Murder* (with Donald Seaman)

A Casebook of Murder

Order of Assassins

Rasputin and the Fall of the Romanovs

Bernard Shaw – A Reassessment

New Pathways in Psychology

The Quest for Wilhelm Reich

*The War Against Sleep – The
Philosophy of Gurdjieff*

*The Lord of the Underworld – A
Study of Jung*

The Craft of the Novel

The Strange Genius of David Lindsay

Frankenstein's Castle

Access to Inner Worlds

Eagle and Earwig (Essays on books
and writers)

Poetry and Mysticism

A Book of Booze

Starseekers

The Brandy of the Damned (Essays
on Music)

Anti-Sartre

The Misfits

Autobiography

Voyage to a Beginning

Fiction

The 'Sorme Trilogy':

Ritual in the Dark

The Man Without a Shadow (retitled
The Sex Diary of Gerard Sorme)

The God of the Labyrinth

Other Fiction:

Adrift in Soho

The World of Violence

Necessary Doubt

The Glass Cage

The Mind Parasites

The Killer

The Philosopher's Stone

The Black Room

The Space Vampires

The Schoolgirl Murder Case

Rasputin: A Novel

Spider World: The Tower

Spider World: The Delta

Colin Wilson was one of the most prolific, versatile and popular writers of the past 50 years. He was born in Leicester in 1931, and left school at sixteen. After he had spent years working in a wool warehouse, a laboratory, a plastics factory and a coffee bar, his first book, *The Outsider*, was published in 1956. It received outstanding critical acclaim and was an immediate bestseller.

He wrote many books on philosophy, the occult, crime and sexual deviance, plus a host of successful novels that won him an international reputation. His work has been translated into Spanish, French, Swedish, Dutch, Japanese, German, Italian, Portuguese, Danish, Norwegian, Finnish and Hebrew.

Colin Wilson died in December 2013.

THE OCCULT

COLIN WILSON
WITH A NEW FOREWORD BY COLIN STANLEY

WATKINS
Sharing Wisdom Since
1893

This edition first published in the UK and USA in 2015 by
Watkins, an imprint of Watkins Media Limited
19 Cecil Court
London WC2N 4EZ

enquiries@watkinspublishing.com

Originally published by Grafton Books in 1979

5 7 9 10 8 6 4

Designed and typeset by Clare Thorpe
Printed and bound in the United Kingdom
A CIP record for this book is available from the British Library

ISBN: 978-1-78028-846-8

www.watkinspublishing.com

ACKNOWLEDGEMENTS

Many of the friends and acquaintances who made valuable suggestions or provided material are acknowledged in the body of this book: A. L. Rowse, Robert Graves, Ronald Duncan, Louis Singer, Dick Roberts, Arthur Guirdham, Wilson Knight, Harold Visiak, J. B. Priestley, David Foster. I would like to add the names of Mark Bredin, Dennis Watkins (whose suggestions about the hanged man card were fascinating if untenable), Russell Turner, Fred Martin, Major George Sully, David Pugh and Richard Cavendish, the editor of *Man, Myth and Magic*. My English editor, Jane Osborn, made many valuable suggestions. My wife Joy prepared the bibliography.

I also wish to express my grateful acknowledgements to the following authors and publishers of books from which I have drawn suggestions and information.

The Bodley Head for J. Cowper Powys' *Autobiography* and *A Glastonbury Romance*; Messrs. Dutton for W. E. Woodward's *The Gift of Life*; Arnold Toynbee and Oxford University Press for *A Study of History*; Robert Graves and Faber & Faber for *The White Goddess* and Doubleday for *Five Pens in Hand*; E. H. Visiak and John Baker Ltd. for *Life's Morning Hour*; A. L. Rowse and Jonathan Cape for *A Cornish Childhood*; Arthur Osborn and University Books for *The Future is Now*; Ivar Lissner and Jonathan Cape for *Man, God and Magic*; Rayner C. Johnson and Hodder & Stoughton for *The Imprisoned Splendour*; Richard Cavendish for *The Black Arts*; J. Eisenbud and William Morrow for *The World of Ted Serios*; J. B. Priestley and Messrs. Aldus for *Man and Time*; Faber & Faber for lines from 'Ash Wednesday' in *Collected Poems, 1909–1962* by T. S. Eliot, and for Warner Allen's *The Timeless Moment*; R. H. Ward and Gollancz for *A Drug-Taker's Notes*; Arthur Koestler and Hamish Hamilton/Collins for *Arrow in the Blue*; Macmillan for the *Works* of W. B. Yeats.

For Robert Graves

CONTENTS

COLIN WILSON AND *THE OCCULT*
A FOREWORD BY COLIN STANLEY

When his now classic study *The Occult* was published in 1971, some critics, fans and scholars of Colin Wilson's previous non-fiction – particularly the 'Outsider Cycle' in which he had created his 'new existentialism' and established himself as a philosopher of some note – were surprised, others downright horrified. It had seemed that after the terrible mauling he had received from the critics and the tabloid press, in the late 1950s, his reputation was recovering somewhat and his career taking an upturn. Many thought this leap into the rather contentious unknown was a retrograde step: both mystifying and likely to be a disaster. Wilson, they felt, was merely jumping onto the occult bandwagon in order to make money.

When the book was suggested, he made no secret of the fact that the occult was not a subject that interested him greatly and when he sought the advice of none other than the poet Robert Graves, asking him whether he should write it, he was told very firmly that he should not. But with a young family to support, he had spent far too much of the 1960s on the arduous American university lecture trail, keeping him away from home for lengthy periods of time. This was to be his first commissioned work, a sign that he had finally 'arrived' as a professional writer. The financial terms from his would-be publishers, Random House in the US and Hodder & Stoughton in the UK (a $4000 advance), were obviously too tempting and so he went ahead.

During the course of his research, he found his attitude to the subject changing:

Although I have always been curious about the 'occult' ... it has never been one of my major interests, like philosophy, or science, or even music. ... It was not until two years ago, when

I began the systematic research for this book, that I realised the remarkable consistency of the evidence for such matters as life after death, out-of-body experiences (astral projection), reincarnation. In a basic sense my attitude remains unchanged; I still regard philosophy – the pursuit of reality through intuition aided by intellect – as being more *relevant*, more important, than questions of the 'occult'. But the weighing of the evidence ... has convinced me that the basic claims of 'occultism' are true.

The completed book, dedicated to Graves, was published on October 4, 1971 with a distinctive dust jacket, in the UK, depicting a large open eye.

Up until then Wilson had always anticipated trends in literature and thought, rather than being one for jumping onto bandwagons. In 1961, for example, he published with Pat Pitman *An Encyclopedia of Murder*, a book which anticipated the boom in true crime studies by almost twenty years. His *The Strength to Dream* – a book on literature and imagination, published in 1962 – heralded the late sixties' obsession with fantasy and science fiction literature. The late sixties also brought about a surge in interest in all things mystical and on this occasion Wilson was not altogether ahead of the game: the pioneers were Louis Pauwels and Jacques Bergier, whose *The Morning of the Magicians* had been a bestseller in France for several years. His publishers clearly wanted Wilson to replicate its success in the English-speaking world and he did not disappoint them: his monumental study went on to be a bestseller and an inspiration to many who read it. So although he lost some readers by taking this seemingly unexpected and bold move into the occult, he gained many, many more.

In fact Wilson had not abandoned philosophy at all. Indeed, he always considered his 'serious' occult books – i.e. 'The Occult

Trilogy'* – to be a logical extension of his 'new existentialism', providing evidence that man possesses latent powers which, if tapped and harnessed, could lead to hugely expanded consciousness and potentially even an evolutionary leap. In a lengthy Introduction to the new Watkins edition of *Beyond the Occult*, published in 2008, he wrote:

> When *The Occult* appeared in 1971, it soon became apparent that many people who had regarded me as a kind of maverick existentialist now believed that I had turned to more trivial topics, and abandoned the rigour of my 'Outsider' books. To me, such a view was incomprehensible. It seemed obvious to me that if the 'paranormal' was a reality – as I was increasingly convinced that it was – then any philosopher who refused to take it into account was merely closing his eyes.

Readers of Wilson's fiction, however, were definitely *not* taken by surprise and had no qualms about his serious foray into the subject; for occult instances and anecdotes abound in all of his novels from the first in the Gerard Sorme trilogy, *Ritual in the Dark* (1960), onwards. For example, in his 1963 novel *The World of Violence* (published in the US as *The Violent World of Hugh Greene*), the young protagonist Hugh, after listening to a piece of music by Beethoven that deeply moves him, sees a ghost (which he calls a 'presence') in the garden and speculates, '... it seems to me that I saw the "presence" in the garden because I was in a disturbed state after listening to the Beethoven, and some new faculty in me had been awakened.' The important phrase here being, of course, 'some new faculty in me had been awakened'. It seems that here we have the germ of an idea that became the focal point of *The Occult*, that is to say 'Faculty X' ('that latent power

---

* Colin Wilson's 'Occult Trilogy' is as follows:
The Occult (1971); *Mysteries: an investigation into the occult, the paranormal and the supernatural* (1978); *Beyond the Occult* (1988)

that human beings possess *to reach beyond the present*'), formulated originally in 1966 and featured in his novel *The Philosopher's Stone* in 1968. Wilson considered 'Faculty X' to be '... the key not only to so-called occult experience, but to the whole future evolution of the human race ... [and] ... it is the possession of it – fragmentary and uncertain though it is – that distinguishes man from all other animals.'

Also in 1963, Wilson's novel *The Man Without a Shadow* (published in the US as *The Sex Diary of Gerard Sorme*), the second in the Gerard Sorme trilogy, appeared in print. It featured Caradoc Cunningham, a larger than life character and practitioner of sex magic, based on the 'Great Beast' Aleister Crowley, who, when he first meets Sorme, impresses him with his telepathic powers. This anticipates the chapter on Crowley in *The Occult* by several years. Wilson then went on to write a short biography, *Aleister Crowley: The Nature of the Beast*, in 1987 (recently reprinted).

In a later novel, *The Glass Cage*, published in 1966, Damon Reade, a William Blake scholar, is approached by the police in the hope that he can help them catch the Thames Murderer, who leaves a quote from Blake beside each victim. Reade has a file of correspondence from Blake fans and decides to take a couple of the weirder letters to an old man in his village who has 'strange powers' and whom he believes will be able to tell intuitively if one of them has been written by the murderer.

And in the final part of the Sorme trilogy, *The God of the Labyrinth* (*The Hedonists* in the US), published in 1970, just before *The Occult*, Sorme researches an eighteenth-century rake by the name of Esmond Donelly. On an increasing number of occasions he finds himself seeing the world through Donelly's eyes, gradually becoming his subject.

So we have devil worshippers, ghosts, telepathy, men with 'strange powers', duo-consciousness, and there are many other such 'occult' instances in the early novels, most of which had been out of print for some time before Valancourt Books set about systematically reprinting them in 2013.

Wilson confirmed his early interest in the subject in the opening chapter of *The Occult*, when he informed us that as a twenty-year-old, living in rented accommodation in London with his wife and young child, forced to work in various dead-end factory jobs – long before the publication of his first book, *The Outsider*, in 1956 – he read all the books on magic and mysticism that he could find in libraries; not just as an escape from his lot but '... because they confirmed my intuition of another order of reality, an intenser and more powerful form of consciousness than the kind I seemed to share.' By the time he came to write the book, in the late 1960s, he had apparently accumulated a library of over five hundred volumes on the subject. And in his 2004 autobiography *Dreaming to Some Purpose*, he revealed that his interest in the subject went right back to his childhood:

> As a child, I had been fascinated by ghost stories. My grandmother was a spiritualist, so I accepted the idea of life after death from the age of six or so.
>
> In the early days of the Second World War, the *Sunday People* had published a series by Air Marshall Dowding, in which he discussed the after-death experiences of an airman, as relayed through a spirit medium. The next world, the dead airman claimed, was not all that different from this one, except that there were no discomforts; grass, trees and sky all looked much as on earth, but when he tried swimming, the water was not wet, so it felt rather like swimming in cotton wool. I read the series avidly every week.
>
> Our local library in Leicester, St Barnabas, had an excellent section on psychical research, and I read all I could find by Harry Price – *The Most Haunted House in England*, *Confessions of a Ghost Hunter*, and *Poltergeist over England* ...

Despite the advice against it, writing *The Occult* turned out to be very advantageous to Wilson both critically and financially. For it was, by and large, received favourably by the critics, sold very well on both sides of the Atlantic and has been translated into many different languages. Cyril Connolly and Philip Toynbee, who were instrumental in turning *The Outsider* into a bestseller in 1956, but had subsequently changed their minds and then ignored his work for fifteen years, relaxed their embargo and came out in support of him again. Indeed, Connolly went on to write:

> I am very impressed by this book, not only by its erudition but by the marshalling of it, and above all by the good-natured, unaffected charm of the author whose reasoning is never too far-fetched, who is never carried away by preposterous theories. Mr Wilson's mental processes are akin to Aldous Huxley.

Alan Hull Walton, writing in *Books and Bookmen*, declared:

> ... in an age of talented mediocrity, [Colin Wilson] is blessed with far more than talent – he is blessed with insight, sincerity, humility, an extraordinarily wide learning (comparable to that of the 'universal man' of the Renaissance), and also manifests something of the breadth of genius of a Goethe. ... His new book ... is by far and away his best work to date, and worthy to be placed on the same shelf alongside William James, F. W. H. Myers' monumental study of *Human Personality* ... and Frazer's *Golden Bough*. ... A review of a thousand words ... cannot do justice to a book of this calibre. ... *The Occult* is a valuable 'must' for anyone with the remotest interest in the future of civilised man.

James Blish in *The Spectator* advised that 'anyone wishing to begin reading in this field might well begin with this book (which also contains a good bibliography)'.

In the US, Joyce Carol Oates praised the work as a 'book of wonders', recommending it as: 'one of those rich, strange, perplexing, infinitely surprising works that repay many readings. Though it contains a great deal of history it is really, like most of Colin Wilson's books, about the future.' And Clifford P. Bendau, in his book on Wilson's work, wrote:

> *The Occult* establishes that Wilson has the ability to research and interpret vast quantities of information. It is apparent that he is able to convey consistent and challenging ideas that prod those who are most comfortable with their established beliefs.

The book's success inspired Wilson's publishers to commission another, *Mysteries: an investigation into the occult, the paranormal and the supernatural*, an equally bulky tome, which appeared in 1978, and then a third, ten years later, *Beyond the Occult*, which summed up his twenty years of research into the subject. The three books amount to a monumental 1,600 pages and also spawned many ephemeral popular illustrated spin-offs – too numerous to mention here individually – but listed entirely in my guide to his 'Occult Trilogy' published by Axis Mundi in 2013.

According to Wilson, the reviews 'had a serious and respectful tone that I hadn't heard since *The Outsider*' and in his 2003 Introduction to the Watkins reprint, he wrote:

> But for me, *The Occult* did a great deal more than make me 'respectable', it also served as a kind of awakening. Before 1970, I had been inclined to dismiss 'the occult' as superstitious nonsense. Writing *The Occult* made me aware that the paranormal is as real as quantum physics (and, in fact, has a great deal in common with it), and that anyone who refuses to take it into account is simply shutting his eyes to half the universe.

Colin Stanley is author of *The Colin Wilson Bibliography, 1956–2010*; *Colin Wilson's 'Outsider Cycle': A guide for students*; *Colin Wilson's 'Occult Trilogy': A guide for students;* and *Colin Wilson's Existential Literary Criticism: A guide for students*.

He has edited *Around the Outsider: Essays presented to Colin Wilson on the occasion of his 80th birthday* and *Colin Wilson, a Celebration: Essays and recollections*. He edits the series 'Colin Wilson Studies', which features essays on Wilson's work by scholars worldwide.

He has written Introductions to new editions of four of Colin Wilson's novels: *Ritual in the Dark, The Man Without a Shadow, The Philosopher's Stone* and *Necessary Doubt*.

INTRODUCTION TO THE NEW EDITION

The publication of this book had the effect of changing my life.

Fifteen years earlier, in 1956, I had had the curious – but not necessarily pleasant – experience of achieving overnight fame. My first book, *The Outsider*, had appeared in May 1956, and was launched with excellent reviews from the most respected critics. Unfortunately, the tabloids were also fascinated by this phenomenon of a twenty-four-year-old working-class writer who had produced a work of philosophy, and I began to figure in the gossip columns.

That same week, another young writer named John Osborne achieved sudden fame with a play called *Look Back in Anger*. He and I were inevitably bracketed together, under the label 'Angry Young Men'. And the sheer amount of silly publicity we received that summer alienated all the serious critics. By the autumn of that year we were being constantly attacked. My own second book, *Religion and the Rebel*, was hatcheted, while Osborne's satirical musical, *The World of Paul Slickey*, aroused such hostility that he was chased down Shaftesbury Avenue by the first-night audience. Everyone was sick of Angry Young Men.

I escaped to Cornwall with my girlfriend Joy, and in due course we started a family. But the intense hostility remained, and my books were often not even reviewed. It was obviously going to take a long time for all the silly publicity about Angry Young Men to be forgotten; it was still dogging me in the late 1960s.

Then, in 1969, my American literary agent, Scott Meredith, wrote to ask me if I would be interested in writing a book about 'the occult' for Random House, in New York. It was not a subject that interested me particularly, but I accepted it because I needed the money.

That autumn I spent some time as a 'Writer in Residence' at the extramural department of an American college in Majorca. We were living in the same village as the poet Robert Graves, Deya. When I asked Graves' advice on writing a book on the 'occult', it came in one word: 'Don't'.

But by then, a commission I had treated almost as a joke had begun to interest me. I had assumed, to begin with, that ghosts were a superstition. Then I discovered that they had been believed in by every civilisation for thousands of years, and began to feel that perhaps my dismissive attitude was a mistake. I began meeting people who had experienced various odd phenomena; one woman told me of her 'Out-of-the-Body' experience when she was suffering from fever in hospital, while my mother had seen some kind of an angel when she was apparently dying from a burst appendix, and had been told that she had to return because 'her time had not yet come'. She lived another thirty-six years.

Even my father, who was not particularly interested in my work – being a non-reader – had a sudden intuition that my book on 'the occult' would be a success, and said so several times in the early 1970s.

As soon as I began to write, I was carried away. Material seemed to fall into my lap. One story that impressed me particularly was told to me by the wife of the Scottish poet Hugh M'Diarmid, who happened to be a communist. Valda M'Diarmid told me that whenever her husband travelled abroad – usually to some place like Moscow or Peking – she always knew when he would be coming home, because their dog would go and sit at the end of the lane for several days in advance. On one occasion, it had known about his return before he did.

This fascinated me. It obviously did the dog no good whatever to know its master was on his way home. It just sat there. But it clearly possessed some natural faculty of 'tuning in' to its master's mind.

I came to formulate a theory of 'the occult': that it is a natural faculty that we all possess, but that human beings have deliberately got rid of because it would be a nuisance.

During the war, a Dutch house painter called Peter Hurkos fell off a ladder and fractured his skull. When he woke up in hospital, he found he could read the minds of his fellow patients, and knew all kinds of intimate details about them. But when he went back to work, he realised the disadvantages of this new ability: he could not concentrate. His brain buzzed continually with unwanted information about his fellow human beings, and he felt thoroughly distracted. It was not until he realised he could make use of this ability as a stage entertainer that he solved the problem of how to make a living.

And he was not simply able to read minds. He could handle a piece of clothing that belonged to someone who had disappeared, and say: 'That girl was murdered' or 'That child was drowned'. And what is even odder, he could add: 'And the child's body will reappear on the tenth of next month', and more often than not, be correct. Yet foreseeing the future ought to be impossible, since it has not yet happened.

The Occult seemed to pour out of me in one long burst. It almost seemed to write itself. The publisher had asked me to write a hundred thousand words – about three hundred pages. But it was obvious that this book would need to be far longer. In fact, the British publisher (Hutchinsons) was so alarmed by the size of the typescript that he suggested I find another publisher. My agent soon found me another who was not worried by its size – Hodder – who, indeed, even offered to let me expand it.

Hodders also decided to issue a pamphlet about me, and to increase my advance, which troubled me. After ten years of poor sales, I was afraid they would lose their money. But they proved to be right. The book was not only widely and respectfully reviewed, but sold excellently. So did the American edition, which immediately went into a Book Club edition.

The English paperback came out in a large, grass-green volume, with some nonsensical quote about it being 'a book for those who would walk with the gods'. But this also sold impressively. When

I went back on a visit to my home town, Leicester, I paid a visit to Lewis's, the department store where I had met Joy in 1953, and discovered a huge rack of *The Occult* paperback, holding at least a hundred copies.

So the book did a great deal for me. I ceased to be stigmatised as an 'Angry Young Man', and became a more-or-less respectable member of the literary establishment. Since I was by then forty, and we had three children, I was rather relieved.

Why do I suppose the book did so well? I feel I owe this partly to a curious historical phenomenon: that in the last decades of every century, there is a sudden revival of interest in the paranormal. In the last decades of the sixteenth century, it was John Dee; a century later (incredibly) Sir Isaac Newton, who was a dedicated alchemist, a century later, Cagliostro, and a century later still, that whole nineteenth-century movement that included Lord Lytton, Eliphaz Levi, Madame Blavatsky, Aleister Crowley and the Golden Dawn. (A book called *The Occult Establishment* by James Webb tells the whole amazing story.)

In the twentieth century, it all started again with a book called *The Morning of the Magicians* by Louis Pauwels and Jacques Bergier, which became a bestseller in the 1960s; then came my own book, in the wake of a part-work called *Man, Myth and Magic*, and then a whole 'magical revival', with a flood of similar books. And while *The Occult* did not go into as many languages as *The Outsider*, it certainly became a close second.

But for me, *The Occult* did a great deal more than make me 'respectable'. It also served as a kind of awakening. Before 1970, I had been inclined to dismiss 'the occult' as superstitious nonsense. Writing *The Occult* made me aware that the paranormal is as real as quantum physics (and, in fact, has a great deal in common with it), and that anyone who refuses to take it into account is simply shutting his eyes to half the universe.

PREFACE

A single obsessional idea runs through all my work: the paradoxical nature of freedom. When the German tanks rolled into Warsaw, or the Russians into Budapest, it seemed perfectly obvious what we meant by freedom; it was something solid and definite that was being stolen, as a burglar might steal the silver. But when a civil servant retires after forty years, and finds himself curiously bored and miserable, the idea of freedom becomes blurred and indefinite; it seems to shimmer like a mirage. 'When I am confronted by danger or crisis, I see it as a threat to freedom, and my freedom suddenly becomes positive and self-evident – as enormous and obvious as a sunset. Similarly, a man who is violently in love feels that if he could possess the girl, his freedom would be infinite; the delight of union would make him undefeatable. When he gets her, the whole thing seems an illusion; she is just a girl …

I have always accepted the fundamental reality of freedom. The vision is *not* an illusion or a mirage. In that case, what goes wrong?

The trouble is *the narrowness of consciousness*. It is as if you tried to see a panoramic scene through cracks in a high fence, but were never allowed to look *over* the fence and see it as a whole. And the narrowness lulls us into a state of permanent drowsiness, like being half anaesthetised, so that we never attempt to stretch our powers to their limits. With the consequence that we never discover their limits. William James stated, after he had breathed nitrous oxide, 'our normal walking consciousness … is but one special type of consciousness, whilst all about it, parted from it by the filmiest of screens, there lie potential forms of consciousness entirely different'.

I formulated my theory of 'Faculty X' on a snowy day in Washington, D.C., in 1966; but the other day, someone pointed out to me that as long ago as 1957 I had told Kenneth Alisop: 'One day

I believe man will have a sixth sense – a sense of the purpose of life, quite direct and uninferred.'* And in 1968 I wrote in a novel devoted entirely to the problem of Faculty X, *The Philosopher's Stone*: 'The will feeds on enormous vistas; deprived of them, it collapses.' And there again is the absurd problem of freedom. Man's consciousness is as powerful as a microscope; it can grasp and analyse experience in a way no animal can achieve. But microscopic vision is narrow vision. We need to develop another kind of consciousness that is the equivalent of the telescope.

This is Faculty X. And the paradox is that *we already possess it to a large degree*, but are unconscious of possessing it. It lies at the heart of all so-called occult experience. It is with such experience that this book is concerned.

Colin Wilson

* *The Angry Decade* (London, 1958), p. 154.

INTRODUCTION

The thesis of this book is revolutionary, and I must state it clearly at the outset.

Primitive man believed the world was full of unseen forces: the *orenda* (spirit force) of the American Indians, the *huaca* of the ancient Peruvians. The Age of Reason said that these forces had only ever existed in man's imagination; only reason could show man the truth about the universe. The trouble was that man became a thinking pygmy, and the world of the rationalists was a daylight place in which boredom, triviality and 'ordinariness' were ultimate truths.

But the main trouble with human beings is their tendency to become trapped in the 'triviality of everydayness' (to borrow Heidegger's phrase), in the suffocating world of their personal preoccupations. And every time they do this, they forget the immense world of broader significance that stretches around them. And since man needs a sense of meaning to release his hidden energies, this forgetfulness pushes him deeper into depression and boredom, the sense that nothing is worth the effort.

In a sense, the Indians and Peruvians were closer to the truth than modern man, for their intuition of 'unseen forces' kept them wide open to the vistas of meaning that surround us.

Goethe's *Faust* can be seen to be the greatest symbolic drama of the West, since it is the drama of the rationalist suffocating in the dusty room of his personal consciousness, caught in the vicious circle of boredom and futility, which in turn leads to still further boredom and futility. Faust's longing for the 'occult' is the instinctive desire to believe in the unseen forces, the wider significances, that can break the circuit.

The interesting thing is that Western man developed science and philosophy because of this consuming passion for wider significances. It was not his reason that betrayed him, but his inability to reason clearly, to understand that a healthy mind must have an 'input' of meaning from the universe if it is to keep up an 'output' of vital effort. The fatal error was the failure of the scientists and rationalists to keep their minds open to the sense of *huaca*, the unseen forces. They tried to measure life with a six-inch ruler and weigh it with the kitchen scales. This was not science; it was crudity only one degree beyond that of savages; and Swift made game of it in the 'Voyage to Laputa'.

Man lives and evolves by 'eating' significance, as a child eats food. The deeper his sense of wonder, the wider his curiosity, the stronger his vitality becomes, and the more powerful his grip on his own existence.

There are two ways in which he can expand: inward and outward. If I am in a foreign country and I get a powerful desire to explore it thoroughly, to visit its remotest places, that is a typical example of outward expansion. And it would not be untrue to say that the love of books, of music, of art, is typical of the desire for inward expansion. But that is only a half of it. For what happens if I suddenly become fascinated by a foreign country is that I feel like the spider in the centre of a web; I am aware of all kinds of 'significances' vibrating along the web, and I want to reach out and grab them all. But in moods of deep inner serenity, the same thing happens. Suddenly I am aware of vast inner spaces, of strange significances *inside* me. I am no longer a puny twentieth-century human being trapped in his life-world and personality. Once again, I am at the centre of a web, feeling vibrations of meaning. And suddenly I realise that in the deepest sense those Indians and Peruvians were right. I am like a tree that suddenly becomes aware that its roots go down deep, deep into the earth. And at this present point in evolution, my roots go far deeper into the earth than my branches stretch above it – a thousand times deeper.

So-called magic powers are a part of this underground world: powers of second sight, pre-vision, telepathy, divination. These are not necessarily important to our evolution; most animals possess them, and we would not have allowed them to sink into disuse if they were essential. But the knowledge of his 'roots', his inner world, is important to man at this point in evolution, for he has become trapped in his image of himself as a thinking pygmy. He must somehow return to the recognition that he is potentially a 'mage', one of those magical figures who can hurl thunderbolts or command spirits. The great artists and poets have always been aware of this. The message of the symphonies of Beethoven could be summarised: 'Man is not small; he's just bloody lazy.'

Civilisation cannot evolve further until 'the occult' is taken for granted on the same level as atomic energy. I do not mean that scientists ought to spend their evenings with an ouija board, or that every university should set up a 'department of psychic sciences' along the lines of the Rhine Institute at Duke. I mean that we have to learn to expand inward until we have somehow re-established the sense of *huaca*, until we have re-created the feeling of 'unseen forces' that was common to primitive man. It has somehow *got* to be done. There are aspects of the so-called supernatural that we have got to learn to take for granted, to live with them as easily as our ancestors did. 'Man's perceptions are not bounded by organs of perception,' says Blake. 'He perceives more than sense (though ever so acute) can discover.' He 'knows' things that he has not learned through schooling or everyday experience, and sometimes it is more comfortable not to know. Osbert Sitwell has a strange anecdote about a palmist:

> Nearly all my brother-officers of my own age had been, two
> or three months earlier in the year, to see a celebrated palmist
> of the period – whom, I remember it was said, Mr. Winston
> Churchill used sometimes to consult. My friends, of course,

used to visit her in the hope of being told that their love affairs would prosper, when they would marry, or the direction in which their later careers would develop. In each instance, it appears, the cheiromant had just begun to read their fortunes, when, in sudden bewilderment, she had thrown the outstretched hand from her, crying, 'I don't understand it! It's the same thing again! After two or three months, the line of life stops short, and I can read nothing ...' To each individual to whom it was said, this seemed merely an excuse she had improvised for her failure: but when I was told by four or five persons of the same experience, I wondered what it could portend ...*

It portended the outbreak of the 1914 war, and the deaths of the brother officers whose life lines came to an end three months after consulting the palmist.

The number of readers who would dismiss this story as a fantasy or a downright lie is probably very small. A larger number may feel that there is some truth in it, but that it has been in some way exaggerated. The majority of people would probably accept that it is more or less true, and all rather odd ... but not very important; at least, they have no intention of thinking about it. And we tend to fall back on this response whenever we are faced with the 'odd': to push it into a compartment of the mind labelled 'exceptions', and forget about it. I hear that Abraham Lincoln had dreams and premonitions of his death for a week before he was assassinated; that is 'odd', but it is also past history, and it may have been exaggerated. I open a weekend colour supplement, and read that for a week before the explosion that destroyed a BEA Comet aircraft on October 12, 1967, Nicos Papapetrou *was* haunted by premonitions, and dreams of death

---

* *Great Morning* (London, Macmillan, 1948), p. 265.

and mourning, so that an hour before take-off, he tried to book on another flight.* That is not past history, but then, Papapetrou was carrying the bomb that accidentally exploded. He was an explosives smuggler and had made six similar trips earlier that year; why did he get premonitions on this one? We shrug, agree that it is very odd and think about something else.

Now, I am certainly not suggesting that we should spend our lives worrying about dreams and premonitions, or patronise fortune-tellers; it is a healthy instinct that makes us ignore them and get on with the practical business of living. But the hard-headed, tough-minded attitude towards such things is a mistake in the most ordinary, logical sense of that term. A mere two centuries ago, the most respected scientists declared that it was absurd to assert that the earth is more than a few thousand years old, or that strange monsters had once walked its forests. When workmen in quarries discovered fossilised sea-creatures, or even the skull of a dinosaur, this was explained as a freak rock formation, nature imitating living forms by way of a joke. And for the next fifty years the hard-headed scientists devoted their time and ingenuity to explaining away the fossils and bones that were found in increasing numbers. Cuvier, one of the greatest zoologists of the nineteenth century, destroyed the career of his colleague Lamarck by stigmatising his theory of evolution as fanciful and unscientific; his own more 'scientific' belief was that all the prehistoric creatures (whose existence was now acknowledged) had been totally destroyed in a series of world catastrophes, wiping the slate clean for the creation of man and the animals of today.

This kind of thing is not the exception in the history of science but the rule. For one of the fundamental dogmas of science is that a man who is denying a theory is probably more 'scientific' than a man who is affirming it.

* *Observer Supplement*, May 10, 1970.

Introduction

In spite of Cuvier, the 'fanciful' ideas of evolution *have* won the day – although, in the form in which they were most acceptable to scientists, they were rigorous, mechanical laws of 'survival of the fittest'. Slowly that is changing, and the latest developments in biology may end by altering our conception of the universe as much as the dinosaur bones altered our conception of the earth. And that is the premise upon which this book is based. The time may not be far off when we can accept certain 'occult' phenomena as naturally as we now accept the existence of atoms.

In order to clarify this assertion, I must speak briefly of the new science of cybernetics. Cybernetics was 'invented' in 1948 by the physicist Norbert Wiener of the Massachusetts Institute of Technology. It is the science of *control* and communication, in machines and animals. (The Greek work *kybernetes* means a steersman or governor.) The floating ball in the lavatory cistern is a simple application of cybernetic control; when the cistern is full, the ball-cock cuts off the water. With a little ingenuity I could devise a similar control to turn off the bath taps when the water reaches a certain level, saving myself the trouble of sitting up in the bath. But in science and industry, the process I want to control may be many times more complicated than bath taps; it may, for example, be some chemical process that might develop in several directions. In which case, I must make use of an electronic computer and 'programme' it to deal with many possible situations. A card with a few holes punched in it is enough to give the computer its instructions and to make it behave like a foreman seeing that a job gets done properly.

Since the late nineteenth century, it has been understood that living creatures derive their characteristics from tiny cells called genes, which are contained in the male sperm and the female egg. The colour of my hair and eyes, and the size of my feet, are all determined by genes. But no one was sure how the genes did this. In the mid-1950s, it gradually became clear that the genes are like a computer card with holes punched in it. The 'holes' are actually molecules of a substance called DNA, linked together in the form of a double spiral, something like two springs twisted together in opposite directions.

The more we know about this computer system that makes us what we are, the more baffling it becomes. Darwin's theory of evolution accounts for the giraffe's neck and the elephant's trunk in terms of accident, just as you might explain a rock worn into the shape of a face by pointing to the wind and rain. Science hates 'teleology', the notion of purpose. The rock didn't *want* to be sculpted into the shape of a face, and the wind and rain didn't want to sculpt it; it just happened. Similarly, biologists hate the heresy known as 'vitalism', the notion that life somehow 'wants' to produce healthier and more intelligent creatures; they just happen to get produced because health and intelligence survive better than sickness and stupidity. But when one realises that human beings are produced by a highly complex computer card, it becomes difficult to avoid slipping into 'teleology' and wondering who programmed the computer.

In 1969, a cybernetician, Dr. David Foster, lectured to the International Conference on Cybernetics at the Imperial College, London, and sketched some of the philosophical implications of these discoveries. He pointed out that from the cybernetician's point of view, it is possible to consider the universe in terms of data and data processing. An acorn, for example, may be regarded as the 'programme' for an oak tree. Even an atom can be thought of as a computer card with three holes punched in it, the holes being (a) the number of particles in the nucleus, (b) the number of electrons orbiting round it, (c) the energy of these electrons expressed in terms of the smallest known 'parcel' of energy, Planck's constant. Dr. Foster goes on: 'Surely it must be obvious that the essential nature of matter is that the atoms are the *alphabet* of the universe, that chemical compounds are *words*, and that DNA is rather a long *sentence* or even a whole book trying to say something such as "elephant", "giraffe" or even "man".'

He goes on to point out that the basic building brick of any electrical information theory is one electrical wave, and a wave consists of two halves, because it is measured from the top of one 'bump' to the bottom of the next trough:

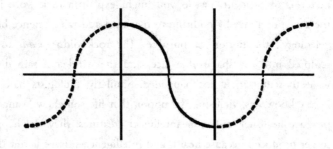

That is, a wave is a 'binary' system, and computers work upon binary mathematics.* This is an important step in his argument, for if we think of 'waves' as the basic vocabulary of the universe, then you can think of life – in fact, of all matter – as being due to waves that have somehow been cybernetically programmed.

What he is saying certainly sounds like 'teleology'. If I saw a complex chemical process being regulated and controlled by a computer, I would infer that someone had programmed the computer. Dr. Foster is saying that, to the eyes of a cybernetician, the complex structures of life around him reveal data processing on a massive scale. This is a matter of scientific fact. And he naturally finds himself wondering what intelligence processed the data?

And now Dr. Foster takes his most controversial step. He explains that 'as an automation consultant, whenever I design a control system for a process it is axiomatic that the speed of the

* See p. 100.

control system must be greater than that of the motions of the process concerned'. For example, you can drive your car because you can think faster than the engine works; if you couldn't, you would crash. But in that case, programming of matter must be achieved by vibrations – or waves – much faster than the vibrations of matter. That is, in cosmic radiations. The universe is, of course, full of cosmic radiations; and, in Dr. Foster's view, these are probably what lie behind the 'programming' of the DNA molecules.

But observe the central point. A wave that carries information is quite different from a wave that doesn't. The information is *imposed* on its structure by intelligence. Dr. Foster's conclusion – although stated with the typical caution of a scientist and hedged around with qualifications – is that the level of intelligence involved must be a great deal higher than our human intelligence. This is also a scientific deduction, not a metaphysical guess. He mentions the Compton Effect in physics, by which the wave length of X-rays is increased by collision with electrons, and the rule deduced from this is that you can make red light from blue light – because its energy is less – but not blue light from red light. 'The faster vibrating blue light is programming for red light, but not vice versa.'

What Dr. Foster is saying is not fundamentally different from the Paley's watch argument. The theologian Paley remarked that when he looks at the works of his watch, he realises that it implies an intelligent maker, and that man is, after all, more complex than any watch. However, Dr. Foster – if I understand him aright – is not trying to introduce God through the back door. He is less concerned with theories about who does the programming than the fact that there *is* programming throughout nature; he is concerned with the question of how the 'information' gets carried to the DNA, and 'cosmic radiation' suggests itself as a plausible assumption. He says, 'One establishes a new picture of the universe as a digitised universe, an information universe, but I think that because of the strong cybernetical influences at work, I prefer to call it The Intelligent Universe.'

It is interesting that Dr. Foster arrives at this Intelligent Universe not by starting from the idea of purpose or God, as religious thinkers do, but simply by considering the facts we now know about the cybernetic programming of living matter. What emerges is a picture of the universe that fits in with the theories of other scientists and psychologists during the past twenty years: Teilhard de Chardin, Sir Julian Huxley, C. H. Waddington, Abraham Maslow, Viktor Frankl, Michael Polanyi, Noam Chomsky. What all these men have in common is an opposition to 'reductionism', the attempt to explain man and the universe in terms of the laws of physics or the behaviour of laboratory rats. The psychologist Abraham Maslow, for example, writes: 'Man has a "higher nature" that is just as instinctoid as his lower (animal) nature …' Dr. Foster's theory of a 'digitised universe' is perhaps bolder than the evolutionism of Huxley and Waddington, but the spirit is fundamentally similar. There is no contradiction.

And all this means that for the first time in Western history a book on the occult can be something more than a collection of marvels and absurdities. Religion, mysticism and magic all spring from the same basic 'feeling' about the universe: a sudden feeling of *meaning*, which human beings sometimes 'pick up' accidentally, as your radio might pick up some unknown station. Poets feel that we are cut off from meaning by a thick lead wall, and that sometimes for no reason we can understand the wall seems to vanish and we are suddenly overwhelmed with a sense of the infinite *interestingness* of things. Ivan Karamazov, in Dostoevsky's novel, tells a story about an atheist who did not believe in life after death, and after his death, God sentenced him to walk a billion miles as a penance. The atheist lay on the road and refused to move for a million years; however, he eventually dragged himself to his feet and unwillingly walked the billion miles.

And when he was finally admitted to heaven, he immediately declared that it would have been worth walking ten times as far just for five minutes of heaven. Dostoevsky catches this mystical sense of a meaning so intense that it surpasses anything we can conceive and that would make *any* effort worthwhile. It is the sense of meaning that spurs man to make the efforts necessary to evolution. While he believes that his boredom and pessimism are telling him the truth about the universe he refuses to make an effort. If, like Ivan's sinner, he could get a sudden glimpse of 'meaning', he would become unconquerable and unkillable; walking ten billion miles would be a joke.

Now, Western science has always agreed that there is plenty to discover about the universe – but it is fundamentally a dead, mechanical universe. You might say that the scientist is nothing more than a glorified accident-investigator. And the accident investigator is himself the product of accident. But man is more deeply moved by meaning than by accident. The French speleologist Norbert Casteret found the underground caves at Montespan exciting to explore; but this was nothing to his excitement when he found the walls covered with paintings of lions and horses, and realised that he had stumbled on the art of prehistoric cave men. Discovery of the product of intelligence is always more exciting than the product of accident.

If David Foster is right, or even half right, then it is the beginning of a new epoch in human knowledge, for science will cease to be the investigation of accident and become a search for meaning. He writes, 'The universe is a total construction of waves and vibrations whose inner content is "meaning" ...' admitting at the same time that our instruments are far too clumsy to decode the meanings carried by high-frequency vibrations. But to believe that the meaning is there, to be decoded, is an enormous step forward, almost the equivalent of the atheist's glimpse of heaven.

And, for present purposes, it also provides a picture of the universe that has room for 'occult phenomena' as well as for atomic physics. In the past, the trouble was always where to draw the line. If you could accept telepathy and premonitions of the future, then why not astrology and fortune-telling and werewolves and vampires and ghosts and witches casting spells? Because if you are going to contradict scientific logic, you may as well be hanged for a sheep as for a lamb, and see how many impossible things you can believe before breakfast.

On the other hand, Dr. Foster's theory agrees with the intuitions of poets, mystics and 'occultists': that there are 'meanings' floating around us from which we are normally cut off by habit, ignorance and the dullness of the senses. So-called esoteric tradition *may* be no more than the superstition of ignorant savages, but it could also be an attempt to explain one of those accidental glimpses of a meaning that goes beyond everyday banality, a moment when the human radio set picks up unknown vibrations. The word 'occult', after all, means 'the unknown', the hidden. Or perhaps these glimpses are not accidental; perhaps the Intelligent Universe is trying to communicate to us.

But whether we want to go this far or not, there is a sense of liberation in being able to accept that the universe is full of meaning that we could grasp if we took the trouble. Bertrand Russell expresses the same feeling in *My Philosophical Development* when he tells how he came to reject the Kantian notion that there is no 'reality' out there: 'With a sense of escaping from prison, we allowed ourselves to think that the grass is green, that the sun and stars would exist if no one was aware of them, and also that there is a pluralistic timeless world of Platonic ideas …'

Man must believe in realities outside his own smallness, outside the 'triviality of everydayness', if he is to do anything worthwhile.

And this brings me to one of the central assertions of this book. As long ago as 1887, Max Müller, the editor of *The Sacred Books of the East*, pointed out* that for all practical purposes our ancestors of two thousand years ago were almost colour-blind, as most animals are today. 'Xenophanes knew of three colours of the rainbow only – purple, red and yellow; that even Aristotle spoke of the tricoloured rainbow; and that Democritus knew of no more than four colours – black, white, red and yellow.' Homer apparently thought the sea the same colour as wine. There are no colour words in primitive Indo-European speech. We can understand why Aristotle's pupil Alexander of Macedon spent his life conquering the world. It must have been a singularly dull world, with no distinction between the red of wine, the blue-green of the sea, the emerald-green of grass and the deep-blue of the sky. But it is understandable, biologically speaking. Life was hard and violent, and the capacity to grasp subtle distinctions of thought or colour would have been of no value for survival. Alexander was energetic and imaginative; what else was there for him to *do* but conquer the world, and then cry when there was no more to conquer?

But the capacity to enjoy 'subtle vibrations' is an important part of our energy-outlets. A man who cannot read is going to have a very dull time as he recuperates in hospital from a serious operation, whereas a man who loves reading may find the inactivity delightful. Boredom is lack of the capacity for registering subtle vibrations. And the definition of a living organism is an organism capable of responding to energy vibrations. These vibrations constitute 'meaning'. Whether I am relaxing in front of a fire, or enjoying a glass of wine; or responding to a symphony, or smelling cut grass as I mow the lawn, I am registering *meanings* and recording vibrations. The important difference between a man and his dog is not only that the dog is colour-blind, but that the man has a wider range of response in almost every field.

* *The Science of Thought* (New York, Scribner's), Vol. 1, p. 299. Also quoted by R. M. Bucke, *Cosmic Consciousness* (New York, 1901), p. 28.

The higher the form of life, the deeper its capacity for registering meaning, *and the more powerful its hold on life*. For Alexander, meaning was bound up with conquest, and when he reached a limit of conquest, he also reached the end of his tether; he had conquered the world at thirty-one; he died at thirty-three.

Evolution is simply the capacity to register meanings that are *already there*. Blue and green existed, even if Xenophanes could not distinguish between them. We are evolving into a universe that becomes progressively more fascinating as we learn to register new vibrations. No doubt in another thousand years, human beings will see a dazzling universe *with a dozen colours that do not exist for us*.

Now, it should be obvious that an increase in 'subtlety' is an *inward* evolution. An apprentice clockmaker begins by repairing large clocks, and slowly graduates to the finest watches. He develops an increasing stillness and concentration, and these are 'inward' qualities.

Man has reached a point in his evolution where he must graduate from clocks to watches, from the large to the subtle. He must turn increasingly inward. That is, he must turn to the hidden levels of his being, to the 'occult', to meanings and vibrations that have so far been too fine to grasp.

I have divided this book into three parts. Although it was originally intended to take the form of a history, I felt that a lengthy preamble was needed – a section in which I could state my own preoccupations and convictions. I have argued that there is a connection between creativity and 'psychic' sensitivity. The creative person is concerned to tap the powers of the subconscious mind, and in doing so, may become aware of forces that are normally inaccessible to consciousness. This is why I have included discussions of the *I Ching* and the Tarot in this section.

The second part is the history that I set out to write. I had the choice of attempting either a history of magic in general, or a history of individual 'mages' and adepts, with the necessary historical background to connect them together. I have chosen the latter course.

The third part of the book is concerned with the subjects that I only had time to touch upon in the second part: witchcraft, lycanthropy and vampirism, the history of spiritualism, the problem of ghosts and poltergeists. The last chapter of the book, 'Glimpses', returns to the subjects of this preface: the metaphysical questions that arise out of occultism; the problem of time; and the nature of 'man's latent powers'.

This is a large book, and as comprehensive a history as I can make it. But it soon became clear to me that it had to be essentially a personal statement of conviction rather than an encyclopedia. There *are* good encyclopedias: notably Lewis Spence's *Encyclopedia of Occultism*. Nandor Fodor's *Encyclopedia of Psychic Science*, and the wide-ranging *Man, Myth and Magic* (which, at the time this book goes to press, has only reached the second of seven volumes). But their disadvantage is that they tend to be a disconnected mass of information. The books of the late Charles Fort have the same fault; he spent his life collecting newspaper reports of weird and unexplainable events to disconcert the scientists, and then failed to disconcert anybody but his admirers because he tossed down a great mountain of facts like a heap of firewood and hoped they would argue for themselves. But facts never do. In this book, perhaps I have argued a little too much, but it seemed to me to be the safer of two courses.

In an early chapter I speak about coincidences; and certainly there have been enough in the writing of this book. On one occasion, when I was searching for a piece of information, a book actually fell off the shelf and fell open at the right page. And items of required information have turned up with a promptitude that sometimes made me nervous. After a while I got used to this, and even began to feel a mild resentment when some piece of information evaded me for more than ten minutes or so. Which seems to demonstrate my point that if the supernatural made too many incursions into human existence, it would end by making us lazy.

My own attitude to the subject has changed during the course of researching and writing this book. Although I have always been curious about the 'occult' – I have five hundred or so volumes on magic and the supernatural – it has never been one of my major interests, like philosophy or science, or even music. While I was by no means entirely sceptical, I felt that most people are interested in the supernatural for the wrong reasons. My grandmother was a spiritualist, and the few spiritualists I met through her did not impress me as particularly wide-awake or intelligent. Some ten years ago the Shakespearian scholar G. Wilson Knight talked to me about spiritualism and lent me books on the subject, and again I could not bring myself to take any deep interest. It was not that I rejected what he said; I had sufficient respect for his intellect in other fields to accept that this was not pure wishful thinking. But I still felt that, compared to the world of philosophy or psychology, there was something *trivial* about all this preoccupation with life after death, as there is about chess or ballroom dancing. There was a smell of the 'human, all too human' about it. Camus expressed the same feeling when he said, 'I do not want to believe that death opens out onto another life. For me, it is a closed door ... All the solutions that are offered to me try to take away from man the weight of his own life. And watching the heavy flight of the great birds in the sky at Djémila, it is exactly a certain weight of my life that I ask for and I receive.' Hemingway, at his best, possessed this same awareness. It is a feeling that our life can offer a *reality and an intensity* that makes most ordinary religious emotion seem trivial and self-deluding. The spiritualist says, 'Surely this life would be meaningless if it came to an end with death?' Camus's reply would be that if he accepts life after death as an *answer* to this meaninglessness, he is losing even the possibility of the moments when life becomes oddly 'real'.

It was not until two years ago, when I began the systematic research for this book, that I realised the remarkable consistency of the evidence for such matters as life after death, out-of-the-body experiences (astral projection), reincarnation. In a basic sense, my attitude remains unchanged; I still regard philosophy – the pursuit of reality through intuition aided by intellect – as being more *relevant*, more important, than questions of 'the occult'. But the weighing of the evidence, in this unsympathetic frame of mind, has convinced me that the basic claims of 'occultism' are true. It seems to me that the reality of life after death has been established beyond all reasonable doubt. I sympathise with the philosophers and scientists who regard it as emotional nonsense, because I am temperamentally on their side; but I think they are closing their eyes to evidence that would convince them if it concerned the mating habits of albino rats or the behaviour of alpha particles.

In the past few centuries, science has made us aware that the universe is stranger and more interesting than our ancestors realised. It is an amusing thought that it may turn out stranger and more interesting than even the scientists are willing to admit.

PART ONE

A SURVEY OF THE SUBJECT

ONE
MAGIC – THE SCIENCE OF THE FUTURE

There is a passage in the Introduction to P. D. Ouspensky's *New Model of the Universe* that never fails to move and excite me:

It is the year 1906 or 1907. The editorial office of the Moscow daily paper *The Morning*. I have just received the foreign papers, and I have to write an article on the forthcoming Hague Conference. French, German, English, Italian papers. Phrases, phrases, sympathetic, critical, ironical, blatant, pompous, lying and, worst of all, utterly automatic, phrases which have been used a thousand times and will be used again on entirely different, perhaps contradictory, occasions. I have to make a survey of all these words and opinions, pretending to take them seriously, and then, just as seriously, to write something on my own account. But what can I say? It is all so tedious. Diplomats and all kinds of statesmen will gather together and talk, papers will approve or disapprove, sympathise or not sympathise. Then everything will be as it was, or even worse.

It is still early, I say to myself; perhaps something will come into my head later.

Pushing aside the papers, I open a drawer in my desk. The whole desk is crammed with books with strange titles. *The Occult World, Life after Death, Atlantis and Lemuria, Dogme et Rituel de la Haute Magie, Le Temple de Satan, The Sincere Narrations of a Pilgrim*, and the like. These books and I have been inseparable for a whole month, and the world of the Hague Conference and leading articles becomes more and more vague and unreal to me.

I open one of the books at random, feeling that my article will not be written today. Well, it can go to the devil. Humanity will lose nothing if there is one article fewer on the Hague Conference ...

When I first read this passage, my own circumstances gave it an added relevance. I was twenty years old, and I had been married for a year. My wife and our son were living in Earls Court, London, our fourth home in a year, and our half-insane landlady was the fourth – and worst – of a series. I was on the dole, and I found this almost as nervously wearing as the various factory jobs I had worked at since I was married. London seemed not merely alien, but somehow unreal. So I understood Ouspensky's feeling of nausea at the prospect of writing on the Hague Conference, and also that craving for *another world* of deeper meaning, represented by books on the occult. There is a passage in Louis-Ferdinand Céline that describes the world as rotten with lies, rotten to the point of collapse and disintegration. I had only to look at the advertisements in the London tube, or the headlines of the daily paper, to see that it was obviously true. Lies, stupidity, weakness and mediocrity – a civilisation without ideals.

That was why I read Ouspensky, and all the other books on magic and mysticism that I could find in the local libraries: not only because they were an escape from the world of factories and neurotic landladies, but because they confirmed my intuition of another order of reality, *an intenser and more powerful form of consciousness* than the kind I seemed to share with eight million other Londoners.

But if, at that time, I had been asked whether I literally believed in magic, I would have answered No: that it was a poetic fiction, a symbol of the world that *ought* to exist, but didn't. In short, wishful thinking. In the first sentence of *Ritual Magic*, E. M. Butler writes, 'The fundamental aim of all magic is to impose the human will on nature, on man and the supersensual world in order to master them.' And if that was a fair definition of magic, then I agreed with John Symonds, the biographer of Aleister Crowley, who said, 'The only trouble with magic is that it doesn't work.' Magic, I felt, was no more than a first crude attempt at science, and it had now been superseded by science.

If I still accepted that view, I would not be writing this book. It now seems to me that the exact reverse is true. Magic was not the 'science' of the past. It is the science of the future. I believe that the human mind has reached a point in evolution where it is about to develop new powers – powers that would once have been considered magical. Indeed, it has always possessed greater powers than we now realise: of telepathy, premonition of danger, second sight, thaumaturgy (the power to heal); but these were part of its instinctive, animal inheritance. For the past thousand years or so, humankind has been busy developing another kind of power related to the intellect, and the result is Western civilisation. His unconscious powers have not atrophied; but they have 'gone underground'. Now the wheel has come the full circle; intellect has reached certain limits, and it cannot advance beyond them until it recovers some of the lost powers. Anyone who has read modern philosophy will understand what I mean; it has become narrow, rigid, logical; and it attempts to make up for lack of broader intuitions with a microscopic attention to detail. It has cut itself off from its source.

And what is, in fact, the source of philosophy – or, for that matter, of any knowledge? It is fundamentally the need for power. You have only to watch the face of a baby who has just learned how to open a door by turning the handle, to understand what knowledge is *for*. In the twentieth century, power has become a suspect word, because it has become associated with the idea of power over other people. But that is its least important application. One of the fundamental myths of magic concerns the magician who seeks political power;

he receives a number of warnings, and if he persists, he is destroyed. Political power strengthens the ego; magical power rises from the subconscious, from the non-personal urge. Ouspensky describes the beginning of his 'search for the miraculous':

> I am a schoolboy in the second or third 'class'. But instead of Zeifert's Latin grammar ... I have before me Malinin and Bourenin's 'Physics'. I have borrowed this book from one of the older boys and am reading it greedily and enthusiastically, overcome now by rapture, now by terror, at the mysteries that are opening before me. All round me walls are crumbling, and horizons infinitely remote and incredibly beautiful stand revealed. It is as though threads, previously unknown and unsuspected, begin to reach out and bind things together. For the first time in my life, my world emerges from chaos. Everything becomes connected, forming an orderly and harmonious whole ...

This kind of language may be off-putting ('horizons infinitely remote and incredibly beautiful'), but it is worth bearing in mind that Ouspensky was trained as a scientist, and he is trying to be strictly accurate. He means exactly that: the sudden sense of *meanings*, far bigger than oneself, that make all personal preoccupations seem trivial. Even Bertrand Russell, the founder of 'logical atomism', catches this feeling: 'I *must*, before I die, find *some* way to say the essential thing that is in me, that I have never said yet – a thing that is not love or hate or pity or scorn, but the very breath of life, fierce and coming from far away, bringing into human life the vastness and fearful passionless force of non-human things.'*

The power to be derived from this 'fearful passionless force' is only

---

* Letter to Constance Malleson, 1918, quoted in *My Philosophical Development*, p.261.

incidentally a power over things and people. It is basically power over oneself, contact with some 'source of power, meaning and purpose' in the subconscious mind.

The ability to become excited by 'infinitely remote horizons' is peculiar to human beings; no other animal possesses it. It is a kind of intellectual far-sightedness that could be compared to a pair of binoculars. We have developed it over two million years of evolution. And at the same time, certain other faculties have fallen into disuse. For example, the 'homing instinct'. In *The Territorial Imperative*, Robert Ardrey devotes an interesting chapter (IV) to this phenomenon. A scientist named Johannes Schmidt made the discovery that every eel in the Western world is born in the Sargasso Sea. In the autumn, the eels of Europe and eastern America make their way down the rivers and end in the Sargasso Sea, between the West Indies and the Azores. The following spring, the baby eels make their way to fresh water; two years later, when they are two inches long, the elvers make their way back home *alone*. Those with 115 vertebrae swim back to Europe; those with 107 vertebrae go west to America. The parents remain behind to die.

The green turtle of the Caribbean performs an equally spectacular feat, swimming 1,400 miles from Brazil to Ascension Island, in the mid-Atlantic, at breeding time. The tiny deer mouse of Wyoming, no bigger than the end of one's finger, can be transported a mile away from home – about a hundred miles in terms of human size and unerringly find his way back to the fifty-yard patch that constitutes home. Homing pigeons return over hundreds of miles. It was once believed that this was the result of hard work by the human trainer, until someone discovered accidentally that baby pigeons return home just as unerringly without any training – and often make better time than the 'trained' adults!

In a few cases, science has been able to explain the homing instinct. Vitus B. Droscher mentions some examples in *Mysterious*

Senses. The blackcap bird navigates by means of the stars – as Dr. Franz Sauer discovered by putting them in a planetarium. Salmon, strangely enough, navigate by a highly developed sense of smell. The eel probably does the same, although this does not explain how baby eels know their way back to rivers they have never seen. Bees and ants navigate by the sun. One scientist at Cambridge University suspects that pigeons navigate by taking an astronomical reading of their latitude and longitude by means of the sun and comparing it with the latitude and longitude of their home territory.

So perhaps there is no need to posit some mysterious 'sixth sense' by which animals find their way home. No doubt there are always 'natural' explanations. But in some cases, it is difficult to imagine what it could be. Scientists in Wilhelmshaven took cats, confined in a bag, on a long drive round the town. They were then released in the centre of a maze with twenty-four exits. Most cats made straight for the exit that lay in the direction of their home. A German zoologist, Hans Fromme, has discovered that the migratory instinct of robins is thrown into confusion when the robins are first placed in a steel strong room. The inference is that robins navigate by sensitivity to some electromagnetic vibration; the current hypothesis is that it originates in the Milky Way, but this is no more than a guess.

But even if this could be definitely proved, would it really constitute an 'explanation' of the homing instinct? We are dealing with degrees of sensitivity that are so far beyond our human perceptions that they are, to all intents and purposes, new senses. *Or rather, old senses.*

There must have been a time when human beings possessed a homing instinct of the same efficiency, for our primitive ancestors hunted their food in huge forests or featureless prairies. There is even more reason for supposing that man once possessed an unusually developed sense of impending danger, for our primate ancestors would otherwise have become extinct in the great droughts of the

Pliocene era, more than five million years ago, when they were struggling for survival against creatures in every way more 'specialised' than they were. Man no longer has a great deal of use for the homing instinct or a highly developed premonition of danger. These faculties have fallen into disuse. But they have not vanished. There seems to be evidence that in circumstances where they are necessary, they become as efficient as ever. Anyone who has read the various books by Jim Corbett, author of *Man-eaters of Kumaon*, will recall a number of occasions when he was saved by his 'sixth sense'.

One example will suffice. In *Jungle Lore*, Corbett describes how he was about to take a bath one evening when he noticed that his feet were covered with red dust. There was a place that lay on his route home where he might have walked through the dust; but he could think of no reason why he should have done so. Eventually he remembered the circumstances. He had walked over a culvert whose parapet was eighteen inches high. As he approached this, he had crossed the road to the other side, walking through the red dust at the side of the road. He crossed the culvert on the right-hand side, then re-crossed the road to the left again as he continued on his way home.

Corbett was baffled; he could not imagine why he had absent-mindedly crossed the road like this. The next day he retraced his footsteps. In the sandy bed of the culvert, on the left-hand side, he discovered the pug marks of a tiger that had been lying there. 'The tiger had no intention of killing me; but if at the moment of passing him I had stopped to listen to any jungle sound, or had coughed or sneezed or blown my nose, or had thrown my rifle from one shoulder to the other, there was a chance that the tiger would have got nervous and attacked me. My subconscious being was not prepared to take this risk and jungle sensitiveness came to my assistance and guided me away from the potential danger.'

How do we explain Corbett's jungle sensitiveness? As a 'sixth sense'? Or simply as some form of subconscious observation? I would argue that it makes no real difference. When Sherlock Holmes deduces that Watson has sent a telegram from the clay on his shoes and the ink stain on his finger, this is obviously what we mean by logical, scientific thinking. It is possible that Corbett's reasons for crossing the road were equally logical, although subconscious. An hour before he set out for home, he may have heard the tiger cough, and subconsciously registered the direction in which it was travelling. A few other small signs – the absence of birds near the culvert, a broken twig – and his subconscious mind was already reaching its conclusions in the best Holmes tradition. But if Corbett remained consciously unaware of all this, then we are dealing with a faculty that may be called a sixth sense, a subconscious faculty by comparison with which our powers of conscious observation are clumsy and inaccurate. We find this difficult to grasp because we use the conscious mind as an instrument of learning. Driving my car has become so natural to me that it might almost be called an instinct; but I had to learn to do it *consciously* first. But it would obviously be absurd to suppose that pigeons learned navigation by the sun in the same manner. There was no conscious process of learning; it was all done at the instinctive level.

We may be able to explain the pigeon's homing instinct in terms that Sherlock Holmes would understand; but it is important to realise that the subconscious mind works with a speed and accuracy beyond our conscious grasp, and that it may work upon data that are too subtle for our clumsy senses. How, for example, do we explain the power of water diviners? I have seen a man with a twig in his hand walking around the field in which our house is built, tracing the course of an underground spring, and distinguishing it clearly from a metal waterpipe. (We later consulted the plans of the house and found that he was completely accurate about the waterpipe.) He denied the suggestion that this was a 'supernormal' faculty, and insisted that he could teach anyone to divine water in less than an hour: 'Everyone possesses the faculty; it's merely a matter of training.' As far as I know, no scientist has ever attempted to explain the power of water diviners, although they are accepted as a commonplace in any country district. And when they *are* finally understood, it will no doubt prove to be something as simple and startling as the salmon's sense of smell, or the robin's sensitivity to stellar radiation. There is no need to draw a sharp distinction between scientific 'commonsense' and powers that would once have been classified as 'magical'. In the animal kingdom, 'magical' powers are commonplace. Civilised man has forgotten about them because they are no longer necessary to his survival.

In fact, his survival depends upon 'forgetting' them. High development of the instinctive levels is incompatible with the kind of concentration upon detail needed by civilised man. An illustration can be found in the autobiography of the 'clairvoyant' Pieter van der Hurk, better known as Peter Hurkos.* In 1943 Hurkos was working as a house painter when he fell from the ladder and fractured his skull. When he woke up – in the Zuidwal Hospital in the Hague – he discovered that he now possessed the gift of second sight; he 'knew' things about his fellow patients without being told. This almost cost him his life. Shaking hands with a patient about to be discharged, he suddenly 'knew' that the man was a British agent, and that he would be assassinated by the Gestapo in two days' time. As a result of his prediction, Hurkos came close to being executed as a traitor by the Dutch underground; he was fortunately able to convince them that his clairvoyance was genuine.

The chief drawback of this unusual power was that he was no longer able to return to his old job as a painter; *he had lost the faculty of concentration.* 'I could not concentrate on anything in those

---

* See *Psychic*, by Peter Hurkos (London, Barker, 1961).

days, for the moment I began to carry on an extended conversation with anyone, I would see visions of the various phases of his life and the lives of his family and friends.' His mind was like a radio set picking up too many stations. From the social point of view he was useless until he conceived the idea of using his peculiar powers on the stage.

Again, science has nothing to say about the powers of Peter Hurkos, or of his fellow Dutchman Gerard Croiset, although these powers have been tested in the laboratory and found to be genuine. Foretelling the future, or solving a murder case by handling a garment of the victim, is obviously a very different matter from Corbett's jungle sensitivity or the homing instinct. But it is worth bearing in mind that until the mid-1950s Schmidt's observations on eels – published as long ago as 1922 – were ignored by scientists because they failed to 'fit in'. Ardrey remarks that the Eel Story was classified with Hitler's Big Lie. That is, no one was willing to tackle the problem until science had reached a stage where it could no longer advance without taking it into account. No doubt the same thing will happen to the observations made on Hurkos by the Round Table Institute in Maine, and those on Croiset by the Parapsychology Institute of Utrecht University.

At this point it is necessary to say something of the course of evolution over the past million years or so. Some eleven million years ago, an ape called Ramapithecus seems to have developed the capacity to walk upright. He began to prefer the ground to the trees. And during the next nine million years, the tendency to walk upright became firmly established, and Ramapithecus turned into Australopithecus, our first 'human' ancestor. What difference did the upright posture make? First of all, it freed his hands, so that he could defend himself with a stone or a tree branch. Secondly, *it enlarged his horizon*.

As far as I know, no anthropologist has regarded this as significant

– perhaps because there are many taller creatures than man. But the elephant and the giraffe have eyes in the sides of their heads, so that their horizon is circular. The ape sees straight ahead; his vision is narrower but more concentrated. Could this be why the apes have evolved more than any other animal? Narrow vision makes for boredom; it also makes for increased mental activity, for curiosity. And when the inventiveness and curiosity were well developed, a certain branch of the apes learned to walk upright, so that his horizon was extended in another way. To see a long distance is to learn to think in terms of long distances, to calculate. Man's ability to walk upright and use his hands, and his natural capacity to see into the distance instead of looking at the ground, became weapons of survival. He developed intelligence because it was the only way to stay alive. And so, at the beginning of human evolution, man was forced to make a virtue of his ability to focus his attention upon minute particulars. No doubt he would have preferred to eat his dinner and then sleep in the sun, like the sabre-toothed tiger or the hippopotamus; but he was more defenceless than they were, and had to maintain constant vigilance.

In the course of time, this ability to 'focus' his attention and calculate became so natural that thinking became one of man's leisure activities. And it 'paid off' to an incredible extent. In a few thousand years, man evolved more than the great reptiles had evolved in several million. He created civilisation, and in doing so, entered a new phase of self-awareness – the phase that human children now enter at the age of six or seven.

Self-consciousness brings heavy losses and enormous gains. The greatest loss is that instinctive 'naturalness' that small children and animals possess. But the vital gain is the sense of force, of power, of control. Man became the wilful animal, the most dangerous animal on the earth, never contented to live in peace for long, always invading the neighbouring country, burning the villages and raping the women. And this endless ego-drive has, in the past ten thousand years, separated him further and further from the apes in their dwindling forests and the swallows that fly south in the winter.

He is not entirely happy with this civilisation that his peculiar powers have created. Its main trouble is that it takes so much looking after. Many men possess the animals' preference for the instinctive life of oneness with nature; they dream about the pleasure of being a shepherd drowsing on a warm hillside, or an angler beside a stream. Oddly enough, such men have never been condemned as sluggards; they are respected as poets, and the soldiers and businessmen enjoy reading their daydreams when the day's work is over.

A poet is simply a man in whom the links with our animal past are still strong. He is aware that we contain a set of instinctive powers that are quite separate from the powers needed to win a battle or expand a business.

And he is instinctively aware of something far more important. Man has developed his conscious powers simply by wanting to develop them. He has travelled from the invention of the wheel to the exploration of space in a few quick strides. But he had also surpassed the animals in another respect: in the development of those 'other' powers. No animal is capable of the ecstasies of the mystics or the great poets. In his nature poetry, Wordsworth is 'at one' with nature in a quite different sense from the hippopotamus dozing in the mud. *Self-consciousness can be used for the development of man's instinctive powers*, as well as those of the intellect. The poet, the mystic and the 'magician' have this in common: the desire to develop their powers 'downward' rather than upward. In the *Symposium*, Socrates expresses the ideal aim: to do both at the same time – to use increased knowledge to reach out towards a state of instinctive unity with the universe. In the two and a half thousand years since then, civilisation has been forced to devote its attention to more practical problems, while the artists and mystics have continued to protest that 'the world is too much with us', and that triumphant homo sapiens is little more than a clever dwarf. If man is really to evolve, then he must develop *depth*, and power over his own depths.

And now, for the first time in the short history of our species, a large percentage of the human race has the leisure to forget the practical problems. And in America and Europe, there is a simultaneous upsurge of interest in 'mind-changing drugs' and in the 'occult'.

The psychedelic cult differs from the drug cults of the early twentieth century, or even the laudanum drinking of De Quincey and Coleridge, in being more positive in character. It is less a matter of the desire to escape from a 'botched civilisation' than a definite desire to get somewhere, to 'plug in' to subconscious forces of whose existence we are instinctively certain. The same is true of the increased sexual permissiveness; it is not simply a matter of disintegrating morals, but the recognition that sexual excitement is a contact with the hidden powers of the unconscious. D. H. Lawrence describes Lady Chatterley's sensations after lovemaking: 'As she ran home in the twilight the world seemed a dream; the trees in the park seemed bulging and surging at anchor on a tide, and the heave of the slope to the house was alive.'

All Lawrence's work is concerned with the need for civilisation to take a new direction, to concentrate upon the development of these 'other' powers instead of continuing to develop the intellect. It is not a matter of sinking into a kind of trance, a passive state of 'oneness with nature', like the cows Walt Whitman admired so much. The nature of which Lady Chatterley is aware as she runs home sounds more like those late canvases of Van Gogh in which everything is distorted by some inner force – by Russell's 'breath of life, fierce and coming from far away, bringing into human life the vastness and fearful passionless force of non-human things'.

In the same way, Ouspensky's preference for reading a book

on magic instead of writing an article on the Hague Conference indicates something more positive than the poet's distaste for politics. At fourteen, Ouspensky is plunged into a state of ecstatic excitement by a book on physics, because it is a contact with the world of the impersonal. But science is a dead end for an imaginative youth; he doesn't want to end up injecting guinea pigs in Pavlov's laboratory. He has a feeling that all the *ways of life* offered by the modern world lead him in the opposite direction from the way he wants to go. In moments of depression he is inclined to wonder if this craving for distant horizons is not some odd illusion, 'the desire of the moth for the star'. But an instinct leads him to search persistently in books on magic and occultism; later, the same desire leads him to wander around in the East, searching in monasteries for 'esoteric knowledge'. (It is ironical that he should have discovered what he was looking for when he returned to Moscow and met Gurdjieff.*)

This sense of 'meanings' that are not apparent to ordinary consciousness is experienced by everyone at some time or another. One may ignore such hints for years, until some event brings them all into focus; or the 'focusing' may happen gradually and imperceptibly. Science declares that life began with the action of sunlight on carbon suspended in water, and that man has reached his present position by a process of natural selection. In that case, the laws of human existence are physical laws, and can be found in any textbook of science. But there occur moments of absurd certainty that seem to transcend the usual law of probability. Mark Bredin, a musician of my acquaintance, described how he came away from a rehearsal late at night and took a taxi home. He was very tired; there was little traffic about along the Bayswater Road. Suddenly, with total certainty, he knew that as they crossed Queensway, another taxi would shoot

* See Part Two, Chapter 8.

across the road and hit them. He was so certain that he was tempted to warn the driver, then decided that it would sound silly. A few seconds later, the other taxi rushed out of Queensway and hit them, as he had known it would. He attributes the flash of 'second sight' to extreme tiredness, when the conscious mind was relaxed and the subconscious could make itself heard.

We may reject the story as exaggeration, or explain it in terms of coincidence'. But the word 'coincidence' solves nothing. For again, everyone has noticed how often absurd coincidences occur. Some years ago, I made an attempt to keep notes of unlikely coincidences, and I find a typical example in my journal for January 1968. 'I was reading Hawkins's *Stonehenge Decoded*, the last section on the standing stones of Callanish, which Hawkins describes as a kind of Stone Age computer. I finished the book, and immediately picked up Bell's *Mathematics, Queen of the Sciences*. It opened at Chapter 6, and I found myself looking at a footnote on Stone Age mathematics. The chances against coming across it immediately after the piece on Callanish were probably a million to one. Again, last night I was reading an account of the Domenech murder case at Moher, in Galway, and noted that the victim had been at Mary Washington College in Fredericksburg, Virginia, where I had lectured recently. Ten minutes later I opened Wanda Orynski's abstracts of Hegel, and saw that the introduction is by Kurt Leidecker of Mary Washington College ... '

There is nothing very startling about these coincidences except the odds against them. I can add another one from the past week. An article in *The Criminologist* referred to a Nebraska murder case without mentioning the name of the murderer; I spent ten minutes searching through a pile of old *True Detective* magazines because I could recall that the man whose name I was trying to remember (Charles Starkweather) was featured on the cover of one of them. I took the magazine back to my armchair and finished the article in *The Criminologist*. It ended with a reference to a murderess named

Nannie Doss, of whom I had never heard. I opened the *True Detective* magazine half an hour later, and discovered that the first article was on Nannie Doss. Oddly enough, as I looked at her photograph, and a caption mentioning the word 'Nannie', I experienced a sudden sense of total certainty that this was the woman I had been wondering about, although it took a few seconds longer to locate her surname in the text.

Similar coincidences are described in a remarkable book, *The Cathars and Reincarnation*, by Arthur Guirdham (which I shall discuss in detail later).* He describes how, one day in 1963, he began to discuss a village called Little Gaddesden, and tried to recall the name of a pub there. Later the same day, he took a book on the Pyrenees out of the public library, and on starting to read it at home, almost immediately came across the name of Little Gaddesden and the pub whose name he wanted to recall. The coincidence – one of several – occurred at the beginning of his strange involvement with a patient whose memories of a previous existence constitute one of the best-authenticated cases of reincarnation that I have come across. (See Part Three, Chapter 2.)

To suggest that such matters are not entirely coincidence is not to suggest that 'hidden forces' were trying to draw my attention to Stone Age mathematics or Guirdham's to the name of a pub. Probably all that is at work is some 'vital sense' of the same order as the eel's homing instinct. The more the mind is absorbed, interested in a subject, the more frequently these useful coincidences seem to occur, as if the healthy mind has a kind of radar system. Distraction or depression will prevent the radar from working, or may prevent one paying attention until too late. The following is from a recent account of a murder case, written by the father of the victim:

It was a squally day of cold-front weather with alternations of

* London, Neville Spearman, 1970.

bright sunshine and sudden rain or hailstorms. My wife and I were at the front of the house, in between the rain squalls, with two painters who were attempting to make some progress on the eaves and window frames. It was necessary to trim down a hedge outside one of the rooms ... At 4 p.m. my wife said: 'Where's Fiona?' Irrationally and unaccountably, we both felt an excess of acute anxiety and fear ...

Until the child was mentioned, both parents were preoccupied with other things, and the alarm signals of the unconscious were unobserved; then, with the question 'Where's Fiona?' they sound clearly, like a telephone that cannot be heard until the television is turned down. The child had been the victim of a sex killer.*

My own experience of 'premonitions' has not been extensive; in fact, I can call only one to mind. On July 16, 1964, an ordinary palmist at a fairground in Blackpool looked at my hand, and warned me that I would have an accident over the next month; she said it would probably be a car accident, and I would not be badly hurt. In mid-August 1964 I decided to take a guest out in a speedboat, although I had a strong premonition of danger. The sea proved far rougher than expected, and when I attempted to land on a rocky beach, a huge wave picked up the boat and dashed it on the rocks, completely wrecking it. No one was hurt, although we spent a bad half hour dragging the badly holed boat out of the heavy sea.

I have had two experiences of apparently telepathic response to another person. My first wife and I had been separated for some months in the summer of 1953, although there were still strong emotional links. One evening, in a cafe in central London, I suddenly felt sick, and had to rush out. I continued vomiting for several hours – in fact, until the early hours of the next morning. A doctor in the

* 'Murder: A Father's Story', by Michael Whitaker, *The Sunday Times*, March 29, 1970.

hospital where I was then working diagnosed the trouble as food poisoning, although I had eaten the same food as the other porters, and they were all well enough. I learned a few days later, however, that my wife *had* been suffering from food poisoning – from a bad tin of corned beef – at the time I was sick; her retching had begun and ended at exactly the same time as mine.

In 1965 I had lectured at St. Andrews University in Scotland, and was driving to Skye. I was feeling particularly cheerful when I set out because the weather was fine, and I was looking forward to stopping at a secondhand bookshop in Perth. But within half an hour of leaving St. Andrews, I began to feel unaccountably depressed. Half an hour later, I asked my wife why she was subdued: she explained that she had had a toothache ever since we left St. Andrews.

It was unfortunately a Saturday, too late to find a dentist in Scotland. On Sunday morning, the gum was now badly swollen. My own depression continued all day. In Kyle of Lochalsh, on Monday morning, we were told that a travelling dentist would arrive at a caravan sometime during the day; I left my wife waiting while I took my daughter for a walk round the town. Suddenly the feeling of oppression lifted. I said, 'Mummy's just had her tooth out.' We arrived back in time to meet my wife coming out of the caravan, minus an impacted wisdom tooth.

When my children were babies, I quickly became aware of the existence of telepathic links. If I wanted my daughter to sleep through the night, I had to take care that I didn't lie awake thinking about her. If I did, she woke up. In the case of my son, I had to avoid even looking at him if he was asleep in his pram. When my wife asked me to see if he was still asleep, in the garden or porch, I would tiptoe to the window, glance out very quickly, then turn away. If I lingered, peering at him, he would stir and wake up. This happened so unvaryingly during his first year that I came to accept it as natural. After the first year, the telepathic links seemed to snap, or at least, to weaken. But when they began to learn to speak, I observed that this was again a delicate and intuitive business – not at all a matter of trial and error, of learning 'object words' and building them up into sentences, but something as complex as the faculty with which birds build nests.* And again there was a feeling perhaps illusory – that the child could pick up and echo my own thoughts, or at least respond to them when attempting to express something.

But, among adults at least, thought-transference must be less usual than feeling-transference. And both of them seem to depend upon the right conditions, a certain stillness and sensitivity. On a still day you can sometimes hear the voices of people miles away

In the above-mentioned experiences of telepathy – if that is what it was – the 'transference' was unconscious and automatic, like the crossing of telephone lines. This gives rise to the speculation whether hatred might be transmitted in the same unconscious manner. My own experience of this has been a doubtful one, and I mention it here only for the sake of completeness. I found myself thinking about it seriously when I read the following in Wilson Knight's book on John Cowper Powys: 'Those who have incurred his anger have so invariably suffered misfortune that he has, as it were, been *forced* into a life of almost neurotic benevolence ... Powys's early ambition to become a magician was no idle dream.' (p. 62)

Before moving to Kensington in the autumn of 1952, my wife and I had lived in Wimbledon, in the house of an old man who suffered from asthma; my wife was his nurse. During the six months we lived in the house, he became increasingly querulous and difficult, until there was a perpetual atmosphere of tension like an impending thunderstorm. I am not given to nursing grudges, but the feeling of being steeped in pettiness, of being prevented from concentrating

---

* A closely similar view of child learning is held by Noam Chomsky, the linguistic philosopher.

on more important things, produced climaxes of loathing in which I wished him dead. In August we returned from a week's holiday to find that he had died of a heart attack.

It was when the situation repeated itself three months later that I found myself speculating idly whether thoughts can kill. The landlady was insanely suspicious, and violent scenes soon became a daily occurrence. Two months later, she visited a doctor, who diagnosed a cancer of the womb. She died shortly after we left the house. I now recalled the peculiar nature of those paroxysms of loathing. On certain occasions, the anger had increased to a pitch that in a paranoid individual would lead to an explosion of violence. But the explosion would be purely mental: a burst of rage and hatred, followed by relief, as if I had thrown a brick through a plate-glass window.

These mental explosions always had a peculiar feeling of authenticity, of reality. By this I mean they seemed somehow different from paroxysms of feeling induced by imagination. I cannot be more specific than this, but I suspect that most people have experienced the sensation.

In his *Autobiography*, Powys writes: 'The evidence of this – of my being able; I mean, and quite unconsciously too, to exercise some kind of "evil eye" on people who have injured me – has so piled up all my life that it has become a habit with me to pray to my gods anxiously and hurriedly for each new enemy.' (p. 480)

The case of Powys is interesting because of the peculiar nature of his genius. Until he was in his mid-fifties, Powys spent much of his life lecturing in America, and three novels written in his early forties are interesting without being remarkable. Then, in his sixties, there appeared a series of immense novels – in bulk and in conception – beginning with *Wolf Solent* and *A Glastonbury Romance*. The most remarkable thing about these novels is their 'nature mysticism' and their incredible vitality; it is clear that he has tapped some subconscious spring, and the result is a creative outpouring that has something of the majesty of Niagara Falls. *A Glastonbury Romance* (1933) is probably unique in being the only novel written from a 'Cod's-eye' point of view. The simplest way of illustrating this is to quote its first paragraph:

> At the striking of noon on a certain fifth of March there occurred within a causal radius of Brandon railway-station and yet beyond the deepest pools of emptiness between the uttermost stellar systems one of those infinitesimal ripples in the creative silence of the First Cause which always occur when an exceptional stir of heightened consciousness agitates any living organism in the astronomical universe. Something passed at that moment, a wave, a motion, a vibration, too tenuous to be called magnetic, too subliminal to be called spiritual, between the soul of a particular human being who was emerging from a third-class carriage of the twelve-nineteen train from London and the divine-diabolic soul of the First Cause of all life.

The abstractness of the language here gives a false impression of a book that is anything but abstract; but it also reveals Powys's desire to see his characters and events from some 'universal' point of view in which the algae in a stagnant pond and the grubs in a rotten tree are as important as the human characters.

One should note the presupposition of this first paragraph, which is present in all Powys's work: that there is a kind of 'psychic ether' that carries mental vibrations as the 'luminiferous ether' is supposed to carry light.

This I would define as the fundamental proposition of magic or occultism, and perhaps the only essential one. It will be taken for granted throughout this book.

What is so interesting about Powys is that he deliberately set out to cultivate 'multi-mindedness', to pass out of his own identity into that of people or even objects: 'I could feel myself in to the lonely identity of a pier-post, of a tree-stump, of a monolith in a stone-circle; and when I did this, I looked like this post, this stump, this stone' (*Autobiography*, p. 528).

It was an attempt to soothe his mind into a state of quiescent identity with the 'psychic ether', with the vast objective world that surrounds us. Everyone has had the experience of feeling sick, and then *thinking about something else* and feeling the sickness vanish. 'Objectivity' causes power to flow into the soul, a surge of strength, and contact with the vast, strange forces that surround us. In a famous passage in *The Prelude*, Wordsworth describes a midnight boating excursion when a huge peak made a deep impression on his mind, and how for days afterwards:

> ... *my brain*
> *Worked with a dim and undetermined sense*
> *Of unknown modes of being; o'er my thoughts*
> *There hung a darkness, call it solitude*
> *Or blank desertion, No familiar shapes*
> *Remained, no pleasant images of trees,*
> *Of sea or sky, no colours of green fields;*
> *But huge and mighty forms, that do not live*
> *Like living men, moved slowly through the mind*
> *By day, and were a trouble to my dreams.* (Book 1)

Wordsworth, like Powys, had acquired the ability to pass beyond his own personality and achieve direct contact with the 'psychic ether', But as he grew older, he lost this ability to transcend his personality and the poetry loses its greatness. Powys never lost his power of summoning a strange ecstasy. In the *Autobiography* he describes how, lecturing on Strindberg in an almost empty theatre in San Francisco, there stirred within him:

> ... that formidable daimon which, as I have hinted to you
> before, *can* be reached somewhere in my nature, and which

when it *is* reached has the Devil's own force … I became aware, more vividly aware than I had ever been, that the secret of life consists in sharing the madness of God. By sharing the madness of God, I mean the power of rousing a peculiar exultation in yourself as you confront the Inanimate, an exultation which is really a cosmic eroticism … (p. 531)

And again, in the Roman amphitheatre in Verona:

Alone in that Roman circle, under those clouds from which no drop of rain fell, the thaumaturgic element in my nature rose to such a pitch that I felt, as I have only done once or twice since, that I really *was* endowed with some sort of supernatural power … I felt it again, only five years ago, when I visited Stonehenge … The feeling that comes over me at such times is one of most formidable power … (p. 403)

There is reason to believe that Powys did not understand the mechanisms of this power. A strange story was related of Powys and his friend Theodore Dreiser:

Dreiser said that when he was living in New York, on West Fifty-seventh Street, John Cowper Powys came occasionally to dinner. At that time Powys was living in this country, in a little town about thirty miles up the Hudson, and he usually left Dreiser's place fairly early to catch a train to take him home. One evening, after a rather long after-dinner conversation, Powys looked at his watch and said hurriedly that he had no idea it was so late, and he would have to go at once or miss his train. Dreiser helped him on with his overcoat, and Powys, on his way to the door, said, 'I'll appear before you, right here, later this evening. You'll see me.'

'Are you going to turn yourself into a ghost, or have you a key to the door?' Dreiser laughed when he asked that question, for he did not believe for an instant that Powys meant to be taken seriously.

'I don't know,' said Powys. 'I may return as a spirit or in some other astral form.'

Dreiser said that there had been no discussion whatever during the evening, of spirits, ghosts or visions. The talk had been mainly about American publishers and their methods. He said that he gave no further thought to Powys's promise to reappear, but he sat up reading for about two hours, all alone. Then he looked up from his book and saw Powys standing in the doorway between the entrance hall and the living room. The apparition had Powys's features, his tall stature, loose tweed garments and general appearance, but a pale white glow shone from the figure. Dreiser rose at once, and strode towards the ghost, or whatever it was, saying, 'Well, you've kept your word, John. You're here. Come on in and tell me how you did it.' The apparition did not reply, and it vanished when Dreiser was within three feet of it.

As soon as he had recovered somewhat from his astonishment Dreiser picked up the telephone and called John Cowper Powys's house in the country. Powys came to the phone, and Dreiser recognised his voice. After he had heard the story of the apparition, Powys said, 'I told you I'd be there, and you oughtn't to be surprised.' Dreiser told me that he was never able to get any explanation from Powys, who refused to discuss the matter from any standpoint.*

Why should Powys refuse to discuss it from any standpoint? *Because he had no idea of how he had done it* and could not describe the process. It depended on the nature of the psychic link between himself and

* W. E. Woodward. *The Gift of Life* (New York, Dutton, 1947). Quoted by Professor Wilson Knight in *The Saturnian Quest*, p. 128.

Dreiser: 'I used to be aware ... of surging waves of magnetic attraction between Dreiser and myself ... which seem super-chemical and due to the diffusion of some mysterious occult force ...' The appearance was probably in Dreiser's own mind; another person in the room would not have seen it.

It may sound contradictory to say that Powys had no idea of how he had projected his 'apparition'; but it is not. For we are now concerned with the fundamental question of *conscious* control of the subconscious mind. All my physical functions, from digestion to excretion, are controlled by my subconscious depths. If I am of a nervous disposition, I may find it impossible to urinate in a public lavatory with other people standing near; no amount of conscious effort can destroy the inhibition; I need to relax and let my subconscious do the work. Stendhal suffered from an embarrassing sexual disorder which he called *le fiasco*. Whenever his sexual excitement reached the point at which he was prepared to make love, he would experience an embarrassing collapse of the ability to do so. No amount of conscious desire to oblige his disappointed partner could make any difference. If I try to remember a name I have forgotten, I again rely on my subconscious to 'throw it up', although in this case I may be able to dispense with its help: I may look up the name in my address book, or get at it by some trick of association of ideas.

There is no reason why a man should not learn the basic 'tricks' of telepathy, or even 'astral projection', as he might train his memory to greater efficiency or get rid of urinary inhibition by auto-suggestion. He would still not be able to explain it, even to his closest friend.

Serious emotional upset can also stimulate the 'psychic faculties'. The case of the playwright Strindberg provides an interesting example. The break-up of his second marriage precipitated an emotional crisis in which he came close to insanity. He suffered delusions of persecution, all of which are described at length in his autobiographical volume *Inferno*. The result was an *unlooked-for* development of psychic powers that parallels the case of Peter Hurkos. In *Legends*, he describes an involuntary astral projection:

> [In the autumn of 1895] I was passing through a dangerous illness in the French capital, when the longing to be in the bosom of my family overcame me to such a degree that I saw the inside of my house and for a moment forgot my surroundings, having lost the consciousness of where I was. I was really there behind the piano as I appeared, and the imagination of the old lady had nothing to do with the matter. But since she understood these kind of apparitions, and knew their significance, she saw in it a precursor of death, and wrote to ask if I were ill. (1912 edition, p. 86)

What is so interesting about this brief account is that Strindberg's power of astral projection was connected with the imagination. He clearly imagined the room in which his mother-in-law was sitting, playing the piano, and the intensity of his imaginative vision somehow 'projected' him into the real room. He had used the 'psychic ether' as he might have used a telephone or closed-circuit television.

In the same volume he describes an event that may have even deeper significance. In the early hours of the morning, in a period of emotional strain he was sitting in a wine shop, trying to persuade a young friend not to give up his military career for that of an artist.

> After arguments and endless appeals, I wished to call up in his memory a past event that might have influenced his resolve. He had forgotten the occurrence in question, and in order to stimulate his memory, I began to describe it to him: 'You remember that evening in the Augustiner tavern.' I continued to describe the table where we had eaten our meal, the position of the bar, the door through which people entered, the furniture, the pictures ... All of a sudden, I stopped. I had half lost consciousness without fainting, and still sat in my chair. I was

in the Augustiner tavern, and had forgotten to whom I spoke, when I recommenced as follows: 'Wait a minute. I am now in the Augustiner tavern, but I know very well that I am in some other place. Don't say anything ... I don't know you anymore, yet I know that I do. Where am I? Don't say anything. This is interesting.' I made an effort to raise my eyes – I don't know if they were closed – and I saw a cloud, a background of indistinct colour, and from the ceiling descended something like a theatre curtain; it was the dividing wall with shelves and bottles.

'Oh yes!' I said, after feeling a pang pass through me. 'I am in F's wine shop.'

The officer's face was distorted with alarm, and he wept.

'What is the matter?' I said to him.

'That was dreadful,' he answered. (pp. 92–93)

We may, of course, dismiss the whole thing as Strindberg's imagination, excited by emotional stress. On the other hand, this event is consistent with the theory of 'psychic faculties' that I have tried to outline, and has the ring of truth. (Strindberg is a remarkably honest man, in spite of his neuroses, as the reader discovers when it is possible to check his version of events against someone else's.) Again, he was exhausted – physically and emotionally. He was pushing himself to his limits as he exerted his powers of persuasion. And, as he remarks in the same book: 'In the great crises of life, when existence itself is threatened, the soul attains transcendent powers.'

One of the most interesting and consistent accounts of these powers is to be found in a book called *Psychic Self Defence* (1930), by 'Dion Fortune', a Freudian psychologist whose real name was Violet Firth. At the age of twenty (in 1911) she was working in a school, under a domineering principal, who took a dislike to her, and (so Violet Firth believed) directed a stream of psychic malevolence at her, using yogic and hypnotic techniques. The result was traumatic, a feeling of bewilderment and misery greater than would be caused by an actual physical attack. A need for self-analysis led her to study psychology (on which she wrote a number of books); later, she came to feel that even the theories of Freud and Jung fail to do justice to the complexity of the human mind, and became a student of occultism. (She had always possessed some degree of mediumistic powers.) She joined the Order of the Golden Dawn (a magical society that will be discussed in the second part of this book), and had further psychic clashes with Mrs. Mathers, the wife of its founder. As a result of these alarming experiences,* she came to believe that the human mind can repel the hostile psychic forces that emanate (often unconsciously) from malevolent people. Even more interesting is the implication that a healthy and optimistic mind repels ordinary misfortune, and that 'accident proneness' or general bad luck are the result of a psyche made vulnerable by defeat or stagnation.

And at this point, I must outline my own basic theory of these powers of the mind.

In Johnson's *Rasselas, Prince of Abyssinia*, there is a scene in which the hero looks at the peaceful pastoral scenery of the Happy Valley where he lives, and wonders why he cannot be happy like the sheep and cows. He reflects gloomily: 'I can discover within me no power of perception that is not glutted with its proper pleasure, yet I do not feel myself delighted. *Man has surely some latent sense for which this place affords no gratification*, or he has some desires distinct from sense which must be satisfied before he can be happy.' (Chapter 2)

The italics are my own. The 'latent sense' is man's evolutionary appetite, the desire to make contact with reality. But that is not all. Who has not experienced this strange frustration that comes in moments of pleasure and fulfilment? As a child, I had this feeling about water. If my parents took me on a bus excursion, I used to

---

* See Part Three, Chapter 3.

crane out of the window every time we went over a bridge; something about large sheets of water excited a painful desire that I found incomprehensible. For if I actually approached the water, what could I *do* to satisfy this feeling? Drink it? Swim in it? So when I first read the passage from *Rasselas*, I understood immediately what Johnson meant by 'some latent sense ... or desires *distinct from sense* which must be satisfied before he can be happy'.

I labelled this 'latent sense' Faculty X. And I came to see that Faculty X has something to do with 'reality'. In *Swann's Way* Proust describes how he tasted a madeleine dipped in tea, and was suddenly reminded of his childhood in Combray – reminded with such an intensity that for a moment he was actually there. 'An exquisite pleasure had invaded my senses ... And at once the vicissitudes of life had become indifferent to me, its disasters innocuous, its brevity illusory ... I had now ceased to feel mediocre, accidental, mortal ...'

Five minutes earlier, he could have said, 'Yes, I was a child in Combray,' and no doubt described it in detail; but the madeleine suddenly meant that he could say it *and mean it*. Chesterton says, 'We say thank you when someone passes us the salt. but we don't mean it. We say the earth is round, but we don't mean it, even though it's true.' We say something and mean it only when Faculty X is awake, that painful reaching-beyond-the-senses. Faculty X is the key to all poetic and mystical experience; when it awakens, life suddenly takes on a new, poignant quality. Faust is about to commit suicide in weariness and despair when he hears the Easter Bells; they bring back his childhood, and suddenly Faculty X is awake, and he knows that suicide is the ultimate laughable absurdity.

Faculty X is simply that latent power that human beings possess *to reach beyond the present*. After all, we know perfectly well that the past is as real as the present, and that New York and Singapore and Lhasa and Stepney Green are all as real as this place I happen to be in at the moment. *Yet my senses do not agree.* They assure me that this place, here and now, is far more real than any other place or any other time. Only in certain moments of great inner intensity do I know this to be a lie. Faculty X is a sense of reality, the reality of other places and other times, and it is the possession of it – fragmentary and uncertain though it is – that distinguishes man from all other animals.

But if the oppressive reality of this place and time is an illusion, so is my sense of being uniquely here, now. 'I am not here; neither am I elsewhere,' says Krishna in the Bhagavad Gita. So that if Faculty X can make Strindberg clearly aware of the reality of a place several hundreds of miles away, is it not conceivable that it might 'transport' him there in another sense?

It would be a mistake to think of Faculty X as an 'occult' faculty. It is not; it is the power to grasp reality, and it unites the two halves of man's mind, conscious and subconscious.

Think: what happens if a piece of music or a smell of woodsmoke suddenly reminds me of something that happened ten years ago? It is like touching the leg of a dead frog with an electric wire. My mind convulses and contracts, suddenly grasping the *reality* of that past time as though it were the present. The same thing happens to Marcel in Proust's novel *Swann's Way* when he tastes a madeleine dipped in tea – his past floods back as a reality. What happens is that our normally lazy and diffused consciousness *focuses*, as I might clench my fist. The tune or smell only provides the stimulus; my inner strength does the rest – *an inner strength of which I am normally unaware.*

A few years ago, psychologists performed a classic experiment with a cat. A wire was connected to the nerve between the cat's ear and its brain, and the other end of the wire was connected to a dial for measuring electrical impulses. When a loud noise sounded near the cat's ear, the needle of the dial swung over violently. Then a cage of mice was placed in front of the cat. It watched them intently. The same loud noise was sounded close to its ear. But the needle did not stir. The cat was so intent on the mice that it ignored the sound – and somehow it 'switched off' the physical impulse between the ear and the brain. *It chose to focus on something else.*

All living creatures have this power to 'focus' on something that interests them, and 'switch off' everything else. Someone accustomed to a modern city probably cuts out as much as 99 per cent of the stimuli that fall on the senses. We all know about this. But what we have not yet grasped is the extraordinary power we possess in being able to focus upon particular aspects of reality. This power *is* Faculty X, but at the moment, we hardly make use of it, unaware of its potentialities.

It is worth asking the question: What is consciousness *for*? When you are deeply asleep, you have no consciousness. When you are very tired, your consciousness is like a dim light that hardly illuminates anything. When you are wide awake and excited, consciousness seems to increase in sheer candle-power. Its purpose is to illuminate reality, to reach out into its recesses, and thus to enable us to act upon it and transform it. It is obvious that our basic aim should be to increase its candle-power. When it is low, reality becomes 'unreal'; as it becomes stronger, reality becomes 'realler': Faculty X.

One of the clearest examples of the working of Faculty X can be found in the tenth volume of Arnold Toynbee's *Study of History*, in which he explains how he came to write that work. He speaks of the sense of 'reality' that suddenly comes to historians: 'The writer of the present Study had an authentic minor personal experience of the kind on the 23rd May, 1912, as he sat musing on the summit of the citadel of Mistra, with the sheer wall of Mount Taygetus bounding his horizon in the western quarter of the compass, towards which he was bound, and the open vale of Sparta stretching away in the opposite eastern quarter, from which he had made his way that morning ...'

'The sensuous experience that activated his historical imagination was not a sound of liturgical chanting; it was the sight of the ruins among which he had wound his way upwards to the peak; and this spectacle had been appalling, for in this shattered fairy city Time had stood still since that spring of A.D. 1821 in which Mistra had been laid desolate ... One April morning, out of the blue, the avalanche of wild highlanders from the Mani had overwhelmed her; her citizens had been forced to flee for their lives and had been despoiled and massacred as they fled; her deserted mansions had been sacked; and her ruins had been left desolate from that day to this ...'

What struck Toynbee on this occasion was not simply the question of 'the cruel riddle of Mankind's crimes and follies', but the total *reality* of the scene conjured up by his imagination. He mentions half a dozen other experiences in which there was this same hallucinatory effect of reality. Reading how one of the proscribed leaders of the Italian Confederacy was refused help by his wife, and committed suicide in front of her eyes, he was 'transported, in a flash, across the gulf of Time and Space from Oxford in A.D. 1911 to Teanum in 80 B.C., to find himself in a back yard on a dark night witnessing a personal tragedy ...' He records similar experiences – all very brief – when reading Bernal Diaz describing the Spaniards' first sight of Tenochtitlan, Villehardouin describing his first sight of Constantinople during the Crusades, a Greek soldier describing how he tried to save a girl from rape. And finally, an experience in which the dividing line between Faculty X and mystical experience becomes blurred:

> On each of the six occasions just recorded, the writer had been rapt into a momentary communion with the actors in a particular historic event through the effect upon his imagination of a sudden arresting view of the scene ... But there was another occasion on which he had been vouchsafed a larger and a stranger experience. In London in the southern section of the Buckingham Palace Road, walking southward

along the pavement skirting the west wall of Victoria Station, the writer once, one afternoon not long after the date of the First World War ... had found himself in communion, not just with this or that episode in History, but with all that had been, and was, and was to come. In that instant he was directly aware of the passage of History gently flowing through him in a mighty current, and of his own life welling like a wave in the flow of this vast tide. The experience lasted long enough for him to take visual note of the Edwardian red brick surface and white stone facings of the station wall gliding past on his left, and to wonder – half amazed and half amused – why this incongruously prosaic scene should have been the physical setting of a mental illumination. An instant later, the communion had ceased, and the dreamer was back again in the everyday cockney world which was his native social milieu ...*

These pages of Toynbee are among the clearest descriptions of the operation of Faculty X that exist, and they underline the point I have tried to make. When I am half asleep, my sense of reality is restricted to myself and my immediate surroundings. The more awake I am, the further it stretches. But what we call 'waking consciousness' is not usually a great deal better than sleep. We are still wrapped in a passive, sluggish daydream. But this is not because there is some natural limit to consciousness, but only because we remain unaware that it can be stretched. We are like dogs who think they are on a chain when in fact they are free.

Faculty X is not a 'sixth sense', but an ordinary potentiality of consciousness. And it should be clear from what I have written above that it is the key not only to so called occult experience, but to the whole future evolution of the human race.

* *A Study of History* (Oxford, 1954.), Vol. X, pp. 130–140.

TWO
THE DARK SIDE OF THE MOON

In the autumn of 1969 I discussed questions of the occult with the poet Robert Graves at his home in Majorca. Graves immediately made a remark that startled me. 'Occult powers are not so rare. One person in every twenty possesses them in some form.'

What interested me so much was the exact figure: 5 per cent. This is also the figure for the 'dominant minority' among human beings. In the early years of this century, Bernard Shaw asked the explorer Henry Stanley how many of his men could take over leadership of the party if he, Stanley, were ill. 'One in twenty,' said Stanley. 'Is that figure exact or approximate?' 'Exact.'

The matter of the dominant 5 per cent was rediscovered during the Korean War by the Chinese. Wishing to economise on man-power, they decided to divide their American prisoners into two groups: the enterprising ones and the passive ones. They soon discovered that the enterprising soldiers were exactly one in twenty: 5 per cent. When this dominant 5 per cent was removed from the rest of the group, the others could be left with almost no guard at all.

Evidence from zoology indicates that the 'dominant 5 per cent' may apply to *all* animals.

The interesting question arises: How far is the biologically dominant 5 per cent the same thing as Graves's 'occult 5 per cent'? There are certainly many reasons for assuming that the two groups are identical. In primitive societies the leaders are also priests and magicians. The men who led hunting parties would again be those who possessed a high degree of 'jungle sensitivity'. What is the power that distinguishes the leader? It is the power to focus, to concentrate the will in emergencies. That is to say, it is a form of Faculty X.

In short, it seems probable that all human beings possess the vestiges of 'occult powers', the powers that spring from their deeper levels of vitality, what the playwright Granville-Barker called 'the secret life'. The dominant 5 per cent are more adept at canalising these powers than most people. The magicians, witch doctors, witches and mediums have been those members of the dominant 5 per cent who have developed their natural powers.

Another interesting sidelight on this matter is shed by recent researches into deep-trance hypnotism, some of which are described in *Mind and Body* by Dr. Stephen Black.* Dr. Black points out that most people can be hypnotised if they co-operate – an un-hypnotisable person would probably be mentally sick – but only a small number of people are 'deep-trance subjects'. Strangely enough, the exact figure is 5 per cent. Deep-trance subjects can be cured of a surprising number of physical ailments by hypnotic suggestion – from asthma to warts. Even 'medium-trance subjects' can be hypnotised into not reacting to a skin test for tuberculosis that would normally cause a raised swelling. Patients who suffered from multiple warts were cured in two stages, one side at a time, to make sure that the warts had not disappeared of their own accord. Warts are believed to be due to a virus infection; yet they vanished without scarring in periods ranging from five weeks to three months.†

Dr. Black's experiments were less concerned with curing specific ailments than with demonstrating that the body can be affected by the mind to an unusual degree; and in this they were remarkably successful. What is at issue, here again, is the hidden power of the subconscious mind, that can be reached and utilised by 'deep hypnosis' in 5 per cent of people. Five per cent of people are capable – potentially at least – of tapping the hidden powers of 'the secret life'.

* London, William Kimber, 1969.
† See article by Sinclair and Gieben in *The Lancet*, October 1959, p. 481.

Graves's concern is less with witches or mystics* than with poets, and his important book *The White Goddess* contains a theory of the nature of poetry that links it not only with the powers of the subconscious, but with traditional magical cults.

According to Graves, there are two forms of poetry: 'muse poetry' and 'Apollonian poetry'. The first is created by 'inspiration, checked by commonsense'; the second with the intellect. He associates 'muse poetry' with the White Goddess of primitive lunar cults. Science, like Apollonian poetry, is an attempt 'to banish all lunar superstitions and bask in the light of pure solar reason'.

Graves's account of the genesis of *The White Goddess* is a remarkable example of what he means by poetic intuition:

The enlightenment began one morning while I was re-reading Lady Charlotte Guest's translation of *The Mabinogion*, a book of ancient Welsh legends, and came across a hitherto despised minstrel poem called *The Song of Taliesin*. I suddenly knew (don't ask me how) that the lines of the poem, which has always been dismissed as deliberate nonsense, formed a series of early medieval riddles, and that I knew the answer to them all – although I was neither a Welsh scholar, nor a medievalist, and although many of the lines had been deliberately transposed by the author (or his successors) for security reasons.

I knew also (don't ask me how) that the answer must in some way be linked with an ancient Welsh poetic tradition of a 'Battle of Trees' – mentioned in Lady Charlotte Guest's notes to *The Mabinogion* – which was occasioned by a lapwing, a dog and a white roebuck from the other world, and won by a certain god who guessed the name of his divine opponent

---

* 'Now I am no mystic: I studiously avoid witchcraft, spiritualism, yoga, fortune telling, automatic writing, and so on' (*Five Pens in Hand*, New York, Doubleday, 1958, p. 58).

to be Vron, or 'Alder'. Nobody had ever tried to explain this nonsense. Further, that both these texts would make sense only in the light of ancient Irish religious and poetic tradition. I am not an Irish scholar either.

Since there has never been any lunatic streak in my family, I could not believe I was going crazy. More likely, I was being inspired. So I decided to check up on the subject with the help of a shelf-full of learned books on Celtic literature which I found in my father's library (mainly inherited from my grandfather, an Irish antiquarian) but which I had never read.

To cut a long story short, my answer to the riddle, namely the letter-names of an ancient Druidic alphabet, fitted the not-so-nonsensical *Song of Taliesin* with almost frightening exactitude; and *The Battle of the Trees* proved to be a not-so-nonsensical way of describing a struggle between rival priesthoods in Celtic Britain for the control of the national learning. You see, I had found out that the word '*trees*' means 'learning' in all the Celtic languages; and since the alphabet is the basis of all learning, and since (as I remembered from Julius Caesar's *Gallic Wars*) the Druidic alphabet was a jealously guarded secret in Gaul and Britain – indeed, its eighteen letter-names were not divulged for nearly a thousand years – well, the possession of the secret must have been something worth struggling about. I had also found out that the alphabet in Caesar's day was called the *Boibel-Loth* because it began with the letters B.L.; and that as a result of the Battle of the Trees, the *Boibel-Loth* had displaced an earlier, very similar, and equally secret Celtic alphabet, the *Beth-Luis-Nion*, whose eighteen letters were explained as references to a sequence of wild trees – induding the Alder. This sequence, I found, served a dual purpose: as an alphabet and as a sacred calendar – the tree consonants standing for the months of which their trees were characteristic; the tree vowels standing for the stations of the Sun, its equinoxes and solstices. It is a calendar which can be proved, by study of the festal use of trees throughout Europe, to have been observed in the Bronze Age (and earlier) from Palestine to Ireland, and to have been associated everywhere with the worship of the pre-Aryan Triple Moon-goddess, sometimes called Leucothea, the White Goddess.*

What Graves came to discover, through research and a series of strange coincidences, was that the Triple Moon-goddess was a universal symbol in pre-Christian poetry and mythology: Greek, Phoenician, Celtic, Roman, Scandinavian, Hindu, even African.

'The most important single fact in the early history of Western religion and sociology was undoubtedly the gradual suppression of the Lunar Mother-goddess's inspiratory cult, and its supersession ... by the busy, rational cult of the Solar God Apollo, who rejected the Orphic tree-alphabet in favour of the commercial Phoenician alphabet – the familiar ABC – and initiated European literature and science.'

The moon goddess was the goddess of magic, of the subconscious, of poetic inspiration. Human mythology has been 'solarised' and then, in the West, Christianised, and the masculine god of reason has usurped an increasingly important place, armed always with the irresistible argument that you can see a thing more clearly by sunlight than by moonlight. But this is untrue. On the contrary, *certain things become invisible in a strong light.* Highly conscious, rational modes of thought are like a wide net through which all the smaller fish escape.

Graves describes how the obsessions with the White Goddess and her sacred tree, the alder, came upon him in 1944, when he was writing a novel about Jason and the Argonauts. On his desk at the

* Lecture on *The White Goddess, Five Pens in Hand*, p. 54.

time was a small brass box with a curious design on the lid. On this box he kept a brass figure of a hump-backed man playing a flute. Ten years later he discovered that the design on the lid of the box represented the African Triple Moon-goddess, Ngame, and that the hump-backed man was the herald of a Queen-mother of an African state who claimed direct descent from Ngame. Back in Majorca in 1946, the coincidences continued to pile up. An antiquarian neighbour had died and bequeathed various small objects to Graves, including a mummy-like figure with a single eye. He later discovered that this mummy was an *okrafo* priest, a substitute-sacrifice to the White Goddess. A carnelian ring he was given by a friend – who knew nothing about the book – had a seal showing the three basic symbols of the cult: a stag, a moon and a thicket.

Even when the book was finished, odd things continued to happen. The first publisher who rejected it died of heart failure shortly afterwards. A second rejected it with a rude letter saying he could not make head or tail of it and he doubted whether anybody else could either; he dressed himself in women's underwear and hanged himself on a tree in his garden.* On the other hand, says Graves, the publisher who accepted it – T. S. Eliot – not only got his money back, but also received the Order of Merit that year. (In the light of the comments on Powys in the previous chapter, one might be excused for wondering how far these events were the work of the goddess, and how far they may have been unconsciously willed by Graves himself.)

Graves remarks: 'Chains of more than coincidence happen so often in my life that if I am forbidden to call them supernatural hauntings, I must call them a habit.' 'Very well: put it down to coincidence. Deny that there was any connection at all between the hump-backed herald on the box ... and myself, who suddenly

---

* Such deaths are commoner than one might suppose. I possess a German volume of legal medicine that contains several such photographs. The actual death from strangulation is usually accidental; the aim is masochistic sexual stimulation. Outsize baby clothes are sometimes used instead of female underwear.

became obsessed by the White Goddess of Europe, wrote of her clan totems in the Argonaut context, and now had thrust upon me ancient secrets belonging to her cult in Wales, Ireland and elsewhere. Please believe me; I was wholly unaware that the box celebrated the goddess Ngame. Or that the Helladic Greeks, including the early Athenians, were racially linked with Ngame's people – Libyan Berbers, known as Garamantians, who moved south from the Sahara to the Niger in the eleventh century A.D., and there intermarried with Negroes. Or that Ngame herself was a Moon-goddess, and shared all her attributes with the White Goddess of Greece and Western Europe. I knew only that, according to Herodotus, the Greek Athene was the same goddess as the Libyan Neith [Lamia, another name of the goddess].'

The White Goddess is an extremely difficult book, complex and bewildering, but the reader who becomes fascinated by its strange, tangled threads soon discovers that Graves is not exaggerating when he speaks of having ancient secrets 'thrust upon him'. He has stumbled upon a whole *knowledge system* as complex as modern physics whose assumptions are those of the 'lunar' rather than solar forces. He has done this by using his poet's intuition to follow clues through apparently unrelated mythologies. The poet Randall Jarrell has asserted that the whole mythology is merely a rationalisation of Graves's cult of the *ewig weibliche*, of his tendency to 'overvalue women at the expense of men' (to which he confesses in one of his poems). It is hard to see how this position can be maintained by anyone who knows the book well; its inner consistency vouches for its genuineness.

It is true that there should not be a conflict between 'lunar' and 'solar' knowledge systems, for all knowledge must be either true or false. One might say that the conflict arises from the narrow dogmatism of 'scientific' modes of thought. Ouspensky expresses it clearly in the passage that follows the long excerpt I have already quoted:

But here, in these books, there is a strange flavour of truth. I feel it particularly strongly now, because for so long I have held myself in, have kept myself within artificial 'materialistic' bounds, have denied myself all dreams about things that could not be held within these bounds. I had been living in a desiccated and sterilised world, with an infinite number of taboos imposed on my thought. And suddenly these strange books broke down all the walls round me, and made me think and dream about things of which for a long time I had feared to think and dream. Suddenly I began to find a strange meaning in old fairy tales; woods, rivers, mountains, became living beings; mysterious life filled the night; with new interest and new expectations, I began to dream again of distant travels; and I remembered many extraordinary things that I had heard about old monasteries. Ideas and feelings which had long since ceased to interest me suddenly began to assume significance and interest. A deep meaning and many subtle allegories appeared in what only yesterday seemed to be naive popular fantasy or crude superstition.*

We have obviously reached a crucial point in the argument. Most readers will be willing to accept the notion that man possesses subconscious powers that are hidden from the conscious intellect. But we are now positing the existence of *external* forces – white goddesses, magical alphabets and so on. Surely this is the point to state firmly that if the deaths of Graves's two publishers were not simply coincidence, then it was the unconscious exercise of the 'evil eye' by Graves himself? And that the strange business of the brass objects on the poet's desk may have been telepathy on the part of Graves, but was certainly not an attempt by the objects to draw

* *A New Model of the Universe,* p. 4.

attention to themselves? For is this not the dividing line between science and superstition? Ancient man thought the lightning was a god; Benjamin Franklin revealed that it was static electricity; and that is exactly what it is.

This is true; but there is more to it than that. And this is the point where another fundamental principle must be stated.

It is easy enough to see that man's logical powers have cut him off from the forces of his subconscious mind. If you start to work out a mathematical problem in the middle of the night, you find it difficult to get back to sleep. Because mathematical calculation involves a peculiar concentration of the *top levels* of your mind, and when you start to calculate you summon up these top levels as Aladdin summoned the slave of the lamp. But sleep depends on the slave going back into his lamp, and allowing the lower levels of the mind to take over. Or, if you think of yourself – your total personality – as a kind of car, then in sleep you *change drivers*.

Human evolution over the past two million years has been the evolution of the conscious driver, the slave of the lamp. Civilisation is highly complex and man needs a highly complex mental organisation to deal with it. Compared to his ancestor of two million years ago, modern man is like a giant corporation compared to a small family business.

The trouble with a giant corporation is that its overheads are so enormous. The electricity bill for the huge office building is enough to run a hundred small businesses. And all its other overheads are in proportion.

The consequence is that *civilised man tends to suffer from subconscious hypertension.*

Consider what happens when a young man gets married and begins to raise a family. He has to think about his future, and a dozen other things besides, until he is like a juggler keeping several balls in the air at the same time. Now, if this thought struck him when he was on his honeymoon, he did not allow it to worry him. On the contrary: fed by powerful streams of subconscious energy aroused by sex, he feels more than equal to it all.

After a few years, there are times when he gets very tired of the juggling act, and wishes he could simply drop all the balls. But of course, since he loves his wife and children, this is out of the question. But there are times when he ceases to put his heart into the juggling, and allows it to become purely mechanical.

What happens now is interesting. Various bills arrive at the end of the month. When he is in a healthy and optimistic condition, he pays them, works out what he has left in the bank, and then begins to think about taking his family out for a picnic on Sunday. But if he is feeling low and depressed, he avoids paying them as long as possible, because he likes the feeling of security produced by the knowledge that his pay cheque is still in the bank. The worries remain permanently as problems at the back of his mind, eating up vital energy as a light you have left switched on eats up electricity. As he feels himself getting more depressed, each additional problem seems to become bigger, and his energy sinks lower. He is now drifting towards what psychologists of fifty years ago called a 'hyperesthetic condition', in which life becomes a series of insurmountable obstacles: every molehill becomes a mountain. His whole psychological being is a series of rooms in which he has left lights switched on, and life becomes a burden. Some people become so accustomed to this state of permanent hypertension that they accept it as their normal condition, and take it for granted that they lose their hair at thirty-five and develop ulcers at forty.

Observe that the basic characteristic of this state is that *you cease to notice things*. Like a man running for a train, you no longer have time to turn your head to left and right. And even when you have caught the train, you don't relax and look out of the window, as any normal child would. The inner tension continues; you try to read a newspaper, or perhaps simply stare blankly in front of you, your mind grinding away at its worries.

Now consider what happens if such a person goes away on a holiday, and suddenly everything seems to 'go right'. It is a sunny morning; he can forget the office for a week or so and simply enjoy the scenery ... It is as if someone had pressed the 'stop' button of a dynamo; the roar of the engine dies, and the silence seems miraculous. It is as if a spring of vitality had suddenly bubbled into consciousness. He has ceased to be passive and depressed. He looks at the scenery with intense interest, or listens with pleasure to the local gossip in the bar of a pub. The inner strain has relaxed. He is no longer wasting his vital energy. And because he is noticing things again, his feedback mechanism begins to work. The pleasure he gets from the sight of a tree in the rain means that his senses begin to reach out, to expect things to be delightful and interesting, which in turn means that his springs of vital energy become more abundant. To look at things *with interest* is to refresh the mind. In *Journey to the East*, Hermann Hesse has the important sentence: 'I ... was responsible for the provision of music for our group, *and I then discovered how a long time devoted to small details exalts us and increases our strength*' (Chapter 1). Precisely. Because when you concentrate seriously upon small details, you release the general hypertension in the rest of your mind, and your vital springs are renewed.

William James also notes that 'bullying treatment' is often the best cure for the 'hyperesthetic state', when all molehills become mountains. The doctor forces the patient to make immense efforts; the first result is acute distress, followed almost immediately by a feeling of relief. Because the hypertension is unnecessary (it is no more than a bad habit), like a child's fear of ghosts, it is a pointless waste of vital energy. Once the mind is snapped out of its state of miserable passivity by a shock, the vital forces begin to work again.

When a human being is healthy, he concentrates on one problem at a time, puts all his sense of purpose into it and maintains a high level of vital feedback from his environment. He does things slowly, with deep interest, and when he begins to get tired, he slows down, and lets his subconscious powers do the work of renewal. He recognises that over-tiredness and the depression and defeat that come with it constitute a vicious circle that must be avoided if he is to be efficient and healthy.

Now, although hypertension is accentuated by modern civilisation, it is not specifically a disease of civilisation. It is a disease of consciousness – that is, of being human. The farm labourer going to work is as likely to ignore his surroundings as the harassed car salesman. And if the inhabitants of some Amazon village are 'closer to nature' than New Yorkers, this is usually at the cost of dirt and ignorance and inconvenience. Hypertension is the price we pay for the symphonies of Beethoven, the novels of Balzac, the advances in medical knowledge that prevent children dying of smallpox.

However, it is not a necessary and inescapable price. It is the result of ignorance, of bad management of our vital economy.

The point to observe here is that although hypertension may not be necessary, it is as widespread as the common cold. It would not be inaccurate to say that *all* human beings live in a state of 'vigilance' and anxiety that is far above the level they actually need for vital efficiency. It is a general tendency of consciousness to 'spread the attention too thinly'; and, like an overexcited child with too many toys on Christmas Day, the result is nervous exhaustion.

What is so interesting in this context are the moments when the tension relaxes, due to auto-suggestion or total absorption in some small task. Yeats describes such a moment, sitting in a crowded London teashop:

While on the shop and street I gazed
My body of a sudden blazed;

And twenty minutes more or less
It seemed, so great my happiness
That I was blessed and could bless.

This is probably a case of auto-suggestion; one can imagine the poet becoming increasingly tense and fatigued as he pushes among the crowds in central London, then sitting down to drink hot tea, as he looks out of the window of Swan and Edgars at the street. Suddenly his dynamos all grow silent, and he looks at the passing crowd with intense interest.

This, in fact, is what constitutes a poet. He is a person who is naturally mentally healthy and resilient, and who frequently experiences moments in which the usual hypertension vanishes, and he is suddenly amazed and delighted to realise how *interesting* everything is. What happens in such moments is that he begins to hear the 'voices of silence'. He perceives that the world is rich with *meanings* that he would ordinarily overlook. I italicise 'meanings' because this is the heart of the matter. The meanings that we perceive when our normal hypertension vanishes are really there. They are not an illusion; they are not purely subjective.

It is true that the word 'interesting' has a subjective ring; *I* decide what is interesting and what isn't. But it has an objective meaning nevertheless. As Sherlock Holmes studies the documents of a case and murmurs, 'Most interesting, Watson,' his meaning could be expressed as 'More complex than appears on the surface'. The sense of meaning that arises in us when hypertension vanishes is a recognition of complexity, of 'interestingness'.

If we think of human evolution as a process of increasing 'complexification' (to use Teilhard de Chardin's expression), then it becomes clear that it also means increased 'hypertension', and that this in turn means an increasing tendency to overlook 'meaning'.

It is important to grasp that the 'meanings' that Ouspensky

began to see in woods, rivers and mountains were not a matter of imagination, or surrender to emotionalism. Graves's 'lunar knowledge' is a reality – a reality of which poets become aware in the moments of stillness. In the Celtic legend of Gwion, cited by Graves, the boy Gwion is employed at stirring a cauldron which contains a magic 'knowledge brew'; three drops fly out and burn his finger, and when he thrusts it into his mouth, he suddenly sees the meaning of all things, past, present and future. In the legend of Siegfried, as set to music by Wagner, drops of dragon blood fall on the hero's hand, burning him; he thrusts it into his mouth, and is immediately able to understand the song of the birds and the 'forest murmurs'. In both cases, the magic brew has the same effect: of inducing the deep inner silence that allows a new perception of meaning.

If we agree, then, that the 'muse poet' or the 'magician' is a person whose mind is able to relax and grasp these deeper levels of meaning, we must also recognise that this is a two-way affair. The meaning is really there, external to his own mind, and his power to 'tune in' to it is only the beginning.

An even more interesting point arises. I have compared man to a car with two drivers: the conscious personality and the subliminal impulses. In civilised man, the role of the subliminal 'driver' is relatively automatic and repetitive compared with that of the conscious 'driver'; he is little more than a maintenance engineer controlling sleep, memory and the functions of the stomach and the bowels. It is the conscious mind that writes symphonies, plans the conquest of space and builds civilisation. But in the 'magical' societies of the remote past, the subliminal 'driver' was just as important. When he took over, it was not merely for the purpose of inducing sleep, but of widening that other kind of knowledge, intuitive knowledge of the 'meanings' that surrounded him like forest murmurs. The magician or mystic aimed at getting somehow deeper *into* nature, *of extending the grasp and power of the subliminal mind.*

Sleep was not a passive condition in which the body recovered from the day's fatigues, but an instrument of investigation, sometimes even an essential preliminary of magic. In ancient Ireland, the choosing of a new king involved the sacrifice of a sacred bull, on which a Druid was gorged until he fell asleep. During sleep, incantations were recited over him, and he would receive 'revelation' of the rightful claimant to the throne.* To the modern mind, such a ceremony immediately suggests fraud practised upon gullible savages. But there are recorded instances of 'sleep magic' that are less easy to explain. In *Pattern of Islands*, Arthur Grimble, who was land commissioner in the Gilbert Islands of the South Pacific, describes the magical ceremony of the calling of the porpoise. Grimble was told that he should eat porpoise flesh to increase his girth. That led him 'to inquire how [he] might come by a regular supply of the rare meat. The long and short of [an islander's] reply was that his own kinsmen in Kuma village, seventeen miles up-lagoon, were the hereditary porpoise-callers of the High Chiefs of Butaritari and Makin-Meang. His first cousin was a leading expert at the game; he could put himself into the right kind of dream on demand. His spirit went out of his body in such a dream; it sought out the porpoise-folk in their home under the western horizon and invited them to a dance, with feasting, in Kuma village. If he spoke the words of invitation aright (and very few had the secret of them), the porpoise would follow him with cries of joy to the surface.'

In due course, Grimble was taken to Kuma. where all the dishes necessary for a feast had been laid out. The fat, friendly porpoise-caller retired to his hut, and for several hours all was silence. The porpoise-caller rushed out of his hut and fell on his face, then stood up 'clawing at the air and whining on a queer high note like a puppy's. Then words came gulping out of him: "Teirake! Teirake!

* See H. R. Hays. *In the Beginning: Early Man and His Gods* (New York, Putnam, 1963), p. 153.

(Arise! Arise!) ... They come, they come ..."' The villagers all rushed into the water and stood, breast deep. Then the porpoises came in: 'They were moving towards us in extended order with spaces of two or three yards between them, as far as my eye could reach. So slowly they came, they seemed to be hung in a trance. Their leader drifted in hard by the dreamer's legs. He turned without a word to walk beside it as it idled towards the shallows ... The villagers were welcoming their guests ashore with crooning words ... As we approached the emerald shallows, the keels of the creatures began to take the sand; they flapped gently, as if asking for help. The men leaned down to throw their arms around the great barrels and ease them over the ridges. It was as if their single wish was to get to the beach.' The 'hypnotised' porpoises were then slaughtered and eaten.

It might be mentioned, in passing, that animals are easily hypnotised. Black describes this in *Mind and Body*, and adds that the phenomenon was described in print as long ago as 1636, when Schewenter observed that if the head of a chicken is pressed to the ground, and a chalk line is drawn from its beak, the bird will remain 'transfixed' until aroused by a loud noise.

The hereditary porpoise-callers of the Gilbert Islands are an example of the development of 'lunar knowledge', and the whole story emphasises a vital point. We are accustomed to thinking of sleep as an uncontrolled and uncontrollable state, in which we lose whatever 'powers' of action and thought we normally possess. Most of our dreams are forgotten on waking. But J. W. Dunne pointed out in his celebrated book *An Experiment with Time* (1927) that we can, with a certain amount of effort, learn to recall dreams. He trained himself to do this by keeping a pencil and paper by the bedside and noting them down every time he woke up in the night. The result was his discovery that dreams often contain pre-cognitive glimpses of events that will happen later. (This will be discussed in Part

Three, Chapter 3.) The 'magic' of the porpoise-callers is a further step in this direction – as was that of the Druids. This also explains the importance attached to dreams by primitive tribes, and why the moon-goddess is the patroness of magical cults.

It may also explain why the White Goddess was regarded as a destroyer as well as an inspirer. Psychedelic drugs, which have the effect of immobilising the 'logical mind', and putting the subliminal powers in the driving seat of personality, can produce revelations of beauty or of horror. The mind that opens itself to 'subliminal meanings' has shed its defences, thrown away its insulation, its 'shock absorbers'. Daylight consciousness has the refuge of common sense, of 'objective reality'. But in subliminal states, the dividing line between reality and one's personal fantasies becomes blurred; and without a certain knowledge and discipline, the mind is at the mercy of its own tendency to morbidity. Graves comments correctly that the nightmare is one of the cruellest aspects of the White Goddess. This should be qualified although Graves may not agree – by saying that the danger arises from the ignorance of her 'devotees', not from any destructive tendency in the Goddess herself.

Another interesting question arises from Grimble's account of porpoise-calling: the comment 'If he spoke the words of invitation aright (and very few had the secret of them) the porpoise would follow …' If it is the power of the dreamer's subliminal self that somehow hypnotises the porpoises, why should the exact form of the words matter? This question obviously involves the whole field of magic rituals and incantations.

The answer is almost certainly: it matters only to the magician, who must believe in the objective validity of what he is doing. Our problem is that we contain two minds, and the conscious mind is so accustomed to its masculine role of dominance that it frequently interferes in the delicate workings of the feminine subconscious. E. H. Visiak, another poet with an abnormally active subconscious mind, described in his autobiography how he worked in a telegraph office and learned to send Morse signals with a key:

I was over-anxious, and fell into a vicious, cramped way of sending. To send properly was delightful. Instead of aching muscles, there was a sensation of free play in manipulating the key, an effortless, flexible cooperation with springing mechanism. One day, while I was practising, my wrist started moving with this delightful freedom. The Superintendent was looking at me in surprise and satisfaction from his desk. I had a glimpse of his benevolently gleaming spectacles, and the power, or knack – whatever it was – was gone, never to return ...*

Visiak's 'cramp' is the hypertension we have been discussing, the conscious mind persistently interfering with the activity of the subconscious 'robot' that deals with these mechanical matters.

Now, the subconscious mind can be trained to respond to certain formulae or symbols. A lover of Wagner only has to hear a bar of the 'Liebestod' to feel his hair prickle. The Hindu saint Ramakrishna could be sent into a state of *samadhi* (ecstasy) by hearing the name of the Divine mother. In *The Waste Land*, T. S. Eliot deliberately uses quotations that have become highly charged with meaning in another context, including quotations from Wagner libretti. Graves states that only true Muse-poetry can produce this prickling of the hair that A. E. Housman declared to be the test of good poetry, and in a general sense, he is obviously right. But the floodgates *can* be made to respond to any 'Open sesame', if one takes the trouble. Teenagers of the fifties experienced the authentic 'prickle' when they saw photographs of the late James Dean. A tune reaches 'top-of-the-pops' status by being played over and over again until it

* *Life's Morning Hour* (London, John Baker, 1968).

arouses a ritual response. Hitler finally had his audiences trained to a point where a certain rise in the tone of his voice could start the emotional orgasm.

The symbol – or form of words – that causes the response is, to some extent, arbitrary. I have read a critic who asserted that Keats's lines 'The moving waters at their priest-like task/Of pure ablution round Earth's human shores' lost their 'magic' when the word 'cold' was substituted for 'pure' in the second sentence. I personally find the line equally effective either way, and conclude that the critic's response – or lack of it – was a matter of habit response.

The inference is that the exact wording of the invitation was of more importance to the porpoise-caller than to the porpoises; it controlled the release mechanism of the power that invited the fishes to the 'banquet'. The wrong wording might have warned the porpoises by releasing his sense of guilt at the deception, or otherwise arousing his conscious 'censor'.

One might summarise this by saying that the conscious mind has the thick skin of a rhinoceros; it is powerful but insensitive. The subconscious mind has 'one skin too few'; it is dangerously sensitive. It needs the masculine conscious mind as a woman needs a husband: for his strength and sense of purpose. And the conscious mind could not subsist without the feminine element, the 'secret life'. But the ideal relation between the two is achieved only when the conscious mind is concentrated upon a single purpose with total commitment. Hence the masculine preference for dangerous sports – mountain climbing, driving racing cars – since the total concentration demanded brings about the union of conscious and subconscious mind, and a new accession of strength. Seduction is similarly motivated; in 'sexual conquest' the male consciousness becomes 'one-pointed', while the union with the female stirs depths of instinctive purpose. But the development of mere will-power is basically futile; it is only the spearhead of purpose. The true 'direction' for consciousness lies in knowledge expansion, a wider and wider grasp of the relations of the actual world, to illuminate and supplement the 'lunar' insights of the subconscious. This is why the development of 'solar' knowledge by Western man must be accepted as a true evolution, in spite of its one-sidedness; it need not remain one-sided.

All this is to say that 'magical systems' – the Hebrew Kabbalah, the Chinese Book of Changes, the Tarot pack, the Key of Solomon, the Egyptian and Tibetan Books of the Dead – should not be regarded as primitive and unsuccessful attempts at 'science', but as attempts to express these depths of 'lunar' knowledge *in their own terms*. The Egyptian and Tibetan Books of the Dead – called in their own languages *Pert Em Hru* (Emerging by Day) and *Bardo Thodol* – are designed to be read aloud to the dying person in an attempt to give the 'subconscious self' a certain control over its strange experiences. To Western ears, this sounds absurd, until we recognise as rational the notion of controlling the 'sleeping self' and its impulses. Then we understand that what the ancient Egyptians and Tibetans were trying to do is not childish and illogical, but a step ahead of any knowledge we possess in the West. (Experiments in deep-trance hypnosis are perhaps the nearest we have come to it.) Anyone who wishes to test this can do so by making an effort to achieve a certain control over his dreams: for example, sleeping on his back to induce a nightmare, and then setting out to *control* the nightmare and prevent it from reaching its normal climax.

The Chinese Book of Changes or *I Ching* is one of the most interesting, and certainly one of the most accessible, of these 'lunar' knowledge systems. It is also unique in being free of harmful aspects; close study of it can do nothing but good. The *I Ching* began as a series of oracles, sixty-four of them, written (according to tradition) by King Wên, founder of the Chou dynasty, more than a thousand years before Christ. These sixty-four oracles were later expanded with 'images' and commentaries on individual lines. (The meaning of this will emerge in a moment.) Confucius and various other scholars wrote commentaries on all this, and the result is the bulky text published in a modern definitive translation in two volumes in 1951.*

On its simplest level, then, the *I Ching* can be regarded as a fortune-telling book like *Old Moore's Almanac*, and no doubt this aspect of it explains the remarkable popularity it has achieved in recent years. But this fortune-telling aspect is based upon a system, and the study of the system is more rewarding and revealing than consulting the oracle.

This system is founded upon the simple opposition of light and darkness, or the positive and negative, called here Yang and Yin. From what has already been said in this chapter, we can immediately hazard the guess that this 'light' and 'darkness' are not supposed to be identified with primitive good and evil, but with the solar and lunar principles. In other words, Yin is not another name for negative qualities and principles, but for the dark 'other side' of the mind.

Yang is represented by an unbroken line, thus: —————; Yin by a line with a break in the middle: ——— ———. Each of the sixty-four 'oracles' is made up of six of these lines, piled on top of one another like a sandwich:

—————

——— ———

—————

—————

——— ———

—————

* Translated into German by Richard Wilhelm, then into English by Cary F. Baynes, with a foreword by Jung. London, Routledge, 1951; New York. Pantheon, 1951.

This happens to represent hexagram 56, Lu, The Wanderer. Each of the sixty-four hexagrams has a title.

Anyone who is mathematically inclined will be able to see how sixty-four hexagrams sprang out of Yin and Yang. If you start off by drawing two lines side by side, one Yin, one Yang, and then see how many combinations you can get by piling new lines on them, sandwich-fashion, you will see that the six lines can be arranged in exactly sixty-four different patterns. I start with two lines:

Now when I add a second line to each, four combinations become possible:

And when I add a third line, eight combinations are possible. In short, I double the number every time I add a new line to the sandwich.

But why sixty-four hexagrams in the first place?

The answer would seem to be that King Wên decided that there were eight fundamental symbols, as follows:

Ch'ien, The Creative, Heaven

K'un, The Receptive, Earth

K'en, Keeping Still, Mountain

K'an, The Abysmal, Water

Chên, The Arousing, Thunder

Sun, The Gentle, Wind

Tui, The Joyous, Lake

Li, The Clinging, Fire

On first acquaintance, the student is inclined to wonder why the set should contain both 'water' and 'lake', which seem to duplicate one another, until it is observed that the symbols go in pairs: heaven, earth; water, fire; mountain, lake; thunder, wind. These are also pairs of opposite qualities: the creative and the receptive; the violent (thunder) and the gentle (wind); the quiescent (mountain) and the joyous (lake); the clinging or constricting (fire) and its opposite, the abyss, emptiness (water). Each of these qualities is represented by a 'trigram' (three lines), and therefore each of the sixty-four 'oracles' is made up of two of the symbols.

King Wên apparently meditated upon these sixty-four combinations of symbols, and interpreted each one as an archetypal situation or condition in human life. For example, if the hexagram represents earth above (at the top of the hexagram) and heaven below, the two can be seen as pressing against one another with equal force, heaven trying to move upward, earth trying to move downward, and perfectly counter-balancing one another; King Wên therefore called this hexagram Peace (or harmony). On the other hand, if heaven is above and earth is beneath, the two move away in opposite directions, without creative contact, and this situation is seen as representing Stagnation or Standstill. This interpretation reveals that we are dealing with the creative drive of the conscious mind and the receptive quality of the subconscious; for when these draw apart, there is, in fact, a condition of vital stagnation.

This may sound fanciful, or simply glib. I can only say that a close acquaintance with the *I Ching* and its symbols soon begins to reveal a remarkable inner consistency, and that such meanings become obvious. At first the landscape is strange and disconcerting; soon it becomes familiar, and everything is seen to be logical. One of the first great minds of the West to recognise this was Leibnitz, who himself cherished a strange dream of creating a 'universal calculus' in which all the truths of philosophy and mathematics should be expressible. He noticed that the way in which the hexagrams are built up constitutes a 'binary' mathematical system; that is, a system that, instead of using the numbers one to ten, and then repeating them, uses only one and two. The binary system is the basis of modern calculating machines and electronic computers. Leibnitz was no doubt mistaken in assuming that King Wên, or the later commentator Shao Yung, knew about binary mathematical systems; but his instinct was correct in seeing the *I Ching* as a distant cousin of his universal calculus. It was Leibnitz who was unscientific; his notion of a mathematical symbolism that could express all 'truth' is absurd; even ordinary language – which is far more flexible – breaks down over quite simple concepts that involve feelings. The *I Ching* is a net woven of altogether finer mesh.

The 'oracle' can be consulted either by means of yarrow stalks, or by throwing down three coins. The yarrow stalk oracle takes a long time; it involves dividing up fifty stalks in various ways, beginning by dividing the heap arbitrarily into two, and then reducing each heap by substracting groups of four sticks from it. The process is too long to describe here, and it would serve no purpose. The coin oracle is simpler. Three coins are thrown down. If there is a preponderance of heads (either three or two) a Yang line is formed. If a preponderance of tails, a Yin line is formed. This is done six times, forming a hexagram, which is then looked up in the *I Ching*. The question to which an answer is required is supposed to be held firmly in the mind throughout this procedure.

The psychologist C. G. Jung justifies all this by a principle that he calls synchronicity, that is, the assumption that 'accidents' and 'coincidences' are, in some way, linked with the unconscious mind – an assumption we have already considered in this book. The answer to the question is known to the subconscious mind – this is the assumption used to explain all prophecy and clairvoyance – and the 'chance' fall of the coins or division of the yarrow stalks can somehow record this knowledge.

It is significant that one of the founders of the psychoanalytic movement, whose professional life had been a continual preoccupation with the subconscious and its symbols, should come to accept such a notion in his seventies. It is said that Confucius also came to the study of the *I Ching* late in life, and once expressed regret that he did not have another fifty years to devote to it. For the real question about the *I Ching* is not whether it is successful as a crude oracle or fortune-teller, but whether, like the myths of the White Goddess, it embodies real lunar knowledge.

But before discussing this aspect of the *I Ching* – as a book of wisdom – I should state that its oracles often possess a weird accuracy that is profoundly disturbing. The story is told of the ruler Li, of the seventh century B.C., who had usurped power, and who consulted the oracle to know whether his son, Ching-Chung, would succeed him as king. The result was the twentieth hexagram, Contemplation, or Seeing into the Distance. The judgement sounds at first baffling:

> *Contemplation. The ablution has been made,*
> *But not yet the offering.*
> *Full of trust they look up to him.*

But both this, and the 'image' that follows, emphasise the 'way of law and ritual'. The judgement speaks of the moment in the religious ceremony when the libation has been poured, but the sacrifice has not yet been made, in which everyone is lost in contemplation and filled with reverence. The 'image' speaks of the king of old who visited the people and gave them instruction – again, this profoundly Chinese notion of the 'right relation' between ruler and ruled. The usurper Li might already have begun to feel twinges of conscience as he read these lines.

There was more to come. If a Yin or Yang line is obtained by throwing three tails or three heads (rather than only two), it is called a 'changing line'; it tends to change into its opposite. In this case, the Yin line in the fourth place was the changing line, and this transformed the hexagram into Stagnation, or Standstill, whose judgement reads:

> *Evil people do not further*
> *The perseverance of the superior man.*

The great departs; the small approaches.

The totality of the judgement here is clearly unfavourable.

The priest who interpreted this oracle for King Li went on to point out that the title of the hexagram also means 'seeing into the distance' – the hexagram is associated with a watch-tower placed on hills – and that this meant that if the prince continued to rule, it would not be in this country, Ch'ien, but elsewhere – the story says that the priest specified the state of Ch'i because its rulers were descendants of the priests of the holy mountain, also implied in the hexagram Seeing into the Distance.

The annals conclude the story by stating that, in fact, Li was himself deposed by his neighbours in the next state, but that the descendants of his son eventually became rulers in Ch'i, as foretold.*

It is worth studying the two hexagrams – twelve and twenty – in the light of this story; they are too long to discuss in detail here, but many other indications of the fate of Li and Ching-Chung can be read into them. Whether one accepts the story or not, it provides insight into the way the oracle is used.

In *Man and His Symbols*, edited by Jung, there is a lengthy account by Jolande Jacobi of the analysis of a repressed, over-intellectual introvert named Henry; Henry was eventually persuaded – much against his will – to try throwing the three coins and consulting the oracle. 'What he found in the book had tremendous impact on him. Briefly, the oracle to which he referred bore several startling references to his dream, and to his psychological condition generally.' The hexagram was number four, Youthful Folly, and contained a warning against entangling oneself in unreal fantasies and empty imaginings. The judgement also forbade consulting it a second time. But two nights later, after a dream in which he saw a sword and helmet

* See Helmut Wilhelm, *Change: Eight Lectures on the I Ching* (New York, Harper, 1960). pp. 95–97.

floating in empty space, he opened the book casually, and came upon the thirtieth hexagram, Li, which has weapons – particularly helmets and swords – for its symbol.

This is the kind of coincidence for which many students of the *I Ching* will vouch, and the effect is usually psychologically shattering. In Henry's case, it was the gradual coming to terms with his subconscious forces, of which the *I Ching* became the symbol, that completed the cure. In the light of what has been said already in this chapter, this is not difficult to understand. His basic psychological problem was a kind of solipsism, a feeling of being trapped in 'consciousness', with a consequent feeling of dissociation from the rest of the world, a constant sense of unreality. For the subconscious mind is the point at which man is truly connected to nature. The historian of occultism A. E. Waite has described how his years of study led him finally to the understanding that there is no true separation between man and the rest of the universe; and how a serious illness that kept him in a semi-conscious state for nearly a month turned this intellectual understanding into deeply felt insight. This, to a lesser degree, is the effect the *I Ching* had on Henry. It also defines the real purpose of all studies of magic and the occult. We know, theoretically, that we possess a 'subconscious' mind, yet as I sit here, in this room on a sunny morning, I am not in any way aware of it; I can't see it or feel it. It is like an arm upon which I have been lying in my sleep, and which has become completely dead and feelingless. The real purpose of works such as the *I Ching*, the Kabbalah, the Key of Solomon is to restore circulation to these regions of the mind.

As to my own personal experience of the *I Ching*, it has certainly disposed me to treat it as perhaps the foremost of all such works. I first came across it in the period I have already spoken of, when I was living in Wimbledon. Obviously, the first thing that any would-be writer consults an 'oracle' about is his future as a writer; he wants a 'long-range forecast'. I took three pennies, and threw them down six times. Each time, there was a preponderance of heads, giving a hexagram made up of six Yang lines, the first one in the book, with a judgement that reads:

The creative works supreme success
Furthering through perseverance.

In the hundreds of times I have consulted it since then, the coins have never given six unbroken lines. Obviously, I was disposed to be convinced. The only other time when I have seen the coins fall in this way was when the oracle was consulted for the first time by the writer Bill Hopkins. He said flippantly: 'If it gives good judgement, I'll believe in it. If it doesn't, I won't.' The oracle fulfilled expectations and produced the first hexagram again.

I clearly recall only one other instance of the book's accuracy from that time. In Wimbledon I consulted it about the old man we were living with, who was charming and extremely difficult by turns. The hexagram obtained was Sung, Conflict, with a judgement that reads:

Conflict. You are sincere
And are being obstructed.
A cautious halt halfway brings good fortune.
Going through to the end brings misfortune.
It does not further one to cross the great water.

This told me exactly what I wanted to know: whether to get out of the place as soon as possible. 'A cautious halt halfway brings good fortune. Going through to the end brings misfortune.' I couldn't think what was meant by the reference to the 'great man' but the text explains that the great man refers only to 'an impartial man whose authority is great enough to terminate the conflict'. The only such man we knew was the brother of my wife's patient; accordingly, we consulted him and explained the problem. He certainly succeeded in smoothing matters over for a short time. As to crossing the great water, we had considered moving across the Thames, back to North London, where I was working. The oracle proved to be right there too. Our move to Earl's Court, after the old man's death, brought a worsening of the situation.

What most impressed me about this particular occasion was the last line; I had obtained three heads; therefore, the commentary applied – nine at the top means:

Even if by chance a leather belt is bestowed on one,
By the end of the morning
It will have been snatched away three times.

One of the old man's most infuriating habits was to give my wife presents when he was in a good mood, and then take them back again, or even give them to someone else. The lines in the *I Ching* apparently refer to being decorated by the king – a leather belt was the equivalent of a medal – but it certainly fitted our situation.

In his preface to the *I Ching*, Jung describes how he consulted it about the question of the new edition which he proposed to introduce to the Western mind. The answer was Ting, the Cauldron, which the commentary describes as a ritual vessel containing spiritual nourishment; i.e. the *I Ching* describes itself as such a vessel. The last 'line', which was a strong one, even prophesied the incredible success that the book has met with in America in the past decade (where it continues to sell almost like the Bible):

The ting *has rings of jade.*
Great good fortune.
Nothing that would not act to further.

(Carrying handles of jade signify that the 'vessel' becomes something that is greatly honoured.)

But for our present purposes, the most important of the 'lines' obtained by Jung was this:

A ting *with legs upturned.*
Furthers removal of stagnating stuff.
One takes a concubine for the sake of her son.
No blame.

Jung interprets this to mean that the *I Ching* refers to itself as a cauldron that has long been out of use (i.e. kept upside down). But the important lines here are the ones referring to the concubine. 'A man takes a concubine when his wife has no son,' Jung comments, 'so the *I Ching* is called upon when one sees no other way out. Despite the quasi-legal status of the concubine in China, she is in reality only a somewhat awkward makeshift; so likewise the magic procedure of the oracle is an expedient that may be utilised for a higher purpose. There is no blame, although it is an exceptional recourse.'

And although Jung does not dot the *i*'s and cross the *t*'s, this is clearly a deprecation of the *I Ching*'s role as a fortune-telling device. It should be an exceptional recourse, not a party game. For the real and permanent significance of the book is not as an oracle but as a book of wisdom.

The first thing noticed by anyone consulting the *I Ching* is its frequent references to 'the superior man'. And its counsels, whether favourable or unfavourable, always include advice for the 'superior man' on how to deal with the situation. And anyone who has ever consulted the *I Ching* in a time of crisis will vouch for the mentally refreshing effect of this approach. 'Life is many days,' says Eliot. But human beings are usually trapped in the present, and respond to problems with a tension and anxiety that treats every problem as a matter of life and death. Johnson once said to Boswell, who was complaining about some trivial anxiety, 'Come, sir, think how little you will think of this in ten years' time.'

And this indicates the significance of the title of the Book of Changes. As I live through the present, all the phenomena of life seem 'real', solid, of permanent importance. In reality, they flow like the surface of a river. The 'I' that looks out through my eyes will be unchanged in ten years' time, but many of these 'permanent' things around me will have disappeared.

The Book of Changes was a great influence on both Taoism and Confucianism. And one might say that the bedrock of the *I Ching* consists of two fundamental concepts, one Taoist, the other Confucian. The Confucian concept is to be found in a saying of Mencius: 'Those who follow the part of themselves that is great will become great men; those who follow the part of themselves that is small will become small men.' The Taoist concept has already been touched upon in speaking of hypertension. Chuang Tzu remarks that a baby can keep its fist clenched all day without getting tired, whereas an adult cannot keep it clenched for more than a few minutes. A drunken man can fall out of a cart without hurting himself. A carpenter whose workmanship was so perfect that it seemed supernatural explained that when he was about to undertake a difficult task, The reduced his mind to absolute quiescence, and guarded against any diminution of his vital powers. After a few days of such quiescence, he no longer cares about the importance of his task (making a musical instrument for the king); he goes into the forest, and his instinct selects the right tree. And in the making of the instrument, he makes no conscious effort but only 'brings his natural capacity into relation with that of the wood'. All Taoist parables have this same content. A butcher who cuts up bullocks with perfect grace and accuracy explains that he does it in the same way – with total quiescence and total concentration – with the consequence that after nineteen years his cleaver is still as sharp as ever.

In Japan this is the fundamental principle of Zen, as readers of Eugen Herrigel's *Zen in the Art of Archery* will know.

That is to say that the master of Tao or Zen places himself in the state that we have already discussed in relation to Powys; the conscious mind with its tensions is lulled; a man's centre of gravity shifts towards the 'secret life'. A celebrated chapter of the works of Chuang Tzu describes the process of sinking into quiescence as 'listening to the music of heaven and earth', listening to the wind or other sounds of nature, as if they were great music, totally absorbed in the thought of their deep significance. The mind begins to respond to the sound of the wind as if it were great music.

This principle of *Tao* has been recognised by modern psychology. For example, Viktor Frankl, the founder of 'logotherapy', tells the story of a school play for which an actor was needed to play the part of a stutterer. A boy was chosen who stuttered badly, but when he got on stage, he found he couldn't stutter. Frankl calls this 'the law of reversed effort'. Stuttering is the result of hypertension, a kind of stage fright – of attaching so much importance to an action that your conscious mind proceeds to interfere, like a stupid sergeant major, and spoils everything. Frankl's principle is simply to persuade your sergeant major to achieve the *opposite* effect by a process of deception, like Br'er Rabbit persuading Br'er Fox to throw him into the prickly briar patch, or Tom Sawyer persuading his friends to whitewash a fence by pretending that he is enjoying it immensely. The stuttering pupil *wants* to stutter on stage; the sergeant major proceeds to interfere, and the opposite effect is achieved. Chuang Tzu's carpenter would work badly if he allowed himself to worry about the Court; he spends several days soothing the sergeant major to sleep before he begins to think about the wood. Frankl cures cases of over-anxiety by telling the patient to deliberately *try* to do what he is so anxious not to do, thus releasing the pent-up emotions and allowing the 'robot' in the subconscious to get on with the job in his own quiet way.

Underlying all this is the recognition that man possesses enormous inner powers which he has *allowed* to become inaccessible through general hypertension and misuse of his mind.

Chuang Tzu's carpenter has simply chosen to contact 'the part of himself that is great' in order to make the musical instrument; he *could* have chosen to 'follow the part of himself that is small', particularly if he is a good craftsman, and perhaps nobody would have known the difference. This is also what Graves means by the difference between Muse poetry and 'classical' poetry; the latter is fundamentally craftsmanship, created by the upper levels of the personality, well made but without inspiration.

Human beings are the only living creatures who have this choice – of following the part that is great, or the part that is trivial. The difference depends upon the unique human faculty of imagination. When an animal is in a dull situation, it becomes dull; the fiercest of all birds, the hawk, becomes quiescent when a black bag is placed over its head. Man's superior consciousness means that he can see further; his sense of purpose stretches into the distance. But we are still 99 per cent animal; few of us bother to develop this unique capacity. We drift along from day to day, becoming bored when things are dull, depressed when immediate prospects look poor, using our powers of foresight and imagination only when confronted by an interesting challenge, and allowing them to lie fallow in between. And this situation, we must admit, applies most of the time to all of us, including the Beethovens and Einsteins. 'Involvement' is our common lot. But what makes us uniquely human are the strange moments of non-involvement. The pressure vanishes. Suddenly we are seeing life from a distance, as if we were gods; seeing it from above, from a bird's-eye view rather than the usual worm's-eye view. In these moments of optimism and affirmation, it seems absurd that we should ever have sunk into a condition of depression or defeat, for it is suddenly obvious that we are undefeatable and indestructible. Every compromise or retreat is seen to be the result of absurd miscalculation. I open casually a book on music and read an account of how the composer Gesualdo found his wife in bed with her lover, and killed her with his sword while his servants killed the lover; then went off to one of his castles and killed his second child, in case he was not the father. In a modern court room, his defence would be one of insanity. But was it insanity? If I try to place myself in his position, I immediately see that it was not insanity – only a blind *involvement* in the situation, like the involvement of a man wrestling with a boa constrictor. Caught in a whirlpool of emotions, he has to make an act of judgement. But most human beings would be incapable of making the correct judgement in such a situation; it is like asking a cabin boy to become captain of a ship in the middle of a storm and expecting him to make the right decisions. What Gesualdo did is not necessarily evil. It would be evil if he had decided in cold blood to kill his wife and child; but he was caught in a storm, his judgements were too immediate, too involved and, therefore, too violent. From the social and moral point of view, it might have been better if he had burst into tears and asked what he had done to deserve such a betrayal; but from Gesualdo's point of view, it would have been equally a defeat.

Thinking about such a situation, one becomes aware of the human lack of detachment; our inexperience and immaturity in the complex problems of the human condition. But it should not be so. We have the 'breathing spaces' when we can take a detached point of view. If it was of life-or-death importance that we learned by these moments of insight, men would quickly become something closer to being godlike. But most of us can drift through life without making any great moral decisions. And so the human race has shown no advance in wisdom in three thousand years.

This is the insight that lies at the heart of the *I Ching*: that man can *choose* not to drift and follow the 'small' part of himself. The method of Tao – of contracting his subconscious powers by minute concentration upon particulars – opens the path to higher evolutionary levels.

Anyone who simply reads and studies the *I Ching* while thinking about its symbols and ideas, and ignoring its powers as an oracle, becomes aware that *this* is its profoundest level of meaning. Like great music, it produces a state of sudden intense delight, of inner detachment, of 'breathing space'. The reader who becomes absorbed in the *I Ching* begins to see it as a whole, and will probably become more skilled in using it as an oracle; like water-divining, this power can be developed simply by making the effort. He will also become aware that the book's power to foretell events is an unimportant by-product of its real purpose.

One final point that must not be overlooked. Richard Wilhelm points out that the primary meaning of Yin is 'the cloudy, the overcast', while that of Yang is 'banners waving in the sun'. Could one devise more basic symbols of the central problem of human existence? Dullness and boredom versus the 'moments of vision'.

THREE
THE POET AS OCCULTIST

The poet is a man in whom Faculty X is naturally more developed than in most people. While most of us are ruthlessly 'cutting out' whole areas of perception, thus impoverishing our mental lives, the poet retains the faculty to be suddenly delighted by the sheer *reality* of the world 'out there'.

Do poets, in fact, possess a higher degree of 'occult' powers than most men?

At the time I was discussing the question of 'occult faculties' with Robert Graves in Majorca, I also met the poet Louis Singer, a contemporary of Graves. Singer's attitude towards such matters seemed to be thoroughly sceptical, although he told me he had once conducted various investigations into spiritualism. I asked him for some account of his experiences; the result was a remarkable fifteen-page document that I shall have occasion to quote several times in this chapter. Singer, like Graves, was fortunate in possessing the poet's faculty of total relaxation; he speaks of 'concentration on nothing, allowing the mind to sink into a passive state'.

Séances failed to convince Singer of the reality of psychical phenomena; but he preserved an open mind, and made efforts to place himself in a receptive mood when alone. A medium had told him that he might expect a visit from her 'control', a spirit-child, in his room:

Now, in the quiet of my room, I awaited her visit with relaxed mind. Of course, nothing happened. I next decided to experiment with a candle. I lighted it and kept it under observation. The flame burned undisturbed. With mind relaxed I watched it, hoping against hope for one of those mystic 'breezes'; but none came. However, suddenly I smelt a beautiful perfume that I had not observed before. In the state of passivity I smelt it without any doubt whatever. I rose and tried to trace it. There was nothing in my room to account for it. Finally I followed my nose. It led me from the top of the house to the basement where the bath was situated. There I found the cause – a piece of scented soap. Here then was my first concrete lesson. In the passive state, when the power of intellection is fully suspended, the senses become hypersensitive. Normally I could not have smelt the soap; abnormally I could.

Here, then, is another example of the sharpening of a faculty beyond its normal powers by a kind of effort at quiescence, the urban counterpart of Corbett's jungle sensitiveness. It was as if his faculties were aware that some extra effort was being demanded of them, but they were not sure what it was; the sense of smell located a scent that it would not normally have bothered to register. Our nervous system contains small gaps – called synapses – whose purpose is to filter out unnecessary sensory stimuli; otherwise we would be aware of every small change in temperature, every faint breath of wind against the face, and the powers of concentration would be greatly diminished.

And this underlines a vital point. It was *through* concentration that Singer regained an abnormally sensitive sense of smell. These faculties, which must be placed in abeyance for practical purposes, were not intended to be permanently repressed. We ought to be able to call upon them at will. Then why can't we? Because we fail to develop the ability to concentrate and to still the mind which would restore them.

But perhaps the most interesting point that emerges from Louis Singer's account of his 'investigations' into spiritualism is the way in which it produced certain definite results, even though his attitude remained 'tough-minded' and critical. At the first séance he attended he convinced himself that most of the 'results' were obtained by everybody's desire to be deceived.

One of the sitters announced she could see lights, I too giving my consent as I was too polite to disagree. Another said she could feel a wind. Again agreement to which I assented. Then for a while, nothing. At last I felt it was my turn, so I remarked it was getting lighter. This met with concurrence. Indeed, one went so far as to remark upon the beautiful lights that played around me. I then suggested a wind. So did everyone present. Later the trumpet miraculously floated into the air, the thin air, and a voice recognised by one sitter as a relative spoke. They were all certain it was not the medium's voice – excepting myself. To me there was not the slightest doubt it was the medium's voice, and not too cleverly disguised ... All I gained from these séances was how suggestible people become under such conditions, and how gullible. Also, how exhausting (pleasantly exhausting) concentration on passivity can be.

I cite this passage to demonstrate that Singer was – and is – unfitted by temperament to be a 'true believer'. When a medium finally produced results that convinced him she was not faking, he had no hesitation in attributing it to telepathy:

Nobody present had ever been in my room, or, for that matter, knew where I lived; yet she described my room in detail, and proceeded to give me advice. I wrote in bed. My hand got between the light and the paper, causing a shadow that strained my eyes. I was in danger of tripping going downstairs owing to the dilapidated state of my bedroom slippers. As to the house itself, she was able to tell me the number of steps leading up to the front door, and that it was the last but one from the end of the street. A house almost opposite had recently been redecorated. Except for the last, I did not know whether the other items regarding the house were true or false. I lived in Danvers Street, Chelsea, which runs into Paulton's Square. The houses are terraces without a break. When I returned home I found she was correct in every detail ... The conclusions I drew from this séance were twofold. (1) Matters I had intended to remedy, e.g. the position of the light when writing in bed and the state of my slippers, communicated themselves to the medium without difficulty, as did the subconscious checks I used in locating the house and recognising it. (2) Any questions that arose from intellection or scholarship could not be answered. Thus the question whether Jesus belonged to the Essenes ... went without reply.

He discovered that he could influence the séance, not only by verbal suggestion but by telepathy. A circular dog's basket suggested to him the shape of a coracle:

... I have, together with most poets, a visual memory that not only is factual but also imaginative ... I immediately visualised a coracle. The chairs were arranged in the customary circle. and by accident one too many was put into position. The medium instructed us to leave it. Some spirit might want to join the circle. It was left, and sure enough a spirit invisible to us occupied it. It was, the medium said, a drowned sailor.

After this, I tried on more than one occasion to dictate what spirit should come through, using the method of visual projection. I was largely successful.

It was at this point I began to toy with the idea of the group mind. Take the example of the coracle and the supposed drowned sailor. Presumably I, without speaking, communicated the idea of a vessel, a very unstable vessel, to the circle. This was seized upon by the medium and the others of the group, supplemented from their own experiences and built up into the drowned sailor ...

He tells other anecdotes of a similar nature, and of occasionally deliberately 'leading them on', to find how much they would swallow. His conclusion was: 'Spiritualists are by and large the most credulous people I have ever met. They believe almost everything connected with so-called supernatural phenomena. Compared to their credulity, the faith that moved mountains seems like scepticism.' Even so, he made observations of definite psychological effects that can only be explained by telepathy: 'One of the aims is to give power to the medium. Thus in a service, the congregation is asked to send out "the right vibrations" ... in séances, this effect is achieved by allowing the mind to direct, or rather to beam on the medium. This is difficult to describe. One feels it going out of one. I developed this technique to some extent, and found that I could not only use it to induce trance condition in the medium, but also to end this condition.'

Louis Singer later joined a 'development circle', where the aim was for individual members to develop mediumistic powers. Singer was unsuccessful. 'I closed my eyes, emptied my mind, even at *times* dozed off, but trance – never!' Even so, he was told by the medium that he had acquired spirit guides, one of whom was a Hindu guru. And when alone with a friend who was also associated with the circle, he decided to try to sink into a trance. 'I said: "Will you observe me, and I'll let the guru come through." She nodded and I closed my eyes and sank into a semi-trance. Suddenly I felt my belly sink in till it seemed to meet my spine. After a short spell I opened my eyes to find Maud gazing away from me to the other side of the room. I felt annoyed. "What are you doing?" I demanded. "You agreed to watch me." "I was," she replied. "You came out of your body and were sitting on that other chair."'

He later developed mild powers of psychometry – the ability to pick up 'vibrations' from objects handed to him. 'I also found I could see the "guides", or secondary personalities, of people, and symbolic pictures or future happenings, but not the distant future. How this came about I have not the slightest idea. I was not conscious of any change in my mind or personality. The only difference between now and formerly was that now I could reach out (metaphorically speaking) and grasp what had previously eluded *me*.'

The only incident that could not be explained in purely telepathic terms was an attempt to duplicate an experiment described by J. W. Dunne in his *Experiment with Time*, in which Dunne 'visualised' the face of his watch while lying in bed, and was able to tell the exact time.* Singer goes on:

On the mantelshelf in my bedroom was a clock with a white metal surround. One morning I had an appointment. I awoke. The room was in absolute darkness ... I tried to repeat the Dunne experiment. I saw the clock in front of my eyes, and decided, as it were, that I could go to sleep for at least another hour, and I did so. When I woke up the second time, I again 'looked at' the clock clairvoyantly, got up, removed the blackout blinds, and confirmed the accuracy of my vision. Now the strange thing was that the surround of the clock in the 'vision' was pale gold ... I then proceeded to analyse my vision as one would a dream. Animals and birds have a built-in time mechanism. They will turn up to the minute when food awaits them ... Indeed, I myself can go happily to sleep, having told myself to wake up at such and such an hour, and wake at precisely that hour. Therefore it was not surprising that I saw the right time clairvoyantly. All that had happened was that my subconscious knowledge of the time had revealed itself in

* See Part Three, Chapter 3.

the projected image of the clock. As to the golden colour of the surround, this could have been an optimistic symbol of the outcome of the experiment. But I must confess I found this explanation to be of doubtful accuracy when I discovered that the clock had been ten minutes fast.

He had seen the time actually *shown by the clock*, not the correct time. The inference is surely that whatever 'powers' he developed were not dependent purely upon telepathic contact with other minds, but could also, so to speak, work directly upon matter.

I have quoted this document at such length because it seems to me to be a perfectly balanced summary of the pros and cons of such experiments in the 'occult'. Singer was a poet, although his disposition tended towards scepticism, and his attempts to develop his powers were, on the whole, successful. What is immediately noticeable here is that actual close involvement in 'occultism' seems to have the effect of *making* things happen, changing the whole life-frame of the experimenter who may, up to that time, have been completely non-psychic. Louis Singer remarks, 'Once one becomes involved in the psychic, there is a certain lack of communication with those who have not had similar experience.' And he goes on to make the important observation: 'Mysticism and spiritualism are arrived at, not by willing, but by *unwilling*. The will has to be abnegated before attainment can be possible. In other words, attainment is involuntary. The actions preceding attainment are instrumental in banishing the will entirely.' However, this should not be taken too literally, for obviously one's capacities *can* be developed, which implies that there is some point in effort. On the other hand, it is also true that a certain passive, negative attitude towards one's own life often seems to induce accident-proneness and a tendency to disturbing coincidences. This becomes very dear in reading Strindberg's late autobiographical writings: *Inferno*, *Legends*, *The Occult Diary*, for example. The normal, rational reader would like to believe that all the strange incidents and coincidences can have a natural explanation, and that Strindberg's paranoia is to blame. For example, he writes:

> Some days ago, as I was going along the pavement, I saw an inn keeper before his door, loudly abusing a knife-grinder who was standing in the street. I did not want to cut off the connection between the two, but it could not be avoided, and I experienced a keen feeling of discomfort as I passed between the two quarrelling men. It was as though I had divided a cord which was stretched between them, or rather as though I had crossed a street which was being sprinkled with water. (*Legends*, p. 94)

One's first reaction is to dismiss it as imagination, something purely subjective. But Gurdjieff, an altogether more reliable and balanced authority, told Ouspensky: 'Have you noticed how, if a man passes quite close to you on a narrow pavement, you become all tense? The same tension takes place between planets ...'*

Strindberg believed that his sufferings and misfortunes were due to an attempt at the practice of black magic. He claims that he had noticed his ability to exercise telepathic influence on absent friends. He was separated from his wife, and wanted to devise a method of bringing about a reconciliation. 'An unwholesome instinct' suggested the idea of using his telepathic powers to make his daughter ill – not seriously ill, but enough to provide the excuse for a visit. He set to work with a photograph of her. He began to experience a feeling of foreboding, and when examining a nut germ under a microscope a few days later, saw that it had the shape of a child's hands clasped in supplication; a friend verified the remarkable resemblance. The attempt misfired; it was the two children of his first marriage who fell ill – a letter describing their illness bore the date of his attempts to

---

* *In Search of the Miraculous*, p. 24.

exercise the 'evil eye'. From this date on, misfortune pursued him, and he was convinced that he had brought it on himself. The catalogue of his 'occult' experiences is so strange that it is tempting to dismiss the whole thing as self-delusion. Incredible coincidences become commonplace, and he is convinced that these are all intended as signs and messages. His coat, placed over the shoulders of a friend, sends the friend into convulsions, and Strindberg believes this is because of his 'electric fluid'. He dreams of an unusual-looking clock, and the next day, sees it in a shop window. He sees a mountain landscape in the corrosion stains on the side of a zinc bath, and later recognises the identical landscape when he visits his wife's home in Austria. He suspects that he possesses the involuntary power of dematerialisation, or becoming invisible. Friends looking for him fail to see him until he touches them and speaks to them. After separating from his third wife, Harriet Bosse, he is convinced that her 'astral body' visits him at night and masturbates him. He also possesses the involuntary power of leaving his body, or 'travelling clairvoyance'* (as it has come to be called). I have already cited two examples of this; on another occasion, he imaginatively transported himself to a scene in his past with such vividness that he actually found himself standing in a garden of his childhood, smelling various flowers and able to touch things; when his wife roused him from this 'trance' by touching his shoulder, he became unconscious and collapsed on the floor. That is to say, his travelling clairvoyance seemed to work in time as well as space.

In trying to decide how much of this is genuine, and how much due to his imagination, we again confront the basic problem: that in such matters, illusion and reality are so thoroughly confused that it is impossible to draw a line. The disposition to expect strange events seems to *make* them happen, and one can only accept that in a large number of cases, they really did happen.

* See Part Three, Chapter 2.

The truth is that we need to revise the simple rationalist approach to such problems. Everyone has met people to whom a particular type of accident or misfortune is always happening. It is almost as if they attract a certain kind of situation or event; and in many cases, one can see they did nothing – consciously – to bring it on themselves. One must simply accept that there are certain types of person to whom certain types of things seem to happen. No rational explanation can cover this completely.

An important point emerges in connection with Strindberg. He was a 'loner'. In the opening sentence of *Inferno* he says: 'With a feeling of wild joy I returned from the northern railway station where I had said goodbye to my wife ... My newly won freedom gave me a feeling of expansion, and elevation above the petty cares of life ...' Living alone, in a single room, in a strange city, produces a strange feeling of almost morbid intensity, like living inside a glass bubble – as anyone who has experienced it will vouch. The great classics of 'loneliness' – Rilke's *Notebook of Malte Laurids Brigge*, Knut Hamsun's *Hunger*, Sartre's *Nausea*, Söderberg's *Doctor Glas*, Amiel's *Journals*, Barbellion's *Journal of a Disappointed Man* – all have this obsessive quality of intensity. Social man is distracted and self-divided. Man-on-his-own generates a kind of single-mindedness whether he likes it or not. And single-mindedness is the first requisite for 'occult' experience, when the powers of the subconscious begin to make themselves felt in consciousness.

But in considering these strange experiences of Strindberg, the dividing line should not be drawn between things that 'really happened' and freaks of imagination, but between events that he somehow 'willed involuntarily' and events in which his subconscious mind played no *active* part. For example, he is insistent that the mountain scenery he saw in the zinc bath corresponded exactly with the mountains near his wife's home at Dornach, which he had never visited. The rationalist explanation would be that he recognised the scenery near Dornach as vaguely similar to images caused by oxidisation of the zinc bath. Strindberg's own explanation would be that 'unseen powers', intent on guiding his destiny, arranged the whole thing to make him aware of their existence. The truth could lie between the two: that telepathic contact with his wife – who was in Dornach at the time he was taking the bath – implanted the picture of the mountain scenery in his mind, and he 'saw' it in the corroded zinc as one sees faces in a fire.

Poets seem to provide a particularly rich field for research into the 'occult', and I have tried to argue that this is because Faculty X is at once the creative faculty and the occult faculty. Robert Graves even goes so far as to contend that all true poems are written in the 'fifth dimension'; but one need not go so far as that, to see that poetry arises out of a certain inner stillness and unity. The historian and poet A. L. Rowse – who, like Graves, is a Celt – also provided me with notes on his own experiences of the para-normal in which this connection is perfectly clear. Rowse, like Strindberg, has always been a 'loner', as his autobiography, *A Cornish Childhood*, makes clear. His poetry is full of a quality of stillness, loneliness:

> *The whole bay brimming with the silent sea,*
> *The call of a curlew, the creaking of a plough …*

or:

> *Evening, Silence, and the questioning of birds.*
> *A bugle blows its erotic note over the city …*

or:

> *The moon, the snow, the light of winter afternoons,*
> *as if one were seeing life go by*
> *from under the sea …*

He writes, in notes entitled 'Telepathy and Such':

> A queer experience of my own comes under the same heading – presentiment, not telepathy.

My undergraduate sitting-room at Christ Church had heavy Victorian sash-windows: each might well have weighed 25 or 30 pounds. One summer evening I was leaning out with the heavy window up, just above my outstretched neck – like a guillotine – when I thought: Suppose if the thing should fall?

I was unwell and, in a black mood, said:

'Let the damned thing fall!'

In a second I forgot, and drew back my head quite casually. In a flash, that moment, the window fell.

What frightened me was not so much that it fell as that I had challenged it to fall, tempted Providence ...

He goes on:

Much about the same time, a period of duodenal illness and strain, in the dead of one afternoon, it suddenly came into my head that if I went all the way down from my rooms to the Library I should see two young men in each other's embrace. I descended, crossed two quadrangles, entered the Library – and there they were!

I didn't know who they were, and have never been presented with such a situation since. I hope I behaved like a gentleman and withdrew quietly; perhaps it was not very gentlemanly of me to have gone, but I acted on suggestion, almost like sleepwalking – and there the situation was!

... I daresay [such experiences] go back to our own earlier animal condition, when all the intuitive element in our makeup was much stronger, and that it has now shrunk very much, become feebler with the development of the upright position and the roof-brain, the reasoning faculties of *homo* (still not very) *sapiens*.

Rowse's assumption that 'animal faculties' include not only abnormally developed senses, but 'second sight', is one that is widely accepted. The Scottish poet Hugh MacDiarmid told me that his wife always knew when he was returning from long journeys – on one occasion as far away as China – because his dog would go and sit at the end of the lane about forty-eight hours before he would arrive home. Telepathy seems to be the obvious hypothesis here, except that on one occasion, the dog sat at the end of the lane before MacDiarmid himself knew he was returning home.

I myself have seen the dog belonging to Eve Farson, wife of the writer Negley Farson, growling at a corner of her bedroom that had once held the basket of the previous dog, now deceased. Eve Farson told me that she had at first kept Albert's basket in that corner, but that his predecessor had 'driven him out' of it so often that she decided to move the basket. And once again, one could explain this by positing some form of animal 'intuition' or telepathy – perhaps even that Eve Farson herself communicated the knowledge of the previous dog to Albert. But no matter how often one calls upon the telepathy hypothesis, there always remain the incidents that cannot be made to fit. Rowse writes:

> In *A Cornish Childhood* I tell the story of my father's youngest brother, Charlie, killed in a mining accident in South Africa. Before leaving home the boy was forever fiddling with our kitchen clock, trying to make it strike, which it had ceased to do, and he couldn't mend it. One day at meal-time, the clock struck out loud, to the surprise of father and mother at table – it was at the time Charlie was killed, they found. They always called it inaccurately (for they hardly knew the meanings of words) a 'presentiment', or more properly, 'a token'.

And this underlines the problem that one encounters frequently in writing about the occult. The assumption of telepathy or

Faculty X can explain a great deal. Rowse says: 'I have found these phenomena far more frequent in periods of illness – perhaps when one's sensibility or receptivity is heightened, and when one's rational controls are lowered.' But pure telepathy can hardly explain the striking of a clock.

The next most likely assumption is that these strange faculties can, under certain circumstances, act directly upon matter, except that we are still dealing solely with human beings – or animals and their subconscious powers. *Not* with any 'unseen power' outside man. This 'minimum working hypothesis' seems to be borne out by a story told by Arthur Grimble in *Pattern of Islands*:

The natives of the Gilbert Islands believed that when someone died, his spirit had to proceed to a sandspit at the northern end of the island of Makin-Meang, a locale known as the Place of Dread. After visiting this halfway house, the ghost could then proceed to paradise, provided that certain rituals performed over his dead body were able to avert the attentions of Nakaa, the Watcher at the Gate, who tried to strangle the spirit in his net.

Grimble persuaded the local constable to take him to see the Place of Dread. The man was, predictably, very nervous, and the visit was hardly a pleasure trip. On the way back, Grimble saw a man approaching: 'Across the arc of a curving beach, I saw him appear round a point. I could follow every yard of his course as he came nearer. My eyes never left him, because my intent was pinned on his getting me that drink. He walked with a strong limp ... He was a stocky, grizzled man of about fifty, clad rather ceremoniously in a fine mat belted about his middle ... I noticed that his left cheek was scored by a scar from jawbone to temple, and that his limp came from a twisted left foot and ankle. I can see the man still in memory ... He totally ignored the greeting I gave him. He did not even turn his eyes towards me. He went by as if I didn't exist.'

Grimble called the constable, who was walking some way ahead, and asked him who the man was. The result was that the constable had hysterics, and rushed back home. Grimble followed him, and promptly complained to the native magistrate about the strange goings-on. They were able to identify the man with the limp. His name was Na Biria, and he had died at the time when Grimble saw him. His body lay at present in a nearby hut. Grimble's first impulse was to insist on seeing the body, to confirm that it was indeed the same man. Then, remembering that any interruption of the rituals might deliver the spirit into the hands of the Watcher of the Gate, he decided against it.

The constable, who had also passed the limping man, had seen no one.

Grimble very rightly doubts the existence of the Watcher of the Gate, or the importance of the Place of Dread as a halfway house to paradise. But the dying man had believed in it, which was enough to project his 'phantasm' along the road to the north. It seems probable that he was still alive when Grimble saw him limping past, and that his thoughts projected his image. Everyone in the islands believed that spirits had to enter paradise via the Place of Dread, and this was enough to produce the 'phantasm'.

This is a tempting hypothesis, since it can be applied to most paranormal phenomena, from poltergeists to witchcraft: the notion that 'magic' is a form of telepathy exercised by the 'group mind' rather than by individual minds.

But does it really simplify anything? How does group telepathy explain the 'prophetic' powers of the *I Ching*? Or Mark Bredin's precognition that his taxi was about to be hit by another one? Or any of the dozens of cases in Arthur W. Osborn's book *The Future is Now*, of which this is a typical example:

The report is by Mademoiselle Dulay, of the Comédie Française.

It concerns the tragic end of the young actress, Mademoiselle

Irene Muza. Mlle. Muza was in a hypnotic trance when she was asked if she could see what awaited her personally in the future. She wrote the following:

'My career will be short: I dare not say what my end will be: it will be terrible.'

Naturally the experimenters, who were greatly impressed by the prediction, erased what had been written before awakening Mlle. Muza from the trance. She therefore had no conscious knowledge of what she had predicted for herself. But even if she had known, it would not have caused the type of death she suffered.

It was some months later that the prediction 'My career will be short' was fulfilled. And indeed, her end was 'terrible'. Her hairdresser had allowed some drops of an antiseptic lotion made of mineral essences to fall on a lighted stove. Mlle. Muza was instantly enveloped in flames, her hair and clothing were set afire and she suffered burns so severe that she died in hospital a few hours later.*

If such cases are to be explained in terms of telepathy and the group mind, then one has to include the notion that the past and future are also somehow accessible to the group mind – Jung's assumption about the *I Ching*.

The thought that the Muza case suggests is one that must have occurred to many people – perhaps when they wake in the middle of the night: that our lives are a kind of gramophone record or film, whose end is, to some extent, pre-determined. I say 'to some extent' because we all have an undeniable sensation of free will in moments of crisis or great excitement. It is an idea that has occurred to many occultists: that life is basically some kind of game, whose pre-condition

* Arthur W. Osborn. *The Future is Now* (with an Introduction by Eileen J. Garrett, president of the Parapsychology Foundation Inc.), New York, University Books, 1961.

is that the players should suffer from amnesia, and then cope as best they can with the series of choices presented over three-quarters of a century. In that case, criminals could be regarded as the losers, those who have made the worst possible choices; the winners would be those who have come closest to overcoming the 'forgetfulness' with which we begin the game. In *The Mysterious Stranger*, Mark Twain made the disturbing assertion that God got tired of being in a lonely, empty universe, and created the whole shadow show of life, in which he is the only real person – the others being robots, made to seem alive. The founder of scientology, L. Ron Hubbard, teaches that men are gods who invented the world as a game, into which they 'descended', and then became victims of their own amnesia, so they became trapped in their game. It is unnecessary to point out that all the great religions hold the view that the essence of man and the essence of God are one and the same. 'I am God, I am God' cried Nijinsky, on the point of madness.

In connection with these glimpses of the future, it is interesting to consider the views of another poet, W. B. Yeats, who also began by accepting telepathy as his 'minimum working hypothesis'. Yeats's interest in the occult was stimulated by Mary Battle, the servant of his uncle George Pollexfen, who possessed second sight. Pollexfen 'would tell how several times, arriving home with an unexpected guest, he had found the table set for three'.

'One morning she was about to bring him a clean shirt, but stopped, saying there was blood on the shirt-front and that she must bring him another. On his way to his office he fell, crossing over a little wall, and cut himself and bled on to the linen where she had seen the blood. In the evening, she told him that the shirt she had thought bloody was quite clean.' (*Reveries*, XVII)

Later, in London, Yeats attended séances and magical conjurations, and joined The Order of the Golden Dawn, led by a strange Scotsman named MacGregor Mathers, whom Yeats met in the British Museum.

It was Mathers, Yeats said, 'who convinced me that images well up before the mind's eye from a *deeper source than conscious or subconscious memory* [my italics]'. Yeats's friend the actress Florence Farr told of how she went for a walk with Mathers, and in a field of sheep he said, 'Look at the sheep. I am going to imagine myself a ram,' with the extraordinary result that the sheep ran after him. Yeats writes:

> He had given her a piece of cardboard on which was a coloured geometrical symbol and had told her to hold it up to her forehead and she had found herself walking upon a cliff above the sea, seagulls shrieking overhead ...

> He gave me a cardboard symbol and I closed my eyes. Sight came slowly, there was not that sudden miracle as if the darkness had been cut with a knife, for that miracle is mostly a woman's privilege, but there rose before me mental images that I could not control: a desert and a black Titan raising himself up by his two hands from the middle of a heap of ancient ruins. Mathers explained that I had seen a being of the order of the Salamanders because he had shown me their symbol, but it was not necessary even to show the symbol, it would have been sufficient that he imagined it.

These 'symbols' that Mathers traced on pieces of cardboard were from the Kabbalah, several books of which Mathers had translated (or adapted) under the title *The Kabbalah Unveiled*. The Kabbalah (of which more will be said later) is a body of ancient Jewish mystical teachings and commentaries on scripture, first written down in the thirteenth century; it asks, How can God, who is presumably perfect and changeless, have got mixed up in the creation of the world? and answers that He put forth ten 'emanations' – called Sephiroth – who actually did the work of creation. Inevitably, the Sephiroth and their creations are all represented by symbols, and these so-called 'kabbalistic symbols' are what Mathers used.

Yeats was by no means entirely convinced by Mathers, who was a strange, cranky figure; he says that when Mathers made some extravagant claim, his friends would make allowances 'as though he were a figure in a play of our composition'* – a polite way of saying that they excused everything by regarding him as a 'character'. But Yeats was baffled by the effect of symbols on the mind. 'It was long before I myself would admit an inherent power in symbols, for it long seemed to me that one could account for everything by the power of one imagination over another, or by telepathy…'†

He was perfectly willing to accept telepathy, and even the power of projecting one's body elsewhere. He tells how, when in Paris, he was on his way out one morning to buy a newspaper, and passed the servant girl, newly arrived from the country. He was thinking, as he passed her, that if such and such had happened, he would have hurt his arm; and he envisaged himself with his arm in a sling. On returning, his host and hostess said: 'Why, the *bonne* [servant] has just told us you had your arm in a sling.'

He also writes: 'One afternoon, about the same time, I was thinking very intently of a certain fellow student for whom I had a message, which I hesitated about writing. In a couple of days I got a letter from a place some hundreds of miles away where the student was. On the afternoon when I had been thinking so intently I had suddenly appeared there amid a crowd of people in a hotel and seeming as solid as if in the flesh. My fellow student had seen me, but no one else, and had asked me to come again when the people had gone. I had vanished, but had come again in the middle of the night and given him the message. I myself had no knowledge of either apparition.'‡

This is similar to cases already cited, and explains why Powys

* *Autobiography*, New York, Macmillan, 1956, p. 187.
† Essay on magic in *Essays and Introductions*, London, 1961, p. 48. Originally published in *Ideas of Good and Evil*.
‡ *Essays and Introductions*, p. 37.

was apparently surprised when Dreiser rang him up to announce his 'apparition'. Yeats's explanation of such phenomena is consistent with what has already been suggested here; he says that 'the greater energies of the mind seldom break forth but when the deeps are loosened' – that is, he attributes it to some strange 'loosening' of the subconscious. He agrees that Florence Farr's 'vision' of the cliff-top might easily have been telepathy, if not pure imagination. And yet there seemed a certain amount of evidence that the symbols produced definite mental images quite apart from the minds involved. 'It was the symbol itself, or, at any rate, not my conscious intention, that produced the effect, for if I made an error and told someone to gaze at the wrong symbol – they were painted upon cards – the vision would be suggested by the symbol, not by my thoughts ...'

So the symbols often seemed to be strangely independent of the minds involved: he speaks of a young Irish-woman who 'thought the apple of Eve the kind you can buy at the greengrocers, but in her trance she saw the Tree of Life with ever-sighing souls moving in its branches instead of sap, and among its leaves all the fowls of the air, and on its highest bough one white fowl wearing a crown'. On arriving home, Yeats consulted Mathers's *Kabbalah Unveiled* and read: 'The Tree ... is the Tree of the Knowledge of Good and Evil ... in its branches the birds lodge and build their nests, the souls and the angels have their place.' He states that he came upon this passage by cutting the pages for the first time, so that it could not have been telepathic transference of his own mental image. Again, a west-of-Ireland bank clerk in whom he induced a trance saw the tree in a walled garden on top of a mountain, observed the souls sighing through its branches and saw apples with human faces, from which came the sound of fighting. The image from the *Zohar* (a book of the Kabbalah) is here supplemented by an image of the Purgatorial mount of Dante, with its walled Paradise on top; the sounds of battle (another girl heard the clashing of swords from inside the trunk) obviously represents what will happen if the apples are eaten. Yeats accounts for all this by speaking of the 'Anima Mundi described by Platonic philosophers', a kind of *racial* memory independent of embodied individual memories, though they constantly enrich it with their images and their thoughts. 'Almost everyone who has ever busied himself with such matters has come, in trance or dream, upon some new and strange symbol or event, which he has afterwards found in some work he has never read or heard of. Examples like this are as yet too little classified, too little analysed, to convince the stranger, but some of them are proof enough for those they have happened to, proof that there is a memory of Nature that reveals events and symbols of distant centuries. Mystics of many countries and many centuries, have spoken of this memory ...' And he defines the real danger of this 'lunar knowledge': 'It is perhaps well that so few believe in it, for if many did many would go out of parliaments and universities and libraries and run into the wilderness to so waste the body, and to so hush the unquiet mind that, still living, they might pass the doors the dead pass daily; for who among the wise would trouble himself with making laws or in history or in weighing the earth if the things of eternity seemed ready to hand?' Aldous Huxley makes the same point in speaking of the effects of mescalin in *The Doors of Perception*: that in a world in which everyone took psychedelics there would be no wars, but no civilisation either.

Yeats, then, takes the next logical step in the argument – a step taken some years later by Jung himself: that there is a racial memory, which works in terms of symbols. This racial memory can be reached by 'hushing the unquiet mind', by reaching a certain depth of inner stillness where it becomes accessible to the limited individual memory.

Yeats goes even further, and suggests that 'magical cures' used by primitive peoples may produce their effect by somehow touching these subliminal depths: 'Such magical simples as the husk of the flax, water out of the fork of an elm-tree, do their work, as I think, by awaking in the depths of the mind where it mingles with the Great Mind, and is enlarged by the Great Memory, some curative energy, some hypnotic command. They are not what we call faith cures, for they have been much used and successfully, the traditions of all lands affirm, over children and over animals, and to me they seem the only medicine that could have been committed safely to ancient hands …' And he concludes: 'I cannot now think symbols less than the greatest of all powers. whether they are used consciously by the masters of magic, or half-unconsciously by their successors, the poet, the musician and the artist.'

Here, then, is a theory of magic that covers all the phenomena described so far in this book, from simple telepathy to the strange complexities of the Druidic tree alphabet and the incarnations of the White Goddess described by Graves.

It is important to understand that an enormous amount of our human experience is really a response to symbols. I speak in *Origins of the Sexual Impulse* of an underwear fetishist who stopped the car when he was driving with his wife, went into a garden and removed a brassiere and panties from a clothesline; he laid these on the ground, and proceeded to go through the motions of copulation with them. Response to the symbol of 'forbidden-ness' – another woman's underwear – was obviously stronger than his response to the actuality of his wife beside him in the car. This is the peculiarity of human beings: that a symbol can gain a hold on the imagination and cause a more powerful response than the actuality that it represents. Control over our deeper powers comes from symbols rather than from straightforward acts of will. Ten minutes before writing this, I was feeling drowsy, having eaten a large breakfast; I opened a book of coloured photographs, and saw one of a wide yellow beach and a deep-blue sea, which instantly produced a sense of coolness, of expansion, as if I had accidentally touched some valve and let the pressure out of a tyre. Symbols can evoke a response even when I am bored and tired, and my senses have lost their interest in 'reality'. Since this has been happening over two million years of evolution, is it implausible to suppose that certain symbols have found a permanent place in the depths of the human psyche? A youth who responds to the picture of a naked woman is responding as 'symbolically' as the fetishist who is excited by her underclothes. Why should it be scientific orthodoxy to accept the 'instinctive' effect of a sexual symbol on the human imagination, and deny those of a religious symbol whose power over the human imagination may be equally deep-rooted?

It is interesting to note that when Yeats came to produce his own attempt at a 'symbolic system', the moon became his central image. Sixteen years after he had written his essay on magic (published in *Ideas of Good and Evil*), Yeats married a Miss Hyde Lees, and four days after their wedding she began to produce automatic writing. In an essay published in *Per Amica Silentia Lunae*, Yeats had asked whether it might not be possible to prick upon the calendar the birth of a Napoleon or Christ. The unknown 'communicator' who used his wife's hand attempted to answer this question by producing a system of symbols, based upon the twenty-eight phases of the moon, and upon two types of men: those who gain power from their combat with circumstance, and those who gain strength from the combat with themselves.

The 'system' is very nearly as complex as that expounded in Graves's *White Goddess*, and a good deal more arbitrary. Or at least, it seems so. The men who belong to each of the twenty-eight phases each have four sets of characteristics: (1) the Will – that is to say, what sort of person they are basically: the hero, the sensuous man, the obsessed man, etc., (2) the Mask – the face he creates to show the world (which is often the opposite of his true character), (3) the Creative Mind – that is to say, his natural creative tendency: intellectuality, emotionality, self-dramatisation, simplicity, etc.' (4) what Yeats calls the 'Body of Fate', which means simply the man's destiny, what the law of the stars decrees for him, so to speak.

The Mask and the Creative Mind each have two possibilities; they can express themselves truly or falsely. For example, Yeats gives as his typical man of Phase Twelve Nietzsche 'the Forerunner'. The Mask he creates to expose to the world is Self-Exaggeration when true, and Self-Abandonment when false. The true expression of his creativity is subjective philosophy, and the false expression is Conflict between two forms of self-expression. This sounds obscure until one tries substituting James Joyce for Nietzsche; then the meaning can be seen: the forerunner whose mask is self-exaggeration (Stephen Dedalus and Shem the Penman), and whose creativity expresses itself ideally as intense subjectivity. In *Finnegan's Wake*, this subjectivity becomes deliberate obscurity of expression: the conflict between the desire to reach an audience and the desire to be secretive and esoteric.

All this sounds more complicated than, in fact, it is. The central idea of the book is very simple: that these four characteristics (or 'faculties', as Yeats calls them) go through various stages of fulfilment, like the phases of the moon. So that, for example, when one turns to Phase Twenty, the Concrete Man, and discovers Shakespeare, Balzac and Napoleon given as examples, it all slowly begins to make sense. The true form of the Mask is fatalism – very apparent in all three – and its false form, superstition. The true form of the Creative Mind is Dramatisation of the Mask – and once again, this is easy enough to grasp in the plays of Shakespeare and novels of Balzac – the dramatisation of fatalism (and occasionally of superstition). Its false form is self-desecration. The Fate of the Concrete Man is enforced success of action – that is, a kind of success that drags him along like a slave behind a chariot and may overwhelm him.

The simplest way to understand *A Vision* is to begin in this way – by studying his examples. It is easier to grasp the significance of a Phase in terms of Parnell or Oscar Wilde or Shelley than by studying its place in the lunar cycle.

These various phases also relate to certain periods of history, which 'throw up' a certain type of dominant figure: Christ, Napoleon, Pascal, Byron.

Whether the reader chooses to accept all this literally is a matter of the individual temperament. Yeats himself ends the Introduction by explaining, disconcertingly, that he does not regard all this as true, but as a 'stylistic arrangement of experience comparable to the cubes in the drawing of Wyndham Lewis'. But a painter *imposes* his own emotional vision upon reality, because 'reality' is all things to all men, and he experiences a compulsion to show what it is to *him*. Similarly, Robert Graves answers the question whether he believes poets to be literally inspired by the White Goddess by saying that, as with the question of whether the Hebrew prophets were directly inspired by God, you can accept it either as metaphor or as fact. And Graves's assertion that '[his] task in writing *The White Goddess* was to provide a grammar or poetic myth for poets' echoes Yeats's ghostly communicants: 'We have come to give you metaphors for poetry.'

But what *is* important is to recognise that *The White Goddess* and *A Vision* are closely allied to the *I Ching* and the Kabbalah: they are attempts to organise 'lunar knowledge', our intuitive sense of 'meanings' behind reality, into some kind of system. To dismiss these attempts as superstition or imagination is to completely miss the point. The kind of knowledge we use to get through a day at the office is logical, conscious knowledge. But we also live on a more intuitive level, and this intuitive knowledge could be compared to the nerves in its sides by which a fish can sense changes in the temperature and pressure of the water. When I am tired and depressed, these intuitions cease to work and I become accident-prone; when I am healthy and optimistic, I sense the ebb and flow of life around me like a fish. A poet in a state of intense 'receptivity' may feel as though he is a spider in the centre of a web, receiving vibrations from all parts of the universe. There is a sense of hidden laws, of 'rules of the game' that are not the laws of chance or of physics. Did the 'system' of *A Vision* come from disembodied spirits, speaking through his wife, or was it the product of Yeats's subconscious mind, after half a century of occult studies? The question is not important. Think of the book as a net that attempts to trap lunar intuitions that evade the nets of reason, and to *induce* the feeling of being a spider in the centre of a web or a fish in its stream. I am willing to believe that Yeats was completely honest in his description of how *A Vision* came to him; but even if it could be proved that he was stretching the truth, it would make no difference to the value of the book. What does it matter who wove the net, if it catches the fish?

All human beings share a common craving: to escape the narrowness of their lives, the suffocation of their immediate surroundings. This, as Einstein says, is why men want to escape from cities, to get into the peace of mountains at weekends. The narrowness of our lives makes the senses close up, until we feel stifled. This also explains why Ouspensky found 'a strange flavour of truth' in books on Atlantis and magic. It is important for us to feel that there is another kind of knowledge, quite different from the logical laws that govern everyday existence, strange realities beyond the walls that surround us. Art, music, philosophy, mysticism are all escape routes from the narrowness of everyday reality; but they all demand a large initial outlay of conscious effort; you have to sow before you can reap.

In comparison, 'magic' or occultism is a simple, direct method of escaping the narrowness of everydayness. Instead of turning outwards, to the world of the great composers or philosophers, the student of the occult turns immediately inward and tries to reach down to his subliminal depths.

This explains why the earliest and simplest forms of magic are symbolic. Not only have symbols a strange power to appeal to the subconscious mind; they are also easy to grasp and to meditate upon. This explains the enormous influence of the *I Ching* over so many centuries. It also explains the popularity of the most important Western system of symbolic knowledge, the Tarot, which must now be considered.

One of the oddest things about the Tarot pack is that there seem to be no legends concerning its origin, although an eighteenth-century philologist, Count de Gebelin, declared that it is fundamentally an ancient Egyptian work called the *Book of Thoth*. But this was before the Rosetta Stone enabled scholars to read Egyptian hieroglyphics; and it must be admitted that subsequent investigation has unearthed no sign of the Tarot pack in ancient Egypt. The Egyptian notion may have arisen from the known fact that the Tarot was used by gypsy fortune-tellers in the fifteenth century. But the notion that it was invented by the gypsies is contradicted by evidence that it was known in Spain, Germany and France at least a century earlier. A painter named Gringonneur made a pack of Tarot cards for the insane Charles VI of France in 1392 – of which seventeen still survive in the Bibliothèque Nationale in Paris. But according to De Givry, in his *Anthologie de L'Occultisme* (1931) there are records of the Tarot in Germany in 1329, a century before the gypsies appeared in Europe.

That a work like the Tarot pack should have no known origin – even a legendary one – may not seem surprising, until one studies the pack. It consists of seventy-eight cards, and can really be divided into two packs: one of playing cards similar to our ordinary pack, except that they have pictures as well as numbers, and twenty-two cards containing various typical symbols of the Middle Ages – the Juggler, the High Priestess, the Hermit, the Pope, the Wheel of Fortune and so on. And these symbol cards remain unchanged through the ages, and their order remains the same. If the pack had been an arbitrary invention of gypsy fortune-tellers, one might expect it to exist in many versions. Count de Gebelin, writing before the French Revolution, declared, for example, that a picture representing the Hanged Man, a man hanging upside down by one foot, is obviously a mistake of early playing-card manufacturers: that the design originally represented Prudence – a man standing on one foot, and reaching out cautiously for a place to put the other – a man with a Suspended Foot, so to speak. But the 1392 Tarot of Charles VI shows a man hanging upside down by one foot, as in all later designs, and this was long before there were such things as printers of playing cards.

Then what does the Hanged Man card *mean*? I have several reproductions of it in different versions, and all have certain things in common. The man hangs from the cross-beam of a gibbet, tied by one foot. The other leg is bent, and its lower part crosses the other leg at right angles, making a tau cross. Oddly enough, the face has no expression of suffering, and there is a golden halo around his head – which, in the Charles VI pack, is simply his hair. Eliphaz Levi, an imaginative occultist of the nineteenth century,* based the twenty-two chapters of his *Dogme et Rituel de la Haute Magie* on the twenty-two trump cards of the Tarot, and has a short section in the twelfth chapter (the Hanged Man is the twelfth card) 'explaining' the Hanged Man as a symbol of Prometheus, whose feet are planted in heaven and whose head only touches earth, 'the free and immolated adept, the revealer menaced with death'. This is all very well, but the hanged man's feet are not in heaven, and neither does his head touch the earth. A. E. Waite, a fellow

* See Part Three, Chapter 6.

'hermetic student' of Yeats's, becomes unusually exalted on the subject in his own book on the Tarot, explaining darkly that we may 'exhaust all published interpretations and find only vanity'. He goes on to explain: 'He who can understand that the story of his higher nature is embedded in this symbol will receive intimations concerning a great awakening that is possible ...,' all of which reveals that although he dismisses Levi as an ignoramus on the subject, he knows no more himself.

Ouspensky has a weird and imaginative chapter on the Tarot in *A New Model of the Universe*, in which he writes prose poems about each of the twenty-two trump cards. He leaves the Hanged Man until last, and then becomes prophetic and Biblical:

And I heard a voice which spoke to me:
'Behold, this is the man who has seen the Truth
New suffering such as no earthly misfortune can
*   ever cause ...'*

And so on for half a page. And in spite of mentions of the Garden of Eden, the sphinx and the abyss, the mystery still remains. What is the card supposed to represent? Why upside down by one foot? In *The Waste Land*, T. S. Eliot has a reference to the Hanged Man, and explains in a note that he associates him arbitrarily with the Hanged God of Frazer's *Golden Bough*; however, a reference to the relevant chapter in *Attis, Adonis, Osiris* reveals that the various gods of mythology who have been hanged were hanged in the normal way, not upside down.

Basil Racoczi, in his book *Fortune Telling*, explains that the hanged man is a 'disciple' who has been hung upside down at a certain stage in his initiation. Gold tumbles out of his pockets. This shows, says Racoczi, that he has not really given up the world, and is in great spiritual danger: the card is a timely warning. There is only one objection to this imaginative interpretation: that some of the earliest Tarots do not show gold tumbling from his pockets, or even show him holding a bag of gold. And if he has just been caught out breaking his initiate's oath, why is he looking so cheerful?

In *The White Goddess*, Graves mentions that the Tarot pack is derived from the twenty-two letters of the full tree alphabet, and that the Hanged Man is associated with its seventh letter, D for Duir, which represents the oak. This might be interpreted as affording some slight clue, since Graves mentions that the word 'Duir' means door, and that the word for oak in many European languages means door: the gibbet on which the hanged man swings certainly looks like a door. And unfortunately, there is no further clue as to why the hanged man hangs upside down.

I dwell upon this problem because such speculation is the best possible introduction to the Tarot pack. It so obviously *means* something. Whoever created it or constructed it meant something quite definite by its symbols. And perhaps one day a historian may discover that some early tribe of gypsies originated in a country where the local duke punished malefactors by hanging them upside down by one foot. But at the moment, the mystery remains impenetrable, and one can only stare with bafflement at the cards, and try to let the intuition work upon them.

This is, in fact, by far the best way of getting to know the Tarot pack: simply to stare at its cards as a child stares at coloured pictures in his favourite book. Tarot packs of earlier centuries are usually in clear, bright, primary colours, so that they can be studied like illustrations in a child's picture book. It helps greatly if the student has a strong sense of the Middle Ages; half an hour browsing through a volume like Joan Evans's *Flowering of the Middle Ages** is an excellent preparation for study of the Tarot. The mind should be full of images of Gothic cathedrals, of medieval

* Thames & Hudson, 1966.

stained glass – which may be the inspiration for the glowing colours of the Tarot – of small towns surrounded by fields, and artisans at their everyday work. Without this kind of preparation, the sceptical modern mind is likely to attach its own associations to cards like the Pope, the High Priestess (Pope Joan) and the Devil. It also enables one to sense when certain images extend further back than Renaissance, or even the Middle Ages. The Moon card, for example, shows a dog and a wolf baying at the moon while from a river (or sea) behind them a lobster climbs on to the land. The moon has a woman's face, and is shedding dewdrops. In the background of the picture, on either side, stand two menacing towers. Somehow the whole picture is out of keeping with the solid world of Chaucerian burghers and knights on tombs with their hands folded in prayer. (It is true that this is one of the few examples of Tarot cards that have changed form radically; the Charles VI pack shows two very Chaucerian astronomers looking at a moon without a face; but this is not to say that the dog-and-wolf card may not be equally old.) Here, very clearly, is a card whose origins go back to pre-Christian times, and that is probably associated with the White Goddess.

But for the most part the Tarot is profoundly medieval in conception, and profoundly Western. It begins with a Juggler – a seventeenth-century Tarot makes him look thoroughly villainous – and ends with a Fool (or Beggar – a man in torn clothes). In between, there is a world of emperors and popes and hermits, and cards symbolising strength, temperance, justice and death. Alliette, one of the commentators on the Tarot, disliked the idea of beginning with the Juggler, and changed its place to number fifteen. As to A. E. Waite, he prefers to change the Juggler into a Magician, 'having the countenance of divine Apollo, with smile of confidence and shining eyes', instead of the villainous-looking confidence trickster of the seventeenth century. He also prefers to end his exposition of the Greater Arcana (the twenty-two trump cards) with the World, a card showing a naked woman surrounded by symbols of the four evangelists, instead of the Fool. In general, Waite's Tarot (with the cards redrawn by Pamela Smith) is a romanticised and sentimentalised version, although the cards never depart far from early originals. The obvious test of any commentator on the Tarot is his understanding of the two cards representing the Sun and the Moon – whether he grasps the distinction between 'solar' and 'lunar' knowledge. Waite does not. Ouspensky comes altogether closer, although this seems to be an imaginative guess rather than true insight.

Apart from the Greater Arcana, there are also the fifty-six cards of the Lesser Arcana, the four suits that have become the ordinary playing cards of today, with its rods (or wands), cups, swords and shekels (or pentacles) changing into clubs, hearts, spades and diamonds. It is worth observing, in passing, that we have here two rod-shaped objects – wands and swords – and two circular objects – cups and money – and since one of the commentators mentions that wands and money were used in medieval methods of divination, it would not be inaccurate to see them as related to the yarrow stalks and coins of the *I Ching*. Each suit has a king, queen, knight and knave, as well as cards numbered from one to ten. Almost certainly, the four suits were meant to represent the four social classes of the Middle Ages: the clergy (chalices), the merchants (money), the nobility (swords), the peasantry (rods).

Although some authorities feel that the Lesser Arcana constitutes a completely different set of cards, with nothing in common with the trumps, they certainly have in common a puzzling symbolism. Each card bears a picture. It may show a series of cups forming a rainbow, or a body pierced by ten swords, or a man oppressed under the weight of ten rods. In Waite's Tarot, the five of wands, for example, shows a group of youths in a field, apparently fighting or playing a war game. In *The Hollow Men*, T. S. Eliot has the lines:

Crossed staves in a field
Behaving as the wind behaves
No nearer ...

This is clearly a reference to Waite's interpretation of the five of wands, where, after speaking of youths brandishing staves, he adds that this is 'mimic warfare ... sham fight ... In this sense it connects with the battle of life'. Waite's five of wands becomes a symbol for Eliot's feeling of the futility of the constant motion that constitutes human existence. On the other hand, Gerard Encausse, who published a commentary on the Tarot under the pseudonym of Papus, interprets the five of wands as 'obstacle overcome by assiduity, victory'. Papus sees the King of swords as an evil man; Waite sees him as a symbol of stern justice.

The Lesser Arcana of the Tarot is, as already mentioned, the source from which modern playing cards are derived. These can also be used for 'divinatory' purposes, and it is interesting to see how closely the meanings of the two packs correspond; it is evidence that the basic tradition of cartomancy (divination by cards) has hardly changed since the fourteenth century. The ten of cups, for example, has a picture of a happy family, and its meaning is contentment and human love. The meaning of the ten of hearts (its corresponding card in the ordinary pack) is Home. Here are a few more correspondences:

Ace of Coins: Felicity. Ace of Diamonds: An engagement.

Five of swords: loss. Five of spades: a funeral.

Three of coins: trade. Three of diamonds: social activity.

Five of wands: mimic warfare. Five of clubs: a lawsuit.

Ace of cups: House of the true heart, content, abode.

Ace of Hearts: Love, marriage.

Four of coins: possession, a legacy. Four of diamonds: a legacy.

When one considers how much individual commentators like to impose their own meanings, it is remarkable that the correspondences remain so close. Papus's Tarot, for example, makes a bid for wide popularity by making the cards tell a story. Cups (hearts) is obviously a love story, with the Ace signifying the beginning of love; the two: 'obstacles deriving from one of the couple'; three: both have fallen in love; four: a third person provokes opposition; five: the obstacle is overcome, and so on. In his explanation of the money cards, he actually reverses the meaning of the four of coins (a legacy) which, he claims, signifies a loss.

The method of consulting the cards – both the Tarot and the ordinary pack – has also remained relatively unchanged. A card is chosen to represent either the person asking the question, or the question itself; in the case of the Tarot, tradition represents wands as blond and energetic, cups as having light-brown hair and a lazy temperament, swords as dark brown and energetic, coins as dark and indolent. This card is placed in the centre of the table; the remaining cards are then shuffled and cut three times by the questioner. What follows depends upon the method favoured by the fortune-teller. Cards may be taken one after the other from the top of the pack – face downwards – and placed in a certain order round the first card. These indicate various influences at work: the general atmosphere of the enquiry, what forces are in opposition, what is the ideal solution, what has gone past, what is in the immediate past, what is in the immediate future and so on. The simplest and quickest way of using the Tarot is to use the Greater Arcana – the twenty-two trump cards – and simply get the questioner to name five numbers below twenty-two, shuffling the remaining cards between each 'call'. The cards are laid out in the form of a cross. The one in the centre represents the synthesis. The card to the left is the 'affirmation' – forces working in favour – and to the right, the negation. Above, the 'discussion' of the problem; below, the solution. The synthesis card, in the centre, should be looked upon as a combination of the other four.

It may seem a long step from Yeats's belief in the subconscious power of symbols to this complicated manipulation of cards; in fact, the reader with a logical turn of mind could hardly be blamed for seeing the whole thing as an amusement for the empty-headed and the gullible. But to dismiss the whole thing on these grounds would be to throw out the baby with the bath water. As with the *I Ching*, consultation of the Tarot depends upon the assumption that the subconscious mind may have more to do with 'chance' events than appears on the surface. It seems to know things that are not apparent to consciousness. In certain moments of peace – or of fatigue – these intuitions can communicate themselves to consciousness; or they may do so quite erratically, for no particular reason, as in A. L. Rowse's sudden intuition that two young men were at present embracing in the college library. If we can accept that the strange events that haunted Strindberg during the second half of his life were not entirely imagined, but were somehow set in motion by the force of his own obsessions, then it is not a long step to accepting that the fall of cards may be influenced by the same obsessions. It also follows that any set of objects could be used for fortune-telling – a watch, a bottle of hair oil, a bar of chocolate, a broken mirror – provided that each object held a definite significance for the fortune-teller. Divination by dominoes and dice is almost as popular as cartomancy, and many primitive tribes use bundles of sticks or beads or teeth. The underlying assumption is that the materials used are no more than the clay which is moulded by the hands of the subconscious 'sculptor'. Auden, in a poem called 'The Labyrinth', writes:

The centre that I cannot find
Is known to my Unconscious Mind;
I have no reason to despair
Because I am already there.

The chief problem is to establish a link between the conscious and subconscious mind; the creator of the Tarot set out to do precisely this. The symbols of the Tarot serve a double purpose: to act as a kind of alphabet, by means of which the subconscious can spell out its meanings; and to stimulate the subconscious by means of their own inherent vitality, rather as a punched card can 'stimulate' an electronic computer. A two-way traffic is intended.

Undoubtedly the most dubious part of card divination is the element of chance. The logical mind finds it hard to swallow that cards taken by chance from a shuffled pack can have any real significance. Strindberg believed that supernatural agencies were trying to 'show' him things when he was struck by some strange coincidence or omen, and this is the real assumption that underlies all 'divination'. It would be interesting to devise new methods of consulting the Tarot that would allow the subconscious mind more direct intervention: for example, placing the questioner in a hypnotic trance and then allowing him to choose a number of cards from a pack of upturned cards; or perhaps persuading the questioner to attempt self-hypnosis. What needs further investigation at the moment is the relation between symbols and the subconscious mind, and the point at which 'cybernetic feedback' begins to occur between the two.

There is one respect in which the Tarot might seem inferior to the *I Ching*. I have explained that although the *I Ching* is a book of divination, it also tries to *raise the mind* above questions about its fate – to make the mind active and self-controlled rather than passively worrying about what the future holds.

And this underlines the fundamental difference of approach between the Tarot and the *I Ching*. The East is naturally more impersonal, more philosophical, than the West. The Oriental mind thinks naturally in terms of spirit and nature, heaven and earth, fire and water; it gazes into the distance. The Westerner lives in a more personal world, with a saviour acting as intermediary between himself and heaven. The symbols of the Tarot are more complex, more personal and more violent than those of the *I Ching*. At first glance the Tarot seems more preoccupied with foretelling disaster than the *I Ching*, which is more interested in teaching the 'superior man' how to become master of his destiny.

Closer study shows that this difference is less important than it appears on the surface. The ominous symbols of the Tarot – the Hanged Man, the Tower Struck by Lightning, Death and the Devil – are intended less as omens of disaster than as shocks to jar the mind out of 'the triviality of everydayness', to induce concentration upon essentials. The Pope, the Last Judgement, the Hermit all focus attention upon 'heaven', as, in another way, do the cards representing the Star, the Moon and the Sun. At the time when the cards were new to Europe, these symbols all had a deep emotional impact, which they have lost since the Reformation. But, as T. S. Eliot pointed out in speaking of Dante's poetry, there is nothing to prevent the modern mind from entering the medieval frame of reference and being as deeply moved by it as Dante's contemporaries were. When the Tarot is grasped in this way – with an effort to understand the inner reality of its symbols – it can be seen as the exact Western equivalent of the *I Ching*: a 'lunar' knowledge system conveyed in terms of interrelated symbols.

PART TWO

A HISTORY OF MAGIC

ONE
THE EVOLUTION OF MAN

If the history of magic is to be understood, we must begin with a discussion of evolution. For if David Foster is right, the evolution of life is not an accident; it has been shaped and guided by forces that possess intelligence and purpose. Magic also assumes the existence of such forces. On the other hand, science insists that the universe can be explained entirely in mechanical terms. If we can show this to be untrue, then we have provided the case for magic with the most solid kind of foundation.

In 1794, Goethe attended a meeting of the Natural Science Society, and there met a man whose works he disliked intensely – the poet Schiller. But as they left the building together, Schiller made a remark that caused Goethe to regard him more sympathetically; he said that he wished that scientists would not make everything so fragmentary and disconnected, because it made them hard to follow. Goethe agreed enthusiastically. 'There is another way of apprehending nature, active and living, struggling from the whole into parts', and he proceeded to expound his view of nature as 'God's living garment'. He ended by explaining his theory that all plants had developed from one original plant. Schiller shook his head. 'That's not an empirical experience. It's just an *idea.*'

In a sense, Schiller was right; Goethe's *Urpflanze* was just an idea. But what Goethe was protesting about was not the method of science, but its preconceptions, with the scientist as a glorified 'accident investigator'. An analogy will make my point clear. The psychologist J. B. Watson believed that all human activities, from sexual intercourse to writing symphonies, can be explained in mechanical terms. Imagine a criminologist investigating a murder case from the Watsonian point of view. A man has insured his wife for a large sum of money, then poisoned her. The psychologist is not in any way concerned with the rights and wrongs of the case, or even with the man's sanity – for to speak of sanity or insanity implies freedom of choice. The criminologist investigates it as he would investigate any other accident: let us say, a bridge that has collapsed during a storm. It is purely a matter of various pressures. In court, the prosecutor asks him: 'But don't you believe that the defendant might have chosen not to murder her?' The criminologist shakes his head. 'There is no such thing as choice. Can a bridge choose not to fall down when the wind pressure is too great for it?' 'But don't you see that throughout his teens, this man deliberately chose the path of least resistance, until his character became completely corrupt?' 'What you have just said is meaningless. You may as well say that water is corrupt for choosing to flow downhill.'

The prosecutor sees the man's life as a series of choices – bad choices in which he has never thought of anything but his own immediate pleasure or gain. It seems clear to him that with a different series of choices, and perhaps a certain amount of help, the man might have become a decent citizen. In other words, the prosecutor sees the man's life as a series of *possibilities*, any one of which might have been realised. The Watsonian psychologist does not even think in terms of possibilities, any more than he wonders why a mountain is not a valley. To him, the 'fact' of the crime, the 'fact' of the criminal, are the realities, and he studies these as a geologist might study a mountain.

Such an attitude may call itself the 'scientific method', but it is obviously not the real thing; it is too dogmatic. Poets such as Blake and Goethe have always objected to this narrow view of science, pointing out that the human mind doesn't work like that. It works by a series of intuitive leaps, not by this negative, cautious plodding. It is possible to stick too close to 'facts'. If I examine a painting through a microscope I shall learn about the texture of the paint, but nothing about the artist's intention in painting the picture. And I *cannot* learn about this intention while I stick to the microscope; I must stand back and see it as a whole before I can understand it.

In 1931, H. G. Wells produced (in collaboration with Julian Huxley) a book called *The Science of Life*, which can be taken as a typical example of this kind of 'science'. And since it offers a sketch of the evolution of life on earth, it provides a clear-cut contrast to the approach on which this book is based.

Wells is very positive that there is no mystical 'life urge', and no purpose behind evolution. Life is a chemical process that somehow originated in the warm seas of the Pre-Cambrian era. It differs from other chemical processes in being somehow self-propagating. It is hard to imagine a chemical process managing to keep itself going indefinitely, although we can imagine, let us say, a snowball getting bigger as it rolls downhill. But when it reaches the bottom of the hill, it stops. A forest fire will spread until it reaches the end of the trees, then it stops. Wells is asking us to accept that life is a kind of forest fire that goes on indefinitely, or a snowball that can roll up hills as well as down.

From this accidental beginning, evolution continues by accident. The horse's speed, Wells points out, is a response to the increasing speed of its devourers. (And conversely, no doubt, the devourers had to increase their speed to catch up with the horse.) The fast horses survived and bred more of their kind; the slow ones died out. And this is the way that evolution has progressed for half a billion years. The method is wasteful but infallible. It depends only on physical laws, not on the will of the individual. Of course, a horse may learn to run faster because it wants to escape jackals, but it cannot pass on its speed to its children; at least, not genetically.

Now, this process of accident may strike the nonscientific reader as unnecessary. My own experience teaches me that life is a purposive process. When I first try to roller-skate or play a trumpet, it seems impossible that I can ever control such a difficult process; it is all I can do to maintain my balance, or get a single squeaky note out of the trumpet. What then happens is that I *concentrate*; I increase my mental pressure, just as I might tighten my grip on a revolver I am about to fire. And slowly I become master of the difficult process. If I make no effort at all, blowing aimlessly into the trumpet and hoping for the best, I shall never learn to play it, or it may take years instead of weeks.

As soon as I have observed the enormous difference between purposeful concentration and aimless drifting, I find it hard to believe that life has reached its present stage by drifting. Eddington said that if a tribe of monkeys pounded aimlessly on typewriters for thousands of years, they would eventually write every book in the British Museum; but we may find that equally hard to believe. It seems obvious that a monkey would not produce an intelligible sentence – by accident – in a year of strumming on a typewriter, and there is therefore no reason to suppose it would produce half a billion intelligible sentences in half a billion years. And we may also find it hard to believe that life has evolved from the amoeba to Beethoven in half a billion years of 'accidental selection'.

Wells's type of argument depends upon a kind of dogmatising scepticism, a pose of refusing to believe anything that cannot be tested and verified. But what he chooses to believe seems oddly arbitrary. He states flatly: 'The molten earth, after throwing off the moon, cooled down gradually ...' Recent examination of moon rock seems to indicate that the moon came from elsewhere. Wells is not to be blamed for not knowing this, but he is to be blamed for the dogmatic tone in which he declares the moon broke off from the earth. Why is he so dogmatic? Because it would be 'fanciful' to assume that the moon came from outer space; it is 'more likely' that it was thrown off by the earth. This makes it a fact. We are all hard-headed scientists here, and there's no mystical nonsense about us ...

But a likelihood is not the same thing as a fact, and an argument that proceeds by a series of hard-headed likelihoods may be as wrong as the wildest guesswork. Moreover, it may miss the whole point, as the microscope misses the point of a painting. Wells admits that he has no idea of where life came from, but it is 'most likely' that it is a chemical process that started in the sea. And since he knows no more about the origins of life than anyone else, it follows that he does not know whether there is a 'mystical life-urge' or whether evolution is purposive. But in the name of hard-headed scepticism, these also become 'facts'. He knows that individuals and races can be highly purposive, but he is not willing to allow purpose to play any part in evolution because our vital characteristics are determined by the genes, and the genes are determined by random shuffling, like a pack of cards. But it seems odd that if my hand and my brain can both be made to obey my sense of purpose, that another part of my body, the genes, should be totally beyond my control. In fact, how *can* I be certain that the genes cannot be affected by the vital forces of my will?

Wells would reply: We have no evidence that they can be, and evolution can be explained purely in terms of natural selection. That, again, makes it a 'fact'.

And so, starting from the 'chemical' picture of life as some sort of self-renewing process, we build up a logical and scientific view of history that explains religion and magic in terms of superstition. The end result is man as we know him today, trapped in his technological civilisation, a victim of forces greater than himself, doing his best to avoid an atomic war. Wells, it is true, took an optimistic view of human evolution; but he called his final postscript to his *Short History of the World* 'Mind at the end of its tether'.

The picture remains depressing only so long as we accept that the 'scientific method' that Wells admired so much is really as reasonable and honest as it looks. It is determined to do without 'teleology', the notion of purpose.

Why is science so opposed to purpose? Because it has suffered so much from it in the past. The savage who believes that the eclipse of the moon is a sign of God's anger is actively blocking the progress of science, for he has closed the question. The Churchmen who burned Giordano Bruno and made Galileo recant were blocking the progress of science. Science has reason to be wary of teleology. But while admitting that a non-purposive science may discover many valuable truths, we may still point out that there is no sound scientific reason for actually *outlawing* the idea of purpose.

Let us consider an alternative to Wells's account of evolution. We may agree that it is just conceivable that life is some sort of 'chemical' process that started in warm seas. But when I think about a chemical process (for example, if I drop a piece of iron into hydrochloric acid, and watch it fizz and dissolve), it seems somehow quite different from a vital process (for example, the way cheese ripens through bacteria in the air). I cannot help thinking of life as a principle of *organisation* inside the purely chemical process that is involved when cheese becomes maggots. In fact, I know that the maggots develop from bacteria in the air; if the cheese is kept in a sterile vacuum, it will remain sterile. It is difficult for me not to think of life as a process that comes from outside the chemicals involved, and which imposes its own organisation on them.

There is, as I have already said, an immense difference between an accidental process and a process upon which I concentrate my sense of purpose. There is even an immense difference between doing something absent-mindedly and really concentrating on it. Life is inseparable from the idea of purpose. It is true that I can easily think of a living creature without much purpose – a cow chewing the cud, Oblomov yawning on his stove – but this is because they are enjoying a breathing space from purpose; earlier effort has *paid* for their relaxation in advance. The simplest living organisms have to fight continually for existence.

Life increased in the warm seas, and developed its own kind of purpose – instinctive purpose – and its own kind of senses. And as the tiny organisms developed into fishes, birds, mammals and insects, they also developed their most important instinct: the community sense. And it is arguable that this community instinct, like the homing instinct and the premonition of danger, was telepathic.

In *African Genesis*, Robert Ardrey mentions an example that seems to me a conclusive argument against total, uncompromising Darwinism: the flattid bug. He was standing with the anthropologist L. B. S. Leakey, looking at a coral-coloured blossom like lilac. Leakey touched the twig, and the flower dissolved into a swarm of tiny insects. A few minutes later the insects re-settled on the twig, crawled over one another's backs, and once again became a coral-coloured blossom, a flower *which does not exist in nature*. Some of the insects were green; some were half green and half pink; others were deep coral; they arranged themselves so as to look like a flower with a green tip.

Now Darwinian selection can explain most examples of 'imitation' in nature; for example, the stick bug, which even has thorns on its back. Random mutation produces a creature that looks rather like a twig, and it survives better than its brothers who look more appetising. And as birds continue to eat the non-imitative bugs, nature 'polishes up' the resemblance. But how can that principle be applied to a whole community? 'Natural selection' works in terms of individuals; we cannot imagine a whole community created by some mass accident of the genes, and then learning, accidentally, to imitate a flower. But if we assume that the flattid-bug community is, in a sense, a *single individual*, a single mind, the problem becomes less complicated.

And if we make this assumption, then we must also drop the idea that the genes cannot be influenced by telepathy. The alternative is to imagine thousands of flattid-bug communities teaching themselves to imitate flowers, but being wiped out in the next generation as their children fail to inherit their colouring, until one day nature kindly takes a hand and allows the trick to become inheritable.

Darwin himself was not entirely convinced that acquired characteristics cannot be inherited. The entomologist Fabre asked him to explain the case of the French *Ammonophilas* wasp, which provides food for its grubs by stinging a caterpillar in its nerve centre and paralysing it. Fabre argues that the wasp must be totally accurate with its sting, for if it stings too deep, it will kill the caterpillar, and if it fails to sting deep enough, the caterpillar will wriggle around and crush the grubs. Fabre points out that the wasp must have learned this trick *the first time*, and then somehow passed it on to its children – otherwise, there would have been no children. Darwin was inclined to agree. Wells (in *The Science of Life*) accuses Fabre of exaggeration, and describes the wasp's accuracy as 'a rough and ready reflex of no great complexity' (basing his criticism on the American variety of *Ammonophilas*); but this makes no fundamental difference to Fabre's argument that the species could not have survived without somehow passing on the trick in the first generation.

Again, we might ask: How did man develop the thickened skin on the soles of his feet? Obviously, by walking on them. But why have *all* men this same characteristic? Do we suppose that there were once men with thin skin on their soles, but they stepped on thorns and died out? That seems unlikely, since having thin soles would not be a great evolutionary disadvantage. On the contrary, it might cause its possessors to become thinkers rather than hunters. Is it not more sensible to assume that man wanted thick soles as a matter of general convenience, and influenced his genes to give him thick soles?

In his Gifford Lectures, *The Living Stream*, Sir Alister Hardy (who was professor of zoology at Oxford and a respectable Darwinian) cites an even odder phenomenon. A flatworm called *Microstomum* has developed a unique defence system. It eats the polyp *Hydra* for the sake of its stinging capsules (called nematocysts). When the *Hydra* has been digested, the stinging bombs are picked up in the lining of the flatworm's stomach, passed through to another set of cells, which now carry them – like builders' labourers carrying bricks – to the flatworm's skin, where they are mounted like guns, ready to fire their stinging thread. It is a curious feature that the stinging capsules do not explode when the flatworm eats the *Hydra*. What is even stranger is that the flatworm does not eat the *Hydra for food*, but only to steal its 'bombs'. Once the flatworm has enough bombs mounted in its skin, it will not touch a *Hydra*, even if starving.

The behaviour of the *Microstomum* is enough to give an orthodox Darwinian grey hairs. How the flatworm learned the trick, and then passed it on to its children by accidental selection – is only the first of the problems. Dr. A. W. Kepner 'was driven to postulate a group mind among the cells of the body to account for the internal behaviour of the *Microstomum*'.

After discussing various similar problems, Sir Alister Hardy takes the immense step of suggesting that telepathy can, in fact, influence the genes, although he is careful to emphasise that this is only guesswork. The analogy he uses – remarking that it is '*only an analogy and not part of the hypothesis*' – is of a painter selecting colours for a painting that is going to be reproduced thousands of times. He may decide to keep varying the colours – the DNA genes – to try to obtain the maximum effect. Sir Alister postulates a 'group mind' among the animals of a species, and the group mind plays the part of the painter. But a painter selects his colours with a view to the overall effect. In short, we are back with the notion of purpose; and, even more important, with the notion that the 'group mind' can directly affect the DNA code.

What all this amounts to is that the accidental selection that Wells insists upon leaves too much unexplained. No one doubts that accidental selection *is* a major force in evolution. But then, no one doubts that various kinds of accident play an important part in the lives of city dwellers; I may accidentally meet a man who gives me a bad cold, or changes the whole course of my life. This does not mean that everything I do, from getting up in the morning to going to bed at night, is without purpose. On the contrary, the accidents take place against a general background of purpose. And the same goes for evolution.

None of the examples discussed above presents the slightest problem for the 'telepathic theory of evolution'. We suppose that life is basically purposive. It organises matter for its own ends, and its aim is to become more complex, more *free*. To begin with, it concentrated on developing telepathic forces – the same forces that enable the flattid bug to understand its place in the 'blossom'. These forces also enabled it to pass on important discoveries to the genes. This 'instinctive mind', the group mind, has many levels. On one level, it organises a group of flattid bugs into a flower and makes sure that some of them are green and some are half green and half coral, and some completely coral. On another level, it organises the cells of the flatworm's stomach to carry stinging capsules to the outer skin. For all we know, the flatworm may be able to 'order' the cells to carry the stinging capsules, just as I am now ordering my fingers to type this page; in organisms as simple as the flatworm, instinctive connections may be more direct. And this speculation emphasises, in turn, that all kinds of processes are now taking place in my own body, although I am apparently unconscious of them. Kepner's postulate of a group mind among the cells of the body applies on every level of life.

The skills developed by birds and animals indicate that life has come a long way towards its objective: power over its material form. But while the homing instinct of birds, the flower-building instinct of flattid bugs, the 'sixth sense' of dogs are very remarkable achievements, they are, in a way, dead ends. For their purpose is mere survival. After nearly half a billion years of evolution, life's chief characteristic was cruelty: baby wasps eating a live caterpillar, a snake eating a live frog. And the power of telepathic communication with its own kind did not involve any sympathy with other species. For all its 'psychic faculties', life remained narrow and vicious.

It had to take the next great step – the most dangerous step yet. It had to discover new ways to conquer the world of matter, which operates by its own complex laws. It had to learn to understand these laws, to grasp them *as generalisations*. The increasing complexity of the forms it was learning to handle meant that it needed a *hierarchic* structure. The boss of a small business can keep in touch with everything himself, but if the business becomes very large, he needs a whole structure of managers, under-managers, foremen, shop stewards and so on. The boss's job is to take an overall view, and leave all the routine jobs to his deputies. Every human being is, in effect, the boss of a giant corporation.

But he *is* the boss. He may not know everything that goes on all the time, but he has an overall idea. And there is nothing to stop him from visiting any office or workshop in the combine. If he wants, he can even take off his coat and repair one of the machines. He no longer has the immediate control that the flatworm has over the cells of its stomach; but if he really needs it, he can get it. If he needs to recover the power of telepathy, or subconscious premonition of danger – 'jungle sensitiveness' – he can re-activate this faculty by an intense effort.

But here is the central point. His chief danger is a kind of *amnesia*. The complexity of the business may strain him so much that he spends all his time worrying ineffectually in his office, staring dazedly at balance sheets and statistics, and wishing he was still just a small family business. *He forgets how much real power he possesses.* When he reaches this stage – becoming 'stale' – it is important for him to get down on the shop floor and roll up his sleeves, to re-contact his simpler, more instinctive self.

And this is a point whose importance goes far beyond this discussion of the occult. We are considering the most important law of human nature. Man is at his best when he has a strong sense of purpose. When my consciousness is doing its proper work – grasping some of the immense complexity of the universe, and calculating how to increase its control and power – its energy flows into the subconscious, and arouses all the forces of the subconscious mind. When conscious purpose fails, everything else slowly breaks down.

Why has man developed consciousness? I suggested the answer in my foreword. He may have lost his animal powers of telepathy. but he has also lost his colour-blindness. When he delights in the contrast of a blue sky with green fields. or the colours of the clouds at sunset, he is operating at a higher level of vitality than any animal can achieve.

And his sense of beauty is the direct outcome of his evolutionary urge. It is related to the power of grasping and mastering complexity. If I look at an old Tudor house set in green lawns and flower beds, with a river at the foot of the garden, my sense of beauty is actually a sense of complexity *and* order. The more wide-awake I feel, the more I 'take in' these chimneys, gables, oak beams, leaded windows, bright flower beds. They give pleasure because they give a sense of the mind's power to control its environment. I may see an equally complex scene from the window of a train – slag heaps, factory chimneys, slum houses – and although it is equally complex, it does not produce pleasure because it seems evidence of the human failure to control the environment, of people who have let life 'get them down'. On the other hand, I may look at a piece of natural scenery that is equally chaotic with jagged rocks, bare hills, a stormy sky – but because I feel no need to control it, it strikes me as beautiful, for I can savour its complexity.

The sense of beauty, then, is a sense of complexity, *and of power over it*. Neither is sufficient without the other. A neurotic sees the complexity, but he feels overwhelmed by it; he lacks purpose. When Alexander the Great cried for fresh worlds to conquer, he possessed the sense of purpose but lacked the sense of complexity; he felt he had come to the end of 'the world'.

Now, ideally there should be a continual 'feedback'. Increased complexity should produce an increased sense of purpose, an increased appetite for life. And the increased appetite for life should stimulate the mind to broaden its limits, to grasp new complexities. What happens in practice is that human beings, even the greatest, reach a certain point where they lose courage. They don't want any more complexity, and their appetite for life also slackens. But it is possible to imagine a human being who has passed this danger point, whose mind reaches out endlessly for new complexities, and whose sense of delight is stimulated to achieve new levels of purpose by the new complexity. If man's mind could reach this point like the 'critical mass' in an atomic explosion – he would become godlike. Think of a schoolboy going for a swim in the river on a hot afternoon: the way the senses feel drunk with the blueness of the sky, the cool smell of the water; the kind of excited ecstasy with which he changes into his swimming costume, somehow afraid that the water will run away before he gets to it. This kind of excitement and affirmation is peculiarly human; the senses reach out eagerly to the world, as if to embrace it. Man often feels this same ecstasy of affirmation as he confronts the universe: sheer delight in its complexity, and the desire to plunge into it with a splash. But, like the schoolboy, he gets tired; the excitement fades. And this failure is purely a lack of self-discipline. An adult can increase his mental stamina by deliberate training, so that, for example, he can listen to a complete Wagner opera without exhaustion.

And this should make clear why we differ so much from the lower animals. No animal possesses that capacity for reaching out ecstatically to grasp the universe. Their instincts are sharper than ours, and they are closer to nature. But they can never know that supreme delight of the imagination taking fire and becoming drunk with its own visions. *That* is what human evolution is about.

But man had chosen a hard, uphill road. It is true that this power to understand the world brought tremendous results. For example, when he learned that wild grass could be sown and cultivated, that wild animals could be tamed and bred for their meat and their skins, life became immeasurably easier. Professor K. A. Wittfogel has estimated, in his book on Chinese economic history, that agriculture can feed between twenty and fifty times as many people as hunting. That means that man has between twenty and fifty times as much leisure. But on the other hand, this new, highly conscious life was narrow and hard, and rather dull compared to hunting and warfare. Romantic modern writers like to declare that peasants are 'closer to nature' than city dwellers; but that is not entirely true. A man like John Cowper Powys has a mystical bond with nature because he has the *leisure* to think and use his imagination. But the Bronze Age peasant worked too hard to be able to cultivate his imagination. And so, although the plough had, in a sense, freed him from his dependence on the day's hunting, it had confined him in a new prison: his home, his fields, his cowbarn.

What happened was inevitable. The men who retained a high degree of their old 'psychic faculties' were rare. Psychic ability springs from a kind of inner stillness, during which the mind becomes clear, like a pond in which the mud is allowed to settle. The men who possessed this faculty became doctors, priests, oracles. This is as true today as five thousand years ago. A recent report on the Huichol Indians of the Mexican Sierra Madre, whose religion is a survival of the pre-Columbian age, describes the shaman, Ramon Medina (who is also, significantly, the tribe's principal artist). Visiting the village of San Andres, the shaman sensed death, and walked to a locked house, where the corpse of a murdered man was discovered in the roof. Norman Lewis comments that the body was discovered 'through what is completely accepted in this part of the world – even by Franciscan missionary fathers – as extra-sensory perception'.*

This power revealed by the shaman could be developed, like water divining, by anybody. It is a perfectly normal part of the make-up of living creatures. But we are unaware of our potentialities, in spite of the increasing interest in 'para-psychology'. One of these potentialities was revealed by the researches of Dr. J. B. Rhine at Duke University. A gambler suggested that the para-psychology team investigate the gambler's superstition that the fall of a dice can be influenced by the human mind. Eighteen series of tests were conducted over no less than eight years. And when this vast amount of statistics was examined carefully, a curious result was discovered. When people were first tested, their score was always a great deal above 'chance'. On the second 'run', the score fell radically, and in the third run, more radically still. In other words, the mind could best influence the fall of the dice when it was fresh and unbored. Repetition of the same old routine gradually blunted its power of 'psycho-kinesis' (PK for short). The figures for these tests, published in 1943, were overwhelming and conclusive.

At first, it might seem that Rhine's results contradict what I have just said: that such powers can be deliberately developed. But the contradiction is only apparent. What the tests *do* seem to prove is that when the mind is 'fresh' – wide-awake and interested – its powers are

* *The Survivors, The Sunday Times*, April 26, 1970.

considerable. Repetition blunts them. But what is boredom? It is a kind of discouragement, a *slacking of the will* due to a feeling that 'it's just not worth it …' What Rhine's results show clearly is that man's 'psychic powers' are greatest when his will is aroused, and fall off radically when it slackens. And if we assume a certain psychic element in accident-proneness. this would also be explained by the result.

Perhaps the most important part of this result is that the scoring falls off *so fast* after the first run. Rhine remarks that when they examined the figures for 123 first runs, there were 134 'hits' above chance. In the 123 second runs, this had dropped to a mere 19, and in the third runs, to only 4. This tells us something of vital importance about human beings. Our powers literally crumble and collapse under boredom. Our human tendency to defeat-proneness, to will-less drifting, has more serious results than we can imagine. It de-fuses our powers.

In modern civilisation, most people are involved in boring routine jobs that seldom stir the will, and certainly not the imagination. The result is inevitable. We are like four-engine aeroplanes running only on one engine. And our natural psychic powers are 'damped' almost to extinction.

But this observation is less depressing than it sounds. For what actually causes the tremendous falling-off in our powers? Boredom, defeat-proneness. But what *is* defeat-proneness? It is basically a frame of mind induced by ignorance. One thinks of the story of the man who hung all night from the edge of a cliff, and when the daylight came, realised there was only a three-foot drop below him. Once he can see clearly, the fear vanishes. In the case of human beings, the defeat-proneness is due to that separation from our subconscious origins. We are 'stranded' in consciousness. Place a man in a completely black and silent room, and within a few days he will go insane, or at least suffer extreme mental strain. Why? For the same reasons that Rhine's PK results fell off so radically after the first test; the will crashes into collapse when it is blinded, and the collapse is out of all proportion to its cause. A little boredom causes total demoralisation.

But the more man learns to shine a searchlight into his lower depths, the more he can understand his actual strength, and the less he is liable to this panic-collapse. Once again, we have to recognise that his most urgent need, at this point in evolution, is to reanimate his sleeping 'psychic' powers.

In this respect, primitive man had one great advantage over modern man: he knew that he possessed them. If, therefore, he wanted to develop them, it was simply a question of the best possible method. The insight must come first; the method follows.

In the remainder of this chapter I want to examine both these aspects – the insight and the method – more closely.

It must be understood first of all that there is no basic difference between 'mystical' experiences and experiences that belong to the realm of magic or the occult. Because his consciousness has evolved too fast, man has lost contact with his real identity. When his inner pressure is low – when he is in a state of boredom or aimlessness – he is aware only of the most superficial level of his identity. The more deeply he feels, the more of himself he is aware of. This is why Yeats says:

When ... a man is fighting mad,
Something drops from eyes long blind,
He completes his partial mind,
For an instant stands at ease,
Laughs aloud, his heart at peace ...

The important line here is: 'He completes his *partial mind*.'

The fundamental problem of human beings was stated with beautiful clarity by L. H. Myers at the beginning of his novel *The*

Near and the Far. Young Prince Jali stands on the battlements of a palace, which he has been travelling all day to reach, and looks at the sunset on the desert. As he does so, he reflects that 'There were two deserts: one that was a glory for the eye, another that it was weariness to trudge. Deep in his heart he cherished the belief that some day the near and the far would meet. Yes, one day he would be vigorous enough in breath and stride to capture the promise of the horizon.' The promise of the horizon – that is the problem, not only for poets and mystics, but for every human being. And our problem is that we have to live with 'reality' constantly under our noses, like a bull in front of which the matador constantly dangles his cloak, never allowing it to see more than a few feet. It is not quite true to say that we are permanently trapped in the present, for we are always getting those 'breathing spaces', these moments when the heart seems to expand with relief and delight.

The odd thing is the strange inability of consciousness to maintain this insight. It is as if some simple element was missing that allows consciousness to become frayed and tangled. When I was at school, we used to learn to make hosiery on machines with banks of needles. Once the machine was knitting the fabric, a heavy weight had to be hung on the bottom of the fabric to prevent it fouling the needles. If one forgot about the weight, and allowed the fabric to reach the floor, the wool immediately climbed up the needles, and within seconds the knitting was a tangled mess. Similarly, when human consciousness 'idles' in neutral, it narrows and loses all sense of values. When this happens, man ceases to reach out, to experience the desire to expand. The sense of 'worthwhileness' fades. And when that happens, any kind of negation and stupidity becomes possible. It might be said that the essential difference between a man of genius and an 'ordinary man' is that the man of genius has a greater power to focus steadily upon his real values, while the ordinary man is always losing sight of his aims and objectives, changing from hour to hour, almost from minute to minute. A criminal is a man in whom this process of 'devaluation' has slipped further.

Why do I spend so much time emphasising the *in*efficiency of human consciousness? Because once this is understood, we catch a glimpse of the potentialities of an efficient consciousness. The great mystics, saints and 'initiates' of the past were simply men who had realised a few of these potentialities. But they were groping instinctively, in a kind of semi-darkness of intuition, like men trying to find their way in a fog. Modern man has the possibility of understanding the mechanism of consciousness, and marching directly towards his objective, with the will flexed to its maximum efficiency.

Man's trouble is not his *inability* to achieve the kind of concentration necessary for maximum use of his powers, but his unawareness of what can be achieved by such concentration. And this recognition leads to a formulation of central importance: 'occultism' is not an attempt to draw aside the veil of the unknown, but simply the veil of banality that we call the present.

The basic mechanism for doing this is very simple. I am normally 'bound up in myself'. If I have nothing in particular to do, I may simply allow my mind to ramble vaguely: to think of some gossip, try to recall the words of a popular song; I may brood on some worry or resentment, or about a programme I saw on television last night. I *choose* what I use my consciousness for. You could say that consciousness is like a box, and I decide what to put in the box.

Now, suppose I am on a walking tour in the Lake District. I see impressive scenery, but I see it through a kind of veil – a veil of myself and my trivial preoccupations. I am allowing the scenery to become associated with mediocre 'vibrations'.

But consider what happens if the scenery I am looking at happens to be associated with a deeper vibration; for example, suppose I am looking at the moors around Haworth Parsonage, and they make me think of *Wuthering Heights* and the tragedy of the Brontës. What *happens* as I experience the sudden vibration of seriousness? Simply that I am rescued from my close-up, personal, worm's-eye view of life; I am reminded that it is bigger, more exciting, more important, more tragic, than I had realised. Or rather, I 'knew' this all the time, but had allowed myself to 'forget' it.

All art does its work in this way – by rescuing us from our self-chosen triviality, to which we are so prone. It is like a deep organ note that makes my hair stir and a shiver run through me. I 'pull back' from life, like a camera taking a long-shot with a wide-angle lens. I quite simply become aware of *more* reality than before.

It is obvious that I can either resist my own tendency to sink into triviality, or accept it and take it for granted. What Shaw calls the period of 'moral awakening' – which occurs in most intelligent people in their early teens, or even sooner – is a deliberate effort to leave behind the triviality of childhood and to focus the mind on greater issues: art, science, music, exploration.

The 'vibration of seriousness' is accompanied by an inner *tightening*, as if slack cables had suddenly taken a weight.

This 'tightening' may occur through a certain effort of the will or imagination, or it may occur spontaneously – that is, without any apparent conscious effort (in sexual excitement, for example).

And it must be emphasised that this inner tightening, the 'vibration of seriousness', is the aim of all religious, mystical and occult disciplines; for when it occurs, man feels his sense of power increase.

It is a sad thought that most people take their triviality for granted; accept that they will remain fundamentally unchanged for the rest of their lives. The first and most important step towards self-transformation is to grasp *intellectually* what I have explained in the preceding pages: that man was not intended for a lifetime of the 'worm's-eye view', any more than a bird was intended to spend its life on the ground. We have a natural faculty for 'pulling back', for seeing things through the wide-angle lens, for switching on to more serious vibrations. For human beings, boredom and depression are abnormal – a failure to grasp their natural powers. My powers are wasted so long as my vision is narrow and personal. They are like a boxer who cannot get any force behind his punches at close quarters. And when my will has become passive through 'close-upness', I fall into a dreamlike state in which illusion and reality are inter-mingled. I become trapped and tangled in my own narrow values, instead of remaining open to values that are greater than myself. For human beings are intended to 'connect' with values outside themselves and to become unaware of themselves as 'personalities'.

Having defined the object of the quest, the next question is the method.

If the major human problem is a certain diffuseness and tendency to make mountains of molehills, clearly the answer must lie in the realm of concentration. This has always been the fundamental religious discipline. But there is an important point to be grasped here. Concentration is exactly like learning mathematics at school: it *can* be a highly disagreeable exercise that provokes nothing but negative emotions. If I hate mathematics, this is almost certainly because I am badly taught, and because I have a certain inner resistance to the subject. A good teacher will get the students so interested and excited that all fear disappears. The famous teacher Trachtenberg. who devised his 'system' in a concentration camp during the war, could turn the worst pupils into enthusiastic mathematicians. And this was because his rules are so simple and easy to remember that students lost their fear of the subject, and took a certain pride in their ability to leap hurdles.

Concentration should also be an entirely pleasurable exercise, pursued for the sheer joy of it. For when it is done correctly, it induces an immediate feedback of delight, that same sense of heightened vitality that is experienced in the sexual orgasm, or when a crisis is suddenly overcome.

What must be grasped here is the *aim* of concentration. Consider the opening scene of *Faust*, in which Faust has worked himself into a state of defeat and despair. The reason is clear: his thinking has become arid and purposeless, and he has sunk into a state of lowered vitality in which further effort brings no feedback. When he is about to commit suicide, the Easter bells ring, suddenly reminding him clearly of his childhood, and 'call him back to life'. He recalls the time when 'heaven's love rushed at me like a kiss', and says:

> *An inconceivably sweet longing*
> *Drove me to roam through woods and fields,*
> *And with a thousand burning tears*
> *I felt a world rise up in me.*

He is back in contact with external reality; he has broken his way out of the glass bubble that surrounded him.

It can be seen immediately that if Faust had decided to throw off his suffocating despair with an effort of concentration, the crucial question would be what he concentrated *on*. The Easter bells immediately directed his efforts to 'reality'; without them, he might have made enormous efforts and only exhausted himself. If a traveller is dying of thirst in a desert, it is important that he direct all his remaining energy in the direction of the nearest oasis.

T. S. Eliot has a similar passage in the sixth section of *Ash Wednesday*, after describing fatigue and resignation:

> *... though I do not wish to wish these things*
> *From the wide window towards the granite shore*
> *The white sails still fly seaward, seaward flying*
> *Unbroken wings*

And the lost heart stiffens and rejoices
In the lost lilac and the lost sea voices
And the weak spirit quickens to rebel
For the bent golden-rod and the lost sea smell ...

Here again we have the Easter bells experience, in this case triggered by the smell of the sea and of golden-rod, and the surge of delight and power: 'Unbroken wings'. This capacity to evoke sheer ecstasy is present in us all the time; but it needs to be understood before it can be controlled. The surge of power that makes 'the lost heart stiffen' is a power that leaps out to *meet* the sense of reality.

This same glimpse can also be achieved through crisis. Graham Greene's whiskey-priest in *The Power and the Glory* experiences total certainty only as he is about to be shot by a firing squad; then he suddenly realises 'that it would have been quite easy for him to have been a saint', and 'he felt like someone who has missed happiness by seconds'. Quite. It is almost funny. We spend our lives peering at things so close-up that we simply fail to grasp their obvious meaning. A kind of laziness drags us down. There is no hurry. Plenty of time. You, who are now reading these words, feel precisely that. There is tomorrow and the day after. But try to focus what happens to the whiskey-priest in front of the firing squad. With a terrible shock he knows that he is *going to die*, now, within seconds. His inner being revolts; his energies surge like a tidal wave. *He makes a more powerful effort than he has made in his whole life.* He is like Sinbad the Sailor hurling the Old Man of the Sea from his shoulders. For a second, he experiences freedom, and then realises with despair that he could have made this same effort in any of the billion-or-so seconds of his previous life ... He has wasted his life in a kind of dream. We are all in this position, all human beings. If you can clearly focus this realisation, you have grasped what the Church means by 'original sin'. We – you and I – are infinitely stronger than we ever realise.

This is what concentration should be focused on. It *can* be nothing more than another form of dreaming. It can also be an attempt to burst the bubble of dreaming.

There is a certain danger in taking the whiskey-priest episode as a starting point for concentration: the danger of a negative outlook. There is no harm in using the imagination to invoke a sense of panic, if the panic succeeds in its effect of breaking the bubble, establishing contact with reality. But if it fails, it can only increase the oppressive anxiety.

The basic method involved here is perfectly ordinary learning, like learning to ride a bicycle or memorise a poem. Every 'peak experience' (to use Abraham Maslow's phrase), every surge of 'contemplative objectivity', shows the mind its own ability to grasp reality by reaching out. The only way to acquire a skill is to keep repeating the attempt until you have learned the knack. Now, it is true that most healthy people have 'peak experiences' fairly often. But they fail to make a determined effort to build on them. They take them for granted, and allow themselves to slip back into their dull, non-expectant state of mind, the old plodding attitude towards existence.

An altogether more sensible approach is to recognise that every time you can induce the Faustian flash of pure affirmation, you are a step closer to being able to do it at will. The closer together the experiences occur, the quicker you can learn. Bear in mind that you are trying to 'pull back' from your worm's-eye view, to get the wide-angle shot of the world. Bear also in mind that Faust, for all his intelligence and perception, is convinced that he has the soundest reasons for despair – until the Easter bells remind him of what 'reality' is really like, blowing away the depression like mist. The 'trick' is not only to take advantage of every flash of optimism, to attempt to amplify it into a 'peak experience', but also to grasp that this is an *objective* exercise, a skill like reading a newspaper, and that it can be practised at any moment when you have nothing else to think about – on a bus, a tube train, walking along a corridor, drinking tea.

This explains the attraction of drugs – particularly psychedelics – for intelligent people. They have an intuition that if a 'peak experience' could be summoned at will, or maintained for half an hour, it would quickly become possible to learn to re-create it without drugs. There is a fallacy here. Most drugs work by reducing the efficiency of the nervous system, inducing unusual states of consciousness at the expense of the mind's power to concentrate and learn. You only have to try to memorise a short list of foreign words when you are slightly drunk to realise this. The mind is usually absorbent, like blotting paper; when you are under the influence of alcohol, it turns into a sheet of glossy paper with no power to absorb. Drugs work by temporarily paralysing certain levels of the mind, like a local anaesthetic, thereby reducing its energy consumption. Worse still, they inhibit 'feedback effects'. When Lady Chatterley feels the park surging beneath her feet like the sea, this is a feedback effect of her intense concentration on her sexual activities: an ecstatic 100 per cent concentration that pumps up enormous subconscious energies from her depths. It is these energies that continue to surge and spread as she returns home. The Kabbalah describes the creation of the world as being a total *concentration* of energy into a single luminous point. (Captain Shotover's 'seventh degree of concentration' in Shaw's *Heartbreak House* is related to it.) All drugs, without exception, produce the reverse of concentration, a relaxation of the mind. In the case of the psychedelics, the nervous system is 'shortcircuited', so that nervous impulses cease to follow their own track, and spread sideways, creating a series of 'feelings'; it is like opening the lid of a grand piano and running your fingers over its strings, producing an effect like a harp. But these 'feelings' have nothing to do with the clear focusing upon reality achieved by the whiskey-priest.

Drugs, then, are the worst possible way of attempting to achieve 'contemplative objectivity'. They increase the mind's tendency to accept its own passivity instead of fighting against it. But any of the more normal 'peak experiences' are an ideal starting point. Sexual intensity is one of the most powerful, since it produces, in effect, a momentary burst of the Easter bells insight, a flash of the power which is a normal human potentiality. This was recognised in India and Tibet by the Tantric yogis, who deliberately utilised sexual ecstasy to create new habit patterns of intensity (for that is what it amounts to). In more recent years a German ironmaster named Karl Kellner was initiated into Tantric yoga in India, and founded the Ordo Templi Orientis (Order of Oriental Templars) on his return to Germany in 1902. This order was founded entirely upon the 'secret' that sexual ecstasy can be used by human beings as a stairway to new levels of power.

Kellner taught a Westernised form of Eastern Tantra worship, which concentrates its attention on the female aspect of the deity under various names and forms (Devi, Radha, Kali, Durga). As Christian ritual involves bread and wine, Tantric ritual involves wine, meat, fish, grain and sexual intercourse (called *maithuna*), and the worship of Durga and Kali (the fierce forms of the goddess) are often associated with violent sexual orgies. This is known as the 'left-hand path'. (The right-hand path, called *Dakshinachari*, is relatively gentle and restrained; it worships the milder goddess Devi.) In all forms of *maithuna*, the 'suspended orgasm' is practised; the important thing is to use the sexual intensity as a ladder to ascend to still greater heights of intensity, focusing upon the illumination rather than upon the sexual pleasure.

In due course Kellner persuaded the English 'magician' Aleister Crowley to become head of the English branch of the Oriental Templars, and for the remainder of his life Crowley placed great emphasis on 'sexual magic', taking to heart the Tantric belief that sexual and magical powers are basically the same thing. Unfortunately, his addiction to heroin and later to gin counteracted the positive effects of his 'sexual magic'.* I shall deal with Crowley more fully in a later chapter. But it may be comented here that Crowley's chief drawback as an 'adept' was an intense self-preoccupation that was the opposite of what I mean by the 'wide-angle lens'. In this important sense, H. G. Wells or Albert Einstein were closer to 'adeptship' than Crowley. In occultism, as in science, intellect and disinterestedness are the cardinal virtues.

Let me summarise the conclusions of this chapter.

Although the science of the nineteenth century called itself 'organised common sense', it was actually based on Descartes' method of doubting everything that could be doubted, and hoping that what was left over would be 'truth'. It decided to make do without the concepts of will and purpose. At the time, this made no serious difference to physics, biology or even psychology. Today, it is beginning to make an important difference. I have tried to outline a scientific view of life in which will and purpose are not excluded.

In essence, this view of man was outlined by F. W. H. Myers, one of the founders of the Society for Psychical Research, towards the end of the nineteenth century.

Myers suggested that consciousness could be regarded as a kind of spectrum. In the middle of the spectrum are the powers we know about – sight, hearing, touch and so on. Below the red end of the spectrum there are organic processes which we somehow 'control'

* I used Crowley (see Part Two, Chapter 7) as the basis of Caradoc Cunningham in my novel *The Man Without a Shadow* (also called *The Sex Diary of Gerard Sorme*), and there is an account of a Tantric sect in *The God of the Labyrinth* (in America, *The Hedonists*). W. Holman Keith's *Divinity as the Eternal Feminine* (New York, Pageant Press, 1960) is an interesting attempt to create a Westernised version of sexual worship. A letter that accompanied my copy of the book indicated that a group in America have put its theories into practice.

without being conscious of doing so – like the *Microstomum* transporting the *Hydra*'s 'bombs' to its skin. But beyond the violet end of the spectrum lie other powers, of which we are almost totally ignorant.

Similarly, Aldous Huxley once made the suggestion that if the human mind has a 'basement' – the Freudian world of instinct and repressions – why should it not also have an attic: a 'superconscious' to balance the 'subconscious'?

The powers of the 'superconscious' *are* within reach of the human will, provided it is fresh and alive. As soon as habit takes over – or what I have called elsewhere 'the robot' – they dwindle. In the same way, general passivity or defeat-proneness or depression will blunt them, just as they also blunt the powers at the lower end of the spectrum. (In a case of one of Maslow's patients, she became so bored with a routine job that she even ceased to menstruate.)

All disciplines aimed at increased use of these powers depend upon a high level of optimism and will-drive.

Which brings me back to my initial assertion that a science – or knowledge system – which has no place for will or purpose is an obstruction to human evolution, and at this particular point in history, a dangerous nuisance.

TWO
THE MAGIC OF PRIMITIVE MAN

In his book *Man, God and Magic*, the ethnologist Ivar Lissner proposes an absorbing thesis: that our primitive ancestors believed in one God, and that they gradually degenerated, through the evil influence of tribal magicians or witches into worshippers of many gods. He argues this from primitive cave paintings, which seem to show the sacrifice of bears and reindeer. Certainly, primitive man's interest in bears is still one of the great unsolved mysteries of anthropology. They were huge and very dangerous, with enormous strength, claws like razors and despite their bulk, incredible speed. To primitive peoples, from the North American Indians to the modern Ainu of Japan and Orochon of northern Siberia, the bear is believed to possess supernatural powers, and may be ritually sacrificed as a messenger to the gods. The bear was one of the most dangerous creatures of the ancient world, yet Neanderthal man went out of his way to hunt it when there was plenty of other prey. The suspicion that there was some magical or religious significance in bear hunts seems to be confirmed by the discovery of a cave in Drachenloch, Switzerland, stacked with the skulls of bears that seem to have been ritually sacrificed. Similar finds have been made in other remote caves; bear skulls placed on altars, or even on a rough-hewn representation of a headless bear. This is indubitable evidence that Neanderthal man – between seventy and eighty thousand years ago – possessed a religion. It is a startling thought. These creatures lived in caves, and were nomadic. They knew about fire, and could make spears by burning sticks to a point; otherwise they had no arts and no culture. Cave art and primitive sculpture belong to the epoch of his Magdalenian successor, Cro-Magnon man. The Neanderthalers lived hard, violent lives, and to judge by their remains, most of them died young. Yet they worshipped a god and made sacrifices to him.

Lissner argues that primitive people were monotheistic on the evidence of their sacrifices. For example, the skeleton of a deer was found in an Arctic lake, held down by a lump of rock, with evidence pointing to ritual sacrifice. But, argues Lissner, the modern Tungus of this area would not sacrifice in this way because each lake and hill has its spirit, and a carcass would offend the lord of the lake. Man probably abandoned this form of sacrifice by submersion when he began to believe that there was a lord of the forest, a lord of the mountains, a lord of the water. How did the change come about? Through the increasing influence of magic and magicians.

We know that Cro-Magnon art, as found in the caves at Lascaux or Montespan or Altamira, was not 'art' in our modern sense, but part of a magic ritual, still practised today by primitive peoples. The Pygmies of the Congo draw in the sand a picture of the animal they intend to hunt, then fire an arrow into its throat; Tungus carve an animal they intend to hunt; Yeniseis make a wooden fish before going fishing, and so on. The Pygmies leave the picture of their quarry, with the arrow in its throat, until they have caught the animal; then they rub some of the animal's blood on the picture and withdraw the arrow. They believe that this ritual establishes some kind of mysterious contact between the hunter and the hunted; now the animal cannot escape. No matter how fast it runs, or where it hides, the hunter moves towards it inexorably, guided by fate. It is the animal's destiny to become his prey.

The 'scientific' attitude to these activities is that they are primitive superstitions, merely a sign of ignorance of cause and effect. If they happen to be successful, this is only because they create a feeling of success in the hunter; it is self-hypnosis. I would argue that this view may completely miss the point. The hunter's mind becomes *totally concentrated* on his prey by the ritual, activating the same powers that led Rhine's subjects to such high scores when they first tried influencing the fall of dice.

What I am suggesting here, and throughout this book, is that whenever man has a strong sense of the *value* of something, he activates his 'powers', the powers that lie beyond the violet end of his mental spectrum. Man has developed to his present stage by learning to do many things mechanically; he learns some difficult skill with a conscious effort, and then passes it on to his subconscious 'robot', which learns to do it efficiently and automatically – riding a bicycle, speaking a foreign language. But to do a thing automatically means that you do not need to *concentrate* on it, and man's increasing use of his 'robot' has meant that he makes less and less use of his faculty of intense concentration. This explains why modern man is inclined to disbelieve in 'powers' beyond the violet end of the spectrum; he hardly ever uses them.

However, these powers operate whenever his sense of values is deeply touched – that is, when he really feels concern about something. After all, the purpose of these faculties is the same as the purpose of all our other powers: to make life run smoothly, to avert catastrophe. The *Journal for the Society of Psychical Research* records a typical case (March 1897) in which a clergyman's wife sent her little daughter to play in the 'railway garden', a walled garden near the railway embankment. 'A few minutes after her departure I distinctly heard a voice, as it were, within me, say, "Send for her back, or something dreadful will happen to her." At the same time I was seized with violent trembling, and great terror took possession of me.' The child was brought back, safe and well. and later that afternoon, an engine and tender jumped the rails and killed three people in the railway garden. The phenomenon can work the other way, as can be seen in a case quoted in *Phantasms of the Living* by Gurney, Myers and Podmore; a Mrs. Bettany described how, as a child of ten, she saw a vision of her mother lying, apparently dead, on the floor of her bedroom. She was on a country walk at the time, and fetched a doctor. They hurried to the bedroom, and found her mother lying on the floor in the position she had seen in the vision; she had had a heart attack, but was saved by the intervention of the doctor. Corroboration of her experience by her father is also published: 'I distinctly remember being surprised by seeing my daughter in company with the family doctor ... and I asked "Who is ill?" She replied "Mamma." She led the way to the White Room, where we found my wife lying in a swoon on the floor. It was when I asked when she had been taken ill that I found it must have been *after* my daughter had left the house.'

The account does not add whether there was a strong bond between mother and daughter, but there undoubtedly was.

Primitive magic was no more than the use of these powers; it was, in the most basic sense, 'sympathetic magic'. Lissner emphasises that the shamans of Siberia (where the word originates) were not 'witch doctors' or magicians, but something closer to mediums. The Manchurian word *samarambi* means 'to excite oneself', while *samdambi* means to dance. The shaman excites himself into a divine frenzy or ecstasy through drum beating and dancing, until he passes into a trance, when his spirit is supposed to have left his body. In his trance he makes the sounds of various birds and animals – he is supposed to be able to understand their language. The anthropologist Mirca Eliade describes shamans as 'specialists in ecstasy', and cites an impressive list of attestations to their powers, including thought-reading, clairvoyance, firewalking and discovering thieves with the aid of a mirror. Lissner describes the tribal ceremony:

A fire burns on the ground. Framed against the night by the red glow of the flickering flames, the shaman begins to move rhythmically, drumming, dancing, leaping and singing. The little bells on his robe tinkle, his iron ornaments clatter, and the Tungus sit there in the dim light, their attention riveted on his every move. The shaman's excitement communicates itself to the circle of spectators, and the larger the audience, the stronger the empathy between them and him. They all know each other, being interrelated and members of the same clan. Drawn together by the combination of night and firelight, they allow the monotonous rhythm of the drums to waft them irresistibly away from the everyday world. The excitement mounts, leaping like a spark from one man to the next, until all are near ecstasy and each is at once performer and spectator, doctor and patient, hammer and anvil.*

Lissner adds: 'I can only confirm Shirokogorov's assertion that those assembled around a shaman experience a satisfaction infinitely deeper than we ourselves do after a musical or dramatic performance.' This is an interesting comment. For after all, what is the purpose of music, of all art? It is an attempt to counteract the effect of the 'robot', what we might call 'the diffusion effect', since it is the opposite of concentration. Human beings have this strong tendency to drift into a state of 'indifference', and so waste consciousness that might be valuably employed. And indifference is like falling asleep; in fact, my sense of values *has* gone to sleep. Any crisis or challenge serves as an alarm clock, to jerk me out of my boredom. But if I listen with total concentration to a Mozart piano sonata, the same effect is achieved. It channels my emotions and mental energies and prevents the 'diffusion effect'.

If the human mind has this innate tendency to 'devalue' reality, then we can immediately grasp the importance of (a) a set of intensely held beliefs (i.e. values), and (b) the kind of concentration and *concern* demanded by primitive magical ceremonies. A Catholic may be transported by the mass, but he still knows that it is a symbolic

* *Man, God and Magic*, translated from the German by J. Maxwell Brownjohn (London, Jonathan Cape, 1961), p. 274.

ceremony, that if a pathologist was called in he would quickly verify that the bread and wine have not become flesh and blood. Even so, he is transported, because the mass concentrates the mind upon a 'reality' more important than the here and now, and this mental act – of putting the present firmly in its place – raises the spirit. The savage believes completely that the shaman's soul has taken leave of his body and is now journeying in heaven or hell. (The shaman of the Altaians has a young birch tree, with notches cut in it, placed in front of him; these represent the various heavens, and as his spirit ascends from one to the other, he describes them in detail from his trance state.) He believes implicitly everything the shaman tells him from his trance. The result must be far more deeply moving and emotionally exhausting than any Wagner opera.

The shaman himself has achieved his priesthood through the most terrifying ordeals, an initiation through pain. Fierce rubbing of his face with an abrasive substance is intended to remove the old skin, and even the second skin is rubbed away, symbolising total rebirth. An Eskimo shaman may have to spend five days in freezing water. Sometimes, the spirit of a dead shaman takes up its abode in the body of his successor; then the new shaman undergoes intense agony and the belief that he has been totally hacked to pieces and devoured by spirits. He 'sees' all this in a trance state, and Lissner states that 'blood-shot patches appear on his body, his clothes sometimes become stained with blood, and gouts of blood discolour his couch of freshly stripped birchbark'. An older shaman has undergone this 'dismemberment' three times. The aim of this initiation is to 'shake the mind awake', to crystallise the will. For the chief problem of human beings is passivity, 'the triviality of everydayness'. If you watch television all evening, or read too long, you feel a 'freezing' of your mind; it congeals; your eyes become capable only of a blank, dull stare. The same is true, to a lesser degree, of all routine existence. The problem is to stir the mind out of its lethargy, to make it *reach out* further. This is why all asceticism begins with stern self-restraint, sometimes self-torment. The thirteenth-century German mystic Suso wore a leather shirt studded with tacks whose points were turned inwards, and for eight years he carried on his back a wooden cross studded with pointed nails; mystical enlightenment came to him suddenly at the end of sixteen years of suffering.

In parenthesis, it is interesting to note that the legend of the northern Siberians declares that the spirits of shamans are born in a larch tree, in nests of varying sizes, and a large bird like an eagle lays iron eggs which turn into shamans. The legend bears a curious resemblance to the Tree of Life, which Yeats describes as a universal symbol (see p. 132).

Lissner argues convincingly that cave drawings of Palaeolithic man – some of them twenty thousand years old – represent shamans performing magical operations, men wearing the masks of birds or skins of bison or deer antlers. Wands or batons found in the caves resemble the drumsticks of the modern shaman. No drums have been found, but this is understandable.

This, then, is Lissner's picture of the life of Neanderthal and Cro-Magnon men, based upon seventeen years of research. In certain ways, they were more primitive than any primitive tribes in the world today. They lived in caves or, later, tents of skin, and they wore animal skins. They worshipped God, and the shamans were their priests; like the Hebrews of the Old Testament, they sacrificed animals to their God. Like any modern priest, the shaman's functions were wholly benevolent: he diagnosed and treated illness, and performed spells to aid the hunters of the tribe.

And then, roughly sixty thousand years ago, changes began to occur. As man became more civilised, it became inevitable that magic should become more important; for man is a creature who craves knowledge and belief, and magic represented his chief form of both. New cults began to spread. At Willendorf in Austria, at Vestonice in

Moravia, at Savignano in Italy, at Lespugue in France, tiny female statuettes have been unearthed by archaeologists. The name 'Venus' has been applied to them. They certainly seem to represent some goddess cult – perhaps the White Goddess herself. Many of them are fat, with enormous breasts, which has led to the suggestion that they might be magical aids to pregnancy; but others are slim. At Brno, a male figure has been found. The artist has concentrated on the body; the face is hardly ever suggested.

And then, just as surprisingly, primitive man stopped making figures of human beings. Why? Because they *were* magical. If you could kill a bison or a reindeer by making its image and performing magical operations, the same applied to human beings. It had become dangerous to represent the human form. The age of magic had begun. If you could kill animals by magic, why not your enemy?

And as man became increasingly obsessed with magic, the number of his gods, and demons, increased. And in the dawn of recorded history – about 3000 B.C. – the civilisations of the Nile valley, the Indus valley and Mesopotamia are riddled with ideas of gods, demons and sorcerers. Some time in this fourth milennium B.C., the human race took its most tremendous leap forward so far – a leap so remarkable that one is tempted to credit the imaginative speculation of Arthur C. Clarke in his *2001* that more intelligent beings from outer space have periodically taken a hand in mankind's development. The Stone Age lasted until sometime between 4000 and 3000 B.C., and man used stone knives, flint spearheads, stone or wooden ploughs. And then man discovered the use of metals. We do not know how it happened. Perhaps someone threw a piece of copper ore into a fire and discovered that a bright, hard metal had flowed out of it. The edges of the metal could be made far sharper than the edges of flint, and were better for skinning animals. At about the same time, some unknown genius – perhaps the legendary Tubal Cain – discovered the many uses of the wheel, both for transport and for making pots. Building bricks were invented. Sailing ships were built. Oxen were harnessed to the plough and the cart. Civilisation as we now know it – *technical* civilisation – came into being. The invention of writing came a few hundred years later, at least, that is the period from which the written records date. Mankind has never known such a comparable advance, unless we count the scientific advance of our own epoch. What caused this sudden surge of achievement was the emergence of large communities. Man was now the most successful creature on earth, and his numbers had increased. He had known the use of agriculture since about 10,000 B.C. But the earth was still covered with forests and deserts. The best places to live were river valleys, or beside the sea. Man crowded together on the banks of the Nile, the Indus, the Tigris and Euphrates, the Yellow River, in conglomerations of tents, mud huts and shacks made of woven reeds. City life brought the advantages and disadvantages with which we are so familiar – disease and crime, and also trade and art. It brought division of labour and time to think. It destroyed once and for all the primeval innocence of the hunters. It emphasised the basic hostility of man to man. In nature there is a law of 'letting alone'; there are few animals that kill for the pleasure of it. A woman collecting sweet berries might hear a bear snuffling around, but she knew it would not attack her unless it was afraid for its cubs. And at nightfall the antelope and the lion drink together, side by side. Hunters from different tribes, meeting one another in the forest, might salute one another and pass on, unless one group had invaded the territory of the other. In the city, a new law of hostility prevailed, and to call it the law of the jungle is unfair to the jungle.

One does not have to believe in Rousseau's 'noble savage' to believe that man's fall from grace came with city dwelling; it is common sense. Some cities might be prosperous and secure, with good land and a strong ruler; but they would be the exceptions. Most cities would be little more than large groups of human beings living together for convenience, like rats in a sewer.

The consequence is obvious, Man ceases to be an instinctive, simple creature. Whether he likes it or not, he has to become more *calculating* to survive. He also has to become, in a very special sense, more aggressive – not simply towards other men but towards the world. Before this time, there had only been small Neolithic communities, whose size was limited by their ability to produce food. If the population increased too fast, the weaker ones starved. It encouraged a passive, peaceful attitude towards life and nature. Big cities were more prosperous because men had pooled their resources, and because certain men could afford to become 'specialists' – in metalwork, weaving, writing and so on. And there were many ways to keep yourself alive: labouring, trading or preying on other men. Unlike the Neolithic community, this was a world where enterprise counted for everything. It would be no exaggeration to say that the 'rat race' began in 4000 B.C.

The more man expanded his activities, the more gods he needed. When he began to sail the seas, he needed to make sacrifices to the sea god; when he set out on a journey, he needed to feel himself under the protection of the god of travellers, and so on. Every new enterprise needed a new god. Man was out to gain control of his environment. And his chief means of achieving this control was still – magic.

In all this ferment and uproar there would be little opportunity for that intense concentration of mind that distinguished the earlier shamans. All religion and occultism that spring from this intense concentration tend to be simple and mystical. They are a recognition of vistas of meaning 'out there', of powers that man can 'plug into' if he directs his mind towards them with strong conviction. All the great religions – Judaism, Buddhism, Hinduism, Christianity, Mohammedanism – are simple in this sense. In the hands of the common people – the nonreligious 99 per cent – they soon lose this simplicity, this clarity of vision, and develop hordes of angels, gods and demons.

This raises another point of central importance to 'magic' – how central was not understood until the emergence of Freud. Primitive people are characterised by a kind of puritanism. The shaman of the Huichol Indians, Ramon Medina, told Norman Lewis that any Huichol who had sexual relations more than ten or fifteen times a year was regarded as a debauchee. Their attitude towards sex, he explained, was based upon the tribe's divine ancestor, the deer, which limited its sexual activity to a brief yearly season. Besides, sexual indulgence wastes vital powers.

This statement may be more accurate than it sounds. Sexual intercourse in itself may not waste vitality, but there *is* an association between self-discipline and survival-qualities. A Huichol boy who was bathing in the freezing river at dawn was reproved by Medina for self-indulgence; three in the morning was the correct time for bathing. 'Such dousings fostered the natural sexual coldness that the Huichols appreciated in their womenfolk,' adds Lewis. Tribal women reflect the virtues demanded by their menfolk; placidity, fidelity, good housekeeping.

In contrast, the city dweller tends to be 'sexier'. The natural outlets of male dominance are hunting and fighting. If these are reduced, an interest in sex naturally replaces them, for the penetration of the female is an act of supreme dominance. The act of making love to a placid, domesticated girl would be less satisfying to this urge than making love to a girl who is more glamorous, independent, challenging. Where a type of human being is demanded by circumstances, it soon appears. Urban culture produced the glamorous courtesan, the 'siren', the woman for whose attention dominant men compete. It becomes a virtue to present men with a challenge. Leonard Cottrell repeats from a Chinese chronicle the story of Emperor Wu's concubine, who was noted for being sullen and difficult to please. She liked the sound of tearing silk, so bales of it were torn in front of her. To gratify her whim, the Emperor lit the beacon fires which summoned his war lords to defend the country against barbarians. Armies arrived at the palace of the Emperor, only to be told that it was all a joke. When she saw the expression on the faces of the lords, the girl laughed – for the first time in her life, according to the story.

Like most ancient stories, this one carries a moral. When the barbarians *did* invade, the beacons were lit, but no one came, and the Emperor was killed and his city destroyed.*

The counterpart of the 'siren' was the Don Juan. The Babylonian epic of Gilgamesh, a thousand years older than Homer, begins by describing how the insatiable sexual appetite of the warrior – and king – Gilgamesh 'leaves no virgin to her lover, neither the warrior's daughter nor the wife of the noble'. His fellow citizens recognise – with Freudian penetration – that he is 'sublimating' a powerful urge to conquer, and beg the gods to create a man strong enough to be his downfall. They create the man-god Enkidu, who first has to be 'humanised' by a courtesan who attends to his sexual education. 'She was not ashamed to take him, and she made herself naked and welcomed his eagerness ...' His eagerness is so great that he makes love to her for a whole week, at the end of which time he is much enfeebled, and his former companions, the beasts of the forest, fail to recognise him. He is also shrunken in stature. (Again we have the notion of primitive peoples that sex is a depressant.) Later, when Enkidu and Gilgamesh have fought, and then sworn friendship, Enkidu finds the gay, debauched life of the city degrading, a drain on his powers, and he and Gilgamesh set out in search of adventure. And when they return, and the goddess Ishtar (the Babylonian Venus)

* Leonard Cottrell, *The Tiger of Ch'in*, Chapter 4.

tries to seduce Gilgamesh, he rejects her; his heroic energies have been diverted into their proper channels, and he no longer cares for this unmanly business of seduction. The whole poem is a protest of the old tribal morality against the sexuality of the town. And its analysis of Gilgamesh's satyriasis has a penetration that suggests that the original Sumerian author was a shaman. (The shamans were also poets and story-tellers; Eliade points out that a shaman has a vocabulary of twelve thousand words, three times that of the rest of the tribe.)

I have argued in this book that man was not really made for civilisation. As an aggressive, highly energetic creature, he finds it difficult to adjust himself to its restraints. He responds to lack of challenge with boredom and a tendency to become slack and demoralised. The sexual instinct remains as powerful as ever, and has to bear an increased weight of frustrated dominance. The result: hypersexuality and sexual perversion. *Gilgamesh*, one of the earliest of written records, sounds almost as decadent as Petronius or Martial where it deals with sex. Except in one respect: homosexuality has not yet appeared. But it is remarkable that homosexuality – rare or nonexistent among primitive tribes – seems to have figured in the history of Western civilisation ever since men began to live in cities. (Experiments conducted by the psychologist John B. Calhoun in which rats were made to live and breed in overcrowded conditions showed that rats developed homosexuality when crowded into 'slums'.)

The same, interestingly enough, may be said of incest. Primitives have strong incest taboos; the Huichols believe that a man who has intercourse with a relative or with someone outside the tribe will become sterile. The taboo on extra-tribal relations is understandable enough: the desire for racial purity. But why a taboo on incest? The anthropologist Claude Lévi-Strauss made his reputation with a book called *The Elementary Structures of Kinship* (1949), in which he advances the interesting theory that incest is tabooed among primitives not because they are afraid of racial enfeeblement, but because savages are obsessed with the notion of gifts. Giving, he says, is an essential social lubricant, a way of fostering community spirit and avoiding war. The natural, selfish response of the male would be to keep pretty daughters and sisters in the family, a private harem: women were property, to be kept or disposed of as the male thought fit. But this would be a source of social tension, says Lévi-Strauss, for the rest of the tribe would feel it unfair that the most attractive girls should be the property of their fathers and brothers. And so the women became the most valuable objects of tribal barter; they were given as 'gifts' to men of other families, who in turn gave their own women. And so women ensured harmony within the tribe, and incest gradually became a taboo. Lévi-Strauss's view is that the incest taboo reveals a kind of 'natural Christianity' in savages: 'It is better to give than to receive …'

I mention this view because it is now generally accepted, and it seems to me demonstrably false. There is no evidence that primitive man was naturally incestuous and reformed out of a desire to keep his neighbours friendly. But if he was, what happened about the ugly daughters, who were not, so to speak, social currency? Were they kept in the family harem? And why should giving away a pretty daughter lessen the tribe's envy? She still had only one husband. If this was the motive for getting rid of her, it would be more sensible to make her the general property of the males of the tribe.

But the real objection, if our line of argument is correct, is that it is far simpler to assume that primitive man knew instinctively that incest would weaken the tribe's genetic purity even more than marriage with strangers. Every child takes half its genes from its father and half from its mother. It may receive a 'recessive gene' from one parent – short-sightedness or some other defect – but the chances are that this will be counteracted by a healthy gene from the other. If blood relatives mate, the chances are higher that the child will get two recessive genes, so that in the long run, incest will breed feebler specimens than normal 'mixed' marriages. If we are right to accept that the genes are somehow influenced by a 'group mind', then the group mind has an excellent reason for creating an instinctive aversion to incest in tribes whose existence depends upon their racial vitality.

When man began to live in cities, the incest taboo was weakened. The brother–sister marriages of the ancient Egyptian rulers have no relevance to this argument, because they were the result of a belief that the kings and queens were gods and therefore not able to mate with ordinary mortals; but according to Suetonius and Tacitus, some of the Caesars indulged in incest purely for pleasure, a piquant variation to stir appetites that had become jaded through too much sexual indulgence.

Now, primitive magic was basically the use of man's hidden powers to influence the hunt, or perhaps the battle. Grimble's description of 'the calling of the porpoises' is a perfect example of primitive shamanism. Under the new, urban conditions, it inevitably became more closely connected with sex. Sexual frustration became increasingly common in the cities. The lords could enjoy their harems; the young nobles could pursue famous courtesans; the poor man still had his overworked wife and large family, and he only had to turn his head to see bare-breasted girls passing in the street. Men were inclined to die younger than women, so there were many sexually frustrated widows. (This is reflected in the story of Ishtar's pursuit of Gilgamesh, as in the story of Venus and Adonis, or even of Joseph and Potiphar's wife.) Bronislaw Malinowsky spent years observing the Trobriand Islanders, and noted the magic rites connected with the launching of a canoe; their purpose was to protect the crew from flying witches who would wreck the boat and eat the bodies of the sailors. Here one can see plainly the sexual origin of the fear of witches. It was believed that if a girl wanted to prevent her lover from becoming unfaithful, she should bake a cake containing her menstrual blood; having eaten it, he would become impotent with other women. The young man who wanted to 'bewitch' a girl had to induce her to drink a potion in which his semen had been mixed. (These magical beliefs persist today as far apart as Sicily and America's Deep South.)

What happened to magic, as it became 'urbanised', was that it became infused with a strong element of nonsense. Cornelius Agrippa, the sixteenth-century mage, declared that women should drink the urine of mules as a contraceptive, because mules are sterile. This would obviously be as effective as most love potions. On the other hand, it would be incorrect to assume that sexual magic was fundamentally no more than crude superstition. Sex is one of the few human functions that has not been successfully 'automatised' by the robot. If I am tired, a beautiful view or a Mozart symphony may fail to stir my interest; but a glimpse of a strange girl taking off her clothes will. That is to say, sex has a certain inbuilt defence against the loss of 'value perception' caused by fatigue or close-upness. This means that it has, so to speak, a 'hot line' to my subconscious mind. Civilisation robbed man of many of his deeper powers; but sex remained unaffected – if anything, it became stronger. The subconscious powers can still be unleashed by sex. It now seems fairly certain that poltergeist phenomena (*poltergeist* means 'rattling ghost') are caused by unconscious sexual disturbances in pubescent girls and boys – particularly girls. Rayner C. Johnson writes:

> One of the most striking features of the poltergeist phenomena is that in an overwhelming majority of cases a young person seems to be the unconscious agent of the effects. In 95% of cases it is a young girl; in 5% a boy or youth, says Price. Moreover, sexual change or shock seems to be frequently associated either with the beginning or the cessation of the phenomena. Puberty and adolescence are thus the periods

favourable to the effects. Price informs us that Eleonora Zugun's power vanished overnight with the first appearance of the menses; that the Schneider brothers were brilliant about puberty, but the effects waned as adolescence advanced; conversely, that Stella C.'s power became marked with sexual maturity; that in the case of Esther Cox, the phenomena which lasted a year were initiated by nervous shock following attempted sexual assault, and that moreover they attained their greatest strength every twenty-eight days ... Price also tells of an interview with the husband of Frieda W., a young Austrian medium, who informed him that at the height of his wife's sexual excitement in their early married life, ornaments would sometimes fall off the mantelpiece in their bedroom; also that during menstruation ... mediumship did not occur.*

Johnson also cites a case of a similar nature that was analysed by Dr. C. A. Meier, Jung's assistant. At the height of the analysis, the patient, in a trance, imagined herself to be penetrating deeper and deeper into a city, which symbolised her problem (presumably sexual, although Johnson does not say so). At the moment she reached its centre, there was a loud report, and a Gothic wooden bench split from end to end.

Robert Graves commented to me that many young men use a form of unconscious sorcery in seducing girls; this is also consistent with the view I am advancing: that since man has become a city dweller, there is a strong connection between his latent 'psychic' powers and his sexuality. Sex can arouse a degree of will-power and intensity that can seldom be found in other departments of civilised life. One only has to see dogs, sleeping out in the worst weather around the house of a bitch in heat, to grasp something of the force of the instinct. Bartok also catches something of it in his ballet *The Miraculous Mandarin*, in

* *The Imprisoned Splendour* (London, Hodder and Stoughton, 1953), pp. 255–256.

which a prostitute lures a mandarin to her room, where he is attacked by two roughs; they smother him, stab him and finally hang him, but he refuses to die until his sexual desire has been satisfied. The mandarin is portrayed as a silent, impassive man, whose desire is expressed only by his burning eyes: a man driven by an enormous will, the archetypal image of the mage.

It is this association of magic with sex that really created the concept of 'black magic'. And this was the second stage in the degeneration of the magical art.

Let us summarise the history of magic, as it emerges from all this.

Primitive man still possessed the supersensory instincts of the lower animals: telepathy, intuition of danger, a 'sixth sense' to guide him to green pastures where the hunting was good. After more than a million years of evolution he had lost most of these powers; for he had, compared with other creatures, become a highly rational being. But the tribal shamans knew how to nurture their powers, and used them for the good of the tribe.

Some sixty thousand years ago, Cro-Magnon man appeared, the highest type of man so far. Magic played a larger part in his life than in that of earlier man. Magic was Stone Age science, and he was the most intelligent creature yet to appear on earth.

The inevitable occurred; the 'white', sympathetic magic of the shamans turned into something more personal. Sorcery came into existence. Sorcery must be clearly distinguished from ordinary magic or witchcraft, which is simply the use of extrasensory powers – that is, telepathy and water-divining are simple forms of witchcraft. Sorcery is the attempt at the *systematic* use of such powers by means of 'spells', potions, rituals and so on. A simple distinction would be to say that witchcraft is fundamentally passive, sorcery fundamentally active.

But perhaps the most important distinction is this. Witchcraft and magic depend upon higher levels of consciousness, a wider grasp of reality than man normally possesses. In this they are closely related to mysticism. Sorcery may depend upon supernormal powers, but it sets out from everyday consciousness, the everyday personality. The characteristic of the everyday personality is its will-to-power: the desire for money, possessions, sexual conquest, position. The mystical urge, on the other hand, transcends all these. A poet enchanted by the freshness of an April shower experiences strange longings, something bursting and struggling inside him, a feeling of the richness and mysteriousness of the universe that makes the ambitions of ordinary men seem stupid and mistaken. It might be argued that *all* men are driven by these urges to self-transcendence: even the politician telling lies to win an election; even the Don Juan telling lies to persuade a girl into bed. That is true. The essential difference is that the poet somehow 'rejects himself'; he is not interested in his personality and its aggrandisement. He would like to become as innocent as clear water. The distinction is important, for it will be raised repeatedly in the course of this book. The difference between a magician and a sorcerer is that the magician is disinterested, like a poet or scientist; the sorcerer wants personal power.

Sorcery came into being sixty thousand years ago, but while men lived simple lives in small villages, it remained an unimportant offshoot of shamanism. With the coming of cities, and the growth of mankind's sexual obsession, it outstripped shamanism and took on an independent existence. From now on, magic and sex remained in close association; it explains the violence of the persecution of witches in the Christian era.

But there is reason to suspect that another important event played a part in changing the history of mankind in the fourth millennium B.C.: the flood.

In the early 1920s, a joint British and American expedition, under the leadership of Leonard Woolley, went to investigate the mound of Tell al Muqayyar, which lies midway between Baghdad and the Persian Gulf; it was the site of the ancient city of Ur, of the Chaldees. The Chaldeans were traditionally the founders of astronomy and astrology; Nebuchadnezzar and Belshazzar were Chaldean kings.

The whole decade of the twenties was rich in archaeological discoveries, dating back to the period of the discovery of writings – 3000 B.C. The treasures discovered were as beautiful and exotic as those discovered in the tomb of Tutankhamen in 1922. But in the summer of 1929, as the digging was coming to an end, Woolley decided to penetrate below a hill that contained the graves of Sumerian nobles (which Woolley called 'the graves of the Kings of Ur'). They discovered clay tablets older than those in the tombs: tablets dating from the discovery of writing. As they continued to dig down, they found more Sumerian pottery, resembling that already found; plainly, Sumerian civilisation had been stable and unchanging over a long period.

And then, to everyone's surprise, they reached a layer of pure white clay. It was over eight feet thick. And on the other side of it, they found more pots and fragments of buildings. The pots were now hand-made, not shaped on a potter's wheel; they were back in the culture of the Stone Age.

The Stone Age was divided from the Bronze and Iron Age by evidence of a flood. Calculations indicated that the flood took place about 4000 B.C., the date of mankind's great change to city dwelling.

In the 1870s a scholar named George Smith was working in the British Museum, examining some of the clay tablets with cuneiform writing that had been found at Nineveh by Rassam, Austen Layard's assistant. These tablets were part of the library of the bloody King Sennacherib of Biblical fame. It was Smith who realised that some of the tablets were part of an ancient poem about a hero named Gilgamesh. I have already mentioned the early part of this epic – one of the greatest works in world literature: how the gods were persuaded to create Enkidu to chasten Gilgamesh, and how the two became friends. Gilgamesh and Enkidu journey to the Cedar Mountain (now known to be between Syria and Asia Minor) and fight with its guardian, the giant Humbaba, whom they kill. On their return, there occurs the episode of Ishtar's attempted seduction of Gilgamesh; when he rejects her, she persuades the gods to send a celestial bull to destroy the city of Uruk. Gilgamesh and Enkidu manage to slay the bull. Ishtar then sends a mysterious disease that kills Enkidu. Gilgamesh is desolated – and suddenly aware of his mortality. He decides to go and consult a man who has been given immortality by the gods – Uta-Napishtim. He journeys to a strange mountain guarded by scorpion men, and penetrates to its heart, a sort of Arabian Nights garden. The goddess Siduri tells him that all men are born to die, but finally consents to help him meet Uta-Napishtim. And it is Uta-Napishtim who narrates to Gilgamesh the story of the flood: how he had been warned by the god Ea that the world was to be destroyed by water, and how he escaped the destruction by building an ark. The gods decided to make him immortal as a consequence.

There is little more of the epic of Gilgamesh – the remainder has not been discovered. On Uta-Napishtim's advice, Gilgamesh finds a plant of Eternal Life at the bottom of the sea; but a snake steals it while he is asleep, and he returns to Uruk sad and empty-handed.

Victorian England was astonished when Smith published his translation of the Flood story from Gilgamesh. Certain tablets were missing, and the London *Daily Telegraph* provided Smith with £1,000 to go and look for the missing fragments. It was a million-to-one chance that he would find them. Amazingly enough, he did, after a mere five days. (Some of the incredible 'coincidences' that have occurred in archaeology are enough to make the most sceptical person believe in the Fates.) Smith unearthed most of the Gilgamesh poem as we know it today; unfortunately, little more has been found, although there have been fragments in the older language of the Sumerians, indicating that the poem records traditions of the previous millennium.

Legends of a flood are widespread throughout world mythology – a flood accompanied by volcanic eruptions, hurricanes and water-spouts. In Greek legend, Deucalion, son of Prometheus, was the sole survivor (together with his wife Pyrrha) of a flood through which Zeus destroyed the world. (The reason given is the same as in the Bible: that the race of mankind had grown utterly corrupt.) Ovid tells the story. So does the Hindu *Rig Veda*, which has Manu building his ark, and alighting on a mountain-top when the flood is over – like Deucalion and Uta-Napishtim. Flood legends are found in the *Popol Vuh*, the 'sacred book' of the Quiche Indians of South America, and among North American Indians. Any reader who doubts the universality of flood legends should look under 'deluge' in the index of Ballou's *Bible of the World*, where he can choose among six different versions, including Persian, Chinese and Hindu.

It is possible, of course, that each of these legends refers to a different flood; it seems unlikely that both China and North America were flooded at the same time. But it is interesting to speculate: *Could* there have been any event in the earth's history catastrophic enough to cause flooding of large areas of the whole globe?

A strange German engineer named Hans Hoerbiger* was convinced that he had the answer, and he numbered Hitler among his followers; even today, the Hoerbiger 'world-ice theory' has thousands of adherents. (In *Morning of the Magicians*, published in 1960, Louis Pauwels declares that he still has a million followers.) Hoerbiger said that it was due to the moon – to the capture of the present moon by our earth. Our moon, according to Hoerbiger, is the fourth that the earth has captured. It was once a small planet that

* 1860–1931.

came too close to the earth – in its inevitable spiral closer to the sun – and became its satellite, creating havoc on the surface of the planet earth in the process.

The 'world-ice theory' (*Welteislehre*) takes its name from Hoerbiger's belief that the universe began when a huge block of cosmic ice somehow encountered a sun. There was a tremendous explosion, which is still continuing. That is why astronomers observe that our universe is expanding, says Hoerbiger. Inevitably, there is no such thing as 'empty space', because an explosion would diffuse its matter all over the universe; what we call empty space is actually filled with rarefied hydrogen and fine ice crystals. (His great idea originated in the days when he was an engineer, and saw molten iron falling accidentally on snow, causing an explosion; he had a sudden powerful conviction that this was how the universe began.)

It will be interesting to see how the Hoerbiger cult will survive the moon landings, for he declared that the moon is covered with a thick layer of ice to a depth of many miles. According to Hoerbiger, the earth's three previous moons have been comets covered with ice that came too close to the earth; a day came when they fell on the earth – for they spiral closer to the earth as the needle on a gramophone record approaches the centre. These giant catastrophes explain the epochs in the earth's evolution – the great Ice Ages, and so on.

Before we dismiss Hoerbiger completely as a madman, it is as well to bear in mind that scientists still have no explanation of some of these changes in the earth's climate. In the past twenty million years, an age of heavy rainfall (the Miocene) was succeeded by twelve million years of droughts and deserts (the Pliocene); then came the Pleistocene, a strange, explosive period with tremendous variations of climate, including four great Ice Ages, which lasted for a million years. In *African Genesis*, Ardrey has an amusing chapter describing the various theories that attempt to account for the four Ice Ages of the Pleistocene, the last of which, Würm, extended from the time of Neanderthal man to a mere eleven thousand years ago. They include comets, the tilting poles of the earth, sudden bursts of solar radiation and Ardrey's own theory that the solar system revolves through a gas cloud every two hundred million years. All the theories can be disproved. And so we still have no definite idea of what has caused the great Ice Ages of the Pre-Cambrian, the Permian and the Pleistocene. Hoerbiger's moon hypothesis is as likely as any. Particularly since it now seems likely that our moon *is* a foreign body captured from outer space.

It is true that Hoerbiger dates the capture of our present moon (which he calls the planet Luna) at about 12,000 B.C. But then, he is quite certain that the capture of Luna caused the Flood. The point is argued in one of the most delightful of crank books, *Atlantis and the Giants*, by the late Professor Denis Saurat (1957). Saurat, a follower of Hoerbiger, seizes on that strange phrase in the story of Noah, 'There were giants in the earth in those days.' There is plenty of geological evidence that giants *did* once exist. In the mid-1930s, the anthropologist G. R. H. Von Koenigswald was shown a tooth from the Kwangsi cave deposits of China (late Tertiary) that seemed to be that of a giant ape, twice the size of the present gorilla; more teeth were later discovered, proving that this was no freak. Then, in the late thirties, near the Javanese village of Sangiran, skull and jaw fragments of human giants were discovered – men twice the size of present-day man. Von Koenigswald described it all in a remarkable book, *Apes, Giants and Man*. It was only the intervention of the war, when Von Koenigswald was interned by the Japanese, that prevented the discoveries from being a worldwide sensation. Von Koenigswald's Meganthropus is about half a million years old.

According to Saurat, a moon gradually approaching the earth would produce giants, for it would counteract the earth's gravitational force. Men – and all living creatures – would become bigger and live longer. (They would live longer because there would be less gravitational wear and tear, heart failure due to overweight, etc.) Hence the legends of Methuselah and other long-lived patriarchs in the Bible. He even uses this hypothesis of longevity to explain Fabre's puzzle of the *Ammonophilas* wasp (mentioned on page 160). If creatures were much more long-lived in those days, the wasp had time to learn to sting the caterpillar in the right places. (I have pointed out that the telepathic theory of evolution provides a better explanation.) The approaching moon would also cause the tides to be sucked into a band around the equator, for they would not have time to retreat. A strange line of maritime deposits running from Lake Umayo, in the Peruvian Andes, and extending for nearly 400 miles southward in a curve to Lake Coipasa, are cited as evidence of this equatorial 'tidal bulge' of thousands of years ago. A great civilisation of giants came into being at Tiahuanaco, near Lake Titicaca, 12,000 feet high in the Andes; their ships encircled the globe – on the 'tidal bulge'. This, says Saurat, explains the resemblances in human culture all over the earth: the cromlechs of Malekula, the megaliths of Brittany and Stonehenge, the resemblances between legends of Greece and Mexico.

There is one slight inconsistency in this theory, which may be overlooked in view of its exciting nature. If the flood of 4000 B.C. was caused by the *capture* of our present moon, not by the explosion of the previous moon as it fell on our earth, then why should there have been giants on the earth in those days? If the earth had no moon to lighten its gravitational pull, there would more likely have been dwarfs on the earth. Or were the giants, perhaps, survivors of the earlier giant races? Saurat declares that the Ruanda tribe of Africa, who sometimes grow to a height of eight feet, are survivors of the giants.

Saurat makes at least one point with which we can agree wholeheartedly. Citing the anthropologist John Layard, who wrote a classic book on the great stone megaliths of Malekula, he suggests that the 'weather magic' of the Malekulan primitives may not have been pure imagination, as Frazer and Durkheim believe, but that the power of the human psyche over nature may have been far more developed in these 'savages'. And in the important essential he agrees with Lissner. Saurat writes:

> For some time it has been fashionable to believe that civilised society has evolved from primitive savagery ... This fashion is now on the wane. We are more disposed to believe that man, as man, emerged very quickly and reached almost at once a state of high intellectual and spiritual development. Then a series of calamities, both moral and physical, overwhelmed him ... and those calamities caused a rapid degeneration in different parts of the earth.

And this underlines the problem in dealing with 'crank' books like those by Saurat, Hoerbiger and Hoerbiger's English disciple H. S. Bellamy. They *are* crank books, because in spite of the impressive weight of evidence they offer – much of it irrefutable – they begin by taking a long leap into pure assumptions. Hoerbiger's obsession with 'cosmic ice' has not, so far, been borne out by space probes, and seems unlikely to be. He does not base his theory on some unexplainable 'fact' that sets him guessing – as Einstein based the theory of relativity on the negative result of the Michelson-Morley experiment to test the presence of the ether – but seems to start from a kind of poetic inspiration, not unlike Graves's 'flashes' about the tree alphabet. On the other hand, his belief that our present moon is an alien from outer space seems to be an inspired guess. And the work of his disciple Bellamy in *Moon, Myths and Man*, showing the remarkable similarities between various moon-catastrophe myths in world mythology, is valuable in its own right. The attitude taken by Martin Gardner, in his delightful classic *Fads and*

Fallacies in the Name of Science – that all this is totally absurd – is hardly justified. The 'science' that Gardner uses as his yardstick is the dogmatic nineteenth-century science that we have already discussed in connection with H. G. Wells. Saurat may leap from 'fact' to 'fact' in the most unorthodox manner: he points out that the ancient Egyptians said that man was taught the art of writing by the gods, then asserts that these gods were actually the highly cultured 'giants' of the pre-Luna phase. But this kind of imaginative guesswork, supported by odd pieces of evidence like the Kwangsi giant and the *Meganthropus* of Java, may be eventually more fruitful than the cautious scepticism of scientists. This is why Ouspensky had his desk drawer full of books on magic and Atlantis, and why he found a 'strange flavour of truth' in them. Man achieves his power over reality by withdrawing from it and recharging his vital batteries by flights of imagination. Otherwise he becomes stale and dehydrated; his attitude towards reality becomes shortsighted and violent. There *is* a flavour of reality in the study of magic and the occult, for it stimulates Faculty X, which is man's direct sense of reality.

I would suggest, then, as a fruitful hypothesis which might well be true, that round about the year 4000 B.C., the earth captured its present moon. It may or may not have had earlier moons – we have no way of knowing, since writing was not invented. The capture of the satellite caused an immense upheaval, volcanic eruptions and tidal waves. A large part of mankind was destroyed. And the tremendous catastrophe had far-reaching psychological effects on the survivors. For thousands of years, man had been a farmer rather than a hunter. He lived in small, secure village communities where there were few changes from century to century. For, as Gerald Hawkins remarks in *Stonehenge Decoded*: 'Primitive tribes do not necessarily welcome radical ideas; they are quite capable of resisting an innovation even if it is demonstrably beneficial, and of putting to death the would-be innovator as a sorcerer. Significant change sometimes depends on force' (p. 35). The flood was an immense shock, stimulating the deepest springs of the will to survive. The security of centuries was at an end. The survivors moved together into river valleys. As in all times of devastation, human hyenas roamed the country, making travel unsafe, raiding what small communities had survived. The city was mankind's instinctive response to the disaster: a huddling together for comfort and protection. And, if we are correct in regarding the moon as the cause of the disaster, then they stared at the new planet in the sky – which glowed red through the disturbed atmosphere – and saw it as an object of terrible significance, a god. Man is a creature with an apocalyptic view who responds best to violent challenge. He had become accustomed to the green, peaceful world that succeeded the last Ice Age (which began 55,000 years ago), a world in which he was becoming the most dominant creature, now that the mammoths and sabre-tooth tigers were extinct. Without the catastrophe he might have continued to live as a nomad or farmer for another five thousand years like his descendants, the aborigines of Australia and New Guinea. The flood shook him out of his sloth.

It is Hoerbiger's belief that it was the flood that destroyed the continent of Atlantis, and this is therefore a convenient place to speak of these legends. The Atlantis myth is derived solely from Plato, who tells the story in two dialogues, the *Timaeus* and *Critias*. Plato's Critias, a real person, explains that his family are in possession of documents written by the statesman Solon, who obtained his information from the priests of Egypt. It certainly looks as if Plato inserted the substance of these documents into the two dialogues in order that it should be preserved; otherwise, the 'myth' seems to serve no particular purpose in the dialogues – it is not intended as a parable or illustrative fable. An Egyptian priest tells Solon that the Greeks are like children as far as historical knowledge goes; they remember only one flood, when there have been many. One of the greatest of these was the one that destroyed the vast continent of Atlantis, which lay beyond the Pillars of Hercules (Gibraltar) and was as large as Libya and Asia together. The destruction was timely, for the Atlanteans had decided to attack Egypt and Athens. All this happened about nine thousand years before Plato. Plato adds that Atlantis held sway over many islands, which makes it sound as though it were a group of islands instead of – or as well as – a continent.

The modern interest in Atlantis began in 1882, when an American called Ignatius Donnelly brought out *Atlantis, The Antediluvian World*, a remarkable work that can still provide hours of fascination. Donnelly asserts that Atlantis was a huge continent lying in the Atlantic ocean, and that its kings and queens became the gods and goddesses of all later mythologies. It was the origin of the Garden of Eden legend. And it was destroyed about thirteen thousand years ago – a date that agrees roughly with Plato and Hoerbiger. Donnelly's book examines the flood legends of the world, and the coincidences of a 'universal culture' that Saurat later drew upon.

Donnelly was followed by a serious and learned student of anthropology, Lewis Spence, who wrote half a dozen books on Atlantis. He enters many strange fields to prove the existence of the submerged continent: for example, he declares that the lemmings of Norway – tiny rodents – sometimes migrate *en masse*, swimming into the Atlantic; they reach a certain point, swim around in circles and then drown. The same is true of flocks of birds, says Spence.

Madame Blavatsky, of whom we shall speak later, took full advantage of the Atlantis legend and incorporated it into her mythology – all dictated by hidden 'masters' living in Tibet. She declared that the Atlanteans were the 'fourth root race' of our planet, which is destined to have seven such races. (We are the fifth, and the third were called Lemurians, who lived on another lost continent, Lemuria or Mu.)

Over two thousand books and articles have now been published on the subject of Atlantis. A theme common to many of them is the notion that the inhabitants of Atlantis destroyed themselves through their use of black magic. This is inconsistent with Plato's view, but is sufficiently widespread to be worth mentioning.

The most recent, and most sane, attempt to solve the problem of Atlantis is that of Professor A. G. Galanopoulos. His theory is based upon a simple fact that was overlooked by earlier writers: that all the figures given in connection with Atlantis are too great. Plato himself expresses doubts whether the Atlanteans could have dug a trench 10,000 stades (1,135 miles) long around the Royal City. The ancients were admittedly capable of enormous works – the Great Wall of China is 1,500 miles long – but on the other hand, a trench of that length would stretch around modern London – Greater London – twenty times! The Royal City of Atlantis would be three hundred times the size of Greater London. This is obviously absurd. But if these figures are reduced by ten, they become altogether more reasonable. The plain on which the Royal City is built becomes 300 by 200 stades – that is, about 34 by 22 miles, an altogether more reasonable size for a city. Similarly, the date given by the Egyptian priest – nine thousand years before Plato (and therefore about 11,500 years ago) – may have been acceptable to Donnelly, Spence and Hoerbiger, but archaeological evidence indicates that the culture of that period was still Palaeolithic (Old Stone Age). Modern man has not yet appeared, and the occasional mammoth, hairy rhinoceros and sabre-tooth tiger were still to be found. The earliest civilisation, that of Egypt, lay six thousand years in the future. But if one knocks off a nought, making it nine hundred years before Plato, the date becomes altogether more reasonable. Athens existed as a fortified town in the Bronze Age (about 2000 B.C.), and there was a high Ievel of civilisation in nearby Crete in 1600 B.C., which at that period was peopled by Minoans.

The sea between Greece and Crete is full of islands, which were once part of Greece itself. The most southerly of these islands is Santorin, which was once circular in shape and some five or six miles in diameter. Around 1500 B.C., there was a tremendous volcanic explosion that ripped apart the island and turned it into little more than the remains of a gigantic crater. Modern Santorin consists of three islands: the largest, Thera, is shaped like a crescent moon; all three islands are covered to a considerable depth with pumice and volcanic rock. The tremendous explosion must have produced a tidal wave like that following the eruption of Krakatoa in August 1883. Greater, in fact, because the Santorin explosion was about three times as large. The eruption of Krakatoa is estimated to be the greatest explosion that has taken place on earth; Rupert Furneaux's book on it states that it was equivalent to a million H-bombs (although one cannot help wondering where on earth he got the figure). Hundred-foot waves swept over islands, killing thirty-six thousand people and washing away whole towns. If the explosion of Santorin was three times this size, then one can begin to understand the Atlantic legend. Crete must have been almost depopulated and its navy destroyed; the explosion seems to account for the mysterious destruction of the palaces at Cnossos and Phaestus at about this time. Greece must have been equally hard hit – and here, possibly, we have the origins of the Deucalion flood legend (although I am inclined to date it 2,500 years earlier, at the same time as the deluge that destroyed Ur). Professor Galanopoulos argues convincingly that Crete was actually the Royal City, while Santorin is the metropolis described by Plato. The empire of Atlantis extended over the many islands of the Aegean. Plato describes the island of the metropolis as having circular canals and one deep channel connecting them. The present-day remains of Santorin show traces of this channel.

But why did Plato multiply all his figures by ten? Professor Galanopoulos has an equally ingenious hypothesis to explain this: a copyist-priest simply mistook the Egyptian symbol for 100 – a coiled rope – for that signifying 1,000 – a lotus flower. He points out that today it would be easy to mix up the English and American billion – one meaning a million million, the other only a thousand million.

No doubt Donnelly and Hoerbiger would reject this solution of the puzzle with disgust;* it is more romantic to believe in a vast Atlantean continent whose people were highly civilised when the rest of Europe was inhabited by Cro-Magnon hunters. But the evidence accumulated by Professors Galanopoulos and Marinatos seems conclusive. Plato has described a Bronze Age civilisation, and Crete was exactly that. When the figures have been reduced by ten, Plato's description of the Royal City and its plain corresponds exactly to Crete. So unless conclusive evidence of a mid-Atlantic continent is unearthed, it would seem that the Atlantis problem is now closed.

In this connection, it is worth mentioning Immanuel Velikovsky, the strange author of *Worlds in Collision* and *Earth in Upheaval*. Martin Gardner dismisses Velikovsky as a crank; but after careful consideration of the evidence, I do not see that one can be as outright as this. Velikovsky believes that an enormous comet swept close to the earth on several occasions, causing great cataclysms, and that it finally became the planet Venus. Gardner rightly points out that Velikovsky leaps from fact to fact without regard to the kind of reasoning that would satisfy a scientist. But the array of facts is

---

* Robert Graves also rejects it in his essay 'The Lost Atlantis' (included in *The Crane Bag*, 1969). His own suggestion, which, he says, is supported by Greek historical tradition, is that Atlantis was to be found in Libya, in the low-lying coastal plain that stretches inland behind the shallow Gulf of Sirte. 'Four thousand years ago, a great part of this region was flooded by salt water from the Mediterranean, but by Solon's day the main surviving evidence of the catastrophe was a group of salt lakes, the largest of them called Lake Tritonis, lying near the foothills of the Atlas. These lakes have since shrunk to salt marshes ...'

impressive and immensely stimulating. One need not take too seriously his contention that it was the action of this comet (which erupted from Jupiter) that coincidentally caused the parting of the Red Sea that saved the Israelites from the pursuing Egyptians, and that, on a later occasion, made the walls of Jericho collapse (again coincidentally). It is as easy to believe that Moses could perform miracles as that coincidences of this magnitude occurred. On the other hand, when he asks what destroyed herds of mammoths in Siberia, or how giant slabs of stone were torn from the Alps to litter the Jura mountains, we are reminded that immense, unexplainable catastrophes have taken place in the history of the earth. Velikovsky devotes a section in *Worlds in Collision* to Atlantis, which, like Donnelly, he believes to have been beyond Gibraltar. (Galanopoulos argues convincingly that the Pillars of Hercules refers to the twin capes of Maleas and Taenarum, now Matapan, in southern Greece.) Unlike Donnelly, Velikovsky also believes that Plato made a mistake and multiplied the date by ten; it should have been nine hundred years earlier, not nine thousand. This is the date he sets for the parting of the Red Sea and the first visitation of his comet.

It sounds as if Velikovsky has merely set up a comet against Hoerbiger's moons as a source of catastrophe, and that the reader might well take his choice; but this is not quite true. We do not know what caused the eruption of Santorin; it was not our present moon. It may therefore well have been Velikovsky's comet. In matters of this sort, where science knows almost as little as anybody else, it is as well to keep the mind open.

Edgar Cayce, a remarkable American clairvoyant and healer, also vouched for the existence of Atlantis. Cayce's Atlantis, like Plato's, was a vast island in the Atlantic Ocean, bigger than Europe, extending from the Sargasso Sea to the Azores. According to Cayce, there were three periods of destruction, from 15,600 B.C. to 10,000 B.C., the first two splitting a single island into three smaller islands;

the third destroying everything. According to Cayce, their civilisation was highly developed, and they possessed some 'crystal stone' for trapping and utilising the rays of the sun. (Cayce died in 1945, long before the laser was invented.) The inhabitants of Atlantis spread to Europe and the Americas after the first two catastrophes – which, says Cayce, explains similarities of features in distant civilisations. The Atlanteans had become totally destructive before the end.

Before this is dismissed as another crank theory, it is worthwhile considering Cayce's success in other spheres. Born in 1877 in Kentucky, the son of a farmer, Cayce wanted to be a preacher, but had to drop this ambition when he lost his voice at the age of twenty-one. A travelling hypnotist put Cayce to sleep and told him to speak in a normal voice. Cayce did; but when he woke up, the laryngitis was back. A local hypnotist now asked Cayce to describe what was wrong with his vocal cords; under hypnosis, Cayce did exactly this, and also prescribed the remedy: hypnotic suggestion to increase circulation in the throat. It was tried, and worked. Layne, the hypnotist, asked Cayce if he could give *him* a reading on a stomach ailment. Cayce allowed himself to be put to sleep, and tried it. His prescribed treatment again worked. Cayce's reputation spread around the town, and he devoted all the time he could spare from his photography business to giving 'readings' to the sick. There were occasional misses, but on the whole the diagnoses were weirdly accurate, and the treatments prescribed effective. He always refused to take money, except occasionally for rail fares to distant towns. Cayce's powers seemed to consist of some kind of 'travelling clairvoyance', the ability to somehow leave his body when under hypnosis, and examine people in other places – the patient did not have to be present, so long as Cayce knew *where* to find him. When he woke up, he could not remember anything he had said in the trance. A highly religious man, he was at first afraid that these powers were diabolic; but the help and comfort he was able to give eventually reassured him.

In 1923, Cayce awoke from a trance in Dayton, Ohio, to be told that he had asserted the reality of reincarnation: that man is born in many different bodies. At that time Cayce did not himself believe in reincarnation; but when his sleeping self had repeatedly affirmed its reality, he came to terms with it, and incorporated it into his orthodox Christian doctrine.

Inevitably, Cayce was asked to give 'readings' of the future. His biographers – and there have been many of them – all assert that these prophecies have been proved accurate again and again. Joseph Millard, for example, cites a whole list of prophecies that have come true: the Wall Street crash, predicted by Cayce in April 1929, six months before it happened, two presidents who would die in office (Roosevelt and Kennedy – Cayce did not mention names, of course), the end of the Second World War in 1945, the decisive tank battle of the war and many others. Cayce also predicted world cataclysms in the period 1958–1998, including the destruction of Los Angeles, San Francisco and America's eastern coastline. (Nostradamus – as will be seen in a subsequent chapter – predicted that 1997 would be the year of some world cataclysm.)

The references to Atlantis began shortly after Cayce first spoke about reincarnation, in 1923. Giving a 'life reading' on someone called David Greenwood, he described a whole series of previous incarnations: in the reign of Louis XIII of France, as a French tradesman who lived in Greece; under Alexander the Great; in Egypt in prehistoric times; and finally, in Atlantis, where he was heir to the throne.

According to Noel Langley (in *Edgar Cayce on Reincarnation*), the Atlanteans, who date back as far as 200,000 B.C. were immensely headstrong, commanded powers of extrasensory perception and telepathy, and had electricity and had invented the aeroplane. Their energy source, the 'Tuaoi stone' or terrible crystal, was eventually so misused by this iron-willed race that it brought about the final catastrophe.

Cayce's descriptions of these later Atlanteans, who were worshippers of Belial, the god of power, make one suspect that his unconscious mind was using them as parables to illustrate a Christian text, Their 'karmic debts' will take many thousands of lifetimes to pay off, he declares. And he seemed to imply that Hitler and Stalin were reincarnated Atlanteans.

Whether Cayce's undoubted powers as a trance-diagnostician also qualify him as a prophet and historian of Atlantis must be left to the judgement of the individual reader. Perhaps it would be safer to wait until the year 1998 has passed without incident before we dismiss him.

Before we pass out of the dim realm of prehistory into the known and recorded history of occultism, in which there is a regrettable amount of charlatanism and pure nonsense, we should bear in mind that *magic relates to the hidden part of the psyche*. It might be called the science of exploring man's hidden powers. It is based upon a strong intuition that there is more, infinitely more, in life than meets the eye or the everyday senses. And when this idea is clearly grasped as an intuition, it produces an enormous and pleasurable excitement, of the sort that a child feels when wondering what he will find in his Christmas stocking, or when he is going to be taken to the fair. Superstition and charlatanism should not be allowed to affect this state of wonder, for it relates to a reality, no matter how absurd its manifestations may become.

It is the recognition of this reality that is the basis of the psychology of Jung. Like Sir Alister Hardy, Jung is convinced of the existence of the collective unconscious. And this leads to what is perhaps his most interesting contribution to psychology: the theory of archetypes. There are certain symbols, he believes, whose meaning can never be pinned down, because, like an electrical cloud, it hangs around them in a fine haze, As the dream reflects my personal life, so the myth represents the life of the race. And the archetypes are symbolic motifs that occur in myths. The hero with a thousand faces, whose history Mr. Joseph Campbell traces in the book of that title, is an archetype. 'A collective image of woman exists in a man's unconscious,' says Jung in *Two Essays on Analytical Psychology*. This image is projected onto the various women he meets, and since it 'corresponds to the deepest reality in a man', it may lead to completely unsuitable relations, for he may be trying to fit the woman into a kind of straitjacket. Frieda Fordham says of the female archetype in her study of Jung: '[she] has a timeless quality – she often looks young, though there is always the suggestion of years of experience behind her. She is wise, but not formidably so; it is rather that "something strangely meaningful clings to her, a secret knowledge or hidden wisdom". She is often connected with the earth, or with water, and she may be endowed with great power. She is also two-sided or has two aspects, a light and a dark …' We have again Graves's White Goddess, or the two aspects of the goddess in Tantric philosophy.

The revolutionary aspect of this theory is Jung's notion that the archetypes float around in the collective unconscious and may turn up in dreams that seem to have little connection with the dreamer's personal problems. (In *Man and His Symbols*, Jung describes the dreams of an eight-year-old girl that are full of such mythological symbols.) Here we have an explanation of Yeats's symbolic Tree of Life with its souls, and the Siberian 'tree of the shamans'.

Describing Jung's theory of the savage mind, Philip Freund says: '[it] is far less developed in extent and intensity than our own. Functions such as willing and thinking are not yet divided in him; they are pre-conscious, which means that he does not think *consciously*, but that thoughts *appear* for him, The savage cannot claim that he thinks; rather, "something thinks in him". [One is reminded of Mahler's remark that it is not the music that is composed, but the composer himself.] The spontaneity of the act of thinking does not lie, causally, in his awareness, but is still in his unconscious. Moreover, he is incapable of any conscious act of will; he must put himself beforehand into the "mood for willing", or let himself be put into it by the shaman's hypnotic suggestion …'* This sounds amazingly like Rudolf Steiner's description of the people of Lemuria (the third 'root race' of mankind), who were unable to reason and lived purely on an instinctive level. (His Atlantis and Lemuria will be considered later.) But in another way, it sounds very much like any of us. Anybody 'wills' better if he puts himself into the mood for willing. Moreover, some external event or suggestion can galvanise my will in a way that seems beyond my conscious power. And this emphasises again that the conscious 'me' suffers from a kind of permanent power-cut. This is because what triggers my will-power are rational calculations and needs, and I seldom put all my heart into them. When some urgency appeals to my deepest reality, the result is a flood of power that amazes me. It may happen in the sexual orgasm. It happened to Nietzsche in a thunderstorm – the sudden overwhelming feeling of well-being. All this emphasises that rational consciousness is a kind of valve that cuts us off from the full power of the life current inside us. Magic is a recognition of this power, an attempt to devise means of tapping it. Ordinary consciousness could be compared to a picture gallery full of magnificent paintings but lit by dim electric bulbs. The moments of intensity are like a sudden burst of bright sunlight that makes a spectator realise just how dazzling the colours are. *Lower states of consciousness do not understand the higher* – just as, according to Dr. David Foster, blue light may be regarded as a cybernetic coding for red light, but not vice versa. Jung's psychology goes deeper than that of Freud or his disciples because he emphasises the superiority of blue light to the red light of rational consciousness.

* Philip Freund, *Myths of Creation*, 1964, p. 69.

I mention the Jungian concepts at this point because they should be borne in mind continually in considering the subsequent history of magic. It would be pleasant to be able to say that the ancient Egyptians, Chaldeans, Babylonians and others possessed an understanding of the occult that has been totally lost since that time. It is not true. The basic traditions of 'magic' were no doubt preserved by natural shamans. But from the point of view of man's inner evolution, the civilisations of the three millennia before Christ are a disappointment. Man was in between two stools. He had lost touch with the old simplicity that made the magic of the shamans effective, but his science was of the crudest kind. As far as organised knowledge went, these three millennia were a Tower of Babel. The Egyptians – the oldest civilisation on earth, as far as we know – had more than two thousand gods. Plato speaks of the tradition of the wisdom of their priests, but what we know of their beliefs – described, for example, in Sir Wallis Budge's *Egyptian Religion and Egyptian Magic* – hardly bears this out. Egyptian magic was based on 'words of power'. They believed that a word or sentence, uttered correctly, had magical effect, and that this magic power could be transferred to amulets or scarabs. Budge relates some typical stories of Egyptian magic. The priest Tchatcha-em-ankh was summoned by King Snefru (who reigned between 2650 and 2500 B.C.) and asked to relieve his boredom; he recommended that the king take a row on the lake in the company of dancing girls dressed in nets. One of the dancing girls lost her turquoise hair-slide in the water. The priest was summoned, and by certain words of power (*hekau*) made a slab of water rise up and lie on top of another; the ornament was found on the bottom of the lake; then the priest ordered the water back into its place.* The magician Teta,

---

* Anyone consulting Sir E. A. Wallis Budge's works on Egypt should be warned that his dating is completely unreliable, being usually about 1,200 years out. He attributes the reign of Cheops (Khufu) to 3800 B.C. instead of about 2600 B.C.

who lived in the reign of Snefru and his son Cheops, knew how to fasten a head on a body after it had been cut off – according to an ancient manuscript. 'Then some one brought to him a goose, and having cut off its head, he laid the body on the west side of the colonnade, and the head on the east side. Teta then stood up and spake certain words of magical power, whereupon the body began to move and the head likewise, and each time they moved the one came nearer to the other, until at length the head moved to its right place on the bird, which straightway cackled.' Teta went on to perform the same miracle on an ox. And the historian Mas'ûdi describes a Jewish sorcerer, a pupil of Egyptian priests, who cut off a man's head and joined it on again, and who also transformed himself into a camel and walked on a tightrope.

There would be no point in speculating whether this was all done by hypnotism. Quite obviously, these people were absurdly credulous; their state of mind was the kind that can still be found in many country villages today. (In a recent British television programme, *The Family of Man*, a woman who specialised in prenatal care described some of the extraordinary beliefs still held by middle-class people in Esher, Surrey: that if a cat jumped up at a pregnant woman's stomach, the baby would be born with some deformity, and that if she found a spider on her, the baby would be born with a 'spider mark' on the same spot.)

People love stories of horrors and wonders. W. B. Yeats tells of a widely believed Dublin story to the effect that Sir William Wilde (Oscar Wilde's father) took out the eyes of a patient and left them on a chair while he went to get a surgical instrument; in the meantime, the cat ate them. In 1969 there was a story about two young thugs who castrated a boy in a public lavatory in central London while the child's mother waited outside; this caused such widespread indignation that a Surrey newspaper printed a denial by a responsible police official. Such a story is invented by someone with a morbid turn of mind, and then circulated purely for its shock value. One can see the same psychology at work in the anecdotes of Egyptian magic recounted by Sir Wallis Budge.

The most interesting thing about Egyptian magic – perhaps the only interesting thing – is its confirmation of Lissner's guess that the reason Cro-Magnon man stopped manufacturing images of human beings is that they were believed to have magical properties. One of Budge's anecdotes concerns a wronged husband who destroyed his wife's lover by making a wax crocodile, which the husband's steward was ordered to throw into the river when the lover went to bathe himself; it turned into a real crocodile and carried off the lover. The wife was burnt to death. Another story concerns King Nectanebus who overcame the navy of his enemies by holding a mock battle with model ships on a large bowl of water. *The Book of the Dead*, a work containing the rituals to be recited over the body of a dead man to ensure his progress in the afterworld, describes how the serpent Apep can be overcome – by making a wax figure of Apep with his name written on it (in green), and drawing the serpent on a sheet of papyrus; these must be burned on a fire of khesau grass four times a day, and then the ashes mixed with excrement and burned again; it was also necessary to keep spitting on the wax image of Apep as he burned. Budge asserts that Aristotle gave Alexander the Great a boxful of wax figures representing his enemies; tradition says that Aristotle taught Alexander 'words of power' to keep these enemies subdued. (Arrian does not mention this in his life of Alexander.) Wax images could be used for less negative purposes: cure of ailments, and for obtaining the love of a woman. Images called *shabti* figures were placed in the tomb with the deceased, and were supposed to work for him and to serve as his scapegoat in the underworld. *The Book of the Dead* gives perhaps the fullest insight into the incredible complexity of Egyptian religious beliefs, for its 190 'chapters' deal with all the perils which the soul of the deceased might encounter in its night-long journey to the underworld (*amentet*). They include spells to ward off various serpents, monsters in human form with tails, crocodiles, giant beetles and jackals – all of these really demons in animal form – and spells to prevent the heart being stolen and the advent of a second death. Compared to the Tibetan Book of the Dead, whose purpose is identical but which recognises that all the perils are products of man's own mind, it is a crude farrago.

Budge remarks accurately: 'From Egypt, by way of Greece and Rome, the use of wax figures passed into Western Europe and England, and in the Middle Ages it found great favour with those who interested themselves in the working of the "black art", or who wished to do their neighbour or enemy an injury.' What he fails to point out is that there is a difference between the shamanic use of an 'image' to direct the mind clearly to its objective, whether to work black or white magic, and the belief that the image itself, inscribed with words of power, possesses magical properties.

The truth is that in spite of their reputation as wise men and magicians, the Egyptians did not possess the single-minded qualities of northern shamans. They had the easy-going Mediterranean temperament. Their fertile land made them prosperous. The rich were very rich; they took pride in personal cleanliness and lived in houses that would still be considered luxurious in modern California. They had a rigid caste system: royalty, nobility, priests, scribes, artisans and so on. Like their riches, their culture was almost accidental, for it depended upon a convenient writing material called papyrus which grew in wide leaves in the river. If they had been restricted to clay and stone, like the Babylonians, the art of reading and writing might have been less widespread.

Papyrus was to Egypt of the second millennium what the paperback book is to the twentieth century. Because of extreme class differences, it suited the rulers to have an elaborate religion (which was based upon the worship of the sun god, Ra). When it suited the upper classes, the religion could be modified, as when the first great queen, Hatshepsut (who ruled at about the time Santorin exploded), gave the god Osiris a partly feminine nature for her own benefit; it was like the Russian rewriting of history. In spite of their military victories and large empire, the Egyptians were lazy, and averse to serious thinking. It took conquest by a barbaric army of 'shepherds' (the 'Hyksos kings' – 1680–1580 B.C.) to stir the Egyptians out of their sloth and turn them into a fighting nation. The battle of Armageddon (or Megiddo) was the first great victory of Thutmose the Third, the husband of the late Queen Hatshepsut, who went on to build an empire like that of Alexander the Great. But the new militarism did nothing to improve the quality of Egyptian intellectual life, unless the monotheistic sun-religion created by the Pharaoh Akhnaton (about 1375 B.C.) is counted as an intellectual achievement. Their science was almost nonexistent, their mathematics remained crude. Like the Chinese, they tended to respect antiquity for its own sake, and so their medicine was a mixture of up-to-date observation and old wives' remedies out of ancient books. Their religion suffered from the same confusion, due to an aversion to discarding any link with the past. They were highly sexed, and the sexual exploits of their gods were nearly as disgraceful as those of the Greeks. Horus loses his temper with his mother, Isis, and chops off her head. His elder brother Set pursues him, and they end by sleeping in the same bed. Set sodomises Horus in the night, but Horus masturbates on a lettuce that Set eats for his dinner, and his sperm makes Set pregnant. (In spite of their embalming skill, the Egyptian knowledge of anatomy was extremely limited.) And so the absurd and Rabelaisian story goes on.

After a few centuries of military victory the old Egyptian laziness reasserted itself, and the nation drooped slowly into luxurious decadence.

I have spoken at some length about the Egyptians because I do not propose to devote more space to the magic of the ancient world. The Sumerians, the Egyptians, the Hittites, the Persians, the Greeks and Romans all embraced a farrago of absurdities not unlike the Egyptian system. The Greeks, having the liveliest intellects of the Near East, also had the least belief in magic, although they believed (like the Egyptians) in dreams and divinations. Their oracles, of which the one at Delphi was the most famous, were virtually shamans; and, like the shaman, she went into terrifying convulsions when inspired. The Persian mages (from whom the word 'magic' derives) will be discussed later in connection with Zoroaster; they were a priest cult like the Egyptian priesthood. The Romans were as superstitious as the Egyptians; Robert Graves's two Claudius novels give a fair picture of their endless preoccupation with auguries, oracles and omens, and their attempts to foretell the future by the flight of birds or the intestines of animals. Apuleius's *Golden Ass* touches on the lighter side of these beliefs – for example, the story of the student Telephron, who agreed to spend the night watching over a dead body to protect it from witches who want to tear off the nose and ears with their teeth. The witches cast a spell over Telephron and eat his nose and ears, replacing them with pink wax; he only discovers this much later when he touches them. There is nothing in the magic of the *Golden Ass* or the Claudius novels that rises above absurdity and superstition. In this respect – belief in omens – the Greeks were little better; the sailing of the whole Attic fleet was delayed in the fourth century B.C. because a soldier sneezed, but their general, Timotheus, laughed them out of it by pointing out that if the gods had really wanted to communicate a warning, they would have made the whole fleet sneeze.

The belief in astrology comes under a different heading. Astrology was generally accepted – and no doubt most of its practitioners were as fraudulent as most ancient 'magicians' – but this should be regarded as a descendant of shamanism rather than as a stepchild of sorcery. There are certain people who are naturally gifted in 'divination', whether by the *I Ching*, Tarot cards or the reading of palms; if such people become astrologers, no doubt their readings can possess frightening accuracy. Ellic Howe points out in *The Strange World of the Astrologers* that some astrologers can produce astounding results, while others, working from the same material (details of the subject's hour of birth) are completely inaccurate. It is a matter of natural talent, and of how carefully these natural intuitive powers have been nurtured.

I have tried to outline the development of 'man's hidden powers' from the dawn of history to its 'Tower of Babel' period, the period of degeneration. When a man's head is full of superstitions and beliefs, he is insulating himself from his natural magical powers. When he melts the wax figure of an enemy, he is putting himself into a trivial and vengeful state of mind that is the reverse of true shamanism, and certainly of any sort of mysticism. There is a negative and stupid side to magic that should be acknowledged and condemned. Ivar Lissner describes how the Ainus of northern Japan carefully rear a bear cub, the women of the tribes suckling it at their breasts. One day it is tied to a stake, and blunt arrows are fired at it to enrage it; it is also beaten with rods. When it has been tormented into a state of exhaustion, it is despatched with a sharp arrow, and ceremonially eaten; the idea is that its soul will intercede for the tribe in heaven. This kind of thing should be classified with a case cited by Budge, in which an Irish labourer, with the help of several cronies, burnt his twenty-seven-year-old wife because he thought she was a witch. Boiling liquid was poured down her throat, after which she was stripped and set on fire with paraffin; she was then forced to sit on the fire to 'drive out the witch' that possessed her. While she died of burns he recited incantations over her, and then sent for the priest to exorcise the house of evil spirits. The husband was sentenced to twenty years in jail, and the cronies to shorter periods. This took place in 1895 in Tipperary.

More than a hundred years earlier, Gibbon, writing about the superstitions of the Romans and their witchhunts with his usual magnificent invective, remarked: 'Let us not hesitate to indulge a liberal pride that, in the present age, the enlightened part of Europe has abolished a cruel and odious prejudice, which reigned in every climate of the globe and adhered to every system of religious opinions.' The self-congratulation was premature.

THREE
ADEPTS AND INITIATES

It would be a long and complicated task to trace the history of magic century by century and country by country. Fortunately there is a simpler method: to consider the lives of the principal figures in the history of Western magic. This is what I propose to do in the next two chapters.

I must begin by repeating my basic general proposition. It is man's biological destiny to evolve Faculty X. All living creatures on the surface of this planet have been trying to do this throughout their history. Man is more than halfway there. A true adept would be a man in whom Faculty X is more developed than in the average.

By this definition, there have not been many true adepts. This does not mean that the great names of magic were charlatans or self-deceivers (although some were). Most of them possessed a high degree of 'intuitive' powers, akin to Corbett's 'jungle sensitivity'. These powers lie at the lower end of man's consciousness – the red end of the spectrum. Faculty X lies at the violet end.

But that is an oversimplification, and I must try to clarify the matter further before proceeding.

Man could be compared to someone who lives in the Grand Canyon, but who is so short-sighted that he cannot see more than five yards. Or to someone who lives in a cathedral, but is surrounded by a kind of curtain, like a fortune-teller's cubicle, that goes with him wherever he walks.

The curtain is 'everydayness'. It is a state of mind rather than an objective reality. The human mind must be thought of as being akin to the radar of bats; we somehow reach out and 'feel' the reality around us. But in my ordinary, everyday existence, I do not need to 'reach out' very far. And I get into the habit of not doing so.

Whenever I am deeply moved by poetry or music or scenery, I realise I am living in a *meaning universe* that deserves better of me than the small-minded sloth in which I habitually live. And I suddenly realise the real deadliness of this lukewarm contentment that looks as harmless as ivy on a tree. It is systematically robbing me of life, embezzling my purpose and vitality. I must clearly focus on this immense meaning that surrounds me, and refuse to forget it; contemptuously reject all smaller meanings that try to persuade me to focus on *them* instead.

And this is why the mage or the adept is a fundamental human 'archetype': he symbolises man's evolutionary destiny. Bulwer-Lytton's description of the mage in *The Haunted and the Haunters* catches his essence: 'If you could fancy some mighty serpent transformed into man, preserving in the human lineaments the old serpent type, you would have a better idea [of him]; the width and flatness of frontal, the tapering elegance of contour disguising the strength of the deadly jaw – the long, large, terrible eye, glittering and green as the emerald – and withal a certain ruthless calm, as if from the consciousness of immense power.' And when he later added a new ending to the story, Lytton extended this sketch into a full-length portrait of a man who seems to be a combination of the Wandering Jew and the Count de Saint-Germain.

But why the hint of menace? Serpents symbolise wisdom, also coldness and deadliness. It is an interesting thought that there are no portraits of 'benevolent supermen' in world literature. There are heroes, usually with fatal flaws, and unbelievable gods. But the nearest thing to a true *superman*, in the original sense of the word, is the character in the American comic strip. Lytton's baleful magician – and his like in the writings of Hoffman, Tieck, Jean-Paul, even Tolkien – is the nearest the human imagination seems to be able to get to the idea of superhumanity. This is to be expected; our lack of sense of meaning means that we understand the negative better than the positive. Can one, for example, imagine a completely benevolent but *equally powerful* Hitler, who wants world domination in order to liberate the poor, to destroy anti-Semitism? No. Benevolent statesmen tend to be idealistic and ineffectual:

The best lack all conviction, while the worst
Are full of passionate intensity ...

Hitler's powers were partially magical, because he was driven by long-range purposes and enormous optimism. The consequence was the automatic development of powers at the 'invisible' ends of the spectrum; the almost hypnotic power over crowds to which so many observers have testified. (Such observers – Lüdecke, Hanfstaengl, Gregor Strasser – were surprised to find that Hitler lacked charisma at close quarters. He 'switched on' his power when he needed it, like a conductor working the orchestra up to a climax.)

Good men tend to mistrust the will and stick to reason. But 'magical' powers cannot be developed without an optimistic effort of will. On the other hand, one does not need to accept the possibility of their development. One of the most amusing cases of the unintentional development of such powers is told of Colonel Henry Steel Olcott, the lifelong associate of Madame Blavatsky. In July 1882, the colonel was in Colombo, Ceylon, trying to encourage a Buddhist revival. (He had left Madame Blavatsky, who tended to dominate him, behind in India.) The local high priest, Sumangala, told him that the Catholics on the island were hoping to convert a place near Kelanie into another Lourdes, complete with a healing shrine. So far, the miracles had failed to occur; but the colonel realised that if mass suggestion got working, they might well begin, and the Buddhists would lose half their congregation. He told the high priest that he had better try working miracles on his own account. The high priest said there would be no point, since he knew he had no powers.

Shortly thereafter, the colonel met a man named Cornelius Appu, who was paralysed in one arm and partially paralysed in one leg. The colonel decided he might as well try out the effect of suggestion, so he made a few mystic passes over the man, and told him that might help.

Later in the day Mr. Appu returned to say he felt better already and ask for more treatment. The colonel made more passes. Cornelius Appu began to improve fast, and told everyone that the colonel was a miracle worker. He wrote out a statement describing his cure – with the hand that had been paralysed. It was published, presumably in a local newspaper. Mr. Appu brought a paralysed friend. The colonel repeated the suggestion treatment, and it worked.

But now, to his dismay, he found himself overwhelmed by hordes of people with every ailment. They came in crowds. And the colonel, although hard pressed, soon found that using his thaumaturgic powers was like riding a bicycle, a matter of confidence and practice. The colonel believed; the sufferers believed; and cures were effected by the dozen. They would interrupt his meals, and force their way in while he was dressing. He records that he had to go away periodically and bathe in the salt water of the harbour, behind his house, where he felt 'currents of fresh vitality entering and re-enforcing my body'. His powers developed to such an extent that one morning, when he was feeling particularly fresh ('it seemed as if I might almost mesmerise an elephant') he cured a young Indian of facial paralysis from the other end of a room, raising his arm and saying in Bengali, 'Be cured.' 'A tremor ran through his body, his eyes closed and reopened, his tongue, so long paralysed, was thrust out and withdrawn, and with a wild cry of joy he rushed forward and flung himself at my feet.'

The colonel developed his power under ideal circumstances. It would not have mattered in the least if he had failed with Cornelius Appu, for he firmly believed he was trying to cure the man by 'selling him the confidence trick'. He continued to believe that it was merely a matter of suggestion, until the powers, allowed to develop naturally and at their own pace, became unmistakable.

This also answers an important question – raised by Louis Singer, and again by A. L. Rowse – of whether powers of mediumship, clairvoyance and so on must develop involuntarily, by not willing, as Louis Singer says. What man calls his 'will' is usually self-divided. This is why, for example, someone can make me itch by merely suggesting that I itch. I don't *want* to itch, and the fear of itching arouses some perverse negative will in me, my unconscious, unused will, which gets tired of sitting still. (I have a theory that it is this negative will that causes many ailments, from ulcers to cancer.) If Colonel Olcott had badly wanted to heal Cornelius Appu, his tension and nervousness would have prevented him calling on his *true will* – the union of conscious and unconscious will, which is the basis of 'magical' powers.

Some fortunate people are still relatively untouched by the civilised disease of self-division, and possess natural thaumaturgic powers. I speak of them in my book on Rasputin:

Most healers agree that the act of healing seems to involve a certain self-depletion, although the powers can be developed to a point where one can be 'recharged' in a very short period [like Colonel Olcott]. Mr. Harry Edwards describes the feeling of a power – a kind of fluid – flowing down his arm and through his fingertips when he touches an affected part of the patient's body. Mrs. Elizabeth Arkle, of Bristol, who also possessed rudimentary healing powers ... has described the same sensation to me. She mentioned that she had to be in good health, psychologically as well as physically, to be able to 'summon' her powers; she experiences the thaumaturgic power as 'a kind of fire' in the areas of the breast or solar plexus. She mentioned that she had only used it with relatives – where the contact, presumably, is stronger – and that on one occasion, when tempted to use it [on her father], she had a strong intuition that it would be wrong, since he was dying. She could not explain why she felt it would be wrong.

Colonel Olcott's description of his dramatic cure of the young Indian is explainable as hypnotic suggestion, like the deep-trance cure of warts, described on page 79. That is to say, hypnotic suggestion produces 'confidence' and awakens the 'true will'. But this explanation cannot be accepted unreservedly. In Cornwall, where I live, the practice of wart-charming is widespread. Our local doctor, when approached by patients with warts, usually sends them to a wart-charmer before he applies his slower remedies. Wart-charmers work in a variety of ways. Some of them 'buy the warts', paying the sufferer a few pence for each wart. (*Not* vice versa; wart-charmers will not take money, and most of them make it a condition of their work that they should not be thanked.) Some insist that it is necessary to rub a piece of 'rusty bacon' on the wart, then bury the bacon. (Where possible, the bacon should be 'stolen', or at least taken without its owner's spoken approval.) Others only need to know the full name of the person to be cured.

The sceptic may feel that we are now entering the realm of old wives' tales and pure absurdity. He would be mistaken. The most startling thing is that cures are almost invariable. They certainly occur with a frequency too great to attribute to chance. For example, the painter and author Lionel Miskin took his whole family to a wartcharmer at Par; they were suffering from warts on the hands. All the warts disappeared in about two weeks. This wart-charmer 'bought' the warts for tuppence each.

But the notion of hypnotic suggestion must be abandoned in cases where it is animals that are cured. Mrs. Betty Bray-Smith of Pentewan had a pony with multiple warts, and was told to approach a wart-charmer on Bodmin Moor, a farmer. She accordingly telephoned Mr. Frank Martin (known as Fred), who was expecting her call. She asked, 'What do I have to do?' 'Nothing,' said Mr. Martin. 'You've done all you have to. The warts will vanish of their own accord now.' They did, during the next two weeks, all except the largest, which had to be removed with silver nitrate.

I was so intrigued by this story, and by other tales of Mr. Martin's powers, that I drove over to his farm to interview him. What I wanted to know chiefly was this: Did he feel that he was projecting some mental power *of his own*, or did he feel he was using 'other forces' outside himself? The latter seemed most likely, since he did not see Mrs. Bray-Smith's pony. However, what Mr. Martin had to tell me left me completely bewildered, for it did not seem to fit either theory. I had been told that wart-charming is an inherited faculty, which can only pass from father to daughter, or mother to son. Mr. Martin told me that he had been given his 'charms' (i.e. certain 'spells' to be repeated) by two old ladies, back in the mid-1930s. He has used them consistently since then, and with a high level of success. He was given several 'charms', including one to stop bleeding, and another to rid of ringworm. The charms are brief incantations, that must end 'in the name of the Father, the Son and of the Holy Ghost'. Since a large number of his 'patients' are sheep and cows, he concludes that it is the charm itself that works, not his own 'powers'. (Sheep and cows are subject to large warts, called in this part of the world 'rigs'.) However it *is* important that the owner of the animal should also believe that the charm will work; Mr. Martin sees the cure as some kind of co-operation between himself and the owner.

He confirms that charms can only be passed on from man to woman, or vice versa; they cannot be 'given' to a member of the same sex. This seemed to imply that once a charm has been 'given', the original owner loses its powers. Mr. Martin verified that most charmers believe this, but said that he himself had given the charms to several people without, apparently, affecting his own powers.

When I asked him how he could explain these powers, he seemed to feel that they were fundamentally of the same nature as those used by Jesus (although far weaker). I pointed out that Jesus was a thaumaturgist: that is, he felt that something was 'taken from him' when he affected a cure. Mr. Martin agreed that his own cures seemed to take nothing from him. (But, he added, his uncle, a man of eighty-four, who was being buried that day, had possessed the power to cure the 'king's evil', scrofula, and had been forced to give it up because it was 'taking too much out of him'. It is interesting to recall that Dr. Johnson was 'touched' for the king's evil by Queen Anne, but Boswell records that it had no effect; evidently the Queen lacked thaumaturgic gifts.) I asked Mr. Martin whether he would consider himself a religious man. After a moment's consideration he shook his head and said he didn't think so. But he emphasised that the impulse behind all such cures must be the impulse to do good. This explains why wart-charmers refuse to take money or even thanks. He explained that he himself often cured people without their knowing anything about it. The important thing was to use the power for good. He described to me an occasion when he had been present at the birth of a calf, and the carelessness of the vet's assistant had caused serious bleeding. The vet remarked that if they didn't get towels quickly the cow would bleed to death. Mr. Martin 'charmed' the cow without saying anything; the bleeding stopped. He did not bother to tell the vet what he had done.

He emphasised the importance of the desire to help. A sceptical friend had remarked: 'If I cut myself now with a knife, you couldn't stop the bleeding. And if you saw a butcher slaughtering a pig, you couldn't stop the pig bleeding.' Mr. Martin agreed, but pointed out that in neither case would it be doing any good. 'But if the butcher cut himself accidentally, I could stop *that* bleeding,' he added.

I found that his most enlightening comments were about his state of mind when he was effecting a cure. He explained that it was a gift, like any other gift – for example, like work. I was puzzled. 'Like work?' 'There are some things you're good at, and some things you're not. For example, if I plough a field, I like the furrows all to run straight, and I really put my mind to it. The same when I thatch a roof – I don't put a lot more effort into it than anybody else, but somehow it all comes right. Now, on the other hand, I can't build walls.' (Cornish 'walls' are part of a 'hedge' or bank of earth, and consist of irregular slabs of stone that use the bank as partial support.) 'I can watch a man building a wall and tell him where he ought to put a certain stone. But I couldn't lay it myself.'

In short, Mr. Martin is speaking of the use of *Tao*, as discussed in an earlier chapter of this volume (pp. 108–9), a kind of stilling of the mind that allows total concentration. It is the use of the 'true will', the instinctive will.

I cannot explain why Mr. Martin's charms work, or why those of dozens, perhaps hundreds, of other Cornish wart-charmers work, except by saying that the Cornish are Celts, and Celts seem to possess a higher degree of natural 'powers' than Anglo-Saxons. I suspect that the 'charms' are less to do with it than a natural thaumaturgic faculty, and that Mr. Martin may not feel that anything has been 'taken out of him' because the cure of warts takes too little for him to notice. As to how he can cure a pony he has never seen, I have no explanation to offer. (When I told him that the largest wart had not vanished, he said that Mrs. Bray-Smith should have phoned him again, and he would have repeated the charm. Some warts and ringworm are tougher than others.)

As a type, Fred Martin struck me as kindly, honest, simple, with a high degree of natural benevolence: that is, the kind of person one might expect to possess natural thaumaturgic gifts. In that case, he may be mistaken when he explains that he cannot cure other ailments – ulcers, for example, and snakebite.

The mention of snakebite raises an interesting question. There *are* a number of Cornish 'charmers' who have the reputation of being able to cure snakebite and control snakes. The master of the local hunt described to me how he had seen one of these charmers immobilising an adder by drawing a chalk circle round it. Mr. Martin spoke of an old lady on Bodmin Moor with similar powers. A child belonging to two visitors was bitten by a viper; they called at the nearest farmhouse to ask if they could telephone a doctor. The old lady who lived there told them she could cure the bite, but that they must first go back and kill the snake. This seemed an absurd request, since they had seen the snake wriggling off into the bracken. The old lady assured them that they would find the snake where they last saw it, and they did. The child suffered no ill effects from the bite.

Anyone who has ever owned snakes knows that they are passive creatures, who soon allow themselves to be handled, and who are very likely to lie still in bracken – or a chalk circle, for that matter. And the late C. J. P. Ionides, the 'snake man', assured me that snakes cannot distinguish between one person and another, and that a tame snake will allow anyone to handle it, so that stories of the 'powers' of Eastern snake charmers are myths. He may well be right; but he was of a determinedly sceptical turn of mind, and would not admit the existence of any unusual 'powers', even in witch doctors or shamans. The stories told of Cornish snake charmers indicate a belief that certain human beings can establish a telepathic power over snakes, similar to the power of Grimble's porpoise-caller. If this is true, then it is an amusing reversal of the notion that it is snakes who possess a hypnotic power. The contrary may be true: that they are good hypnotic subjects, at the mercy of the stronger psychic powers of man.

It would be a mistake, however, to imply that such powers are confined to simple, unsophisticated people, as the following passage demonstrates; it is from a letter written by Aldous Huxley (December 8, 1915):

I went on to dine with the Gilbert Murrays, where I was lucky enough to see one of Gilbert's thought-reading performances. He is considered one of the best telepathists going – at any rate, he was astonishing on Sunday. He was best, of course, with his daughter, with whom he generally does it. With her he can describe scenes in books he has never read. He did two on Sunday – one out of Conrad's new book [*Victory*], which he got almost word for word as his daughter described it and one out of *Sinister Street*. He feels the atmosphere of the thought: thus as soon as he came into the room the time his daughter had thought of *Sinister St.* – a scene of undergraduates talking together – he said 'How I hate these people' – the aesthetic young man being very hostile to him. He tried one with me, which came off extraordinarily well considering I was a stranger. I had thought of the following scene: the Master of Balliol listening to an essay on *The Egoist*, a book he has not read. Gilbert Murray stood holding my hand about half a minute, then began to laugh and said 'Oh of course, it's the old Master of Balliol being embarrassed. I'm not very clear about what, but I think it's a conversation about a new poet' – which is close enough for a first attempt with an unfamiliar mind. He can't exactly describe the process – it seems to be a kind of smelling out of thought, of detecting it in the atmosphere.

But it might be more accurate to say that the process is closely allied to what happens when I try to *remember* some scene or event that partly eludes me; a half-picture forms in my mind, a few tantalising threads of association, but not the whole thing. Which raises again a point I made earlier: that our own mental processes are quite as 'occult' and mysterious as the powers of thaumaturgists or telepathists. One might say that Murray 'remembered' what was going on in Huxley's mind – or used exactly the same mechanisms that we use in trying to recall something, but reached into Huxley's mind instead of his own.

Another point worth noting. Murray's response 'How I hate these people' might easily have been conveyed by the same telepathic process to the people he was talking about. And since we have already discussed the suggestibility of the average person, the self-division that makes us think about something we don't want to think about, it is not difficult to see how a person with some telepathic ability could exercise 'the evil eye'.

In short, we must recognise that the powers we have been discussing are *commonplace*. They exist far more widely and generally than we choose to acknowledge.

How can we summon these powers? It would be more to the point to ask: What *prevents* us from summoning them? The answer is: the blinkers, the narrowness, the fact that my consciousness is occupied with trivial issues such as why my car uses so much oil and whether a certain girl is being unfaithful to her husband. The only infallible way to develop these powers is for human beings to systematically turn away from triviality, to reject the near and concentrate on the far.

Man must develop *positive consciousness*. He has reached his present position on the evolutionary scale through his power to turn his mind into a microscope and concentrate on small things. But this has made him a victim of the small and the negative. Human history is the history of childishness, of silly quarrels for small reasons. Like the housewife in *Under Milk Wood* who says, 'Before you let the sun in, mind it wipes its shoes,' we have become slaves of our amazing capacity for detail. Such a woman obviously does not really enjoy being alive. She is trapped in her own negativeness. So are we all.

I know of only one religion that has made this recognition its foundation: Zoroastrianism, the religion of the ancient Persians. The Persian scriptures, the Gathas, state that the Supreme Being, Ahura Mazda, created two twins, *who produce reality and unreality*. Reality and unreality are seen as the essential elements from which the world is created. They are not positive and negative, but both are equally positive. It was only later that they degenerated into Good and Evil. (Later still, there was a further degeneration, when Ahura Mazda, the first cause, was identified with the Good, and his enemy Ahriman with the devil.) For reality is meaning – out there – and unreality is human *subjectivity*, our tendency to get enmeshed in our self-chosen values. We derive our power to act, to work, to concentrate, to evolve, from this same subjectivity, so it cannot be regarded as negative or evil. It becomes negative through human stupidity and defeat-proneness.

The Magi, from whom the word 'magic' is derived, were the priests of this ancient religion. I would suggest, then, as a hypothesis that can never be proved or disproved, that the original Magi derived their magic powers from 'positive consciousness' – from the recognition that subjectivity is only good so long as it keeps itself open to the reality of meaning outside itself.

Positive consciousness is a happy, open state of mind. A man in love has positive consciousness – especially if he has just discovered that the girl returns his feelings. It is a sense of the marvellous *interestingness* of the world. We still use the word 'magic' in this sense – talking about 'the magic of summer nights', 'magic moments' and so on. This is not a misuse of language; that is what real magic is about.

The little we know of the Magi is derived almost entirely from the *History* of Herodotus, much as our knowledge of Atlantis depends entirely on Plato. Herodotus, writing in the fifth century B.C., a few decades before Plato, was speaking about the later stages of the Magian religion. Even so, he is struck by the purity of their faith: 'They have no images of gods, no temples, no altars, and consider the use of them a sign of folly ... Their wont, however, is to ascend to the summits of the loftiest mountains, and there to offer sacrifice to Zeus, which is the name they give to the whole circuit of the firmament. They likewise offer to the sun and moon, to the earth, to fire, to water, and to the winds ...' The Persians later developed the worship of the sun-god, Mithras, who is a saviour with much in common with Jesus (and whose religion in later centuries almost supplanted Christianity in Rome).

All the references in Herodotus are incidental, so we learn only that the Magi were skilled in the interpretation of dreams, and that they were a powerful caste who continued to dominate Persian life even after an attempt to seize power led to mass executions – presumably because daily life was unthinkable without them.

The Magi were the descendants of the shamans of the Neolithic, but with one important difference. The shaman derived his power from *mana*, the magical force that permeates nature. The Magi were also 'adepts' and scholars. They knew something of mathematics and astrology, both of which had originated not far away in Mesopotamia, and were skilled in divination. Their religious beliefs owe something to the Hindus; they certainly believed in the transmigration of souls. From the few references to them that are scattered in the classical writers, it seems fairly certain that the Magi began as an order of Wordsworthian nature mystics. Friedrich von Schlegel speaks of their 'primitive veneration of nature', and says that they were not a priestly caste but an 'order' divided into grades of apprentice, master and perfect masters.* Eliphaz Levi, perhaps not the most reliable of authorities, speaks of 'secrets that gave them mastery over the occult powers of nature' (that is to say, they were shamans), and citing Pliny and Lucius Pison as his authorities, declares that they could produce electricity. They existed long before the birth of their 'avatar' Zoroaster (or Zarathustra) in the seventh century B.C., and from the evidence of the early Gathic hymns and later Zendavesta (supposedly written by Zoroaster), it is clear that the religion changed from nature worship to something closer to the religions of Mesopotamia, with their angels and demons. Later still, it degenerated into fire worship. By the time of Cyrus (who died in 529 B.C.), the great founder of the Persian empire, the Magi had also degenerated into a ruling cult, like the priests of Egypt.

But in their early days they were an order of worshippers and philosophers, like the Greeks who celebrated the Orphic and Eleusinian mysteries, or like the Jewish order the Essenes. Perhaps the most puzzling feature of the order is that they had no temples. If Herodotus is correct in saying that they performed their worship on mountaintops, then we must take these two facts in association to indicate that the Magi were nature mystics in the fullest sense of the word – the sense in which the seventeenth-century cobbler Jacob Boehme was a nature mystic. This description of Boehme's second 'illumination' catches its essence:

> Boehme's glance was attracted by a polished pewter dish that reflected the sun. Suddenly a strange feeling overpowered him, for it seemed as if he were looking into the very heart of nature and beholding its innermost mystery. Startled and desiring to banish such presumptuous thoughts, he went out on the green. The vision persisted and became even more clear. The grass and flowers were stirred with strange living forces.

* *Philosophy of History*, Bonn, p. 224.

Over nature the veil of matter grew thin and half-revealed the
vast struggling life beneath.*

Boehme's vision can be interpreted in a number of ways, but all come
back to the same thing: the sense of overpowering *meaning* in nature.
Boehme spoke of the 'signature' of things, meaning their inner
symbolic essence, which makes it sound as if he caught a sudden
intuitive glimpse of Dr. David Foster's notion of a universe of coded
information in which all living things are the expression of a vital
intelligence.

There seems to be no doubt that the Magi were a mystical order
of exceptional purity, the natural link between the shamans of the
Stone Age and the confused magical cults of the urban civilisations.
They were the expression of man's need to escape his animal destiny,
to 'see beyond the veil'.

And this provokes the question: Why? Man is not naturally a
mystical creature. He farms, he breeds children, he fights wars; if he
worships nature, this is only out of the superstitious belief that the
elements are gods.

I am inclined to believe that the answer lies in war. All the early
poems are about battles. Homer was writing the *Iliad* at about the
same time the Magi were composing the Gathic hymns in Bactrian,
the language of eastern Persia. It was a violent and cruel world,
and the Eastern temperament tends to lack humane fellow-feeling.
Herodotus tells the story of King Astyages, the grandfather of Cyrus,
who dreamed that his daughter's child would overthrow him. He sent
one of his servants, Harpagus, to kill the child; Harpagus handed him
over to a herdsman instead. Later, when he discovered that Cyrus was
still alive, Astyages took a horrible revenge on Harpagus; he invited
him to a feast, asking him to send his thirteen-year-old son to help

---

* Howard Brinton, *The Mystic Will*, London, 1931, p. 47. Brinton is paraphrasing
Boehme's biographer, Von Frankenberg.

prepare it. At the feast, Harpagus ate his fill of meat; Astyages asked him if he had enjoyed it, and Harpagus said he had. A covered bowl was then placed in front of Harpagus; when he removed the cover, he discovered the head and limbs of his son; he had been eating him. Herodotus records: 'The sight ... did not rob him of his self-possession. Being asked by Astyages if he knew what beast's flesh it was that he had been eating, he answered that he knew very well, and that whatever the king did was agreeable: Later, Harpagus engineered Cyrus's victory over his grandfather.

The first part of the story sounds apocryphal – too much like the story of Oedipus and other legendary heroes. But it is a historical fact that Cyrus overthrew his grandfather with the aid of Harpagus, who was sent out to repel Cyrus's army, and joined it instead. So it seems likely that the story of Harpagus is true. It demonstrates the barbarous temper of these Eastern potentates. (Astyages also ordered the execution of all the Magi who had persuaded him to spare Cyrus.) Living in a world like this, surrounded by violence and ambition, watching the degeneration of urbanised humanity, it is not surprising that the descendants of the shamans turned away from it all and immersed themselves in the mystical peace of nature.

In this connection, we should also speak of the religious 'mysteries' of Greece, particularly those of Orpheus and Eleusis, and of the Hebrew sect of the Essenes, who arose some centuries later. For all these have important characteristics in common with the Magi of Persia. The Orphic religion was supposed to have been founded by the legendary singer Orpheus – roughly contemporary with Zoroaster – who also travelled with the Argonauts and soothed their quarrels with his songs. Various poems attributed to him describe the creation of the world from a cosmic egg, and speak in detail of life after death. Like the later Christians, his followers seem to have believed that all non-Orphics were doomed, for Plato quotes one of their myths to the effect that the uninitiated will be forced to spend eternity trying to fill a sieve with water by means of another sieve. (The Greeks had a strong feeling about the horrors of futility, as evidenced also in the legend of Sisyphus, who has to roll a rock uphill and watch it roll down again.) Nothing is known about the Orphic mysteries of initiation, but much can be inferred from what we know of those of Eleusis, since the two religions often intermingled, and Eleusis was used for the Orphic rites. Eleusis, a town fourteen miles west of Athens, was the place where Demeter, the corn goddess, was finally united again with her daughter Kore (or Persephone), who had been stolen by Hades. (Curiously enough, both goddesses were often identified with Diana, Graves's White Goddess.) The Eleusinian mysteries began with a cleansing in the sea, then the imparting of occult knowledge, then an initiation that involved certain tests – probably wandering through underground passageways with carefully prepared 'surprises', rather like the ghost train on a modern fairground – and finally with the garlanding of the initiate. (Anyone who knows Mozart's *Magic Flute* can form some idea of the 'ordeal' part of the mysteries.) All this guaranteed that the initiate would spend eternity comfortably in the Elysian Fields.

The Essenes, the Jewish sect of the third and second centuries B.C., also had solemn initiatory rites, and the aspirant had to remain a novice for a year. They were then tested for two more years. They were fundamentally a 'purist' religious group, who later moved into the wilderness near the Dead Sea, and were responsible for the Dead Sea Scrolls. Like the Orphics, they preached a life of strict purity and the unlawfulness of killing anything. In *Jews, God and History*, Max Dimont states flatly that John the Baptist was an Essene, and that Christianity was fundamentally an offshoot of the Essene faith. This may well be true. The French mystical writer Edouard Schuré believes that Jesus was initiated into the Essene faith.

What all these sects have in common is the sense of solemnity and awe induced by their sacred mysteries. The Greeks and the Romans took their religion fairly lightly, and the Jews were less bigoted than the New Testament would have us believe (the Pharisees were, in fact, easygoing and tolerant, while the Sadducees were political realists who did not believe in immortality or resurrection). Anyone who has read Pater's *Marius the Epicurean* will remember the delightful account of the religion of Numa in the first chapter, and its relaxed, pastoral atmosphere. (Numa was a legendary emperor of Rome who, according to Eliphaz Levi, could control lightning.)

The mysteries were a different matter. Their aim was to raise the mind beyond everyday triviality to steady contemplation of the miraculous character of nature. The method was to make the aspirant identify himself with the story of Demeter and Kore or Orpheus, in much the same way that a good preacher can make his congregation identify themselves with the passion of Jesus on Good Friday. The story of Demeter is dramatic enough for this treatment – her daughter being seized and raped by the god of the underworld as she gathered roses, crocuses, hyacinths and violets in the fields; Demeter's long search, during which time she posed as a mortal and became a nurse in the house of the king of Attica, at his palace in Eleusis. (She decided to make the king's newly born son immortal, but was caught by the queen as she was about to put him into the fire, and forced to reveal her identity.) Her grief makes the earth barren until Pluto agrees to allow Kore to return to earth every year. The myth explains the seasons, and the initiates took it literally. The mysteries began with a ritual fast, then with an all-night vigil, in which the candidates for initiation sat, veiled, on stools covered with sheepskins. During this time they would meditate on the rape of Kore and the sorrow of Demeter, the long search and so on. In this oral part of the initiation, all this was driven home by sacred drama and 'sermons'. The 'tests' followed; they were probably terrifying and perhaps genuinely dangerous. After all this came the dramatic climax; Demeter's sorrow in her temple at Eleusis, the fields barren of all vegetation, the restoration of her daughter, upon which she causes a field of ripe corn to shoot up. At this point in the celebrations, the worshippers are shown a ripe ear of corn. And, as with the rituals of the shamans, the dramatic effect must have been shattering. The worshippers look outside, at the fields of swaying corn and the ripe orchards, and it seems a revelation. From this time on, the name of Demeter or Kore makes a shiver run over the scalp.

The Orphic mysteries, which would also be celebrated at Eleusis, used the story of Orpheus in the same way, emphasising his sorrow at the loss of Eurydice, the descent to the underworld, his second loss of her when he looks over his shoulder, breaking his promise to Pluto (or Hades); his death, from being torn to pieces by Thracian Maenads.

What we do not know is the nature of the secrets imparted to the initiates, which were certainly of a magical nature. Even the Essenes, who were an ascetic religious order, had 'magical' secrets; the Jewish historian Josephus says, 'They studied with great diligence certain medical writings dealing with the occult virtues of plants and minerals.' And for the Greeks, as for the Magi, nature was a living thing, a veil concealing strange secrets. Each tree, each flower, each colour,* had occult significance. (Graves devotes two chapters of *The White Goddess* to an exposition of the occult significance of the various trees.) There was some significance in each of the flowers that Kore was picking before she was raped.

As to Orphism, it soon blended with the worship of the god

---

* I have already mentioned the hypothesis that the Greeks could see a smaller range of colours than we can, and this seems to be confirmed by colour-lore. Apart from black and white, the only colours with special significance are red (danger, war), blue (aristocracy and the virtues connected with it), yellow (wealth or power), green (fertility). Black and white signify mourning and innocence, of course. Yellow may also signify vindictiveness.

Dionysus, who originated in Thrace, and who was worshipped there in the form of a bull. Dionysus was quickly accepted in seventh-century B.C. Greece, because he was exactly what the Greeks needed to complete their pantheon of gods; under the name Bacchus he became the god of wine, and his symbol was sometimes an enormous phallus. Frazer speaks of Thracian rites involving wild dances, thrilling music and tipsy excess, and notes that such goings-on were foreign to the clear rational nature of the Greeks. But the religion still spread like wildfire throughout Greece, especially among women indicating, perhaps, a revolt against civilisation. It became a religion of orgies; women worked themselves into a frenzy and rushed about the hills, tearing to pieces any living creature they found. Euripides' play *The Bacchae* tells how King Pentheus, who opposed the religion of Bacchus, was torn to pieces by a crowd of women, which included his mother and sisters, all in 'Bacchic frenzy'. In their ecstasy the worshippers of Bacchus became animals, and behaved like animals, killing living creatures and eating them raw.

The profound significance of all this was recognised by the philosopher Nietzsche, who declared himself a disciple of the god Dionysus. He spoke of the 'blissful ecstasy that rises from the innermost depths of man', dissolving his sense of personality: in short, the sexual or magical ecstasy. He saw Dionysus as a fundamental principle of human existence; man's need to throw off his personality, to burst the dream-bubble that surrounds him and to experience total, ecstatic affirmation of everything. In this sense, Dionysus is fundamentally the god, or patron saint, of magic. The spirit of Dionysus pervades all magic, especially the black magic of the later witch cults, with their orgiastic witch's sabbaths so like the orgies of Dionysus's female worshippers, even to the use of goats, the animal sacred to Dionysus. (Is it not also significant that Dionysus is a horned god, like the Christian devil?)

The 'scent of truth' that made Ouspensky prefer books on magic to the 'hard facts' of daily journalism is the scent of Dionysian freedom, man's sudden absurd glimpse of his godlike potentialities. It is also true that the spirit of Dionysus, pushed to new extremes through frustration and egomania, permeates the work of De Sade. As Philip Vellacot remarks of Dionysus in his introduction to *The Bacchae*: 'But, though in the first half of the play there is some room for sympathy with Dionysus, this sympathy steadily diminishes until at the end of the play, his inhuman cruelty inspires nothing but horror.' But this misses the point about Dionysus – that sympathy is hardly an emotion he would appreciate. He descends like a storm wind, scattering all human emotion.

All this is the background of the first 'great initiate' of recorded history, Pythagoras. It is true that the legendary Egyptian founder of magic, Hermes Trismegistus ('Thrice Greatest Hermes'), is supposed to have preceded him; but it is doubtful whether Hermes actually existed (the Egyptians identified him with the god Thoth, who gave men the art of writing) and the documents relating to him belong to the post-Christian era. Pythagoras was born about 570 B.C. – a remarkable era, for it was at about this time that the Buddha was born in India, and Confucius and Lao Tse in China.

Nowadays we tend to associate Pythagoras with early science and mathematics; but this is a mistake. He was primarily a religious mystic who was interested in everything. He wanted to understand the world because he believed that its principles were basically mystical or occult, and that mathematics demonstrated this. According to the common conception, a number is just a number – an abstraction; but Pythagoras knew that numbers have as much individuality as mountains or human beings. He defined a friend as 'My other "I" – like 220 and 284.' What he meant by this was that 220 can be divided by 1, 2, 4, 5, 10, 11, 20, 44, 55, 110, and these add up to 284. The divisors of 284 are 1, 2, 4, 71, 142, and these add up to 220. So 220 and 284 are 'amicable numbers'.

This was how Pythagoras's mind worked – by analogy. (This is true of magicians in general, with their motto 'As above, so below'.) His interest in numbers and in science was not a desire to construct a chain of logic or inference, but the feeling that each separate fact might be a symbol of something much bigger – that facts might reflect bits of heaven, like broken shards of a mirror.

Pythagoras was born on the island of Samos, the son of a merchant. The tyrant of the island, Polycrates, seems to have taken a liking to Pythagoras, and sent him with a recommendation to his friend the pharaoh Amasis of Egypt, asking that Pythagoras be initiated into the Egyptian mysteries.

There is a story of the pharaoh Amasis and Polycrates that affords an insight into the curious fatalism of that era. Polycrates was known as a singularly lucky man. Amasis felt that this kind of thing could not last, since the gods do not allow men to be happy for too long. He advised Polycrates to inflict some minor form of suffering or inconvenience on himself, as a man in danger of apoplexy might drain off a small quantity of blood from his veins (the simile is Grote's). So Polycrates took a particularly valuable ring and threw it into the sea. A few days later a fisherman brought him a present of a fish – and the ring was found in its stomach. Amasis became convinced that nothing could now avert ill-fortune. In fact, it was greed that brought about Polycrates's downfall: an envious Persian lord on a neighbouring island lured him there with promises of gold, and then tortured him to death in a manner that Herodotus says was too disgusting to mention. Significantly, the daughter of Polycrates dreamed of the catastrophe beforehand and did her best to persuade her father not to go. Here again we note these characteristic elements of that period in human evolution: cruelty, envy, prophetic dreams and a superstitious and pessimistic fatalism that turns out to be disquietingly accurate.

After some ordeals, including circumcision, Pythagoras was initiated at Thebes; he learned Egyptian, says Diogenes Laertius, and associated with Chaldeans and with Persian Magi. From them he learned about astronomy – the Chaldeans invented the signs of the zodiac in this era – and about numbers. (The famous 'theorem of Pythagoras' about the square of the hypotenuse was probably learned from Egyptian priests.) However, the Persian king Cambyses invaded Egypt, and Pythagoras was sent by him to Babylon, where he spent another ten years or so, studying the Mesopotamian mysteries. In all, he was away from his homeland for thirty-four years, and during that time he must have encountered sages from India or China, for there is a strong element of oriental mysticism in his later philosophy, as well as a belief in reincarnation that he elaborated into metempsychosis, the belief that the soul may pass into the body of other creatures, including animals.

Back on Samos, Pythagoras discovered that his patron Polycrates had changed for the worse; in fact, the regime had taken on a repressive character. He moved to Crotona in southern Italy. His personal magnetism was so great that he collected many disciples, but he also aroused envy and enmity; even his brother-philosopher Heraclitus had sarcastic things to say about him. An enemy raised the populace against him in Crotona and some of his followers were slaughtered. This seems to indicate that they had become a powerful influence in the city. (Edouard Schuré says that Cyton, the man who caused the uprising against Pythagoras, was a rejected pupil.) Diogenes Laertius says that Pythagoras was killed in Crotona. burned in a house to which the mob had set fire. Porphyry says he escaped and went to Metapontum, where he died at the age of eighty.

During the thirty years he spent in Crotona, Pythagoras became one of the great intellectual influences on the Mediterranean world. He brought Eastern mysticism to the West. His school was a school for mystics, and the initiatory rites were long and challenging. Pythagoras was a philosopher rather than a magician; in fact, he invented the word 'philosopher'. But his highly mystical philosophy was one of the great influences in the history of magic.

Having said this, it must be admitted that his philosophy was striking and original rather than profound. He was apparently amazed to discover that there is a relation between the four principal notes of the Greek musical scale and the distance between them, as measured on the string of the lyre. One delightful legend records that he was passing by a blacksmith's shop, in which four smiths were striking anvils of different sizes and producing four different notes. Pythagoras had the anvils weighed, and found that their weights were in the proportion 6, 8, 9, 12. He then stretched four strings from the ceiling, and hung the four anvils from them – or four weights of the same proportion. The strings, when plucked, produced these same notes.

Pythagoras built up a whole mystical philosophy of numbers upon this discovery, or so the story goes. On the lyre string the distance between the notes was 3, 4 and 6, and the notes themselves could be worked out in the proportions 1 : 2 (octave), 3 : 2 (fifth) and 4 : 3 (fourth). The four numbers involved (1, 2, 3, 4) add up to ten, a sacred number. This discovery sounds absurdly simple to our sophisticated ears; but it must be remembered that few people in those days could count beyond ten, and that the art of multiplication was still unknown, even to the Egyptians. It struck Pythagoras as a revelation that these four notes – which, when played together, sounded so harmonious – should be explainable in terms of whole numbers. His mind leapt to the startling idea that perhaps all the harmony of creation is due to numerical secrets of the same sort. Creation starts with the 'divine, pure unity', number one, then develops to the 'holy four', and the first four digits beget ten, the sacred number, from which everything else springs.

In the same way, you can make up a triangle of dots by putting four dots for the bottom row, three dots for the next, two dots for the next and one dot for the apex. (The Greeks seem to have recorded numbers by the primitive method of dots.) This proved to the Pythagoreans that the triangle is also a mystical symbol. If you make up several of these triangles, each one with an extra row of dots, you notice that any of these triangles, added to the one before, makes a 'square'. That is to say, a triangle made up of three dots, added to a triangle made up of six dots, makes nine dots, which is three times three.

All this sounds like a harmless arithmetical game. But we are using the hindsight of centuries of science. In order to understand the full impact of Pythagoras on the Mediterranean world of his time, we must put off sophistication and travel back 2,500 years. There were various 'mysteries' – of Orpheus, Eleusis, Egypt, Babylonia – and some interesting views on life, death and the gods. But no one had ever made an attempt to unite all this into one magnificent structure of knowledge. Pythagoras knew about numbers; he knew about music; he knew about magic; he knew about astrology; he knew about the gods of Egypt and Chaldea and Persia and India. The Pythagorean 'mysteries' were based on those of Orpheus, who, by this time, was somehow identified with Dionysus. Dionysus is the life-force itself, formless and overpowering. Apollo is the god of art, of order, of harmony. He is not really the opposite of Dionysus – only death is the opposite of life. He represents a more complex and ordered form of Dionysus, an attempt of the formless energy to express itself as visible beauty, in opposition to ugliness and chaos. Apollo is a universal god – the Horus of the Egyptians, Mithras of the Persians, Marduk of the Babylonians. How does Dionysus become Apollo? Through ordering matter *harmoniously*, in accordance with secret laws of proportion, like the one Pythagoras stumbled on in music.

This was the essence of Pythagoras's vision, and in spite of its inaccuracies, it is fundamentally a true vision – truer, perhaps, than we shall encounter anywhere else in the realm of magic. Instinctively Pythagoras understood the upward evolutionary movement of life, away from animal instinct and 'jungle sensitiveness' towards *distance vision*, the ability to grasp far horizons of reality. Unlike his contemporaries Thales, Heraclitus and Parmenides, and unlike Aristotle later, he never lost his secure grasp on the mystical, the 'one' – what Hindus would call Brahman – but he tried to understand the 'one' by the use of his intellect.

The result was sometimes sense, sometimes nonsense. He believed, says Diogenes, that the air close to the earth is stagnant, and that therefore every living creature on the earth is subject to disease and death; but the upper airs are always in motion, and ought therefore to be able to confer immortality. An interesting guess, but wide of the mark. His view of sex was jaundiced, although he had a wife and at least one daughter; he advises sexual intercourse in the summer, not winter, but adds 'that the practice is pernicious in every season, and is never good for the health'. The pleasures of love, he said, make a man 'weaker than himself'.

This may indicate that Pythagoras was a shaman, whose powers were diminished by sexual intercourse. His contemporaries believed all kinds of interesting legends about his magical powers. The story is told that he tamed a wild bear by whispering in its ear, and called down an eagle from the air to perch on his wrist. When he and a disciple were watching a ship entering harbour, and the friend speculated what treasure was on board, Pythagoras foretold correctly that its cargo was two dead bodies being sent home for burial. His life is so surrounded by magical legend that there is no way of knowing whether he was really a medium, or simply a mystical philosopher. His contemporaries seem to have had a habit of ridiculing him in epigrams, and one chronicler asserted that Pythagoras's legendary descent to the Underworld to converse with the dead was a fraud; he had actually hidden in a cave for several weeks, getting his mother to write him news of what was happening in the world so he could pretend to have learned by supernatural means. He may well have had a touch of the charlatan – most 'great initiatees' did, as we shall see. The charlatanism of Pythagoras – his claims to remember previous incarnations, and so on – may have been, like Gurdjieff's, an attempt to create the right atmosphere for the reception of his ideas. He lived to a considerable age – Diogenes Laertius says ninety – and seems to have been a remarkably strong and healthy man, who once startled everybody by winning the boxing championship at the Olympic games.

We may note, in passing, that the Greeks seem to have lived to a greater age than most races. The Bible sets three score and ten as the average of human life. Pythagoras divides life into four stages: youth to the age of twenty, manhood to the age of forty, middle age to sixty, old age to eighty. In the Middle Ages, average life expectancy was about forty. I have elsewhere* advanced the theory that 'intellectuals', especially mathematicians, live longer than any other type of man.

If we can never be certain whether Pythagoras possessed occult powers, there can be no doubt whatever in the case of his most famous disciple, Apollonius of Tyana, who lived in the first century A.D., and whose life was written a century later by an accomplished Greek named Philostratus. This 'life' is full of absurdities and wonders, but it is possible to discern through them all a natural medium with powers of prevision. Like Pythagoras, much of his life was spent in travel, and his philosophy, expounded in a series of long speeches in Philostratus, is a compound of Pythagoras and of Hindu, Babylonian and Egyptian magical lore. Philostratus wrote

* *The Philosopher's Stone.*

the book to please Empress Julia, wife of Severus, and seems to have based it on the memoirs of Damis of Nineveh, a disciple and friend of Apollonius. (It was this same Empress Julia who commissioned Diogenes Laertius to write his *Lives of the Philosophers*, from which I have quoted.) The result is the usual curious mixture of realism and myth. It is not too difficult to draw the line. We are told that Apollonius was a god, the son of Proteus, and that one of his calumniators, Tigellinus, withdrew the charges (of impiety against Nero) when he recognised Apollonius as a god. On the other hand, it is perfectly clear that Apollonius spent a great deal of his life defending himself against charges of being a black magician, and that he was, in fact, a travelling philosopher and medium who was certainly not widely regarded as a god, or even a real mage. (In those superstitious times, people would have been very chary of offending a real 'magician'.) And there is one human touch that sounds too genuine to have been invention. When Apollonius consulted the Delphic oracle to ask if his name would be remembered in the future, she answered that it would be, but only because he would be so reviled. On leaving the temple, Apollonius tore up the paper – hardly the reaction of a philosopher. (But the oracle proved to be correct. Because various enemies of Christianity later tried to set Apollonius up as a rival to Jesus, he became known mainly as an antichrist.)

The stories told of his magical powers sound as if they might have come out of *The Golden Ass*. In Rome he raised from the dead a young lady of aristocratic connections whose death had caused the whole city to mourn. (The ancients were naturally unaware that severe brain damage occurs within hours of death, so that a person who had been miraculously revived would be an imbecile; the same objection, of course, applies to the raising of Lazarus.) When his friend and disciple Menippus of Corinth introduced him to his (Menippus's) future bride, Apollonius instantly recognised her as a vampire (or Lamia – Keats wrote a poem of that title about the episode). Menippus refused to believe his warnings, but Apollonius came to the wedding, and with a few magical passes caused the guests and the feast to vanish – all were illusions conjured up by Lamia – and made the bride admit that she intended to eat Menippus. (Keats, the sentimentalist, makes Lamia a lovelorn snake who becomes a woman to win her lover; Apollonius, the cold-hearted philosopher, exposes her, destroying their happiness.)

A slightly less fantastic story describes how Apollonius warned the people of Ephesus of a forthcoming plague; fortunately he recognised an old beggar as the plague carrier and persuaded the populace to stone him to death, upon which the old beggar turned into a black dog. The truth of the story may well be that Apollonius recognised, in some instinctive way, that the beggar carried the plague, and had him stoned to death as the lesser of two evils.

The kind of calumny with which Apollonius had to contend all his life is illustrated in the account of his trial before the emperor Domitian. An enemy named Euphrates accused him of plotting against Domitian and killing a shepherd in order to discover from his entrails the date of Domitian's downfall. (It must be remembered that the Romans believed in divination by entrails – but they were usually those of an animal.) Apollonius voluntarily presented himself at Rome to answer the charge, confident, apparently, that it was not his destiny to die at the hands of the emperor. His defence was that he had never, at any time, practised sacrifice, and that he had spent the night in question sitting beside a dying disciple, Philiscus of Melos. He explains that he is a philosopher, and seems to deny that he has magical powers. He also says that he would happily descend to Hades to rescue the spirit of Philiscus. Since one of the legends told of him is that he *did* descend to Hades (like Pythagoras), it seems likely that this part of the story, at any rate, is genuine. We gain a glimpse of Apollonius as he really was:

a philosopher, a natural medium and something of a seer. His prophetic powers were probably undeveloped. Otherwise. it would hardly have been necessary for him to consult the Delphic oracle on his future reputation; the fact that he thought of consulting her at all on such a subject proves that he possessed his share of ordinary vanity. On the other hand, he was basically a man of good will, who used his powers to benefit other people. Philostratus tells a story of a father who had four unmarried daughters, all needing dowries. Apollonius persuaded him to spend what money he had to buy an olive orchard; it brought forth an excellent crop of olives when everyone else's olives failed. This suggests that Apollonius possessed some of the old power of shamans to make the land fruitful. He later told the father of buried treasure on his land. Presumably he did not know of the treasure originally, otherwise he would have told him of it sooner; he probably 'divined' it in the course of working his fertility charms in the olive grove.

The divining of buried treasure is less fantastic than it sounds; in fact, it is an ordinary branch of dowsing, In his book *Witches*, the antiquarian T. C. Lethbridge describes how he was investigating Viking graves on the island of Lundy – they turned out not to be Viking after all – when his companion suggested that he should try dowsing for volcanic dykes, which are normally detected by a magnetometer. Lethbridge was led blindfolded over the clifftops. holding a twig. 'Every now and then the twig would turn violently in my hands for a few paces and then stop.' His companion then took off the blindfold and told him that he had located every one of the dykes. There are probably thousands of people who, like Lethbridge, are natural dowsers without knowing it. Apollonius was a dowser. We shall never know the exact nature of his other mediumistic powers because the truth about him is overlaid with tall stories about his magical abilities. It is easy enough to recognise the absurdities, but less easy to get at the truth behind them.

FOUR
THE WORLD OF THE KABBALISTS

Apollonius of Tyana lived during one of the most remarkable epochs in human history. For quite suddenly, the whole of the Mediterranean world was covered with communities of people who wanted to turn their backs on the life of the cities; who experienced an acute craving for contemplation and knowledge of the infinite. Like the Essenes, they moved into the wilderness and formed their own communities. They were not Christians, and the Church came to refer to them as the Gnostics, and to denounce them as heretics. With its usual thoroughness, the Church destroyed most of their written records, and left hostile and distorted accounts of them in theological writings.

This mass exodus to the wilderness is a strange phenomenon. It might be regarded as the third great evolutionary step taken by the human race. The first was the creation of cities round about 4000 B.C. The second was the religious movement that swept across the Western world in the seventh century B.C. – the era that produced Zarathustra, the Buddha, Lao Tse and Confucius, Orpheus and Pythagoras and Dionysus, and the mystery cults that sprang up all over Greece and its neighbours. There had been great religions before – and great temples, like Stonehenge, built between 1900 and 1600 B.C. – but these earlier religions were the worship of a heterogeneous gallery of nature gods or local deities. What started to happen in the seventh century B.C. was quite different: it was a real religious movement that spread in ripples over the civilised world, reaching Gaul and Britain in the form of Druidism. (The date is not known, but it was probably around 400 B.C.)

The movement spent its force; a civilised scepticism took its place in Greece and Rome. And then, in the century before the birth of Jesus, a new wave began to gather force. It was a reaction against pagan scepticism and Roman imperialism. While Judas Maccabeus was conducting his guerrilla campaign against the Romans, the Essenes withdrew to the shores of the Dead Sea and developed a mystical Judaism. A hundred years before Jesus the Essenes paid homage to a man known simply as The Great Teacher. His name has not come down to us.

Then came Christianity, and with it, the birth of Gnosticism. They should not be regarded as antagonistic, but as different expressions of the human craving to escape the futility of human existence. Christianity gained its ascendancy by preaching the End of the World and the Kingdom of God. It declared flatly that the end of the world would occur *within the lifetime of people who were alive at the time of the Crucifixion*; a great battle would take place – Armageddon, named after the battle won by Thutmose III of Egypt – and everyone who was not a Christian would sink into eternal death, while the Christians would live forever on an earth that had been restored to its original Eden state. This was a powerful argument, and it helps to explain the enormous success of Christianity. But it is not the whole reason for its success; otherwise, Christianity would have died out when the End of the World failed to arrive in the first century A.D. There was a deep and genuine craving for 'meanings' beyond those of everyday life, with its dreary, everlasting struggle for subsistence. Sensitive men have always felt that the everyday world is a repetitive bore. At the time of Jesus the whole civilised world was convulsed by the feeling of loathing and rejection of the kind that can be found in Eliot's *Waste Land* and *Hollow Men*.

And this is expressed in Gnosticism even more clearly than in Christianity. There were dozens of Gnostic sects, and their beliefs varied widely. But the basic one was this. The world was not created by God, but by a stupid and conceited demon (or Demiurge).

God is above Creation; he is referred to as the Alien, the Abyss, the Non-Existent. This latter epithet means that God is totally beyond everything we mean by existence. He dwells in the realm of the Pleroma – mystical Plenitude. (This God forms the basis of the doctrines of the Kabbalah, and later of Boehme's mystical system, in which God is called the *Ungrund*, or 'groundless'.) But there was some kind of basic split in this Alien Godhead, and a Fall took place. The end result of this Fall (which some of the Gnostics believe to be due to Sophia, the feminine figure of wisdom) is the Demiurge (or archon) who created the universe. This archon is the 'God' of the Old Testament – the figure Blake called Old Nobodaddy – and the identification is made clear in Gnostic writing by putting into his mouth sayings from the Old Testament. Time is a counterfeit substitute of eternity. The Demiurge created another six archons to help him with creation. He is totally ignorant of the Divinity from which he has fallen, and believes himself to be the only God. The seven archons created man, whose state is doubly tragic because he is trapped in a world created by a deluded God.

However, there is a spark of hope. Something in man rejects this false world, and longs for its true home. One sect of Gnostics, called the Ophites (from the Greek *ophis*, serpent) believed that the snake in the Garden of Eden was an agent of divine goodness who gave man forbidden knowledge so that he could set out on the long road to saving his soul. The chief characteristic of the Gnostic doctrine is its tendency to make heroes of the villains of the Old Testament – Cain, Esau and so on. The Gnostics disliked Judaism, with its narrow, bigoted values, even more than they disliked the degenerate religions of Greece and Rome.

Man, then, finds himself in a prison; but because of the help of the wise serpent (who plays the same role that Prometheus plays in Greek legend), he has a chance of escape, through knowledge. (Gnosis equals knowledge.) Man's true home is the Divine Light.

(The concept of light plays an important part in the doctrines of Orpheus and Pythagoras too.) By the use of his will and intellect, he will eventually achieve freedom.

(One of the most perfect expressions of Gnostic attitude can be found in David Lindsay's masterpiece *A Voyage to Arcturus* (1920), although it is doubtful whether Lindsay was acquainted with Gnosticism.)

A later sect of Gnostics called themselves Manichees – followers of Mani. They went even further in believing that all that belongs to the world is evil, while all that belongs to the spirit (*pneuma*) is good. They believed that sex is bad simply because it prolongs the evil of procreation, and that a dying man is lucky to be escaping this world. (They might help a dying man on his way by starving him, or even suffocating him.)

It can be seen that in basic respects Gnosticism agrees more closely with modern evolutionism than Christianity does. Knowledge was not man's Fall, but his salvation. And although this meant primarily 'knowledge of the divine' (theosophy), it certainly did not in any way exclude scientific knowledge. On the contrary, Gnosticism is permeated with the doctrines of Pythagoras – his number mysticism as well as his belief in reincarnation and the soul's pilgrimage from body to body.

At this point it is necessary to speak at greater length of the Kabbalah (also spelt Cabala and Qabalah), since it seems reasonably certain that it derives from the doctrines of the Gnostics. There are two major books of the Kabbalah, the *Sepher Yetzirah*, or Book of Formation, and the *Zohar*, or Book of Splendour. Waite believes the first part to have been written in the second century A.D., although Richard Cavendish, more conservative, places it between the third and sixth centuries. Tradition declares that 'its fundamental doctrines go back as far as Abraham, and there can be no doubt that they represent a very early stage of Jewish mysticism. The *Zohar* was written down, in Aramaic, in Spain around 1275 by a Kabbalist named Moses de Leon. The importance of the Kabbalah lies in this: it is one of the oldest systems of mystical thought in the world; it was regarded for many centuries as *the* key to all the mysteries of the universe; and it was an influence on practically every philosopher and religious thinker from the founder of the Essenes to Roger Bacon. Madame Blavatsky called her own bewildering compilation of esoteric occultism *The Secret Doctrine*, but for most thinkers of the Middle Ages and Reformation the words 'secret doctrine' had only one connotation: the Kabbalah.

The basis of all cabalism is a diagram known as 'the sacred tree', which consists of ten circles joined by twenty-two lines (see p. 263).

The ten circles are the Sephiroth, or emanations of God. This is basically a Gnostic diagram: that is to say, it represents the Creation as a fall from ultimate godhead to the earthly kingdom. The soul begins its journey downwards, progressing through ten 'spheres', like the layers of an onion, ending in a state of amnesia in the earthly body. Mysticism is, of course, the attempt of the soul to achieve union with God again. The Kabbalah asserts that this cannot be done in one single leap, but that the soul has to make its way back up through the nine spheres above it, starting by detaching itself from the earthly body. (The doctrine of the Astral Body is fundamental to cabalism: the notion that man possesses a 'spirit body' of roughly the same shape and extent as his earthly body, which can detach itself and move upwards.) Like the Tibetan and Egyptian Books of the Dead, the Kabbalah is a guide book for the soul in its path upward. Like the *I Ching*, it is also a book of wisdom that can be studied for its own sake. Some influential occultists also assert that the twenty-two Tarot cards are pictorial representations of the twenty-two paths, so that the Tarot is essentially a kabbalistic document.

The essence of the Kabbalah is easy to grasp; an intelligent student can do it in half an hour. Once this basic pattern is understood,

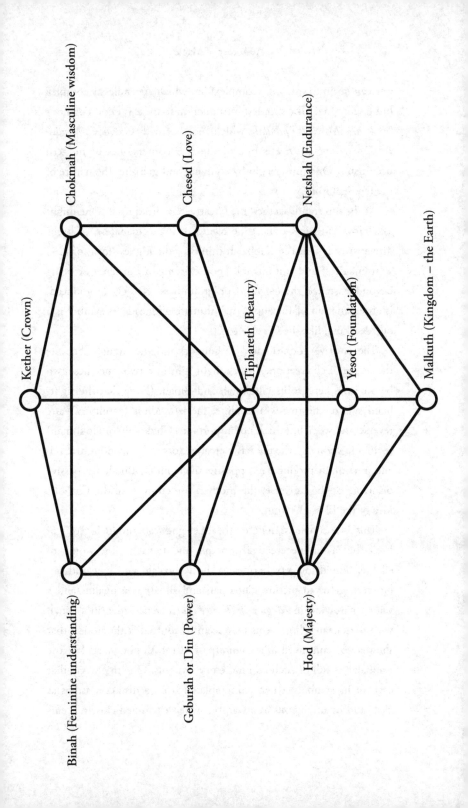

one can begin to study the complexities, which are endlessly complex but fascinating. (The simplest introduction to these is Dion Fortune's book *The Mystical Qabalah*, which together with Crowley's *Magick in Theory and Practice* is one of the two cornerstones of modern occultism.) One must begin by studying and grasping the nature of the ten Sephiroth.

At the top stands Kether, the Creative Godhead itself. One might ask: How can the Godhead be regarded as an emanation of itself? The answer is that the Kabbalah thinks of the highest form of God as unmanifest and unthinkable, non-existent in the sense of being beyond existence, the *Ungrund*, or 'groundless'. Kether, the godhead, is an emanation of En Soph, this ultimate godhead. Its symbol is a bearded king, like the Greek Zeus.

The creative godhead had a thought, and the thought became the origin of all creation. This thought split into two, and these two became the Sephiroths Chokmah and Binah. (Note that the right-hand side of the tree is masculine; the left side is feminine. Waite reverses the order, but this is not important.) Chokmah (or Hokhmah) is the life-giving spirit, the basic creative force, the wisdom of God, and it naturally produces its opposite, the feminine Binah, the passive principle of the universe, the mother, something like the Catholic idea of the Blessed Virgin.

This is the first triangle of the tree, godhead producing out of itself the masculine creative principle and the feminine womb of all life. Sexual imagery permeates the Kabbalah, and it would not be sacrilegious to picture Chokmah and Binah as a phallus and a vagina. Crowley, in *Magick in Theory and Practice*, identifies Binah with the Great Whore. This may seem to contradict the notion that she may be conceived as a counterpart of the Virgin Mary; but the Kabbalah is full of such contradictory symbols. One might say that each of its symbols, when contemplated from a distance, seems as clear and unambiguous as a star, but when examined closely, seems to be made of a smoky mist that changes its form continually. This is reflected in some of the names given to Binah in Dion Fortune's table of correspondences: Ama, the dark sterile mother; Aima, the bright fertile mother; Khorsia, the throne; Marah, the great sea. She is also the yoni (vagina), kteis (European term meaning the same thing) and chalice, while her 'spiritual experience' is a Vision of Sorrow,* recalling the Virgin.

The next triangle of the tree is in some ways the most interesting. Here the male, Hesed (or Chesed), is protective love, the essential quality of the father. This is associated with receptive intelligence, and the force that creates civilisation. His 'planet' is Jupiter, and the Greek god who corresponds to him is Neptune (Poseidon), the sea god. But his wife, strangely enough, seems anything but female. Geburah (or Din) is associated with Mars, war, and with the deadly basilisk, and with cruelty and violence. Perhaps she is best understood as Kali, the destructive Divine Mother of Hindu mythology, who is simultaneously the living mother of the universe and the symbol of anarchic violence. Her colours are red and black, as well as the orange of fire. She is justice in its harshest aspect. Her correspondences include the sword, the spear, the scourge and the chain. Her positive characteristics are energy and courage.

Tiphareth, the third point of this second triangle, reconciles the two opposites; it is tempting to think of it as Jesus, for one of its symbols is the crucified god. But the symbol almost certainly pre-dates the Christian era; it is probably connected with the hanged god of Frazer. Tiphareth is beauty, and a glance at the diagram will show that it is in direct line of descent from the supreme godhead, Kether. Its astrological symbol is the sun. It is to be regarded as a plane of springing vitality and warmth.

* Four Tarot cards are also assigned to her – the three of each suit – and students of the Tarot will find Dion Fortune's book an invaluable key, with its parallels between the Tarot and the Kabbalah. She uses Crowley's Tarot correspondences.

In the next triangle (Netshah, Hod, Yesod) we have descended to attributes of this world and humankind. Netshah is endurance and victory, and may be regarded as the symbol of the instinctive life of nature, with its boundless energies and power of self-renewal. 'It is by means of dance and sound and colour that the Netzach angels are evoked,' says Dion Fortune. Netshah is described in Julian Grenfell's lines:

And life is colour, warmth and light
And craving evermore for these ...

Its female counterpart, Hod (glory or majesty), is the sphere of the mental faculties, particularly imagination and intelligence. Cavendish states that it also has an evil side – reason and logic – which the Kabbalah distrusts. So Hod may be thought of as combining Blakeian qualities of vision and imagination with the narrowness of logical positivism.

The 'son' of these two Sephiroth is Yesod, the sphere of the moon (we are back to Graves's White Goddess). Oddly enough, one of the symbols of Yesod is the male genitals. (The whole tree is sometimes regarded as forming a man – an idea Blake borrowed for his prophetic books – and the Sephiroth also correspond to parts of the body.) Yesod is the sphere of magic. (Observe that it combines the deep forces of nature – Netshah – with intelligence and imagination, a clear statement of the forces behind magic.) Its Tarot cards are the four nines, representing great strength, great happiness, material gains and also despair and cruelty, the negative aspects of the goddess.

The last of the Sephiroth is Malkuth, the Earth. It is associated with the rainbow and with the fruitful forces of nature. Its symbol is a young girl, crowned and throned, and its names include Malkah, the queen; Kallah, the bride, and the Virgin. This is the world of generation, of the energies of spring, the peculiar intoxication that some young women exercise unconsciously. (Frank Wedekind calls his Lulu *Erdgeist*, or earth spirit.) William Blake catches its essence – innocence, pure joy – in *The Book of Thel*. Its negative virtue, significantly enough, is inertia.

These, then, are the ten Sephiroth, the heart of the Kabbalah, the ten aspects of God. Connecting the ten are twenty-two paths, corresponding to the greater arcana of the Tarot. The Sephiroth themselves are also regarded as paths, making thirty-two in all. Each path has many symbols and correspondences – I have been able to indicate only a few of these. The serious student of the Kabbalah studies the Sephiroth and their attributes, tracing the relations between them. No doubt the Kabbalah was originally a purely devotional system, meditation upon the ten aspects of God. It combined with astrology and other forms of divination until it became a complex but beautiful and symmetrical web of correspondences. Jewish religion tends to be harsh, dogmatic and pedantic, with its rules and disciplines; the Kabbalah is its mystical and devotional side. It is certainly one of the most beautiful and satisfying studies in the whole realm of occultism.*

The realms of the Sephiroth – which are divided into four worlds corresponding to the triangles (Atziluth, Briah, Yetzirah, Assiah) – can be explored intellectually, or through mystical disciplines, which Dion Fortune calls 'travelling in the spirit vision'.† Occultists believe that the soul, or astral body, can be free from the physical body by disciplines of concentration akin to yoga. It can then attempt to make its own way along the thirty-two paths, and

---

* Readers interested in further study are recommended to begin with Richard Cavendish's account in *The Black Arts* and to pass on to Dion Fortune's *Mystical Qabalah*, the most readable book on the subject. Madame Blavatsky's *Secret Doctrine* is a treasure house of kabbalistic lore, connecting the Kabbalah with Eastern doctrines. Waite's *Holy Kabbalah*, an exhaustive and exhausting compendium, should not be approached until a thorough grounding has been obtained; otherwise early discouragement is likely.

† For further discussion of 'projection of the astral body', see Part Three, Chapter 3.

the kabbalistic tree is a guide book, complete with warnings and instructions. Dion Fortune explains that if an 'astral traveller' sees 'a horse (Mars), or a jackal (Luna) in the sphere of Netzach (Venus), one would know there was a confusion of plane and the vision was not reliable. In her sphere one would expect to see doves, and a spotted beast, such as a lynx or leopard.' Cavendish explains:

> The Kabbalist explores the strange country he has entered and speaks to any of the figures which approach him, but he must be cautious. The figures may try to deceive and ensnare him … In this mysterious world the aspiring Kabbalist needs guide-posts to help him find his way about and avoid pitfalls. The guide-posts are provided by the system of correspondences, which lists the creatures, plants, colours, jewels, scents and symbols associated with the Sephiroth and twenty-two paths … If the occult traveller believes he is in the region of Netshah, the sphere of Venus, and he sees a horse or a jackal, he knows that something has gone wrong. The horse belongs to Mars, the jackal is a beast of the moon … If he is working up the twenty-second path, which leads from Malkuth to Yesod, and he meets a figure in a scarlet robe, he knows he has strayed from the way. The path belongs to Saturn, and the colour of Saturn is black.*

Other branches of the Kabbalah deal with gematria – a system by which Hebrew words are converted into numbers, and then into other words of the same number – and the Names of Power, the secret names of the angels and demons of each sphere which can be used in magical conjuration. The most important of these names is the Tetragrammaton, the name of Jehovah (YHVH), which makes its appearance in all the *grimoires*, or books of magical conjuration.

* *The Black Arts*, p. 97.

Names, like symbols, are believed to possess magical properties, and the most popular form of talisman is a small piece of paper with the name of a protective angel written on it. In his delightful book on the Golden Dawn, *Ritual Magic in England*, Francis King describes a 'new system of magic' invented by an occultist named A. O. Spare. 'Like all magicians,' says King, 'he believed that any desire deeply felt in the inmost centre of human consciousness was capable of fulfilment.' The magician's desire is compressed into the shortest possible sentence, then letters are crossed out until every letter appears only once; the remaining letters are combined to form a sign or sigil, which the magician allows to sink into his subconscious by staring at it intently. The subconscious then does the rest.

King describes one of Spare's experiments in symbolic magic. He announced his intention of causing freshly cut roses to fall from the air, and waved various symbolic drawings around, repeating the word 'roses', with his face contorted. At this moment the overhead plumbing exploded, deluging Spare and his companion with sewage.

Apollonius of Tyana may have been a Kabbalist; he was certainly closely connected with Gnosticism. His name is often coupled with that of the founder of a major school of Gnosticism, Simon Magus (or Simon the Magician), who gave his name to the Simonians. Because of the assiduity of the Christians in destroying all documents of the sect, we know little about him. He is referred to in the Acts of the Apostles (Chapter 8) as a magician of Samaria who was regarded by the people as a wonder worker. According to the Acts, he was converted to Christianity. The little we know about him is derived from the writings of various Church Fathers who were hostile to him. (They even gave his name to a sin, simony, because of a legend that he offered the apostles money to confer magic powers on him.)

Through the mist of legend and exaggeration, we can discern the outline of a man with mediumistic powers and a Pythagorean love of knowledge. He learned magical 'secrets' from the priests of Egypt, and from Persian Magi. (The latter, of course, were also the 'three kings' who attended Jesus's birth in the manger.) He was a pupil of the Arab Dositheus, whom the Clementine Fathers claim to have been a false Messiah; however, he seems to have been, in actuality, nothing worse than the founder of a sect of Gnostics. That Simon was a medium of unusual powers is clear from two of the magical feats attributed to him: the ability to make his body float in the air, and the ability to make heavy furniture move without touching it.

These powers bring to mind the most remarkable of modern mediums, Daniel Dunglas Home, of whom I shall speak later.* Browning portrayed Home as the fake medium 'Mr. Sludge', but this is totally unfair. Not only was Home never 'exposed' or shown to have used trickery, but scientific observers repeatedly verified that he could float through the air and make heavy items of furniture move. This was not done only on one or two occasions but on hundreds of occasions over some forty years. Home also performed these feats in broad daylight, and with none of the medium's usual paraphernalia. Unfortunately, these things happened in the era before the foundation of the SPR (Society for Psychical Research) and before snapshot cameras were invented. When heavy tables tilted, objects on them remained stationary, as if glued to their surface. Home asserted repeatedly that he had no idea how these things were done; he was only some kind of radio set that picked up strange powers.

If, then, we accept that Simon Magus was able to move heavy furniture and 'levitate' – and dismiss the stories that assert he could make himself invisible or turn himself into an animal – we have another example of a Pythagorean figure, balancing himself between intellectualism and 'magic'. (He is also said to have been able to pass

* See Part Three, Chapter 2.

unharmed through fire; Home could handle red-hot coals when in a trance.) Like Goethe's Faust, he is said to have conjured up Helen of Troy and fallen in love with her. His Christian antagonists claim that the woman was a prostitute named Helena, whom he purchased from a brothel in Tyre. It is significant, however, that Simon Magus called her also 'Selene', the moon goddess: enough to make one suspect that what was really at issue here was a clash between doctrinaire Christianity and the older worship of the White Goddess.

Eliphaz Levi, with his usual imaginative inaccuracy, writes: 'Simon became passionately enamoured of his servant [Helen]; that passion, at once weakening and exalting, restored his cataleptic states and the morbid phenomena that he termed his gift of wonders. A mythology full of magical reminiscences combined with erotic dreams, issued fully armed from his brain; he undertook pilgrimages, like the apostles, carrying Helena with him ...'

All that can be said for this is that it fits in with the legend of Simon Magus fostered by the Church. According to this legend, Simon is basically a tragic figure, a black magician whose magic was mostly illusion – being inspired by the father of lies himself. He wants power and acclaim, but lacks the necessary purity and high-mindedness (hence his offer to buy magical powers from the apostles). The legend has it that he went to Rome and became a favourite of Nero's, using fraud, trickery and hypnotism to establish himself. He hypnotises one of Nero's guards into believing that he has decapitated him (Simon Magus) when he has actually only decapitated a ram, and thus convinces Nero that he can rise from the dead. He becomes Nero's court magician, and the Jews in Rome embrace his Gnostic doctrines. To aid his deluded fellow countrymen, the Apostle Peter goes to Rome and challenges Simon to a magical contest. Simon conjures up huge dogs that rush towards Peter, but he makes them vanish by holding out a loaf of holy bread. Simon then levitates himself, and flies out of the window; but

St. Peter falls on his knees, and brings him down with a well-aimed prayer. Simon dies of two broken legs, and Peter is thrown into prison by Nero. (He will escape, of course, since he holds all the cards.)

There is little to be learned from this Christian version of the story, except that the choice of a ram as the animal to represent Simon, and his relationship with the siren Helen, seem to indicate that the Christians associated Simon with pagan eroticism. The Gallic bishop Irenaeus, in a refutation of Gnosticism, says the Simonians believed that wisdom (Sophia) was made prisoner on earth by the seven archons and subjected to every kind of indignity, including being imprisoned in a female body and forced to become a prostitute in a brothel. Can the Helen episode be coincidence? Or did the Simonians worship woman as the incarnation of the 'eternal womanly' and perhaps account for the ecstasy of sexual intercourse by reference to her divine origin? The Christian habit of destroying the records, so reminiscent of Hitler and Stalin, means that we shall never know. Our knowledge of the Gnostics remains vague and general: we know that the Simonians 'practised magic', that the Therapeuts practised some form of spirit healing, that the Cainites took a sympathetic view of Judas and that Cerinthus, leader of the Cerinthians, may have been the author of the *Apocalypse* that is usually attributed to St. John. There can be little doubt that the Gnostics preserved many of the traditions and ideas of the Orphics, and are therefore in the direct line of descent of the Western magical tradition of the Middle Ages.

The historian Gibbon found it difficult to restrain his sarcasm when writing about the early history of Christianity, remarking that 'the laws of Nature were frequently suspended for the benefit of the Church'. And when one studies the relevant documents, it is difficult not to feel the same. Christianity was an epidemic rather than a religion. It appealed to fear, hysteria and ignorance. It spread across the Western world, not because it was true, but because human beings are gullible and superstitious. Sienkiewicz's *Quo Vadis* shows us a community of great souls defying the might of Rome because they possess a higher truth than the pagans. But it would be more accurate to think of the early Christians as a mass movement akin to Billy Graham-ism or the Jehovah's Witnesses. There is something offensive in the way they praise themselves with the unintelligent enthusiasm of a television advertisement. Hordes of demons are invented in order to demonstrate that the saints can get the better of them with a few prayers. In the story of the magician Cyprian (later St. Cyprian) in *The Golden Legend*, the Devil boasts at length, 'I threw the heavens into confusion; I cast down angels from on high; I deceived Eve … I stained the earth with blood … I prompted the crucifixion of Christ,' and so on. 'Not knowing, poor wretch,' adds the chronicler, 'that the power of Christ is insuperable.'* This is typical of the tone of early Christian writers. They seem unaware that by giving their saviour the attributes of a comic-strip superman, they are removing any sporting interest from the conflict, and making people with a spark of independence feel like siding with the Devil. Cyprian wants the Devil to help him woo a girl called Justina, who has become a convert to Christianity and a confirmed virgin; although all Antioch is stricken with a plague (which the girl defeats in its sixth year by praying), she remains proof against the Devil's assaults; the Devil confesses that 'the crucified one is greater than all, and Cyprian decides to become a Christian.

This is not intended as an indictment of Christianity as such; a religion is judged by its highest manifestations, not its lowest. All propaganda is meant to appeal to the feeble-minded; Christian hagiography is no exception.

Christianity should be judged by its mystics, not by its 'religious

* Quoted by E. M. Butler, *The Myth of the Magus*, Oxford, 1948, p. 89.

caterpillars' (to borrow a phrase of Marlow's). Perhaps the most fundamental objection to Christianity is Nietzsche's: that it exalts negative virtues. St. Augustine labours the contrast between the City of This World and the City of God through about a thousand pages of his major work. His attack on the earthly city carries conviction; he portrays its pride, its vanity, its short-sightedness and expediency – in short, its slavery to the merely personal. One expects the City of God to be a city governed by the drive towards the impersonal by creativity and vision. Instead, Augustine talks about self-sacrifice, obedience, humility, chastity. It is all negative. Under the circumstances, it is not surprising that the early Christians spent most of their time squabbling among themselves, burning 'heretics' and inventing nonsensical stories about demons. To read any early Christian tract – for example, John Cassian's *Institutes of the Monastic Life* (about A.D. 400) is to plod through long discussions of faults and sins – carnal impulses, covetousness, vainglory, pride and so on. He describes *accidia* – Oblomov's disease of boredom – and prescribes manual labour as the antidote. Monks who spent most of their time in this negative frame of mind were turning their minds into stagnant pools.

Mankind had reached a point in its evolution where the emphasis swung from the body to the soul. Augustine was right to regard Plato as the most important pagan forerunner of Christianity, for Plato was the first to express the idea that the soul spends its time trying to free itself from the body, and that therefore death is a 'consummation devoutly to be wished'. The earlier Greeks had never seen the soul as somehow the antagonist of the body; *pneuma* was the breath of life, but the ghost that descended to the nether world was a more or less exact replica of the body, the principle that animated it, not its enemy. Quite suddenly, after a mere four thousand years of civilisation, man became soul-conscious, aware of a part of his identity that went beyond the body and his everyday affairs.

So far, his needs had been simple: food, drink, security, comfort, a certain amount of excitement. Now he was developing what might be called 'meta-needs', the need for a widening and deepening of consciousness. He did not understand this; he did not possess the concepts to grasp what was happening. As to Jesus himself, he had certainly never preached the war of the soul against the body. He preached universal love, the principle of mutual aid. His discovery was common sense rather than metaphysical; it was the economic principle of division of labour. If ten men each make the parts of a motor car, they can build a dozen motor cars a day. If each man tried to make a motor car on his own, he would be lucky to make one a week. Jesus was a visionary who foresaw the kingdom of God on earth, and who wanted to persuade men to behave like gods and not like animals. He had no dislike of the body as such and was perfectly prepared to eat with publicans and sinners. It was St. Paul who invented the religion of salvationism that depended on self-torment, and that thrived on hysteria and emotionalism. It happened to fit the need of the human race at that point in evolution for rejecting the 'lower self' that lives and dies like an animal. It is arguable that St. Paul's 'crosstianity' was one of the greatest disasters that has ever befallen the human race: a great black shadow of intolerance, a super-totalitarianism that makes communism seem harmless by comparison. What Western man needed at that point was a positive religion. The religions of Greece and Rome failed because they lacked seriousness and intensity. Mankind was haunted by a vision of freedom. The human race was in the grip of civilisation neurosis. Man's instincts could remember the days when he lived by hunting the bear and mastodon on wide savannas. He was like a child in its first year at school, looking back nostalgically to days of freedom. The craving took the form of a nostalgia for a return to some kind of golden age. Christianity quite simply outbid its rivals in offering him a dream that more or less fitted. The Greek religion of Demeter or Orpheus might have been a serious rival, but it had lost its vitality over the centuries and, in any case, believed in reincarnation. The idea of being endlessly reborn on earth was far less satisfying than the idea of sitting at the right hand of Jesus on a paradise-earth. The religion of Mithras, the sun-god, was almost identical with Christianity in its tenets – the 'saviour', an eternity of bliss (or woe for the nonbelievers) – and at one time it almost replaced Christianity in the Roman empire; but it lacked the savage proselytising zeal of the more totalitarian Christians and was eventually stamped out by them with the usual thoroughness. It should be remembered that the Dionysian religion had gained such a hold partly because it made such terrifying threats – its opponents driven insane and made to devour their own children and so on. Modern communism uses the same techniques (as portrayed, for example, in Koestler's *Darkness at Noon*) – savage threats along with promises of delightful reconciliation for the repentant sinner. Christianity, with its gallery of devils and demons and incubi – in whom it was a sin to disbelieve – used the same baleful methods, and its murderous stranglehold was not broken until the age of Galileo and Newton.

Christianity was a disaster; it would have been better if the great religion of our era had been more positive, something closer to the worship of Orpheus or Dionysus. But in the historical sense, it was still a huge step forward for the human race. For the first time in its violent history, a large portion of mankind believed completely in a dogma that was *unconnected with its everyday life*. This is of quite peculiar importance. For, as we have already observed, everyday life traps man in a small box called the present. And it destroys his long-range purpose as effectively as the black hood destroys the savageness of the hawk. Confined to the dull, unchallenging present, he turns into a vegetable. If the best is to be got out of him, he needs to be driven by purposes that galvanise him out of his passivity. Only a few men, like Alexander and Napoleon, are fortunate enough to be rescued from their boredom by the beckoning of great events. The rest of us, if we want to transcend the 'triviality of everydayness', have to create our own purpose, or look around until we find one. Most people never do. So although much can be said against Christianity, we must recognise it had one virtue that outweighed all the faults. It turned the great mass of humankind into creatures with a certain purpose. If they believed literally in demons, they also believed literally in angels and in heaven.

The first ten centuries of Christianity mark the nadir of the Magician. Everyone believed in magic, of course, but it was regarded as the province of the Devil. This must have been hard on natural mediums and witches, although the great witch scares were still some centuries ahead. A legend that came to exert enormous influence on the Middle Ages concerned a priest named Theophilus. Apparently a poor-spirited creature, he declined the offer of a bishopric because he was afraid of the responsibility; but the man who *did* accept it persecuted him until the worm turned. Theophilus approached an evil old Jew (the Jews by this time were the universal scapegoat), who conjured up the Devil. Theophilus agreed to deny Mary and Jesus (who, the Devil explained, were 'offensive to him'), and in exchange, his fortunes were reversed, his rival was unseated and he became bishop in his place. But he now began to worry about his eternal salvation, and prayed to the Virgin to help him. She eventually obtained God's pardon for Theophilus, who confessed his sin publicly, and died shortly afterwards in an atmosphere of sanctity, having burned the diabolic pact.

For some reason, this absurd story touched the imagination of Christians for a thousand years (E. M. Butler mentions the dates A.D. 600 to 1600). It was the first story of its kind: a servant of the

Church dabbling with the Devil, comes close to eternal damnation (a thought that made everyone shudder with horror), but ends by appealing to the Blessed Virgin, who has already become the symbol of tenderness and mercy in the Church. The story could be endlessly elaborated: the humiliations of Theophilus at the hands of his successful rival, the magical tricks of the Devil to unseat the rival, his fear and repentance. It 'had everything', as a Hollywood producer might say. And it started the great tradition of similar stories, which reaches a climax in the Faust legend. The old religion of the shamans was now totally forgotten. If anyone had discovered those Stone Age drawings of horned magicians in caves, it would have been regarded as proof that the men of old were in the power of the Devil before Jesus came down to save the human race.

Christianity ceased to be a religion of the oppressed after the conversion of the Emperor Constantine (A.D. 312); the Christians were suddenly 'top dog', and they proceeded to oppress with an efficiency that Nero would have envied. The Library of Alexandria – which contained, among other things, Aristotle's own collection of books – was burned down on the orders of the archbishop of Alexandria (backed by the Emperor Theodosius). Knowledge was evil; had not Adam been evicted from Paradise for wanting to know? Besides, the scholars of the Library were suspected of practising alchemy, the attempt to transmute base metals into gold and to discover the philosopher's stone, the secret of eternal life. Alchemy eventually gained a kind of respectability by declaring that its search for the philosopher's stone was a symbol of the Christian's search for mystical union with God.

Only one remarkable emperor tried to make a determined stand against this poisonous, negative religion that was conquering the West: Julian, known as 'the Apostate', Constantine's nephew. A gentle scholar, so retiring that he escaped assassination by Constantine's sons, he made a determined attempt to get rid of Christianity on his accession to the throne in 361. His ambition was to restore the pagan worship of the gods, and substitute Mithraism for Christianity as the official religion. In his letter to Sallust, *On the Sovereign Sun*, he speaks of the 'strange longing for the solar rays' that possessed him as a child, and adds that of his own accord, without the help of books or teachers, he learned 'divination by means of the heavenly bodies', i.e. astrology. Unfortunately, Julian, the man of peace, made the mistake of trying to become a warrior, and died on an expedition to Persia, only two years after he came to the throne. His old school friend the bishop of Constantinople (Gregory Nazianzen) wrote two 'invectives against Julian'; since Julian had shown him great kindness, he was forced to invent malicious motives to explain it. At all events the death of Julian was a tragedy for the Western world; if he had lived as long as the Emperor Augustus, the world would have become a better and saner place. Ibsen, in his play *Emperor and Galilean*, grasped some of Julian's importance, and the play should be read by all who are interested in the philosopher-emperor. (The other great philosopher-emperor, Marcus Aurelius, had also persecuted the Christians two centuries earlier, and this has always been held against him; but the truth seems to be that balanced, rational minds like Julian's and Marcus Aurelius's were affronted by the mixture of superstition and hysterical emotionalism in Christianity.) The thought of a long-lived Julian is one of the most regrettable might-have-beens of Western history.

It would certainly have made an immense difference to the history of magic. Pagans had no horror of magic, for they did not associate it with the Devil (or his pagan equivalent – Set, Ahriman and so on). Under Christianity, magic became Black Magic, and its power derived from demons, instead of from man's own hidden faculties. As far as magic is concerned, Christianity is an enormous red herring. 'Magic' is a natural human faculty and can be developed like any other faculty. But under Christianity, manifestations of mediumship, second sight and the rest were regarded as evidence of possession by demons or angelic intervention. The 'initiate' became either a holy man or a sorcerer. A monk who happened to possess mediumistic powers might find himself burnt alive or canonised.

An example of the latter is St. Joseph of Copertino, the 'flying monk', whose feats are well attested by many witnesses. Giuseppe Desa was born in Apulia, Italy, in 1603, a strange, sickly boy who became known as 'Open Mouth' because his mouth usually hung open; one commentator remarks that 'he was not far from what today we should call a state of feeble-mindedness';* a bishop described him as *idiota* (although the word meant innocent rather than idiotic). He was subject to 'ecstasies' and, even as a teenager, given to ascetic self-torments that undermined his health. At the age of seventeen he was accepted into the Capuchin order, but dismissed eight months later because of total inability to concentrate. Not long after, the order of Conventuals near Copertino accepted him as a stable boy, and at twenty-two he became a Franciscan priest. He continued to starve and flagellate himself, acquiring a reputation for holiness. Then one day, in the midst of his prayers after mass, he floated off the ground and landed on the altar in a state of ecstasy. He was unburned by candle flames, and flew back to his previous place.

Sent to see the Pope, he was again seized by such rapture that he rose in the air. His flying fits seem to have been always associated with the state that the Hindus called *samadhi*, ecstasy. His levitations ceased for two years when a hostile superior went out of his way to humiliate and persecute him; but after a holiday in Rome as the guest of the superior of the order, and an enthusiastic reception by the people of Assisi, he regained his good spirits and sailed fifteen

* E. J. Dingwall, *Some Human Oddities*, London, 1947.

yards to embrace the image of the Virgin on the altar.

He seems to have been a curious but simple case; floating in the air when in a state of delight seems to have been his sole accomplishment. The ecstasy did not have to be religious; on one occasion, when shepherds were playing their pipes in church on Christmas Eve, he began to dance for sheer joy, then flew on to the high altar, without knocking over any of the burning candles. Unlike Daniel Dunglas Home, St. Joseph seems to have been able to control his flights. On one occasion, when he had flown past lamps and ornaments that blocked the way to the altar, his superior called him back, and he flew back to the place he had vacated. When a fellow monk remarked on the beauty of the sky, he shrieked and flew to the top of a nearby tree. He was also able to lift heavy weights; one story tells of how he raised a wooden cross that ten workmen were struggling to place in position, and flew with it to the hole that had been prepared for it. He was also able to make others float; he cured a demented nobleman by seizing his hair and flying into the air with him, remaining there a quarter of an hour, according to his biographer; on another occasion, he seized a local priest by the hand, and after dancing around with him, they both flew, hand in hand. When on his deathbed, at the age of sixty, the doctor in attendance observed, as he cauterized a septic leg, that Fr. Joseph was floating in the air six inches above the chair. He died saying that he could hear the sounds and smell the scents of paradise.

What are we to make of such phenomena? It would be convenient if we could dismiss the whole thing as a pack of lies or as mass hysteria or hypnosis. We can certainly dismiss 95 per cent of the miracles attributed to the saints in this way without a twinge of conscience. (A typical example: St. Dunstan of Glastonbury is reported to have changed the position of the church by pushing it.) But the evidence cannot be dismissed; it is overwhelming. His feats were witnessed by kings, dukes and philosophers (or at least one philosopher – Leibnitz). When his canonisation was suggested, the Church started an investigation into his flights, and hundreds of depositions were taken. He became a saint 104 years after his death.

E. J. Dingwall, an arch sceptic in such matters, concludes an account of the friar by admitting that 'our knowledge of these things is far from adequate'.

Fr. Joseph flew. There can be no possible doubt about that. It would be pointless to ask, 'How do we explain it?' because we cannot even make a start on understanding the mechanisms involved. Home attributed his flights to spirits, rather than to his own powers. Fr. Joseph's flights undoubtedly proceeded from his own powers. The most sensible attitude is to assume that all human beings are potentially capable of flying and performing the other feats of Fr. Joseph. This is totally consistent with the view I am expounding in this book. There is a fundamenal error in the way human beings grasp the world. We think of the mind as a helpless imponderable in a world of solid matter, a mere passive observer. We take a negative view of ourselves and the world, unaware of the extent to which we control things that merely seem to 'happen'. *I* control all my physical processes, from digestion to the disposal of my waste products, by a subconscious will. Next time you urinate, try to observe the 'mental act' by which you 'unlock' the release mechanism, and you will observe that it is a kind of 'will' that involves *not willing* with your upper conscious levels. Yet it is certainly an act of will, not something that happens involuntarily. Mages and mediums are people who have accidentally acquired the power of using this 'unconscious will' to an unusual extent. They are often very simple people – like St. Joseph of Copertino – because in simple people the personal consciousness, and its will, are often undeveloped.

It is amusing to record that Leibnitz's patron and travelling companion, the Duke of Brunswick, was converted to Catholicism by the flights of Fr. Joseph – amusing because we can be almost certain that there was no connection between Fr. Joseph's beliefs and his mediumistic powers.

Another amusing touch that might provide ammunition for a sceptic is that although Fr. Joseph wore no underwear (except metal chains and such things), his flights never exposed the congregation to embarrassment; his garments were controlled by his hidden powers, or perhaps by ghostly hands, anxious to preserve his modesty.

In writing of a thing like this, one becomes aware of the total pointlessness of scepticism. It is like insisting that black is white or that two and two make five. We can talk about 'degrees of certainty', and insist that we can never 'know' whether something is true. But the weight of the evidence is such that we know that Joseph of Copertino was able to fly when he was in ecstasy as well as we know that Napoleon died on St. Helena. There is room for a tiny doubt – there is a story that Napoleon escaped from St. Helena and was accidentally shot to death in the grounds of Schonbrunn Castle in Austria,* for that matter. But when one faces the weight of evidence, it is no longer possible to take a sceptical or neutral attitude. The only important question is: What does it *mean*? And it is then that one realises that the real reason that human beings prefer not to think about a monk who could fly is that they can't think of an explanation. And while men will devote their whole lives to problems like squaring the circle or trisecting an angle, they seem to experience no similar compulsion to solve problems connected with the 'occult'. In 1923, Thomas Mann, who was then one of the best-known writers in Europe, wrote an essay called *An Experience in the Occult*, in which he described attending a séance with the medium Willi Schneider, a nineteen-year-old dental assistant. Mann held Schneider's wrists during the séance, and describes his strange twisting and sweating,

* See Frank Edwards, *Stranger than Science*, Chapter 45.

like a woman in labour – or the Delphic Oracle. Then handkerchiefs and bells flew round the room, a music box was played and the keys of a typewriter struck by the spirit-fingers of a guide called Minna. Mann testifies: 'Any mechanical deception or sleight-of-hand tricks were humanly impossible.' He wrote as an open-minded sceptic, who had taken no interest in the occult before his experience, and who took none after. He merely described flatly what he had seen, and his own theory was that the phenomena were caused by the mind of the medium, somehow turning its dreams (Schneider was in a trance) into objective realities. In view of the unimpeachable nature of Mann's testimony, one might imagine that journalists all over the world would begin to speculate how these phenomena were caused. But no one did – at least, outside 'spiritualist' circles. If the witnesses had been the Pope and the archbishop of Canterbury, it would have made no difference. It would not 'fit in', and any divorce scandal involving a member of the aristocracy is more newsworthy than an indigestible fact.

The challenge *is* to make these phenomena 'fit in' – as Einstein made the Brownian movement and the Fitzgerald contraction fit in by evolving the theory of relativity. Mann's own attempt at an explanation is expressed in these words: 'It was Hegel who said that the idea, the spirit, is the ultimate source of all phenomena; and perhaps supranormal physiology is more apt than normal to demonstrate his statement.' One might enlarge on this by saying that human beings have no idea of the extent to which they are unconsciously involved in the phenomena of their lives. We can accept the notion that my subconscious mind can make me forget an umbrella in a house I want to revisit; but not that it might, under certain circumstances, make the umbrella fly through the air.

Whether the forces that made St. Joseph float like a balloon and threw a felt ring in Thomas Mann's face were 'telekinetic', or whether St. Joseph and Willi Schneider somehow provided the energy for extra-human agencies, is a matter upon which no opinion can be ventured at this stage. But that these forces are, potentially, in the control of every human being, there can surely be no doubt.

Our ordinary human powers are odd enough. For example, anyone who has suffered from catarrh or head colds will know that a blocked sinus can be cleared by a certain kind of mental effort. Try it as an experiment. You are lying in bed on your left side, and your left sinus is blocked. Turn on to your right side, and then try to unblock the sinus by an act of concentration. It involves a kind of self-hypnotism: you imagine the point of blockage and imagine it clearing; if it starts to clear, you make additional efforts. How is this done, physiologically speaking? Not by muscles, obviously. The explanation is probably that you cause an increased flow of blood to the area.* Here, then, is an example of a 'faculty' which we all possess, but which no one bothers to develop, because it seems unimportant. But carry the experiment a stage further. Next time you feel the onset of a mild sore throat, try the same concentration treatment: focusing the source of infection and 'leaning on it', so to speak. My own experience is that this can also be made to work. (After all, we are familiar with the opposite effect; you feel a cold coming on; you go to sleep, and when you wake up, it's suddenly far worse – as if the switching off of the will had allowed the cold to make headway.) Once this trick has been learned, it is interesting to devise new experiments to test your control over your body – for example, warming cold hands or feet through concentrating (a more difficult feat, but worth persevering in). All of which seems to suggest that our powers are greater than we assume, and that we fail to grasp this through a *habit* of passivity, of drifting with the current.

Willi Schneider's mother mentioned that they would have to

---

* Which, it might be recalled, was how Edgar Cayce cured his own loss of voice.

vacate their flat because the neighbours were complaining about the strange goings-on: fists knocking on walls, disembodied hands lifting things, even a ghost showing itself in the dining room. Daniel Dunglas Home was thrown out of the home of his foster parents for similar reasons. More than a century before the remarkable feats of Joseph of Copertino, there occurred in the Dominican Friary at Berne, in Switzerland, a series of events that show much the same pattern; but in this case, they ended less satisfactorily for the friars than in the case of the flying monk.

Johann Jetzer was born in the village of Zurzach in Switzerland in about 1483. There are certain factors in common with Joseph of Copertino: the extreme poverty of his childhood, lack of schooling, early religious inclinations. He succeeded in saving enough money to persuade the Dominicans at Berne to accept him as a lay brother in 1506. He made a good impression, spending his days in prayer and fasting. But within a short time, strange disturbances began. One night, Jetzer was awakened by the ghost of a Dominican friar with a black face, who pulled the bedclothes off the bed, and explained that he was suffering on account of his sins. Jetzer was admitted to the order as a friar in 1507, and the manifestations increased. A large stone fell on the floor, doors opened and shut on their own, voices were heard, and the ghost appeared again, identifying himself as a former prior of the order who had fallen into bad ways and been murdered, since which time he had been in purgatory. He asked Jetzer to have masses said for his soul, and to scourge himself until the blood flowed. No one in the monastery took this amiss; there was nothing unusual in a spirit asking to be relieved from its well-deserved torments. The masses were said; Jetzer continued to see the spirit, who was noseless and earless (having had these organs removed when he was murdered), and the poltergeist phenomena continued to occur when the ghost was due. Finally, the ex-prior appeared complete with nose and ears, to thank the monks for delivering his soul from purgatory; he was now in a state of bliss.

To have a spirit from heaven on visiting terms was an honour for the monastery; and it might also be turned to the profit of the Dominicans in general. For the Dominicans and the Franciscans were engaged in a controversy about whether the Virgin Mary, like her son, Jesus, was conceived by supernatural means, and was therefore free of original sin. The Franciscans said she was; the Dominicans said not. Jetzer was told to ask his ghostly visitor, Fr. Heinrich Kalpurg, which opinion he favoured. The ghost said he *thought* the Immaculate Conception of Mary was true, but he would send along St. Barbara to verify it. St. Barbara arrived the following Friday and took a letter prepared by the lector of the priory, which she said she would deliver to the Blessed Virgin herself. Not long after, the Virgin appeared in Jetzer's cell, dressed in white and accompanied by St. Barbara and two small cherubs. She was able to tell Jetzer that the Dominicans were right and the Franciscans wrong; she was conceived in a perfectly normal way. (The Church declined to accept her word for it, and more than three centuries later made it an article of dogma that she had been conceived miraculously.) She appeared on a number of subsequent occasions, and performed such actions as worshipping the host (thereby proving she was not a demon in disguise) and tearing up a tract that asserted her Immaculate Conception.

The ecclesiastical authorities were approached for their advice on these strange events, and they advised caution. However, the monastery benefited from the gossip about the Virgin's visit.

But now things began to go wrong. Next time the Virgin appeared, accompanied by two angels, she picked up a wafer of the holy sacrament and declared that it would change into the flesh of her son. She replaced the wafer, now red in colour, on the table. Something made Jetzer suspicious – even though, according to him, the Virgin and the adult-size angels were suspended in the air; he leapt up and seized her hand, whereupon the white host fell from it; she had merely switched wafers by sleight-of-hand. Worse still, Jetzer recognised the hand as that of the lector, a man named Stephan Boltzhurst. The two angels turned out to be the prior, Johann Vatter, and the subprior, Franz Ueltschi. Jetzer rushed out and asked a prior from another monastery to come and witness the scene, but the visiting prelate decided not to interfere in matters that did not concern him. The next day the prior explained that the deception had been deliberately arranged to test Jetzer's powers of observation; Jetzer accepted this explanation. The Virgin appeared subsequently and confirmed the prior's explanation. She ended her visit by piercing his feet, his right side and one of his hands.

It seems to have occurred to the prior that it would now be most convenient if Jetzer were to die in his odour of sanctity, and thereby preclude the possibility of anti-climax. At all events, Jetzer became suspicious about a bowl of soup, and gave it to some wolf cubs that lived in the grounds of the priory. These died, and the subprior explained that they were probably unused to the rich spices used in the soup.

Soon after, the Virgin and St. Cecilia came to Jetzer's cell; he seized the hand of the Virgin and recognised the subprior, who again explained that they were testing his powers of observation.

The image of the Virgin in the chapel began to weep tears of blood, and then statues of Jesus and the Virgin talked to one another: He was heard asking why she wept, and she explained that it was because the honour due to Him alone was being bestowed on her – another explicit statement about the Immaculate Conception. But a neighbouring priest climbed up to examine the statue of the Virgin and declared that the tears were made of red paint.

The ecclesiastical authorities decided it was time for an investigation. Jetzer was taken before the image of the Virgin, who proceeded to instruct him in what he should say. He saw the picture of the Holy Trinity moving slightly, and looking behind it, he found the lector crouching there. Shouting that they were a pack of rogues, Jetzer dragged him out. But the prior was anxious enough about the investigation to make another attempt to convince Jetzer. St. Bernard of Clairvaux came to Jetzer's cell in the dusk and told him what to testify. But as the saint was gliding – or, Jetzer says, floating – out of the window, Jetzer observed that it wore the sandals of their own priory. This made him suspicious, and he leapt up and gave the spectre a shove, whereupon it fell out of the window and on to the flags below. Jetzer recognised the prior again.

On a subsequent occasion, the subprior and procurator, Steinegger, appeared dressed as the Virgin and St. Catherine of Siena. Jetzer was so angry he wounded the procurator in the leg with a knife, whereupon Ueltschi shouted, 'Hit the damned rascal in the face,' and Steinegger implemented the suggestion with enthusiasm. A free-for-all followed in which a window was broken.

All these strange events took place in a few months of 1507, the year Jetzer was admitted to the order. In October the examination began at Lausanne, and to begin with, it looked as though Jetzer meant to stand by his colleagues, for he affirmed the reality of the various apparitions of the Virgin. Then one day in November, he changed his mind, asked the bishop's protection and told the full story, as it has been recounted above.

The scandal rocked Switzerland. Jetzer was unfrocked. The Pope decided that a trial was required to clear the good name of the Dominicans, and this began the following July. When the four accused – the prior, subprior, lector and procurator – affirmed their innocence, they were tortured until they changed their minds. The prior held out longest; but finally, exhausted by suffering, he allowed his confession to be written down. They were not accused merely of fraud, but of a pact with the Devil, and Jetzer gave details of a séance at which several grey-bearded phantoms were called up.

The four accused were handed over to the secular arm, and in due course burned at the stake. Jetzer was banished; and only the vaguest details of his subsequent history are known: he married, took up his trade of tailoring and died in his native village in his mid-thirties.

E. J. Dingwall,* upon whose account I have drawn, is of the opinion that Jetzer was as guilty as the other four, and was perhaps even the sole guilty one. He reduces the case to the question: Was Jetzer deceiver or deceived? He does not consider the third possibility which seems to me, on the whole, most likely: that Jetzer was a medium who involuntarily caused strange things to happen when he entered the priory – perhaps, like Joseph of Copertino, in a deeply emotional condition because his lifelong wish was about to be satisfied. The apparition of the earlier prior could have been the result of an over-stimulated imagination, although this is by no means certain. It is difficult to tell at what point the prior decided that the miracles should be prolonged – that is, whether the first appearances of St. Barbara and the Virgin were genuine, in the sense of being due to Jetzer alone, or fraudulent. It is certainly suspicious that when Jetzer was given the stigmata, only one hand was pierced, suggesting that he may have performed the operation himself.

Assuming that Jetzer was basically sincere, and that at least the early phenomena were genuine, do we then conclude that the Virgin and the sinful prior really entered Jetzer's cell? This, it seems to me, would be contrary to common sense. Jetzer was probably unaware that he was responsible for the phenomena, but his unconscious mind directed them. Dingwall even reinforces this supposition by citing the strange case of the Abbé Vachère, who lived at Mirebeau, near Poitiers. The Abbé, born in 1835, was a highly respected member

* *Very Peculiar People*, London, 1950.

of the Church, well liked by the Pope himself, and approaching his sixtieth year when the phenomena began. A picture of Jesus in his private chapel showed drops of reddish moisture that seemed to ooze from its surface – in particular, from the hands and feet of the Saviour. The phenomenon occurred so often that the Bishop of Poitiers asked him to send the picture to Poitiers for examination. But when it was out of the Abbé's presence, it ceased to bleed and shed tears. As soon as it returned to Mirebeau, it started again.

The Abbé was helping some workmen who were building Stations of the Cross near his home, and pinned up another picture of Jesus in the workmen's shed; to his own amazement and embarrassment, it also began to bleed. This was too much for Rome; he was excommunicated for the Bishop of Poitiers had decided he was a fraud. The Abbé was naturally shattered. He visited friends at Aix-la-Chapelle, and a statue and picture belonging to his hostess began to bleed. The blood was analysed and found human. One sceptical investigator climbed into the Abbé's house when he was away and looked at the picture; it was dry, but during the time he spent in the room, it began to bleed; the sceptic went away convinced that the bleeding was genuine.

Although several independent investigators were convinced of the reality of the phenomena, the Church was embarrassed, and refused an investigation. The Abbé died in 1921, at the age of sixty-eight; his death was due to apoplexy. As soon as he died, the phenomena ceased.

In this case, Dingwall accepts that there was probably no fraud; he agrees that the Abbé himself produced the phenomena unconsciously. That is to say that, as in all other cases of 'miracles', the phenomena may be genuine, but they prove nothing whatever about religion, but only about the beliefs of the people concerned. Joseph of Copertino was canonised; Jetzer was defrocked and banished; Vachère was excommunicated. It would have been just as logical if all three had been canonised or burned. The case of the Abbé Vachère proves only that in the twentieth century the Church had become as cautious and nervous as the men of science in dealing with the unexplainable.

All this emphasises the difficulty of drawing a dividing line between normal and paranormal phenomena. In such famous cases of demoniacal possession as the Aix-en-Provence nuns and the Loudun nuns (brilliantly described in Aldous Huxley's *The Devils of Loudun*), one can be quite certain that the 'demons' were nonexistent in the ordinary sense, but the possessed nuns believed in them. In both these trials, a priest was accused of causing the bewitchment that made the nuns roll on the floor, shrieking and blaspheming: in the Aix-en-Provence case, Fr. Louis Gaufridi; in the other, Fr. Urbain Grandier. In both cases, the priest had taken advantage of the intimacy of the confessional to seduce young girls who later became nuns. Gaufridi's accuser was the teenager Madeleine de la Palud, who at one point admitted in court that her accusations were 'all imaginings, illusions, without a word of truth in them', and that she 'swooned for the love of Gaufridi'. She then began to quiver with erotic frenzy, her hips moving up and down with the movements of copulation. Both Gaufridi and Grandier were tortured and burned to death. The antics of the possessed nuns went no further than blaspheming, making lewd suggestions, rolling on the ground in a way that displayed the part of the body that was the root of the trouble. Although their possession enabled the nuns to roar in strange voices like demons, it conferred no other unusual powers on them, and in the case of the Loudun nuns, tests to see whether the demons had given them the gift of extrasensory perception were unsuccessful. But if the psychological disturbance had been greater, the results might well have been positive. The dividing line between normal and paranormal had been reached, but not crossed, by the possessed nuns.

The belief in hordes of spirits and demons may be considered the chief contribution of Christianity to the study of magic. Josephus mentions a book of spells and incantations for summoning demons that was in use as early as the first century A.D. Its author was supposed to be King Solomon, who figures in occult mythology as a great magician. A magical work known as *The Key of Solomon* ranks next to the legendary *Emerald Tablets* of Hermes Trismegistus as the most celebrated of magical texts. It exists in many forms, and the reason for this is curious and significant: the text had to be copied out by hand by each person who wished to use it; a printed text would have no virtue.* This makes it as clear as could be that the basic necessity for the performance of magic is the mind of the magician himself. He must enter into a deep, intimate relation with the text, for it is *his* powers that are going to be used. In the same way, the magician must make his own magical instruments, including pen, ink, water-sprinkler, inkwell, sand-shaker, incense, candles, and forge his own knives, sword, hatchet and so on. He must furnish these weapons with engraved wooden handles. He must also choose and inscribe his own wand and staff. The handles of the knives had to be made of boxwood, and the branch had to be cut at one blow; presumably the would-be magician went on making tremendous swipes until he either lopped off a branch or broke the sword. Before commencing his magical operations, the magician must fast for nine days and observe all kinds of rules. The ritual begins with the tracing of a magic circle with the knife; it must then be inscribed with symbols from the Kabbalah. A lamb has to be slaughtered and skinned, and its tanned skin used as parchment for inscribing magical symbols, such as pentacles.

The ritual invocation itself lasts about an hour, and includes threats to the spirit if they fail to appear. But by this time, according to the *Key*, they should have appeared – some dressed like soldiers, others like noblemen, finally the King himself, accompanied by

---

* A belief that is also accepted by most modern 'witches'.

magicians. At this point, after identifying himself, burning incense and showing symbols to the King (presumably the Devil, or at least a minor potentate of hell), the magician can ask what he wants: whether it is information about the future or the aid of the demons in performing sorcery. The name of God and Jesus is repeated many times to keep the spirits subdued. Finally, they must be dismissed courteously, with still more invocations. The magic circle must not be broken, or the magician might be torn to pieces by demons.

Benvenuto Cellini, in his memoirs, has a remarkable passage describing how a certain necromancer-priest performed these rituals in the Colosseum in Rome.

> He gave the pentacle to his necromancer friend to hold, and he put the rest of us in charge of the fire for the perfumes. And then he began his incantations. All this lasted for over an hour and a half. Several legions [of demons] appeared, till the Colosseum was filled with them. I was busy with the precious perfumes, and when the priest saw so many devils, he turned to me and said: 'Benvenuto, ask them something.' So I asked them to bring me together with my Sicilian girl, Angelica. We were given no reply at all that night; but I was more than satisfied with what I had seen.*

Understandably. And on a subsequent occasion, the results were even more startling and impressive. The necromancer said that they needed an innocent young boy to get the best results, so Cellini took his shop boy, a twelve-year-old named Cenci.

> The necromancer began to make terrible incantations, calling up by name a whole host of major demons and commanding them by virtue and power of the uncreated, living and eternal God, in Hebrew, as well as in Latin and Greek. The result was

* Translated by George Bull, Penguin Classics, p. 121.

that in a short space of time the Colosseum was filled with a hundred times more demons than there had been on the previous occasion.

We assume Cellini could not actually see them, for he does not say so. He certainly couldn't hear them, for when the necromancer told him to ask about the Sicilian girl, Cellini did not hear their reply; it was the necromancer who told him that he would be with her within a month. (This proved to be accurate.)

At this point, the boy Cenci, who apparently *could* see them, became panic-stricken, and his terror affected the others, including the necromancer, whose voice shook so much that he was not able to sound the right note of command in dismissing them. He decided to do it by the less polite expedient of burning asafoetida, a resin that burns with a stink like garlic and onions. One of the acolytes contributed his own assistance by filling his trousers. 'The tremendous stench and noise made the boy lift his head a little, and when he heard me laughing he plucked up courage and said that the demons were running away like mad.' However, as they walked home the boy saw two or three demons following them, bounding along on the rooftops or the ground.

Cellini's story does not end there. The priest-necromancer persuades him to join him in consecrating a book to the Devil which will enable them to discover buried treasure. He assures Cellini that the demons will keep their promise about the girl, but adds that he will be in great danger first. Cellini then gets involved in a quarrel in the street, and throws a handful of mud at his opponent; the mud contains a sharp stone, and the man falls unconscious, his head bleeding. One of Cellini's rivals for papal favours passes by, sees what has happened and tells the Pope that Cellini has murdered one of his favourite craftsmen. The Pope orders that Cellini be hanged immediately, and he is forced to flee to Naples. There he finds his

Sicilian girl, and they spend a delightful night. In the night, Cellini remembers that his night with the demons took place precisely one month ago. 'So anyone who meddles with spirits should bear in mind what tremendous risks I ran.'

When Cellini's book first reached print – two hundred years after his death in 1551 – there were many who felt that it was mostly lies and braggadocio. Since that time, historical research has revealed the accuracy of so much of it that many reputable authorities – A. J. Symonds and E. M. Butler, for example – now believe that Cellini was remarkably truthful.

Assuming that his account is basically accurate, we may either dismiss it on naturalistic grounds – after all, Cellini does not say that he actually saw or heard anything unusual – or accept that *something* took place in the Colosseum, even if it was not what the necromancer claimed. The ceremony was, in effect, a séance, and something certainly seems to have been conjured up. The necromancer had no doubt it was demons. Aldous Huxley remarks of Fr. Surin, the exorcist in the Loudun affair: 'The notion that ESP might be a natural faculty, latent in all minds and manifest in a few, never seems, for a single instant, to have entered his head … Either the phenomena of telepathy and clairvoyance did not exist, or they were the work of spirits whom one might presume … to be devils.'

The insistence on the magician personally copying the manuscript offers the important clue. Otherwise, the modern reader is bound to dismiss all the lengthy preparations and incantations as superstitious mumbo jumbo. What practical difference can it make that the sword should be of 'virgin iron' and wrapped in white silk? Obviously none, if we think in terms of mechanical operations of nature; the sword is not going to trigger any natural process or chain reaotion. Then what is the purpose of these complex operations. if not to delude the gullible?

The answer is surely: to drive the mind to make an *abnormal* effort, to summon its hidden powers. The aspirant must put his whole *will* into the ritual, trying to use it like a sledge-hammer, preventing the usual leakage of energy. The long preparatory fast is intended to induce the same feeling of seriousness as the fasting and cleansing that precede the Orphic and Eleusinian mysteries.

But in order to understand the underlying spirit of the magic that flourished so unexpectedly in the sixteenth century (and the years 1500 to 1600 undoubtedly were the century of magic), it is necessary to understand something of the mysticism that inspired it. For it cannot be stated too often that the essence of magic and the essence of mysticism are one and the same; the crucial difference is that magic lies at the lower end of the spectrum, mysticism at the higher. Both magic and mysticism are an attempt to get into tune with an 'inner force'. Plotinus (A.D. 205–270) was not a Christian, but his influence on Christian mystics was enormous; he compared human beings to the choir standing around a choir master but with their attention distracted by things going on about them, so they fail to sing in tune or in time. He held that creation was a series of steps leading away from the One (or God); he called those steps emanations. (The Kabbalists later borrowed his ideas, as William Blake was to borrow from the Kabbalah.) This is definitely a non-Christian view, for Plotinus's evil is a negative thing, depending upon how many steps you have taken away from the One; it is like someone walking away from a lighted house at night, moving further into the darkness of the garden. But why should people walk away, unless tempted by the Devil? Because, says Plotinus, we are empty-headed, and easily distracted. The philosopher is the man who determinedly ignores distractions and multiplicity, and tries to see back towards the One. 'Such,' he concludes, 'is the life of gods and of godlike men; a liberation from all earthly bonds, a life that takes no pleasure in earthly things, a flight of the alone to the alone.'

This is the intoxicating idea at the heart of mysticism; and in spite of the apparent difference of aim, it is not far from the divine intoxication of the Dionysians. It is the feeling that this banal world in which we appear to be stuck *can be escaped*. We are all in the position of some dazed person wandering around after an accident, not knowing where he is going to – only half-conscious. A mystic is a man who has partly 'come to'. He has caught a glimpse of what life and death are really about.

One of the earliest and most influential of Christian mystics was Dionysius the Areopagite, who was supposed to be the Dionysius who was converted by St. Paul, but almost certainly wasn't. His mystical works are meditations on the theme of God, whom he defines, after the manner of Plotinus and the Kabbalists, as a kind of divine darkness and emptiness. How can this God be the personal God of the Christians? Dionysius explains that God is the cause of goodness and beauty while remaining behind and above them. His enormous appeal and influence prove again that the creature who had not long ago been a kind of ape had developed 'divine longings', like a caterpillar trying to turn into a butterfly. All the mystics emphasise the deep peace and silence of the mystical experience. St. Catherine of Siena talks of merging with an 'ocean of rest'. Meister Eckhart begins his first sermon by quoting the Wisdom of Solomon: 'For while peaceful silence enwrapped all things ...' although it has no particular relevance to the sermon. St. John of the Cross says that illumination comes 'in silence and rest, far from all things tangible or natural'. Gertrude of Helfta describes how her illumination occurred when she 'sat down by a fishpond and contemplated the loveliness of the place; the limpidity of the flowing water, the deep green of the surrounding trees, the free flight of the birds and especially the pigeons, but above all the solitary calm of the secluded site filled me with delight'. The 'subconscious tension' I have discussed in

Chapter 2 disappears; the mind ceases to be blurred and turbulent. An immense peace springs up in the depths of the mind like a cool spring; and with a sudden shock, man catches a glimpse of his potentialities.

It is only one step from the tradition of 'esoteric Christianity' to the world of the alchemist and the astrologer. Albertus Magnus (1206–1280) writes: 'The alchemist shall live in loneliness, remote from men. He must be silent and discreet ...' He must also choose 'the right hour for his operations' – that is, when the heavenly bodies are propitious. And a later philosopher and occultist added, in a letter to Cornelius Agrippa: 'To the vulgar, speak only of vulgar things; keep for your friends every secret of a higher order ...' This was Trithemius, a man who, according to tradition, took shelter in a Benedictine monastery in a snowstorm, and became so enamoured of the peace and privacy that he joined the order, later becoming the abbot of the monastery.

Magic shares another fundamental principle with mysticism: the notion 'As above, so below' (attributed to Hermes Trismegistus). In mysticism, this means that the soul and God are one and the same. In magic, the principle is altogether more complicated. Man is the 'microcosm', whose symbol is a five-pointed star (or pentacle); the universe is the macrocosm, and its symbol is the six-pointed star (or two triangles interlaced – the symbol of Solomon). The occultists of the Middle Ages and the Reformation saw man and the universe connected by thousands of invisible bonds. (Paracelsus, for example, believed there was a connection between the seven organs of the body and the seven planets.) To use a modern analogy, one might say that the relation of the individual to the universe is like the relation of the white corpuscles of the blood to the whole man: they are separate organisms, yet they are certainly not independent; their purpose is geared to that of the whole body. Man may feel separate from the rest of the universe, but he is not, according to occult doctrine; there are a thousand 'correspondences' between man and the macrocosm. Paracelsus would have found nothing strange in David Foster's notion of an 'intelligent universe' in which cosmic rays may carry coded information that can influence the genes; it was exactly what he meant by 'As above, so below'.

This, then, was the conception that underlay all the magic of the 'hermetic century', 1500 to 1600. *Man is an organ in the body of the universe.*

The common magical beliefs fitted in with this notion. St. Albertus Magnus himself, a revered theologian rather than an occultist (he was canonised in 1931), explains at length how various precious stones can be used for medical and moral purposes: the amethyst increases concentration; the emerald induces chastity; the agate strengthens the teeth and drives away phantoms and snakes. Among herbs, betony produces the power of prophecy, and verbena is a love charm. Feverwort could cure fever; liverwort, diseases of the liver. Another widespread belief was that if a man received injury from any physical object – a knife, hatchet, stone, etc. – the object should also be treated for the injury it had caused. A hatchet with which a butcher cut himself was covered with the same salve as his wound and hung behind the door; when the butcher experienced pains one day, it was found that the hatchet had fallen on the floor.

All this sounds so absurd as to be hardly worth mentioning. But to dismiss it would be a mistake. For the oddest thing is that such remedies often worked. They still do. A neighbour of mine in Cornwall, an old countryman, told me a story of how his dog had been cured of an adder-bite by a 'charmer'. But before he took the dog to the charmer, he tied a piece of holly bark under its collar – the dog had been bitten on the jaw – to stop the poison spreading. The next morning, the dog's head was badly swollen, but the poison had not spread to the rest of the body.

Why should such a preposterous remedy work? Presumably for the same reason that the charm also worked on the dog, and for the same reasons that the prayers of Christian Scientists often work. Mary Baker Eddy's teacher, Phineas Quimby, asserted that healing powers are more common than we suppose; in fact, that like the power of dowsing, *everybody* possesses them to some degree.*

And what of that other foundation stone of magic, belief in the stars? How can this be reconciled with common sense? Again, we must begin by recognising that astrology *can* produce remarkable results. Johannes Kepler, the founder of modern astronomy, had a grumpy dislike of astrology, perhaps because he was forced to produce a yearly 'almanac' as part of his duties at Graz in the last decade of the sixteenth century. His first almanac contained prophecies of an intense cold spell, and of an invasion by the Turks. In 1594 the cold was so intense that many died of it, and the Turks devastated the country from Vienna to Neustadt. Kepler wrote: ['The heavens] act on [a man] during his life in the manner of the loops which a peasant ties at random around the pumpkins in his field; they do not cause the pumpkin to grow, but they determine its shape …'

The science of men like Albertus Magnus, Cornelius Agrippa and Paracelsus may have been crude and defective, but it was based on this instinctive recognition of the psychic links between man and nature. The science of Newton, Huygens and Priestley was incomparably more accurate, but it had lost belief in the invisible links. Man was merely a conscious intelligence in an alien universe. Kierkegaard expressed the feeling two centuries later when he wrote: 'Where am I? Who am I? How did I come to be here? What is this thing called the world? … And if I am compelled to take part in it, where is the director? I want to see the director …' There was the sense of being cast up, helpless, high and dry.

* Spiritualists believe that 'spirits' are actively engaged in healing and protecting.

The occultists of the sixteenth century, for all their absurd superstitions, knew something that Kierkegaard had forgotten.

The two great occultists of the sixteenth century, Cornelius Agrippa and Paracelsus, were not 'initiates' in the esoteric sense of the word. Both were wandering scholars rather than philosophers. Of the two, Paracelsus was the greater intellect.

Agrippa's real name was apparently Henry Cornelis, and he was born in Cologne in 1486. An early biographer, Henry Morley, asserts that he came of a noble family called Von Nettesheim; others take a more sceptical view and assert that he called himself Agrippa von Nettesheim after the founder of Cologne (and after a village near Cologne). At all events, his parents were sufficiently well-off to have him educated at the newly formed University of Cologne.

He was a natural mystic, preferring Plato to Aristotle, and studying the neo-Platonist philosophers – Plotinus, Iamblichus, Porphyry and Proclus. He had something in common with the last, for Proclus (410–485) was a wealthy and handsome young Greek who intended to become a lawyer, but was bitten by the bug of philosophy and devoted his life to its study; he was the last great Platonist. Proclus asserted that human consciousness can, in a kind of divine madness, leap into the One at the heart of all things and become united with it. Agrippa was deeply influenced by this view, which he also found in the Kabbalah, whose major section, the *Zohar* (Book of Creation), was written down by a Spanish Jew, Moses de Leon, around 1280. Both Proclus and the Kabbalah talk about a number of 'emanations' from the ultimate godhead, and about a complex path that the adept can follow in order to approach the godhead.

Agrippa was bitten. Unfortunately he lacked the temperament of the philosopher. In most respects, he was a Renaissance man, dynamic, adventurous, endlessly curious. He possessed the longing for mystical illumination without possessing the temperament for it. His life is basically tragic. Besides, the age in which he lived was too extrovert and turbulent to allow much peace to a man of his temper.

In his late teens, Agrippa made a considerable impression at Cologne. He was a good linguist and an omnivorous reader. (Printing had been invented just before his birth.) When he became coutt secretary to the king of Rome and Germany, Maximilian the First, it looked like the start of a brilliant career. But the Holy Roman court was hardly the place for a scholar; Maximilian used him as a spy, and sent him, at the age of twenty, to Paris. At the University of Paris, he made contact with a few kindred spirits, occultists and philosophers. There he met a Spanish nobleman named Gerona, who was on his way to see Maximilian. Gerona was in trouble; there had been a revolt of peasants, and he had been thrown out of his estate in Catalonia. Agrippa decided to help him.

The story of how he did this, or tried to, provides some of the most exciting pages of Morley's biography, and deserves to be outlined here to give some idea of Agrippa's resourceful character. He devised plans whereby Gerona's chief stronghold, the Black Fort, could be retaken by cunning. The plan succeeded, and as a consequence, Agrippa became unpopular with the peasantry. There was a general revolt, and it looked as though Agrippa would be cut off in a stronghold at Villarodona. Three miles away, in rugged mountain territory, there was a half-ruined tower that stood among bogs and pools of stagnant water. Agrippa decided he could defend this better than Villarodona, and moved there before the rebels arrived. There was a mountain behind it, and it was approached up a narrow valley, which they blocked with overturned carts. The infuriated peasants, determined to have the blood of 'the German', made unsuccessful attempts to break the barrier, then decided to starve out the garrison. Two months dragged by.

One of the garrison was a good climber; he scaled the rocky walls above them, and reached the mountaintop. From there he could see a lake known as the Black Lake, on the other side of which there was a monastery. The abbot would certainly help them if they could get a message to him, but they had no boat, and the only way to do this was to go through the rebels, since the lake was surrounded by wall-like cliffs.

Agrippa disguised a youth to look like a leper, staining his skin with the juice of the milk-thistle and other herbs and then painting it with leprous spots. A letter was hidden in a hollow of the boy's staff and a bell hung round his neck. At night he was led across the marshes by his father, who knew the road; it was necessary to approach the encamped peasants from another angle if they were not to guess where he came from. Stammering and slavering, he walked among them, and they all retreated as far as possible. Later, he returned in the same way, carrying instructions from the abbot. That night, the garrison prepared to move out. Towards dawn, they fired a volley at the peasants to show they were still there, then retreated quietly, and followed their guide up the steep mountainside. They rested at the top and ate breakfast, looking anxiously across the lake. At 9 a.m. they saw two fishing boats coming towards them, and they fired off their guns, as a signal to the boats and a gesture of defiance at the rebels. The descent to the lake took most of the day, down a rocky gully; they knew they couldn't be caught now. That evening, August 14, 1508, they ate their first good meal for two months in the monastery.

But the mission had hardly been successful. Gerona had somehow been captured by the peasants, and presumably killed. So Agrippa's courage and resourcefulness had been wasted. And this was typical of his life. He was not born for real success.

There would be no point in detailing Agrippa's travels around Europe – Barcelona, Majorca, Sardinia, Italy, Avignon, Lyons, Dole, Chalon-sur-Saône, then back to Dole, where Agrippa lectured on the system of the Hebrew scholar Reuchlin, another Kabbalist.

Agrippa was fascinated by the Kabbalah, not only by its mystical aspects but by its 'magical' doctrines; particularly the number science known as Gematria. In Hebrew, letters all have a numerical value. The letters in a word were added up, and any other word that added up to the same number was regarded as being related to the first. So that if a practitioner of Gematria wanted to know whether a certain girl would make a suitable wife, he would add up the letters of her name, and if the sum was the same as the letters of 'whore' or 'spendthrift', it was too bad for her. If she was also an adept in Gematria, she might point out that they also added up to 'wisdom' or 'virtuous'. Luther and his enemies spent a great deal of time turning one another's names into insulting epithets by Gematria.

Agrippa's exposition of these secrets at the University of Dole gained him many admirers, a degree as Doctor of Divinity and some kind of salary. He fell in love, and seems to have hoped to settle down under the patronage of Maximilian's daughter Margaret of Ghent; he even wrote an essay called *The Nobility of Women* to flatter her. But his interest in the Kabbalah made him enemies among narrow-minded monks, and a Franciscan friar denounced him from the pulpit when Margaret was in the congregation. As usual, Agrippa's luck ran out, and he moved on to England.

By this time, he had written his major work, the three-volume treatise *On Occult Philosophy*, although this had to wait more than twenty years for publication. It is a remarkable work for a man of twenty-four. He begins by stating clearly that magic is nothing to do with sorcery or the devil, but with various occult gifts – prophecy, second sight and so on. A typical chapter of the first volume is entitled 'Of Light, Colours, Candles and Lamps, and to what Stars, Houses and Elements several Colours are ascribed.' The 'houses', of course, refers to the signs of the zodiac; each planet has two, one for the day and one for the night. But his central belief is stated at the beginning of the sixty-third chapter: 'The fantasy, or imaginative power, has a ruling power over the passions of the soul, when these are bound to sensual apprehensions.' That is to say, when my passions are bound up with physical things, rather than with ideas, my imagination begins to play a large part in my feelings. Some slight depression sends my spirits plummeting; I become a victim of a seesaw of emotion. The next sentence is slightly obscure, but expands this idea: 'For [imagination] does, of its own accord, according to the diversity of the passions, first of all change the physical body with a sensible transmutation, by changing the accidents in the body, and by moving the spirit upward or downward, inward or outward ...' This is a remarkable sentence to have been written in 1510. It not only recognises the extent to which human beings, especially stupid ones, are the victims of auto-suggestion, but also that these moods affect the body *directly*. There is always present in hermetic literature this suggestion that man's body is more dependent on his will than he ever realises. Agrippa goes on to point out that lovers can experience such a strong tie that they feel one another's illnesses. People can die of sadness, when the will becomes inoperative. These doctrines of Agrippa might be compared with the assertion of Paracelsus, seven years his junior, that 'Resolute imagination is the beginning of all magical operations,' and that 'It is possible that my spirit ... through an ardent will alone, and without a sword, can stab and wound others.' The talk of Gematria and correspondences may or may not be nonsense (there is probably more in it than meets the eye); but we are here dealing with men who are magicians because they are shamans, possessors of psychic powers. It is true that we do not possess direct evidence of this: no anecdotes revealing powers of prophecy or second sight. There are plenty of anecdotes about the magical powers of both Agrippa and Paracelsus, but nothing that can be taken seriously. It must be remembered that we are dealing with a remote epoch when popular credulity was unfathomable; a story had to be fantastic to raise an eyebrow. The kind of events that would interest the Society for Psychical Research – prevision, spectres of the living, thaumaturgy, telepathy – would have been dismissed as too dull to be worth re-telling. All the stories about Agrippa that have come down to us are sensational. He paid innkeepers in gold coins that looked genuine enough but which turned into shells later. He had a black dog as a familiar, and one day fearing that he had sunk too far into the Devil's clutches, ordered it to leave him, whereupon it rushed out and leapt into the River Saône. He summoned the spirit of Tully to deliver one of his orations before the elector of Saxony, and the spirit reduced everybody to tears.

One of the best-known stories tells of how Agrippa left the key of his workroom with his wife. A student lodging with them begged her for the key until she gave it to him; he went into the room and looked at the book of spells that lay on the table. As he was reading, a demon appeared, and asked why he had been summoned. The terrified student could only stammer, and the demon seized him by the throat and strangled him. When Agrippa returned he realised that he would be accused of murdering the student. Whereupon the demon was conjured up again, and ordered to restore the dead man to life for a short time. The student, now apparently alive and in good health, walked up and down the marketplace several times, then suddenly collapsed and died of a heart attack. However, close examination of the body revealed that he had been strangled, and Agrippa was forced to flee from the town.

Such stories tell us nothing about Agrippa, although the last one reflects accurately the bad luck that pursued him all his life. Two wives died, and the third proved disastrous, leaving him emotionally shattered and financially ruined. His clashes with the priesthood – he was violently anticlerical, having had many experiences of the ignorance and jealousy of monks – drove him out of many towns where he might have expected to settle down to a life of peaceful study. At different times he lectured on theology at Cologne, on occultism at Pavia, and became public advocate at Metz, where his defence of a peasant woman on a charge of sorcery led to a clash with the inquisitor that forced him to leave. His hopes of advancement from Margaret of Ghent fell through; an appointment as physician to the queen mother of France, Louise of Savoy, was even more disastrous; he spent most of his time trying to collect his salary, and was confined to Lyons from 1524 to 1526 without money and without permission to leave. It is hardly surprising that he eventually began to feel persecuted. He wanted the quiet life of a scholar, with a pleasant domestic background. He was a genuine mystic, and as he got older, began to feel that magic was a waste of time and that only theology was worth studying. Although he decided not to publish his book on the occult until 1531, he was known as a magician, and his reputation among priests and clerics was bad. In 1530 he published at Antwerp a book, *On the Vanity of Sciences and Arts*, a curious, nihilistic work, whose central thesis is that knowledge only brings man to disillusionment and recognition of how little he knows. It reads like an anticipation of Faust's speech in Act I of Goethe's play. The only worthwhile study, says Agrippa, is theology and scripture. He was undoubtedly sincere. Life had dealt him some hard blows. His second wife died of the plague in Antwerp; his book on the vanity of science outraged his patron, Charles V, who had given Agrippa an appointment as a chronicler of history, and Agrippa was thrown into jail and declared a heretic. The publication of his *Occult Philosophy* only worsened the situation, for it looked like a complete retraction of all he had said in the previous book, and gave him a reputation for inconsistency. Back in Cologne, he fell foul of the Inquisition; he went to France, but made some bitter remarks about the late queen mother and was jailed again. He died in Grenoble in 1535, not yet fifty years of age, worn out and defeated, hated by half the monks in Europe. It was a sad end for the disciple of Plotinus and Proclus, whose deepest desire was for a life of meditation and philosophy, but whose adventurous and impatient temperament drove him to travel like the Wandering Jew.

It may be mentioned, in passing, that one of the legends of Agrippa concerns a visit paid to his alchemical laboratory in Florence by the Wandering Jew himself. (In David Hoffman's *Chronicles of Cartaphilus, the Wandering Jew*, the date is given as 1525.) Cartaphilus begged Agrippa to show him his childhood sweetheart in a magic mirror. Agrippa asked him to count off the decades since the girl died so that he could wave his wand for each decade; when the Jew reached 149, Agrippa began to feel dizzy; but the Jew went on numbering them until the mirror showed a scene 1,510 years earlier, in Palestine. The girl, Rebecca, appeared, and the Jew was so moved that he tried to speak to her – which Agrippa had strictly forbidden. The mirror immediately clouded over and the Jew fainted. On reviving, he identified himself as the Jew who struck Jesus when he was carrying the cross, and who has been condemned to walk the earth ever since.

Another legend declares that Agrippa was able to show the Earl of Surrey his beautiful mistress, Geraldine, in the same magic mirror.

Agrippa's own claims to have contacted the dead and summoned spirits for divination seem to indicate beyond doubt that he was a gifted medium rather than a 'magician'. He describes, for example, how to use a sieve for vaticination (prophecy); it must be suspended from a pair of forceps or pincers, and these in turn must be pivoted between the two index fingers of two assistants. This can be used for establishing the identity of criminals; the names of all suspects must be repeated in the presence of the sieve, which will begin to swing when the guilty person is named. Another method, Agrippa says, is to balance the sieve on a pivot and spin it; it should stop when the guilty person is named. 'More than thirty years since, I made use of this manner of divination three times,' says Agrippa. 'The first time was on the occasion of a theft that had been committed; the second on account of certain nets or snares of mine used for catching birds, which had been destroyed by some envious one; and the third time in order to find a lost dog which belonged to me and by which I set great store. In every said attempt I succeeded; yet I stopped notwithstanding after that last time for fear lest the demon should entangle me in his snares.'* If this method of divination actually worked, as Agrippa claims, then it was clearly a matter of mediumship, and it is interesting that Agrippa believed the 'spirits' he summoned to be demons, as did Cellini's necromancer-priest.

The career of Paracelsus resembles that of Agrippa in many respects, although he was less of an adventurer, more a single-minded student of medicine and science. He was brilliant; he was also noisy and belligerent (the word 'bombast' is derived from his name, Bombastus).

Philippus Aureolus Paracelsus, whose real name was Theophrastus Bombastus von Hohenheim, was born in the village of Einsiedeln, near Zurich, in Switzerland, in 1493. He was the son of a doctor, William Bombastus von Hohenheim. The child was frail and so weak that he was not expected to reach adulthood. He studied at Basel, then went to Würzburg to study under the abbot Trithemius, whose occult books fascinated the aspiring physician. Like Agrippa, he was a romantic, passionately attracted to the idea of discovering the Philosopher's Stone or the Elixir of Life or the Grand Catholicon, a remedy that was supposed to be good for any illness.

At the age of twenty-two, Paracelsus – as he now called himself, after the Roman physician Celsus – worked for a year in the silver

---

* Quoted by De Givry, p. 300.

mines of the Tyrol, then decided that he wanted to see more of the world and began a period of wandering that lasted for nine years. His aim, he declared, was to acquire medical knowledge by seeing the widest possible range of patients.

It is important to realise that Paracelsus never thought of himself as a magician or occultist. On the contrary, his temperament was thoroughly empirical and toughminded. He believed in alchemy and astrology because they seemed sensible, scientific things to believe in; but he was intensely sceptical about remedies that involved any form of 'magic', sympathetic or otherwise. This disposition was reinforced when he met in Paris a very remarkable man, Ambroise Paré, who was to become one of the great geniuses of medicine. Paré was never prepared to do what had been done before merely because everyone took it for granted. When he went to war as an army surgeon in 1537, wounds were cauterized by pouring boiling oil into them. Paré decided to try an ointment of egg yolk, rose oil and turpentine, and discovered that wounds treated with this healed faster; he concluded, correctly, that more soldiers had died of shock and exhaustion than of their wounds. When limbs were shattered by cannon shot, it was the custom to allow them to gangrene, then hack them off with a saw; Paré tried tying the bleeding arteries with ordinary thread, and discovered that when the bleeding was stopped, the soldier recovered more often than not.

All this happened some years after his first meeting with Paracelsus, but the attitude was already formed; he and Paracelsus exerted a mutually beneficial influence. The wanderings continued, according to his biographer John Hargrave: Italy, Germany, Denmark – where Paracelsus gained experience of war in King Christian II's campaign against Sweden – even Russia. He was a natural healer: that is, he had more than a touch of the thaumaturgist. He wrote, 'Magic is a teacher of medicine preferable to all the written books.' But his definition of magic is a 'power that comes direct from God' and somehow conferred on the doctor. It is a kind of instinct for healing. And this instinct, says Paracelsus, is based upon the knowledge that man is the 'microcosm' of nature. Health is based upon some kind of harmony between man and nature. There is a fundamental principle of life which the alchemists call 'azoth' and symbolise by a red lion. The word also means 'essence'. Azoth can convert all metals into gold. There is a story told by Sudhoff that Paracelsus cured the daughter of an innkeeper who had been paralysed from the waist downwards since birth with teaspoonfuls of wine and his 'azoth of the red lion'. Whether this means that he cured her by 'mental power' rather than medicine is not clear, but it seems likely, in view of his statement that a good physician depends on a natural 'magic'. Paracelsus also gave the name 'azoth' to his sword, of which he was so fond that it was said he slept width it in his bed.

In 1524, he settled for a time at Basel, where he was appointed to the chair of medicine. He commenced his tenure by ordering his students to light a bonfire and throwing into it the works of Galen, Avicenna, Rhazes and other noted physicians of antiquity, shouting that they were all less gifted than the hairs of his beard. The rest of the professors of the school of medicine denounced him as a charlatan and exhibitionist, and tried hard to get him expelled from the university; but the authorities stood by him. He was noisy, eccentric, dogmatic – 'always drunk and always lucid', says one authority. He had a remarkable talent for invective, and told his colleagues: 'You are nothing but teachers and masters combing lice and scratching. You are not worthy that a dog should lift his hind leg against you. Your prince Galen is in hell, from whence he has sent letters to me, and if you knew what he told me, you would make the sign of the cross on yourselves with a fox's tail.' His language was always colourful.

His fortunes fluctuated at a dizzying rate. He had cured the publisher Frobenius of a septic leg, which the publisher's physicians had wanted to amputate, and his treatment of Erasmus for gout and kidney trouble led the great scholar to write 'I cannot offer thee a fee equal to thy art and learning.' But when he cured a prominent citizen, Canon Lichtenfels, who had offered a fee of a hundred gulden, the canon declined to pay up, and Paracelsus had to take him to court. Although he was clearly in the right, his enemies somehow influenced the verdict, which went against him. Paracelsus was never a man to take insult lying down; he produced a remarkable stream of execration, in which the mildest epithets were 'wormy lousy sophists'. It was contempt of court, and Paracelsus decided that the best way to stay out of jail was to leave Basel. His enemies rejoiced; they had always been certain that he would go too far.

Like Cornelius Agrippa, Paracelsus was a split personality. His medical and scientific genius were beyond question. But he was also a showman. His manners were bouncy and vulgar; his clothes were usually creased and shabby; he was a fat, bald man who often became red in the face. Agrippa was born unlucky; Paracelsus made his own bad luck by losing his temper so easily. In Strasbourg he was asked to dispute with Vendelinus, a defender of Galen. Vendelinus was long-winded and pompous, but Paracelsus played into his hands by snorting, 'I will not condescend to answer such rubbish,' and stalking out. Naturally, Vendelinus's supporters asserted that he was unable to reply. Another instance: the margrave of Baden was on the point of death from dysentery, which had completely exhausted him. Paracelsus gave him a potion which, he claimed, contained semi-precious stones ground to powder, and then put him to sleep with laudanum; the margrave woke up feeling better. He was so delighted that he handed Paracelsus a jewel for payment. It was not a very valuable jewel, but princes are capable of meanness. Instead of taking it with simulated gratitude and allowing the margrave to spread the story of the remarkable cure, Paracelsus lost his temper and declared that he usually sent in an account for his services, and that he was grossly insulted. Princes do not like being spoken to in that way; the natural result was that the margrave decided that his own doctors were correct when they said that they had cured him before Paracelsus came on the scene, and that there was not time for Paracelsus's remedies to work, and so on. Paracelsus wore the jewel around his neck as a reminder of the ingratitude of princes; he would have done better to forget it.

His defender Frobenius was no longer alive to support him; he had died as a result of a stroke that came from ignoring Paracelsus's advice about overstraining his heart, but Paracelsus was blamed for his death. He left Basel, and became a wanderer for the rest of his life. His character did not improve. He brooded on his wrongs and tongue-lashed his opponents at every opportunity; he continued to drink too much, and dressed like a tramp. His indignation made him pour out manuscripts, but he found it difficult to persuade publishers to print them. (Most of his works came out long after his death.) For some reason he was refused admission to the town of Innsbruck. After thirteen years of this kind of life, he was tired and discouraged, like Agrippa, whose last years had been just as harassed. The Prince Palatine, Archbishop Duke Ernst of Bavaria, invited him to come and stay in Salzburg; the Duke was a student of the occult. Paracelsus arrived in April 1541. It seemed to be a perfect haven, the place he had been searching for all his life. But the sudden relaxation after fourteen years of hardship and insult was the worst thing that could have happened to him; he died in September, at the age of forty-eight. One story claims that he was poisoned, another that he was pushed from the top of a cliff; the truth is probably that he was worn out.

Paracelsus was greater than Cornelius Agrippa for only one reason: his deeper insight into the nature of the strange relation between body and mind. 'Man is not body. The heart, the spirit, is man. And this spirit is an entire star, out of which he is built.

If therefore a man is perfect in his heart, nothing in the whole light of Nature is hidden from him ... The first step in the operation of these sciences is this: to beget the spirit from the inner firmament by means of the imagination.' Again and again there is this insistence on the power of imagination. He distinguishes it clearly from 'phantasy', or mere daydreaming. Man is a small model of the universe, but seen as if in a mirror. Vast spaces stretch *inside* him – the 'inner firmament' – and he identifies imagination with this inner firmament. In a state of imaginative inspiration, these inner spaces seem to open up, giving rise to a sense of freedom, of other realities. Some centuries later, Aldous Huxley was to recommend the use of psychedelic drugs to explore these inner spaces. Paracelsus knew nothing of such things; but he believed that the inner firmament has its fixed laws, like the firmament of the heavens: not merely laws but *meanings*. (A law is something rigid and mechanical; a meaning is something *put there*.) Man's problem is to grasp these meanings by means of intellect guided by imagination. Imagination is the explosive flare that lights up the inner spaces, revealing meaning.

This is the inner core of truth in Paracelsus. The personality that enclosed it was coarse and egotistic. If Agrippa's chief fault was self-pity, Paracelsus's was self-assertion and anger.

And this is to say that both possessed natural 'occult faculties', but neither approached the upper end of the spectrum – freedom from personality. Agrippa was moving closer to it towards the end of his life, with his increasing absorption in mysticism. But the times were not propitious. Europe was dominated by men of action – Luther, Charles V, Maximilian – and the thinker had to don the disguise of the charlatan to make his mark. Rabelais, Leonardo and Michelangelo were more or less at home in it; St. John of the Cross and St. Teresa found refuge in religious orders; for Agrippa and Paracelsus, there was no refuge.

It is necessary at this point to say something more about alchemy, although it is difficult to dispute the view that it is a pseudo-science, the crude forerunner of chemistry. But it cannot be entirely dismissed.

Dalton suggested in 1808 that matter is made up of small particles called atoms. But it was not until towards the end of the nineteenth century that scientists discovered ways to explore the atom. When they did, they made the discovery that all materials in the universe are made up of the same building bricks: protons and electrons, the proton being 1,836 times heavier than the electron. An atom is like a small solar system. The 'sun' at its centre is made up of a block of protons and neutrons (a neutron is a particle that combines proton and electron), while the 'planets' that circle in their orbits are the electrons. Each atom has the same number of protons as electrons, the protons being charged positively, the electrons negatively. And the difference between gold and silver is nothing to do with the amount of air, fire or water in it, or with its 'azoth', but simply that gold has seventy-nine protons in its centre and seventy-nine electrons circling round it, while silver has only forty-seven of each.

Transmutation of the elements is taking place all the time; the element radium with an atomic number 88 (the number of protons in its nucleus – neutrons don't count) gives off radiation known as alpha or beta rays, until it turns into lead, with an atomic number 88. The same is true of all the other radioactive elements. By bombarding elements with streams of neutrons, physicists can sometimes knock off a few protons or electrons and turn one element into another. But this can only be done with elements that are very close together in atomic number. In theory it should be just possible to change gold into mercury by adding one proton and electron to it, or transforming it into platinum by knocking off one proton and electron. Needless to say, this could only be done in such tiny quantities, and at such vast expense, that it is hardly a practical solution to the problem of the alchemists.

It would seem, then, that we should be able to dismiss alchemy as pre-scientific chemistry, and leave it at that. And if we insist on sticking to a rationalist standpoint, there is no alternative. However, fairness compels us to admit that this would be the easy way out. As always in these occult matters, we come to the conclusion that they may be exceptions to the laws of nature.

For example, the Dutch physician Helvetius (whose real name was Johann Frederick Schweitzer)* wrote a circumstantial account of an encounter with an alchemist. Helvetius was a man of good reputation, who became physician to William of Orange, and historians of chemistry are generally agreed that he was above suspicion. If he was tricked, that is another matter; but no one has suggested how it could have been done. The nineteenth-century historian of chemistry Hermann Kopp prefers to keep an open mind about the case.

Helvetius's account is given additional weight because his own attitude to alchemy tended to be sceptical, and he would certainly have been indignant to be called an occultist.

In his book *Of a Transmutation* he tells how a stranger came to his house on December 27, 1666, wanting to discuss the making of fireworks; he describes him as a small man with a plebeian accent from northern Holland and a pockmarked face. The stranger told Helvetius that he admired his treatise against the 'sympathetic powder' of Sir Kenelm Digby,† and asked Helvetius if he had ever come across the Grand Catholicon, the universal remedy for all ills; Helvetius said he hadn't. The stranger then asked him if he would recognise the Philosopher's Stone if he saw it, and produced an ivory

---

* Not to be confused with the famous French encyclopedist, Claude Adrien Helvetius (1715–1771), the sceptical author of *On Man*.

† Digby, an 'accomplished cavalier', declared that his powder, iron sulphate, could cure a wound if it was placed on the bloody bandage, without being brought into contact with the wound.

box containing three small lumps of stone the colour of sulphur. Helvetius begged for a little of it 'for remembrance' but the stranger declined. Helvetius managed to scrape off a grain of the 'stone' with his nail, and later tried dropping it onto melted lead. The result was that 'almost the whole mass of lead flew away, and the remainder turned into a mere glassy earth'.

The stranger discoursed at length, on this first occasion, about the use of semi-precious stones to cure diseases. He also made a drink from warm rain water, laminated silver and a white powder, which he and Helvetius shared, the result being that Helvetius felt pleasantly tipsy; the stranger declined to comment on the drink, but went on to describe how his 'master' had taught him how to transmute lead into gold.

On his second visit, three weeks later, the stranger took Helvetius for a country walk, and talked of the Elixir of Life and other matters. Helvetius tried to persuade him to stay at his house, but 'he was of so fixt and steadfast a spirit that all my efforts were frustrate'. The stranger finally gave Helvetius a tiny crumb of the sulphur-coloured metal; when Helvetius complained about the smallness of the amount, the stranger asked for it back, cut it in half and threw the other half into the fire, saying that Helvetius still had enough for his purposes.

Helvetius thereupon confessed what had happened when he stole a fragment of the stone on his nail, and showed the stranger (whom he calls Elias) the crucible; the stranger told him he should have wrapped it in wax before dropping it in, so it would not vaporise instantly on contact with the hot lead.

So far, the story sounds like a confidence trick. The stranger goes away again and promises to return the next day; but he fails to do so, and never comes again. The natural sequel would be that Helvetius tries the fragment of philosopher's stone and nothing happens. In fact:

I cut half an ounce, or six drams, of old lead, and put it into a crucible in the fire, which being melted, my wife put in the said Medicine made up into a small pill or button, with presently such a hissing and bubbling in its perfect operation, that within a quarter of an hour, all the mass of lead was totally transmuted into the best and finest gold, which made us amazed as if planet struck … I could not sufficiently gaze upon this so admirable and precious work of nature; for this melted lead … showed us the most rare and beautiful colours imaginable; yea, and the greenest colour, which as soon as poured into an ingot, it got the lively fresh colour of blood; and being cold, shined as the purest, most refined and resplendent gold.

A goldsmith confirmed that it was pure gold. Not content with relating these wonders, Helvetius goes on to declare that a quantity of this gold, mixed with silver and nitric acid, produced still more gold.

In 1782, a young man named James Price inherited a large sum of money, and bought a country house at Stoke, near Guildford in Surrey. Later in the year he announced that he had discovered how to transmute metals, and asked a number of distinguished men to come and check his claim. A group that included Lord Onslow, Lord Palmerston (not the Prime Minister but his father) and Lord King watched him turn mercury into silver by heating it with a white powder, and mercury into gold by heating it with a red one. The ingots thus made were tested and found to be genuine and were shown to the king, George III. But Price said that he could not prepare more of his powders without damage to his health. The Royal Society pressed him very hard, and the resulting controversy seems to have unhinged his mind; he committed suicide by drinking cyanide in front of three members of the society who had been sent to examine his claims.

The career of Alexander Seton, a Scottish alchemist, is perhaps the most startling of all. He lived in a seaside village near Edinburgh – perhaps Port Seton – and in 1601 was involved in rescuing Dutch mariners whose ship was wrecked nearby. In the following year, he went to see the pilot, James Haussen, at Enkhuizen, near Amsterdam. The friendship was a warm one, and Seton finally revealed to Haussen that he could manufacture gold, and proved it by making gold of a piece of lead by adding a powder. A little of this alchemical gold was given to a doctor named Van der Linden, whose grandson, a historian of chemistry, relates the episode. Seton then proceeded to travel around Europe, and his next chronicler was a German professor from Strasbourg, Wolfgang Dienheim. Dienheim was a sceptic about alchemy; Seton invited him and Jacob Zwinger, a Swiss savant, to witness another exhibition of gold-making by means of a lemon-yellow powder. Dienheim and Zwinger were convinced, and Dienheim wrote of the episode.

In Strasbourg, Seton seems to have caused trouble to a goldsmith named Gustenhover. At all events, Gustenhover was presented with a quantity of powder by a stranger who made experiments at his house in Hirschborgen; Gustenhover proceeded to make gold. He demonstrated his abilities before the members of the city council, who were even allowed to carry out the experiment themselves.

Unfortunately these events came to the knowledge of Rudolph II, Emperor of Germany, whose seat was at Prague; Rudolph, an untalented king, was an avid occultist. He sent for Gustenhover and demanded the secret; Gustenhover told him he had used up all the powder. The king refused to be convinced, and Gustenhover, after an unsuccessful attempt to escape, spent the remainder of his life in jail.

Seton spent the next year travelling around Europe; his mission seems to have been to convert sceptics to alchemy, and according to the stories contained in his *Life*, he was entirely successful. In 1603 he married the daughter of a Munich burgher, eloping with her to Krossen, the seat of the elector of Saxony. This proved to be a major error. The elector asked for demonstrations of his skill, then asked for the secret; when Seton refused, he was tortured and kept in jail.

A student named Michael Sendigovius contrived his escape. He had friends at court and was allowed to visit Seton. When the guards had been lulled by his frequent visits, Sendigovius managed to make them drunk one night, and escaped with Seton. Together with Seton's wife, they fled to Cracow. Seton declined to part with his secret, even to his rescuer; but when he died, worn out by his sufferings, a few months later, he left the remainder of his powder to Sendigovius. Sendigovius married Mrs. Seton, and had a highly successful career as an alchemist, dying in Parma at the age of eighty-four (in 1646). He never discovered the secret, and when the powder was exhausted, became a charlatan. But in the financial sense he was in every way luckier than Seton, and was given a country estate by King Sigismund of Poland. He published some of Seton's works under his own name, and these works continued to be reprinted for the next two centuries.

These accounts are harder to defend or explain than anything else in this book, and the temptation to dismiss them is very strong. Helvetius may have had a reputation as an honest man, but perhaps he also had a touch of the charlatan. Price's suicide makes it look as though he had used fraud to deceive his noble witnesses. I first came across his story in a popular volume called *Unsolved Mysteries* by Valentine Dyall. I looked up James Price in J. M. Stillman's *Story of Alchemy and Early Chemistry* and could not find it; nor could I find any reference to Price in any other reference book.

I concluded that Mr. Dyall had found the story in some volume of doubtful authenticity. However, reading the book on alchemy by E. J. Holmyard, whose *Elementary Chemistry* is still one of the best school textbooks, I found an account that bears out Mr. Dyall in most details, except his assertion that 'experienced chemists were allowed to examine the entire laboratory', etc. Holmyard states clearly that the various noble lords were untrained in science. But there is no reason to suppose they were not watching the whole process closely. As to the life of Seton and Sendigovius, its sources are hardly as authentic as that of Helvetius, and no sceptic would have difficulty pulling it apart.

Assuming that we are not disposed to pull it apart, what explanation can be offered? The account of Seton's life given by Lewis Spence in his *Dictionary of Occultism*, which paraphrases the *Life* of Seton, declares that Seton refused to give Sendigovius his secret because 'it was impossible to him as an adept to reveal the terms of the awful mystery'. That is to say, it was not purely a matter of chemical preparation, but of magic. And magic, I have suggested, depends basically upon the summoning of 'spirits' by natural mediumship. If we can accept that 'spirits', or some other strange power (perhaps mental), caused Daniel Dunglas Home to float in and out of windows, allowed him to handle red-hot coals and prevented objects from slipping off tilted tables, it is perhaps not a great step to believe that, for a different type of medium, they might convert mercury into gold.

It is worth bearing in mind that the psychologist Jung regarded alchemy as the predecessor of modern *psychology* rather than of chemistry. And in the autobiographical *Memories, Dreams, Reflections* he makes it clear that he regarded the discovery of alchemy as one of the greatest intellectual adventures of his life, one that was heralded by a whole series of premonitory dreams. He admits that when he first attempted to read a sixteenth-century alchemical treatise, his first reaction was: 'Good Lord, what nonsense! This stuff is impossible to understand.' But gradually he came to realise that he 'had stumbled upon the historical counterpart of [his] psychology of the unconscious'. Over ten years of close study, he came to see that alchemy is a great deal more than an attempt to make gold. It is an attempt to penetrate the Mystery itself – the mystery Jung came to identify with the Unconscious – and to discover the laws of the secret working of the universe. Alchemy was the distinctive form taken by magic in the seventeenth century; the Philosopher's Stone it sought was nothing less than man's ultimate control over death. In modern terminology, we might say that it was man's attempt to learn to make contact, at will, with the 'source of power, meaning and purpose' in the depths of the mind, to overcome the dualities and ambiguities of everyday consciousness.

It would be missing the point to say simply that Jung regarded alchemy as a symbolic form of psychology, in which the manufacture of gold becomes a symbol of the 'transformation of the personality through the merging and blending together of the noble and base elements, the conscious and the unconscious' (although this phrase is Jung's own). He would hardly have spent a decade studying this subject unless he felt that it had something important to teach him. Alchemy, Jung believed, was less concerned with chemical processes than with psychic processes, the transformation of the personality. All men have certain moments in which they feel like gods or supermen – as when Nietzsche described himself as feeling 'six thousand feet above men and time'. A divine secret slumbers in matter; in attempting to liberate it, says Jung, man takes upon himself something of the role of Redeemer. (This feeling – of the significance hidden behind the changing face of matter – is obviously close to David Foster's 'information universe', a concept that Jung would have appreciated.) The secret sought by the alchemists was, according to Jung, the secret of the transmutation of *consciousness* into the godlike state, ultimate 'individuation'. He associated it also with the aim of the yogis – and it is significant that unusual 'powers' over matter are regarded by Hindus as a natural by-product of the spiritual transformation of the yogi – as with the alchemists.

Jung's view of alchemy is certainly the profoundest that has appeared in the twentieth century, and his essays on the subject are among the most fascinating, and convincing, that he ever wrote. It is now no longer possible for an intelligent person to dismiss alchemy entirely as the product of superstition and ignorance.

And what of that much maligned subject, astrology? Here the objectors seem to have an irrefutable case. The ancients based their calculations upon the assumption that there are seven planets: Mercury, Venus, Mars, Jupiter, Saturn, the Moon and the Sun. They included the Moon and the Sun, but were unaware that the earth is a planet. They were also unaware, of course, of the existence of Uranus, Neptune, Pluto and the asteroids, those fragments of a planet that exploded between Mars and Jupiter. (One might add that the existence of this lost planet was predicted by Bodes Law, after which a careful search revealed its fragments – surely a conclusive demonstration of the superiority of the laws of science over those of astrology?) How can one take seriously a 'science' that declares that Mars exerts a warlike influence because the planet happened to be named after the Roman god of war?

But the case for astrology is stronger than it looks. If we admit the existence of some form of 'pre-vision' or second sight, then we are accepting that certain human beings possess unusual powers of intuition – even of intuiting the future. (This whole question of the nature of time will be discussed in the final chapter.) Any psychiatrist will confirm that many people are affected by the full moon, and that there is nothing in modern psychiatric or medical theory to account for this. If the moon can affect us, then why not the other planets?

As to the objection that the astrological characteristics of a planet are derived arbitrarily from mythology, the astrologers would deny it flatly. The planets were named after various gods and goddesses because their influences had been observed to correspond; Venus was named after the love goddess because she was observed to exert an influence in matters of love. In this way, Mars came to be named for warlike influences; Mercury for intelligence and ability (the 'winged messenger of the gods'); Jupiter for the fatherly qualities – protectiveness, good humour, love of order; Saturn for evil and failure; the Sun for creativeness; the Moon for imagination, poetry and the other qualities of the White Goddess. The moon is also associated with instability and change – hence lunatics.

Astrology, then, is based upon the same system of 'lunar knowledge' as the *I Ching*, the tree alphabet and the Kabbalah, and it is no more an 'exact science' than palmistry. Like palmistry, it depends upon an almost mediumistic faculty. In his remarkable book *Urania's Children*, Ellic Howe describes his own teacher in astrology, Mrs. Phyllis Naylor, and goes on: 'The mathematical side was easily learned but I could not catch Mrs. Naylor's skill in describing the psychological characteristics of the people (whom I knew well) whose horoscopes I had produced for her inspection. She had no idea of their identity.' Howe goes on to tell how he was challenged by a professional astrologer to describe what had happened to him on two particular days of his life – a challenge no other astrologer had been able to meet. Using the 'Hamburg system', Howe succeeded so well that the astrologer gave him a testimonial admitting that 'had I not known otherwise, prior knowledge might have been suspected'.

And this, most astrologers would agree, is the essence of astrology: not a complicated mathematical system or a system of beliefs, but a knack, like water-divining, of seeing the connections between character and planetary influences. As with mediumship and divining, we can only say that it *does* work, and that no one has the least idea why. It is a lunar system, and refuses to conform to the methods of ordinary science. Ellic Howe's book is largely devoted to Karl Ernst Krafft (1900–1945), an astrologer who attempted to prove astrology statistically by studying thousands of horoscopes of well-known men, and demonstrating that the major events of their lives and the exact dates of their deaths could be predicted from their natal horoscope. His vast *Treatise on Astro-Biology* (1939) is crammed with facts and figures, and looks as impressive as a government blue book. Mr. Howe's conclusion is that although it certainly does not read like the work of a madman, 'it has no scientific importance whatever'. And yet Krafft was a highly talented astrologer. On November 2, 1939, he sent a letter to a Nazi intelligence chief predicting that Hitler's life would be in danger from an explosive between November 7 and 10. On November 9, there was a bomb attempt on Hitler's life in the Bürgerbräu beer hall in Munich that killed seven people and wounded sixty-three. Krafft himself was eventually a victim of Hitler's purge against astrologers (who were supposed to have influenced Hess's flight to England), and died en route to Buchenwald in January 1945.

The 'hermetic century' produced three men whose names have become almost synonymous with magic: Agrippa, Paracelsus and Nostradamus. None of them were magicians. But of the three, Nostradamus has the greatest claim to occult powers.

Michael Nostradamus was born at St. Remy, in France, in the year 1503, of Jewish-Christian parents. His grandfathers on both sides were physicians and astrologers to 'Good King René' of Anjou, who lived at Aix, in Provence. Michael's father was a notary. His maternal grandfather, being out of a job after the death of King René, devoted himself to the education of his talented grandson, and Michael learned Greek, Latin, Hebrew, medicine and astrology. When this grandfather died, the other one took over Michael's education. It was decided that he should become a physician, and he was sent to study at the university at Montpellier. He passed his exams without difficulty. And no sooner was he qualified than plague broke out in Provence, and he was able to demonstrate his medical skill. It proved to be as remarkable as that of Paracelsus. He was a born healer. And he seemed unafraid of the plague that killed the townspeople of Montpellier by the hundreds. From 1525 until 1529 he travelled around, helping to combat the plague, and on his return to Montpellier, finally received the doctor's degree that he had earned four years before. For the next two years he practised and taught in Montpellier; then he set out again on his travels. Unlike Agrippa and Paracelsus, Nostradamus was not a flamboyant personality; there was an instinct in him, derived from generations of persecuted Jews, for bowing to the storm and keeping himself in the background. For this reason, he gained more material success than either of his remarkable contemporaries.

He settled in the town of Agen, and became a close friend of Scaliger, one of the most famous scholars in Europe. There he decided to marry. His practice prospered. Then the plague broke out again, and killed his wife and two children. He moved on again. Accusations of heresy followed him, for he had been rash enough to quote the commandment about brazen images when watching workmen casting a statue of the Virgin.

There followed eight years of wandering – it seems to be a tradition among magicians of the sixteenth century. It was now that his odd powers began to operate. He began to get flashes of second sight. In Italy he saw a young man named Felix Peretti, a swineherd who had become a monk; Nostradamus is said to have fallen on his knees and hailed Peretti as 'His Holiness'. It was after the death of Nostradamus that Peretti became Pope Sixtus V.

Another story concerns a Seigneur de Florinville, with whom Nostradamus was lodging, who asked Nostradamus to prophesy what would happen to two piglets in the farmyard; Nostradamus replied that a wolf would eat the white one and they would eat the black one. The seigneur ordered his cook to kill the white one for supper that evening. But as the pig lay in the kitchen, ready for roasting, a young wolf cub kept as a pet began to make a meal of it. The cook killed the other pig and served it at supper. As they ate supper, de Florinville told Nostradamus that he had disproved his prophecy about the pigs; Nostradamus contradicted him and the cook was sent for. Under the stern eye of his master the cook admitted what had happened. The sceptical de Florinville was convinced.

In 1544 Nostradamus was again called upon to fight the plague, this time in Marseilles. In November, floods cut off St. Remy, and bodies of men and animals spread the plague still further. In 1546, he went to Aix-en-Provence to fight the plague. It is almost impossible for us nowadays to conceive of the horrors that were commonplace in the Middle Ages and after. The city of Aix was almost deserted; the gates were closed, the streets full of unburied corpses, the churches empty, the law courts and parliament inoperative. What Nostradamus could do in a situation like this is not clear, although it is certain that he understood the importance of disinfectant and fresh air. (It must be remembered that it was not until the nineteenth century that doctors understood about germs; before that, a doctor who had just dressed a septic wound might go on to deliver a baby without bothering to wash his hands.) At all events, he did so well that he was voted a pension. He went on to Salon and performed the same services there. And in 1547 he decided to settle in Salon. He married again, bought a house and spent the remainder of his life – nineteen years – practising medicine and writing his 'prophecies'. He married a widow, and they moved into a house in a narrow, dark street. A spiral staircase led up to the top-floor room that Nostradamus made into a study. From there he could look out over the narrow roofs of the town, which was dominated by the old castle built on a steep rock. In this setting he worked peacefully, and built up a European reputation as a mage and prophet. A student and disciple, Jean de Chavigny, moved into the house, and became Nostradamus's biographer.

Eight years after moving to Salon. Nostradamus published the first edition of his prophecies, which he called *Centuries* because the prophecies, each contained in four-line stanzas, were printed in lots of a hundred. The stanzas are extremely obscure. Moreover, they are not printed in any kind of order. Nostradamus was afraid of being accused of witchcraft. If his harmless comment about the statue of the Virgin could be construed as heresy, what might happen when he prophesied the rise and fall of kings and popes? Nostradamus leaned over backwards to explain that he was in no sense an 'occultist', telling his son – then only a few months old – in the preface that he had burnt all his books on magic in case they might be abused by seekers after power. But James Laver, the author of one of the best books on Nostradamus, states his conviction that Nostradamus used magical methods for his divinations.

Certainly the quatrains are odd enough. What could make a man sit down and produce hundreds of stanzas like this:

Bestes farouches de faim fleuves tranner;
Plus part du champ encore Hista sera.
En cage de fer le grand fera treisner,
Quand rien enfant de Germain observera (II, 24)

(Hunger-maddened beasts will make the streams tremble; most of the land will be under Hister; in a cage of iron the great one will be dragged, when the child of Germany observes nothing.)

Did Nostradamus know what he meant by 'Hister', or was it a name that simply 'came' to him, as it were? Since the Second World War, there has been a tendency to assume that Hister means Hitler. James Laver believes that 'the child of Germany observes nothing' means that he observes no laws of decency in combat – which certainly fits Hitler. On the other hand, Robert Graves is of the opinion that Hister means the Danube (Ister). 'He was concerned about Venice, which was in a very low condition in Nostradamus's youth, but made a glorious recovery at Lepanto.'* Graves's interpretation seems to me the more likely, particularly since, in another stanza, Nostradamus mentions 'the Rhine and Hister', obviously referring to two rivers.

En lieu bien proché non esloigné de Venus,
Les deux plus grands de L'Asie et D'Afrique,
Du Ryn et Hister qu'on dira sont venus
Cris pleurs a Malta et costé Ligustique (IV, 68)

(In a place not far from Venus the two greatest ones of Asia and Africa, of the Rhine and Hister will be said to come; cries and tears at Malta and on the coast of Liguria.)

The third Hister stanza says:
La liberté ne sera recouvrée,
L'occupera noir, fier, vilain, inique,
Quand la matière du pont sera ouvrée
D'Hister, Venise faschée la republique.

(Liberty will not be recovered; it will be occupied by one who is black, proud, low-born and iniquitous; when the matter of the bridge is open, of Hister, Venice is greatly annoyed at the republic.)

* Letter to the author, December 4, 1969.

Laver interprets these as follows. He admits he does not know what is meant about the place not far from Venus, but suggests that the two greatest of Asia and Africa means Japan and Mussolini (who had invaded Abyssinia), *du Ryn et Hister* means 'of the Rhine and Hitler' – all referring to the Axis Pact – and that the last line refers to the bombing of Malta and Genoa. The second stanza says that liberty will not be recovered; the proud, dark, wicked man (Hitler) will occupy it; the 'bridge' refers to the Pope, Pontifex Maximus (pontifex is a bridge), and these lines refer to the concordat, between Mussolini and the Vatican in 1928. The Republic of France is displeased.

Graves suggests a simpler interpretation. The place not far from Venus is a place not far from Venice. The bridge referred to is a bridge across the Danube (Ister) – i.e. interference in Italy and the south (Malta) by Charles V of Austria when he became Charles I of Spain. The republic that is greatly annoyed is Venice.

If the same stanzas can be interpreted as referring to both the sixteenth and the twentieth centuries, it may be felt that Nostradamus's prophecies are somewhat lacking in definiteness. This is certainly true when one considers individual prophecies; but it must be admitted that he is altogether more impressive when one considers the number of 'hits' in his whole output. Laver acknowledged that he began to be impressed when he read:

Du nuict viendra par la forest de Reines,
Deux pars, vaultorte, Herne la pierre blanche,
Le Moyne noir en gris dedans Varennes:
Esleu Cap. cause tempeste, feu, sang, tranche.

(By night will come through the forest of Reines two married persons, by a tortuous valley [circuitous route]; Herne the white stone; the black monk in grey into Varennes; Elected capet; causes tempest, fire, blood and cutting.)

Varennes only appears once in French history, and this stanza may therefore be regarded as a test case. It is connected with the attempted flight of Louis XVI of France and his wife, Marie Antoinette, after the French Revolution. On June 20, 1791, the King and Queen disguised themselves and fled, escaping by way of the Queen's apartment, the King in grey, the Queen in white. They were recognised by the postmaster of Chalons, and as a consequence, arrested at Varennes. They spent the night at the shop of a grocer named Sauce, and then were returned to Paris, where in due course both were beheaded. (*Trancher*, to slice, is used for beheading.) Louis was of a monkish temperament, and he was an elected king because he was the first French king to hold the title by will of the Constituent Assembly rather than by Divine Right.

There are too many 'hits' in these four lines for them to be dismissed as chance. Two people, one in white, one in grey, coming to Varennes by a devious route: then tempest, fire, blood and *tranche*, which, as Laver observes, sounds like the thud of the guillotine. There are also a few misses, or at least, unexplainable phrases and words. There is no forest of Reines, even though Charles A. Ward, in his book on Nostradamus, assures us that this is what the road to Varennes is called. But it is strange that he should speak of *Reines* (queens) when a queen *is* involved in the incident; one edition of Nostradamus (Le Pelletier) prints *forest* as *fores*, Latin for 'door'. They escaped by the Queen's door. (And it is true that Nostradamus mixes Latin and French as he feels inclined.) What of 'Herne the white stone'? This is supposed to be one of the epithets applied to Marie Antoinette – Laver says *Herne* is an anagram of 'queen' (*reine*). Tempest, fire and blood is an apt description of the Reign of Terror.

In another quatrain, Nostradamus refers to a mitred husband (using the word 'part', as he used *deux 'pars'* above for 'married couple'), and speaks of a traitor called Narbon and a seller of oils called Sauce. Sauce, as already mentioned, was the grocer in whose house the King and Queen were confined at Varennes, while the Count of Narbonne *was* a traitor, a minister of the King's who intrigued with the rebels.

If all this sounds amazing, it should be borne in mind that it is not unique. Laver quotes Maistre Turrel of Autun, an astrologer who lived at the same time as Nostradamus, as actually mentioning 1789 as the year of 'great and remarkable changes and altercations', and upheavals regarding sects and the law, and adding that this period will last for twenty-five years – which takes us to 1814, the year of Napoleon's downfall. And another astrologer, Richard Roussat, published in 1550 (five years before Nostradamus's *Centuries*) a book, *On the Changes in the Times*, in which he quotes the passage from Turrel (proving its authenticity), and giving a date 243 years from the time he wrote the book (i.e. 1792) as the date of 'the future renovation of the world'; although the Revolution started in 1789, the revolutionary calendar was inaugurated in 1792. And Jean Muller's *Liber Mirabilis*, published in 1524, gives 1788 as the date of immense changes that will 'bring ... sad destinies ... all the empires of the universe will be overthrown and everywhere there will be great mourning'. Admittedly, his way of writing 1788 is as follows: 'When a thousand years have been accomplished after the Virgin gave birth, and when seven hundred more years have passed, the eighty-eighth year will be very astonishing,' etc. But the date specified is quite definite. Nostradamus speaks for the 'vulgar advent', in his preface addressed to his son, and gives an approximate date in the mid-1700s.

On the whole, Nostradamus's prophecies concerning the Revolution, the execution of the King and Queen, and the rise of Napoleon, are the most impressive and convincing examples of his power of pre-vision. This is not surprising. Nostradamus was a Frenchman; the majority of his prophecies concern French history. The Revolution was the major event in French history; it is logical that he should devote more space to it than to lesser events. Reading straight through the prophecies, it is hard not to feel a kind of awe; there are simply too many things that coincide. If one comes upon a stanza that mentions the republic, 'reds' and 'whites', and speaks of a torrent full of litter, it is reasonable to suppose that he is referring to the Republic established by the Revolution, to the republicans and royalists (who were called reds and whites} and to the torrent of the Revolution.

Quand la lictiere du tourbillon versée,
Et seront faces de leurs manteaux couvers,
La republique par gens nouveaux vexée,
Lors blancs et rouges jugeront à l'envers.

(When the litter of the whirlpool is poured out, and their faces shall be covered by their cloaks [the cloak of legality under which the horrors were perpetrated?], the republic will be vexed by new men, and their reds and whites shall hold opposite opinions about one another.)

It may be well to remind readers briefly of the course of the French Revolution. In many respects it resembles the Russian Revolution of 1917. The King was a fool; his queen, Marie Antoinette, a spendthrift and a snob. At a time when the King should have been making concessions to the common people, she wanted to prevent anyone but an aristocrat being an officer in the army or a member of the government. But her extravagance brought the country to a point where it was necessary to levy new taxes on the landowners, and the landowners protested so loudly that the King had to agree to set up a kind of parliament made up of nobles, clergy and 'the Third Estate', the commoners. When this parliament showed signs of wanting to curtail the King's freedom, he tried to disband it, then to get his soldiers to scatter the rebellious commons by force. The soldiers refused, and the King had to climb down and grant the concessions. He moved foreign troops to Paris and prepared to break his promises. At this, the people revolted, and the result was national bloodshed – peasants burning the houses of the landowners and murdering their families. But the King remained safe. The National Assembly began the work of reforming the law. And everything might have blown over quietly if the King had not made his foolish attempt to escape. For everyone knew that he intended to rejoin his loyal troops in the east and crush the Revolution. His capture was the turning point, and the turning point in French history.

At this juncture the 'new men' arose to vex the republic; their names were Robespierre, Danton and Marat – the Jacobins, redder than the reds. And when France became embroiled in a war with Austria and Prussia, and the Prussian Duke of Brunswick announced he meant to restore full powers to the French king, it was the end of Louis. The mob took over. All 'gentlefolk' were arrested, then mobs invaded the prisons and thrust them out, one by one, to be massacred by the crowds outside. The Duke of Brunswick changed his mind after a minor battle at Valmy, and retreated. The republic was proclaimed, the King and Queen tried and executed. France declared war on England and set out to make Europe republican. In Paris the guillotine rose and fell with a monotonous thud. Robespierre took over after the murder of Marat by Charlotte Corday. The chemist Lavoisier and the poet André Chenier were guillotined for being aristocrats; moderate 'reds' (Girondins) were guillotined for being moderate; Danton himself was guillotined for objecting to the bloodshed. Robespierre became a Stalin who inaugurated purge after purge. Finally, when he hinted at another massive purge, the Assembly turned on him and arrested him and his followers. His supporters in the *Hôtel de Ville* rescued him. His enemies surrounded the *Hôtel*. Some of

Robespierre's companions tried to leap out of the windows and injured themselves horribly on the railings; Robespierre himself had his lower jaw shot off, and went to the guillotine after seventeen hours of agony, his face wrapped roughly in a dirty bandage. The Revolution was completed. The stage was set for the rise of Napoleon.

In the light of this history, Nostradamus's number of 'hits' can be seen more clearly. One of the earliest acts of the Revolution was to replace the provinces of France – Normandy, Burgundy and so on – with 'departments'.

Faux exposer viendra topographie
Seront les cruches des nomumens ouvertes,
Pulluler socte, saincte philosophie,
Pour blanches noires, et pour antiques vertes.

(Topography will be falsified; urns and monuments shall be opened; sects swarm, religious philosophy; for white, black; new unripe things (green) replace the antique.)

The burial place of French kings at St. Denis was violated and their ashes scattered. (Observe that Nostradamus writes *nomumens* instead of 'monuments', another example of his curious anagrams.) Sects certainly 'pullulated'. Laver thinks that *saincte philosophie* means that the rationalistic philosophy of Voltaire will replace religion. But on the contrary, the rationalist Hébert and his party were guillotined, and Robespierre preached like a religious maniac. So *saincte philosophie* probably means precisely that.

The French clergy were legislated out of existence, and their money and goods used to finance a new currency:

Las! qu'on verra grand peuple tourmenté,
Et la loi saincte en totale ruine;
Par autres lois toute la Chrestienté
Quand d'or d'argent trouvé nouvelle mine.

That is an exceptionally clear quatrain: 'the great people tormented, holy law in total ruin, all Christianity under "other laws", when a new gold and silver mine is found': the goods of the clergy.

> *D'esprit de regne munismes descriés,*
> *Et seront peuples esmeus contre leur Roy;*
> *Paix, sainct nouveau, sainct loix empiréss,*
> *Rapis onc fut en si très dur arroy.*

(The ramparts [*munismes* – Latin *munimen*] shall be decried, people shall rise against their anointed king [*esmeus* instead of *esleu*]; peace, a new saint, sacred laws made worse; Paris [*Rapis* – another anagram] was never in a worse state.)

The 'peace' that comes after the people have risen against their king was the 'breathing space', when it looked as if all might return to normal again; the 'new saint' is probably Robespierre, with his ranting against atheists, and his Festival of the Supreme Being celebrated by his order in June 1894.

> *A soustenir la grand cappe troublée,*
> *Pour l'esclaircir les rouges marcheront;*
> *De mort famille sera presque accablée,*
> *Les rouges rouges le rouge assommeront.*

The *grand cappe troublée* means the troubled king. Nostradamus always refers to the king as capet or cap., with a full stop after it. The reds march to sustain him – the Girondins, the moderate reds; by death his family will be almost wiped out; the red 'reds' will destroy the reds. I personally find this last line one of the most convincing in Nostradamus. '*Les rouges rouges le rouge assommeront*'; no better brief summary of the course of the Revolution could be made.

It would be supererogatory to go on quoting the dozen remaining stanzas that seem to refer clearly to the Revolution; they can be found in Laver's book, or in Charles Ward's *Oracles of Nostradamus*. But there is one that I cannot resist quoting.

Des principaux de cité rebellée,

Qui tiendront pour liberté ravoir,

Destrancher masses, infelice meslée,

Crys, hurlements a Nantes piteux veir.

(Of the principal citizens of the rebellious city, who tried to recover liberty, masses beheaded, unhappy melée, cries, howls at Nantes pitiful to see.)

Many cities of France were shocked by the brutality of the Jacobins in Paris, and rebelled in the name of a moderate republicanism. Lyons executed its Jacobin leader to defy Paris. Nantes also attempted to throw off the yoke of Paris. So did Marseilles and Bordeaux. In due course, all paid very heavily for their boldness. But Nantes was unfortunate in falling under the domination of a madman named Carrier. He seems to have been literally insane. He talked droolingly of blood. He had fits during which he rolled on the floor and yapped and howled like a dog. His task – to punish Nantes – was a sadist's delight, and he extracted every drop of pleasure from it. He hated children – 'They are all whelps' – and had five hundred of them taken to the meadows outside the town and slaughtered – shot down, then clubbed. He found the guillotine too slow to kill off the 'rebels', and he may have felt worried that his execution of children might cause a revolt against him – some of the victims were so small that their necks would not reach across the block, and the blade sliced their heads in two. Then the executioner himself died of horror after executing four young sisters. Carrier devised a new method: *noyades*, drowning. A barge filled with prisoners was hauled into the middle of the river, then a hole staved in its bottom.

Men with hatchets waited until the last moment to make sure no one managed to free his hands and scramble out of the hold. A barge or raft would hold more than a hundred at a time. The sexual basis of these outrages is proved by another of Carrier's innovations, 'republican marriages', in which a naked man and woman were tied together face to face and then drowned together. Swinburne wrote a sensual poem about it, but it is doubtful if the couple experienced much sexual stimulation. One man did escape – a poultry dealer named Gustave Leroy – by managing to cling to the bottom of a barge that stuck on a sandbank. When Robespierre fell, Carrier was put on trial, and Leroy told of how he had been one of 105 people to be towed out in a barge. One of them had asked a guard for a drink of water, and wondered why the guards roared with laughter. Carrier and his fellow butchers were guillotined.

In the face of all this, it is difficult to see how the stanza about the principal citizens of rebellious Nantes, who tried to recover freedom and who were beheaded, can refer to any episode but this. Even the 'unhappy melées' (or mixtures) sounds like the 'republican marriages'. It would admittedly be even more convincing if he had referred to the drownings: but in another stanza, he speaks of the horrors of the Revolution as being 'fire, *water*, iron and rope', and says 'those who engineered these things shall die by them'. He ends with the astonishing line: 'Except one who will spread ruin throughout the world' – Napoleon.

Considering that all the things he foretold were in the future, it seems strange that Nostradamus's obscure stanzas aroused any interest during his lifetime. In fact, they made him immediately famous. They are, in any case, so full of prophecies of fire, plague, blood and torment that they no doubt satisfied the universal desire to hear about catastrophe.

The queen of France in 1555 was Catherine de Medici, who was an enthusiastic student of the occult. She had good reason to be.

A remarkable prophet named Luc Gauric or Gauricus had foretold the death of her husband, Henry II, in a duel. And Gauric's fame as a prophet was as great as that of the younger Nostradamus. Gauric worked by the stars, but there seems to be no doubt that he possessed occult gifts of the same type as Peter Hurkos's in our own time. He cast the horoscope of Giovanni de Medici, son of the great Lorenzo, and foretold correctly that he would become pope. (Giovanni became Leo X, the pope with whom Luther clashed.) In Scotland, Gauric told the Archbishop of St. Andrews that he would die on the scaffold – as he did, victim of Protestant enemies. On another occasion, his frankness brought unpleasant consequences. He told Giovanni Bentivoglio, tyrant of Bologna, that he would die in exile. The tyrant ordered five 'drops' on the *strappado* – a form of torture in which the victim's hands were tied behind him, and then the victim was hoisted into the air on a pulley and allowed to drop. Before he reached the floor the rope was jerked upward again which usually had the effect of dislocating the shoulders. It took Gauric some years to recover, but he had the satisfaction of seeing Pope Julius II drive the tyrant out of Bologna in accord with his prophecy. He even prophesied the exact date of the death of Pope Paul III – November 20, 1549.

Gauric had made a double prophecy concerning Henry II of France. First of all, he predicted that he would witness a duel when he came to the throne. The duel took place between Gui Sabot Jarnac and François la Châtaigneraie in 1547, and the King was present to see Châtaigneraie killed. The second part of the prophecy was that the King himself would die as a result of a duel. This seemed unlikely enough, but Catherine de Medici decided to doublecheck with the new prophet of Salon. Nostradamus went to Paris and impressed Catherine, although there is no record of what passed between them. Nostradamus had already foretold the manner of the King's death in the *Centuries*:

Le lyon jeune le vieux surmontera,
En champ bellique par singulier duelle:
Dans cage d'or les yeux lui crevera,
Deux classes une, puis mourir, mort cruelle.

(The young lion shall overcome the old, in the field of war in single fight; in a cage of gold he will pierce his eyes, two wounds one, then die a cruel death.)

In 1559, the two daughters of Henry II married: one to Philip of Spain, one to the Duke of Savoy. Henry took part in the tournament held in celebration – forgetting, apparently, the prophecy about a duel. When he was jousting with the young Gabriel, Comte de Montgomery, Henry's eyeball was accidentally pierced by the shattered stump of his opponent's lance, which penetrated the gilt visor of his helmet – the 'cage of gold'. It took him ten days to die: certainly a cruel death. Montgomery had to escape to England to escape the Queen's wrath. The phrase *deux classes une* is obscure; Laver believes it to refer to a splinter of the lance that penetrated the King's throat, while Ward translates it 'the first of two loppings', assuming *classe* to be the Greek *klasis*, lopping, *une* as the Latin *una*, first; the second 'lopping' referring to the murder of his son Henry III by the monk Jacques Clément.

Another stanza seems to refer to Catherine herself:

La dame seul au regne demeurée,
D'unic esteint premier au lict d'honneur;
Sept ans sera de douleur esplorée,
Puis longue vie au regne par grand heur.

(The lady shall remain to rule alone; her unique spouse dead on the field of honour; after mourning seven long years, she will live and reign long.)

Catherine mourned her husband for seven years, and lived and reigned for another thirty years, or at least, played an extremely active part in the affairs of France. Henry II was succeeded by Francis II, a sickly youth, whose horoscope Nostradamus had cast at the request of the king. Nostradamus has a stanza that declares that the eldest son of the widow shall die before he reaches the age of eighteen; his next eldest brother will be affianced even younger. Francis died of blood poisoning six weeks before his eighteenth birthday. His neurotic brother, Charles IX (only ten at the time), was affianced to Elizabeth of Austria at eleven. In his fourteenth year the king paid a visit to Nostradamus at Salon, accompanied, of course, by his mother. Catherine asked Nostradamus to draw up a horoscope of her younger son, the Duke of Anjou, and Nostradamus told her he would succeed to the throne. But he was even more interested in young Henry of Navarre, who was also in the royal train. He asked to see him naked, but the boy was afraid he was going to be beaten, and refused. Nostradamus went into his bedchamber early the next morning and examined him; he stated that Henry would one day become king. This makes it seem clear that Nostradamus's predictions, or some of them, were not based on astrology, but upon some kind of intuition or second sight. He may have wanted to examine marks on the boy's body – the record does not specify. In fact, Charles IX, the king responsible for the Massacre of St. Bartholomew, died of tuberculosis in his mid-twenties; Henry III, who succeeded him, was stabbed by the monk Jacques Clément, as he sat in the lavatory; Henry of Navarre, a Protestant, succeeded to the throne. All this is foretold with some precision in Nostradamus. The massacre of the Huguenots, Protestants, on the Eve of St. Bartholomew, is also foretold by Nostradamus:

> Le Noir farouche quand aura essayé
> Sa main sanguine par feu, fer, arcs tendus,
> Trestous le peuple sera tant effrayé
> Voir les plus grans par col et pieds tendu.

Noir is Nostradamus's usual anagram for *roi*, king. Charles was certainly a ferocious king; he insisted on disembowelling the game himself when out hunting, and had a curious habit of blowing out the brains of any pigs or donkeys he met with. During the massacre, he was leaning out of the window of the Louvre with an arquebus shouting 'Kill! Kill!' 'The ferocious king, when he has tried out his hand with fire, iron, arquebus, all the people will be afraid to see the greatest man hung by his neck and feet.' Admiral Coligny, leader of the Huguenots, was the chief target of the massacre; Catherine had persuaded her son that he must be killed, and Charles finally shouted hysterically, 'All right, but kill every other Huguenot in France at the same time.' Coligny was dragged through Paris and hanged upside down from a gibbet. (It is interesting to speculate whether this might have had anything to do with the Hanged Man card in the Tarot, but the dates make it unlikely.)

Nostradamus's health began to break down; in his sixties his gout changed to dropsy. He foretold his own death with his usual precision:

De retour d'Ambassade, don de Roy mis au lieu,
Plus n'en fera, sera allé à Dieu,
Parens plus proche, amis, frères du sang,
Trouvé tout mort près du lict et du banc.

(On his return from his embassy, the king's gift put in its place, he will do no more, being gone to God; by close relations, friends, blood brothers, he will be found near the bed and bench.)

Nostradamus had been sent to Arles as the representative of Salon; on his return, he was found dead near the bed, lying on the bench he used to hoist himself into bed. He was buried upright in the wall of the church of the Cordeliers, at his own request.

The *Centuries* has continued to be studied ever since. One of its most disquieting prophecies declares:

Like the great king of the Angolmois
The year 1999, seventh month,
The Great king of terror will descend from the sky,
At this time, Mars will reign for the good cause.

Some take this to mean the end of the world, while others think it may mean an invasion from outer space. The *grand Roy d'effrayeur* sounds unpleasantly like a hydrogen bomb. The great king of the *Angolmois* is almost certainly Genghis Khan – *Angolmois* is another of Nostradamus's anagrams for Mongolians. Perhaps he is warning against the 'yellow peril'. Laver is of the opinion that Nostradamus may be following a notion familiar in the Middle Ages that the world would last seven thousand years; it was assumed to have been created in 4000 B.C. (Archbishop Usher gives the date as 4004 B.C., based on a careful calculation of all the ages given in the Bible.) The Millennium is the last thousand years of the earth's existence, so Nostradamus may have calculated July 1999 as the beginning of the end, rather than the end. It may be worth the while of world statesmen to make special efforts for peace in mid-1999.

FIVE
ADEPTS AND IMPOSTERS

After the great sixteenth century, there is a falling off in the quality of magic. The reason is anybody's guess. All things go in cycles. There are great ages of poetry, of painting, of music, of science. In the year Cornelius Agrippa was born, there appeared a book called *The Hammer of Witches* (*Malleus Maleficarum*) by two Dominicans, Jakob Sprenger (1436–1495) and Heinrich Kramer (1430–1505), which Rossell Hope Robbins calls 'the most important and most sinister work on demonology ever written'. The authors were, respectively, dean of Cologne University and prior of a monastery. The book went into sixteen German editions, eleven French, two Italian and at least six English. Dr. Faust, who became such an interesting hero of legend, lived at the beginning of the century, for Trithemius mentions him contemptuously in a letter written in 1507. Faust was to replace Theophilus in the public imagination; but where Theophilus had been a poor creature who sold his soul to the Devil in a fit of despair, Faust was the satanic hero, twisting his moustaches and committing mischievous villainies. Theophilus captured the imagination of six centuries because the idea of traffic with the Devil was so terrifying. The sixteenth century found it rather piquant, rather exciting; Faust aroused a kind of secret admiration.

What was happening – as we can now see, in retrospect – was that the Church was losing its grip. The human imagination was growing up; the age of science was approaching. An intelligent, cultured country gentleman named Reginald Scot wrote *The Discovery of Witchcraft* in the 1580s; he took the point of view of a thorough-going sceptic who declared that 'all spiritualistic manifestations were artful impostures' and that witches were an invention of the Inquisition. Some of his anecdotes are ribald and delightful – as, for example, the story of a young man who was unfortunate enough to lose his sexual member while fornicating. He went to a witch, who told him she knew of a tree in which there was a nest full of spare penises. 'And being in the top of the tree, he took out a mighty great one and showed the same to her, asking her if he might have the same. Nay, quoth she, that is our parish priest's tool, but take any other thou wilt ...' The nest, apparently, contained twenty or thirty tools, lying in provender – undoubtedly oats – upon which they fed. 'These are no jests,' Scot says seriously, 'for they be written by ... judges.' King James I called the book 'damnable', and wrote his *Demonologie* to refute it; but even with a king's name to recommend it, the book never achieved the popularity of Scot's work.

Scot was mistaken in his belief that all spiritualistic manifestations are due to fraud or to mental disturbance on the part of the witnesses. But after so many centuries of total credulity, it was a healthy sign. As to King James, he had been converted to a belief in witches by the North Berwick case, in which a young girl who possessed natural gifts for 'spiritual healing' was tortured by her master until she confessed that she was aided by the Devil; under further torture she implicated a number of other people. Those she named were so respectable – a school-teacher, John Fian; a cultured, elderly lady, Agnes Sampson; two other women of sound reputation, Euphemia Maclean and Barbara Napier – that it seems likely she chose them because she hoped they would quickly show the absurdity of the charges. But the only way to stop inhuman tortures was to invent tales of witch's sabbaths, and implicate more innocent people. This they all did, until seventy people stood trial. King James himself supervised some of the torture, especially when Agnes Sampson invented a wild story about sailing to sea in a sieve to try to wreck the king's ship. Most of the seventy were burned, some without the usual mercy of being strangled beforehand. James wrote his *Demonologie* as a consequence of this experience. It is an ironical twist that James's passion for interrogating witches finally led him to agree with Reginald Scot that it was mostly fraud and illusion; in the last years of his reign, witchcraft trials almost ceased. It may be said in extenuation of James I that he was a neurotic homosexual of weak character whose Scottish common sense finally triumphed over his superstitious credulity.

The life of Dr. John Dee, one of the most sympathetic (if not remarkable) figures in the history of magic, spanned five reigns: Henry VIII, Edward VI, Queen Mary, Queen Elizabeth and James I. Dee is almost unique among 'magicians' in possessing absolutely no occult faculties – he said so repeatedly himself. He was a kind of mystic, although not of a particularly high order. For his obsession was knowledge, scholarship, learning. He was like some earlier H. G. Wells, consumed by a thirst to know everything. Like all true poets and magicians, he was driven by a vision of a reality quite different from the commonplace world in which we live out our lives. Paracelsus and Agrippa were doctors who studied magic because it was a part of their profession; both had a streak of charlatanism. Dee studied magic because he was a poet, for whom it seemed to offer a key to another form of existence; there was nothing of the charlatan about him.

Dee's father, a Welshman, was a minor official at the court of Henry VIII; Dee was born in London on July 13, 1527. Cornelius Agrippa was an embittered wanderer around Europe at the time; Paracelsus was about to be driven out of Basel by his enemies; Nostradamus was a young doctor, without a degree, who also travelled through Europe, fighting the plague. In due course Dee himself would become something of a wanderer, although never homeless.

Dee attended the Chantry School at Chelmsford. It was a

peaceful little market town surrounded by green meadows, with a brown, slow-moving river. Dee loved browsing through books and manuscripts. He was charmed by the Catholic ritual (for England was by no means all Protestant). And his appetite for knowledge was kept sharp by the narrowness of the school curriculum. At that time, and for another century, even the universities were thoroughly unambitious. Instead of reading, writing and 'rithmetic, they taught grammar, logic and rhetoric. Latin was taught, but hardly any Greek. Students were in the charge of a tutor, who was so much *in loco parentis* that he could beat them if necessary. Academic standards were low in England; there was little to prevent a student spending his seven years drinking and womanising; after all, no English gentleman could really find much use for Latin and logic, or even geography and mathematics, when he took over the family estates.

So when Dee went to St. John's College, Cambridge, at the age of fifteen, he had no reason to feel that he had found his spiritual home – as Bertrand Russell did in the 1890s. But at least the opportunities were there if he wanted them. He did, intensely. He allowed himself only four hours a night for sleep. He even studied Greek. The university authorities soon became aware that they had a prodigy among them, and at the age of nineteen, Dee was made a fellow of Trinity, and an under-reader (assistant professor) in Greek. He was already an enthusiastic astronomer.

The atmosphere of Cambridge stifled him; at the first opportunity, he went to the University of Louvain, one of the best in Europe, where Cornelius Agrippa had been. Inevitably, Dee read Agrippa's *Occult Philosophy*, and was excited and impressed by the notion that magic and alchemy were not merely diabolic studies, but a practical aid in the mystical quest for God. Magic was in bad repute in England, a suburban backwater as far as culture was concerned; but on the Continent it aroused intelligent interest. It must be remembered that magic and science were closely linked at that time; even mathematics was regarded as a 'magical' study, with Pythagoras as its prophet. Magic meant for Dee what science meant for H. G. Wells three centuries later. It was what he had always dreamed of: a magnificent, wide field of study, with no visible limits. He quickly gained a reputation to match Cornelius Agrippa's.

When he went to Paris in 1550, his reputation preceded him, and at Rheims he gave a course of lectures on Euclid that were free for anyone to attend. He was so popular that he was offered a professorship; but he felt that more exciting things awaited him, and returned to England, where the ten-year-old Edward VI had succeeded Henry VIII. He was granted a pension by the King, and immediately sold it for two rectorships.

In 1552 he met the occultist Jerome Cardan, who was a 'witch' in the precise sense of the word: that is, he possessed a high degree of second sight and other occult faculties. There seems to be no reason to suspect Cardan of lying, when he declares (in his memoirs) that he could project his spirit outside his body. He also makes the interesting assertion that he could, from childhood on, 'see' imaginary things with a sense of total reality. As a child, he says, he could not control this faculty, but later he learned how to select things he wanted to 'see'. All this conforms to the picture we have already built up of the natural visionary, a man with some kind of chemical imbalance that has the effect of a dose of a psychedelic drug on his nervous system. All this was accompanied by a semi-hysterical lack of self-control, so that he would argue for the sake of arguing, whether he believed what he said or not, and find himself compelled to speak of things that he knew would offend people. He believed himself to be accompanied by a familiar spirit, and was an unusually talented astrologer and prophet. He certainly qualifies as one of the most remarkable psychological curiosities of all time.

Cardan was a major influence on Dee, who began to think in terms of spirits who might be contacted to aid him with his researches. His problem now, and for the rest of his life, was money. He was convinced that if he could try his own approach to alchemy – the use of spirit-forces – he would soon solve the problem of the Philosopher's Stone. But alchemy cost money. His hopes of royal preferment were dashed when Edward VI died at the age of sixteen, and the country was plunged into political crisis. Edward named Lady Jane Grey as his successor to the throne, and Dee's patron, the Earl of Northumberland, proclaimed her queen. She was the granddaughter of Henry VII; Henry VIII's eldest daughter, Mary, had other ideas, and Northumberland and Lady Jane Grey lost their heads. The following year, Sir Thomas Wyatt, son of the poet, led a rebellion to protest against Queen Mary's proposed marriage to Philip of Spain; he wanted to put her younger sister, Elizabeth, on the throne instead. He also failed and was executed, and Elizabeth was placed under arrest.

Having married the heir to the Spanish throne, Mary earned herself the nickname of Bloody Mary by burning large numbers of Protestants. As far as Dee was concerned, the only thing that could be said in favour of all this burning was that while people thought about burning Protestants they forgot about burning witches. He was called upon to cast Queen Mary's horoscope. Perhaps his foreknowledge of her early death gave him the idea of contacting her younger sister, who would be the next queen, and who was then a captive at Woodstock. He visited Elizabeth and cast her horoscope too. He also showed her the horoscope of her elder sister; for after all, was not Mary's fate entangled with Elizabeth's? But Mary's spies took the view that this was a little too like political plotting. Dee was arrested and thrown into jail, charged with treason. He had the upsetting experience of seeing a fellow prisoner, Barthlet Green, burned for heresy, although he seemed a harmless, gentle soul. It was lucky for Dee that

Mary was fond of her younger sister; otherwise he might have paid the penalty of coming between the present and future queens. Dee was released in 1555. But it had been a near thing.

Mary died three years later, and Elizabeth became queen. The first thing she did was to ask Dee to calculate the most favourable day for the coronation, and Dee suggested January 14, 1559. Now it looked as if Dee was firmly established at last; he was more or less the royal astrologer. It was unfortunate that Queen Elizabeth I was tight-fisted, and Dee's finances failed to improve. He became a kind of general errand boy, travelling to the Continent on missions for the Queen, and for her minister Burleigh and Sir Francis Walsingham, head of the Queen's spy system. Like Agrippa, Dee found himself hurled into intrigue. For a bookish, peace-loving scholar, it must have been a considerable strain. In Amsterdam in 1563 he discovered a book called *Stenographia* by Trithemius, a work on magic, alchemy and the meaning of numbers; it influenced Dee's own work on magic, *Monas Hieroglyphica*, which he finished in twelve days after reading Trithemius. Commentators have been puzzled by the remark of Lord Burleigh, the secretary of state, that it was 'of the utmost importance for the security of the realm'. Why? It deals in ciphers, which might have been valuable in spying; and Dee was already obsessed by the idea of discovering buried treasure by means of the spirits – which would certainly have benefited the realm. The only other possibility is that Dee thought he had a certain method of forestalling the plans of England's enemies through astrology. If so, no one believed in it enough to finance it; Dee remained the errand boy and occasional consultant on magical affairs.

After various Continental wanderings, Dee returned to England in 1564, and moved to his mother's house at the Thameside village of Mortlake, where he returned to his magical studies. In 1574, when he was forty-seven, he married, but his wife died a year later. That he was still in royal favour is shown by the fact that the Queen paid an informal call on the day of his wife's death; she wanted to see his 'magic glass', which seems to have been nothing but a convex mirror. When she heard there was a death in the house, she refused to come in, but examined the glass in a nearby field.

Two years later, Dee married Jane Fromond, lady in waiting to Lady Howard of Effingham, some years his junior. They settled in his mother's house at Mortlake, and she soon produced the first of the eight children she would bear him. When his mother died in 1580, she had already given him the house. For a few years, Dee's life was idyllic. He cast horoscopes to eke out his income. He made maps for the Queen, had a great deal to do with plans for naval defence (so that he must be given some of the credit for the defeat of the Armada in 1588) and made calculations for a new calendar. His interest in occult matters never slackened, and in his *Spiritual Diary* he records dreams, and tales of spirit rappings and other manifestations. But his new obsession was crystal gazing – the idea that long gazing into any kind of clear depth can induce a semi-trancelike state, in which the future can be foreseen and spirits reveal themselves.

Dee's chief trouble was that his mind was too discursive and active for the kind of serene contemplation necessary. What he needed was someone with occult faculties – a 'scryer' (or descryer). In 1581 Dee had a brief experience of seeing something in the crystal, but he does not specify what it was. In 1582 he found a youth named Barnabas Saul, who became his scryer for a few months; however, Barnabas got into trouble with the law, for reasons that are not recorded, and was questioned about his occult activities. He preferred to denounce Dee rather than face the prospect of further entanglement with the law – which had stringent statutes against witchcraft – so Dee lost his natural seer.

Two days later, Dee was visited by a swarthy, good-looking young Irishman named Edward Kelley, who talked about occult matters, and mentioned that he was a natural scryer. There is no reason to disbelieve him, although he seems to have been an objectionable young man in many ways; he was an apothecary's apprentice turned forger and coiner – for which he had lost his ears. (Occult faculties often seem to be accompanied by instability of character.) Dee explained that he was not a magician, since the word 'magic' held evil associations for him. Before his sessions of crystal gazing, he always prayed for divine help. Kelley agreed; he fell on his knees and prayed solemnly. Then he peered into the crystal. In less than a quarter of an hour, he was describing to Dee the figure of a cherub that he could see in its depths. Dee instantly identified it, from his kabbalistic knowledge, as Uriel, the angel of light. The angel could not communicate, being imprisoned in the crystal, so to speak. But Dee felt this was the beginning of a new epoch in his life: the Philosopher's Stone was already within reach. He immediately invited Kelley to move into the house. Dee's wife, on being introduced to the ear-less Irishman, was less enthusiastic; she had an intuition that things would not go well. And she never took to Kelley thereafter. But, as an obedient wife, she accepted him. Not long afterwards, Kelley decided to marry a local girl; for now that his wanderings were temporarily at an end, he experienced the need for someone to share his bed. The evidence seems to show that he always had a secret hankering after Jane Dee, who was closer to his own age than to her husband's. But she regarded him with mistrust.

It is a pity that there is no detailed record of what happened in the Dee household after Kelley's arrival in 1582. All we know is that Kelley, in spite of a touch of charlatanism, possessed the Irish gift of second sight, and that very soon he was seeing and hearing spirits every day. Since he could hear them now, it must be assumed that they spoke in audible voices. Reading Dee's own account, in the light of our more detailed knowledge of such things, it is almost certain that Kelley went into a light trance and contacted spirits like any modern medium. There were various 'guides'; one was called Medicina. These guides brought along other spirits. Dee, with no experience to guide him in these matters, assumed that all were angels. One woman asked Dee if he thought she was a jeweller's wife, because she wore jewellery; Dee replied that he was certain she was a messenger of Jesus, because Jesus had purchased 'the jewell of eternal life with the jewell of his precious blood'. The spirits must have found him a tiresome old crank. However, like most of the spirits who appear at modern séances, they seemed to have nothing very profound or useful to impart. After many months, Dee was as far as ever from the Philosopher's Stone or the secret of divining buried treasure. And Kelley found the quiet, scholarly household a strain after his adventurous life, and was subject to fits of violent rage, which the gentle Dee put up with. Kelley also complained that the spirits addressed him in foreign languages. He sneaked off whenever he could, on the pretext of seeking treasure, and no doubt found the brothels and ale houses of London more congenial than the Mortlake house. The spirits knew what he was up to, and often denounced him – in his presence, of course – to Dr. Dee, calling him 'a youngling, but old sinner', and telling Dee that his own 'sight' was perfecter than Kelley's, because purer.

In November 1582, Dee had a vision of a child-angel floating outside the window, holding a crystal egg. He identified this with Uriel. Then the Archangel Michael appeared and told Dee not to be afraid of it, but to pick it up. Since this crystal ball is now in the British Museum, there is presumably something behind the story, although I know of no precedent in occult history for spirits actually making gifts of 'spiritual' objects.

In 1583 a Polish nobleman, Count Adalbert Laski, was introduced to Dee. He was a servant of Henry III of France – whom we have already met in connection with Nostradamus – and he wanted Dee to foretell the king's future. He also thought Dee might give him advice, through the spirits, about his own claim to the Polish crown, vacated by Henry of Anjou when he became Henry III of France. Laski became such a regular visitor at Dee's house that Dee, who was always in debt, had to apply to the Queen for money to entertain him. Laski was so impressed by Dee and Kelley that he urged them to accompany him to Prague, to visit the king of Germany, the occult student Rudolph II. Dee disliked the idea, but Kelley cheered up at the prospect of travel, and even stopped having tantrums for a while. In 1585, Dee and Kelley, accompanied by their wives, and Dee's three children, set out on a Continental journey which was to last four years.

On the whole, it was a frustrating four years. Kelley was getting above himself; he had picked up magical jargon from Dee, and was now inclined to represent himself as the master. He claimed to be the owner of a rare alchemical manuscript and a 'powder of projection' (i.e. a powder for changing base metals to gold), which he had found at Glastonbury, the legendary home of Merlin and King Arthur.

They continued to converse with spirits and see visions, and Jane Dee produced more babies. Dee was kindly received by the great King Stephen Bathory of Poland at Cracow, but ordered out of Prague by King Rudolph, who explained that the Pope had accused him of necromancy. Count Wilhelm Rosenberg, viceroy of Bohemia, invited them to his castle at Tribau, and there Dee spent a peaceful eighteen months, although Kelley again became quarrelsome. When Kelley decided that he had had enough of descrying spirits in the crystal, Dee tried his eight-year-old son Arthur, but the boy saw nothing. Kelley agreed to try again, and this time had an amazing message. The guide Madimi had ordered him and Dee to share their wives in common. Jane Dee had hysterics, then became furious. When the child-angel Uriel confirmed the counsel, Dee added his persuasions, and wrote: 'There is no other remedy, but as hath been said of our cross-matching, so it must needs be done ... She showed herself prettily resolved to be content for God his sake and his secret purposes to obey the admonishment.' This sounds clear enough. although Dee's biographers all seem intent on preserving decency by insisting that the scandalous episode never took place, or at least, never reached the carnal stage.

Kelley now decided that nothing further was to be got by prolonging the partnership, and he and Dee finally separated. Dee returned to England; Kelley achieved some sucess as an alchemist and scryer, but seems to have died in prison not many years later.

Dee returned to England in 1589, and he was to live until 1608, to the age of eighty-one. But the remaining years of his life were, on the whole, disappointing. In his absence, his house had been broken into, and many of his books and instruments destroyed. The Queen finally granted him the wardenship of Christ's College at Manchester, then little more than a village, but he found it a frustrating post, and altogether less of a sinecure than he had hoped. His wife died of the plague there. He continued to write – his unpublished writing would occupy many volumes – and wrote about his dreams in his Diary. When the Queen died in 1603, Dee knew that his hopes of further preferment were at an end; James I had no use for a reputed sorcerer. The best he could hope for was to be left in peace.

His new scryer, Bartholomew Hickman, had visions of the angel Raphael, who uttered comforting messages and foretold that Dee would finally discover the secrets he had spent his life searching for. But the vision was probably inspired by Dee's own wishful thinking, for he died at Mortlake in 1608, still no nearer to the object of his life's quest. As his biographer G. M. Hort remarks, he cannot claim to rank among the world's successes. His main significance is that he was one of the first great occultists to make constant use of spirit communication; he was the founder of modern psychical research, two hundred years before his time.

By 1600, the age of magic was over. The voice of sane scepticism was making itself heard: in Rabelais, in Montaigne, in Ben Jonson. Montaigne was revolted by the burning of witches, and remarked: 'A brilliant and sharp clarity is needed to be able to kill people; our life is too real and substantial for supernatural, fantastic incidents.' No one, I think, not even an occultist, would disagree with him. The problem here is simply *what human consciousness is aware of.* William James, in *The Varieties of Religious Experience*, contrasts the 'sick soul', who is always too aware of the misery and suffering in the world, and the clear-eyed optimist, whose temperament rejects misery instinctively. The same thing applies to matters of the occult. A busy, energetic sort of person has no time for the supernatural, and his temperamental rejection of it makes him feel that his world of practical clear-cut issues is the only real one. It is a healthy instinct. We should bear in mind that nearly all children dislike the supernatural, except in ghost stories. This is not necessarily fear, but an instinctive need to confront a clear, simple world in which they can make decisions and shape their lives. Anyone who has ever learned to love science can understand this. There is something cold, hard and exhilarating about science, like a snowball fight on a frosty day; it seems to open up vistas of control and conquest. By comparison, the world of the occult is misty and damp, reminding man of his ignorance and encouraging him to adopt a passive attitude towards his existence.

With the age of Rabelais and Shakespeare, then of Newton and Milton, the human intellect reached a new stage in its evolution. There was a sense of potentialities, of exciting horizons. The discovery of America in 1492 was a symbol of this change. The Roman church was tottering under the blows dealt it by Luther and Henry VIII. It is true that Galileo was forced to recant the view he expressed in 1632, that the earth went around the sun, but in the year of his death (1642) Newton was born, and it no longer mattered greatly what the Pope and his cardinals said. With the publication of the *Principia* in 1687, science had taken a greater step forward than magic had taken since its birth in ancient Egypt and Chaldea. When one considers the involved absurdities of Cornelius Agrippa, John Dee and Trithemius, then turns to this magnificent, complex structure of ideas in which everything is true, it becomes possible to see why magic had ceased to be important.

The truth is that the rise of science was in no way a blow against occultism. On the contrary: it meant that occultism could free itself from the pseudo-science of Agrippa and Paracelsus and concentrate upon its real concerns.

The greatest occultist of the eighteenth century, although he belongs to the history of religion rather than magic, was born in the year after Newton published the *Principia*. Emanuel Swedenborg was a natural medium, although his powers developed late in life. In his early years he studied science and mathematics; at twenty-eight, he became assessor of the Swedish Board of Mines, and wrote a work on the smelting of metals. He studied astronomy and physiology. But he was an intensely frustrated man. Soon after he became an assessor, he fell in love with a Miss Pelhem, and was accepted by her; but she decided she did not care for Swedenborg after all, and broke off the engagement. Swedenborg was highly sexed, and it must have been a blow on every level: of pride, of emotion and of purely masculine sexuality. (In his book on *Conjugal Love* he shocked his followers by stating that concubinage and the keeping of mistresses are excusable under certain circumstances – a remarkable statement for the son of a bishop.) He was equally frustrated intellectually, for his scientific views, many of which were far ahead of his time, were ignored by Sweden's academies. He escaped his frustrations through hard work. In 1713, at about the time of his disappointment in love, Charles XII asked him to solve the problem of transporting five ships across fifteen miles of dry land (he was besieging the Danes in the fortress of Fredrikshald); Swedenborg did it in seven weeks. He was later involved in building the docks at Karlskrona and in building the canal that was to connect the North Sea to the Baltic (and which had to be abandoned when Charles XII was killed in battle). Swedenborg's energy was enormous; he wrote books on algebra, astronomy, minerals, economics, the tides, salt mining and on anatomy.

All this practical work starved the religious side of his nature, and in 1744 this burst out like a torrent. It began with a dream in which he heard a roaring wind that seemed to pick him up and fling him on his face. He began to pray, and then saw Jesus in front of him. After a cryptic conversation, which ended with Jesus saying, 'Well, then, so,' he woke up. This was only one of a series of strange dreams and hallucinations (or visions). He began having ecstatic trances, and the perpetual sexual itch suddenly ceased to trouble him. There followed visions in which he paid visits to heaven and hell. He announced in his books that the after-world is very much like this one in all basic particulars, and that people remain much as they were when they were alive. But since it is less substantial than this world, their states of mind are far more important, and heaven and hell are these states of mind. In such works as *The True Christian Religion*, *Heaven and Hell*, *The Divine Love and Wisdom*, he describes circumstantially conversations with angels, devils and people who have 'passed over'. And this leads us to the heart of the Swedenborg problem. Most of his contemporaries dismissed him as a madman or a liar. And his twentieth-century critics – E. J. Dingwall, for example – have been inclined to take a Freudian view and to regard his 'visions' as eruption of his repressed sexuality. There is a good case for this view. In 1748, when he was sixty, he woke up believing that his hair was full of small snakes, and attributed this to the departed spirits of certain Quakers. His view of the Quakers suggests a definite touch of paranoia; against all the evidence, he asserted repeatedly that their worship was vile and indecent, and that they practised wife-swopping. This seems to indicate a capacity for self-delusion and a sexual obsession.

On the other hand, when one turns to his writings, it becomes difficult to take this 'reductionist' view. His obsession with Biblical exegesis may bore the modern reader, and as far as style goes, he is certainly no Pascal or Newman; but it is all sane and lucid enough – refreshingly so. There are no flashes of genius in his work, but there is a balanced and deeply serious mind. When challenged by sceptics about his views, he remained calm and serious, never losing his temper, or even his sense of humour.

And although these views seemed wild and strange to his own contemporaries, they have received a great deal of support since then. Spiritualism did not exist in the eighteenth century; it came into existence in the 1850s. By the end of the nineteenth century there was a considerable body of literature that purported to have been dictated by 'spirits' (such as the *Spirit Teachings* of Stainton Moses), and these have continued to swell ever since.* The general tone of much of this literature is nauseatingly pietistic; but it must be admitted that it has a remarkable inner consistency; when one considers how easily religious sects develop their own doctrines and dogmas, this agreement is surprising. Its descriptions of 'the other

---

* 'Spirit teaching' may be briefly summarised as follows. Man is not 'saved' by the death of Jesus on the cross; he must save himself by his actions during his life. All thoughts and actions are registered on the 'spirit body', so that after death, a man is known for exactly what he is. One's actions are all important; a naturally good agnostic will achieve a higher status than an uninspired but punctilious churchgoer. 'Compensation' must be made for evil in the after-life, but there is no hell – it is a mental state. There is no upward limit to the progress of which the soul is capable, and which continues in the other world. These views are common to Swedenborg and to modern spirit teaching.

world' correspond closely to Swedenborg's. Sceptics may take the view that this is because Swedenborg influenced the spiritualists. Spiritualists deny this on the ground that the sheer variety and quantity of spirit writings – in many languages, and written over a century – disprove it. The only other logical explanation is the Jungian one that Swedenborg's visions were explorations of the racial psyche, expressions of archetypal symbols, and that the same is true of modern spiritualism. Without taking sides, we can only point out that the evidence in Swedenborg's favour is stronger today than it was in his own time.

On the other hand, what can one say about his book *Earths in the Universe*, in which he states that most of the planets have inhabitants, and then goes on to describe them in a way that suggests a painting by Hieronymus Bosch? The atmosphere of the moon is different from that of the earth so that moon-men speak from their stomachs instead of their lungs, with an effect like belching; the Martians have faces that are half black and half tawny; they live on fruit and dress in fibres made from tree bark. If Swedenborg was a medium, we can only assume the spirits were pulling his leg. Or, what is more likely, his imagination was so highly developed that he mixed up his dreams and fantasies with his authentic insights.

The Freudian, or reductionist, explanation cannot be entirely dismissed. Swedenborg *was* sexually frustrated; some of his religious experiences can be paralleled in any textbook of abnormal psychology. He was in his late fifties when his explosive psychological forces finally achieved a certain balance. But this recognition should not blind us to his genuine religious inspiration and the importance of his basic ideas. There was nothing of the charlatan about him, and his life does not show the parabolic rise and fall that seems characteristic of 'magicians'. Of the genuineness of his occult powers there can be little doubt.

Count Höpken, one of his contemporaries, tells the best known of these:

> Swedenborg was one day at a court reception. Her majesty asked him about different things in the other life, and lastly, whether he had seen or talked with her brother, the Prince Royal of Prussia. He answered no. Her majesty then requested him to ask after him, and give him her greeting, which Swedenborg promised to do. I doubt whether the Queen meant this seriously. At the next reception, Swedenborg again appeared at court; and while the Queen was ... surrounded by her ladies of honour, he came boldly forward and approached her majesty ... Swedenborg not only greeted her from her brother, but also gave her his apologies for not having answered her last letter; he also wished to do so now through Swedenborg; which he accordingly did. The Queen was greatly overcome, and said: 'No one but God knows this secret.'

On July 19, 1759, a great fire took place in Stockholm. Swedenborg was three hundred miles away at the time, in Gothenburg, a guest at a party. At six in the evening he told the guests that the fire had just broken out; two hours later, he told them that it had been extinguished only three doors from his home. This was confirmed two days later when a messenger arrived from Stockholm, verifying every detail of Swedenborg's description.

In 1761, Mme. de Marteville, the widow of the Dutch ambassador, asked Swedenborg for his help. A silversmith was demanding payment for a silver tea service, and she was certain her husband had paid for it before his death. However. she could not find the receipt. She asked Swedenborg if he could 'contact' her husband. Swedenborg said he would try. A few days later he told Mme. de Marteville that he had spoken to her husband, who said that the tea service *had* been paid for, seven months before his death, and that the receipt would be found in the bureau drawer. Mme. de Marteville replied that the bureau in question had been thoroughly searched. Swedenborg then described a secret compartment in the bureau that contained some private correspondence and the receipt. Both receipt and correspondence were found where Swedenborg had described them.

E. J. Dingwall, in a penetrating article on Swedenborg,* points out that the evidence for these three incidents, and for certain others of a similar nature, is confused and conflicting. This may well be so, but unless we intend to dismiss all these stories as fabrications or, at least, exaggerations, there is no point in dwelling on minor differences between versions written by different witnesses at different times. There have been many other mediums who have performed similar marvels. If the basic proposition of this book is correct – that the occult faculty is latent in everyone, and can be developed by anyone who really wants to – then it is likely enough that the three stories are fundamentally accurate. Swedenborg had the first important qualification for acquiring second sight and/or mediumship: lack of self-division, a wholehearted obsession with 'things spiritual'. But, like any other medium, Swedenborg was far from infallible, as his curious words about the Quakers demonstrate. When Swedenborg was asked by a friend if he could foretell the future, he replied flatly that only God knew the future. If he meant this as a general proposition, and not merely as a denial of his own powers, then he was again mistaken. The evidence for pre-vision is as abundant as for other forms of mediumship. Dingwall points out that another visionary named Humphrey Smith prophesied the Fire of London six years before it happened. So, for that matter, did the astrologer William Lilly, who was actually summoned before a committee investigating the Great Fire on suspicion of knowing more about it than he should because he had foreseen both the fire and the plague

* *Very Peculiar People*, London, 1950.

– and published his prediction – the previous year.

The real importance of Swedenborg lies in the doctrines he taught, which are the reverse of the gloom and hell-fire of other breakaway sects. He rejects the notion that Jesus died on the cross to atone for the sin of Adam, declaring that God is neither vindictive nor petty-minded, and that since he is God, he doesn't need atonement. It is remarkable that this common-sense view had never struck earlier theologians. God is Divine Goodness, and Jesus is Divine Wisdom, and Goodness has to be approached through Wisdom. Whatever one thinks about the extraordinary claims of its founder, it must be acknowledged that there is something very beautiful and healthy about the Swedenborgian religion. This feeling of breezy health is the basic reason for its enduring popularity. Its founder may not have been a great occultist, but he was a great man.

The new spirit of science meant, in effect, that a Paracelsus or John Dee could no longer exist. If Paracelsus had been born two centuries later, he would have been an eminent doctor and scientist, not a magician. As to the occultists themselves, they could no longer claim that science was on their side. Which meant, in effect, that they had to lay claim to extra-scientific knowledge. They had a choice: charlatanism or mysticism. And from the year 1700 onward, there is no 'magician' who lacks a streak of charlatanism.

This certainly applies to one of the most interesting transitional figures, Franz Anton Mesmer, who is falsely credited with having invented hypnotism (with which 'mesmerism' has become synonymous). His is one of the most curious stories in the history of occultism.

Mesmer's life should have been comfortable and uneventful. His parents were well-off; he was born in Switzerland on May 23, 1734, and took a degree at the University of Vienna at the age of thirty-two. The subject of his dissertation seems a throw-back to the age of

Paracelsus: *The Influence of the Planets on the Human Body*, written, of course, in Latin. He was a man of compelling personality. A rich patient, some years his senior, fell in love with him, and he married her and moved into her fine palace on the outskirts of Vienna. He also owned a luxurious townhouse at 261 Landstrasse.

The theory advanced by Mesmer in his thesis is of considerable interest. He believed in a kind of psychic 'ether' that pervades all space, and that the heavenly bodies cause tides in this fluid. These ever-moving tides produce health. If something checks their action in individuals, the result is sickness. In other words, health is man's natural condition; sickness is a kind of blockage. Man must rely on 'instinct' rather than reason, an instinctive oneness with nature. If a 'blockage' has occurred in a patient, the best way to cure it is to bring on a crisis which will sweep it away.

These theories interested a Jesuit named Professor Maximilian Hehl. He had been consulted by a wealthy English lady, who was passing through Vienna in 1774, because she had stomach cramps, and believed that a magnet could cure them; she had left hers at home. Hehl made her the magnet, which she laid on her stomach; her cramps vanished. Was it possible that the magnet was moving Mesmer's 'etheric fluid' around the body? He made this suggestion to Mesmer, who began trying the effect of magnets on his patients. Amazingly, they seemed to work. So the body *did* possess 'tides'.

Not long afterwards, Mesmer was bleeding a patient. (In those days it was the common cure for most ailments.) He observed that the flow of blood increased when he approached, and lessened when he moved away. The conclusion was clear; his own body must be a kind of magnet. Man possesses 'animal magnetism'. In 1775 Mesmer published a pamphlet about his discoveries. The medical profession was sceptical, but patients were anxious to try the new treatment, and Mesmer's practice increased. He would lay magnets on the patients, or simply his hands, and the pains would vanish.

What happened is clear enough. Mesmer believed that the magnets – and his hands – moved the stagnating 'magnetic fluid' in his sick patients: his patients also believed it. So when they felt relief, Mesmer had reason to believe that he had produced it. And, like Colonel Olcott, he began to develop healing gifts, the latent healing gifts that every human being possesses.

Mesmer's fame increased suddenly through an accident. A hypochondriac baron, Haresky de Horka, suffered from 'spasms' that doctors were unable to cure; finally, one tired and sarcastic doctor told him that he should try Mesmer, meaning, no doubt, to intimate that since the baron's troubles were imaginary, a quack could do them no harm.

Mesmer went to the baron's estate at Rokow. He had slipped several large magnets between his clothes to 're-charge' himself, for he believed that animal magnetism and the metallic kind are one and the same. For several days, the baron failed to respond to treatment, and the spasms continued. Mesmer, certain of his powers, persisted, and on the sixth day, the results began; as the baron writhed in asthmatic paroxysms, Mesmer held the baron's foot. The paroxysms abated. He held his hand; they started again. Clearly, Mesmer had finally got the measure of the baron's etheric fluids and was learning to make them flow back and forth as he wanted. After an hour of this, the baron felt fine. The cure became the gossip of Vienna, and the medical profession cursed their sarcastic colleague who had helped establish a charlatan.

Mesmer devised an apparatus to distribute the magnetism; a number of jars of 'magnetised water', with magnets immersed in it, were connected with steel bands, and the whole arrangement placed in a wooden tub half full of iron filings and water. A metal nozzle could be used to spray the magnetic power round the room. Trees in the garden were magnetised; so was the fountain. Patients lay around in the garden by the dozens, holding hands, and receiving the waves of magnetic power. The results continued to be remarkable.

Mesmer's downfall in Vienna came through a young blind pianist named Maria Theresia Paradies, a protegee of the Empress. Mesmer, unaware that her blindness was purely physical in origin – due to a detached retina – offered to cure her if she could come and live in his house. The Empress gave permission. The girl was naturally enthusiastic. And after a few weeks, she became convinced that she could see dimly. All Vienna discussed the case. But there were doubters, who pointed out that when Mesmer treated women patients they dressed in a loose smock and his hands carefully kneaded their breasts and thighs. Why were his resident patients all pretty girls? Why did he neglect his ailing and elderly wife? A Professor Barth was appointed to examine Maria Paradies, and he pronounced emphatically that she was still blind. The girl's father was influenced by Barth and the Jesuit Hehl, now an enemy of Mesmer's, to go and drag her away from the house of sin. The girl refused to go, even when her mother slapped her into a state of exhaustion. Finally, the Imperial Morality Police intervened, and Mesmer decided to flee Vienna before he was arrested. The girl returned to her parents. It is said that Mesmer had, in fact, helped improve her condition, and that Barth admitted this privately to Mesmer. However, the blindness certainly returned when the treatment was discontinued.

Mesmer went to Paris, and immediately became a craze. A century before Freud, he had discovered the importance of the sexual element in hysterical illnesses. He would enter his treatment room in a lilac silk dressing gown, carrying a long magnet, which he would point at patients as he passed. He would go into the next room and begin to play a magnetised piano. The patients would form a chain – men alternating with women – and press their thighs to increase the magnetism. Soon people would have convulsions, and collapse on the floor. Since magnetism was performed with hands, and the thighs were a sensitive area, they had every opportunity of trying out their animal magnetism on one another, all in the cause of medical science. Assistants would take away some of the more violently affected to the Crisis Room, where further animal magnetism was applied to bring on a climactic convulsion. Everyone believed totally in Mesmer's theories, for only ardent belief could justify these orgiastic activities. It was a delightful way of loosing repressions, and the treatment was understandably successful. Mesmer's fame spread throughout France. He instructed pupils in his methods, and established centres in many major cities. When conflict with the authorities began, it was Mesmer who was in the strong position. The king, Louis XVI, offered Mesmer a pension for life if he would promise to remain in France, but pointed out that he ought to allow a medical commission to examine proofs of his claims before a contract was signed. Mesmer declined to furnish proofs, and refused to sign a contract. He asked for a guaranteed half million francs for research, and threatened to leave France if it was not provided without strings attached. His aristocratic patients begged the king to give way, but Louis dug in his heels. On the day his ultimatum fell due, Mesmer left France – this was on September 18, 1780. His followers immediately started a fund, each contributing a hundred louis d'or for the privilege of being a shareholder in a new magnetic company. When the fund reached 350,000 louis d'or, far more than he had demanded, Mesmer agreed to return to France, and his activities continued as triumphantly as ever.

The King was understandably irritated by this behaviour, and finally succumbed to the demands of his Medical College to set up an independent commission of enquiry. In 1784 several doctors observed with fascination the violent convulsions of the patients, and concluded that although Mesmer certainly possessed strong powers of suggestion, there was no evidence of a magnetic fluid.

For Mesmer, this was the end of the boom. His fortunes declined gently. He was satirised and jeered at. A doctor went to him with a fake story of illness, allowed Mesmer to 'cure' him, then published an account of it all, claiming that it revealed Mesmer's inability to diagnose illness. Since the tide was against Mesmer, no one pointed out that most doctors could be taken in by the same methods. A concert given by Maria Paradies did nothing to improve the situation; she was as blind as ever. Mesmer had the courage to attend, and to ignore the whispers and comments of the audience, who all knew the story.

He stayed in Paris throughout the Revolution, but finally felt that his life was in danger and fled. He lost all his money. An attempt to set up practice in Vienna was foiled again by the police, who promptly banished him over the border. He was nearly sixty; he was tired, and the attacks had lowered the self-confidence that was the basis of his type of healing. He managed to live comfortably – a man with such a reputation could never lack for wealthy patients – and finally retired near Constance. He declined an offer from the King of Prussia to set up a Mesmer Institute in Berlin, whereupon the King sent a doctor to learn his secret, and the doctor was appointed professor of mesmerism at the Berlin academy and placed in charge of a hospital devoted to its methods. His last years were peaceful, and he died in 1815, just before his seventy-ninth birthday.

It may be felt that he was of no significance in the history of occultism. But this is not true. In important respects, he might almost be a reincarnation of Paracelsus. He recognised the importance of the spirit, the imagination, and felt that the universe is pervaded by meaningful influences. Most of his results can be explained in terms of hysteria, release of repression, auto-suggestion and so on. But what is important is that he understood that illness is not natural, but some kind of blockage of natural forces – a kind of mental stagnation. His instinctive desire was to set the vital forces in motion again. If the treatment had been entirely a matter of imagination, it would not have worked as well as it did. He did not understand the forces he was using, but he recognised their existence.

The discovery that he should have made, and is generally credited with having made, was stumbled upon by one of his disciples, the Marquis of Puységur, who was one day trying to 'magnetise' a shepherd boy by stroking his head when he observed that the young man had fallen asleep. Shaken, the boy remained insensible. The Marquis shouted 'Stand up,' and to his surprise, the boy stood up, without opening his eyes. When asked questions, he replied. When told to walk or sit down, he did so. Finally, when he woke up, he had no memory of what had happened. Puységur called the phenomenon 'spasmodic sleep', and it was for an Englishman, James Braid, to call it hypnotism in 1843. Braid realised that hypnotism is basically due to a narrowing of the attention until the mind is in a state of what he called mono-ideism (single-idea-ism). That is to say, the hypnotic trance is the reverse of what I have called Faculty X. It follows that since we are so seldom in that 'awakened' state when the mind is somehow aware of the reality of other times and other places, we are nearly always in a state of consciousness approximating the hypnotic trance.

If the fifteenth century is the century of magic, the eighteenth is the least magical of all. Magic reached its lowest point, and its three most noted practitioners – Cagliostro, Saint-Germain and Casanova – were adventurers rather than occultists.

To include Casanova among the 'magicians' may cause surprise; but he was, in fact, a serious student of the Kabbalah and astrology; and although he thought of himself as an imposter, his powers of prophecy often surprised and worried him. His *Memoirs*, besides being the world's greatest autobiography and the most complete picture of Europe in the eighteenth century, are also the best possible introduction to the forms taken by occultism in the 'age of reason'.

Giovanni Jacopo Casanova, who later added the spurious title Chevalier de Seingalt, was born in Venice in April 1725, son of an actor of Spanish descent and the beautiful daughter of a shoemaker, with whom he eloped. Young Giovanni was so sickly that he was not expected to live. A nosebleed continued so long that he was taken by his grandmother to a witch, who locked him in a box while she performed noisy incantations. The bleeding stopped. The witch burned drugs, gathered the smoke in a sheet and wrapped it around him. Finally, she told him that a beautiful lady would visit him that night. In the night, Casanova saw a beautiful fairy come out of the fireplace into his room – fire-grates were large in those days – who rubbed ointment on his head, speaking in a foreign language. His symptoms vanished during the next month, and he became a healthy and precocious boy.

Before we dismiss this story as evidence of Casanova's fecund imagination, it is worth bearing in mind that, like Cellini, he often sounds less truthful than he actually is; where it has been possible to check his stories against other sources, they have proved to be remarkably accurate. The witch was probably genuine, even if the fairy was a dream resulting from her suggestion.

In his teens Casanova became an abbé, but his enthusiasm for the opposite sex was his downfall; he was thrown out of the house of his patron, a senator, when he was caught with the senator's ward 'looking into the difference in conformation between a boy and a girl'. After more similar indiscretions, he left the Church for the army, then became a fiddler in a theatre and joined a band of daredevils who spent their nights looking for trouble.

One evening, he made the acquaintance of a senator named Bragadin, who suffered an apoplectic fit on the way home in a gondola. Casanova installed himself as a nurse; when the senator's two closest friends told Casanova he might go home if he wanted to, Casanova replied, with his natural theatrical instinct: 'If I go he will die; if I stay, he will get well.' Strangely enough, the prophecy proved accurate; in the night, Bragadin almost succumbed to a mercury poultice that his physician had put on his chest; Casanova removed it and washed his chest, whereupon the invalid fell into a peaceful slumber. The following day, the doctor resigned the case and left his patient in the charge of Casanova, who proceeded to quote medical authorities he had never read, and prescribed the correct treatment – rest and diet – by instinct.

Then came the fateful day: 'M. de Bragadin, who had the weakness to believe in the occult sciences, told me one day that, for a young man of my age, he thought my learning too extensive, and that he was certain I was the possessor of some supernatural endowment: Casanova, never one to fly in the face of providence, admitted that he was a Kabbalist and possessed the *Key of Solomon*. He found them easy to deceive. They asked him incomprehensible questions, and his 'oracle' gave incomprehensible answers, which they professed to find enlightening. 'I saw how easy it must have been for the ancient heathen priests to impose upon ignorant and therefore credulous mankind.'

He was given a generous allowance and treated like a son of the house. He took to gambling – his chief source of income throughout his life – and soon after, engaged in his first major deception as a magician. The motive seems to have been pure vanity and the spirit of mischief. In Mantua a young man persuaded him to go and look at the collection of antiquities owned by his father, among which was a knife, said to be the one with which St. Peter cut off the ear of the high priest's servant. (Luke states that it is a sword.) Casanova, amused by the credulous old gentleman, assured him that he was possessed of a fortune, since the knife had magical powers – it could be used to locate all the buried treasure in the Pope's dominions. However, its sheath was also needed, and fortunately Casanova knew the man who owned the sheath. He manufactured a sheath out of an old boot, which he showed to the antiquarian. He now offered himself as the magician who could unearth the treasure for them. The son had a letter from a man who thought there was treasure on his land, which was part of the papal estates. As he brought out the letter, Casanova managed to glimpse the name of the village – Cesena. He set up his 'oracle' – numbered cards made into 'pyramids' – and extracted the answer that the treasure in question was buried somewhere near the Rubicon. A map was consulted, and it was found that the Rubicon ran through Cesena. The old man and his son admitted the identity of the village, totally convinced they were dealing with a magician.

In Cesena, Casanova was introduced into the household of a wealthy peasant, George Franzia. The eldest daughter, a girl of fourteen named Javotte, was pretty, which was what Casanova had hoped. An adventure without sexual involvement would not have been to his taste.

He was a master in the art of obtaining confidence by various means. He told the old man that they must observe strict secrecy, for fear of the Inquisition. When he asked why it was that the inquisitors were more powerful than a magician, Casanova explained that it was because monks had more devils under their command.

He told them that Javotte would be their means of obtaining the treasure, because a pure virgin was necessary. Then, on successive days, he instituted a ritual bathing of members of the family: first the father, then the brother, and then – the whole point of the proceedings – Javotte. He explains that he did not expect to make her fall in love with him: 'but one finds a compensation in the complete control obtained over a woman'. He bathed her himself, and she responded to his caresses until 'her ardent fire was at last quenched by the natural result of that excitement'. On drying her, Casanova came close to destroying the virginity that was essential to his magic, but fortunately his own excitement also reached a harmless climax before he succumbed. The following morning, it was the girl's turn to bathe him, and she proved as expert at caresses as Casanova himself. She slept in his room, and from that night onward they slept together, although he continued to 'respect the essential point'. He decided that her virginity could remain intact until the night after the incantations.

He mentions passing a part of the following night observing some of the strange signs that had made Franzia certain the treasure was buried on his land. Heavy blows came from under the ground at intervals, and the cellar door opened and closed regularly, as if by invisible hands. He admits that he was unable to explain this, but concludes that 'there was some unknown roguery at work'.

When the hour came, he says: 'I throw off all profane garments. I clothe myself in the long white robe, the work of a virgin's innocent hands. I allow my long hair to fall loosely. I place the extraordinary crown on my head, the circle *maximus* on my shoulders, and, seizing the sceptre with one hand, the wonderful knife with the other, I go down into the yard. There I spread my circle on the ground, uttering the most barbarous words, and after going round it three times I jump into the middle.' A thunderstorm began to brew up, and Casanova experienced a fleeting regret that he had not thought of predicting that something of the sort might take place. But as the sky was split with lightning, he suddenly began to wonder if there wasn't something supernatural going on after all. And as the storm increased, he became convinced that if he was to escape with his life. he must remain in the magic circle.

The amusing consequence is that Casanova ended by being convinced that the innocence of the virgin was under the special protection of God, and that if he dared to violate it, 'the most rapid and terrible death would be my punishment'. And so he explained to Franzia that the seven spirits guarding the treasure had made him agree to delay digging it up, and gave him a long document describing the location and extent of the treasure. It is typical of Casanova that he later returned to present Javotte with a pair of expensive bracelets. In spite of his rogueries, he was fundamentally a good man.

There would be no point in relating his other exploits as a 'magician'. The ancient and gullible Madame D'Urfé believed in him implicitly, and he explains typically that 'if I had thought it possible to lead back Madame D'Urfé to the right use of her senses I would have made the attempt, but I felt sure her disease was without remedy, and the only course before me seemed to abet her in her ravings and profit by them'. He accordingly took part in remarkable ceremonies whose aim was to cause Madame D'Urfé's soul to pass into the body of a baby, so she could live all over again. The passage describing the ceremony is inimitably funny, and affords some insight into the kind of charlatanism employed by other 'magicians' besides Casanova; but it is too long to quote here.

On falling in love with a beautiful Englishwoman, Justiniana Wynne (whom he calls Mlle. X. C. V.), he made use of the name of Paracelsus to produce the desired result. She was pregnant by a lover who had deserted her, and told Casanova that she had a recipe for an 'aroph' that would terminate her condition; it was 'a kind of unguent composed of several drugs, such as saffron, myrrh, etc. compounded with virgin honey'. Casanova, whose advances had already been rejected, immediately added that the preparation became infallible if it was mixed with fresh male semen, and offering himself as the means of introducing the aroph into the mouth of the womb. 'We looked – I like a medical student about to perform an operation, and she like a patient, with this difference, that it was the patient who arranged the dressing. When she was ready – that is, when she had placed the aroph as neatly as a skull-cap fits a parson, she put herself in the proper position for the preparation to mix with the semen.' It is sad to relate that, in spite of dozens of applications of the aroph to the mouth of the womb, Paracelsus's recipe failed, and Miss Wynne eventually had the baby in a convent.

Casanova possessed a natural 'occult faculty'. When some of his absurder prophecies came true, he would experience for a moment the superstitious awe he felt in the thunderstorm; once, when he made a careless slip in consulting the pyramid-oracle, the answer obtained struck him as utterly wild; but it proved to be correct. In Dux, where he spent his declining years, he stated that a certain cat would have six black kittens, and the cat had precisely that number.

His occult faculty accounted for his amazing luck during his first forty years; a 'sixth sense' made him say or do the right thing, as when he found himself announcing that if he stayed with Bragadin, he would live. The same thing applies to his relations with women. If the *Memoirs* were a novel, it would explain why there is an odd similarity about his sexual exploits; the author would be recording his own fantasies. Some commentators have questioned Casanova's veracity on precisely these grounds: that the same type of girl, the same type of situation, keep recurring. For readers with more insight, and sympathy, this is precisely what assured his basic veracity. In real life, the same type of thing *does* keep happening to people with a definite personality. Casanova, with his punctilious good manners and his genuine protectiveness and generosity towards women, was always meeting a type of impressionable girl who, within days or even hours, was saying, 'Do what you like with me, I am yours.' It is typical that his own daughter fell in love with him – without, of course, knowing his identity.

This curious psychic radar began to fail him in his late thirties, when his passion for a beautiful courtesan, La Charpillon, led him to commit various follies, none of which brought him any closer to his goal. She was one of his few total failures; she set out to humiliate him, and succeeded. The superb confidence that had for years brought him the luck of a sleepwalker was cracked. And from now on, although he still had his triumphs ahead of him, he was on the downhill slope of defeat. It is interesting to reflect that precisely the same thing happened to Mesmer during his later Paris period. The confidence went; and what is a mesmerist without confidence? Casanova lived to be seventy-three, dying two years before the end of the century he had dramatised so brilliantly; but something of the essential Casanova died in London with his passion for La Charpillon.

In the long-drawn-out frustration of his last days, Casanova kept his soul alive by writing his *Memoirs*; but when Count Marcolini at Dresden refused to allow even the first volume to be printed, he lost heart and broke off the writing at the point where he had reached his fiftieth year. How great is the loss may be a matter of some dispute, for the remaining years of his life might have left the reader with a bitter taste in his mouth. But there is one cause of regret for all students of the occult: that Casanova did not describe his second meeting with one of the most baffling men of the age, the 'Count Cagliostro'; he might have cleared up a mystery that must now remain unsolved. Everyone has heard the name of Cagliostro; for most people, it has sinister and dubious associations, rather like that of Rasputin. Few people, even among the well-informed, knew very much about him, for even the basic facts of his life are in doubt. The only thing we know with any certainty is that he died tragically in the prisons of the Inquisition in 1795, probably strangled by his jailer. Opinions as to his powers and abilities cover the whole spectrum, from Carlyle's 'King of Liars' and 'Great Quack Face' to Lewis Spence's 'One of the great occult figures of all time'.

Even his identity is still a matter for argument. In her book on the Diamond Necklace affair, Frances Mossiker remarks: 'Those who consult the encyclopedias will find it stated as categorical fact that Count Alessandro di Cagliostro was "Giuseppe Balsamo of Palermo". It is enough to shake one's faith in reference books, in view of the fact that the basis for such identification must rest for eternity on the evidence of an anonymous letter to the Paris police ...' But Miss Mossiker ends by more or less acknowledging that Cagliostro and Balsamo are probably the same person. W. R. H. Trowbridge denied it emphatically in his book on Cagliostro, asserting that although Casanova met Balsamo, whom he describes unflatteringly, he never met Cagliostro. F. Ribadeau Dumas, the author of *Cagliostro, Scoundrel or Saint?* has the highest possible opinion of Cagliostro, but accepts that he was Balsamo. Goethe was sufficiently fascinated by Cagliostro to pay a visit to Balsamo's family when he was in Palermo – a full account of the visit can be found in Funck-Brentano's *Cagliostro and Company* – but he portrays him as a swindler in his play *The Grand Copht*.

But Goethe's interest in Cagliostro is a clue to the truth that probably lies behind all these contradictions. It was not, I think, the interest of the artist in the scoundrel – the interest that made Thomas Mann write a book about a confidence man. It was a recognition of a fundamental similarity between the two of them. Shaw remarked that no man is at home in society until he has found his natural place, either above or below the one he is born to. Cagliostro and Goethe were both born far below their natural places; both ended up hobnobbing with princes and cardinals, and gaining universal respect on the strength of inborn genius. And there *was* a natural genius, a natural strength in Cagliostro, that made itself felt. A hostile witness, the Baroness D'Oberkirch, met him at Cardinal Rohan's at Saverne, and describes him: 'While not actually handsome, his face was the most remarkable I have ever seen. His eyes, above all. They were indescribable, with supernatural depths – all fire and yet all ice. It seemed to me that if any two artists sketched him, the two portraits, while having some slight resemblance, might yet well be totally dissimilar. Ambivalent, he at once attracted and repelled you; he frightened you and at the same time inspired you with insurmountable curiosity.' Casanova had described him about ten years earlier as 'short and badly hung, and his face bore all the indications of daring, impudence, sarcasm and imposture'. But this sounds like hindsight sharpened by jealousy. Baroness D'Oberkirch says: 'Cagliostro was possessed of a demonic power; he enthralled the mind, paralysed the will.' This is no vulgar adventurer; it is a man of real force.

When Cagliostro was in the hands of the Inquisition, his biography was written by one of its hirelings. Naturally, it portrays him simply as a scoundrel and cheat; Carlyle and all other hostile commentators have followed this Inquisition biography, whose avowed aim is to cut its subject down to size. The obvious question arises: If Cagliostro was such a contemptible rogue, how did he achieve such influence over so many people? Carlyle replies: Because he was one of the greatest cheats that ever lived. And this crude and simplistic view simply denies the remarkable power to which so many people have testified.

If it is accepted that Cagliostro was, in his way, a man of genius – that is, of an intelligent vitality far above the average – the contradictions begin to vanish, and the story of his life takes on a shape and direction that is absent from Casanova's.

It is fairly certain that he was born Giuseppe Balsamo, son of a poor family of Palermo, in 1743. Goethe describes the family as simple but warm-hearted peasants, living in a single room. His father died when he was young, and since his disposition was naturally explosive, he soon became ungovernable. He was sent to the seminary school of San Rocco, but ran away several times; he was then enrolled as a novice in the Benfratelli of Cartegirone. One day, in a burst of anticlerical exuberance, he shocked the brothers by improvising freely on the sacred text he was supposed to be reading aloud at supper, substituting the names of notorious prostitutes for those of the saints. This achieved the effect he had been aiming for: he was thrown out. He now took lessons in drawing, for which he showed unusual talent. His skill with the pen and brush extended to copying letters, theatre tickets and anything else that would bring a profit.

He was naturally attracted to the occult, and to alchemy and astrology. It is not certain where he acquired his basic knowledge. But Sicily has always had a strong tradition of witchcraft and occultism, and no doubt instruction was easy to come by. He possessed a natural degree of second sight. This is evidenced by the story told by Baroness D'Oberkirch, who describes how Cagliostro, immediately after seeing her for the first time, suddenly announced: 'You lost your mother a long time ago. You hardly remember her. You were an only child. You have one daughter, and she will be an only child. You will have no more children.' Pressed to answer by Cardinal Rohan, the offended Baroness, who objected to being addressed so familiarly, finally admitted that he was right about herself. His prediction about her daughter also came true.

The stories of his rascalities at this period all stem from his Inquisition biographer, and may therefore be suspect. The most famous of them states that he gained the confidence of a miserly goldsmith, and convinced him that he could make gold. The incantations took place in a remote field at midnight, and at the crucial moment, ruffians dressed as demons rushed out and knocked the goldsmith insensible. When he recovered his senses, Balsamo managed to convince him that the demons had made off with the large amount of gold they had brought with them for purposes of magical conjuration. The same source adds that Balsamo was himself robbed by two accomplices in Calabria, and reached Rome, at the age of seventeen, completely destitute. He managed to live by his artistic talents. Goethe tells a story of how Balsamo forged some documents at the request of the Sicilian marquis, and was thrown into prison in consequence. The enraged marquis went to see the judge, and met the prosecuting counsel in his anteroom. He ended by knocking him down and jumping on him. The judge was so impressed by this display of conviction that he freed Balsamo on the spot.

Whether the forgery story is true or not, it is certain that he continued to study occultism, and became the laboratory assistant of a Greek named Altotas, who, among other things, had discovered a process for giving flax fibres the glossy feeling of silk. They travelled in Egypt, and called at Malta, where they made the acquaintance of the grand master of the Knights of Malta, a man named Pinta. Pinta was an enthusiastic amateur of alchemy, and welcomed the two adepts. Balsamo so impressed him that he later gave him letters of introduction to distinguished men in Rome and Naples. In Rome, as a dashing young artist of twenty-six, Balsamo was fascinated by a beautiful fourteen-year-old girl, daughter of a copper smelter who lived in an alley named after the local church of the Trinita de Pellegrini, in a slum quarter. Lorenza Feliciani was illiterate but dazzling, and in spite of some opposition from her father, she married Balsamo.

It was in the following year that Casanova met them at Aix-en-Provence in the south of France. He says that they were assumed to be people of rank because they had distributed alms generously on entering the town. They had made a pilgrimage to St. James of Compostella in Italy, and then to Our Lady of Pilar in Spain, and were now going back to Rome. Lorenza, who impressed Casanova as modest, devoted and honest, said that the alms they had given were the excess from the money they had received at the last town, where they had begged them. Balsamo asked Casanova to take up a collection for them at the table d'hôte, and Lorenza asked him to give them a letter of introduction for Avignon. Later, Balsamo proved his skill as a forger by making such an exact copy of the letter that Casanova himself swore that the copy was his original letter. He warned Balsamo to be careful, or his talent might cost him his life.

From this story, it is clear that Balsamo had found a jewel in his wife. With her gentle beauty, she made a far more favourable impression than Balsamo could have created alone.

Whether the pilgrimage was undertaken for religious reasons is a different matter. Balsamo was a man who had something inside him that wanted to get out. He could not have settled down to copper smelting in Rome. He felt the world held something important in store for him, and he meant to keep moving until he found it.

They seem to have returned to Spain, for Lorenza later recounted how the viceroy in Barcelona tried to seduce her, and then, when she repulsed him, tried to get her arrested as an unmarried woman living in sin. In Madrid, Balsamo worked for the Duke of Alva. In the following year they came to London, and Balsamo worked as a painter and decorator for a while with a fellow Italian. And there is a story that he extorted a hundred pounds from a Quaker who fell in love with his wife and was caught by him in a compromising position. It is certain that he went to prison for debt, having failed in a lawsuit against someone who owed him for pen drawings. Lorenza persuaded a philanthropist named Sir Edward Hales (whom she later called 'Sir Dehels') to get her husband out of jail. He did more than this; he gave Balsamo a job decorating the ceiling at his home near Canterbury. Balsamo was not used to this kind of work, and when the ceiling was ruined, they left for France.

Lorenza describes an acquaintance they made on the boat. 'On the passage to France we made the acquaintance of M. Duplessis, the Steward of the Marquis de Prie, who showed us all kind of civilities. And when M. Balsamo showed him some of his works, he appeared surprised. "You will make your fortune in Paris," he said. "I am an advocate at the Parliament, and I know many lords; don't distress yourself, I'll present you to the king. You won't have to go on your travels again. Your wife is very pleasant, very pretty, very charming. I'll do all I can to set you up in Paris.'"

Balsamo must have guessed that Duplessis was more interested in Lorenza than himself, but the prospect of finally settling down to a prosperous existence no doubt made him prefer to ignore the danger and hope for the best.

They were destitute when they arrived in Calais, but M. Duplessis offered Lorenza a seat in his carriage.

"'And what of my husband?" I [she] said.

"'Can't he wait a little at Calais? He will come on later.'"

She declined. So Duplessis offered Balsamo the use of a horse. The long ride to Paris must have been hard on his seat. Meanwhile, M. Duplessis was whispering declarations of love in Lorenza's ear. 'Thus tormented against my will, I was several times tempted to stop and leave M. Duplessis, in order to escape the solicitations and actual violence he showed me … but knowing the irritable and fiery nature of my husband, I feared to inform him of what was going on …' In Paris, M. Duplessis let them stay at the house of the Marquis de Prie. Balsamo was naturally more tired than his wife and retired to bed, while she went to an opera with M. Duplessis. This continued for two months, and it seems that Lorenza finally ceded her virtue one night when her husband went to visit an apothecary. But having made Lorenza his mistress, Duplessis now wanted her to separate from her husband. She was won over to the extent of moving into apartments in the Rue St. Honoré. Balsamo went mad with jealousy and rage – a reaction that throws doubt on the story of his deliberate complicity in his wife's seduction. He applied to the king for redress. It was granted, and in February 1773 Lorenza went into the women's gaol of Sainte Pélagie, where she made the statement that has been quoted. She spent nearly a year in prison, while her repentant husband tried to get her out. When she was released in December, his fortunes had taken a turn for the better. A skin lotion containing borax had made him money, and he had become instructor in alchemy to two amateurs of the subject. They decided to return to Italy, this time in style. Balsamo now called himself the Marchese Pellegrini – taking the name of the church near his wife's home. They visited Balsamo's family in Palermo, and he rented a house there for a time. Unfortunately the goldsmith he had swindled was still alive, and had Balsamo imprisoned. W. R. H. Trowbridge asserts that Goethe's story of the Sicilian marquis, who effected Balsamo's release by jumping on the prosecuting attorney, belongs to this period rather than to his early *Wanderjahre*.

In 1776, Balsamo returned to London and changed his name to Cagliostro, which happened to be the name of an uncle in Palermo. Two important events took place on this second visit to England. He was admitted to the Lodge of Freemasons. And he was fleeced by confidence tricksters who thought he had a manuscript containing an infallible system for predicting the winning numbers in a lottery. The story is obscure, although it seems fairly well authenticated. Cagliostro may have predicted certain winning numbers through his power of second sight, but he did not want to continue doing it. There were lawsuits involving a necklace, and, as Carlyle puts it, 'the most accomplished swindler of the swindling eighteenth century was … hobbled, duped and despoiled by the aid of the masterly fictions of English law'. It is impossible to know how far Cagliostro was to blame.

Altogether more important, from the point of view of his future, was his admission to the Esperance Lodge of Freemasons, at the rooms of the King's Head in Gerrard Street, Soho, on April 12, 1777. He called himself 'Joseph Cagliostro, Colonel of the 3rd Regiment of Brandenburg', and his wife also became a mason.

The freemasons are a 'secret society' of a religious nature, whose basic tenet is the brotherhood of man. Originally a society of stone-workers who travelled around Europe wherever great buildings were being erected, with a system of secret signs for recognising one another, it became the home of occultists, alchemists, astrologers and so on. Readers of *War and Peace* will remember Peter Bezukhov's encounter with the freemasons when he is in a state of pessimism and exhaustion. Although Tolstoy was not himself a mason, he states their aims with clarity and sympathy. First, the notion of brotherhood: 'No one can attain to truth by himself. Only by laying stone on stone *with the co-operation of all* [my italics] by the millions of generations from our forefather Adam to our own times, is that temple reared which is to be a worthy dwelling place of the Great God.' This notion of a long secret tradition is of fundamental importance: 'The first and chief object of our Order, the foundation on which it rests and which no human power can destroy, is the preservation and handing on to posterity of a certain important mystery, which has come down to us from the remotest ages, even from the first man – a mystery on which perhaps the fate of mankind depends. But since this mystery is of such a nature that nobody can know or use it unless he be prepared by long and diligent self-purification, not everyone can hope to attain it quickly. Hence we have a secondary aim: that of preparing our members as much as possible to reform their hearts, to purify and enlighten their minds, by means handed on to us by tradition ...' He goes on to describe their third aim: the regeneration of mankind. (This is the one that appeals most to Peter.) Then he details the 'seven steps of Solomon's temple'. (There is a close connection between the idea of masons and temples, inevitably.) They are discretion, obedience, morality, love of mankind, courage, generosity, love of death. Peter is enjoined to meditate continually on death, and he finds this the most difficult proposition to swallow.

Tolstoy's description of the initiation rites should also be read by anyone who wants to understand the attraction of freemasonry. To a non-mason, these are bound to sound absurd; the aspirant wears a slipper on one foot and a boot on the other, and is led blindfolded through passages, led along certain carpets to the accompaniment of knockings with mallets and swords, made to hold a pair of compasses against his breast, confronted by men in robes pointing swords at him, made to kneel 'at the gates of the temple' and so on. At one point, Peter suddenly wonders if it is all a practical joke. Frank King, in his book *Cagliostro, the Last of the Sorcerers*, summarises Cagliostro's initiation briefly:

> The ceremony was very similar to that which is performed in Masonic Lodges today with the addition of several harmless but undignified scenes which were intended to impress the candidate. Thus Joseph was hauled up to the ceiling by a rope and allowed to dangle, signifying his helplessness without divine aid. He was stabbed with a dagger, the blade of which collapsed into its handle, to emphasise the fate which would be his should he betray the secrets of the Order. He had to kneel, divested of his clothing, to show his subservience to the Master of the Lodge.

It can be seen that the freemasons are direct descendants of the Orphics and Pythagoreans. The aim of the initiation is to produce an immense sense of significance and reverence. It is not surprising that, at the end of it all, Tolstoy's hero 'felt as if he had returned from a long journey on which he had spent dozens of years, had become completely changed, and had quite left behind him his former habits and way of life'.

This also makes it clear why the freemasons have always been persecuted, particularly in Catholic countries. The Church may feel that Protestantism and its various sects are bastard offshoots of the parent tree, weak imitations that can never be a real challenge because they cannot offer a real *alternative* to the immense apparatus of Catholicism. The freemasons were virtually setting up an alternative church that claimed far greater antiquity than Catholicism. The man who joined it felt himself a member of *the* fundamental Secret Society, guarding the most ancient mystery. The problem of any organised religion is always the same: how to imbue its followers with such a profound sense of purpose that old habits and personality patterns are permanently remoulded. The freemasons did this by using the techniques of the Mysteries of ancient Greece. The initiate would emerge from all this with a sense of being in a neat and orderly universe, where his aims and purposes are suddenly quite definite. A tradition dating back to Adam stands behind him. The notion of the brotherhood of man gives him a new sense of belonging to the human race. What is more, the world is full of brother masons – actively benevolent brothers who will not allow him to sink. This is, of course, an extremely important part of the attraction of any religion, for the craving for security and 'territory' is deeper even than the religious instinct; at least, it demands to be satisfied first in most people. The real power of the Catholic Church in the Middle Ages lay in monasteries, where the monks were given this basic 'security of tenure', so to speak.

I have discussed freemasonry at such length because it is impossible to explain the remainder of Cagliostro's life without it. Up to now, he had remained an adventurer on much the same level as Casanova, an artist driven from pillar to post by adversity, by a fate that seemed to take pleasure in tormenting him and kicking his feet from under him. The wandering life produces a sense of pointlessness and contingency, a slow erosion of self-respect. Cagliostro was thirty-four; he had been wandering for nearly twenty years; the life of adventure had lost its charm. This was like coming home. Its emotional effect was as profound as on Peter Bezukhov. The transformation was total. He had been thrown a lifeline, and he lost no time in scrambling ashore. From then on, freemasonry was his life's work.

Moreover, since he himself was a born magician, was he not naturally one of the priests of this religion? His business was not to be a simple follower, like the valet and the ageing alchemist who had been received into the London lodge at the same time as himself. He was a grand master by right. If he had joined the Catholic Church he would have set out to become pope, feeling that was his natural position. And his fellow Catholics would have found his pushiness hard to tolerate. The masons didn't mind it in the least. There could be no doubt about the genuineness of his conversion; he would obviously be a powerful proselytiser. Just as Italy was the original home of Catholicism, so England was the parent country of freemasonry, for although it had not been its original home, it had been the source of the great revival of freemasonry in the sixteenth century. And where was the original home of freemasonry? Cagliostro knew the answer: almost certainly, Egypt. What is the world's earliest great architectural monument? The pyramids. Is not the Great Pyramid of Cheops full of secret measurements embodying arcane secrets? Masons later built the Temple of Solomon, but that was long after, a whole two millennia later (Cheops was about 2900 B.C.; Solomon belongs to the tenth century B.C.)

Cagliostro claimed that on his visit to London he picked up at a bookstall a manuscript on the subject of Egyptian magic and masonry by one George Gaston. Whether this is true or not is unimportant. Cagliostro either discovered or invented 'the Egyptian rite', an even more ancient and solemn rite than that of the modern masons. He devoted the remainder of his life to establishing the Egyptian rite. This was by no means an alternative to already established rites of freemasonry; it was a higher order, and only freemasons could qualify for it. As far as freemasonry was concerned, the idea was a good one. A still higher order of adepts could only broaden their base and extend their influence.

The founders of Egyptian masonry were the prophets Elijah and Enoch; the latter was known as the Grand Copt, or Copht. In due course, Cagliostro promoted himself from agent of the Grand Copt to the Grand Copt himself. He also added some impressive mystifications to his claims. The pupils of the prophets never die; like Elijah, they are eventually transported bodily into heaven. They have twelve lives, and after each, rise up from their ashes like the phoenix. Cagliostro began to drop hints that he was thousands of years old. His wife, although she continued to look twenty even in her thirties, dropped hints about an officer son serving in the army. There can be no doubt that Cagliostro continued to be something of a confidence man. But his aims were no longer personal. He saw freemasonry as the supreme good for the world; it was his task to spread the word. The rites of freemasonry are symbolic, like the Catholic mass. Cagliostro's claims about the prophet Enoch and the phoenix were simply an extension of this symbolic truth; their aim was to create the right frame of mind, to raise men above their old selves. The absurd miracles of the saints and martyrs are intended to have the same effect.

What is more important, the psychological change that took place in Cagliostro, and the new lack of self-division, had the effect on his 'occult powers' that we might expect. They increased suddenly. There are few stories about Balsamo's power of second sight or healing; there are dozens about Cagliostro's. He had a remarkable faculty of clairvoyance, and was inclined to use young children as mediums. He would breathe upon the child's chin and forehead, and then make mystic symbols on his forehead and hand. The five-year-old son of Marshal von Medem was made to stare at his hand, and his father asked him what his sister was doing. The Countess von der Recke describes what happened in her memoirs: '... he described her as placing 'her hand on her heart as though in pain. A moment later, he exclaimed: "Now she is kissing my brother. who has just come home." On the Marshal declaring this to be impossible, as this brother was leagues away, Cagliostro terminated the séance, and with an air of the greatest confidence ordered the doubting parent to "verify the vision". This the Marshal immediately proceeded to do; and learnt that his son, whom he believed so far away, had unexpectedly returned home, and that shortly before her brother's arrival his daughter had had an attack of palpitation of the heart.'

Cagliostro now had a mission – and a way of making a living. Now, when he entered a European city, he made for the Masonic Lodge, made speeches about the Egyptian rite and initiated members into it. He seems to have gone to Venice, Berlin, Nuremberg and Leipzig. In Leipzig, at a banquet given in his honour, he prophesied that if the lodge failed to adopt the Egyptian rite, its master would feel the weight of the hand of God before the end of the month. When the master, a man named Scieffort, committed suicide not long afterwards, the masons of Leipzig followed Cagliostro's advice. His tour of Europe became a triumphal procession from lodge to lodge as his reputation preceded him. Trowbridge, his warmest defender, admits that 'he did not hesitate to recruit his followers by imposture when without it he would have failed to attract them', but adds, with undoubted accuracy, that there is not a single authenticated instance in which he derived personal profit by imposture. The impostures seem to have been mostly in the matter of clairvoyance. The solemn Egyptian rite of initiation, which included long speeches in foreign languages by the Grand Copt, ended with a ceremony in which a young boy or girl (called *pupilles* or *colombes*) practised clairvoyance by gazing into a bowl of water. It appears that Cagliostro was not above bribing the *pupille* or *colombe* in advance. On one embarrassing occasion, after a highly successful séance, the *colombe* announced that it had all been fixed in advance, and Cagliostro had to brazen his way out of it.

His stay in Courland seems to have been typical of what happened in most places. The head of the lodge, Marshal von Medem, and the marshal's eldest daughter, Countess von der Recke, were deeply impressed by the Grand Copt. His exhibition of clairvoyance through the five-year-old son, mentioned above, was successful. So were séances where invisible angels kissed the child medium – the kisses all being clearly audible. At séances Cagliostro also gave remarkable performances of thought-reading; he possessed the same kind of power that Gilbert Murray later displayed. He correctly foretold that the countess had recovered from an illness, and would be found at a certain hour writing at her desk. However, the countess was a mystic with Swedenborgian leanings, and all this spiritualism struck her as morbid. When Cagliostro, like Casanova, began to speak of how to recover buried treasure with the aid of spirits, her faith in him began to collapse, and he decided it was time to move on.

The next stop was St. Petersburg. But here his luck ran out. It was here that his *colombe* suddenly betrayed him after a successful séance. His wife also, it seems, betrayed him with the Empress Catherine's lover, Potemkin, which pleased neither the magician nor the Empress. Her doctors, two Scotsmen named Rogerson and Mouncey, also prejudiced her mind against him. Licking his wounds, he moved on to Strasbourg.

It was here that his fortunes took a steep turn for the better. He was already a rich man, and he entered Strasbourg on September 19, 1780, preceded by six liveried servants on black horses, and driving in his black japanned coach covered with magic symbols. Crowds lined the route; they had been waiting all day. He did not move to a luxury hotel, but to a small room over a tobacconist's in a poor quarter, where he proceeded to distribute alms and cure the sick. There can be no doubt whatever that, charlatan or not, Cagliostro tried to live by the highest principles of masonry. Just as, ten years earlier in Aix, he had given away his excess money to the poor, so now he set out to practise philanthropy on a grand scale.

He had developed another typical characteristic. Perhaps because he was so often snubbed by the aristocracy as a charlatan, he was inclined to refuse to treat them, or even to meet them if they came to his door. This is understandable. He felt he was working for the regeneration of mankind; he was an idealist; why should he gratify the idle curiosity of self-opinionated aristocrats? When the philosopher Lavater, a friend of Goethe, asked to meet him, Cagliostro replied: 'If your science is greater than mine, you have no need of my acquaintance; if mine is the greater, I have no need of yours.' Lavater persisted, and later became the warmest of Cagliostro's defenders.

It is now that Cardinal de Rohan enters the story. He was a strange man, a prince of the family of Bourbon, tall, handsome, rich, enormously charming. In spite of his position in the Church, he loved wine, hunting and the opposite sex. The sorrow of his life was that the queen, Marie Antoinette, disliked him. Her mother, Maria Theresa of Austria, had taken a strong dislike to him when he was ambassador to Austria, and his dreams of becoming the Richelieu, the Mazarin, behind Louis XVI, were receding further every day. He had another sorrow, even more curious: he was in love with the Queen. He had met her for the first time ten years earlier, when she came through Strasbourg (of which Rohan was the bishop), a girl of fifteen en route to join her husband. She was very beautiful, with ash-blonde hair and a perfect complexion, and a slim figure that would later become plumper. When the cardinal-bishop administered communion to the kneeling princess, he found himself envying the husband who would shortly claim her virginity. But, oddly enough, this was not to be. In bed with his beautiful young wife, the future king of France became impotent. In his diary he wrote 'Nothing'. What was worse, the situation soon became common knowledge all over Europe. Louis's doctors said that the trouble was physical not psychological and that it could be cured by a scalpel; but the King (he came to the throne in 1774) was afraid of pain and declined. So for the next six years, he clambered on to his wife every night, and the result continued to be 'Nothing'. It must have struck the cardinal as a sinful waste, and deepened his morbid preoccupation with the lovely ash blonde.

It was ten years after the meeting that the cardinal-bishop of Strasbourg heard about the miracle worker who was now living in the town. He sent a note to Cagliostro, and was promptly rebuffed, in the same manner as Lavater. Cagliostro replied that if he was ill, he would cure him; if he wasn't, then he had no need of a doctor, nor the doctor of him. The cardinal, unoffended, declared that he had asthma and asked Cagliostro to attend him. The two immediately impressed one another. The cardinal told the Abbé Georgel that he saw in Cagliostro's face 'a dignity so impressive that he felt himself in the grip of an awesome religious experience'. It was the cardinal-prince who became the acolyte and disciple, and who was flattered when Cagliostro told him one day, 'Your soul is worthy of my own. You deserve to be the confidant of all my secrets.' The Baroness D'Oberkirch, like many others, reacted unfavourably to the idea of an adventurer gaining so much influence over Rohan, yet found him hypnotically fascinating. Baron de Gleichen has left an accurate portrait:

> Cagliostro was small, but he had a very fine head which could have served as the model for the face of an inspired poet. [In fact, Cagliostro's bust gives him a strong resemblance to William Blake.] It is true that his tone, his gestures and his manners were those of a charlatan, boastful, pretentious and arrogant, but it must be remembered that he was an Italian,

a physician giving consultations, self-styled Masonic grand master, and a professor of occult sciences. Otherwise his ordinary conversation was agreeable and instructive, his actions noble and charitable, and his healing treatments never unsuccessful and sometimes admirable: he never took a penny from his patients.

And Cagliostro *was* fabulously successful in Strasbourg; both as an occultist and a doctor. Sometimes it was simply warmth and confidence that produced their effect, as when he was successful in delivering a baby for a woman who had been given up by midwives. He decided the baby was still alive, and soothed her and gave her confidence, admitting afterwards to Gleichen that the result was due to luck rather than skill. He cured the Marquis de Lasalle of a gangrened leg. When the cardinal's uncle, the Prince de Soubise, was dangerously ill, the cardinal took Cagliostro along to see him without disclosing the Grand Copt's identity. The prince had been given up by his regular doctors. but Cagliostro had him up and about within three days. It was this cure that improved his reputation with the aristocracy.

His séances in Strasbourg were equally impressive, and he gave indubitable proofs of second sight and telepathy: reading the contents of a sealed envelope, predicting what people were doing in other places and successfully avoiding traps set for him by the unbelieving (when a widow asked a question about her husband, the *colombe* remained silent until the woman admitted the trick).

He impressed the Baroness D'Oberkirch by telling her one day that the Empress of Austria had just died; it took three more days for the news to reach Strasbourg. The baroness, while fascinated by Cagliostro, was determined to resist him, continuing to believe that he wanted some favour of her – an introduction to the Grand Duchess of Russia? (She could not have been aware that

Cagliostro had left St. Petersburg under a cloud.) She told Rohan that she was convinced Cagliostro wanted to fleece him of money; the cardinal replied by showing her a diamond-and-gold ring worth 20,000 francs, which he claimed that Cagliostro had made in front of his own eyes. This convinced her.

There can be little doubt that Cagliostro had no intention of swindling anyone. He had plenty of money. (No doubt the ring had been given him by some freemason admirer, or by someone he had cured.) What he wanted now was simply to consolidate his position, to become the friend of princes, to regenerate the human race. He had no need to be a swindler now. He had proved his powers, and even if the cardinal broke with him, he still had his freemasons. (His own Egyptian lodges all sent him small contributions.)

As to Lorenza, now a beautiful woman in her mid-twenties, she was the toast of the town. The Inquisition biographer states that she gave herself to many of her admirers, in exchange for money, of course. A more reliable source states that while she was capable of flirting and keeping them happy with smiles, she remained faithful to her husband. This is undoubtedly true; they were living in the public eye, and a liaison would have ruined her; besides, her husband had already forgiven her twice; his patience might not extend to a third time.

It was a pity that Cagliostro did not remain in Strasbourg, where he might have lived out the remainder of his life in comfort. But the hatred of the doctors made him uncomfortable, although he fortunately discovered in time a spy they had planted in his household. He went to Naples to nurse an old friend who was dangerously ill, then to Bordeaux and Lyons. Then he obeyed the cardinal's insistent demands, and went to Paris. The eve of his downfall had arrived. And, in another sense, the eve of the French Revolution.

The decade between 1770 and 1780 had not been a happy one for

Rohan, for the Queen had become his enemy, and blighted his career. When her husband became King, she had the cardinal – or bishop, as he was in those days – dismissed from his job as ambassador to Austria. She also tried hard to prevent him from being made cardinal, grand almoner, administrator general of the Sorbonne and abbot of St. Waast in Arras, and although she failed in each case, she managed to make her royal displeasure felt in a hundred minor matters. The crueller she became, the more infatuated became her admirer. (It might be supposed that sexual frustration was the underlying cause of her disapproval of the dashing cardinal; but she had ceased to be a virgin on July 20, 1777, when the King had finally risen to the occasion; a week later she was able to assure her mother that 'the essay has been repeated'. She later produced two sons and a daughter.)

The cardinal's eye for a pretty woman was his misfortune. In Strasbourg he had met a charming adventuress who called herself the Countess de la Motte Valois, who claimed to be a descendant of Henry II. She had married a handsome but impecunious army officer named La Motte. In Paris, she called on the cardinal, now grand almoner of France, to see if he could not do something to help restore her family's ancestral lands, or perhaps get her husband a commission in the king's regiment. The cardinal liked her; he liked her so much that her second visit lasted until the early hours of the morning; she was too grateful for the purse of gold he had given her to object when he began to unhook her dress. Oddly enough, the fifty-year-old cardinal fell violently in love with this young girl in her mid-twenties, and wrote her a number of indiscreet letters. It was the cardinal who made sure she was introduced at court. And, according to the Countess de la Motte, her misfortunes had soon made her a bosom friend of the Queen's. Rohan was delighted. It was the opportunity he had wanted for years. He begged his attractive mistress to use all her influence with Marie Antoinette. And he was overjoyed when the countess assured him that the Queen was softening towards him.

In fact, the countess was hatching a plot to get rich. She believed, mistakenly, that the cardinal was a very rich man. (In fact, he was a spendthrift, and a fire at his mansion near Strasbourg had cost him a fortune.) The scheme was simple. It was known that the Queen, herself a talented spender, coveted a diamond necklace that had been made by two jewellers named Boehmer and Bassenge; but the price – 1,600,000 livres – was too much even for her.* Jeanne de la Motte's plan was to persuade Rohan to purchase the necklace for the Queen, then she would make off with it. The cardinal was not expected to make the Queen a present of the necklace – only to buy it secretly for her, or rather, to pledge his credit for it.

It was all fatally easy. The countess undertook to deliver letters from the cardinal to the Queen, and she forged the Queen's replies. The cardinal naturally expected some sign of the Queen's approval; the countess and her husband hired a young courtesan, Nicole D'Oliva, to impersonate the Queen at a secret meeting in the gardens of Versailles. The cardinal was allowed to kiss her slipper, and seems to have had no suspicions.

Now, Cagliostro's only part in this absurd business was as Rohan's confidant. He had been in Lyons and Bordeaux during the period when the cardinal was negotiating for the necklace, so he had the perfect alibi. He had even warned the cardinal against Jeanne de la Motte at an early stage. But he does seem to have encouraged the cardinal's hopes of advancement through the Queen, and the Inquisition biographer says he conjured up an image of the Queen in a bowl of water for the cardinal's benefit. The most damaging thing that can be said of Cagliostro in this whole affair is that his occult gifts were clearly not working at all between 1784 and

---

* A livre in those days was roughly equivalent to an English shilling or American quarter, so the necklace cost $400,000, or £100,000.

1785, when the whole thing blew up. Did no star tell him that a tidal wave was about to burst over so many people?

It came in July 1785, when the first payment – of 400,000 francs – fell due on the necklace, and the cardinal received the request from the jewellers. *He* passed it on to the Queen through the Countess de la Motte; The countess forged a letter from the Queen saying she could not meet the payment. The cardinal was astounded, and then alarmed when the jewellers pointed out that in that case he would have to meet it himself. The countess had expected this, of course, and she had expected him to pay up quietly. This happened to be impossible; the cardinal could only raise an immediate 30,000 francs. The jewellers declined to give him the three months' leeway he asked for, and applied direct to the Queen, who thought they had gone mad. Boehmer saw the King, who naturally demanded an explanation from Rohan himself. And it was at this point that the Queen interfered just once too often. She was so indignant that her name had been taken in vain that she demanded the instant arrest of Rohan. It would have been more sensible to hush the whole thing up: a public scandal could do no one any good. Instead, Rohan, Cagliostro, the countess and her lover Villette (who had taken part in the forgeries) were all arrested. The countess's husband was in London, where he had been disposing of the jewels.

The result of Marie Antoinette's decision was the eventual destruction of practically everyone involved in the case. Rohan and Cagliostro were acquitted, but Rohan was ruined, and Cagliostro had become a laughing stock. The countess was ordered to be whipped naked in public and branded. Nicole D'Oliva and Villette were acquitted, the latter banished. Marie Antoinette had been a popular queen before the case; now, although her innocence was established, she was booed and hissed by the Paris mob whenever she went out in her coach. Jeanne de la Motte, an endlessly fluent liar, managed to convey the impression that she was the victim of the Queen and cardinal, who had been having a love affair. When whipped and branded, she struggled like a fury and bit through the leather of the executioner's tunic, drawing blood. The crowd sympathised with her. She escaped to London, but the line of her destiny was also plunging steeply. She wrote a *Story of My Life*, in which she lied as brilliantly as ever, declaring herself the victim of Cagliostro, Rohan and the Queen. She quarrelled with her husband, who got tired of her love affairs. She quarrelled with her lover, who got tired of her tantrums. The money for the necklace seems to have vanished very quickly – she had lived with immense extravagance in the six months before she was found out – and she was perpetually hounded for debt. Attempting to escape her creditors, she climbed out of a window, and fell three floors to the pavement, fracturing her hip, splintering her arm and losing an eye. She lingered on for several weeks – long enough to express grim satisfaction at the news of the King's arrest at Varennes, and died before her thirty-fifth birthday. By that time, Cagliostro had been in the Inquisition's prisons for two years, which also caused her some satisfaction. Even the girl Nicole D'Oliva, who had impersonated the Queen, died at the age of twenty-eight. The cardinal died fairly comfortably in Baden in 1803.

It was Cagliostro, the innocent bystander, who came off worst of all. Before his arrest, he was rich, famous and widely respected. Incarceration in the Bastille completely unnerved him. Besides, he was frantic with anxiety for his wife, who was arrested with him. After seven months, she was released, and received universal sympathy. Cagliostro stayed in jail for nearly a year. He took it very badly. And he made a ridiculous impression at his trial, 'swaggering, dashing, in a gold-embroidered green taffeta coat', his hair hanging in greasy ringlets to his shoulders. When the judge asked him who he was, he replied in the voice of a ham actor: 'I am a noble voyager, Nature's unfortunate child,' which drew a burst of laughter. He had prepared a 'life story', which seems intended as a deliberate mockery. In it he claimed to be of noble birth, although he had no idea of his parentage, and that he was brought up under the name of Acharat in Arabia, and had apartments in the palace of the Mufti Salahaym, head of the Mohammedan religion; travels in Asia and Africa follow; he meets his Master, Althotas, who dies in Malta, pressing his hand. And so on. Cagliostro seems to have totally lost his judgement. It was time to be quiet, dignified, restrained, if he wanted to emerge from this with a shred of reputation. Instead, he played the mountebank.

After the trial, he went to London, banished by the King. He tried to sue the governor of the Bastille for the return of large sums of money and other items stolen when he was arrested, but lost the case. He was still sufficiently rich to send Nicole D'Oliva, whose beauty had made a great impression at the trial, seven hundred crowns. In London he addressed a *Letter to the French People*, which immediately achieved large sales in Paris. It was another nail in the coffin of the old order. The letter also has a prophetic ring, in view of future events; he declares that he will not return to Paris until the Bastille is pulled down and made into a public promenade, and prophesies that the French will have a prince who will abolish *lettres de cachet* (arbitrary orders of imprisonment or banishment) and will convoke the States-General (parliament); 'he will not be satisfied with being the first of his ministers; he will aim at being the first of Frenchmen'. But to state that Cagliostro prophesied the Revolution and Napoleon is going a little too far. He did not say the Bastille *would* be made a public promenade – only that he would not return until it was. However, it is arguable that his letter did much to bring about that result not long after. It was the King himself who convoked parliament, even if the last sentence quoted fits Napoleon.

London was no refuge. The British freemasons were not interested in the Egyptian rites, while the *Courier de L'Europe* published an exposé of Cagliostro that is quite as vindictive as the Inquisition biographer's account, revealing his true identity as Giuseppe Balsamo. Cagliostro and Lorenza moved to Basel, then Turin, where the police instantly ordered them to move on. They tried to settle in a small village in the Austrian Tyrol, Roveredo, but were again ordered to move on. In Trent in Austria he found another alchemist cardinal willing to become his patron, but the Emperor ordered him to leave Austrian soil. His wife had lost her beauty, although only in her early thirties, and as their fortune dwindled, was forced to sell her diamonds. Cagliostro finally made his supreme mistake and returned to Rome, attempting to propagate freemasonry under the nose of the Pope. In 1789 he was arrested, and never again gained his freedom. The Vatican hinted at vast plots by French revolutionaries to overthrow the Church, and doubled the guard around the Castel Sant' Angelo. Cagliostro's trial was undoubtedly intended as a declaration of war on freemasonry. The freemasons replied to the Inquisition biography with a pamphlet that made a far greater impact, and convinced the Pope that he was wise to have rid himself of the dangerous freemason. Cagliostro was transferred to the Castel San Leo, where the cells were made of old dried-up cisterns or cut out of solid rock; here he was almost literally buried alive in darkness. He died in 1795, at the age of fifty-two. His wife died in a nunnery in 1794, still under forty. When French soldiers took the San Leo prison in 1797, they searched for Cagliostro, intending to treat him as a revolutionary hero; but he was dead.

This remarkable man was, indeed, the last of the magicians, and nearly two centuries after his death he remains as misunderstood as during his lifetime. In spite of the broad streak of charlatanism in him, he was undoubtedly a genuine magician. He regarded himself as a man with a mission, and he pursued it single-mindedly. He loved good living, but he was also incredibly generous – perhaps the most basic sign of a fundamentally good man. As he himself pointed out at his trial, there is no reliable evidence that he ever harmed anyone during his extraordinary career, and there can be no doubt that he did much good. It is curious that his career, like that of so many others we have considered – Agrippa, Paracelsus, John Dee, Casanova, Mesmer – reached a certain apex and then went into a runaway decline. This seems to be a characteristic of all magicians; it can also be seen in Madame Blavatsky, Aleister Crowley and Rasputin.

I have deliberately left one of his most remarkable predictions to the end, because it involves the complex science of numerology. This was made at a masonic gathering during his final period in Paris, at the home of the orientalist the Count de Gebelin.

Cagliostro explained to the assembly that each letter in the alphabet has a numerical value – a kabbalistic doctrine. He demonstrated the system, analysing the names of Catherine de Medici, Henry III and Henry IV of France, showing how, when the letters of their name were added up, the result could be 'read' like an astrological chart. He went on to try the result on the names of Louis XVI and Marie Antoinette. The King's prediction stated that he must beware of dying on the scaffold before his thirty-ninth year; 'he is condemned to lose his head for being guilty of war'. Marie Antoinette would be 'unfortunate, unhappy in France, a queen without throne or money, wrinkled prematurely through grief, kept on a meagre diet, imprisoned, beheaded'. Cagliostro based his numerology upon the system of Cornelius Agrippa, which is based upon the Hebrew alphabet. In this, the numbers from one to eight have the following letters associated with them:

1: A, I, Q, J, Y
2: B, K, R
3: C, G, L, S
4: D, M, T

5: E, H, N
6: U, V, W, X
7: O, Z
8: F, P

The system for 'finding someone's number' (no doubt the slang phrase comes from this) is to take the letters of his Christian name and surname, and add them all together, thus:

C O L I N W I L S O N
3 7 3 1 5 6 1 3 3 7 5

These numbers add up to 44. The two digits 44 add up to 8. The number corresponding to my name is therefore 8. If the digits had added up to 48, then the second addition would have produced the number 12; in that case, a third addition must be made to produce 3 (one plus two).

The signification given for the various numbers is as follows:

One: a number signifying directness, ambition, power. Its possessor is a pioneering, inventive personality, unlikely to have many friends or close associates. Capable of kindness and generosity, but also of ruthlessness. The poet Yeats summarised the personality of number one in the lines:

There is not a fool can call me friend.
And I may dine at journey's end
With Landor and with Donne.

It will be found that the letters of William Butler Yeats add up to one. In this case, the middle name is included, because Yeats was known as W. B. Yeats, not as William. Oddly enough, if the letters of his most common nickname, Willy Yeats, are added up, they also come to one.

Two: this is the reverse of the previous number, signifying a well-balanced, gentle disposition. Richard Cavendish speaks of it as an evil and female number in *The Black Arts*. People with the number two make good subordinates or helpers, but may be over-sensitive, too easily depressed. Just as the negative aspect of number one is extreme self-assertion, refusal to admit one is in the wrong (what A. E. Van Vogt calls 'the right man' – a man who will assert he is right in the teeth of all the evidence), so the negative aspect of number two is deviousness or vacillation.

Three: the number of versatility and plenty, a traditionally lucky number. ('Three times lucky.') People with the number three are gay, charming, adaptable, talented, lucky, but inclined to be 'other-directed', living too much for the approval and liking of other people.

Four: this is the 'square' number of the Pythagoreans, indicating endurance, firmness of purpose, calmness. In its negative aspect it means dullness, 'square' in the modern slang sense. Since it is the number of the earth, it may also indicate powerful underground fires that sometimes break through in the form of earthquakes or volcanoes.

Five: this is a number of magic, the pentacle. Fives are lovers of adventure. They are also lucky, but inclined to instability, erratic, full of nervous energy, inclined to be boastful, lovers of women and often of alcohol.

Six: this is the number of dependability and harmony. At their best, sixes are kindly, peace-loving, stable, and lovers of home and family; at their worst they tend to be trivial, too obsessed with detail, fussy. Since six is divisible by both two and three. it has affinities with the qualities of both these numbers.

Seven: another magical number, the number of mystery and mysticism. Sevens may be psychic; they are usually introverted, more interested in an inner reality than in the external world. Aloof, self-controlled, dignified. In their negative aspect, they may be simply out of touch with reality, incompetent, vague.

Eight: this is an auspicious number, signifying drive and success. Eights have affinity with fours and twos; they are solid, four-square, capable of long efforts and great concentration. In their negative aspect, this may amount only to stubbornness and persistence in the wrong course of action, in which case the positive characteristics become negative, and success becomes failure.

Nine: this is the royal number, associated with a high degree of creativity (the nine muses) and spiritual achievement. Nines are visionaries and poets at their best, wildly volatile at their worst, given to intense romanticism.

Anyone who tries out this system will have some striking successes. I have pointed out that Yeats makes an ideal number one. The letters of Bernard Shaw make a nine, and, interestingly enough, Richard Cavendish adds that nines are always falling in and out of love, and quotes Cheiro to the effect that nines often undergo many operations by the surgeon's knife. Both fit Shaw remarkably closely.

However, it must be admitted that failures are likely to be as frequent as the successes. Try to think of a typical 'three' – versatile, lucky, charming, a lover of people. Felix Mendelssohn seems to fit the bill precisely. But the letters of his name add up to four, the 'square'. William Blake would surely be a nine, or at least a seven; instead, this most visionary and introverted of men is a five: the number of adventure and boastfulness, which suits Casanova or Cagliostro more than Blake. But Casanova is an eight, and Cagliostro is a one. This latter cannot be coincidence, for the letters of Giuseppe Balsamo add up to six, a number more suitable to Dickens's Mr. Brownlow or Wells's Mr. Polly. Oscar Wilde, who might also be expected to be a three, is an eight, signifying drive and will-power. It is true that he achieved tremendous success, and then tremendous failure, but this seems due to vacillation rather than unshakable purpose.

A more modern system of numerology writes out the numbers from one to nine, then writes the alphabet under them, thus:

1: A, J, S
2: B, K, T
3: C, L, U
4: D, M, V
5: E, N, W
6: F, O, X
7: G, P, Y
8: H, Q, Z
9: I, R

Further information can be extracted from a name by adding up the sum of its vowels, which indicates the inner nature of the person concerned. Addition of the consonants gives the external personality, the social façade.

It goes without saying that there is more to numerology than this; for example, most numerologists also make use of astrology, and vice versa – the two sciences are closely connected. Cagliostro's procedure must have been extremely complicated to draw such detailed answers from the 'oracle'. One is tempted to dismiss the whole thing as just another apocryphal story about a 'magician'. But there are well-authenticated stories of similar prophecies, which leave no doubt that such detailed prophecy is possible under propitious circumstances. Jacques Cazotte, a royalist and author of the romance *Le Diable Amoureux*, prophesied the revolution in some detail in 1788 at a dinner given by the Duchesse de Gramont. Cazotte, an occultist, apparently had a burst of what can only be called inspiration, in which he was able to foretell the future of many people present. He told Condorcet that he would take poison to cheat the executioner, that Chamfort would cut his own veins but die months later, that the astronomer M. Bailly would die at the hands of the mob, that the

Duchesse de Gramont would die on the scaffold and that the only victim of the executioner who would be allowed a confessor would be the King himself. An atheist, Jean de la Harpe, was thoroughly sceptical, and wrote the whole thing down; Cazotte prophesied for him that he would become a Christian. He became a monk, in fact, and the prophecy was found among his papers after his death in 1803. A century later the whole matter was subjected to close examination by Dr. Walter Borman, who found abundant evidence for the prophecy in letters and journals of the period. Even the Baroness D'Oberkirch mentions it in her memoirs, published in 1852: she describes an evening in which it was discussed in her salon, and a medium who had been brought there by the Marquis de Puységur (the discoverer of hypnotism) was questioned about it; the medium went into even more detail about the fate of various people actually present, all of which was again proved accurate.

Now, it is true that there is a great difference between numerology, with its fixed rules, and prophecy, which may be due to Dunne's 'serial time' or any other cause; but again, it must be pointed out that there are no exact sciences of prediction, whether by the stars, numbers, hands or anything else; everything depends upon the innate talent of the diviner; Cagliostro used numbers rather than consulting them.

Before leaving Cagliostro, a word should be said about his healing powers. In a sense, an adventurer like Cagliostro or even Casanova is potentially the ideal thaumaturgist. The nature of illness is bound up with negation. Human beings have the power to close their senses and focus upon unimportant matters – for example, I can spend a morning poring over my cheque-book stubs, until my mind feels oddly dehydrated. The reason children experience so much of the 'glory and the freshness of a dream' is that they have not yet acquired this power to narrow the mind; since they have no great responsibilities, they have no need for it. But now we reach the point of crucial importance. This useful power to focus upon detail can easily create a flood of emotional negation. (Anyone who has made the mistake of thinking about money worries in the middle of the night knows this.) It is for the same reason that a man balanced on his toes is easily pushed over. The mind needs to have a kind of penumbral area that is aware of other times and other places to keep it healthy: Faculty X.

Now, intelligent people can usually cure themselves of a tendency to negativity. Wordsworth's *Intimations of Immortality* ode offers a perfect example; using his mind and his memory he jerks himself out of his negative mood until the mind is wide open again. Narrowness is like catarrh or a bad cold in the head; it produces a blocked-up feeling. Wordsworth's 'timely utterance' has that effect of clearing the sinuses so one can breathe freely again.

Most illnesses bring with them a feeling of helplessness and depression that reinforces the illness, and not many people have Wordsworth's highly developed power of getting the mind out of reverse and into forward gear. The power of a breezy adventurer like Cagliostro stems from his positiveness. The winds of heaven blow through his mind because he is used to meeting adversity and triumphing; the very energy of his demeanour is a reminder of how good the world is, how much can be achieved by effort; he acts on his patients like the sound of the Easter bells on Faust, bringing the breath of far-off things.

All this makes it sound as if Cagliostro's chief asset was a good bedside manner; but it goes deeper than that. As the many descriptions of him make clear, he could radiate a compelling force that cannot be reduced to cheerful mannerisms. It was this force that was sapped by the Bastille experience. Instead of withdrawing to some quiet place, where he could slowly recuperate, until like Wordsworth he had restored his strength and optimism, he launched into controversy and litigation. All he had to do was sit tight for two more years, and he would have been again picked up by the tide of history and made into a revolutionary hero, as Cardinal Rohan, in fact, was. His downfall must be blamed upon unsound judgement; it was an avoidable tragedy.

If the stature of Cagliostro increases upon careful examination, the reverse is true of the other 'great magician' of that period, the Count of Saint-Germain. Kurt Seligman's chapter on him begins: 'Who was he and where did he come from? The riddle has never been solved. The dates of his birth and death are unknown. Incredible things are claimed of him. Frederick the Great called him the man who cannot die; and the count himself asserted that he had lived two thousand years … He would speak familiarly of a chat with the Queen of Sheba and of wonderful happenings at the marriage of Cana …'

Potentially, he sounds the most exciting magician of all. But Seligman seems to have been unaware of the researches of Gustav Berthold Volz in the twenties. These revealed that although Saint-Germain was infinitely more sophisticated and cultured than Cagliostro, he was fundamentally little more than a fine actor. When the reports of contemporaries are examined, it does not even appear that he displayed more finesse than Cagliostro; he was a boastful self-advertiser. Casanova, who was easily impressed by genuine intellectuality, immediately spotted him for a charlatan, and took pleasure in queering his pitch when they were both on diplomatic missions to the Hague. But he did not have to do a great deal; Saint-Germain's own lack of tact quickly brought about his downfall, and he had to fly to England.

Only one 'mystery' remains: his origin. And it should be borne in mind that in those days it was not particularly difficult for that to remain a mystery. Communications were bad, and most registrations of births and deaths were confined to the parish records. The account that states that Saint-Germain was the son of a tax collector of San

Germano, and that he was born in 1710, is probably correct. Nothing whatever is known of his life before the 1740s, when he seems to have appeared in Vienna and become acquainted with various members of the aristocracy, among them Counts Zabor and Lobkowitz. He also met there the French Marshal de Belle-Isle, who brought him to France. By 1758 – by which time he would be in his late forties – he had become an established favourite of Louis XV and his mistress Madame de Pompadour (for whom the famous Diamond Necklace was originally intended).

Casanova, who met him at about this time, describes him as one of the most remarkable conversationalists he had ever met – and this is a considerable compliment from a man whose own talents were impressive. He describes Saint-Germain as a scholar, linguist, musician (he had an extremely pleasant singing voice), chemist, and as very good-looking (which Casanova himself was not, being swarthy and hook-nosed). He was a 'perfect ladies' man', flattering them and offering them a wash that would prevent wrinkles which he claimed to be expensive but which he gave away. He probably came to the king's attention through Madame de Pompadour.

Saint-Germain's 'gimmick' was that he claimed never to eat, but to live on some strange food or elixir that he compounded himself. He would sit through society dinners, keeping the table amused by his conversation, declining all food and drink. He would explain in a smiling way that he was a great deal older than he looked, but deny that he was, as some people claimed, five hundred years old. Casanova says he would assert calmly that he was three hundred. Saint-Germain's knowledge of history was considerable, so that he was able to report conversations of historical personages in such a way that it sounded almost as if he *had* been present himself. If asked whether he had been present, his answer would be an enigmatic smile. He developed mystification to a fine art.

What were his real achievements? He was a fine linguist, and seems to have discovered interesting processes for dyeing silk and leather. Altogether the evidence would seem to indicate that the love of his life was chemistry; whenever he could persuade a rich patron to offer him food and lodgings, he immediately set up a laboratory. The mid-eighteenth century was the pre-chemical age; Priestley, Cavendish, Lavoisier, belong to the later years of the century. But then, Saint-Germain seems to have been fascinated by minerals and dyes rather than by the question of the composition of air or water. His chemical knowledge was genuine; his charm and culture were genuine. A theatrical streak made him want to astonish as well as please; hence the hints about being present at Cana, and the affectation of eating only some magical food. (The simple answer is probably that he was a vegetarian, a natural ascetic who disliked the guzzling and boozing that went on at the tables of the rich.*)

In spite of his boastfulness, which made Count Warnstedt describe him, as late as 1779, as 'the completest charlatan, fool, rattle-pate, windbag and swindler', his style was less exuberant than Cagliostro's, and he could give the impression of being quiet, modest and well balanced. As E. M. Butler remarks,† his relations with his patrons often 'held elements of discipleship' – that is, he aimed to interest the intellect as well as the sense of wonder in his patrons, and tended to assume the role of teacher. Strangely enough, he was a materialist, who stated that his only interest was the good of mankind.

Any man, even the most consistent, can appear to be many different persons in the eyes of different observers, and a man as mercurial and deliberately enigmatic as Saint-Germain is bound to arouse wide differences of opinion. He forced his acquaintance on his last patron, Prince Charles of Hesse-Cassel, much against the prince's will, and yet ended by winning him over so completely

* T. H. White's *The Age of Scandal* presents an interesting picture of the astounding eating habits of this period.
† *The Myth of the Magus*, p. 199.

that the prince was shattered by his death (in 1784) and wrote, 'He was perhaps one of the greatest sages who ever lived ...'

His known life seems to have been lived under the protection of a series of such patrons. After the diplomatic mission for Louis XV failed (he was supposed to put out feelers for a peace between France and England) due to the intervention of the French foreign minister, the Duke de Choiseul (who detested him), he fled to London, then later bought an estate in Holland, now calling himself Count Surmont. He came close to making a fortune by interesting people in high places in his various chemical processes, which included dyeing and 'the ennobling of metals'. He was forced to vanish at a certain point, taking 100,000 gulden with him, but the factories he set up nevertheless seem to have prospered. He seems to have spent the next ten years or so in Russia, and again made friends in high places, including Count Alexei Orlov, one of the chief engineers of the palace revolution that placed Catherine the Great on the throne and the hero of the battle of Chesmé (1770), in which the Russian fleet defeated the Turks. E. M. Butler believed that he probably aided the Russian war effort actively; he was made a Russian general, calling himself General Welldone. Back in Nuremburg in 1774, he impressed the Margrave of Brandenburg, Charles Alexander, and his standing was further improved when he was publicly embraced by Orlov. He told the margrave that his real name was Prince Rakoczy, and that he was the last of the line, preserving his incognito in order to avoid assassins. In 1775, the margrave learned that the remaining three Rakoczys were dead, and that the retiring, studious guest at his castle at Triersdorf was really the adventurer who went under many aliases, one of which was Saint-Germain. Taxed with this, Saint-Germain had no alternative than to admit it, but asserted that he had never disgraced any of his many aliases, and that he had only adopted them to throw would-be assassins off the scent. He insisted that he *was* the last Rakoczy. The margrave disbelieved him, and the ageing Saint-Germain resumed his travels in 1776. Frederick the Great ignored a letter asking for patronage, although there is some evidence that Saint-Germain had worked for him as a secret diplomat (i.e. a spy) in France during the period of his involvement with the French royal family. (It was this suspicion that made Choiseul his enemy.)

In Leipzig, the grand master of the Prussian masonic lodges, Prince Frederick Augustus of Brunswick, subjected him to close scrutiny, and concluded that he was not a mason. (Saint-Germain claimed to be a mason of the fourth grade, but said he had forgotten all the secret signs.) Fortunately Saint-Germain found his last patron, Charles of Hesse-Cassel, in 1779, and spent the last five years of his life peacefully under his protection. He owned to being eighty-eight when he met the prince, although he was probably only in his late sixties. Lodging in a damp room gave him rheumatism, and he began to suffer fits of depression in his last years. After his death, at the age of about seventy-four, many people refused to believe he was dead. Respectable witnesses claimed to have seen him over thirty years later, and another story asserted that he had declared that he would spend eighty-five years in the Himalayas before reappearing in Europe. Madame Blavatsky declared he was one of the Hidden Masters in Tibet.

Perhaps the last word on him should be spoken by a not-entirely-hostile witness, the Prussian Ambassador to Dresden, Count Alvensleben, in 1777:

> He is a highly gifted man with a very alert mind, but completely without judgement, and he has only gained his singular reputation by the lowest and basest flattery of which a man is capable, as well as by his outstanding eloquence, especially if one lets oneself be carried away by the fervour and enthusiasm with which he can express himself ... Inordinate vanity is the mainspring driving his whole mechanism ... he

is stimulating and entertaining in society, as long as he is only narrating. But as soon as he tries to develop his own ideas, his whole weakness shows itself ... But woe to him who would contradict him!*

And so the legend of the man of mystery explodes with a hollow pop when examined closely. In the twentieth century there would be no need for all this mystification and imposture; Saint-Germain would become a brilliant industrial chemist, or perhaps turn his eloquence to some purpose on television. In the century that starved Mozart, and nearly killed Bach and Handel with overwork, he had to fight to keep alive. It was a bad century for magicians.

* E. M. Butler, op. cit., p. 204.

SIX
THE NINETEENTH CENTURY – MAGIC AND ROMANTICISM

In the first years of the nineteenth century there died a man whose name deserves to be better known to students of mysticism and the occult: Louis Claude de Saint-Martin, the 'unknown philosopher'. His immense significance is that he was midway between the traditional mystics of the East or West and a new evolutionism. His philosophy is informed with an extraordinary air of optimism. Man is fundamentally a god, says Saint-Martin, not a worm. In this atmosphere of health and light, his work resembles Swedenborg's. As the epigraph of my book *The Stature of Man*,* I quoted a passage that catches the essence of Martinism; speaking of the idea that the earth is a mere speck in the universe, he says:

> It is perhaps this wrong connection of ideas which has led men to the still falser notion that they are not worthy of their creator's regard. They have believed themselves to be obeying the dictates of humility when they have denied that the earth and all the universe contains exists only on man's account, on the ground that the admission of such an idea would be only conceit. But they have not been afraid of the laziness and cowardice which are the inevitable result of this affected modesty. The present-day avoidance of the belief that we are the highest in the universe is the reason that we have not the courage to work to justify that title, that the duties springing from it seem too laborious, and that we would rather abdicate our position than realise them in all their consequences. Where

* In England, *The Age of Defeat* (1959).

is the pilot that will guide us between these hidden reefs of conceit and false humility?

After studying the bewilderingly eventful lives of Casanova, Cagliostro, Saint-Germain, John Dee and the rest, it is a relief to come across a man to whom almost nothing happened. He was born at Amboise, in Touraine, in the same year as Cagliostro – 1743. His family were aristocrats of reasonable wealth, and although his mother died soon after his birth, his stepmother proved an excellent substitute, and he adored her. His family were devout Catholics, and he was sent to the college of Pontlevoi while still very young. It was there that he discovered a book on self-knowledge by Abadie, and it seems to have exercised an enormous influence on his mind. He studied for the law, and in due course was called to the bar. But he felt nothing but distaste for the affairs of everyday life, and managed to persuade his father to allow him to abandon the bar for the army. It may seem an odd choice, but he no doubt reasoned that an army commission in times of peace is something of a sinecure and after the seven years' war and the treaty of Paris, Europe was more or less at peace in 1766, the year Saint-Martin entered the army. In this he proved to be correct, for he was able to devote a great deal of time to study while his brother officers were out drinking.

At the age of twenty-four, when he was with his regiment in Bordeaux, Saint-Martin met the man who was to be the major influence in his life, Don Martines de Pasqualles de la Tour. Martines was a Rosicrucian of a peculiar kind. The Rosicrucians were a secret society bearing many resemblances to the freemasons, but their emphasis was on occultism; they were said to be followers of Paracelsus. Most of the legends about their origins seem to be fabrications (they can all be found in A. E. Waite's *Brotherhood of the Rosy Cross*). But the notion of this mystical brotherhood, the thought of a worldwide society of magical adepts, seems to have satisfied some demand in the imagination of the seventeenth and eighteenth centuries. There were many small Rosicrucian societies all over the continent, many of them affiliated with the freemasons. Don Martines was a member, perhaps the founder, of a curious group of masonic Rosicrucians called the Elect Cohens. Martines had already established an order of so-called *Illuminés* in Paris; Illuminism was another form of Rosicrucianism, but associated with political aims. (It would be roughly correct to say that the Illuminists were to the Masons and Rosicrucians what the Jesuits were to the Catholic Church.)

Martines was something of a Cagliostro figure. He claimed to be a magical adept who had attained a very high level indeed. The ceremonies of his group included incantation in the manner of the Key of Solomon and a complex number mysticism, which differed in many basic respects from that mentioned in the last chapter. But all this magic was held to be only the means of attaining ultimate mystical illumination – which is no doubt why Don Martines liked to call his group *Illuminés* although they were non-political.

Saint-Martin was initiated into the Elect Cohens in the second half of 1768. The effect was as deep as Cagliostro's induction in the freemasons. Saint-Martin became a dedicated man. Three years later, in 1771, he left the army and devoted the remainder of his life to mysticism. And although the master withdrew to Santo Domingo in the West Indies, dying in 1774, and although Saint-Martin became poverty-stricken as a consequence of the French Revolution, there was no deviation from this life-long endeavour to bring to the world this vital insight that man is somehow a god who has forgotten his heritage and come to accept that he is a beggar.

In Saint-Martin, this position does not involve the belief that there is no God; on the contrary, his philosophy is completely God-oriented. Being profoundly religious, he accepted the religion in which he had been brought up, but, like Swedenborg, interpreted Jesus and the Virgin in his own way. His mysticism was deeply influenced by Jacob Boehme, for whom his respect was so enormous that he placed him next to Jesus himself.

But the core of his philosophy is his belief in the importance of man. He comes very close to Sir Julian Huxley's statement that man is now the managing director of evolution in the universe when he writes: 'The function of man differs from that of other physical beings, for it is the repair of the disorders of the universe.' This notion of 'repairing' is of central importance in his philosophy, and it explains the importance he attached to Jesus as the archetypal repairer. What fascinates Saint-Martin is that man keeps having quite clear flashes of godlike faculties. It is as if some dormant power wakened up in him. 'Man possesses innumerable vestiges of the faculties resident in the Agent which produced him ...' This must not be taken as just another assertion that the kingdom of God is within us. It is far more exciting than that. If you believed that the engine of your car was completely dead, due to some fundamental fault, and you casually pushed the starter, expecting nothing, and the engine gave a cough and a roar, then stopped again, you would be excited because you would realise there is *nothing fundamentally wrong with it, after all.* Without realising it, man possesses immense powers. He is 'engendered from the fount of wonder and the fount of desire and intelligence'. And his most vital faculty is his imagination – imagination in the sense that Paracelsus used the word, the faculty for reaching beyond himself, beyond his everyday life. Man wears blinkers; imagination is the power to see beyond them. Most men sit dully, like sheep in a field, imagining that 'there's nothing to be done', that everyday reality is a kind of prison from which there is no escape except through drugs, drink or suicide. In fact, the doors are open. Man's chief trouble is his curious passivity, which is like hypnosis. The beginning of his 'salvation' are the glimpses of freedom that come in times of crisis or in moments of sudden ecstasy.

Blake had spoken of the 'five windows that light the caverned man', the five senses, but added that there is one through which 'he can pass out what time he will'. Saint-Martin wrote: 'The soul leaves the body only at death, but during life, the faculties may extend beyond it, and communicate with their exterior correspondents without ceasing to be united to their centre.' He is speaking about Faculty X. At every moment, man is freer than he realises.

Saint-Martin produced most of his books under the pseudonym 'the unknown philosopher'. Living in a time of violence and of aggressive rationalism, he wanted to avoid drawing too much attention to himself; besides, he was convinced that his writings would appeal only to a small audience. In this he was wrong. By the time he died, at the age of sixty (his health was always frail), Martinism was a European movement like Swedenborgianism or freemasonry, and it continued to exercise considerable influence after his death. (The freemason who converts Peter in *War and Peace* – a real person called Bazdéev – was also a Martinist.) It is a pity that he has been forgotten in our own century, for his ideas are more relevant than ever.

Unlike Cagliostro, Saint-Martin had no political influence on his time; by no stretch of the imagination can he be called a harbinger of the Revolution. But he was a vital influence on a far greater revolution, the great movement called Romanticism. Romanticism, the new spirit created by Goethe, Schiller, Hoffmann, Wordsworth, Shelley, Berlioz, was the artistic expression of the mysticism of Claude de Saint-Martin. Underlying it all are those 'glimpses', those moments when the engine starts up for a moment.

Romanticism is based on moments of ecstasy. And what is ecstasy? Perhaps the least controversial definition would be: a sudden bubbling up and overflow of pent-up emotion. And when a man experiences ecstasy, all commonness disappears; he is rocked in a cradle of delight, and life is almost unbearably sweet. It is in such moments that he realises what a poor thing his skinny, starved everyday consciousness is.

The Romantics were driven by the spirit of magic, which is the evolutionary spirit of the human race. And it was Fichte who noted the basic paradox of Romanticism: 'To be free is nothing; to become free is heavenly' (*Frey seyn ist nichts; frey werden is der Himmel*). When you have freedom, you yawn and take it for granted, because man's will is mostly in neutral gear; when you suddenly become free after a long period of misery and bondage, everything is delightful and life seems infinitely rich. It is the same when you suddenly get something you want very badly; even the most mediocre male gets a glimpse of the immensity of freedom as a girl yields to him for the first time. This is why Casanova and Frank Harris and the author of *My Secret Life* spent their lives in pursuit of sex; they were after the flashes of lightning that reveal man's freedom.

The romantic with the most powerful obsession with magic was E. T. A. Hoffmann, known to most modern readers through Offenbach's opera *The Tales of Hoffmann*. In him it is possible to see at once the weakness and the peculiar strength of the Romantics. Their chief weakness was that they did not think. But their strength was an ability to be carried along on a flood of emotion that took them a long way towards mystical insight. The Romantics used the imagination to release pent-up frustrations and to conjure up the kind of world they would like to live in. Agrippa, Paracelsus, Cagliostro were unhappy wanderers; the Romantics were wanderers in the world of imagination:

> *I travelled through a land of men,*
> *A land of men and women too,*
> *And heard and saw such dreadful things*
> *As cold earth wanderers never knew.*

wrote William Blake in *The Mental Traveller*.

In his masterpiece, *The Golden Pot*, Hoffmann creates a weird farrago of myth, magic and alchemy. Everything that happens to its hero, the student Anselmus, is the wish-fulfilment fantasy of a frustrated magician. A clumsy, preoccupied young man, he sits beneath a tree on the river bank and hears magic snakes whispering to him of love and another reality. The eccentric Archivist Lindhorst hires him to copy magical manuscripts for him, and he realises that Lindhorst is a salamander, exiled from Atlantis for falling in love with a green snake. The snakes in the tree are Lindhorst's daughters, and the youngest, Serpentina, is in love with the student. However, so is the daughter of the dean of the university, Veronica, who expects Anselmus to rise one day to the rank of privy councillor.* There is the fundamental situation: the tug of war between the world of magic and the boring real world, which is disappointing, whether it is offering you success or drudgery. The world thinks Anselmus insane; what could be the objection to settling down with a beautiful girl, and accepting a comfortable job through the good offices of her father? And can he trust the strange visions conjured up by the half-mad Lindhorst, with his wild talk about how the youth Phosphorus embraced a white lily and fought with a black dragon? When the university registrar interrupts Lindhorst with a request that he tell them a true story instead, Lindhorst declares that this is the truest story he can possibly tell them. It corresponds to a deeper level of reality than this dreary, repetitive world. And in the end, Anselmus has the courage to choose Lindhorst and Serpentina rather than Veronica and the rank of privy councillor. And in most of Hoffmann's stories, this decision would lead to tragedy; but in this, his most fantastic tale, he allows Anselmus and Serpentina to live happy ever after in Atlantis.

In this story occurs one of Hoffmann's most striking symbols.

---

* Highest rank in the Civil Service.

At one point, Anselmus finds himself corked up in a glass bottle standing on a shelf. In other bottles there are Church scholars and law clerks, and they all look perfectly happy. When he asks them how they can be so cheerful, confined in a glass bottle, they reply that he must be joking; they are standing on the Elbe bridge looking down into the water, and later on they intend to go and have a drink in the tavern. The episode plays no real part in the story, and has obviously been inserted because Hoffmann thought it so important. Most people are unaware that they are imprisoned in a glass bottle; they are convinced they are free. It is the misfortune of the man of deeper perceptions to realise that he is imprisoned.

But this image also points to the central fault of all the Romantics: they are pessimists and defeatists. They see no way out of the glass bottle except into the unreal world of imagination, which weakens its devotees and makes them unfit for real life. With the exception of Goethe, the Romantics seem unaware of that other form that ecstasy takes: the violent, raging appetite for more life. There are moods in which the whole world seems so beautiful that man feels he can plough through life like a tank, smashing down every obstacle. Our usual state is one of poor appetite; we are like a man recovering from a long bout of retching, feeling that he never wants to eat another large meal. In moments of intensity he develops an enormous appetite, and feels as if he could keep on eating for a week. Everything in the world is fascinating, including an old tramp blowing his nose in the gutter and the smell of gasworks beside the canal.

This is ultimately the reason that we have to reject the Romantics. Wrapped in self-pity, they fail to stay the course. It seems to be almost a law that we have to accept one unsatisfactory extreme or another: the magician who gets too involved in the world, or the Romantic who is afraid to get involved.

But at least the Romantic revival brought a magical revival with it. The nineteenth century was a noisy, industrial century, a century of dirt, smoke, bad drains, sooty chimneys, but also of railways, canals, exploration, of good beef and good beer, of the Great Exhibitions of Paris and London, the Crystal Palace, the England of Dickens and Cobbett, the France of Flaubert and Maupassant. It was perhaps the most energetic century in mankind's history. And in all the frantic money-making and empire-building, 95 per cent of mankind was pushed against the wall. Hence the revival of magic, which is fundamentally a revolt against coarse-grained reality.

The country in which this first occurred was France. Strangely enough, the man who gave it impetus was that arch-historian of money-makers and go-getters, Honoré de Balzac. Balzac had a strong mystical leaning, which emerges in such works as *Louis Lambert*, *Seraphita* and *The Quest for the Absolute*. But for Louis Lambert, as for Balthasar Claës, the hero of the last novel, the quest of the absolute ends in death, not in triumph.

In 1810, when Balzac was only eleven years old, there was born in Paris the man who was to become the source of the modern revival of magic, Alphonse Louis Constant, who wrote his books under the name of Eliphaz Levi. The parish priest was impressed by his intelligence and was instrumental in having him sent to St. Sulpice. In due course, Constant became a priest; but within a few years he was thrown out of the priesthood for preaching 'doctrines contrary to the Church' – exactly what these were has not come down to us. In his late twenties, a literary friend, Alphonse Esquiros, took him along to hear a strange prophet called Ganneau, an aged man who wore a woman's cloak and babbled about the creation of the universe and the fall of man to a group of disciples. Constant describes him in the *History of Magic*: 'a bearded man of majestic demeanour ... He was surrounded by several men, bearded and ecstatic like himself, and in addition there was a woman with motionless features, who seemed like an entranced somnambulist. The prophet's manner was abrupt and yet sympathetic; he had hallucinated eyes and an infectious quality of eloquence. He spoke with emphasis, warmed to his subject quickly, chafed and fumed till a white froth gathered on his lips.' The entranced woman was Ganneau's wife, whom he believed to be a reincarnation of Marie Antoinette (he believed that he was a reincarnation of Louis XVII). After Ganneau's death, his wife continued to be convinced that she was Marie Antoinette, becoming indignant only if anyone questioned it. Constant and Esquiros, who had gone to Ganneau's attic to laugh, were overcome by his eloquence and became his disciples.

I have quoted Levi's description of Ganneau, not because it is of any historical importance, but because it gives something of the flavour of Paris in the mid-century, all the talk of ecstasy and occultism and revolt. Levi even has an extraordinary story of a disciple of Ganneau's called Sobrier, who one day in 1848 began shouting on a street corner, advising the people to march to the Boulevard des Capucines and express their dissatisfaction directly to the ministers. Finally, half Paris was marching behind him, whereupon he slipped away. The mob stopped before the Hôtel des Capucines; someone fired a shot at them, and suddenly the revolution had started. Sobrier had played his part in history in an almost trancelike state.

At thirty Constant married a girl of sixteen, Noémie Cadiot, who bore him two children and subsequently left him. He was drawn increasingly to the study of magic, although he made some sort of a living on the edge of the literary world. In 1856 there appeared his *Dogma and Ritual of High Magic*, one of the books Ouspensky kept in his drawer when reporting the Hague conference. This was followed by a *History of Magic* and a number of other books on occult subjects. Disciples and pupils gathered round him, and he died at the age of sixty-five, in 1875, having started a magical revival virtually single-handed. He admits that his own inspiration was *Louis Lambert*, Balzac's study of a brilliant, highly strung young mystic.

It must be admitted that Levi's books do not inspire confidence. For what he is claiming is, unfortunately, a lie:

> Behind the veil of all the hieratic and mystical allegories of ancient doctrines, behind the darkness and strange ordeals of all initiations, under the seal of all sacred writings, in the ruins of old Nineveh or Thebes, on the crumbling stones of old temples and on the blackened visage of the Assyrian or Egyptian sphinx, in the monstrous or marvellous paintings which interpret to the faithful of India the inspired pages of the Vedas, in the cryptic emblems of our old books on alchemy, in the ceremonies practised at reception by all secret societies, there are found indications of a doctrine which is everywhere the same and everywhere carefully concealed.

This passage reveals a highly romantic imagination, and little else. It is not true that there is a 'secret doctrine' known only to adepts. The Stone Age shamans did not possess a secret doctrine, only a curious oneness with nature and a contact with man's subconscious powers. There is no secret doctrine apart from science, as we have clearly seen in the course of this book. Pythagoras, Agrippa, Paracelsus, thought of themselves as scientists, and they also happened to possess a certain degree of shamanistic power. This is not to deny that 'magical ceremonies' *work*; they do. Raynor C. Johnson mentions a description by George and Helen Sandwith of fire-walking in Fiji, an annual ceremony. 'The essential feature appears to have been that those who participated had to be fully charged with some unknown type of energy (presumably generated on the aetheric level), and ten days of ritual preparation were devoted to this. Numerous tests were made before the culminating event: their flesh was pierced by skewers without the feeling of pain or loss of blood, and they were lashed without pain being felt or weals appearing. The same energy appears to have remarkable therapeutic powers, and the case is described of the almost instantaneous healing of a Hindu girl whose legs had been paralysed from birth.* For the fire-walking ceremony, forty tons of logs are burned, and the heat is so great that their faces had to be shielded from scorching at twelve feet. One of the fire-walkers remarked to the Sandwiths: 'This is something that really works; it is not just talk and promises.' The evidence for such feats is beyond dispute; but it does not prove that the ten days of ritual preparation involved some secret doctrine; whatever the ritual, its aim is to put the shaman in contact with the 'aetheric energy' that Johnson mentions. (He also mentions that tragedies *have* occurred due to insufficient preparation.)

And so Eliphaz Levi's books are based on a false premise. Even A. E. Waite (who translated them) – himself not the most reliable of historians of magic – feels impelled to warn the reader that Levi uses his imagination too much. His aim is to impress his readers with his own knowledge of the 'secret doctrines', of the Kabbalah, etc. In fact, he knew little or no Hebrew. In short, he is another in the long line of magical charlatans. This is not to say that he is no more than a confidence man. He studied magic and believed in it, and even E. M. Butler, who remarks that his so-called science 'becomes more transparently bogus with every page one turns',† is willing to accept his account of raising the spirit of Apollonius of Tyana, as described in Chapter 13 of *Transcendental Magic*. According to Levi, a mysterious lady, an adept, showed him her magical 'cabinet', and asked him to evoke the spirit of Apollonius to ask it a question. The 'cabinet' was a room in a turret, with concave mirrors, a marble altar, a copper tripod and a white lambskin rug. He observed a vegetarian diet for three weeks before the invocation and had to fast completely for the last seven days; during all this time he

---

* *Nurslings of Immortality*, 1957, p. 117.

† E. M. Butler, *Ritual Magic*, 1949, pp. 283 et seq.

meditated on Apollonius and held imaginary conversations with him. At the end of twelve hours of magic incantations (all detailed in the appendix of *Transcendental Magic*), the shade of Apollonius appeared in a kind of grey shroud. It vanished several times, apparently objecting to the sword Levi was wearing, and at one point touched his arm, which remained numb for days. It answered his two questions telepathically, prophesying death for the subjects of both. Afterwards, Levi says, 'something of another world had passed into me; I was no longer either sad or cheerful, but I felt a singular attraction towards death, unaccompanied, however, by any suicidal tendency'. He claims to have invoked the shade on two subsequent occasions and learned two important kabbalistic secrets. He adds, however, that he does not believe the shade was necessarily Apollonius, but that the whole manifestation was a kind of 'drunkenness of the imagination'. Bearing in mind Paracelsus's concept of the imagination, we need not take this to be a total disclaimer of a genuine occult experience; in fact, he adds that he 'did see and ... did touch, apart from dreaming, and this is sufficient to establish the real efficacy of magical ceremonies'. And at the beginning of the chapter on necromancy, he remarks sonorously: 'Eliphaz Levi Zahed, who writes this book, has evoked, and he has seen.'

Levi exerted a considerable influence upon the novelist Bulwer-Lytton, who became something of a disciple, and the description of the magician in *The Haunted and the Haunters* is a fanciful portrait of Levi; there are also echoes of him in *A Strange Story*, *Zanoni* and *The Coming Race*, the first of which is a classic of occultism and suspense that has been oddly neglected in our own time. One of the focal points of Levi's magical doctrine is the notion of the 'astral light', Levi's name for the invisible magical ether that we have encountered in other occultists, and which he describes as 'a force more powerful than steam'. In Lytton's novel *The Coming Race*, this appears as *vril*, a magical form of energy. (It is an amusing thought that the manufacturers of Bovril beef extract borrowed Lytton's word and united it with a cow to form the name of their product; Levi's astral light lives on.)

It was Bulwer-Lytton who made the idea of occultism fashionable in England, and was chiefly responsible for the magical revival that involved Mathers, Yeats, Crowley, Waite, Dion Fortune et al. The revival might have started fifty years earlier if a certain Francis Barrett had been a better writer; in 1801, Barrett published a large study of ritual magic called *The Magus*, whose portraits of demons may still be found in most histories of magic and witchcraft, and in an advertisement at the end of the book, appealed for students and disciples to help him create a magic circle. But the book is dull, if informative, and cannot bear comparison with Levi. The Reverend Montague Summers, that credulous historian of witchcraft and vampirism, asserts that Barrett *did* succeed in founding a circle and that Cambridge subsequently became something of a magic centre as a consequence.

What should by now be quite clear is that the spirit of magic underwent a complete transformation in the nineteenth century. With Paracelsus it had been a science. With Cagliostro it became the instrument of his religion of the regeneration of mankind. But with Levi and Lytton it became a romantic literary property, surrounded by dense clouds of incense. Goethe's Faust turns to magic because he is sick of his human limitations, and he wants to explore those moments of godlike intensity that Saint-Martin wrote about. Nineteenth-century man found himself high and dry in a materialistic and boring world. In the Middle Ages, devils were a reality that everybody accepted without question – hence the morbid fascination aroused by the legend of Theophilus. Now the shadows were gone; the common daylight made everything hard and clear. And the romantics looked back nostalgically to the age of demons and incubi, altogether more stimulating to the imagination than railways and paddle steamers. The universal complaint was boredom. In *Obermann* (1804), Etienne de Senancour created a Byronic hero who broods among the mountains of Switzerland upon man's inadequacy and his own failure to establish contact with the magnificence of Nature. The real problem of life is not its misery but its meaninglessness. He remarks that cloudy weather makes him feel sad, but when the sun comes out it strikes him as 'useless'. He feels tired and without desire; he is neither happy nor unhappy – even unhappiness would be a relief from the dullness. A hundred and fifty years before Samuel Beckett, Obermann sits waiting for Godot. This feeling of futility and boredom was the foundation of the occult revival.

But what about the feeling that man possesses godlike powers – the feeling that is obviously based on reality, if the claims of the Fiji fire-walkers are true? How is it that the most intelligent men – like Obermann, and like Matthew Arnold, who wrote a poem about him – are crippled by a feeling of helplessness, of contingency, of being a mere plaything of forces greater than themselves? There can be only one answer. Because they are mere rationalists, obsessed by the 'scientific view of nature'. Men like Bulwer-Lytton and Eliphaz Levi recognised this instinctively and took steps to combat it. Hence the 'magical revival'.

But the really explosive impetus for the revival came from America. A completely new epoch in the history of occultism opened on the evening of March 31, 1848, in the house of the Fox family in the town of Arcadia, Wayne County, New York. For some time the family had been disturbed by rapping noises, and on this evening, the two Fox girls, aged twelve and fifteen, asked the mysterious knocker to repeat noises made by snapping their fingers. The 'spirit' did so. Twelve days later, a roomful of neighbours heard a man called William Duesler ask the 'spirit' questions, which were answered by raps. The spirit said that it had been murdered for money, and buried in the cellar. Digging in the cellar later produced some decayed human remains, which were presumably those of the pedlar who had been murdered by a previous tenant of the house. It was then discovered that the Fox sisters seemed to incite rapping noises wherever they went. A relative of the Foxes later declared that it was all fraudulent – produced somehow by the girls cracking their double-joints – but by that time, 'spirit rapping' had caught on and spread all over America. Undoubtedly, much of it *was* fraudulent. Equally certainly, much was genuine.

These phenomena will be discussed more thoroughly in the third part of this book; they are mentioned here only to introduce one of the most flamboyant figures in the history of occultism: Helena Petrovna Blavatsky.

She was born Helena Hahn, the daughter of a Russian colonel, in 1831, and she was the cousin of Sergei Witte, later prime minister and friend of Rasputin. She seems to have been an explosive madcap. Married at sixteen to a man twenty-four years her senior, she deserted him after a while – the marriage still unconsummated – and began her wanderings around the world. Count Witte said she became a bareback rider in a circus, taught the piano in Paris and London, became assistant to the medium Daniel Dunglas Home for a while, managed an artificial flower factory in Tiflis and periodically turned up at her home in Ekaterinoslav looking plumper and stranger than ever. She had been beautiful as a young girl, with curly dark hair, a large, sensual mouth and great azure eyes. She soon put on weight, reaching sixteen and a half stone (232 pounds) in middle age; but no matter how much her bulk increased, she never lost a gentle, feminine, appealing quality – it comes out even in her last photograph. She also travelled, according to her own account, in Mexico, Texas, India, Canada and Tibet – the last was almost impossible for a woman to enter, and she was turned back twice. The circus job seems to have ruined her sex life; she fell off a horse and displaced her womb which, a doctor certified later, made abstention unavoidable; she later declared: 'I am lacking something, and the place is filled up with some crooked cucumber.' Returning to Italy from Greece in her fortieth year, the *Eumonia* blew up, and only seventeen of its four hundred passengers survived; she described limbs and heads falling around her as she swam.

She enters the history of occultism some two years later. It is true that she seems to have acquired some reputation as a medium in Russia, but details are lacking. In 1873, she went to America, and found the country in the grip of the spiritualist craze. It had progressed a long way since the Fox sisters had produced rappings twenty years earlier. Now the spirits turned tables, made articles of furniture fly around the room, played musical instruments and even materialised at séances. Two brothers named Eddy were the most prominent materialisation mediums, and it was at their farm near Chittenden, Vermont, that Madame Blavatsky met a bearded lawyer who possessed the honorary rank of colonel – Henry Steel Olcott. Olcott was a bearded, gentle, naïve American, with eyes that tended to look in opposite directions. He was much taken with Madame Blavatsky, whose character was certainly striking. She was enormously vital, direct of speech (as the remark about the 'crooked cucumber' demonstrates), a nervous chain-smoker who often soothed her nerves with marihuana (which was not illegal in those sensible times), and capable of colourful and imaginative profanity. The bumbling, serious-minded colonel found her a magnet. He wrote about her in the newspaper for which he was correspondent, and saw much of her when she returned to New York. Other newspapers interviewed her because she was good copy. There was no romantic involvement with the colonel; in fact, she married a young Georgian named Michael Bettanelly, seven years her junior, on his promise that he should not try to invade her bed. When he failed to keep it, they separated. She was breezily indifferent to the existence of her Russian husband, Vice-Governor Blavatsky. She is admittedly on record as saying that sexual love is 'a beastly appetite that should be starved into submission'.

Madame Blavatsky had definite mediumistic powers. Throughout her life, acquaintances spoke of strange knocks and rappings that occurred in her presence. The colonel was glad to call upon her help when it was a question of investigating mediums suspected of fraud – for example, a couple named Holmes, who were accused of hiring a Mrs. Eliza White to impersonate a 'materialised spirit' called Katie King. The famous socialist Robert Owen was much taken with Katie King and gave her presents of jewellery, which Katie took back with her to the spirit world. With Madame Blavatsky's help, Olcott was able to tell his readers – in a book called *People from the Other World* – that the Holmeses and Katie King were undoubtedly genuine.

It was clear to HPB, as she became known to her admirers, that her future was tied up with spiritualism. The trouble was that it was already becoming less fashionable; and a spiritualist newspaper she helped to launch soon failed. She and the colonel started a Miracle Club, which was basically simply another séance group, but this did not prosper. The colonel was a total believer in HPB's powers, and he contributed greatly to her support in the year after he met her. Occasionally when he was with her, notes dropped out of the air detailing her needs, and she explained that they were from certain secret Mahatmas she had met in Tibet, spiritual adepts who would one day regenerate the world. The colonel always followed their instructions. There was also a Brotherhood of Luxor – in these early days, HPB tended to emphasise Egypt rather than Tibet – whose members sent messages to the readers of *The Banner of Light*, the spiritualist newspaper that publicised her doings in exchange for a certain amount of financial support.

It was one of the Luxor Brotherhood who suggested that the colonel should leave his wife and three children and move into the same building as Madame Blavatsky. The marriage was not entirely happy and he was glad to follow the suggestion.

It was on September 7, 1875, that Madame Blavatsky embarked on the career that was to make her world-famous. A certain Mr. Felt had lectured to a small study group about the hermetic secrets embodied in the measurements of the pyramids. He explained that those secret 'laws of proportion' could also invoke spirits, although, he added, the spirits he had seen showed no sign of intelligence. The colonel suggested that perhaps they ought to form a society to study this kind of thing. HPB nodded vigorously. And during the next week they thought of a name for it – the Theosophical Society.

The word was not invented by HPB. It had been in use, as a synonym for mysticism, for centuries; for example, Bishop Martensen refers to Jacob Boehme's system as a 'theosophy' in his classic book on Boehme (1882). But after HPB, theosophy meant primarily a curious system of Eastern and Western mysticism, 'secret doctrine' and spiritualism. As soon as the society was formed, HPB set out to write its bible. She wrote endlessly, day after day, chain-smoking and occasionally glancing up to read some book held out for her by spirits. The result, *Isis Unveiled*, came out in two volumes in September 1877 and sold amazingly well. An incredibly erudite work, blending doctrines from the Kabbalah, Cornelius Agrippa, Pythagoras, Buddhist, Hindu and Taoist scripture, *Isis Unveiled* can still be studied with enjoyment, if only for the extraordinary boldness of its conceptions. We have already touched upon her doctrine of 'root races' in discussing Atlantis. The first root race lived near the North Pole and they were invisible, being made of fire-mist; the second, living in northern Asia, were just visible – they invented sexual intercourse; the third root race were the ape-like giants of

Lemuria, who communicated telepathically and could not reason in our sense; the fourth were the Atlanteans, who were destroyed through black magic; we are the fifth (and according to the occultist Lewis Spence, we are also heading the way of Atlantis); the sixth root race will evolve from the present human race and will live on Lemuria (in the Pacific) again; after the seventh root race, life will leave our earth and start up on Mercury. Buried in all these remarkable assertions there is the vitally important notion that man is in a privileged position. It is true that his spirit is trapped in an unprecedented weight of flesh; but he possesses the will and intellect to cope with it. He *could*, with confidence and courage, become godlike.

For three years, the Theosophical Society more or less flourished in America. Then HPB decided that interest was declining, and that they should go to India. An odd coincidence prompted this decision. In 1870 the colonel had met an Indian named Moolji Thackersey on shipboard; seven years later the colonel happened to be talking to a friend who had just returned from India, and he asked him if, by any chance, he had met Thackersey. His friend had indeed; he even had his address. Olcott wrote to him about the Theosophical Society; Thackersey wrote back about a new Indian religious movement called the Arya Samaj, started by a remarkable teacher called Swami Dayananda Sarasvati. Olcott also wrote to the Swami, and soon the Theosophical Society had accepted the idea of amalgamation with the Arya Samaj. And when, not long after, Daniel Dunglas Home made some slighting remarks about Madame Blavatsky and her society in one of his books, she decided to leave the treacherous and unspiritual West and seek light in India.

The trip began badly – seasickness, heat and a large bill for expenses from the president of the Bombay Arya Samaj, which made HPB erupt into a volcano of profanity. All the same, they had made the right choice.

India was getting tired of British domination. These cultured Westerners who thought that the wisdom of India was preferable to the technology of the white man were a great moral boost. Swami Dayananda found them naïve and too interested in occult phenomena, but the rest of Bombay accepted them with enthusiasm. Their magazine, *The Theosophist*, sold better than it had ever done in America. The tide was all in their favour, even though there were aspects of India they found jarring. One old gentleman of high rank brought a pretty ten-year-old girl into the room, and HPB smiled charmingly; but when he said: 'Allow me to present you to my little wife,' she roared, 'You old beast, you ought to be ashamed of yourself.'

Her occult powers seemed to increase. She caused a shower of roses to fall on the heads of a company of scholars and pandits, made a lamp flame rise and fall merely by pointing at it and materialised a cup and saucer at a picnic. On this last occasion, two Englishmen suggested that Madame Blavatsky might have buried the cup and saucer in the place where they had been found, and HPB was so angry that 'she seemed to take leave of her senses'. Nevertheless, she agreed to provide further proof of her powers – or rather, the Mahatmas' – that evening. She asked their hostess if there was anything she particularly wanted, and the hostess mentioned a brooch lost some years ago. After asking her to envisage it clearly, HPB announced that the Masters had deposited it in a flower bed outside. The company went into the garden, dug among the flowers and unearthed the brooch.

A new disciple, A. P. Sinnett, asked if he might be allowed to correspond with the Mahatmas, and HPB said it might be possible. Sinnett gave her a letter to be transmitted, and a few days later he found a reply on his desk from a master who called himself Koot Hoomi Lal Singh. Another disciple, A. O. Hume, wrote to Koot Hoomi, and also received an answer. The letters from Koot Hoomi continued until there were enough of them to publish in a volume.

(They are at present preserved in the British Museum in seven volumes.) Sinnett and Hume certainly had no doubt whatever that the letters came from a secret master in the Himalayas. On one occasion, they asked him whether it would not be possible to establish direct contact with him instead of having to use HPB as a mailbox. The result, after this letter had been handed, sealed, to HPB, was a violent scene in which her profanity reached a new level of colourful inventiveness.

The colonel went to Ceylon and became converted to Buddhism, to Swami Dayananda's disgust. The colonel could not see any important difference between these various Eastern religions. The Swami insisted on disaffiliating the Arya Samaj from the Theosophical Society, and even came to refer to HPB and Olcott as a couple of charlatans. I have already spoken of his sudden development of thaumaturgic powers in Ceylon (pp. 229–30). This, and the publication of a work called *A Buddhist Catechism*, which achieved remarkable popularity, gave the colonel a certain independent standing in the society. HPB was not entirely happy about this either.

But her downfall was the result of her generous and open nature. In Cairo in 1872 she had met a certain Emma Cutting, who subsequently married a one-eyed Frenchman named Coulomb. After various business ventures failed disastrously, Mme. Coulomb read in the Ceylon newspaper that HPB had founded a theosophical society in Bombay. She wrote to her; HPB replied warmly. The Coulombs went to Bombay, and were soon installed as HPB's housekeepers. This was a mistake. Mme. Coulomb was a sour, trivial-minded woman who stored up grudges. She began by adoring HPB and ended by hating her. In 1884, five years after her arrival in India, it seemed that HPB was firmly established as the leader of one of the most influential movements in the country. (Olcott, an indefatigable traveller, had set up branches throughout India and Ceylon.) Her position seemed impregnable. She decided it was time for a visit to

Europe. She stayed with Lady Caithness, another occult enthusiast, in Nice, and borrowed her flat in Paris. She went to London, and cheerfully agreed when the Society for Psychical Research asked if they might investigate her claims. Then, back in Bombay, Mme. Coulomb blabbed. She chose a Christian missionary, editor of the *Christian College Magazine*, as the recipient of her confidences. He was only too delighted to pass on her revelations to his readers; the Christian missionaries had been HPB's bitterest opponents ever since she arrived. Mme. Coulomb showed him letters from HPB that made it clear that many of her effects had been achieved by fraud. She claimed that she had made a model of Koot Hoomi and walked around with it on her shoulders on moonlit nights, and that she had caused Mahatma letters to be 'precipitated' at the dinner table by the simple expedient of dropping them through cracks in the ceiling from the room above. The scandal was enormous; a report was immediately telegraphed to the London *Times*. An American spiritualist, Henry Kiddle, added fuel to the flames by pointing out that Koot Hoomi had stolen several paragraphs from one of his published lectures. Koot Hoomi replied, in due course, that he had somehow caught the words floating through the psychic ether, and written them down without thinking.

The Society for Psychical Research had intended to publish a more or less favourable report, but these events made them think again. They sent an investigator to India. But when he was finally admitted to the room which had contained the 'shrine' – a cedarwood cabinet in which Mahatma letters had often been precipitated – he found it empty, and the walls newly replastered. For some faithful disciple, wishing to demonstrate that fraud was impossible, had slapped the rear wall of the shrine, saying, 'You see, it's perfectly solid,' when, to his dismay, a panel had shot open, revealing another panel in the wall of HPB's boudoir. They were convinced that all this had been deliberately planted by the treacherous Coulombs – and indeed, it was true that M. Coulomb was a carpenter – and so removed the shrine to another room, and subsequently burnt it.

Inevitably, under the circumstances, the report of the Society for Psychical Research was distinctly sceptical. Madame Blavatsky, who was at the time suffering from a complication of diseases due to her great weight, retorted angrily that the phenomena would continue after her death – which would certainly not be long now.

But it was not the end yet. HPB recovered and rushed back to India, determined to sue the missionaries. Her legal advisers told her not to; a 'magician' is always at a disadvantage in a court of law when faced by sceptics, for the trial is bound to turn into a debate on the reality of the magician's claims. The missionaries thereupon decided to force the issue by issuing a writ for libel against an old general who had called Mme. Coulomb a liar and a thief. This would also have had the effect of raising all the same issues in court. Madame Blavatsky was forced to flee back to Europe. She had fulfilled the magician's destiny of triumphant rise and sudden downfall.

She travelled through Italy, Switzerland and Germany. She was dying of Bright's disease. She decided to write another book that should clarify the obscurer points of *Isis Unveiled* and began *The Secret Doctrine*. Again, the manuscript pages piled up as her pen raced over the page. (The published version is over 1,500 pages long.) She told W. B. Yeats, who had met her on her second visit to England: 'I write, write, write, as the Wandering Jew walks, walks, walks.' Yeats noted a quality that is not apparent to readers of her works: her sense of humour. She told one serious disciple that the earth had another globe stuck on it at the North Pole so that it was shaped like a dumb-bell, and the disciple swallowed it without blinking. HPB reminded Yeats of an old Irish peasant woman. He records that her cuckoo clock hooted at him when he was alone with it, although it was not ticking and there were no weights on it. When HPB took a strong dislike to a priggish female guest, she described how her master had cured her of rheumatism in the knee by placing a live dog, which he had cut open, over the knee.

Perhaps Yeats's funniest story about her concerns a 'female penitent' who became' entangled with two of HPB's more serious male followers. HPB spoke to her sternly: 'We think that it is necessary to crush the animal nature; you should live in chastity in act and thought. Initiation is granted only to those who are entirely chaste.' And after several more minutes of this, she concluded: 'I cannot permit you more than one.'

But when another young lady, a Miss Leonard, successfully seduced a budding Mahatma called Mohini Chatterjee (of whom Yeats wrote a poem), HPB became so angry that she wrote her a thoroughly libellous letter and had to apologise.

The manuscript of *The Secret Doctrine* was a huge pile of jumbled papers. Various friends read it and said it was incomprehensible. She told them to get to work on it; so the book was typed, then rearranged. The book came out in 1888. Annie Besant, who had been a Fabian and Bernard Shaw's mistress, reviewed it, and wanted to meet the author. Her first reaction was aversion: but when HPB said, 'Oh, my dear Mrs. Besant, if only you would come among us,' she melted. She subsequently became the leader of the Theosophical Society. It would not be inaccurate to say she became a Theosophist on the rebound from Shaw – the recent end of their affair had hurt her deeply. Years later, when her adopted son Krishnamurti met Shaw in Bombay, Shaw asked how she was. 'Very well, but at her great age, she cannot think consecutively.' 'She never could,' said Shaw.

HPB died on May 8, 1891, in her sixtieth year. She had been seriously ill for at least six years, and in spite of a complication of heart disease, kidney disease and rheumatic gout, her enormous vitality not only kept her alive but crackling with sparks. Her biographer, John Symonds, is not exaggerating when he calls her 'one of the most remarkable women who ever lived'. She was larger than life-size.

Aleister Crowley believed he was a reincarnation of Eliphaz Levi; if so, Madame Blavatsky must have been a reincarnation of Cagliostro. She had the same charisma, the same adventurousness, the same mixture of humour, roguery and genuine psychic ability.

As to this last, there can hardly be any doubt. She could not have held so many disciples entirely by means of confidence trickery. She was a medium in the same sense that Home was, and in the sense that many adolescent children are. Phenomena happened when she was around. Her companion in later years tells of how she went into HPB's room one night to turn out a lamp that was burning. She turned it out and got back into bed – the room was divided by a screen – when the lamp was lit again. She turned it out again, and this time watched until the last spark had vanished; suddenly, it lit again. The third time she did it, she saw a disembodied brown hand turning up the wick. When she finally succeeded in waking the sleeper, HPB explained she had been in her astral body, conversing with 'master', and that the sudden awakening was dangerous; it almost caused her heart to stop.

The first time she met Sinnett, he remarked that they had tried spiritualism but couldn't even get a rap; she replied, 'Raps are the easiest thing to get,' and raps immediately began to sound all around the room.

Olcott and various other theosophists actually saw Koot Hoomi and other masters under circumstances that rule out HPB's interference. And on several occasions, the masters left behind souvenirs of the visit – a silk handkerchief, for example. It is true that Olcott and the other disciples may have been lying. But on other occasions, the possibility of trickery seems much reduced. Major-General H. R. Morgan was being shown the 'shrine' when Mme. Coulomb knocked off a china tray and smashed it. While

M. Coulomb was trying to repair it with clay, the general remarked that surely the masters ought to be able to restore it if they thought it important? The tray was placed in a cloth in the shrine; a few minutes later, it was found in its original unbroken state with a note saying cryptically that the Devil was not as black as he is painted.

W. B. Yeats tells of how he saw some kind of light floating around the portrait of Koot Hoomi (which HPB had painted 'under guidance'); it vanished when he approached. HPB remarked, 'I was afraid it was mediumship but it was only clairvoyance.' The difference, she explained, was that if it had been mediumship, the light would not have gone away as Yeats approached.

Swami Dayananda was undoubtedly correct when he criticised the theosophists for being interested chiefly in 'phenomena'. The Hindu ascetics insist that any advanced yogi can produce phenomena, and that they are a waste of time, a red herring across the path of spiritual advancement. The works of the theosophists which include such notable classics as Annie Besant's *The Ancient Wisdom* and Sinnett's *Esoteric Buddhism* – are full of references to the Upanishads and Buddhist scriptures, but anyone who turns from theosophic literature to the original scriptures soon realises that there is an abyss of difference; the purity of the religious impulse has been lost in transition. It is not that Hinduism lacks its preposterous tales of miracles. Paramhansa Yogananda's *Autobiography of a Yogi*, a recent work by a man who died in 1952, contains stories as extraordinary as anything in the lives of the medieval saints. There are not only stories of telepathy and 'projection' of the astral body to distant places, but of the creation of a magic palace in the Himalayas, and the overnight healing of a yogi's arm when it has been almost severed from his body. Even so, Yogananda's book breathes the true spirit of Hinduism, and can create the peculiar spiritual intoxication that can also be found in the Gospel of

Sri Ramakrishna and the Bhagavad Gita. By comparison, *The Secret Doctrine* is on the level of children's fairy tales, a muddy torrent carrying all kinds of strange objects on its surface. Again we feel strongly that interest in occultism often involves a certain immaturity.

This becomes even clearer when we consider the magical revival in France that followed the death of Eliphaz Levi. Levi's chief disciple was the young Marquis Stanislas de Guaita, who wrote poems in the manner of Baudelaire and took morphine. Together with another young student of the Kabbalah, Oswald Wirth, Guaita formed an order of Rosicrucians in Paris. He wrote a curious work in several volumes called *The Serpent of Genesis*, with the subtitle *The Temple of Satan*, in which he violently attacked a 'false prophet', Eugène Vintras, and 'a base idol of the mystical Sodom, a magician of the worst type, a wretched criminal', called Joseph-Antoine Boullan.

The two objects of this attack occupy a prominent place in the history of French occultism in the nineteenth century. Pierre Michel Eugène Vintras was a Norman peasant and visionary who achieved something of the same celebrity as Swedenborg. He was born in 1807, and in 1839 he became manager of a cardboard-box factory at Tilly-sur-Seule. One evening he had a curious experience. A ragged old workman knocked on his door and addressed him by his Christian names, Pierre Michel. He got rid of the old man by giving him ten sous, but the old man apparently did not leave the building. Puzzled, Vintras asked a workman to help him search. He did not find the old man, but he found a letter and his ten sous. He now became convinced the old man was an angel. The letter was not addressed to Vintras, but he read it all the same. What he read impressed him very deeply. For the letter concerned the pretender to the French throne, Louis XVII, son of the king who had been executed.

Historical evidence seems to indicate that the son of Louis XVI and Marie Antoinette died in captivity at the age of ten, in 1795.

The unfortunate child had been kept locked in a dark room for six months, his food pushed through the grating in the door, and eventually died of scurvy. But no one seems to have seen the body and it was rumoured that he had escaped. Even the *Encyclopedia Britannica* admits that this is just possible. At all events, he was never heard of again. But in 1832 a German forger called Karl William Naundorf settled in France and announced that *he* was the missing heir to the throne. He was expelled in 1836, but by then he had many enthusiastic supporters. Naundorf's followers, who called themselves the Saviours of Louis XVII, declared that France was about to enter a period of terrible calamities (which proved to be true enough), and that these could only be averted when Louis XVII returned to the throne. Then a golden age would begin, a period of unparalleled prosperity, spiritual and material.

The letter Vintras read was full of these prophecies about the exiled Naundorf. Convinced that the angel who delivered the letter had been St. Michael, Vintras instantly declared himself to be a convert to the pretender's party.

He was a powerful ally, for he now began having apocalyptic visions, which he communicated so convincingly that he soon had hordes of followers, including a scholar called Charvoz, the curé of Mont Louis.

Vintras set up a chapel in the cardboard-box factory, and on the altar placed a number of hosts which, he said, had been sent to him by various disciples who had rescued them from desecration. (At this period, there was a certain amount of stealing of consecrated wafers from churches, presumably for use in black magic ceremonies.) And a miracle occurred; the hosts began to bleed. Medical tests verified that the blood was genuine and human (although it should be borne in mind that it was not until 1900 that Uhlenhuth discovered the method of testing a blood sample to establish its origin). Like the Abbé Vachère, of whom we have already spoken, Vintras seemed to have the odd ability to cause blood to materialise out of thin air. He was undoubtedly slightly insane, and his 'visions' have many parallels in the annals of medical psychology. For example, he describes a dream in which his 'chapel' was full of demons and monsters while the voice of the devil invited him to become one of his 'elect'; the Virgin Mary, whose face hovered above an abyss, confirmed that he was damned. In spite of such nightmares, he continued to preach the 'work of mercy', and the followers of Naundorf, who had 'probably engineered the first visit from the 'angel', had no reason to regret their decision to recruit him.

However, his publicist, the Abbé Charvoz, disregarded his advice to proceed with caution, and announced the miracle of the bleeding hosts in a widely distributed pamphlet. The authorities became nervous; a bishop denounced Vintras, and in 1842 Vintras and an agent of Naundorf's called Ferdinand Geoffroi were arrested and charged with fraud. They should have been acquitted, since the old ladies whose money they were accused of embezzling stated publicly that they had given the money of their own free will and had no regrets. Nevertheless, Vintras was sentenced to five years in prison, and Geoffroi to two. An appeal was dismissed. It was while Vintras was serving his sentence that an ex-disciple named Cozzoli published a pamphlet called *The Prophet Vintras* denouncing the sect as a cover for sexual perversions, and alleging that Vintras performed black masses and masturbated on the host while he prayed. A police investigation of these charges exonerated Vintras. He came out of jail in 1845, the year that the pretender Naundorf died in Holland, and went to London, where his sect continued to flourish. He now declared himself to be an incarnation of the prophet Elijah, as Cagliostro had done before him, and even the Pope's declaration that the sect was heretical did not diminish his widespread influence. He returned to France in 1863, consecrated a number of 'priests' in his Church of Carmel and died in December 1875.

One of these 'priests' was a dubious character called Boullan. Boullan, born in 1824, was a defrocked priest. The summary of his life that is given by Robert Baldick in his biography of Huysmans sounds too fantastic to accept without reservation. But Baldick, a fellow of Pembroke College, Oxford, asserts that 'a study of the priest's private papers, recently discovered in a remote French village by M. Pierre Lambert, and of a "confession" which he wrote in the prisons of the Holy Office, leaves no doubt that these reports of his depravity were well founded'. Boullan founded a religious community near Paris in 1859, and taught that sexual intercourse was a road to salvation. His disciples believed that they had copulated with Cleopatra and Alexander the Great, as well as with saints and archangels. In 1860, says Baldick, Boullan sacrificed a child borne him by a nun, the co-founder of the society, in some Satanic rite. As a result of these activities, he was imprisoned until 1870, when he returned to Paris, only outwardly repentant, and founded a dubious magazine called *Annals of Sanctity in the 19th Century* devoted to occult matters and accounts of Satanism. The basis of his teachings was still, apparently, sexual, and he taught his disciples how to dream they were having sexual intercourse with the saints of Jesus Christ by means of auto-suggestion. The Archbishop of Paris finally intervened, and Boullan was defrocked. Vintras, now in the last months of his life, was in Lyons. Boullan became his disciple. And when Vintras died later that year, Boullan, to the indignation of other members of the Church of Carmel, declared that Vintras had appointed him his successor. The result was a schism in the church. Boullan was finally accepted by a minority in Lyons, and settled there under the care of a housekeeper, Julie Thibault. She participated in a ceremony called the Union with Life, which seems to have been, to put it mildly, Dionysian in character. Boullan taught that since Adam and Eve fell through sex, man must learn to regenerate himself by the same means; sexual intercourse with people on a higher spiritual level than oneself raises one to their level – hence the importance of hallucinatory acts of intercourse with Jesus and the Virgin. Since Boullan was also on a higher spiritual plane than the female members of his congregation, it followed that he could give them a start on the upward path.

It was this sexual doctrine that Stanislas de Guaita, Levi's disciple, denounced in *The Temple of Satan* (1891). He said that it amounted to incubism and succubism – intercourse with male and female demons – and that Boullan's doctrine that one should help 'inferior beings' by copulating with them could be used to justify bestiality. Guaita and Wirth decided that Boullan should be exposed the year after he succeeded Vintras – 1886 – and they wormed their way into his confidence, and that of his housekeeper, by pretending to be humble seekers after knowledge. Boullan was naturally cautious – he kept his sexual doctrines secret, to be communicated only to trusted adepts – but he finally expounded them to his new disciples. Guaita and Wirth then revealed that they were wolves in sheep's clothing, held some kind of mock trial in Boullan's absence and finally informed Boullan that he had been found guilty and condemned.

Boullan naturally assumed this meant that the two Rosicrucians meant to kill him by magic. He now recalled bitterly that he had taught them some particularly murderous spells. If these were now flying through the psychic ether between Paris and Lyons, he would obviously have to counteract them with spells of his own. Guaita and Wirth (who later wrote on the Tarot) were joined by two other Rosicrucian adepts – a poet, Edouard Dubus, and a highly eccentric novelist who called himself Sar Peladan. The battle went on for several years, with both sides experiencing inexplicable fits of oppression and nerves which they set down to the incantations of the other.

The novelist J. K. Huysmans had become well known for his remarkable novel *À Rebours* (*Against the Grain*), about a rich young man, Des Esseintes, who detests the banality of everyday life, and locks himself in his villa, surrounded by exquisite food, liqueurs, pictures and books to live a life of the imagination and senses. Des Esseintes is one of the greatest symbols of the romantic revolt against 'the world'. ('As for living, our servants can do that for us.' said Axel, in Villiers de l'Isle-Adam's play.) Huysmans had begun as a follower of Zola and the naturalist school, but his sympathies were closer to the aestheticism of Oscar Wilde. (*À Rebours* becomes the bible of Dorian Gray in Wilde's novel.) He became increasingly fascinated by Satanism and decided to write a novel about it. First, he had to collect his material, and it was necessary to meet a Satanist. He heard about Boullan, and wrote to him in Lyons, asking for information, and offering to represent him in his novel as 'the Superman, the Satanist … far removed from the infantile spiritualism of the occultists'. (For some odd reason, believers in magic were violently opposed to spiritualism.) Boullan, glad of such an ally, welcomed Huysmans to Lyons. He told him the whole story of the battle against the 'black' Rosicrucians, explained that his own magic was strictly white and gave him all kinds of strange information. Huysmans kept faith; the novel *Là Bas* (*Down There*) appeared in the spring of 1891, with a flattering portrait of Boullan as the misunderstood white magician Dr. Johannés (a name Boullan had assumed), who performs miracle cures and un-bewitches people who have been bewitched by black magicians.

Là Bas is not a good novel; it is hardly a novel at all. But it is a very remarkable document that throws light not only on the psychology of French magicians of the nineteenth century, but upon the nature of 'black magic' in all ages.

There is very little plot. The writer Durtal, Huysmans himself, is engaged on a life of Marshal Gilles de Rais, the sexual pervert who derived pleasure from killing children, and excerpts from Gilles's biography are interspersed throughout the book. One senses a curious immaturity in Huysmans's interest in Gilles; when he describes him disembowelling children and masturbating on their intestines, he is not really aware of the horror of the subject; it strikes him as bizarre, freakish and therefore fascinating.

Durtal receives passionate letters from an unknown woman. The letters (which Huysmans had actually received from a female admirer) make it clear she is neurotic and hysterical, but Durtal, bored and weak-minded, is intrigued, and decides he is in love with the unknown. He eventually discovers that she is Hyacinthe Chantelouve, wife of a rather sneaky Catholic historian. There is a typical scene in which she finally agrees to give herself to him and undresses; Durtal has an immediate sense of anticlimax and finds the act of lovemaking sickening.

He discovers that she knows a priest who performs the black mass, the sinister Canon Docre (based on a Belgian abbé, Louis Van Haecke), and persuades her to take him to one. The black mass scene is obviously the high point of the novel. It has a remarkable feeling of authenticity. The altar boys are ageing poufs, covered with cosmetics. The chapel is dingy and damp, with cracked walls. The face of Christ on the cross is painted so that it laughs derisively. Canon Docre pours out Swinburnian invective on the Crucified: 'Thou hast forgotten the poverty thou didst preach, thou hast seen the weak crushed ... thou hast heard the death rattle of the timid ...' The women then begin to have convulsions in the manner of the Loudun nuns. One of the aged choir boys performs an act of fellatio on him. Docre ejaculates on the host and tosses it to the convulsed women; he also apparently defecates on the altar. Huysmans's language is not explicit, but ordure obviously plays a central part in the mass. Durtal finally drags Mme. Chantelouve away; she takes him to a room in a cheap bar, where, in spite of his protests, she possesses him. As far as Durtal is concerned, that is the end of the affair.

What comes out so clearly in the description of the black mass is the desire of the participants to *shock themselves* out of their normal state of dullness. One of the most curious features of all such ceremonies – witch's sabbaths and so on – is this emphasis on ordure and dirt. In Huysmans, it becomes clear that the whole thing, far from being horrifying and sinister, is merely an expression of bourgeois frustrations. Parents demand that children keep clean, therefore it gives a sense of wickedness to wallow in dirt. The 'blasphemies' sound completely harmless to anyone who is not a Catholic and who does not accept that disbelief in the divinity of Christ involves eternal damnation. The convulsions are intended to afford the same kind of relief as pornography. I have commented earlier on the element of deliberate nastiness that some pornographers throw in as a final touch of naughtiness; this is also present at Huysmans's mass: 'Another [woman], sprawling on her back, undid her skirts, revealing a huge and distended paunch; then her face twisted into a horrible grimace, and her tongue, which she could not control, stuck out, bitten at the edges, harrowed by red teeth, from a bloody mouth.' The Devil's realm is supposed to be ugliness. But the reader can sense an element of self-contradiction in Huysmans's account. So much ugliness and unpleasantness can hardly make the mass sound wicked, for who would want to witness anything so nauseating? So he takes care to mention that there are attractive women present, 'Junonian brunettes', even a young girl. And in doing so, he reveals the paradoxical absurdity of Satanism. The element that makes the black mass attractive is perfectly normal, healthy, pagan sex. The driving force behind it is the sexual repression that is inevitable in all civilisation, where leisure gives everyone time to daydream about sex. The ugly crones with bitten tongues are an attempt to disguise this truth. A mere twenty years after *Là Bas*, D. H. Lawrence was undermining the whole foundation of this kind of infantile diabolism by emphasising that sex is a liberating activity; the penis is 'the rod that connects man to the stars'. After sexual intercourse a healthy couple should experience something of the 'oceanic feeling' that characterises mysticism, and this oceanic feeling is an intuition of the godlike, not the demonic. If Huysmans's diabolists had possessed any powers of self-observation, they would have noted that they experienced a sense of release, of 'cosmic consciousness', after their orgy, and that this is inconsistent with their professions of diabolism. Diabolism is an artificial antithesis, conjured into existence by bigotry and frustration – not a genuine expression of man's revolt against the godlike.

This conclusion is underlined by the weakness and immaturity that Huysmans reveals in his self-portrait as Durtal. His troubles arise out of boredom, inactivity. It is boredom that makes him work himself into a state of romantic fervour when he receives the letters from the unknown. When he discovers that the unknown is a society hostess whom he has met, he feels a mixture of disappointment and pleasure: disappointment because Hyacinthe is less alluring than his imaginary 'unknown'; pleased that she is, after all, quite sexually desirable. When she denies herself to him he begins to want her frantically. His moment of greatest pleasure occurs when she kisses him when her husband is in the next room. As soon as she surrenders he is revolted, and the morning after their depressing adultery, thinks longingly about chastity. As an excuse for not sleeping with her again, he tells her that he has a mistress and an ailing child, and is so touched by his own lie that he comes close to tears. Durtal is an addition to the long line of weak heroes in French literature: Obermann, Constant's Adolphe, Stendhal's Julien, Balzac's Rubempré. The only objection is that Huysmans was not aware of this; he thinks that Durtal's torments – which finally draw him back into the Church in *La Cathidrale* – are the agonies of sensitivity and intelligence, not of mere self-indulgence and lack of discipline.

I have dwelt on *Là Bas* because it makes it possible to see the great 'magical battle' between Boullan and Guaita for the futile and rather silly business it really was. The Abbé Boullan died on January 3, 1893, at the age of sixty-nine, the day after writing an ominous letter to Huysmans. 'At 3 o'clock I awoke suffocating … From 3 to 3.30 I was between life and death.' The numbers 8, 9, 3, in the year boded evil, he said. Mme. Thibault, who later became Huysmans's housekeeper, wrote to him the same day telling him that after dinner, Boullan had struggled with congestion of the lungs, and then died suddenly. It was fairly obviously angina pectoris and a heart attack; it was not the first. But Huysmans immediately decided that the Rosicrucians had killed Boullan with their spells, and accused them of it in letters to newspapers. Guaita and Wirth declared flatly that there had been no spells at any time – no doubt telling the truth. Guaita fought a duel with Huysmans's friend Bois, who had also accused him, but neither was hurt. The horse taking Bois to the duel came to a halt, trembling – no doubt telepathically sensing its rider's fear – and his pistol failed to fire; naturally, he attributed both these occurrences to Guaita's magic. Dubus, the Rosicrucian poet, boasted that it was *his* magic that had killed Boullan; but he himself died shortly afterwards, after telling Huysmans that he was pursued by voices. Guaita died in 1898 from an overdose of drugs.

It may be doubted whether anyone tried actively to cast death-spells. If Guaita was, as Baldick asserts, only twenty-seven when he died in 1898, then he was only fifteen when he and Wirth inveigled the secrets of the Union with Life out of Boullan in 1886; it sounds more like an adolescent prank than a calculated act of hatred. Huysmans may have added fuel to the flames with his novel, but since it does not directly attack the Rosicrucian group, it cannot have made all that much difference. If the 'magical battle' hastened Boullan's death, it was because he worked himself into a state of nerves about it. It is doubtful, in any case, whether Guaita or any other member of the Rosicrucian group possessed the kind of nervous vitality necessary to project malice telepathically, in the way that John Cowper Powys believed he could.*

Huysmans records Durtal's future course, and his own, in three subsequent novels, *En Route*, *La Cathédrale* and *L'Oblat*. These volumes, like *Là Bas*, can hardly be called novels; they detail Durtal's path into the bosom of the Church – he ends as a Benedictine oblate – with lengthy discussions of medieval theology and the lives of the saints. The reader does not get a sense of a solution of Durtal's problems, because Catholicism is not the solution. Durtal is self-divided, unhappy, thoroughly dissatisfied with his life and with himself. It is an evolutionary craving that drives him, the desire to achieve the 'violet end' of the spectrum of consciousness, and he fails.

At the British Museum Reading Room I often saw a man of thirty-six or thirty-seven, in a brown velveteen coat, with a gaunt resolute face, and an athletic body, who seemed, before I heard his name, or knew the nature of his studies, a figure of romance. Presently I was introduced ... He was called Liddell Mathers, but would soon, under the touch of 'The Celtic Movement', become MacGregor Mathers, and then plain MacGregor. He was the author of *The Kabbalah Unveiled*, and

---

* The *Daily Express* for July 22, 1970, reports the suicide of a thirty-five-year-old gardener, who became convinced that an ex-girlfriend had bewitched him. His landlady told the inquest: "'About eighteen months ago he was introduced to a girl who was involved in black magic. He went out with her for a week, and she told him she belonged to a cult and that she had killed three men. She said she could put a curse on him. I told him to give her up, and he did.'" ... Mr. Harrington began to brood, and spent six weeks in hospital receiving treatment for nerves. Last Friday she returned from shopping and found him hanging from the banisters ... "He told me about a nightmare he had that shattered his nerves. He said he dreamed of a man upside down on a crucifix in a field.'" The parallel with Boullan needs no underlining.

his studies were only two – magic and the theory of war, for he believed himself a born commander, and all but equal in wisdom and in power to that old Jew. He had copied many manuscripts on magical ceremonial and doctrine in the British Museum, and was to copy many more in Continental libraries, and it was through him mainly that I began certain studies and experiences, that were to convince me that images well up before the mind's eye from a deeper source than conscious or subconscious memory. I believe that his mind in those early days did not belie his face and body – though in later years it became unhinged, as Don Quixote's was unhinged – for he kept a proud head amid great poverty. One that boxed with him nightly has told me that for many years he could knock him down, though Mathers was the stronger man, and only knew long after that during those weeks Mathers starved.

I have quoted Yeats at length because the portrait of Mathers contains all the essential elements of the magician. There is the poverty, the driving will-power, the obscure sense of destiny, the romanticism that makes him change his name from Liddell to MacGregor. It is tempting to say that he is a man born in the wrong age, an adventurer who finds the nineteenth century too tame; but since, as we have seen, Agrippa and Paracelsus were no better off, this cannot be maintained. The 'old Jew' Yeats refers to is Ahasuerus, the Wandering Jew. Yeats was fascinated by the passage in Shelley's *Hellas* describing the old Jew living 'in a sea cavern 'mid the Demonesi', and he became a Theosophist – joining the Dublin circle that gathered around George Russell (A.E.) – 'because they had affirmed the real existence of the Jew'. This idea of a lonely superman, possessing more-than-human power and wisdom, is an immense attraction to people who, like Yeats, detest their own age.

Mathers introduced Yeats to a small group of Christian Kabbalists called The Hermetic Students, and soon after, they decided to call themselves 'the Order of the Golden Dawn'. Mathers talked mysteriously of an unknown master who had instructed him to found the Hermetic Students – perhaps Saint-Germain himself. The truth seems to be that Mathers had been a Rosicrucian and had been asked by a fellow Rosicrucian, Dr. William Woodman, to interpret a manuscript he had bought in the Farringdon Road. It turned out to be a ritual of ceremonial magic, and it mentioned a magical society in Germany. Mathers, Woodman and a Dr. Wyn Westcott, the London coroner, wrote to the German society and were given a charter to found their own group. Mathers, being of a dictatorial nature, ended as its sole leader. According to John Symonds the German order seems to have been influenced by Madame Blavatsky, for it believed in secret masters in Tibet.*

The Golden Dawn had lodges in Edinburgh, Paris, London and Weston-super-Mare. Mathers claimed to have established contact with the 'secret chiefs' in Paris, and his authority was increased by his discovery in the Bibliotheque de L'Arsenal of a grimoire called *The Book of Sacred Magic of Abra-Melin the Mage*, printed in 1458.

Mathers became the curator of a private museum owned by Frederick J. Horniman in 1890, but in 1891 he quarrelled with his employer and was dismissed. Horniman's daughter, Miss Annie Horniman, made him an allowance of £443 a year, and he moved to Paris. His wife, the daughter of the philosopher Bergson, was also a 'seer'. He left the actress Florence Farr in charge of the Order, and began performing 'Egyptian Rites' in Paris – he even hired the Bodinière Theatre and charged admission to see them. (It is not clear whether these had any connection with

* Although in Crowley's *Confessions*, it is more likely that the 'secret chiefs' were German magicians, and one was certainly a Frenchman of Scottish descent.

Cagliostro's Egyptian rite but it seems likely.) Probably he left Florence Farr in charge because he felt that a woman was less likely to take advantage of his absence to increase her own authority. If so, the idea was unsound; there were others in the order who were finding his autocratic manner a strain: for example, Dr. Westcott, one of the original founders. Rumbles of revolt were heard, and they increased when Mathers showed a tendency to want to introduce his new Egyptian rites to the London society. And at this point, says Joseph Hone, in his biography of Yeats, Mathers precipitated a break by 'seeking the support of a dreadful young man, who broke into the rooms of the Order and took possession of a book containing much secret matter'. When Hone's book came out in 1942, the 'dreadful young man' was still alive and so could not be mentioned by name. It was Aleister Crowley, the reincarnated spirit of Eliphaz Levi. His intervention was the beginning of the end for the Order of the Golden Dawn, which now disintegrated gently. A new order, the Stella Matutina, declared that it would not tolerate mystagogues; but without mystagogues, it failed to maintain the interest of its members.Mathers died in 1918, overcome, according to the first edition of Yeats's autobiography, by powerful magical currents emanating from Crowley.

In his excellent book *Ritual Magic in England* (1970), Francis King describes the subsequent history of the Golden Dawn. Mrs. Mathers became head of one of the branches of the Order, but failed to hold it together. That remarkable occultist Dion Fortune broke away and formed her own Temple; she later alleged that Mrs. Mathers launched murderous 'psychic attacks' on her, and actually succeeded in killing one errant member. In 1934, a Crowley disciple named Frances Israel Regardie joined the Stella Matutina and then proceeded to publish its secret rituals in a four-volume edition; this betrayal apparently pushed the society into the final stages of collapse. The magical banners and instruments of the

A.O. (another branch) were buried in a clifftop garden on the south coast; in 1966, the crumbling of the cliff deposited them on the beach, and several magical groups instantly laid claim to them. This event seems to conclude the history of the Golden Dawn.

SEVEN
THE BEAST HIMSELF

There is an element of exhibitionism in all magicians; after all, the desire to perform magic is fundamentally a desire to impress other people. In Crowley, it so outweighed his other qualities that most of his contemporaries dismissed him as a publicity seeker. And since the English have a peculiar horror of immodesty, he came to be regarded as the embodiment of every anti-English vice. Seven years after his death – in 1954 – the Finchley Public Library declined to purchase a copy of John Symonds's biography of Crowley, or even to try to borrow it from another branch. The friend of mine who tried to order it was told that libraries are intended to circulate literature, and that by no stretch of imagination could Crowley be associated with literature.

It cannot be denied that the librarian had a point: Crowley was a mountebank. In spite of this, he deserves serious consideration. for he was a magician in the original sense – a mage rather than an 'occultist' or 'spiritualist'. His character was flawed and complex, but his career certainly followed the parabolic course of rise and downfall that seems typical of magicians.

He was born Edward Alexander Crowley on October 12, 1875, the year that saw the death of Levi and Vintras, and the creation of the Theosophical Society. His father, Edward Crowley, had made his fortune from Crowley's Ales, and retired to devote his life to preaching the doctrines of the Plymouth Brethren. They lived in Leamington, a still, peaceful town not far from Stratford-on-Avon; '... a strange coincidence', he remarked later, 'that one small county should have given England her two greatest poets – for one must not forget Shakespeare.' In his autobiography, which he calls *The Confessions of Aleister Crowley*, he makes it clear that much of his later 'diabolism' was a revolt against the religion of his childhood. Like Huysmans's diabolists, he associated sex with sin. He wrote later: 'My sexual life was very intense ... Love was a challenge to Christianity. It was a degradation and a damnation.' He also remarks contemptuously of the members of the Golden Dawn: 'They were not protagonists in the spiritual warfare against restriction, against the oppressors of the human soul, the blasphemers who denied the supremacy of the will of man' – a phrase that brings to mind the doctrines of Saint-Martin. It was his mother, he said, who first said that she thought he was the Beast from the Book of Revelation, whose number is 666.

This makes it sound as if his childhood was repressed and embittered. In fact, his autobiography makes clear that he had affectionate and indulgent parents, and was rather a spoilt little boy. Boys tend to imitate their fathers, and his father, he says, was a born leader of men, so his spirit grew unchecked. His father died when he was eleven, and his natural wildness increased. He seems to have been the kind of schoolboy who smokes in lavatories and loves breaking his sister's toys. At the age of eleven he went to a private school for the sons of Brethren at Cambridge, and it was here that the spirit of revolt seems to have been sown in him. It happened immediately after his father's death – up till this time he had been happy enough there – so presumably he was suffering from some kind of emotional shock. More important, he was approaching puberty, and he was always powerfully attracted by sex. His mother was so puritanical that she violently quarrelled with Crowley's cousin Agnes because she had a copy of a book by Zola in her house (moreover, a perfectly harmless one, *Dr. Pascal*). So when a servant girl showed an interest in him, Crowley lost no time in getting her into his mother's bedroom and possessing her on the bed. The motivation here is clear enough. He was fourteen at the time. His career almost came to a premature end on Guy Fawkes night, 1891, when he tried to light a ten-pound home-made firework, and was unconscious for ninety-six hours. He went to public school at Malvern in the following year, then on to Oxford, where he lived lavishly and published his own poems. He discovered rock climbing, and for many years this was to satisfy his adventurous temperament. He was not a good poet because he lacked verbal discipline; a few lines of one of his poems will give an idea of his qualities:

I sate upon the mossy promontory
Where the cascade cleft not his mother rock,
But swept in whirlwind lightning foam and glory
Vast circling with unwearying luminous shock
To lure and lock
Marvellous eddies in its wild caress …

There is a certain impressionistic power; but it has no originality; it might have been written eighty years earlier. Perhaps everything came too easily: he had charm and wealth, he was a born mountaineer, a fluent poet, a successful lover; so his occasional setbacks produced a torrent of rage and self-justification instead of an effort at self-discipline.

In his late teens he came across Mathers's *Kabbalah Unveiled* (which is, in fact, basically a translation of the *Zohar* taken from a Kabbalist called Rosenroth), which fascinated him precisely because it was all so incomprehensible. Next came A. E. Waite's compilation on ceremonial magic, *The Book of Black Magic and of Pacts*. Waite was later a member of the Golden Dawn, and Crowley refers to him with typical unfairness: 'The author was a pompous, ignorant and affected dipsomaniac from America, and he treated his subject with the vulgarity of Jerome K. Jerome, and the beery, leering frivolity of a red-nosed music-hall comedian …' There follows a passage that illustrates what was wrong with Crowley as a stylist: '[Waite] is not only the most ponderously platitudinous and priggishly prosaic of pretentiously pompous pork butchers of the language, but the most voluminously voluble. I cannot dig over the dreary deserts of his drivel in search of the passage which made me write to him ...' (*Confessions*, p. 127). It is true that Waite is an appalling stylist, but he is never as bad as this. (Readers of Symons's *Quest for Corvo* will recognise a style of invective much like Rolfe's.)

Apart from Swinburnian poetry, Crowley also produced a cycle of poems about a sexual psychopath who ends as a murderer (*White Stains*) and a sadistic, pornographic short novel called *Snowdrops from a Curate's Garden*, which shows close affinities with Sade, psychologically as well as stylistically.

Through a student of chemistry, Crowley was introduced to an 'alchemist' named George Cecil Jones, and through Jones to the order of the Golden Dawn. He was disappointed by the mediocrity of most of the members, and found the ceremonies commonplace. Nevertheless, he was admitted, and given the name Brother Perdurabo (one who endures to the end). He was of the lowest of the society's ten grades, and began working hard to rise in rank.

The oddest fact of all is that Crowley was a born magician. Perhaps the explosion that almost killed him at sixteen had awakened his faculties – like Peter Hurkos's fall from a ladder. He possessed a remarkable sense of direction that made him compare himself to Shetland ponies that can find their way through bogs and mists. These instinctive, animal faculties – 'jungle sensitiveness' – were strongly developed in him. He mentions that he can never remember mountains he has climbed, yet can recognise every pebble if asked to repeat the climb – '... my limbs possess a consciousness of their own which is infallible'. Hostile critics have dismissed his 'magic' as wishful thinking; he was a romantic who wanted to believe in magic as Yeats wanted to believe in fairies; as Huysmans said, 'to find compensation for the horror of daily life, the squalor of existence, the excremental filthiness of the loathsome age we live in'.

This misses the point. What Crowley realised instinctively was that magic is somehow connected with the human will, with man's *true will*, the deep instinctive will. Man is a passive creature because he lives too much in rational consciousness and the trivial worries of everyday. Crowley, with his animal instinct and his powerful sexual urge, glimpsed the truth expressed in Nietzsche's phrase 'There is so much that has not yet been said or thought'. This should be borne in mind as a counterbalance to the natural tendency to dismiss him as a mountebank. If an ordinary, rational person tried to perform a magical ceremony, he would be thinking all the time: This is absurd; it cannot work. And it wouldn't. In moments of crisis or excitement, man 'completes his partial mind', and somehow knows in advance that a certain venture will be successful. William James remarks that a man can play a game for years with a high level of technical perfection, and then one day, in a moment of excitement, something clicks, and *the game begins to play him*; suddenly, he cannot do a thing wrong. Crowley states all this clearly in the important twentieth chapter of his autobiography, of which the following are the key passages:

> I soon learned that the physical conditions of a magical phenomenon were like those of any other; but even when this misunderstanding has been removed, success depends upon one's ability to awaken the creative genius which is the inalienable heirloom of every son of man, but which few indeed are able to assimilate to their conscious existence, or even, in ninety nine cases out of a hundred, to detect ... The basis of the [misunderstandings] is that there is a real apodictic correlation between the various elements of the operation, such as the formal manifestations of the spirit, his name and sigil, the form of the temple, weapons, gestures and incantations. These facts

prevent one from suspecting the real subtlety involved in the hypothesis. This is so profound that it seems almost true to say that even the crudest Magick eludes consciousness altogether, so that when one is able to do it, one does it without conscious comprehension, very much as one makes a good stroke at cricket or billiards. One cannot give an intellectual explanation of the rough working involved … In other words, Magick in this sense is an art rather than a science.

Here Crowley is very close to Paracelsus. His meaning is not always quite clear, but the total drift is plain. Magic is to do with a subconscious process, and the actual ceremonies and rituals are not 'apodictically related' to it, as treading on a rake is apodictically related to it hitting you on the head. It is interesting that he should use the word 'apodictically', later used by Edmund Husserl to mean 'beyond all question'; for Husserl was the first to grasp clearly that all conscious processes are 'intentional' and that therefore man's vision of himself as a passive creature in an active universe is false. His consciousness is so far removed from the power house that drives him that he can no longer hear its roaring, and makes the mistake of believing that consciousness is flat, passive, mirror-like.

Let me try to state this as plainly as possible. If a child whips a top, he is aware of the immediate relation between his whipping and the spinning of the top; if he stops whipping, the top slows down. Man has become so complicated that he is unaware of the relation between his will-power and the spinning of the top called consciousness, and minor discouragements tend to get so out of proportion that he forgets to whip it. Crowley had some intuitive sense of the powers of his hidden will, what Paracelsus meant by imagination, and he turned to magic with an instinct rather than an intellectual impulse. With much the same obscure feeling of *potential power*, Hitler turned to mob-oratory and Rasputin turned to faith-healing. Madame Blavatsky also possessed it to a remarkable extent, without possessing the self-discipline to go with it. The same is true of Crowley, to an even greater degree. But he cannot be understood without recognising that he *did* possess it.

When he became an ally of Mathers in Paris, Mathers sent him to London to try to regain control of the order of the Golden Dawn. Crowley had his own grudge against them: they had refused to allow him to ascend to a higher grade. The result was the dissolution of the Golden Dawn, and legal problems.

Yeats wrote irritably to Lady Gregory: 'Fortunately [Crowley] has any number of false names, and has signed the summons in one of them. He is also wanted for debt …' He added that they had refused to grant Crowley a higher grade because 'we did not think that a mystical society was intended to be a reformatory'. This view of Crowley is by no means unjustified. He shared with Mathers a curious weakness: the desire to pose as an aristocrat. Mathers was given to dressing in kilts and calling himself the Chevalier MacGregor or the Comte de Glenstrae. Crowley took a flat in Chancery Lane shortly after joining the Golden Dawn, cultivated a Russian accent and called himself Count Vladimir Svareff. He explains in his autobiography that he did this in the interests of psychological observation; he had observed that his wealth gained him a certain respect from tradesmen, and he now wanted to see how much lower they would bow to a Russian nobleman. When he moved to a house on the shores of Loch Ness, he called himself Lord Boleskine, or the Laird of Boleskin, and imitated Mathers in adopting a kilt. Here he concentrated upon the magic of Abra-Melin the Mage, whose ultimate aim is to establish contact with one's Guardian Angel. Crowley states that he and Jones (the alchemist) had succeeded in materialising the helmeted head and left leg of a healing spirit called Buer in London, and that on another occasion an army of semi-materialised demons spent the night marching around his room. In Scotland the lodge and terrace of Boleskin House became peopled with shadowy shapes, the lodgekeeper went mad and tried to kill his wife and children, and the room became so dark while Crowley was trying to copy magic symbols that he would have to work by artificial light, even when the sun was blazing outside.

After the quarrel with Yeats – who, according to Crowley, was 'full of black, bilious rage' because Crowley was a greater poet – the Laird of Boleskin went to Mexico, where his concentrated effort almost succeeded in making his image vanish in the mirror. This in itself makes quite clear what Crowley was out to do: to discover new horizons of the will. This raises the question: But in that case, why did he need *magic*, if his effects were produced by the will? And the answer underlines the central point of this book. The will cannot operate *in vacuo* – at least, except in certain moments of pure self-awareness. It needs a whole scaffolding of drama, of conviction, of purpose. When a patriot talks about his country, he does not mean the view out of the bathroom window, although that is certainly a part of his country. In order to get that patriotic glow, he needs to think of the Union Jack or Old Glory, and accompany it with some definite image of green fields or some battlefield of the past. When Crowley sat alone in his room in Mexico City, it was not enough to stare in the mirror and will; he had to think of the great 'secret doctrine' of magic, and see himself as the lonely 'outsider' with his sights fixed on the stars, and a quite definite aim: to establish contact with this Guardian Angel, as Abra-Melin the Mage had done before him. For the same reason, he picked up a prostitute because of the 'insatiable intensity of passion that blazed from her evil inscrutable eyes' that had 'tortured her worn face into a whirlpool of seductive sin'. Since the unfortunate woman lived in a slum, she was probably merely half-starved, but the image of the 'scarlet woman' was important to define Crowley's *self-image* clearly – the Nietzschean explorer, marching away from the warm camp fires of humankind into the cold outer wastes of the mysterious universe. And since he liked to dramatise himself as the Beast from Revelation, then a half-starved hag – no doubt a good Catholic and an affectionate mother – had to be the Whore of Babylon. But the point to observe is that *it worked*. With all his absurd Swinburnian gestures, he succeeded in capturing the fluid will and preventing it from ebbing into the sand of forgetfulness and self-depreciation. That was the aim.

'Meanwhile my magical condition was making me curiously uncomfortable. I was succeeding beyond all my expectations. In the dry pure air of Mexico, with its spiritual energy unexhausted and uncontaminated as it is in cities, it was astonishingly easy to produce satisfactory results. But my very success somehow disheartened me. I was getting what I thought I wanted and the attainment itself taught me that I wanted something entirely different. What that might be it did not say. My distress became acute ...' He sent out an 'urgent call for help from the Masters', and a week later received a letter from George Jones that contained exactly what he needed. It can be seen that his 'quest' differed from that of any Christian or Eastern mystic only in mere form; he was on the same journey outward. Instead of the Upanishads or *The Cloud of Unknowing*, he studied the Kabbalah with its notion of the universe as ten spheres connected by twenty-two paths. The sceptic may shrug, but is this more absurd than believing that Jesus died for Adam's sin, or that Mohammed is the prophet of God? The 'results' produced by a religion are not based upon the *apodictic* truth of its dogmas, but the dogmas are indispensable to the results, and the results are real.

The twenty-fifth chapter of the *Confessions*, in which all this is described, leaves no doubt of Crowley's sincerity, or of the reality of his misery; he was not driven by exhibitionism, but by an obscure craving for reality. Oddly enough, it was his old mountaineering companion Eckenstein who was able to show him the next step. He advised him to give up magic, and simply develop a power of immense concentration. He saw immediately that Crowley's trouble was still the fluidity of his will and sense of identity. And it is to Crowley's credit that he immediately followed Eckenstein's prescription and spent months in what amounted to yogic training.

There followed more mountain climbing – up Popocatepetl – travels to San Francisco, then Ceylon, and a love affair with a married woman that resulted in a book *Alice, An Adultery*. In Ceylon he found his close friend Allan Bennett, a student of Buddhism and colleague from Golden Dawn days; Crowley's generosity had been responsible for sending Bennett to Ceylon. Bennett was later the founder of the British Buddhist movement, and he was one of the few people of whom Crowley was consistently fond. He spent months teaching Crowley all he knew of Eastern mysticism; after his months of thought control under Eckenstein, it came as a revelation. It is extremely interesting that Crowley, speaking of this period, emphasises the importance of a scientific approach to mysticism. 'A single unanalysed idea is likely to … send him astray.' And he makes a vitally important point that reveals that his insight was genuine: the fundamental principle of yoga 'is how to stop thinking … The numerous practices of yoga are simply dodges to help one to acquire the knack of slowing down the current of thought, and ultimately stopping it altogether.' We return to the concept I have emphasised throughout this book; of *stillness*, of preventing the energies from flowing away like water down a drain.

Bennett had been a private tutor to the solicitor-general in Ceylon; he now decided that it was time to renounce the world and become a Buddhist monk. Crowley went off and hunted big game, penetrated a secret shrine at Madura, explored the Irrawaddy River in a canoe and finally visited Bennett in his monastery, where, he claims, he saw Bennett floating in the air and being blown about like a leaf.

Crowley, now in his mid-twenties, was still basically a rich playboy and sportsman. In 1902 he was one of a party that attempted to reach the summit of Chogo Ri (or K.2), the world's second highest mountain, in the Karakoram range of India; but bad weather and illness frustrated the expedition.

Back in Paris, he called on Mathers, hoping that his new accomplishments would win Mathers's respect; but Mathers was not in the least interested in yoga, and only admired himself. Their relations became several degrees colder. Crowley became something of a figure among artistic circles in Paris, and Maugham portrays him in *The Magician*, one of his least successful novels.

He returned to Boleskin, and became friendly with a young painter, Gerald Kelly (who later became Sir Gerald Kelly, president of the Royal Academy). At Kelly's family home, Strathpeffer, he met Kelly's unstable sister Rose, a girl with a pretty face and a weak mouth. Already a widow, she had involved herself with a number of men who all wanted to marry her, and had encouraged them all. Crowley's quirky sense of humour suggested the solution: marry him, and leave the marriage unconsummated. She could have his name, and be free of her admirers. They were married by a lawyer the next morning. But Crowley was not a man to pass up the opportunity of performing his 'sexual magic' on another woman. Besides, there was an element of masochism in Rose that appealed to the touch of sadism in him. Their decision to keep the marriage platonic lasted only a few hours. The rage of Gerald Kelly and Rose's other relations delighted Crowley, who loved drama of any sort. He took Rose back to Boleskin – and had to quickly cancel an arrangement whereby a red-headed tart he had picked up should become his housekeeper – and then to Paris, Cairo (where they spent a night in the Great Pyramid) and Ceylon. It was here that Crowley shot a bat, which fell on his wife's head and dug its claws into her hair; that night, Rose had a nightmare that she was a bat, and clung to the frame of the mosquito net over the bed, howling; when he tried to detach her she spat, scratched and bit. Crowley described it as 'the finest case of obsession that I had ever had the good fortune to observe'.

It should now be fairly clear what was wrong with Crowley, and why he, like other magicians, carried inside him the seed of his own downfall. The self-centred child who disliked his mother (he describes her as 'a brainless bigot') had almost no capacity for natural affection. It is this that makes him a 'monster'. He liked Bennett and Eckenstein because they impressed him, not because they touched any chord of affection. In Mexico he came close to disinterested study of a subject that might have raised his whole personality to a higher level; but life was too easy – it was too much of a temptation to indulge the schoolboy in himself. In Boleskin he had written to a society for the suppression of vice complaining that prostitution was conspicuous in Foyers. They sent a man to investigate, and finally wrote saying they could not find any sign of prostitution in the small Scottish town; Crowley then wrote back, 'Conspicuous by its absence, you fools.' His marriage to Rose was fundamentally another schoolboy prank. The serious part of him was not getting a chance to develop. In Cairo, when he and Rose returned there, he dressed himself in robes and called himself Prince Chioa Khan, declaring that an Eastern sultan had given him the rank. He told Rose's parents that any letter not addressed to Princess Chioa Khan would be returned. When her mother addressed an envelope to the 'princess', but added an exclamation mark, Crowley returned it to her unopened. He could be extremely exasperating when he wanted.

There now occurred the event that Crowley thought the most important of his life. Rose was pregnant, and Crowley's attempts to invoke 'sylphs' (spirits of air) for her benefit put her into a peculiar mood. The most sensible explanation is that she had received the imprint of Crowley's personality so deeply that she found herself in telepathic contact with him and expressed notions that floated around in his subconscious. She told him that he had offended Horus, of whom, he says, she knew nothing. In a museum she showed him a statue of Ra-Hoor-Khuit, one of the forms of Horus, and he was impressed to find that the number of the exhibit was the number of the Beast in Revelation, 666. Rose (whom he now called Ouarda) now began to instruct him on how to invoke Horus; the ritual did not seem to make sense, but he tried it. The result, he assures his readers, was a complete success. Not only did he hear from Horus, but from his own Guardian Angel, whom he had been trying to invoke for so many years. His name was Aiwass. Horus told him that a new epoch was beginning (and many occultists would agree with this – Strindberg was saying much the same thing at the same time). Then Crowley was ordered to take his Swan fountain pen and write. A musical voice from the corner of the room then dictated *The Book of the Law* to him, assuring him that this book would solve all religious problems and would be translated into many languages. It goes further than any previous scriptures, Crowley says, in proving conclusively the existence of God, or at least, of intelligence higher than man's, with whom man can communicate.

What is one to think of all this? *The Book of the Law*, with its fundamental assertion 'Do what thou wilt' (borrowed from Rabelais and William Blake), seems to be an attempt to write a semi-biblical text like *Thus Spake Zarathustra*, and the style is rather like Oscar Wilde's biblical-pastiche prose poems: 'Be goodly therefore; dress ye all in fine apparel; eat rich foods and drink sweet wines and wines that foam! Also, take your fill and will of love as ye will, when, where and with whom ye will ...' This is quite plainly Crowley, the man with a hangover from the Christianity of his childhood, speaking, and sounding rather like his contemporary Gide in *Les Nourritures Terrestres* written seven years earlier. On the other hand, there can be no doubt whatever that Crowley himself attached enormous importance to the work. It was his own Koran, and he was the chosen prophet. All great religions, he says, can be expressed in a single word: in Buddhism, Anatta; in Islam, Allah. In Crowleyanity the word was Thelema, the name of the abbey ('Do what you will') in Rabelais. And for the rest of his life, Crowley began all his letters with the assertion 'Do what thou wilt shall be the whole of the Law'. The epoch of Gods and demons is over; the new epoch opens in which man must cease to think of himself as a mere creature, and stand firmly on his own feet. This *would* be humanism, except that humanism, while placing man on his own feet, sees him as 'human, all too human', the thinking reed. Crowley sees him as a potential god, gradually coming to understand his own powers. It must be admitted that the conception is profound. It is true that Saint-Martin had expressed it more than a hundred years earlier, and Shaw would express it again in *Back to Methuselah* twenty years later; but it reveals Crowley as a great deal more than a brainless charlatan. He had created a fundamentally Nietzschean morality: 'We should not protect the weak and vicious from the results of their own inferiority'; 'To pity another man is to insult him.' As to sin: 'Strong and successful men always express themselves fully, and when they are sufficiently strong no harm comes of it to themselves or others.' There is nothing original about Crowley's book; Shaw's *Man and Superman*, written at the same time, is a greater work in every way. But it is still Crowley's major achievement, and when he had finished it, he may well have felt that he had at last produced his masterpiece, a work that towered above his plays and poems, and that it was worth devoting his life to making it known.

Back in Paris, Crowley wrote Mathers a letter declaring that the Secret Chiefs had appointed him head of the order. 'I did not expect or receive an answer. I declared war on Mathers accordingly.' He insists in his autobiography that he himself did not understand *The*

Book of the Law, hated parts of it, and only slowly recognised it for the immense revelation it was.

At Boleskin again, he prepared a collected edition of his works in three volumes, and he later offered a large money prize for the best essay on his works. He was pathetically anxious to be accepted as a major writer. Malevolent magical currents swept from Paris – Mathers was obviously out to get him – and killed off his dogs, and caused a workman to go berserk and attack Rose. Crowley invoked forty-nine demons, which Rose apparently saw, and sent them off to torment Mathers. Rose bore him a small daughter, whom he called Nuit Ma Ahathoor Hecate Sappho Jezebel Lilith.

The next major event was another mountaineering expedition, this time to Kanchenjunga. The briefest way to deal with this is to quote the account given by Showell Styles in his history of mountaineering *On Top of the World*:

> In 1905, a small expedition took up the challenge [of Kanchenjunga] … Three competent Swiss climbers and one Italian – Guillarmod, Reymond, Pache, and De Righi – chose as their leader an Englishman, a skilled mountaineer named Aleister Crowley. Crowley was perhaps the most extraordinary character who ever took to the mountain sport. He was ostentatiously careless and inhuman in all he did, styled himself 'the Great Beast of the Apocalypse', and practised Black Magic and Satanism. The party advanced up the Glacier and reached a height of 20,400 feet on the face below the main peak and to the west of it; and here, at Camp VII, the Swiss called a conference at which Crowley was formally deposed from leadership because of his sadistically cruel treatment of the porters. Crowley refused to accept this. The expedition was then called off, and all except Crowley started down for the lower camps. There was a slip which set off an

avalanche. All of them were swept down and buried under the snow. Guillarmod succeeded in freeing himself and digging out De Righi, while Reymond (who had escaped the worst of the fall) came to his aid. Together they dug feverishly to try to rescue the deeply buried Pache and the three porters who were engulfed with him, at intervals shouting to Crowley to come and help them. But Pache was dead, and the porters too.

Crowley had heard the frantic calls for help but had not troubled to come out of his tent. That evening he wrote a letter, later printed in an English newspaper, commenting that he 'was not over-anxious in the circumstances to render help. A mountain accident of this kind is one of the things for which I have no sympathy whatever.' Next morning he climbed down, keeping well clear of his late companions who were toiling to recover the bodies, and proceeded to Darjeeling by himself. As a Satanist, it seems, he was doing rather well.

And Kanchenjunga remained unattempted for another quarter of a century.

Styles's account is inaccurate in only one minor detail; Reymond stayed with Crowley, but went to the rescue of the others when they shouted.

In Calcutta, Crowley describes how he was attacked in the street by a gang of pickpockets, but that, far from feeling afraid, he felt like a 'leopard', the master of the situation. He managed to fire his revolver with perfect calm, and then 'made himself invisible'. He explains that this is not literally true; it was simply that he possessed some odd power of causing a blank spot in the minds of people looking at him – like a conjuror. (Strindberg, we have seen, believed he also possessed this power.)

The next day Rose and the child arrived, and Crowley admits, 'I was no longer influenced by love for them, no longer interested in protecting them …' He took them to China, where he smoked opium, and 'got his own back' on some rebellious coolies by underpaying them and escaping down-river with his rifle pointed at them. After four months of this, he instructed Rose to return to England by way of India, to pick up the luggage in Calcutta, while he returned by way of New York. On arrival back in Liverpool he heard that the baby had died of typhoid in Rangoon.

Rose produced another baby not long after – Lola Zaza – who almost died of bronchitis soon after her birth. Crowley took the opportunity to order his mother-in-law out of the sick-room, and assisted the hag 'down the stairs with my boot lest she should misinterpret my meaning'. But the marriage to Rose was virtually over; Rose had become a dipsomaniac, and later went insane. This was a pattern that was to recur with people who became too intimate with Crowley.

His first disciple was a 'classic case of persecution mania' named Lord Tankerville, whom he calls Coke in the autobiography. With Tankerville he travelled in Morocco and Spain – Tankerville presumably paying, for Crowley's fortune was beginning to run out – but Tankerville ended their association with the remark: 'I'm sick of your teaching – teaching – teaching – as if you were God Almighty and I were a poor bloody shit in the street.' But he soon found another disciple, Victor Neuberg, a poet. He published more poetry, a book praising himself called *The Star in the West* (a fulsome account of Crowleyanity by a soldier, J. F. C. Fuller, later a major-general), which won the £100 prize for the best essay on his works, and a bi-annual journal of magic called *The Equinox*. Crowley also decided to start his own magical society, which he called the Silver Star or A:A, and made use of the rituals from the Golden Dawn. He knighted himself, explaining that he had acquired the title in Spain for services to the Carlist cause, and shaved his huge domed head. Rose was now going insane and he divorced her. Symonds says that Crowley often entertained mistresses in their home, and occasionally hung her upside down by her heels in the wardrobe.

In 1910 he discovered the use of mescalin, and devised a series of seven rites. which he called the Rites of Eleusis, and hired Caxton Hall for their performance on seven successive Wednesdays. Admission was five guineas, and the aim was, he said, to induce religious ecstasy. His latest mistress, an Austrian violinist called Leila Waddell, accompanied the group on the violin. *John Bull* reviewed them with hostility, and another magazine, *The Looking Glass*, devoted several issues to attacking Crowley. It was the beginning of the persecution that was to last for the rest of his life. It cannot be maintained that it was undeserved. His life was becoming a series of mere events, like the lives of all the other magicians we have considered. Mathers tried to prevent the publication of the third issue of *The Equinox* because it contained a full description of the secret rites of the Golden Dawn, which Crowley had taken an oath never to reveal. The judge found in favour of Mathers. Crowley performed some magic from the book of Abra-Melin, and appealed; this time he won, and duly published the secrets.

But he had passed the high point of his life. From now on, although he lived until 1947, it was all downhill. The promise had gone, and the pattern was set: magical ceremonies, mistresses, frantic attempts to raise money, newspaper attacks on him and attempts to justify himself in print. In 1912 he met the German adept Theodor Reuss, who accused him of giving away occult secrets. The secret Crowley had given away in one of his books (called *Liber 333, The Book of Lies*) was that sex could be used magically. Reuss was a member of the Ordo Templis Orientis, which has been mentioned in an earlier chapter. Reuss ended by authorising Crowley to set up his own branch of the order, and Crowley set about performing sexual magic with diligence, sodomising Victor Neuberg in Paris in 1913 as part of a magical ceremony. He also practised sexual magic with a companion of Isadora Duncan's, Mary D'Este Sturges, and they rented a villa in Italy for that purpose. He also took a troop of chorus girls to Moscow – they were called the Ragged Ragtime Girls – and had a violent affair with another 'starving leopardess' of a girl, who needed to be beaten to obtain satisfaction. Crowley claims it was his first relationship of this sort, but it was not the last. Physical sadism was another taste he acquired. He opened a Satanic Temple in a studio in Fulham Road, and an American journalist described the number of aristocratic female disciples who frequented it. Crowley had now filed his two canine teeth to a sharp point, and when he met women, was inclined to give them the 'serpent's kiss', biting the wrist, or occasionally the throat, with the fangs. Symonds also mentions that he had a habit of defecating on carpets, and explaining that his ordure was sacred, like that of the Dalai Lama.

The Great War caught him in Switzerland, now aged thirty-nine. He claims that he tried to persuade the British government to employ him, and was refused. He decided to go to America. After a year of various unsuccessful magical activities, he thought up a new role – the anti-British Irishman. He was not, of course, Irish; he had never even been to Ireland. But this did not matter. He made a speech to the waves at the foot of the Statue of Liberty and tore up his British passport, or what he claimed was his British passport. After this, he began to write virulent anti-British propaganda for a newspaper called *The Fatherland* (subtitled *Fair Play for Germany and Austria-Hungary*). In his autobiography he triumphantly explains the reason for this: he was trying to *help* Britain by making his propaganda so absurd that it would provoke the opposite effect.

Admiral Sir Guy Gaunt, then head of Naval Intelligence in America, undoubtedly put his finger on the real motive when he wrote to John Symonds: 'I think you describe [Crowley] exactly when you refer to him as a "small-time traitor". As regards his activities, I think they were largely due to a frantic desire for advertisement –

for he was very anxious to keep his name before the public somehow ...'

But this does not completely explain it. There was also Crowley's increasing disgust with England, the country in which he felt an exile, that refused him recognition on any terms.

Crowley describes his period in America as a period of poverty and humiliation. Humiliated or not, he seems to have managed to live fairly well. A report in a New York paper, *The Evening World* (quoted by Symonds), describes a fairly luxurious studio in Washington Square. It must be remembered that Crowley was always fairly expert at getting money from disciples. An American writer on witchcraft, William Seabrook, who was introduced to Crowley by Frank Harris, says that Crowley had a cult with followers and disciples. He also says of their ceremonies: 'They were Holy Grail stuff, mostly. Some of their invocations were quite beautiful.'

Seabrook, who had met Gurdjieff and noted the tremendous power he seemed to exude, remarked that Crowley was also a man of power. And this should be borne in mind as a counterbalance to Symonds's accurate but overcrowded account, which gives the impression that Crowley had reached a kind of dead end. What always distinguished Crowley from the disciples who came and went was a remarkable inner strength. It was this that preserved him from the disaster that overtook so many of them. He would eat and drink until he became bloated, and then deliberately starve himself down to a healthy weight again. Seabrook tells an amusing story of how Crowley one day announced that it was time he went off to spend forty days and nights in the wilderness. Seabrook and some other friends decided to stake Crowley, who was broke. They also found him a canoe and a tent. When they went to see him off, they discovered that he had spent every penny of the money on huge tins of red paint and ropes. He told them that, like Elijah, he would be fed by the ravens. Crowley spent the forty days and nights painting in huge red letters on the cliffs south of Kingston the inscriptions: EVERY MAN AND WOMAN IS A STAR and (inevitably) DO WHAT THOU WILT SHALL BE THE WHOLE OF THE LAW. He was fed by neighbouring farmers, who presented him periodically with eggs, milk and sweet corn. He returned to New York looking healthy and cheerful.

Seabrook goes on to tell one of the oddest stories about Crowley's powers. When Crowley said he had gained greater power through his vigil, Seabrook asked for a demonstration. Crowley took him along Fifth Avenue, and on a fairly deserted stretch of pavement, fell into step with a man, walking behind him and imitating his walk. Suddenly Crowley buckled at the knees, squatted for a split second on his haunches, then shot up again; the man in front of him also buckled and collapsed on the pavement. They helped him to his feet, and he looked around in a puzzled manner for the banana skin.*

The incident makes Crowley sound like Till Eulenspiegel; it seems typical that he should demonstrate his power by making a respectable banker fall down.

Towards the end of his American period, Crowley discovered yet another 'scarlet woman'. A woman named Renata Faesi called on him with her younger sister Leah, a thin girl with a broad mouth, sharp teeth and flat breasts. Apparently 'something clicked' as soon as they saw one another, and Crowley seized her and began to kiss her violently, to Renata's astonishment. 'It was sheer instinct,' says Crowley. Fairly soon he was taking off her clothes to paint her in the nude – the painting was a ghoulish object called *Dead Souls* – and in due course Leah Hirsig, also called The Ape of Thoth and Alostrael, became pregnant.

In December 1919, Crowley returned to London. But he was not happy in England. He now suffered from asthma and bronchitis

* I have used this incident in my novel *The Sex Diary of Gerard Sorme*, in which Crowley is one of the central characters.

every winter, and periodic indulgence in all kinds of drugs, from mescalin and hashish to cocaine, heroin and opium, had lowered his physical resistance to the English cold and damp. His former pupil Victor Neuberg had married and settled down, but he remained obsessed by Crowley for the rest of his life.* Crowley had cursed him when they separated before the war, and Neuberg had been a nervous wreck for a long time afterwards. (He still attributed his ill health to Crowley's curse.) There was no one else in London from whom Crowley could get money. Fortunately, at this critical juncture, he received a legacy of £3,000. (He had spent the £30,000 left him by his mother years before.) He decided to make for warmer climes, and after some preliminary wandering, Crowley and Leah Hirsig chose a farmhouse at Cefalù in Sicily. They were also accompanied by a nursemaid, Ninette Shumway (who had quickly become Crowley's mistress), Ninette's two-year-old son and by the two children Crowley had by Leah, a boy called Dionysus and a newly born girl, Anne Leah, whom he called Poupée. Crowley, now in his mid-forties, seems to have developed a few normal human feelings. He wrote in his diary: 'I love Alostrael [Leah]; she is all my comfort, my support, my soul's desire, my life's reward ...' (He was certainly passionately fond of the Poupée, whose health had been feeble from the beginning.)

At first, life at the farmhouse, which he called the Abbey of Theleme, was idyllic, with bathes in the sea and long hours of meditation and sex magic. Crowley covered the walls with paintings of people having sex in every position, and painted his studio – which he called the Chamber of Nightmares – with demons. He was convinced that an adept could only become free of the need for drugs by taking them freely and mastering the need for them; so piles of cocaine were left around for anyone to take like snuff, while heroin

* See *The Magical Dilemma of Victor Neuberg*, by Jean Overton Fuller (London, 1965).

was supplied by a trader from the mainland. But the jealousy of his two scarlet women tended to spoil things. Symonds describes a typical scene:

> On the day the sun entered the sign of Taurus, i.e. the 20th April [1920], The Beast celebrated this event by an act of sex-magic in which both his loves participated. In the middle of this, a violent quarrel broke out between Sisters Alostrael and Cypris [Leah and Ninette], and the latter, bursting into tears, snatched up a thin cloak to cover her nakedness and ran out into the rain and the darkness. The Beast wandered over the mountainside looking for her, afraid she had fallen over the precipice. After calling her name for an hour (her little son Hermes helped by yelling from the Abbey window), he found her and dragged her back. Meanwhile Alostrael had been at the brandy and was now drunk. She greeted Sister Cypris with a curse and the fighting began again. With difficulty Crowley persuaded Concubine Number Two to go to bed. Then Alostrael, as if to have the last word, began to vomit and throw a fit.

Crowley tried hard to convince his womenfolk that possessiveness was an evil, and that they had to rise above such triviality, but they were unconvinced. However, they continued to submit to magical ceremonies – for example, Leah allowed herself to be possessed by a goat, whose throat was then cut as a sacrifice. An American film star, Elizabeth Fox, announced her imminent arrival, and Crowley looked forward to possessing her; however, she proved to be a disappointment – Crowley likened himself to the girl who went out to meet a dark, distinguished gentleman and found it was a one-eyed negro. The mathematician J. N. W. Sullivan arrived with his wife, Sylvia, and liked Crowley; they talked all night. Sylvia liked Crowley too; he managed to get her to stay on twenty-four hours after her husband left, and they practised sex magic together.

But life at the Abbey was becoming too complicated with personal clashes and quarrels. The child Poupée died after a long illness, and Crowley was genuinely shattered. A young American, an ex-naval officer named Godwin, arrived, and Crowley named him Brother Fiat Lux. But the strain of life in the Abbey proved too much for him. Another disciple, an Australian businessman named Frank Bennett, arrived, and Crowley asked Fiat Lux to let Bennett have his room. The result was tantrums and violence; Fiat Lux returned to America with less sanity than he left with.* On the other hand, he was triumphantly successful with Frank Bennett, who, like the young Crowley, had been the victim of a repressive upbringing. When Crowley explained that the sexual organs were the image of God, and that the best way to free the hidden powers of the subconscious mind is through sexual magic, the revelation was so startling that Bennett rushed to the sea and swam frantically. After more discussion that night, he walked barefoot in the mountains, then, after a day of bewilderment, went into a trance-like state of pure delight as he began to grasp this idea of the importance of allowing the subconscious to express itself. This was not, of course, Crowley's problem; in fact, Crowley's problem was the reverse of this – his

---

* In *Ritual Magic in England*, Francis King reveals that Godwin returned to America, and founded the Choronzon Club in 1931 – Choronzon being a demon. Godwin rejected Crowley's practice of 'magical masturbation' and replaced it with what he called Dianism, and what is usually called the Karezza, sexual intercourse continued indefinitely without orgasm. (It had been 'invented', as far as America was concerned, by J. H. Noyes, founder of the Oneida Community.) The aim of the Karezza is to produce long-drawn-out ecstasy or intoxication. Francis King says that Godwin is still operative on the West Coast. Another Crowley disciple, Jack Parsons (who founded Cal. Tech.), apparently ran the Amencan O.T.O. from a huge house in Pasadena, mixing magic with nuclear physics, and attracting official misgiving. Ron Hubbard, the founder of Dianetics, has described how he was sent in to investigate by Naval Intelligence and caused the group to disperse.

subconscious was always bursting uninvited into consciousness, producing his exalted states and visions of the masters. Crowley's problem was self-discipline.

At all events, Bennett's clear recognition that his ordinary self-consciousness was only half the picture, that his subconscious self was equally a reality, acted as some kind of release that plunged him into ecstasy, and he went back to Australia full of the gospel of the Beast.

As to Crowley, the problem of self-discipline was becoming increasingly oppressive. The doses of heroin he took would have killed a normal man. Periodically he forced himself to take the 'cold turkey cure', simply depriving himself of the drug for days, and on the first occasion, after a long period of intense depression and misery, again began to paint and write with the old excitement. But he usually went back to drugs, apparently determined to learn to take them or leave them as he wanted. The result was long periods of lassitude and increasing insomnia, which had troubled him for years. Besides, he had spent the £3,000 legacy, and was broke again. In Cefalù there were no rich disciples to borrow from; on the contrary, a steady stream of visitors needed feeding.

J. N. W. Sullivan suggested that he write his memoirs; Crowley approached Collins, and got a £60 advance on a book called *Diary of a Drug Fiend*, then dashed off the novel at top speed. It was a remarkable achievement, even if not well organised enough to be a good novel. It is about an aristocratic couple who become slaves of heroin, then meet Crowley, retire to his Abbey, and are miraculously cured and 'saved'. The book appeared in 1922, and was violently attacked by James Douglas in the *Sunday Express*. Douglas revealed that the Abbey was a real place, and denounced Crowley as a seducer of youth. Crowley was not entirely displeased at this eruption of publicity; but the book was allowed to go out of print, and Collins changed their mind about publishing Crowley's autobiography – or 'autohagiography', as he preferred to call it – even though they had given him an advance of £120.

In London, Crowley met an excitable and slightly unbalanced young man named Raoul Loveday, an Oxford graduate, who was married to a pretty model. Loveday had read Crowley's works, and within hours he was an enthusiastic disciple. When Crowley returned to Cefalù, Loveday and his wife, Betty May, followed, even though her misgivings were strong. Betty May hated Thelema; she hated the inadequate food, the lack of lavatories, the obscene paintings and, above all, her husband's total infatuation for the Beast.

Loveday's stay at Thelema was to last just over three months and be terminated by death. Both he and Crowley were ill with some kind of liver complaint much of the time – probably hepatitis, due to bad water. In February 1923, Crowley decided that a cat was to be sacrificed. He hated cats, and this one had scratched him deeply when he tried to throw it out of the room. When he found it in the scullery again, he made the sign of the pentagram over it with his magic staff, and ordered it to stay there until the hour of the sacrifice. Crowley's power was working. The cat became transfixed. Betty May carried it away, but it came back to the same place, and sat petrified, refusing food.

Loveday was selected to perform the sacrifice. The cat was placed on the altar; incense was burnt; magical invocations went on for two hours. At the end of this time, Loveday slashed the cat's throat with a knife; but the blow was too light, and it rushed around the room howling. It was caught again, etherised, and then Loveday was made to gulp down a cup of its blood. He subsequently collapsed and took to his bed. Crowley consulted his horoscope, and observed that he might die on February 16 at four o'clock.

Violent quarrels with Betty May followed; she left the Abbey in a fury after calling Ninette a whore, but came back the next day at her husband's request. On the 16th, at the time Crowley had predicted,

Loveday died. Betty May now recalled that when they had married, he had dropped the ring as he was about to put it on her finger – a bad omen; and in a photograph of the two of them, taken at St. John's College, Oxford, there was the ghostly outline of a young man whose arms were stretched above his head – the exact position in which Loveday died.

Back in England, Betty May talked to the *Sunday Express*, and the British public was shocked and delighted with more revelations of the Beast's immorality. *John Bull* also joined in the attacks. By the time these appeared, Crowley himself had been laid low by the same illness as Loveday, and was semi-conscious for three weeks before he began a slow recovery. But the adverse publicity had its effect on the new ruler of Italy, Mussolini; shortly afterwards, Crowley was ordered to vacate the Abbey of Thelema and get out of the country.

Now an ex-disciple reappeared in his life: Norman Mudd, an ugly young man who had known Crowley as long ago as 1907 at Cambridge. Mudd had been introduced to Crowley through Neuberg. But when Crowley's unsavoury reputation and pornographic books got him banned from the college where he had been a student, their friendship went into cold storage. Mudd became a professor of mathematics in South Africa, but, like Neuberg, he could not forget Crowley. Now, when Crowley was being attacked by the British press, he appeared at the Abbey of Thelema, presented his life's savings to Crowley and begged to be taken back as a disciple.

Crowley moved to Tunis, hoping that the Italian government would change its mind. Leah went with him, and also, presumably, their five-year-old boy, who now smoked cigarettes all day long and declared that he would become the Beast when his father died. Ninette had borne Crowley another daughter, and Crowley's horoscope for her ended 'She is likely to develop into a fairly ordinary little whore'. Norman Mudd joined them, and he and Leah became lovers. Crowley didn't mind; Leah was supposed to be the Whore of Babylon. Now in her forties, she was looking haggard and old. Crowley was too preoccupied trying to shake off his illness. His drug addiction was impossible to shake off, and he had to accept it. He spent days moping in the hotel, trying to write volume one of the 'hag' – the autohagiography. He had acquired a small Negro boy, with whom he performed acts of sex magic. Crowley's homosexuality began as an act of defiance of convention rather than of actual preference, but it seems to have become another habit.

Crowley deserted his little party – Mudd, Leah, the Negro boy – and went to France. He lunched with Frank Harris in Nice, and Harris managed to raise 500 francs for Crowley to get to Paris, although Harris himself was broke and at a loose end. (Crowley recorded in his diary that Harris was insane, and referred to *My Life and Loves* as the autobiography of a flea.) Mudd and Leah meanwhile starved in Tunis. In Paris, Crowley staggered around, dazed with drugs. Perhaps one of the most shocking sentences in Symonds's *The Great Beast* reads: 'He had tried everything and now at the age of fifty, when he could only proclaim the law of Thelema, he realised that what he really wanted was a job, some congenial work …' He was thrown out of the hotel where he was living on credit.

Leah and Mudd somehow managed to get to Paris, where Mudd was pressed into writing a pamphlet defending the Beast: an open letter to Lord Beaverbrook, proprietor of the newspaper that had caused all the trouble. Mudd staggered to London, where he took refuge overnight in the Metropolitan Asylum for the Homeless Poor. Crowley and Leah moved to Chelles-sur-Marne for a few months. But Crowley was getting tired of his scarlet woman, who seemed to lack his own incredible ability to survive under any conditions. When a rich American lady named Dorothy Olsen fell under his fascination, Crowley appointed her his new scarlet woman, and deserted Leah. Leah's sister had gone to Cefalù and taken away the child Dionysus, now six, to America; Leah, instead of being grateful, was furious and hysterical. Mudd returned to her, and they starved in Paris while Crowley and his new mistress travelled towards the sun in North Africa. Crowley usually managed to fall on his feet.

Both Leah and Norman Mudd became extremely bitter about the Beast, although it is not quite clear why. There was nothing to stop them finding work and continuing life together. But Crowley's defection seemed to break something inside both of them. It was not the end yet, although Leah became a prostitute for a while, and later a waitress. As to Mudd, although he was dirty, unshaven and in a state of moral collapse, his chief worry was still that Crowley might be unfaithful to *The Book of the Law*. Even Crowley's new love ran out of money after a few months of supporting him in the style to which he was accustomed, and had to write to American friends to borrow money. But Crowley was now recovering his powers, and his luck was taking a turn for the better. Theodor Reuss, the head of the German order of the O.T.O. (Ordo Templi Orientis), had died, and his successor, a Herr Traenker, turned to Crowley as one of the elect. Admittedly, the German branch was shocked to read *The Book of the Law*, with its Swinburnian anti-nomianism. All the same, the Germans paid Crowley's maor debts in Paris, and even paid the fares of Crowley, Dorothy, Leah and Norman Mudd to Gera, in Thuringia. Leah and Mudd remained in Germany after Crowley left. Both of them came to hate Crowley, and Leah wrote him a letter renouncing her vows of obedience. What eventually happened to her is not known, except that she had another baby by another member of Crowley's order. (Ninette, still back in Cefalù, had also had another baby by a local peasant.) As to Mudd, nothing much is known of him except that he committed suicide by drowning in Guernsey, in the Channel Islands, in 1934, clipping the bottoms of his trousers with bicycle clips and then filling them with rocks before he walked into the sea. Crowley had come to reject his most faithful disciple by then; he had written to Leah earlier: 'I shall be very glad when the 42nd misfortune from that one-eyed man is over.'

Crowley was now definitely past his peak, at least as a magician. As a public figure he was notorious – 'the wickedest man in the world' – but this was hardly an advantage. It meant that no prosperous publisher would touch the *Confessions*, and when a small press (with the magical name Mandrake) brought out the first volume, their salesmen were unable to get orders from bookshops. Not only was Crowley ordered out of France in 1929, but his two chief disciples, an American secretary (known as the Serpent) and his latest mistress, Maria Teresa de Miramar, were not even allowed to enter Britain, and were turned back at Tilbury. It was to get Teresa into Britain that Crowley took the startling step of marrying her on August 16, 1929, in Leipzig. He was due to lecture in Oxford early in 1930, but was banned. He tried to present an exhibition of his paintings, at a house he rented in Langham Place, but another attack on him in *John Bull* made the owner cancel the lease. The marriage with Maria quickly turned into a cat-and-dog fight and dissolved, but there were always plenty of other women eager to become his scarlet woman. The latest was a German girl called the Monster, Hanni F——, who was only nineteen. They went to Lisbon together. ('God once tried to wake up Lisbon – with an earthquake; he gave it up as a bad job.') But Hanni suddenly began to get a feeling of claustrophobia; the magic depressed her; she deserted Crowley and returned, to Lisbon, leaving for Berlin the next morning, with a certain amount of help from the American consul. To be deserted was a shattering experience for the Beast; he pursued her to Berlin and a reconciliation took place. Before leaving, he left a suicide note at the top of Hell's Mouth, a high cliff, and pinned it down with his cigarette case. The result was a flattering uproar in the world's press; it would certainly have been a neat ending to the story if the world's wickedest man had killed himself. But after lying low in Berlin for a few days, he attended the opening of an exhibition of his paintings. Hanni F—— was presumably with him; at all events they were reconciled, and she had now become a satisfactory magical assistant. Crowley asserts that she became a skilled 'scryer' and saw the Devil looking at her out of the crystal. Their sex magic was successful to the extent of making her pregnant. Eventually, she left him, taking his *Book of Lies*; with his usual vengefulness, Crowley remarked: 'I'm glad I can brand her as a thief.' He had also persuaded her to write a letter to the helpful American consul in Lisbon implying that she meant to accuse him of raping her; schoolboy humour and schoolboy malice were the dominant traits of his non-magical personality.

His wife, Maria, went insane and was interned in Colney Hatch. Symonds states that Hanni F—— also went insane. But it would, perhaps, be unfair to reach the conclusion that anyone who got mixed up with Crowley went insane. The explanation is a great deal simpler. Whatever else one can say against Crowley, he was certainly a powerful, dominant personality, and he attracted weaklings, as all strong people do. But Crowley himself was weak to the extent of needing the admiration of these weaklings, instead of avoiding them, as *The Book of the Law* suggests. They wasted his time, but he had nothing better to do with it. Hanni was neurotic from the beginning, and this is why she attracted him. The same is true of Dorothy Olsen, of Maria de Miramar, of his first wife Rose, of Leah Hirsig – in fact, of every woman of whom we have any detailed record. He liked the kind of woman with whom he could fight. His next mistress, whom Symonds calls Gertrude S., stabbed him with a carving knife on one occasion. When Gerald Hamilton (Isherwood's Mr. Norris) was staying with Crowley in Berlin, he came in one day to find Gertrude tied up on the floor, with a note beside her saying that she was not to be released. On another ocasion he found Gertrude naked on the floor and Crowley asleep. When he asked Crowley if she was ill, Crowley said, 'What, hasn't that bitch gone to bed yet,' and dealt her a tremendous kick that started another bout of scratching and screaming. These bouts usually ended when the local doctor was called in and administered a sedative. Crowley liked masochistic women.

As far as magic is concerned, the rest of Crowley's life is an anticlimax. The major event of the thirties was the law case against his old friend Nina Hamnett. Crowley developed a belated taste for litigation when he saw a copy of his novel *Moonchild* displayed in a shop window with a note stating that his first novel (*Diary of a Drug Fiend*) had been withdrawn after the *Sunday Express* attack. This happened to be untrue; it had simply gone out of print. Crowley sued the bookseller, and got £50. This apparently gave him the idea of suing Nina Hamnett, a Soho character who had referred to him as a black magician in her autobiography, *Laughing Torso*. She had raised the idea only to dismiss it, mentioning also a rumour that a baby had disappeared at Thelema. Crowley knew Nina Hamnett had no money, but her publisher, Constable and Co., certainly had, and they would have to pay. So he set a law case in motion. Whether he expected to succeed is a matter for speculation; his counsel warned him that if the prosecution got hold of a copy of *White Stains* he wouldn't stand a chance. (*Snowdrops from a Curate's Garden* would have been more to the point, a piece of wildly humorous pornography in the manner of Apollinaire's *Debauched Hospodar*.) None of his friends were willing to appear for the defence. And when a number of witnesses had described Crowley's magical activities, the judge (Mr. Justice Swift) stopped the case, declaring that he had 'never heard such dreadful, horrible, blasphemous and abominable stuff as that which has been produced by the man who describes himself … as the greatest living poet'. The jury found against him, and he was bankrupted. This was less serious than it sounds, since he had no assets anyway. The publicity was (naturally) tremendous, and this may have been all Crowley wanted.

The case reveals that Mudd was right to fear that Crowley might become fundamentally unfaithful to *The Book of the Law*. For Crowley's life had at least been an admirably consistent protest against 'the Protestant ethic' and bourgeois hypocrisy. Since it had been his lifelong aim to shock people like Mr. Justice Swift and his jury, it was somewhat inconsistent to hope to arouse their moral indignation on his behalf.

It is difficult to think of Crowley as pathetic; but this is the word that summarises the Crowley John Symonds knew in his last years. Symonds met him after the war, when he was living in a boarding house called Netherwood at the Ridge, Hastings. The photograph of him at this period shows a thin old gentleman dressed in tweeds, smoking a pipe and looking like any retired colonel. He was more interested in heroin than food, which explains the loss of weight. Symonds says that he sometimes took as much as eleven grains a day, when the normal dose would be one-eighth of a grain. All sense of direction had gone. He was a bored old man who found the lonely evenings frightening. Perhaps this is the final comment on Crowley. Such 'powers' as he possessed came naturally; they were due to an overactive subconscious mind. But he never *developed* any real inner strength: the strength to be creative. And for the last quarter of a century of his life, he was a drug addict and an alcoholic. Louis Singer told me a typical story of Crowley's later years. He asked a friend, Eileen Bigland, if he could stay with her, because he had to do some writing. Each day she went into the nearby town to do her shopping. Rather to her surprise, Crowley asked to come with her; he would wander off on his own, and meet her in a café when she had finished. At the end of two weeks he left. Mrs. Bigland's daughter reported that the lavatory cistern was making an odd noise, and when investigated, it proved to contain fourteen empty gin bottles, one for each day of his stay. Her wine merchant later confirmed that Crowley had called in every day and collected a bottle of gin, which was booked to her account. Throughout his life, Crowley had no hesitation about imposing on friends and taking whatever he wanted. The irate wife of one of his disciples pointed out to him in a letter that he had spent £15,000 of her money in expensive cigars, cognac, cocktails, taxis, dinners and mistresses, and concluded 'God Almighty himself would not be as arrogant as you have been, and that is one of the causes of all your troubles'. The analysis is accurate. From the beginning to the end of his life, Crowley possessed a rather silly arrogance, a lofty, theatrical view of his own value that seems to derive from Oscar Wilde and the aesthetics of the nineties. This explains why he could turn on faithful disciples like Norman Mudd and Leah Hirsig, totally convinced that some action of theirs had forfeited their right to his divine condescension.

But there was, equally, a positive side to Crowley. This emerges in Seabrook's account of Elizabeth Fox's experience at Thelema. She was the 'film star' who somehow avoided becoming Crowley's mistress. Seabrook says that before she came to Cefalù she was in a depressed condition due to too much night life and bath-tub gin. Crowley dismayed her by telling her that she must begin with a month's solitary meditation in a lean-to shelter on the cliff-top. When she objected, he pointed out that there was a boat leaving the next day. To comply, she had to meditate naked, except for a woollen burnoose that could be utilised on chilly days. The shelter was completely empty; the latrine was a lime pit outside the 'tent', 'She would have, said Master Therion, the sun, moon, stars, sky, sea, the universe to read and play with.' At night, a child would quietly deposit a loaf of bread, bunch of grapes and a pitcher of water beside her.

She decided to give it a try. The first days confirmed her fears. Sun, moon and sea are all very well, but if you feel bored, they are boring. For the first days she felt nervous and resentful. By the nineteenth day, her chief sensation was boredom. And then, quite suddenly, she began to feel 'perfect calm, deep joy, renewal of strength and courage'.

There is nothing strange in all this, although few people know it. The mind must be made to stop running like a wrist-watch. It must be persuaded to relax and sit still. Its hidden fountain of strength must be persuaded to flow. This is the secret of the Hindu ascetics who sit still for years. It is not a penance, but a continuous trickle of deep delight. What is more, this is an *automatic* process. Our subconscious robot will adjust to any conditions if it is given long enough. It adjusts to stillness, so that the stillness ceases to cause boredom. For you have boredom when nothing is happening inside you. And nothing happens inside you when the outside world keeps the mind distracted. If the outside world is stilled for long enough, the inner power-house begins to work. This is a matter that must be discussed at length in considering the greatest magician of the twentieth century, George Gurdjieff. But Crowley knew about it. This was why he spent his forty days and nights up the Hudson. It is a pity that he had forgotten all about the secret when he most needed it, at the end of his life.

Even after death Crowley succeeded in creating an uproar. In his seventy-second year, he began to run down, and the bronchitis was more troublesome than usual; he died on December 5, 1947. Louis Wilkinson, the novelist (and close friend of the family magicians the Powys brothers), read aloud his *Hymn to Pan* at the funeral service; it is as gleefully and shamelessly phallic as one might expect of Crowley. The Brighton Council stated that it would take all steps to see that such an incident was never repeated.

EIGHT
TWO RUSSIAN MAGES

Occult powers seem to be a matter of national temperament. Second sight and telepathy come naturally to the Irish. The Germans seem to produce more gifted astrologers than other nations.* The Dutch have produced two of the most gifted clairvoyants of this century: Croiset and Hurkos. Russia tends to produce mages – men or women who impress by their spiritual authority; no other nation has a spiritual equivalent of Tolstoy and Dostoevsky, or even of Rozanov, Merezhkovsky, Soloviev, Fedorov, Berdaev, Shestov. Certainly no other nation has come near to producing anyone like Madame Blavatsky, Gregory Rasputin or George Gurdjieff. Each is completely unique.

Rasputin seems to possess the peculiar quality of inducing shameless inaccuracy in everyone who writes about him. Even that sober historian of magical rites E. M. Butler manages to pack a dozen or so in the three pages she devotes to him in *The Myth of the Magus*. This is an example: 'The frenzy he induced in himself and his worshippers, the intoxicated state of ecstasy, the scourging, the debauches, the mixture of cruelty, love and lust are a debased demoniacal, indeed maniacal Slavonic edition of the Dionysiac rites of Greece.' Everything in this sentence is false, at least as applied to Rasputin. Neither is it true, as she states, that the word *Rasputin* means dissolute; if it did, he would no doubt have had the sense to change his name early in his career. It means a crossroads, and happens to be as common as Smith in the village where he was born, Pokrovskoe.

* See Ellic Howe's *Urania's Children: The Strange World of the Astrologers*, 1967.

The truth about Rasputin is simple and unsensational; yet in its way, as remarkable as anything we have considered so far. Unlike most magicians, he had nothing whatever of the charlatan about him. He was a religious mystic of the same type as Boehme or Saint-Martin. Son of a Siberian peasant, probably the distant descendant of Siberian shamans, Rasputin became a carter in his teens and acquired a reputation as a brawler. One day he drove a young novice to a monastery, and was so impressed by the place that he stayed for four months. Then he went back to his life of drinking and womanising. Around 1890, when he was twenty, he married a girl four years his senior. Their baby son died, and Rasputin again heard the call of religion. After seeing a vision of the Virgin beckoning to him, he set out on a pilgrimage to Mount Athos in Greece. And when he returned, two years later, he was a changed man. He built a small oratory in the back yard and spent his days in prayer. His reputation as a holy man spread around the district, and soon he was holding services and preaching to rapt congregations of villagers. The village priest was naturally resentful, and told the bishop of Tobolsk that Rasputin held orgiastic rites, and that he was a member of the Khlysty, the Russian equivalent of the American Shakers or Snake Handlers. This story has been gleefully seized on by all his biographers, who rival one another in fantastic invention. Naked women dance around a huge bonfire while Rasputin roars: 'Sin, because only through sin can you become holy'; then men and women roll on the ground and copulate with the nearest person, while Rasputin possesses his sisters one after the other (Rasputin had no sisters). Even Aldous Huxley was taken in by this journalistic nonsense, and repeats it in his essay on Rasputin. Nothing is more certain than that Rasputin's prayer meetings were in every way harmless. The bishop of Tobolsk had them investigated and found nothing to take exception to. It is quite possible that Rasputin may have embraced any female disciples who wanted closer contact;

he was still in his early twenties, and his Christianity was permeated by a Whitman-esque mysticism, the feeling that 'everything that lives is holy'. But he was no charlatan or swindler; throughout his life he gave away the considerable sums of money presented to him by admirers.

In the course of his wanderings he began to develop remarkable thaumaturgic powers. In my own book on Rasputin,* I have pointed out the parallels with Mary Baker Eddy and her teacher, Phineas Quimby. Quimby believed that all human beings possess these powers, and that it is simply a matter of developing them. He also believed that healing can be performed at a distance as easily as at close quarters. This was because he thought that he was healing by the power of God – or, more specifically, of Jesus. This was also true of Rasputin. His cures depended largely upon kneeling by the bedside of the sick person and praying. Praying had the effect of releasing powers of optimism, 'positive consciousness'; he felt the success of such an operation as a sense of outgoing power, inner relief. And although it would not be true to say that Rasputin could not have healed unless he was a religious man – healing is a natural power, like water divining or telepathy – he certainly required a capacity for 'inwardness', for calling upon instinctive depths of emotion, that is closely akin to music or poetry. A cynical charlatan could not have done it.

By the time he came to St. Petersburg, in his mid-thirties, Rasputin had developed great power. In Russia the profession of holy man (or *staretz*) is as respectable as in India, or as it was in Europe in the Middle Ages. The wave of spiritualism had spread from America across the world, and by 1900 it was all the rage in Russia. Russia, in any case, was in a peculiar, mystical frame of mind, which was due directly to its history of political repression. Ever since Ivan

* *Rasputin and the Fall of the Romanovs*, London and New York, 1964.

the Terrible, Russian tsars had been absolute rulers, and most of them were cruel in a casual, thoughtless kind of way. Even in the reign of Alexander I, one of the great liberal tsars, murderers were flogged to death. Sir Robert Porter, an English observer, described in 1809 seeing a man flogged until he was like a mass of butcher's meat, after which his nostrils were torn off with pincers. The Russian was accustomed to the sight of pain and death, and it increased his natural mystical tendencies. Political oppression – which meant that a man could be sent to Siberia for expressing a liberal sentiment – and widespread poverty meant that idealism could only find expression in art or religion.

The St. Petersburg to which Rasputin came in 1905 was probably the mystical centre of the world. It was full of occultists, spiritualists, astrologers and disciples of Tolstoy, Dostoevsky and Soloviev. The Tsarina herself was known to be interested in spiritualism. Rasputin had no difficulty in getting into the drawing rooms of the aristocracy, where his blunt peasant manners and air of power soon won him a crowd of disciples.

The parallels between the history of pre-revolutionary France and pre-revolutionary Russia are so numerous that it is hard to believe in the 'blind chance' theory of history. Like Louis XVI, Tsar Nicholas II was a weak, basically amiable character who had inherited centuries of absolute monarchy. Like Louis, he married a foreigner who was totally lacking in all political sense while driven by some inner demon to meddle in politics. Russia also had no parliament, but when Nicholas came to the throne, there was an increasing agitation to set one up on the English model. And Nicholas, like Louis XVI, vacillated, agreeing to call parliament (or the Duma, as it was called), and then trying to dissolve it.

But Rasputin, unlike Cagliostro, became an influence at court. The Tsarevitch, the son of the Tsar, suffered from haemophilia, inherited from the family of his great-grandmother, Queen Victoria.

Haemophilia is a disease in which the blood is unable to clot, so that the smallest cut becomes a dangerous haemorrhage. All hopes for the future of the Romanov family were pinned on the boy Alexey, for he had arrived after his mother had produced four girls. When, some time in 1907, the boy bruised himself badly and sank into a fever, someone whispered to the Tsarina that there was a miracle worker called Rasputin who might help. Rasputin was sent for; he prayed fervently beside the bed; and before he left the room, the boy was breathing normally and sleeping peacefully. This, at least, is the story told by most 'biographers'. The most cynically inventive of these, Heinz Liepman (whose book is almost literally 50 per cent fiction),* tells the story of how Rasputin was drinking heavily with gypsies when the Tsar's messenger arrived on horseback, asking for the miracle worker: amid deep silence, Rasputin falls on his knees and prays, then tells the messenger, 'The crisis is past. The boy will recover,' and makes his leisurely way to the palace.

The truth seems to be that Rasputin had met the Tsar and Tsarina at least two years before this crisis is supposed to have taken place, in 1905. When the house of the prime minister, Stolypin, was blown up by a bomb and his children injured, the Tsarina offered him Rasputin's services; this was in 1906.

Rasputin cured the boy on at least two more occasions. In 1912, when Rasputin was in disgrace because of the machinations of his enemies at court, Alexey slipped when getting out of a boat and badly bruised himself. Fever set in. A few days later, the doctor had despaired of his life. The Tsarina's closest confidante, Anna Vyrubov, was asked to telegraph Rasputin, who was some thousands of miles away in Pokrovskoe. He telegraphed back, 'The illness is not as dangerous as it seems. Don't let the doctors worry him.' As soon as

---

* After I had pointed out that the book was full of invented 'facts' and quotations, my publishers wrote to Liepman and asked him to comment on the allegations; he replied that he had written the book so long ago that he had forgotten the details.

the telegram arrived, Alexey's condition took a turn for the better. Again, in 1915, the boy was accidentally thrown against the window of a train, and his nose began to bleed. This time, Rasputin deliberately delayed putting in an appearance for twenty-four hours, by which time the boy was in a fever. He explained to the chief of police that he wanted the Tsar to stew in his own juice for a bit. But as soon as Rasputin entered the room, the bleeding stopped. Whether Rasputin possessed a 'charm', like the Cornish healers I have discussed in an earlier chapter, or whether his thaumaturgic powers had developed to a point where he was absolutely confident of their efficacy, it seems certain that he knew he could stop the bleeding instantly.

It is not entirely clear why Rasputin made so many enemies at court. When writing my biography of him in 1963 I accepted the story – repeated in every book about him, and in all histories of the period – that Rasputin became involved in politics and would use his influence over the Tsarina to get his friends appointed to government posts. Subsequently, a disciple of Rasputin's, Dr. Elizabeth Judas of New York, told me flatly that there was no evidence whatever that Rasputin was involved in politics. This seemed such an astonishing statement, in view of all the history books, that I set out to disprove it by searching through all the original papers I could find, including the correspondence between the Tsar and Tsarina during the crucial years. Dr. Judas seems to be correct; there is very little evidence that Rasputin played the central role in Russian politics that is generally assumed. He advised the Tsar on the conduct of the war, and was generally ignored, and his influence over the Tsarina remained as enormous as ever. But of the diabolical schemer portrayed by Sir Bernard Pares there is no sign in these papers.

Why, then, was he so hated by so many? The first and most bitter of his enemies was a monk called Illiodor, who began as a friend of Rasputin's, then devoted all his energy to causing his downfall.

Illiodor was a religious fanatic who modelled himself on Savonarola; his sermons brought him immense influence. In 1911 he and Rasputin clashed, and Rasputin was summoned before Bishop Hermogen of Saratov, his one-time supporter, to justify himself. Illiodor, it seems, accused him of drunkenness and sexual debauchery. Rasputin seems to have been roughly handled, and he went to the Tsar with his own version of the story; the Tsar immediately banished Illiodor and Hermogen.

The story told by Maria Rasputin in her book on her father is that Illiodor had raped, or tried to rape, a neurasthenic woman who came to him for confession, and that the woman had asked Rasputin to help her obtain justice. This version is almost certainly untrue for a simple reason (of which I myself was not aware when I wrote my book): that Illiodor was homosexual. And this piece of information makes the puzzle suddenly fit together. In December 1909, Rasputin had spent some time visiting Illiodor's 'spiritual fortress', a monastery he was having built near Tsaritsyn. Rasputin showed an inclination to hug Illiodor's more attractive parishioners. After this, Illiodor went to Pokrovskoe with Rasputin, and Rasputin told him about his own early debaucheries in graphic detail (Rasputin made much of the sinfulness of his early life). Illiodor was younger than Rasputin, and more of a natural ascetic; Rasputin, unaware that Illiodor's indifference to women was not entirely a matter of superhuman purity, took pleasure in twitting him about it. By 1911, when Illiodor's cautious admiration had turned to intense dislike, Rasputin had no doubt discovered Illiodor's secret. He was not noted for tact or discretion, particularly when he had been drinking his favourite sweet Georgian wine. This probably explains Illiodor's gradual loss of influence at court – the Tsarina was as prudish as her grandmother about such matters – and the estrangement between himself and Rasputin that led to the clash of 1912.

It should also be borne in mind that the Tsarina was hated by her husband's courtiers. Like Marie Antoinette, she was known as 'the foreigner', and at the beginning of the 1914 war, it was generally believed that she was on Germany's side. It was she who regarded Rasputin as a father figure and treated him as a saint. In effect, all the Tsarina's enemies became Rasputin's.

At all events, Rasputin was at the centre of a vortex of vicious gossip, plotting and counterplotting. Stories about his drunkenness led the Tsar to banish him from court several times.

There was one time in which Rasputin may be said to have meddled in politics. He had on two occasions strongly advised the Tsar against going to war about the Balkans, which were claimed by Austria. In June 1914, as everyone knows, Franz Ferdinand was assassinated at Sarajevo by a young Bosnian patriot, and as a consequence, Austria declared war on Serbia. The world's destiny was in the hands of the Tsar, for he now had to make up his mind whether to stand by Serbia and declare war on Austria, or let the Balkans solve their own problems. This was the point where Rasputin's advice would have made all the difference between war and peace. Unfortunately Rasputin was not around to give advice; he had also been stabbed by a would-be assassin in his home village of Pokrovskoe, and was hovering between life and death for weeks.

When I was writing my book on Rasputin I noted the coincidence – that Rasputin and Archduke Ferdinand had been struck down at about the same time – and tried to find the actual date when Rasputin had been stabbed. The accounts seemed to differ; the most reliable historian, Sir Bernard Pares, seemed to think it was on Saturday, June 26, 1914. But Maria Rasputin's book on her father states quite definitely that they all arrived at Pokrovskoe on the Saturday, and that it was the following day, Sunday, when Rasputin was stabbed. This was made even more likely by the fact that he was stabbed after he returned from church. So Rasputin was stabbed *on the same day* the Archduke was shot. Maria Rasputin gives the time as shortly after two in the afternoon.

I now looked up the assassination of the Archduke Franz Ferdinand. He had felt certain he was going to die even before visiting Sarajevo, telling his children's tutor: 'The bullet that will kill me is already on its way.' Shortly after ten o'clock that morning, a home-made bomb was thrown at his motor-car, but the Archduke and his wife were uninjured. They attended a ceremony in the town hall, leaving half an hour later. It was on the drive back through Sarajevo, at about eleven o'clock, that Gavrilo Princip, a consumptive young student, leaned forward and fired two shots, killing the Archduke and his wife. The carriage was travelling slowly because it had taken a wrong turning, and was now turning back on to its correct route.

Sarajevo and Pokrovskoe are, of course, on different lines of longitude, so the time in the two places differs. I set out to work out the difference. There are 50 degrees of longitude between Sarajevo and Pokrovskoe. It is a simple sum, because the earth passes through 360 degrees when it does a complete turn in twenty-four hours. That is: 180 degrees in twelve hours, 90 degrees in six hours, 45 degrees in three hours. So to turn through 50 degrees, it takes exactly three hours and twenty minutes. The Archduke Ferdinand was murdered shortly before eleven. Rasputin was stabbed at 2.15, and 10.55 in Sarajevo was exactly 2.15 in Pokrovskoe. The man whose death caused the First World War, and the man who could have averted the war, were struck down at the same moment. The coincidence is as extraordinary as any I have come across.

Rasputin was finally murdered on the night of December 29, 1916. He felt strong forebodings of death, and wrote a curious letter, which was shown to the Tsarina soon after it was composed, saying that he felt he would be dead by January 1, 1917; and that if he was killed by the Russian peasantry, Russia would remain a prosperous monarchy for hundreds of years; if, however, he was murdered by the 'boyars' (aristocracy), their hands will remain soiled with his blood for twenty-five years, and no nobles will remain in Russia; the Tsar and his family will die within two years.

It sounds like a fabrication; but Sir Bernard Pares saw a facsimile of the letter and was inclined to accept its authenticity; he is the most sceptical and balanced of historians of the period. Twenty-five years, of course, takes Russia to the German invasion (June 1941), which may certainly be reckoned a turning point in Russian history, if not the date when all nobles finally vanished from Russia.

Rasputin was invited to the house of the wealthy Prince Yussupov at night, and given poisoned cakes and wine. The cyanide, which should have rendered him unconscious within a minute and killed him in four (its effect is fundamentally that of suffocation, preventing the blood from carrying oxygen), seemed to have no effect. Yussupov shot him too. But when he came back with the other conspirators for the body, Rasputin got up, and burst through a locked door into the courtyard. He was shot again, then battered with an iron bar. Finally, he was dropped into the river through a hole in the ice. When his body was recovered, it was found that he had died of drowning. The crime writer Nigel Morland was told by an acquaintance of Rasputin's that he suffered from alcoholic gastritis, which thickens the lining of the stomach and would prevent cyanide from being absorbed quickly. A more likely explanation is that Yussupov was lying when he claimed to have poisoned Rasputin. No poison was found in the body. Yussupov lived for the rest of his life on the reputation of being 'the man who murdered Rasputin', and was prone to fly to law whenever anyone described the incident in such a way as to show him in an unfavourable light. Not long before his death, he even stated in court that Rasputin had been a German spy – a story he must have known to be nonsense, since it had been exploded by half a dozen biographers since Rasputin's death. Yussupov, like Illiodor, was a homosexual, and his hatred of Rasputin may have had some curious sexual basis.

Rasputin's prophecy, like Cagliostro's, was remarkably accurate; the revolution came in the following year. The Tsar and his family were kept prisoners, like Louis XVI and Marie Antoinette, for a year, and executed in the Ekaterinburg cellar on July 16, 1918. The parallels with the French royal family continue, for the story quickly went about that one of them – the Grand Duchess Anastasia – had escaped. In 1922 a girl who had made a suicide attempt in Berlin was 'recognised' as Anastasia by another woman in the ward, and admitted her identity. Various exiles from the Russian court recognised Anna Anderson as Anastasia, but her claim was not legally allowed – the Tsar had deposited large sums of money in foreign banks, all of which would go to Anna Anderson – and a German court has only recently dismissed her final appeal for recognition. Maria Rasputin met her in America in the late sixties, and is reported to have declared her belief that Anna Anderson was the Grand Duchess Anastasia (whom she had known well as a child).

There were also at least two false Alexeys – the Tsarevitch – but neither of them gained anything like the credence accorded to Anastasia.

Rasputin, like Crowley, was a natural mage. He did nothing to develop his powers; it is even doubtful whether he had any control over them. And this applies, by and large, to every 'magician' I have discussed in this book. It is because it does not apply to George Ivanovitch Gurdjieff that he is probably the most interesting of all magicians. He possessed certain powers to begin with, and he spent a lifetime carefully developing them. There can be no doubt that he achieved a large degree of Faculty X.

The key to Gurdjieff's teaching lies in the word 'work'. A typical story will make it clear. A. R. Orage, a noted literary figure in the London of pre-1914, and editor of *The New Age*, decided to sell his newspaper and become a pupil of Gurdjieff. He then went to Gurdjieff's Institute for the Harmonious Development of Man at the Prieuré des Basses Loges in Fontainebleau. Gurdjieff handed him a spade and told him to dig in the garden. Orage was out of practice, and soon found digging so exhausting that he used to go to his room and try to restrain tears of fatigue and self-pity. It seemed that he had made an appalling mistake. He decided to make a still greater effort, and suddenly found himself intensely enjoying the digging.

The story* clearly has much in common with Elizabeth Fox's account of her month's meditation under Crowley's orders. What happens is simple. We fall into a habitual mode of life, which means that our day-to-day activities become so repetitious that the 'robot' in the subconscious mind can go off-duty. There are no sudden emergencies to keep him alert. So one's inner world becomes as habitual and predictable as one's outer life. The problem is to persuade the robot to start fertilising consciousness with bursts of 'newness', so that one can develop. The best way to do this is through discomfort, one's first reaction to which is misery and pain. When this self-inflicted misery has gone on long enough, the robot has to take some action to counteract it. The *additional effort* is important in breaking through, for it convinces the robot that this is serious. One's inner life ceases to be barren and repetitious. The inner spring is flowing again.

The ascetic practices of saints obviously work on the same principle.

From birth until the age of twenty-one, we grow physically and in every other sense. Changes take place inside us without our volition. Then it stops. We are so used to the changes taking place

* Taken from the anonymous *Teachings of Gurdjieff, The Journal of a Pupil* (London, 1961), p. 28.

'automatically' that we find it difficult to stop expecting automatic growth to continue. It doesn't, and most people slowly ossify. If growth is to continue, unusual efforts must be made in order to stimulate the robot into providing 'newness'. This is the core of Gurdjieff's work. Its first aim was to defeat man's natural laziness, his tendency to relax and 'switch off'. Orage, describing what happened when he made the 'extra effort' at gardening, says, 'Just then, *something changed in me.*' He had learned the basic secret; that there is no good reason why we should not continue developing, in this inner sense, all the time, so that something continues to 'change' every day.

Gurdjieff was born in 1873 in Alexandropol, in the Transcaucasus, so that although his parents were Greek (his surname was actually Gorgiades), his nationality was Russian. In his book *Meetings with Remarkable Men* he summarises the salient features of his early years. His father was an *ashokh*, a 'bard'. One of the poems he 'sang' was about Gilgamesh. When he read in a magazine that the tablets of the Gilgamesh epic had been found at Nineveh, he experienced enormous excitement at the idea that a poem sung by his father should have been handed down verbally for thousands of years. It was the beginning of a suspicion that perhaps other forms of knowledge had been handed down through the ages – secret teachings. Certain curious events stimulated in him the feeling that there *was* secret knowledge to be obtained, if he only knew where to look. A neurasthenic young man in the village was able to predict the future with astonishing accuracy; he did this by sitting between two candles and staring at his thumb nail until he went into a trance and would see the future (of whomever he happened to be enquiring about) in his nail. He foretold correctly that Gurdjieff would develop a painful sore spot on his right side – it was a carbuncle that had to be removed – and that he might have a gun accident (he was shot in the leg when hunting). One evening, companions suggested 'table turning', and the leg of the table rapped out correctly the age of each one of them. Oddest of all, perhaps, was the phenomena connected with a sect called Yezidis, a tribe in the Mount Ararat region, sometimes known as devil worshippers. He saw a Yezidi boy crying, unable to escape from a circle that mischievous children had drawn around him. Subsequently he verified this fact by experiment, and records that it took himself and another strong man to pull a Yezidi woman out of a circle drawn around her. As soon as she left the circle by this forcible means she lapsed into a trance; placed back in the circle, the normal consciousness returned. The Yezidi is confined to the circle as if by walls of glass; if not put back into it after being dragged out, the trance state lasts from thirteen to twenty-one hours. The Yezidi priests could restore consciousness in such a case by means of an incantation.

One day a young man well known to Gurdjieff died after a fall from a horse. The night after he was buried, he was seen trying to re-enter his home. His throat was cut, and the body was taken back to the cemetery. It sounds as if the man had not actually been dead when he was buried, but the neighbours were convinced that his body had been possessed by an evil spirit, perhaps a vampire.

Gurdjieff began to read everything he could find on occultism in an attempt to explain these phenomena. He visited monasteries. On a pilgrimage to a nearby wonder-working shrine, he saw a young man who was completely paralysed down one side crawl uphill, fall asleep beside the shrine and then wake up cured. He saw a girl dying of consumption cured overnight by drinking rose hips boiled in milk after the Virgin had told her in a dream that this would cure her. And he saw a special service for rain, in which all the churches of the town participated, followed by an immediate downpour.

Gurdjieff took a job as a stoker on the local railway, and when he was asked to accompany an engineer to survey the route of a proposed railway, Gurdjieff managed to make a great deal of money by approaching the mayors of the towns that the railway was scheduled to go through, assuring them that their towns were not on the proposed route but that he could 'fix' it for a sum of money. Gurdjieff had no objection to making money by dubiously legal means, and he tells with relish a number of similar stories in his book. He used the money to set out with a friend, Sarkis Pogossian, trying to find the remaining members of the ancient Sarmoung Brotherhood, which, Gurdjieff says, was established in Babylon in 2500 B.C.

It was Pogossian who, according to Gurdjieff, told him the great secret about work. Pogossian never merely relaxed; he always swung his arms rhythmically, marked time with his feet or moved his fingers. He explained to Gurdjieff that he was trying to accustom his whole nature to love work, to get rid of its laziness. Evidently he possesed a strong sense of the futility of wasted time. He told Gurdjieff, 'I am convinced that in this world no conscious work is ever wasted ...'

The moral sounds obvious; but it should not be underestimated. Crowley, like most 'magicians', wasted his life, moving restlessly from one futile activity to another. Why? Because he was driven by the negative desire to escape boredom, to escape the feeling that if he stopped moving, life would also stop. It is a negative feeling of the emptiness of life that drives them. Pogossian's belief that all work ultimately 'pays off' is obviously the perfect antidote to this attitude, and the secret needed by magicians.

Pogossian and Gurdjieff got mixed up in a fight in Smyrna, and the English sailors on whose side they fought somehow got permission for them to travel on a warship to Alexandria. Here Gurdjieff went on to Jerusalem, while Pogossian travelled to England and trained as an engineer. In Egypt he met Prince Yuri Lubovedsky, who seems to have introduced him to the idea of 'work on oneself'.

A Persian dervish later told him that he was wasting his time practising Hatha Yoga, and explained that the body is a complex machine: 'If you know every small screw, every little pin of your machine, only then can you know what you must do.'

Gurdjieff travelled widely for the first forty years of his life. According to his own account, he visited monasteries all over Europe and Asia, and even joined an expedition to look for a hidden city in the Gobi desert. (It turned back when one of its members died from the bite of a wild camel.)

It was shortly before the First World War that Ouspensky met Gurdjieff. Ouspensky was another 'seeker' who had visited the East looking for secret knowledge. He was disappointed. But when he came back to Moscow, he felt that the search had, for the time being, reached a dead end. He gave a few lectures on his travels, and was told that he ought to meet Gurdjieff. He found a small, black-moustached man with a face like a rajah, who answered his questions about hidden knowledge precisely and carefully with no attempt at mystification.

Gurdjieff's basic point was simple and startling. Man is such a bundle of impulses and emotions that he can hardly be said to exist in any meaningful sense. He changes from hour to hour, almost from moment to moment; he is a helpless victim of the events that carry him along. He wanders around in a kind of hypnotised state. In fact, he is, in a quite literal sense, asleep all the time. He has occasional moments of intensity, flashes when he glimpses what he could be, the freedom of which he is potentially capable. But in no time at all, his mind has gone back to sleep again, and he is again living a routine, habit-filled existence, his mind entirely occupied by trivialities to which he attaches far more significance than they deserve.

Is it possible to 'wake up'? Ouspensky wanted to know. It is, said Gurdjieff, but it is very difficult. Because the habit from which we are trying to escape is like a powerful current, and after trying to swim against it for a few minutes, we gradually lose strength and go to sleep again. It is necessary to follow a precise method of escaping.

Man is a machine. If he is to learn to rise above his 'mechanicalness' ('living and partly living', as Eliot says) he must understand the machine.

The essence of Gurdjieff's doctrine can be summed up in an image taken from that remarkable novel *The Haunted Woman*, by David Lindsay. A woman goes to buy a house from a man she has never met. They are, on the whole, indifferent to one another, having, apparently, little in common. But as she walks alone across the hall, she sees a flight of stairs leading to an upper region of the house. When she goes up them, she finds herself in a part of the house that ceased to exist a long time ago; the scenery outside the window is different. And when she sees herself in a mirror, she is also different, somehow more mature and developed; she has 'realised herself'. The 'self' she is looking at in the mirror is the person she might have become, to so speak, if circumstances had been ideal for the development of her inner qualities.

Her host, the man from whom she may buy the house, also wanders up the stairs, and finds her there. He is also changed, and these two 'realised' people fall in love. However, when they descend again to the lower part of the house, they have totally forgotten everything about the upper storey, which now no longer exists. And when, accidentally, they again find themselves together in the upper storey, they rack their brains for some method by which they can overcome this amnesia, and *remind themselves* about the other regions of the house.

Lindsay has created an image of the basic problem of the artist and the mystic. In the moments of 'higher consciousness' there is always a feeling of 'But *of course*!' Life is infinitely meaningful; its possibilities are suddenly endless, and 'normal consciousness' is seen as being no better than sleep. For, like sleep, it separates man from *reality*.

When man gets this feeling of 'reality', he knows that nothing in the world could be so important as keeping it. He tries every possible method of reminding himself not to forget, not to stop fighting to achieve it. What is more, in this state of intensity, it becomes clear that it can be achieved. He sees now as something that is self-evident that he possesses a *true will*, the ability to focus clearly on an objective and then to achieve it in the most economical way. But then he descends back to his lower storey, and can only remember dimly that he had a vision. The sleep comes back.

The main trouble is a kind of listlessness, a tendency to waste time and consciousness, like a person staring out of the window at the rain and yawning, wondering what to do next. On the other hand, the moment Paris saw Helen of Troy, his whole being was gripped by an objective. Loyalty, honour, gratitude to his host, all ceased to matter, as a kind of tornado shook his soul.

That is to say, an *objective* (Helen of Troy) arouses immense depths of will and energy.

The revelation that strikes a man in the moods of 'waking consciousness' is that this objective is always there. All he has to do is *learn to see it*, and everything else follows; his true will awakens.

Now, Gurdjieff, in his travels, had made the simple discovery we have already mentioned: that any unusual effort, any new beginning, has this effect of shaking the mind awake. I am normally quite out of touch with 'reality', almost as out of touch as when I am asleep and dreaming. I look at that tree, but I don't really see it, or believe in its existence. My mind is elswhere – like half listening to someone who is talking and half thinking about something else. The result is a kind of double-exposure effect in my consciousness, a certain blurring. Any crisis or sudden touch of ecstasy makes me put twice as much effort into perception, and whatever I am looking at suddenly comes clearly into focus, like the slight touch on the wheel of a microscope or pair of binoculars that makes things appear clear and sharp.

But life is largely routine: ritual, as Lionel Johnson said. I don't set out on some exciting journey every day. I cannot rely on such things to keep my mind awake. I do not meet a Helen of Troy every day, and what is more, unless I propose to waste my life like Casanova, I cannot rely on the pleasant 'shocks' of sexual desire to keep waking me up.

Sometimes, music or poetry has this effect of awakening my mind to reality, causing that broadening of inner horizons, the *widened sense of reality*. But that doesn't always work either.

We need, so to speak, a reliable alarm clock.

The answer to this is simpler than one might suppose. It is simply a matter of getting the 'robot' habituated to producing larger quantities of energy than necessary.

Gurdjieff's basic method therefore consisted of 'work'. The first thing that happened to a new student at the Prieuré was that he was told to join a working party. They might be making a road, cutting down trees, breaking stones, diverting a stream, milking cows. The anonymous author of the Gurdjieff *Journal* had an experience common to all. He 'worked' well, but with a certain resentment. Gurdjieff sent one of his right-hand men, Dr. Stjoernval, to explain that the student was failing through resentment to economise energy. He should work like a labourer, not like a machine. He advised him to make a list of foreign words and learn them as he worked, and also try to 'sense' his body and be aware of its activities. The moment he ceased to work in a negative, 'withdrawn' frame of mind, and 'involved' himself *and his will* in the work, he began to find it deeply satisfying.

This aspect of Gurdjieff's teaching could be called 'applied Taoism'. He laid great stress on the importance of learning to work, and told Ouspensky that a man who could make a good pair of shoes was potentially a better student of 'the work' than an intellectual who had written a dozen books. Similarly, when a woman novelist told Gurdjieff that she felt more conscious when she was writing, he replied, 'You live in dreams and you write about your dreams. How much better for you if you were to scrub one floor consciously than to write a hundred books ...' The clashes between Confucius and Lao Tse in the Taoist scriptures immediately come to mind. (See p. 108.)

What Gurdjieff did at his institute was to turn bored, egotistic, confused people into well-balanced machines, too busy to think about themselves. His exercises allowed the student's natural capacities to operate again. He spoke of man's three 'centres', the intellectual centre, the emotional centre, the 'moving' (or physical) centre, and said that each works with its own energy. When man is working at top pressure, each centre works in harmony with the others. When man is unbalanced, as he tends to be in modern civilisation, centres work lop-sidedly and often become exhausted.

But it is not only the habit of civilisation that makes most people lop-sided and inharmonious. They get the habit of indulging negative emotions, and these temporarily damage them, as a fire damages a building. One of the most interesting things about Gurdjieff as a person was his apparent freedom from negative emotions. The best example of this is a story told by Seabrook. In the 1920s, Gurdjieff decided to write down his ideas in the form of a vast book called *All and Everything, Beelzebub's Tales to His Grandson.* He decided to apply his principle of 'work' to the book, and deliberately wrote it in an incredibly long-winded and complicated style, to force his readers to make an enormous mental effort to grasp his meaning. Beelzebub, flying around the earth in a space ship, tells his grandson about the 'three-brained beings' on the planet earth, and their peculiar tendency to treat fantasy as reality. This is because a commission of archangels got worried about man's developing powers and planted in him an organ called Kundabuffer, whose purpose is to keep him from achieving 'objective consciousness'. This is obviously a legend of original sin, like Plato's legend of the gods cutting man in two.

Seabrook was asked to ask a number of intelligent friends to supper to hear chunks of the magnum opus. These included Lincoln Steffens, two pragmatist philosophers from Columbia, and J. B. Watson, the founder of behavioural psychology, who also believed that man is a machine, but firmly disbelieved that he could turn himself into anything else. Gurdjieff's disciples proceeded to read at length. Seabrook writes:

Late in the evening, Mr. Steffens and John Watson began whispering. Presently Mr. Watson said: 'Either this is an elaborate and subtle joke, whose point is completely over our heads, or it's piffle. In either event, I don't see that much can be gained by hearing more of it. I propose, if Mr. Gurdjieff is agreeable, that we now converse for a while.'

So we all relaxed and conversed, and presently supped, with equal amiability on the part of both hosts and guests. Mr. Gurdjieff was more brilliant, and more witty, than the manuscript had been. He was so agreeable, so keen, so affable, that Steffens, Watson, Montague, and all the rest of them took him into their complete confidence and explained unanimously their conviction that – unless he was trying to put over a cosmic joke of some sort whose point had not yet become manifest – his future did not lie in the field of authorship. Gurdjieff suggested that his purport might be too deep for our limited comprehension.

Presumably Gurdjieff's reason for wanting to read aloud to a group of American intellectuals was the desire of the author to reach an audience – that is, vanity played some small part in it. But the rebuff only had the effect of making him more witty and friendly than ever.

Fritz Peters, the author of *Boyhood with Gurdjieff,* has some interesting stories that make a similar point. One Russian emigré called Rachmilevitch was peculiarly irritating; he grumbled non-stop. One day when the pupils were all planting lawns, he threw down his hoe, told Gurdjieff he was insane and marched off. Gurdjieff sent Fritz Peters, a boy of twelve, after him, and Rachmilevitch was brought back. Later that evening, Gurdjieff made everyone laugh by telling them that Peters had found Rachmilevitch sitting up a tree (which was true). This time, Rachmilevitch marched out and returned to Paris. Gurdjieff went to Paris and persuaded him to return. He explained to Fritz Peters that Rachmilevitch had one valuable quality – he irritated the hell out of everyone. And this prevented people falling into a routine!

Gurdjieff placed a Miss Merston in charge of the institute while he was away, and she and Peters soon clashed; his chickens got into her garden and scratched up flowers. She threatened to wring the neck of the next one that did this, and carried out her threat. Thereupon Peters dug up and destroyed some of her favourite flowers. This was reported to Gurdjieff on his return. He pointed out to Peters that the chicken had been eaten, so it had served some purpose, whereas the destruction of the flowers had been pointless. But he also told Miss Merston that she had failed him by wasting his time with such trivialities.

On another occasion, when Miss Merston had drawn up a long list of everybody's misdemeanours when Gurdjieff was away, Gurdjieff startled everyone by handing out money for each misdemeanour committed (Peters received by far the most). But the rebuff had the effect of making everyone sorry for Miss Merston, so that she ceased to be a dragon.

Perhaps the most amusing story concerns a special occasion when Miss Merston served tea to everyone. Every time she bent over to hand someone a teacup, she farted gently, and said, 'Pardon me.' Everyone was slightly embarrassed, but Gurdjieff was delighted; he proceeded to draw attention to the explosions of wind, comparing them to the report of a toy gun, and remarking on her politeness in excusing herself after each fart. Again, the result was to reduce Miss Merston's 'dragon' status and make everyone like her.

There are many stories of this kind of attitude towards 'difficult' people; in each of them Gurdjieff displayed what Shaw called 'natural Christianity'. But in another sense, it was not 'natural'. The natural reaction to such people is to ignore them or quarrel with them. After the affair of the flowerbed, Gurdjieff told Peters that both he and Miss Merston had merely *reacted* to one another in a purely mechanical way. Gurdjieff's response to difficult people was a deliberate exercise of freedom.

The physical work at the Prieuré was only the beginning. The real work was bound up with dancing. Again, Seabrook gives one of the most striking accounts. In 1924, Gurdjieff took forty of the Prieuré students to New York, where they put on displays.

What excited and interested me was the amazing, brilliant, automaton-like, inhuman, almost incredible docility and robot-like obedience of the disciples, in the parts of the demonstrations that had to do with 'movement'. They were like a group of perfectly trained zombies, or like circus animals jumping through hoops ringed with fire, or like the soldiers of Christophe who marched without breaking step off the parapet of the citadel on that sheer mountainside in Haiti. They did things, without suffering any apparent hurt, almost as dangerous as dropping off a cliff, and certainly more dangerous than leaping through fiery hoops.

The group consisted of young and youngish women, most of whom were handsome and some of whom were beautiful; and of men who looked as if they had come, and probably did, from the best British and continental homes and universities. I met some of these disciples and they were almost without exception people of culture, breeding and intelligence. The demonstrations, I imagine, were to show the extent to which the Gurdjieff Institute ... had taught them supernormal powers of physical control, co-ordination, relaxation, etc. And there was no fake about it, ... because if they hadn't learned supreme co-ordination, they'd have broken their arms and legs, and maybe their necks, in some of the stunts they did. But what I felt the demonstrations showed, even more than their control over themselves, was the terrific domination of Gurdjieff, the Master. At his command, they'd race, spread out at breakneck speed from left to right across the stage, and at another low command from him, freeze in full flight as if caught by a race-track camera. Once I saw Gurdjieff push a dancer who had been 'frozen' by his command in an attitude of difficult equilibrium. The dancer tumbled and rolled over several times, then rolled upright and back again, apparently without volitionally *assuming* it – in the original frozen position.

Gurdjieff himself, a calm, bull-like man, with muscles in those days as hard as steel, in immaculate dinner clothes, his head shaven like a Prussian officer's, with black luxuriant handlebar moustaches, and generally smoking expensive Egyptian cigarettes, stood casually down in the audience, or off to the side beside the piano ... He never shouted. He was always casual. Yet always in complete command. It was as if he were a slave-master or wild-animal tamer, with an invisible bull-whip swishing inaudibly through the air. Among his other qualities, he was a great showman, and a climax came one night which literally had the front row out of their seats. The troupe was deployed extreme back stage, facing the audience. At his command, they came racing full-tilt towards the footlights. We expected to see a wonderful exhibition of arrested motion. But instead, Gurdjieff calmly turned his back, and was lighting a cigarette. In the next split second, an aerial human avalanche was flying through the air, across the orchestra, down among empty chairs, on the floor, bodies pell-mell, piled on top of each other, arms and legs sticking out in weird postures – frozen there, fallen, in complete immobility and silence.

Only after it had happened did Gurdjieff turn and look at them, as they lay there, still immobile. When they presently arose, by his permission, and it was evident that no arms, legs or necks had been broken – no one seemed to have suffered even so much as a scratch or bruise – there was a storm of applause, mingled with a little protest. It had almost been too much.*

Seabrook quotes Gurdjieff as saying, 'If we live calm, monotonous days and peaceful nights, we stultify. We had better torture our own spirit than suffer the inanities of calm.'

He adds: 'His disciples therefore were awakened at all hours of the night, suddenly, and had learned to remain "frozen" in whatever positions they had chanced to stand or fall in when leaping out of bed.'

The gymnastic exhibitions were not the only part of the displays. There were also 'tricks' that Seabrook describes as being similar to those practised by Houdini, thought-reading, etc. The audience were warned that there would be 'tricks, half-tricks, and true supernatural phenomena'. Half-tricks, it was explained, depended on an abnormal sensitivity. An object is hidden and a blindfolded man takes the hands of various people in the room, without speaking to them, and 'reads their minds', so that he finds the hidden object. In fact, says Gurdjieff, he does not read their minds, but is highly sensitive to the pressure of their hands, which make slight involuntary movements of the muscles which indicate where the object is hidden.

Genuine telepathic phenomena also seemed to occur; a pupil would sit among the audience and be shown some object; he would then telepathically 'transmit' the name and shape of the object to

---

* *Witchcraft, Its Power in the World Today*, 1942, Part III, Chapter 3.

pupils on the stage. Even more startling, the pupil in the audience would transmit to M. de Hartmann, the pianist, the name of an opera – any opera – and he would play an extract from it. An artist pupil sketched animals 'transmitted' by the pupil in the audience.

These could, of course, have been 'tricks'. But Gurdjieff himself possessed strong telepathic powers – of which I shall speak in a moment. It may well be that he was able to convey these to some of his pupils.

As can be seen from Seabrook's account, the dances were so complex and difficult that they required an almost yogic training. Gurdjieff claimed to have collected them from various Oriental sources: dervishes, Essenes, Buddhists and so on. Kenneth Walker, in his own account of Gurdjieff, *Venture with Ideas* (perhaps the finest introduction to Gurdjieff), mentions that the dances involved learning to do different things with different limbs. Anyone who has ever tried rubbing his stomach in a circle and waving the other hand straight up and down will see the difficulty involved here. The dances certainly had the effect of releasing Walker's hidden energies. He records that he often left his Harley Street surgery exhausted, then drove a considerable distance to the Gurdjieff group meeting; but after several hours of 'exercises', he felt totally wide-awake, brimming with energy.

Everyone has noticed this phenomenon at some time. No matter how tired you are, some sudden excitement or crisis can snap you into full alertness. We possess two types of will. I have elsewhere used the illustration of a bullet. The bullet is driven by an explosion of cordite. But the cordite, although powerful, is quite harmless and inexplosive on its own. At the end of the bullet there is a tiny cap of a substance called mercuric fulminate, which explodes instantly on contact. The hammer of the gun explodes the fulminate, and the fulminate explodes the more powerful cordite. Man possesses a fulminate will and a cordite will. If I am doing some routine job, like mowing the lawn, I use my cordite will. But it burns rather dully. If something really excites me or arouses my sense of urgency, it is the fulminate will that explodes, and that produces a roar of power from the cordite will. The fulminate will is tied up with the imagination and sense of purpose, and these in turn detonate my ordinary will-power and vitality.

But sudden emergency is not necessary to produce the same effect. Any hard and unusual work causes me to 'warm up' until finally my consciousness broadens. This is the basis of the Gurdjieff disciplines.

Gurdjieff's 'system' is highly complex; but there would be no point in trying to summarise it here. Planets are regarded as living beings. Different worlds exist on different levels of materiality (this sounds like Madame Blavatsky) and have different vibrations. Man's chief business is actually to produce a kind of psychological vibration that 'feeds' the moon. Ouspensky's book *In Search of the Miraculous*, one of the most thorough expositions of Gurdjieff's ideas, is full of tables of 'octaves', 'worlds', 'triads', 'elements' and so on. It is an interesting but not important question whether Gurdjieff learned this during his travels, or whether he invented it as a kind of framework for the theoretical side of his 'system'. He speaks of seven centres in all: intellectual, emotional, moving (physical), instinctive, sexual and two more called 'higher thinking' and 'higher emotional'. He explains that the centres tend to work with one another's energies and take over one another's functions. 'It is a very great thing when the sex centre works with its own energy.' It then becomes akin to the higher emotional centre. Everyone can understand this statement; for example, D. H. Lawrence's descriptions of the gradual improvement in the sexual relation between Mellors and Lady Chatterley showing the sex centre learning to use its own energy instead of working on emotional or (worse still) thought energy. When the sex centre works with its own energy, sympathy and tenderness are involved;

sex ceases to be a kind of mutual masturbation. But then if anyone takes the trouble to analyse this statement phenomenologically, he will see that it is untrue. Sex can be bad because my mind is elsewhere, because I am worried, because, in short, I am involved in a world of fantasies. When I am properly *balanced*, when my mind is aware of the objective reality, sex is likely to produce maximum intensity and insight.

However, this is unimportant. We may take a sceptical view, and say simply that Gurdjieff was a psychologist of singular brilliance and insight, on a level with Nietzsche. The important thing is that he grasped the basic problem and tried to remedy it.

The core of his system concerns levels of consciousness. Man has potentially four states of consciousness, says Gurdjieff. First of all, there is sleep, when you are wrapped in your own private world. Then there is waking consciousness, or so-called waking consciousness. which you appear to share with other people. But we are not really sharing a common consciousness. We each remain wrapped in our own blanket of subjective fantasy. And into this semi-sleeping state there burst occasional moments of intensity-consciousness, when we seem to wake up. Gurdjieff calls this self-remembering. He demonstrates by a simple exercise how difficult this is to achieve. If you close your eyes, you sink into a subjective inner world in which you think only of yourself. If you look at your watch when someone asks you the time, you forget yourself, and become aware only of your watch. But try looking at your watch, *and also being aware of yourself looking at it*. You will find that you can only do this very briefly. After a moment, your attention slips, and you either forget your watch and become aware only of yourself, or forget yourself and become aware only of the watch.

All the moments that we remember for the rest of our lives, the moments of sudden intense happiness, are moments of self-remembering. I seem to wake up, and have a feeling of 'What *me*, *here?*' I am as aware of the place as of myself being in it. And such states may last for half an hour or so.

Beyond self-remembering there is a fourth state called 'objective consciousness', that is, a constant state in which the mind actually perceives objective reality all the time. This is seldom or ever achieved by human beings, even in flashes.

One of the chief aims of the 'work' – either manual labour or dancing – was to induce increased self-consciousness, the possibility of achieving self-remembering for long stretches.

In my own terminology: habit leads the robot to economise on the energy it sends up to my conscious mind. This in turn leads my conscious mind to find life rather dull. In fact, the dullness is *inside* me, but I think that the world itself is to blame, so I allow my consciousness to become even duller and lazier. This means that the robot sends even less energy. And so the vicious circuit continues. If, on the other hand, I can somehow induce in myself a state of optimistic expectation, I cause the robot to pour more energy into consciousness, and the more energy he releases, the more the world strikes me as delightful and interesting. If I am at all self-observant, I will also recognise that this state of wide-awakeness, intense aliveness, is due to effort on my part. Once I clearly grasp this, the old vicious circle – whereby we can get used to *anything* – is broken. It could be quite permanently broken, and then a new form of man would appear.

Gurdjieff's system was based upon the same insight as Freud's and Edmund Husserl's: that although man appears to himself to be a very simple, straightforward being – a mirror-like consciousness – he is actually an immensely complex machine with many levels. Like the top gear in a car, consciousness is our weakest level. It is unfortunately the only level that many of us are aware of. Our real strength lies on other levels. The evolutionary problem is for us to become aware of these other levels.

The essence of personal evolution is the actual *heat* generated by mental effort. Gurdjieff distinguishes between what he calls 'personality' and 'essence'. Most actors have a great deal of 'personality', because they take the trouble to develop it. But it is only a surface layer. 'Essence' is inner strength, true 'personality'. Gurdjieff says that one of the few men he had ever known who possessed true essence was a Corsican brigand, who used to spend all day peering down the sights of his rifle in the hot sun, waiting for passing travellers; the strength and endurance caused that inner fusing called essence.

Two years after meeting Gurdjieff, Ouspensky had begun to develop the 'mental muscles' for longer periods of self-remembering. To begin with, his efforts at self-remembering had tended to slip into total forgetfulness. He speaks of a long effort at self-remembering as he walked through Petrograd, and the 'strange emotional state of inner peace and confidence that comes after great efforts of this kind', and then of suddenly *waking up* two hours later, and remembering that he has completely forgotten to remember himself. Here, it can be seen that the plunge from a higher form of consciousness to a lower one is exactly like a black-out. In the summer of 1916 the 'miracle' began to happen; he describes it in Chapter 13 of *In Search of the Miraculous*. In a house in Finland, after a session during which he had been savagely sarcastic to everyone, including Ouspensky, Gurdjieff suddenly began to speak to Ouspensky telepathically. 'I heard his voice inside me, as if it were in the chest, near the heart.' Gurdjieff put questions without speaking, Ouspensky answered them, and it continued for half an hour.

The experience also demonstrated, to Ouspensky's satisfaction, that Gurdjieff was by no means infallible, in spite of his occult knowledge. After two hours of walking in the forest, struggling with conflicting emotions, Ouspensky says, 'I saw that Gurdjieff was right; that what I had considered to be firm and reliable in myself in reality did not exist. But I had found something else. I knew that he would not believe me, and that he would laugh at me if I showed him this other thing. But for myself it was indubitable and what happened later showed I was right.'

Later, in bed, Gurdjieff's voice again spoke in his chest, and Ouspensky replied mentally. They carried on a conversation from different parts of the house.

The following morning, at breakfast, the mind-reading act continued, Ouspensky began to brood on a problem about the 'ray of creation'; Gurdjieff told him – speaking normally – to leave it for now, because it was too far ahead.

Ouspensky says that he was in a strange emotional state for three days, and although Gurdjieff told him that he was now no longer asleep, he felt this to be untrue; he was undoubtedly 'asleep' at times.

What had happened is that long effort had broken through to Ouspensky's psychic faculties, the red end of the spectrum. This is why he felt that he had not achieved full 'wakefulness'.

On the way back to Petrograd, Ouspensky, alone in the compartment, not only talked to Gurdjieff but saw him. And back in Petrograd, Ouspensky had the impression of seeing 'sleeping people': 'suddenly I saw that the man who was walking towards me was asleep ... Although his eyes were open, he was walking along obviously immersed in dreams, which ran like clouds across his face. It entered my mind that if I could look at him long enough I should see his dreams ... After him came another also sleeping. A sleeping *izvostchik* [cab driver] went by with two sleeping passengers. Suddenly I found myself in the position of the prince in "The Sleeping Princess". Everyone around me was asleep.' After a few weeks this strange state passed off and Ouspensky returned to 'normal' consciousness. This again demonstrates that what he had experienced was not true waking-consciousness, although it was certainly more awake than everyday consciousness. It was some kind of accidental return to 'jungle sensitiveness', to the occult faculty of animals. But as a result of this period, he also reached new depths of intuition. He explains his sudden clear perception that violent means, to achieve anything whatever, are always a mistake. They always produce negative results. This is not, he says, a moral conclusion, like Tolstoyan non-resistance, but a practical one. This is obviously the reason for Gurdjieff's patiently creative attitude in his personal relations, the refusal to give way to the impulse to destroy or dismiss.

The Revolution forced Gurdjieff to leave Russia. No doubt he would have been 'liquidated' fairly quickly as an organiser of 'secret' groups. In London, Ouspensky himself began to teach groups what he had learned from Gurdjieff, and his group finally provided the money for Gurdjieff to buy the buildings at the Prieuré. Ouspensky and Gurdjieff had ceased to work together. In fact, there was a total opposition of temperament. Ouspensky was a scientist by nature – dry, precise, abstract (although this is not to say that he was a mere 'intellectual'). Gurdjieff was a Walt Whitmanesque type of character, in some ways not unlike Rasputin. He was not a saint. He liked good food, and drank a lot of Armagnac. When he was settled at Fontainebleau he moved in his mother, brother and sister, and the anonymous author of the *Journal* remarks that he was a patriarchal figure. An aphorism on the wall in the study house said: 'It is a sign of a good man that he loves his father and mother.' He was, as Orage said, a 'complete man'. When the men bathed communally, they had a ritual of telling dirty jokes, and Gurdjieff would make them line up to examine the degree of sunburn of their behinds. His wife died at the Prieuré, and Gurdjieff took a mistress, who was soon pregnant. He was, apparently, capable of sleeping with attractive female pupils, and I myself have met a professor at an American university who told me he was one of Gurdjieff's natural sons, and by no means the only one. In *God Is My Adventure*, Rom Landau tells a story of an American woman novelist, who sat next to Gurdjieff's table in a restaurant. Gurdjieff suddenly began to inhale and exhale in a peculiar way, and the woman went pale. She said that she had caught Gurdjieff's eye – 'I suddenly felt as if I had been struck right through my sexual centre. It was beastly!' Even Crowley did not possess the capacity to cause instantaneous orgasms in strange women.

Landau also mentions that he stumbled upon proof that Gurdjieff had been in Tibet; an Arab writer, Achmed Abdullah, said he had met Gurdjieff in Lhasa, when Gurdjieff was an agent of the Russian secret police.

On his return to France after his American trip, Gurdjieff had a serious motor accident that almost killed him. There was something odd about this accident. Fritz Peters has described Gurdjieff as an insane driver who would not last two minutes on a modern road. Before leaving Paris for the Prieuré he told Mme. de Hartmann to order the mechanic to carefully check his car; he was peculiarly insistent. He then told her to take a train back to the Prieuré instead of coming with him. No one knows exactly what happened; a passing gendarme found the wrecked car by the side of the road, and Gurdjieff, badly injured, lying beside it covered with a blanket, with his head on a pillow. The gendarme said it seemed impossible that a man so badly injured could have moved that far. Only Gurdjieff's fantastic vitality saved his life. Had he somehow foreseen the accident? Or was it, in some odd sense, deliberate? He was not usually an accident-prone man.

On the other hand, neither was he a superman. Fritz Peters describes a trip to Vichy with Gurdjieff driving. Gurdjieff insisted on driving too fast on the wrong side of the road. Peters was supposed to map-read, but Gurdjieff went so fast that they usually shot past turnings. He always refused to turn back, so they had to find new routes all the time. He declined to stop for petrol, and would drive until the car ran out. Then one of the two boys had to walk to the nearest garage, and bring a mechanic too, since Gurdjieff was convinced that it could not be mere lack of petrol that had made the car stop. (It is not clear why he didn't keep a can of petrol in the boot.) He always arrived at hotels so late that they had to knock the proprietor up. In the Vichy hotel, his behaviour was wildly eccentric, and he introduced the boys as the sons of Henry Ford and Vanderbilt.

Out of this Vichy trip sprang another curious proof of his occult knowledge. He invited a Russian family to the Prieuré. They had a daughter. Gurdjieff told the assembled pupils that he would now demonstrate an Eastern method of hypnotism, which depended on the subject's susceptibility to music, especially to certain chords. At a certain climactic chord, he said, the girl would go into a trance.

The Russian family came into the room, and the girl sat beside Gurdjieff. During the music, played by Hartmann at the piano, she was obviously moved, and at the climactic chord, seemed to faint. It took a long time to bring her round, and the Russian family were so alarmed that it cost a considerable effort to persuade them to stay. After this, Gurdjieff persuaded the girl to perform the demonstration several times. Peters says that her hysteria when she came out of the trance was too obviously genuine for the whole thing to be a 'put-up job'.

Neither is there any need to look for 'alternative explanations' in the case of Gurdjieff. He had learned to push his senses to new limits through various disciplines and studies. As a consequence, he had gained certain occult powers. Whether these powers were of any importance is another matter. Probably he did not think so himself.

He differed from all the other magicians we have considered in one obvious respect. He was free from the usual magician's destiny of sudden rise and slow downfall. Compared to him, Paracelsus, Agrippa, Dee, Crowley, Madame Blavatsky, seem to be talented eccentrics, lacking in self-discipline and the sense of self-preservation. The author of the *Journal of a Pupil* describes a meeting between Gurdjieff and Crowley, but it is clear that they had nothing to say to one another. He says, 'Crowley had magnetism, and the kind of charm that many charlatans have; he also had a dead weight that was somehow impressive' – that is, Crowley *was* a 'man of power'. 'His attitude was fatherly and benign, and a few years earlier I might have fallen for it. Now I saw and sensed that I could have nothing to do with him.' He does not describe the tea, except to say that Gurdjieff kept a sharp watch on Crowley, and says, 'I got a strong impression of two magicians, the white and the black – the one strong, powerful, full of light; the other also powerful, but heavy, dull, ignorant.' This seems to be a fair estimate.

Gurdjieff's life was controlled, ordered. Perhaps the only quality he shares with most magicians – apart from the natural occult faculty – is the *need* for disciples. The real difference between the mage and the mystic (or saint) is that the saint has no business with other people. On the other hand, Gurdjieff insisted that a group of people can achieve more than one person working alone. Ouspensky himself was interested to discover that his own teaching had the curious effect of *teaching him things he did not know before*. That is to say, his *awareness* deepened as he taught. This may also have been true of Gurdjieff.

Gurdjieff called his method 'the fourth way'. The first three are the way of the fakir, the way of the monk, the way of the yogi. That is, the way of physical discipline, the way of emotional discipline, the way of intellectual discipline. The fakir treats his body as the circus ringmaster treats the performing animals; the monk concentrates on prayer, on achieving *samadhi* through deep love and devotion; the yogi tries to work directly with consciousness, expanding it by certain exercises and disciplines. Gurdjieff sometimes called his fourth way 'the way of the cunning man'. But essentially, it is a way of *knowledge*; scientific knowledge. Man must set out to *learn*, and accept nothing on trust. (This explains why teaching was so important to Gurdjieff and Ouspensky.) How does this differ from the way of yoga? I might put it this way. At school I learned to solve mathematical problems by means of log tables or formulae like the binomial theorem; but as often as not, I could not work out the logarithm of a number myself without the tables, or explain to someone how the binomial theorem was invented. So there is a million miles of difference between a clever schoolboy who comes top of the class in mathematics, and a mathematical prodigy like Bertrand Russell who was devouring Euclid for pleasure at the age of nine. The difference is that Russell becomes a *creative* mathematician, while the brilliant schoolboy remains merely a competent calculator. Gurdjieff's problem was to convince his pupils of this: that loving and continuous efforts put into 'the work' will not only give a man a new degree of freedom, but will make him a *creatively* free personality, while the fakir, the monk and the yogi remain somehow statically free.

All the emphasis in his work is laid on the idea of being. He insists that most people do not exist, or hardly exist at all: they are little more than wisps of vapour held together by a body. Asked whether there is life after death, Gurdjieff replied that such wisps of vapour do not survive because there is hardly anything to survive. Asked whether there is such a thing as destiny, Gurdjieff replied that only a person with essence has a destiny; other people are merely subject to the law of accident.

At its simplest level, Gurdjieff's 'work' is an attempt to gain control of one's own life rather than being a leaf tossed around by the wind. At the beginning of the 1914 war, Ouspensky was impressed by the sight of a lorry loaded with crutches – crutches for limbs that had not yet been blown off. Such a sight raises the immediate question: But cannot something be *done* about it?

Gurdjieff's reply would strike a social reformer as pessimistic. Nothing can be done, because a war is a situation in which several million machines fight several other million machines, 'reacting' helplessly to one another. A criminal or a sex maniac often argues that he was carried away by an 'irresistible impulse', and this is precisely why criminals are among the lowest members of the human race. We are *all* carried along to some extent; the highest type of human being would be the one who is not a mere leaf in the gale of his emotional reactions. The aim of the 'work' is to *put on weight*, psychic weight, until you are a heavy stone rather than a leaf, and the wind cannot move you.

In her book *The Unknowable Gurdjieff*, Margaret Anderson describes how an intellectual woman writer spent only a day at the Prieuré, asking intellectual questions all the time. The Gurdjieff pupils naturally ignored her request to 'put it in a single phrase', although one of them did say, 'It is a method for preventing your past from becoming your future.' The woman left in a state of spiteful annoyance, having decided that the whole thing was a bluff. Fourteen years later, Margaret Anderson met her again, and realised that she had not changed in the least. Every word and every gesture was *predictable*. Her past had become her future, in spite of her intellectuality.

On the other hand, the very title of Margaret Anderson's book – *The Unknowable Gurdjieff* – underlines the chief fault of the 'Gurdjieff movement' (which still exists). Her contention is that Gurdjieff is so profound as to be ultimately unknowable. It was J. G. Bennett, one of Ouspensky's most brilliant followers, who coined the phrase. Gurdjieff is undoubtedly the greatest 'magician' dealt with in this book; but he is not beyond human understanding. Neither is he uniquely original. In his essay 'The Energies of Man', William James talks about the phenomenon of 'second wind': why, on some days, we feel dull and washed out, 'as though a sort of cloud weighed upon us', and why this 'cloud' can often be dispersed by deliberately driving yourself to painful effort. The exhausted runner gets second wind, proving that he was not exhausted after all. James also speaks about neurasthenic patients, to whom life has become a whole series of insurmountable obstacles, and how a psychiatrist jars them out of it by forcing them to make efforts, which at first are agonising, and then are succeeded, quite abruptly, by a feeling of relief. James is pinpointing the problem Gurdjieff deals with, and prescribes precisely the same course of actions, 'shocks' or abnormal efforts. What is more, James is more deeply concerned with the problem of *why* our minds get narrower and narrower, until life is a series of obstacles; Gurdjieff nowhere analyses this important problem. Again, in the preface to *Back to Methuselah*, in a section headed 'And the greatest of these is self-control', Shaw emphasises that this is the difference between a man and an animal, and in the play itself, he tries to show human beings who have gradually achieved this higher degree of self-control. Shaw goes further than Gurdjieff in believing that this higher degree of self-control would prolong human life indefinitely. That Gurdjieff died at the age of seventy-six is evidence that he had not acquired a high degree of this self-control. (Kenneth Walker warned him a year before that he was eating and drinking too much, and would soon be dead if he did not stop; Gurdjieff ignored him.)

Gurdjieff was a very great man; but he was not unknowable – neither was his system an unsurpassable ultimate in human knowledge. There are even vital matters upon which he was relatively ignorant. Let me try to define these.

The most important realisation of all is Husserl's recognition that human consciousness is *intentional*. As I go through conscious, everyday life, I am unaware of the amount of *deliberate work* I am putting into 'living'. So much of life seems to 'just happen', so much seems to be 'given', that I get into a habit of thinking of myself as a passive object, acted upon. This is as absurd as if I tried to write with a pen *without putting any pressure on the nib.*

Ask yourself why a holiday often produces an increasing state of 'positiveness', of optimism and well-being and the feeling that life is immensely interesting? Because the change makes you *put more interest* into the act of consciousness, of seeing and doing. Why did Sartre feel so free during the war when he might be arrested at any moment? Because the danger made him keep *alert* – that is, put more interest into seeing and doing. Normal consciousness is shy and lazy and mole-like, hardly putting any effort into living. We allow habit to tempt us into devaluing experience. It is too easy to forget the values we have fought for. Why does Paris feel such ecstasy as he lies naked beside Helen for the first time? Because he has fought and plotted and schemed for this moment, and now it has arrived, he means to savour it to the last drop. But unless he is a very remarkable person, he will be taking her for granted when he has made love to her a thousand times. We have to live 'close up' to life, to see it from a worm's-eye view, and we *forget* the wider bird's-eye view.

What can be done about this 'forgetfulness of existence' (to borrow Heidegger's phrase)? At the end of *All and Everything* Beelzebub tells his grandson that what man really needs is an 'organ' by which he can be constantly aware of the exact date of his own death. This would stop men wasting their lives as if they were immortal. This solution is precisely the same as the one offered by Heidegger in *Being and Time*: live with a constant awareness of death.

The injunction is useful, but not very helpful. Hemingway, for example, tried to live up to it, and still died a pathetic alcoholic.

To grasp the meaning of intentionality is to grasp the solution. Every moment of 'intensity consciousness', every 'Paris-in-Helen's-arms' moment, gives us a clear glimpse of the very simple answer.

Our normal more-or-less-bored state of everyday consciousness arises from the habit of devaluing the world. Instead of saying 'How fascinating', we yawn and say 'That's old stuff ...' But the law of intentionality says that the less you put into perception, the less you get out. And it becomes a vicious downward spiral.

There is, however, an important point without which this cannot be fully understood. If someone were to ask me to do a crossword puzzle, I might reply, 'No, crosswords bore me.' If he then said, 'But this is a special crossword puzzle. Its solution will tell you exactly where a million pounds worth of gold is buried in your back garden,' my whole attitude would change – provided of course, I believed him, or even half believed him.

The Paris-in-Helen's-arms moment reveals the *objective* meaningfulness of the world. It also reveals that consciousness need not be so barren. Everyday consciousness tends to be narrow because we have to take a worm's-eye view of life if we are to be efficient. But we make it worse by a dull, passive, discouraged attitude towards it. It is like having a capacious bag, and using it only to carry a single pencil. In moments of intensity we realise that far more can be *got into* consciousness – other times, other places. There is no good reason, for example, why I should not remember my whole childhood as vividly as Proust remembered *his* when he tasted the madeleine dipped in tea.

Man's trouble is not so much the narrowness of his consciousness (which is important and necessary) as that he lives perpetually on a far lower level of *value* than the universe merits. Poetry, music, sexual delight, holidays, disappearance of crisis, can raise him momentarily to a higher level. But since he is ignorant of the fundamentally *intentional* nature of his response to existence, he tends to fall back into passivity and forgetfulness. At present, his 'devaluing tendency' is unconscious. First of all, he must grasp his 'devaluing tendency' consciously. Then he must begin a conscious, disciplined process of revaluation.

I must emphasise that everything depends upon understanding the intentional mechanisms of consciousness. Once these are grasped you are working in the daylight. Until they are grasped you are fumbling in the dark.

Gurdjieff's remarkable achievement was to understand that most of our limitations are arbitrary, due to habit. William James says, 'There seems no doubt that *we are each and all of us to some extent victims of habit neurosis* ... We live subject to arrest by degrees of fatigue which we have come only from habit to obey. Most of us may learn to push the barrier further off, and to live in perfect comfort on higher levels of power.' James instances an officer in the Indian mutiny who performed astonishing feats of endurance when the lives of many women and children were at stake. Now, there can be no doubt that all of us would live on a far higher level of vitality if we could choose more interesting and adventurous lives. But the whole point of civilisation is to rob life of the element of danger and risk, and we cannot have it both ways. Gurdjieff's discovery was that this is not a real setback. We are intelligent creatures with minds, and we can devise disciplines that are as exciting as any physical danger. These disciplines can make our evolution – which has so far been a matter of accident and natural selection – conscious and deliberate.

An interesting problem arises: the black-room problem. If a human being is placed in a completely black and silent room, his mind is totally destroyed in a matter of days or weeks.

The reason is obvious. Even when surrounded by physical stimuli, our value sense gets eroded too easily. We let ourselves sink into the downward spiral. It is even more so in the black room. Man's habitual negative, devaluing tendency now has the run of his mind, unchecked by sudden bonuses of delight or glimpses of misery and danger that restore the sense of reality. It is like placing a man with a persecution complex among people who *do* rather dislike him.

Man's sense of values is sick and enfeebled. However, this statement should not be taken as an excuse for cultural despair. To diagnose our 'original sin' as clearly as this is to already be within easy marching distance of the solution.

Now, it is certain that a Gurdjieff pupil could stand the black room longer than the average person, simply because the neurotic tendencies to self-pity, egoism, destructiveness, have been partly erased. But since the Gurdjieff system depends so much on 'exercises', on 'work' in a purely physical sense, the black room would present a very formidable obstacle. The only final answer to the black room is to develop the 'value muscle', the ability to 'pull back' and take a bird's-eye view. Man becomes godlike not merely through effort, but through values. Gurdjieff's Corsican brigand may possess 'essence', but that is only the first requirement. Intelligence, imagination, creativity, are equally important. And these spring into being from the value sense.

How is all this connected with 'occult faculties'? At this point, the answer can be stated with some degree of precision.

Faculty X is a vivid sense of the reality of other times, other places. I possess a book of pictures of Cornwall as it was a hundred years ago, and to look at the old cobbled streets of Penzance or St. Austell produces in me a kind of shock of wonder, like catching the breath with delight. Suppose we discovered some method of taking the mind back into the past, so that I could see the cobbled street in three dimensions and hear the people who walked along it in those days. Suppose someone could invent some occult method whereby I could actually be present at the execution of Charles I, or watch the boy Mozart playing his own concerto to Marie Antoinette, or glimpse the face of Jack the Ripper as he walks under a street lamp. The sense of wonder would now be so intense, the mental energy aroused so enormous, that I could never be the same person again. Deeper levels of my being would be permanently shaken into life, never to fall asleep again. For having glimpsed such wonders, I could never sink back into my previous state of un-wondering sloth.

This new sense of wonder would be quite different from Ouspensky's strange excitement during the three weeks that he became 'telepathic'. Ouspensky's telepathy *happened to him*; this intensity would be something *I do myself*. I would control it, by my knowledge.

Ouspensky declared that during his telepathic period, he could clearly *see* the futility of violent methods of achieving anything. Gurdjieff's anonymous pupil said he could instinctively feel that he should not get mixed up with Crowley. The 'psychic radar' begins to operate when the mind overflows with energy, and the mind overflows with energy when its perception of values is clear and intense. The achievement of any degree of Faculty X would animate all the so-called psychic faculties, the red end of the spectrum. These occult powers should be a function of the sense of purpose. This does not mean that *all* the occult faculties would wake up – only those that are important. For a man with a strong sense of purpose, the faculty for avoiding accidents is important, certainly more important than telepathy. Gurdjieff's faculty was apparently inoperative when he drove from Paris to Fontainebleau that day.

I am reasonably convinced that we could, at this point in our evolution, deliberately develop a great many faculties that have so far been accidental. I will give only one example of this. The following is an account of an experiment in will-power conducted by a group that included Professor M. Welford, who teaches psychology at Leicester University. Professor Welford writes:

> In my early twenties I was systematically reading-up as much as possible on chiromancy, divination by means of playing cards, and telepathy. A group of four, all at Leicester University College (as it then was), all young men, and all closely

associated for several years at school – and as obsessed bridge players – were involved in the experiment. The fourth person I can't remember, but the second was a friend I had known for five or so years (and who eventually shot himself) and the third was a typically volatile, fluent and amiable Jew, with whom I had very considerable success in fortune-telling by cards and palmistry.

(1) a series of cards was dealt, face up, on a table, while the 'receiver' was out of the room. The transmitters agreed which card was to be chosen, and brought the subject into the room. He would hold his hand loosely over the cards (eyes shut or open) and allow his hand to be moved towards the cards at the transmitters' directions which was given by a series of carefully pre-arranged sequential directions piecemeal, very like 'talking a plane down' when the pilot is incapacitated or blinded by fog.

(2) In a room roughly ten feet by ten feet, and full of furniture and other articles (ashtrays, trinkets, pipes, books on shelves and window sill), the transmitters would sit, having decided upon the objective to be reached while the receiver was out of the room. A typical programme would be: 'Pick up the pipe on the coffee table and place it to the left of the vase on the window sill.' The receiver was brought in, and disoriented while blindfolded, and then 'guided' to the target piecemeal, movement by movement (as described in [1] above), as though directing a machine. E.g. 'turn left – stop – move forward – stop – lower left hand – move to right – grasp – lift –' and so on.

The receiver emptied his mind and remained poised but passive. The transmitters concentrated on projecting the 'orders' as powerfully as possible. The atmosphere was tense, exciting and strangely still. Exhaustion usually followed.

The chief difference between this and Rhine's experiments with cards is that Rhine's assistants were trying to transmit images, pictures, while Professor Welford's group were trying to transmit orders, impulses. And here it was not a statistical matter – how many times the receiver guessed right – but a matter of immediate and visible results. There is no 'magic' involved, only a faculty that we all possess. This explains the mindreading part of the demonstrations of Gurdjieff's pupils; intense work had got them all 'in tune', awakening their 'receivers'. It also explains the 'miracle' of telepathy between Gurdjieff and Ouspensky. In an ordinary group of more or less sceptical people, the telepathy would not be successful because of a lack of concentration and conviction; the highly complex Gurdjieff exercises broke down this barrier of indifference.

The question of why his pupils suffered no damage when they all fell off the stage is even more interesting. If I am deeply and powerfully concerned to perform some action *perfectly*, or to avoid something that I very much want to avoid, I draw a deep breath, so to speak; I prepare to *pour* energy into the task. In doing most jobs, my boredom level is fairly high. If I am tightening a nut on a machine, I may waste a great deal of energy because I am not willing to get up and readjust my position until I am at the best angle for gripping it with the spanner. In most of my actions, I decide in advance how much energy it is worth putting into it, like a mother telling a child, 'Don't spend more than five shillings …' Gurdjieff's aim was to force his pupils to pour energy into their dancing, not to economise in any way, to aim at absolute perfection. The vast amount of effort turned the dancing into an instinct, and when instinct is operating powerfully, the chance of accident is immediately diminished. It is almost as if the stores of poised energy create a psychic armour.

The achievement of Gurdjieff was to raise such matters as these from the realm of 'magic' and the occult to the realm of scientific common sense. He did this by creating a framework of psychological knowledge big enough to embrace them all. His influence has not yet made itself felt; but when it does, he will be seen as an innovator of the same rank as Newton, Darwin or Freud.

This section on Gurdjieff would not be complete without some mention of Subud, the 'religion' that was embraced by Gurdjieff's chief English follower, J. G. Bennett. For it was Bennett's assertion that Subud was the logical end-product of the Work, and that its founder, Pak Subuh, was the forthcoming Avatar, the Awakener of Conscience, who is described in *All and Everything* under the name Ashiata Shiemash. It is true that Gurdjieff's Ashiata is described as having lived near ancient Babylon; but Bennett convinced himself that it was intended as a hint of the coming Messiah. In his book *Concerning Subud* he also describes travels in the East, and meetings with sheiks and holy men who all foretold that he, John Bennett, was to become the English John the Baptist of a new Saviour. This is no exaggeration; Bennett apparently believes that Subuh is 'the second coming', heralding the end of the present age in earth history.

Subuh, who was born in 1901 in Indonesia, came to England in 1957, and was installed at Bennett's home, Coombe Springs, where a flourishing movement soon sprang up. The film star Eva Bartok, a former Gurdjieff pupil, came there shortly before Subuh's arrival, suffering from an internal complaint that necessitated a serious operation; she was pregnant and expected to lose the baby. Subuh's wife administered the *latihan*, a form of meditation, to her, without spectacular result. After nineteen days, when Miss Bartok was about to enter the hospital for her operation, Subuh himself took a hand. Bennett describes the bedroom as 'charged with energy that annihilated all personal feeling', and says that those present had a telepathic experience of fear and physical pain, slowly displaced by growing faith in the power of God. Afterwards Subuh declared that

Miss Bartok would not need an operation; her doctors verified this, and the baby was born normally. The resulting publicity helped to spread Subud throughout the Western world. But Bennett's hope that all Gurdjieff's followers would join Subud was frustrated. Many of them felt, understandably, that the essence of Gurdjieff's system was its logical, scientific nature, and that Subuh, whether a genuine Avatar or not, had nothing whatever to do with it.

The essence of the method called Subud (Bennett denies that it is a religion or a belief) is the latihan. What is the latihan? It is an 'opening up' of the mind that permits divine energies to perform their work of transformation. Followers of Subud have to be initiated into the latihan by a 'helper', and at first it has to be 'taken' in a group. Later, after the practice has been established, the latihan can be taken at home. Each latihan lasts about half an hour, and followers of Subud practise it about three times a week.

The essence of the latihan is *inner stillness*, the opening of the heart to *meaning*. It would seem, then, that it is simply another name for the basic mystical experience. For example, Powys's ability to somehow enter into the essence of trees and rocks was a form of the latihan. It is not an exercise or a form of prayer; the only 'action' involved is the initial act of submitting the mind to the force, which should thereafter produce a kind of chemical reaction on the soul.

The latihan is not only the basic mystical experience; it is also the basic poetic experience. Wordsworth begins the *Intimations of Immortality* ode by describing a state of inner confusion and discouragement; he then opens his mind to nature, deliberately induces positive consciousness, until he can write 'and I again am strong'. Subuh, a greater spiritual dynamo than Wordsworth, can apparently initiate this state in other people and transmit his own 'positive consciousness' directly. Bennett points out that the latihan differs from ordinary meditation or relaxation exercises in that it does not lead to drowsiness; like Gurdjieff's exercises, it makes the mind more awake. Poetry has this same effect, like adding a pinch of yeast to grape juice; an inner ferment begins, a *cleansing* process.

The latihan, then, is one of the basic forms of mystical discipline, perhaps *the* basic form. The importance of the 'helper' should be clear; the starting point of the latihan is the transcendance of the usual self-division, and this is difficult for a self-divided person without help, without a feeling of definite purpose induced by someone else. For the same reason, it is more difficult to hypnotise yourself than to allow yourself to be hypnotised.

Nevertheless, it must be stated clearly that latihan is *not* the logical consummation of Gurdjieff's exercises. Gurdjieff aimed at a strengthening of man's 'true will'. His starting point was that there is something *wrong* with man, as there might be something wrong with any machine – a car or a watch, for instance. The first necessity is to understand the machine. This is not the way of the monk, the fakir or the yogi, but the fourth way. Gurdjieff calls it 'the way of the cunning man', but it might just as accurately be called the way of the engineer, the man who understands the machine. Subuh's way is essentially the way of the saint or monk, the opening of the soul to God. It is the way of Ramakrishna, of Sri Ramana Maharshi, of Sri Meher Baba, and it has found a more recent exponent in the Maharishi who gained so much influence over the Beatles. It is difficult to see how Bennett, who had known Gurdjieff since 1920 and who regarded him as the most remarkable man he ever met, could arrive at the conclusion that Subud is a direct continuation of the Work. It is an important alternative road, leading in the same direction; but it is not at all the same thing. Gurdjieff was aiming at a kind of 'yoga for the West', at utilising the typical Western qualities – scientific analysis, intellectual precision, practical ability, driving energy – for *psychological* purposes. Subud is essentially a religious method. Gurdjieff himself would have viewed it with the warmest approval; but it would not have taught him anything he did not already know.

Bennett himself apparently came around to this opinion; he left Subud four years after joining.*

---

* Andrew Haydon, a Subud member, gave me the following information: 'He [Bennett] felt the latihan was not enough and wanted to practise Gurdjieff exercises. On asking Pak Subuh's advice, he was told that it was his choice, but Subuh felt that it was unnecessary for further work, and asked Bennett to retire as a helper. But the final breach was over a clash of personalities on a committee dealing with practical needs of Subud.'

PART THREE

MAN'S LATENT POWERS

ONE
WITCHCRAFT AND LYCANTHROPY

I have mentioned already that in the occult tradition women are regarded as evil. In numerology, the female number 2, which represents gentleness, submissiveness, sweetness, is also the Devil's number. The Hindu goddess Kali, the Divine Mother, is also the goddess of violence and destruction. Women tend to 'think' with their feelings and intuitions rather than with the logical faculty. A female assessment of a situation or a person is likely to be more accurate and delicate than a man's, but it lacks long-range vision. One might put it crudely by saying that women suffer from short-sightedness, and men from long-sightedness; woman cannot see what lies far away; man cannot see what is close. Thus the two are ideal complements. The association of woman with evil arises from the situation in which the female assumes the male role, when a short-term logic is applied to long-term purposes. William Blake portrays the situation in his 'prophecy' *Europe*. Los is the male god of poetry, the sun and time: his consort, Enitharmon, is inspiration, the moon and space. But although they are the ideal 'man and wife' in eternity, they often fail to understand the other's nature in the realms of time. Blake seems to believe that 'female reason' came to dominate Europe soon after the Crucifixion, and continued to do so for 1,800 years, until the revolutions in America and France reasserted the healthier, *more impersonal* masculine will. But as a result of this female domination, all the less pleasant aspects of Christianity came into being – the idea that sex is sinful, sickly schoolmarmish notions of virtue and of eternal reward in 'an allegorical abode where existence hath never come'. Creativity and adventurousness are stifled, for the female obsession with security makes them seem dangerous. Whether this situation is evil in itself, it certainly creates evil; the revolt of men like Sade and Crowley is the violent male reaction against this stifling female idea of goodness, and the triviality and spite that are its negative aspects. According to Blake, Christianity became a negative and female religion, a kind of landlady's religion of prohibitions and 'thou shalt not'.

If all this is true, if Blake and the occult tradition are correct in their view of women, the result is a *completely new insight* into witchcraft. Why do we always think of witches as women? The word applies to both men and women; but the idea of a man with magic powers conjures up a picture of a wizard or warlock, someone like Merlin or Tolkien's Gandalf, or perhaps Lytton's serpentine magician. The word 'witch' arouses visions of women on broomsticks, stirring cauldrons with toads and henbane, or offering obscene homage to the Devil. Why this association of ideas?

At this present point in human history, evolution is aiming at Faculty X. Human beings are partly animal; we are tied down to the present moment, like cows. But we also have a remarkable capacity that is not possessed by any other animal. Consider that passage in Dickens's *Christmas Carol*, where Scrooge thinks about himself as a schoolboy, remaining behind in the schoolroom and reading the *Arabian Nights* with its visions of far cities and sultans' palaces, Ali Baba and Sinbad. In such a moment he realises how far his own life has gone wrong. The human mind was meant to take wings and escape the mere present moment, soar away to other times and places.

If intelligent and vital people are denied this 'holiday' from everyday triviality, their creativity takes the form of an increasingly burning resentment against the life that imprisons them, and against its moral standards. But it is not only the human imagination that craves release; the human will needs aims and desires to stimulate it.

The result can be seen in the famous case of Isobel Gowdie, the Auldearne witch, who suddenly decided to 'confess' in 1662, and created a legend that retained its power for centuries. She seems to have been an attractive, red-headed girl who married a Scottish farmer, whose remote farm was near Auldearne, in Morayshire. Life on the farm was dull and she remained childless. Her husband was an unimaginative boor. Isobel claims that she met a 'man in grey' on the downs, and that he baptised her as a witch that same evening in Auldearne church; this was in 1647. She went on to describe witches' sabbaths – with covens of thirteen witches – and her power to transform herself into a hare or cat. Significantly, her confessions are obsessively sexual; she had intercourse with demons at the sabbaths, and with the Devil himself; she even had intercourse with one of her demon lovers while lying in bed beside her sleeping husband. The sperm of these demons, she said, was icy cold. The Devil used to beat the witches, who were, of course, naked.

The picture that emerges is of an imaginative and highly sexed girl being driven half insane with frustration, until she evolves a whole fantasy about the powers of evil. It is a basically masochistic fantasy, in which she is baptised in her own blood, sucked from her by the Devil, and then is beaten and sexually possessed by demons. Eventually her whole life is dominated by this fantasy, which is reinforced by her strong masochistic tendencies; her sexual perversion develops until it becomes a kind of sweet poison, made all the more potent by the rigid Presbyterianism, the Calvinistic Bible-thumping, that dominates the community. She can have no doubt that she has sold herself to the Devil, for the fantasies that possess her day and night are diabolic: the Devil swishing his scourge through the air, and violating her with his immense, scaly penis, which produces pangs as excruciating as childbirth, yet at the same time indescribably pleasurable. After fifteen years of this, she is suddenly seized by a terrifying, an almost unthinkable idea. It is like the urge that drives some men to expose themselves to children, or that made Peter Kürten go back to the scene of his sadistic murders to savour the horror of the crowd. Why not make her fantasy *public*, shatter everybody by telling them what has been going on in their stolid, sabbatarian community? The idea appeals to her masochism. And why not involve other people in the community? – not, of course, out of spite, but merely because this would make it altogether more convincing. She confesses; the fantasies pour out of her in the six weeks between April 13 and May 27, 1662, and she gloats as she sees the shock they produce. They strip her and examine her minutely for devil's marks, and she finds it all deliciously voluptuous.

It is not clear what happened to her, or to the other Auldearne witches she implicated: one authority says she was burned, and her ashes scattered; another declares that the records are incomplete, and that she may even have been released eventually. Probably she was executed. The case is remarkable chiefly for its detail – that is, for the fertility of Isobel Gowdie's imagination.

But this is not to assert that all witchcraft from the thirteenth to the eighteenth centuries can be reduced to terms of imagination and sexual frustration. We know that a large percentage of people have occult powers, and always have had. These range from the ability to 'read character' to the ability to cause 'supernatural' happenings. Such powers are more common among simple country people than people in towns. We also know that when the will and imagination are gripped with some strong idea, reality often seems to conform to it. There is no need to doubt Crowley's story about the dictation of *The Book of the Law*; it is equally certain that it was not the god Ra-Hoor-Khuit who contacted Crowley's wife and finally dictated the book to Crowley. Crowley's belief in magic was a deeply emotional obsession, the channel through which springs of creativity found their way to the surface. There are plenty of parallel stories of 'inspiration', from the prophecies of Nostradamus to those of Joanna

Southcott at the end of the eighteenth century. Joanna Southcott's reputation as an inspired prophetess ended in 1814, when she announced to the world that she was about to bear Shiloh, the Prince of Peace, in a virgin birth, and actually showed every sign of pregnancy – except a baby.) Strindberg's autobiography *Inferno* reveals the way that an obsessional conviction about supernatural powers seems to cause events that confirm the reality of the powers. According to William Blake, a firm persuasion that a thing is so makes it so. Once the imaginative pattern has been set, and has stirred the creative obsessions, the rest follows.

It is worth noting that most of the male magicians we have considered in this book have been, on the whole, benevolent: Agrippa, Dee, Cagliostro, Saint-Germain; even Crowley asserted that his magic was strictly white, and there are no stories of his harming anyone through magic. When Powys discovered that he was harming people with his psychic blasts of anger, he became 'neurotically benevolent'. Women, on the other hand, are more prone to personal obsession, and, in the case of 'natural witches', to the misuse of their power – not for personal advantage, but for the disadvantage of their enemies.

All this suggests a theory of witchcraft that differs fundamentally from the two hypotheses that have so far held the field. The first, represented by the 'Reverend' Montague Summers, holds that the Devil and his hordes of demons are real, and that witches are genuinely in their power. The second, to be found in Rossell Hope Robbins's *Encyclopedia of Witchcraft*, holds the whole thing to be a delusion. The view I am here suggesting is that witches and their powers are real enough; the Devil and his powers are not. Montague Summers, that dubious and romantic clergyman, is not entirely wrong when he says that most witches deserved what they got. This is not to say that they deserved to be tortured and burned; no one does. But many of them may have believed themselves to be servants of the Devil. It is significant that all the 'magic' described by Isobel Gowdie is inspired by malice: the witches dug up the body of an unchristened child and buried it in a farmer's manure heap to destroy his crops; stuck pins in a clay image to destroy the local laird's children; ploughed a piece of land with a miniature plough drawn by toads to make it sterile. Whether or not Isobel Gowdie really took part in such magical exercises is a matter for argument; but there can be no doubt that many witches did. And in many cases, perhaps the majority, their spells must have been effective.

There is another aspect that must be taken into account. In small, lonely communities, superstition itself can create a kind of 'magical ether' that may increase the effectiveness of the spells. This can be seen in a case of our own century, the 'witchcraft murder' of Charles Walton in February 1945 at Lower Quinton, Warwickshire. Walton, a seventy-four-year-old labourer, was found under a willow tree lying on his back, with a pitchfork driven through his throat and into the ground; a cross had been slashed on his ribs, starting at the throat, and the bill-hook that had been used was still lodged between his ribs. Fabian of the Yard, who was sent to Lower Quinton, at first had every reason to suppose it an open-and-shut case, since if Walton had enemies, everyone in the district would know about it. Fabian's team took four thousand statements and sent twenty-nine samples of clothing, hair and blood to the police laboratories for analysis, but all to no effect. People were tense and unhelpful. They waited a whole day to question a man, who peered out of his door and remarked, 'He's been dead and buried a month now – what are you worried about?'; then shut the door firmly.

The inference seems fairly clear: many people in the area know about the murder, and are not telling. Lower Quinton is in the middle of witchcraft country. A few miles away, on a high ridge, stand the Rollright Stones, a monument probably as old as Stonehenge and undoubtedly the site of witches' sabbaths in the past.

It is a country of wooded hills, winding roads, limestone cottages and sinister names: the Devil's Elbow, Upper and Lower Slaughter; Meon Hill itself, in whose shadow the murder occurred, has a sinister reputation for witchcraft.

Donald McCormick, who wrote a book on the case, recounts a conversation in the village pub, in which one of the locals stated that he knew of two witches still living in the area, while another claimed that he had married a witch, who later left him. The dead man himself had had a reputation for second sight. As a boy he had seen a black dog for three nights on Meon Hill; on the third night it had changed into a headless woman, and the following day his sister had died. He bred large toads, and there were many of them in his garden when he died. Fabian himself saw a black dog running down Meon Hill, followed closely by a farmhand; but when he asked the farmhand about the dog, which had run out of sight, he went pale and asked, 'What dog?' That afternoon, the police car ran over a dog. The next day a heifer died in a ditch – the second since Fabian's arrival.

The murder of Charles Walton is still unsolved, but it is possible to make an 'informed guess' as to what happened. Walton was believed to be a witch, and his solitary habits increased the impression. He bred toads – an odd occupation – and a local inhabitant told Donald McCormick that he sometimes harnessed the toads to a toy plough and allowed them to run in fields. Isobel Gowdie claimed to have used the same method to cause poor crops. The farmers certainly *had* poor crops the previous year; many of them complained to Fabian about it. It was 1945, the last year of the war, and for the past five years, southern Warwickshire had been exceptionally isolated – no foreign visitors to Stratford or Evesham, low gravity beer in the pubs and not much of that. In 1944 there was a bad harvest; 1945 began warm and wet; but *somebody* believed that Charles Walton and his toads would ensure another bad harvest. Southern Warwickshire has its own traditional methods of dealing with witches. There is a belief that if a witch is 'blooded' – made to bleed – her power is neutralised. In 1643 Parliamentary forces saw an old woman walking on the river at Newbury, and shot her, after slashing her forehead to drain her of her power. (Robbins suggests she was walking on stilts.) In 1875, seventy years before the murder of Charles Walton, a village idiot named John Haywood became convinced that an old woman called Ann Turner (or Tenant) had bewitched him; he pinned her to the ground with a hay fork, and slashed her throat and chest in the form of a cross with a bill-hook; this was only a few miles away from Lower Quinton – in Long Compton.

That Walton was a witch is doubtful; that locals believed he was is almost certain. To understand the murder, and how presumably decent people could condone it, one has to make an effort of imagination, and carry the mind back to the warm January and February of 1945, in an out-of-the-way village suffering the effects of five years of war. Walton was killed on February 14, which was not only St. Valentine's day and Ash Wednesday, but the day on which the ancient druids made their sacrifices. (The druidic date was February 1, but their calendar was two weeks behind ours.) The sacrifice was for ensuring good crops. Walton's murder was probably planned months in advance, perhaps the previous autumn, and the date fixed. It seems fairly certain that it was believed that his 'familiar' was a black dog, for a black dog was found hanged on Meon Hill a few days after the murder. And if anyone experienced remorse about the killing of a harmless old labourer, it probably vanished as the year advanced, and the harvest *was* bad, in spite of the good weather. McCormick quotes one old countryman: 'Crops should have been the best ever with early spring. There's no reason for bad crops. Summat's wrong when crops go against nature.'

The Lower Quinton case is not particularly interesting for its own sake, but it enables us to understand something about witchcraft in Europe. For the 'European witch-craze' (as Professor Trevor-Roper calls it) is a baffling phenomenon that has never been satisfactorily explained. The Middle Ages did not believe in witches; the official Church doctrine, expressed in the 'canon Episcopi', stated that anyone who believed in witches 'is beyond doubt an infidel and a pagan'.

The change in attitude began in the eleventh century, with the rise of a powerful sect called the Cathars. Doctrinally speaking, the Cathars were descendants of the Gnostics and Manichees, whom we have discussed in an earlier chapter. They believed that the Old Testament God was a demon, that the world was the creation of the Devil, the Monster of Chaos. They accepted that salvation could be obtained through Jesus, but apparently insisted that Jesus had not actually been crucified on the cross; his earthly form was a phantom, for how could the essence of goodness be embodied in matter, which is evil by nature? Like the Manichees, and the later Russian sect called the Skoptzi, the Cathars believed in sexual abstention, on the grounds that anything that prolongs physical existence is evil.

The amazing thing is that Catharism gained such immense and widespread acceptance. Originating, apparently, in the Balkans in the tenth century, they spread slowly over Europe. A sect of Cathars near the town of Albi, in southern France, became known as Albigenses. In various forms, this new Gnosticism spread as far as Constantinople (where they were known as Bogomils) in the east to northern France, where the first Cathar bishop was established in 1149. By the end of the twelfth century there were eleven Cathar bishops, six of them in Italy itself.

No doubt the misery and disease of the late Middle Ages helps to account for this success. Prosperous countries are content with an easy-going religion; where there is poverty and misery, something sterner and darker is required. This is why Presbyterianism later made such an appeal in Scotland, and why Methodism flourished among the bleak and rainy villages of Cornwall. There is also something in the Manichean doctrine that appeals to the deep romanticism in human nature, the feeling that this world is hell and that man's happiness lies in 'another sphere'.

When Count Raymond VI of Toulouse became a Cathar, the Pope decided it was time to do something about it, and called for a crusade. To many knights and barons of France, this was like being asked to a boar hunt; it would only last forty days (the standard specified time for a crusade), and there was sure to be plenty of rape and plunder. A vast army swept down on southern France, and whole towns were wiped out, heretics and faithful alike. Simon de Montfort (father of the De Montfort who formed the first English parliament) was the most brutal of these plunderers, and stayed on in Toulouse, causing a bloody war. The infamous Inquisition was born in Toulouse in 1229, and its most determined agents were Dominicans, who travelled around and reported heresy wherever they found it. The full story of the horrors of these years has never been told, and perhaps this is just as well. The Church was determined to stamp out this heresy at all costs. A cynic might take the view that cardinals dining on roast boar and good Italian wine felt threatened by the bleakly ascetic doctrine of the Cathars. At all events, the Cathars and Albigenses were bloodily stamped out; the few survivors withdrew to remote mountain villages, as did the Waldenses under similar persecution more than two centuries later. Dominic (later St. Dominic), founder of the Friar Preachers, who established his headquarters at Toulouse in 1215, vowed to dedicate himself to destroying Catharism by 'persuasion addressed to the heart and mind', but his secret police – for this, in effect, is what the Dominicans were – soon got the bit between their teeth, and saw Devil worshippers in every shadow. It was these Dominican 'preachers' who discovered that the Devil had changed his tactics; having lost his army of Cathars, he set out to create a secret army of evil old women, dedicated to his service and to the secret overthrow of the Church. Possibly they were not entirely wrong. Extreme cruelty and persecution is bound to produce an 'underground' dedicated to destroying the oppressors through secret means. And so we must think of the earliest 'witches' as a Cathar Resistance Movement, a kind of heretical I.R.A. This is not as absurd as it sounds. It is true that there had always been witches – in small numbers. But they were, so to speak, private practitioners. The Cathars believed that the God who created this world is a demon who had managed somehow to wrest his power from the Ultimate Godhead, which is far above such trivialities as creation. This is a comfortless doctrine. To whom are you to pray when in extreme distress? Not to the Supreme Being; why should he care what one of his fallen aeons has been up to? That leaves the wicket aeon himself, the Monster of Chaos, Old Nobodaddy. Perhaps some of the Cathar women, who had seen their husbands and children murdered, *did* pray to the Monster of Chaos for revenge. Two centuries later the Cathars no longer existed, but the Dominican inquisitors were fulminating against witches, whom they called Waldenses, who met together at Sabbaths or 'valdesia'. (The Waldenses were also called Vaudois after the Alpine village of Piedmont where they established themselves.) In the Pyrenees, witches were called *gazarii* (obviously derived from Cathars).

The Dominicans kept asking the Church to give its official sanction to the crusade against witches, but the Church, remembering that the 'canon Episcopi' denied the existence of witches, held out for another century. Then, unfortunately, a superstitious paranoiac, John XXII, became pope. He was convinced that his enemies were plotting to kill him by magic; so it was he who finally gave way to the Dominican demand that 'sorcery' itself should become a crime, quite apart from the question of heresy. This was in 1326, in

Super illius specula. It is significant that this same Pope had declared heretical the Franciscan doctrine of the poverty of Christ; anything to do with poverty was suspect.

Even so, the witchcraft epidemic began slowly. It started in the Pyrenees and the Alps – the territory of the Albigenses and Waldenses. The pattern emerged very early. In the first secular trial for witchcraft at Paris, in 1390, a woman called Jehane de Brigue was accused of sorcery by a man she had cured when on the point of death! Jehane explained that she was not a witch, but that she had simply used charms, taught to her by another woman, which included 'In the name of the Father, the Son and the Holy Ghost' – from which it is clear that the fundamentals of 'charming' have not changed in six hundred years. Under threats of torture, confined in an icy and filthy dungeon over the winter months of 1390–1391, Jehane finally 'confessed' to having a demonic familiar named Haussibut. Ruilly, the man she had cured, told the court that Jehane attributed his illness to bewitchment by his mistress, by whom he had two children. Under threat of torture, Jehane confessed that it was actually *she* who had bewitched Ruilly, at the request of Ruilly's wife, Macette, who wanted to pursue a love affair with the local curate. Macette was then also arrested, tortured on the rack, and confessed. It is not explained why Jehane bewitched Ruilly, and then saved him. Jehane and Macette were executed. There were undoubtedly many cases in which white witchcraft – the natural application of 'occult powers' – led to torture and execution. In 1618 a vagabond named John Stewart had a vision of a ship sinking near Padstow in Cornwall; he was in Irvine, in Scotland, at the time. When the news came that a ship from that area *had* sunk at Padstow, Stewart was arrested and charged with second sight. A woman who had muttered curses about someone on board the ship was arrested as a witch, and under torture she implicated two other women and the eight-year-old daughter of one of them. The child confessed that she had seen a demon dog that emitted light while her mother and Margaret Barclay, the accused witch, moulded wax figures. Margaret Barclay was strangled and burned, although she withdrew the confession that had been forced from her under torture. One woman she accused died after a fall from the church roof; she was escaping from the belfry. Another 'confessed', but withdrew her confession, and declined to forgive the executioner at the end. John Stewart managed to strangle himself with his own bonnet ribbon while awaiting execution.

After the publication of the *Malleus Maleficarum* (already referred to on page 345) in 1486, the new science of printing played its important part in the expansion of the witch craze. Any writer with a vivid imagination could reckon on achieving a degree of celebrity with a description of the demons evoked by witches. Professor Trevor-Roper points out that the majority of these 'demonologists', who caused such incalculable suffering, were harmless, scholarly characters; Rémy was a Latin poet and a historian, yet when he died in 1616 he had sent nearly three thousand victims to the stake. Boguet and De L'Ancre are both mild scholars and Latinists.

The witch craze was so horrible and so widespread that the human imagination cannot encompass it. We find it hard enough to envisage Hitler's murder of six million Jews over less than ten years, so it is quite impossible to imagine a campaign of torture and murder lasting for four centuries. It is true that witchcraft executions were on a smaller scale than the Nazi atrocities; but it must also be remembered that each witch was tortured individually. Rossell Hope Robbins seethes with moral indignation: 'The record of witchcraft is horrible and brutal; degradation stifled decency, the filthiest passions masqueraded under the cover of religion, and man's intellect was subverted to condone bestialities that even Swift's Yahoos would blush to commit. Never were so many so wrong, so long ...' But after reading a dozen or so pages of his *Encyclopedia of Witchcraft*, the student feels that these words err on the side of mildness.

For atrocities on this scale, there can be no single cause. It was partly political; countries came first under Protestant, then Catholic domination and when the Church wanted to punish a Protestant populace, it sent Dominican inquisitors. Catholic reconquest caused witch purges in the Rhineland, Flanders, Poland, Hungary. It was the Church's way of taking revenge on Protestants. It could also be used by a prince or baron as a method of taking revenge on rebellious subjects – a safe way, that would not lead to further rebellion.

But the psychological motivations are equally important. The beginning of the witchcraft craze corresponded with the Black Death and the Hundred Years' War. When people are oppressed and miserable, violence becomes a psychological necessity. And violence is always associated with sex, particularly in puritanical and repressive societies. Witches were made to confess to intercourse with demons, and minutely examined for the witch's mark (a spot on the body insensitive to pain). Franz Buirmann, appointed witch-seeker by the Prince-Archbishop of Cologne in the 1630s, apparently used his position to seduce women who would otherwise be inaccessible. A Frau Peller who refused his advances was the wife of a court assessor. Buirmann acted swiftly; she was arrested one morning and was under torture by the afternoon; the hairs were all shaved off her body and head, and the torturer's assistant was allowed to rape her while he did this. Buirmann, looking on, stuffed a dirty piece of rag into her mouth to stifle her cries. She was burned alive in a hut filled with dry straw, all within hours. Buirmann had been placed in a position where he could act out sexual-sadistic fantasies. It sounds like an episode from a novel by Sade.

With all the talk of demons, witches' sabbaths, torture, the smell of burning flesh, witchcraft became a darkly alluring obsession. Its equivalent nowadays would be the particularly violent sex crime, which is nearly always followed (a) by imitative crimes, (b) by confessions from cranks. The murder of Elizabeth Short, the Black Dahlia, in Hollywood in 1949 was followed by six similar murders in the Los Angeles area and twenty-nine confessions to the crime. The particularly horrible nature of the murder – she had been hung upside down, tortured, then cut in half – had made it front-page news for weeks. Lonely men, brooding on the newspapers in stuffy lodgings, finally decided that it would be worth the risk. And in the same way, lonely, bored women like Isobel Gowdie, living narrow and comfortless lives, found the lurid pamphlets about intercourse with demons terrifying and increasingly fascinating. And since they believed that the air is full of invisible demons, it would not be long before they were convinced that their wishes were known to the Devil. A sexual dream would confirm this.

But why did all this happen after the Reformation? The Middle Ages may have been the ages of faith, but they were also ages of war, poverty, disease and belief in demons. All the conditions were there. Except one. The peculiarly human condition of *freedom of imagination*. In the Middle Ages, this had not yet evolved. Man plodded about his daily tasks, and did not see far beyond them. What happened after 1450 was not only a social but an evolutionary change, one of those periodic ripples that seem to run across the human race like wind across corn. Gilles de Rais, a baffling figure, signals its arrival in the first half of the century. His spirit wants to burst its prison, to commit crimes that no man has ever dared to commit, to establish contact with the Devil himself, to become the wealthiest and most powerful prince in Christendom. The peasants whose children he stole were patient, plodding, cowlike creatures who finally forgave the torturer. But during the next century, the unrest that drove Gilles to demonism reached the peasantry, and was amplified by their boredom. Why, asks Dr. Margaret Murray, are the accounts of the witches' sabbaths so remarkably similar, whether they come from France in the fourteenth century or Austria in the fifteenth or Spain in the sixteenth or the Netherlands in the seventeenth? Why is the Devil always described as a huge, goatlike man (or, less frequently, as a huge toad) who speaks with a hoarse voice 'like someone speaking through a bung hole', who makes the witches kiss his nauseating behind, and whose embraces are icy cold? It must be more than mere imagination, or some of the stories would vary, making the Devil hot, or sweet-smelling, or pleasant-voiced. Montague Summers takes this to be evidence for the reality of the Devil; Dr. Murray does not go as far as that; she only suggests that the sabbaths *were* a reality, and that the Devil was probably impersonated by an enormous man wearing a mask and a cloak, and who used an artificial phallus that squirted cold milk. She certainly has no doubts that such sabbaths took place, and neither have even the most sceptical historians. What happened then, it seems, is that the witch craze produced a hysteria that created precisely what it was trying to destroy. This is a peculiarity of the human imagination that is only now being recognised by psychology: that when it is denied active, creative expression, it seeks out any powerful stimulus, no matter how terrifying or negative. The human mind craves movement, any movement. Sartre describes, in one of his early books, the case of a young girl who had been educated in a convent, and then married to a professional man. Left alone all day in the apartment, she began to experience an absurd compulsion to go to the window and summon men like a prostitute. Goethe has a classic story called *The Honest Attorney* in which a virtuous young wife, left to herself, finally becomes insanely obsessed with the idea of comitting adultery – precisely because the idea would normally horrify her. What is at work here is the same principle as in hypnotism. Boredom or emptiness allows the mind to fill up with unused energy, producing a painful sensation like an overfull bladder. An excessive degree of self-consciousness is created. This produces the usual effect of preventing the instincts from doing their quiet, unobtrusive work; the feelings are frozen. The desire for strong feelings – the most basic of human psychological needs – becomes a kind of panic; guilt and misery are preferable to boredom. What the mind really craves is the sense of vastness and wide-openness, of other times and other places, of *meaning*. What the inquisitors were doing was to create a body of myths and symbols that were *supercharged* with meaning and that consequently exercised an overwhelming gravitational pull on imaginative and bored women. The Devil literally finds work for idle hands and idle minds.

I would regard this as the most important element in the witch craze, more important than ecclesiastical politics, or even the persecution of harmless 'natural mediums' and clairvoyants. And if this is so, then it must also be recognised that the inquisitors and judges were not as blameworthy as we now believe. They knew little or nothing about the symptoms of sexual hysteria. And the symptoms of demonic possession were often very convincing indeed, as we have seen in the case of the Loudun nuns. Let a modern liberal rationalist try to put himself in the position of some ordinary parish priest of the seventeenth century, reading a pamphlet describing the possession of a girl called Elizabeth Allier. When the nun, who is twenty-seven, goes into fits that any modern psychologist would recognise as sexual hysteria, and speaks in a hoarse, masculine voice, the Dominican friar François Farconnet repeats exorcisms and questions the demons; they give their names as Orgeuil and Boniface and explain that they entered the girl on a crust of bread when she was seven, and intend to stay there until she dies. The incantations continue over Saturday and Sunday, and finally, when the friar exposes the sacrament and orders, 'Go, then, miserable creatures,' the girl twists into extreme convuisions, her tongue sticks several inches out of her mouth, and the devils declare hoarsely, 'I go, Jesus.' From then on (we assume), the girl is cured. No one is hurt, no one is tortured or burnt; it is just a case of a holy friar freeing a poor girl from two evil spirits. Would even the most sceptical parish priest be justified in doubting that demons really do exist and that he should warn his congregation solemnly about the importance of saying grace before meals, and making the sign of the cross over anything you happen to eat between meals? Moreover, although it is true that many witch confessions are produced by torture, many of them are voluntary, by women who know that their only chance of saving their souls from eternal punishment is to allow their bodies to be committed to the flames.

It is true that there are sceptics – like Johann Weyer (the pupil of Cornelius Agrippa), Reginald Scot, Friedrich von Spee, himself a witch-judge who changed his mind about witches – but how can one take such people seriously? They assert that witches do not exist, that accounts of spells and second sight are old wives' tales, when everyone in the parish knows that the grocer's wife dreamt of her father's death the very night it happened and that horses shy up at the spot where two witches were buried in unhallowed ground. This kind of scepticism is really an incapacity for religious feeling; it would be capable of dismissing the virgin birth itself as superstition.

And, of course, such reasoning is fundamentally correct. But the evidence for demons and witches' sabbaths *was* of a kind that no reasonable, unbiased mind could reject. Some witches undoubtedly could blast crops with their curses. Thousands of old women could foretell the future and charm warts. What the inquisitors – the sincere and religious ones – failed to see was that all this is no reason for torture and burning; that, in fact, the torture and burning have the effect of increasing the grip of the Devil on the human imagination.

We must also take into account the stimulus of torture and

burning on the human imagination. Man has not been civilised for long – a few thousand years. Christianity does not come naturally to the strong and enterprising. Prosperous merchants and stolid farmers long for peace and a quiet routine, but the born soldier dreams of winning glory in battle, and the born criminal dreams of burning cities and raping the women. It is significant that the really violent manifestations of the witch craze date from the *end* of the Hundred Years' War (1453), almost as if it were a substitute for war. And they come to an end in the latter part of the eighteenth century, just before the new era of wars and revolutions plunge Europe into mass bloodshed again.

The witch craze rolled over Europe in a series of waves, each one followed by a period of calm. There were times when the persecutions became so bloody that there was a spontaneous revolt against them. By the beginning of the sixteenth century, the craze was reaching a climax, particularly in Germany, where its most sadistic manifestations seem to occur. If the appointed inquisitors showed themselves too tolerant, they were likely to be burned as witches. This happened to Dietrich Flade, who was Vice-Governor of Treves and Rector of the University; he exerted his influence to restrain witch hunters, and did his best to get condemned witches banished instead of burned. His leniency opened him to the suspicion of being on the Devil's payroll, and a witch hunter named Zandt literally 'framed' him by bribing condemned witches to shout that Flade was a witch himself. (In exchange for this, they were strangled before being burned.) In spite of his eminent position, Flade was arrested, and finally strangled and burned. In Bamberg in 1628, Vice-Chancellor George Haan was similarly accused of being too lenient with witches, and he and his wife and daughter were all burned, in spite of an order from the Emperor himself for their release. In the case of Haan, this might be considered poetic justice, for he had been one of the accusers of the burgomaster Johannes Junius, whose last letter to his daughter before his execution is one of the most moving documents in the history of witchcraft:

> And then came also – God in highest heaven have mercy – the executioner, and put the thumbscrews on me, both hands bound together, so that the blood spurted from the nails and everywhere, so that for four weeks I could not use my hands, as you can see from my writing.
>
> Thereafter they stripped me, bound my hands behind me, and drew up on the ladder. Then I thought heaven and earth were at an end. Eight times did they draw me up and let me fall again, so that I suffered terrible agony. I said to Dr. Braun: 'God forgive you for thus misusing an innocent.' He replied: 'You are a knave' …
>
> Now, my dearest child, you have all my acts and confessions, for which I must die. And it is all sheer lies and inventions, so help me God … If God send no means of bringing the truth to light, our whole kindred will be burned …

Other eminent citizens were tried and executed; their property, valued at 220,000 florins, went to the Bishop-Prince, Gottfried Johann von Dornheim. (His cousin, bishop of Würzburg, burned nine hundred witches between 1623 and 1631). Tortures included crushing by heavy weights, the ladder (a form of strappado, dislocating the arms from their sockets), baths in boiling water (which killed six people in 1630), forcible feeding on herring cooked in salt, and then refusal of water, needles driven into the quick of the nails up to their heads and – perhaps most effective for procuring confessions – prevention of sleep for days or weeks. Punishments included the cutting off of hands, and the tearing off of female breasts with red-hot pincers. Eventually the Emperor Ferdinand himself was forced to intervene and order that the trials be made public and confiscation of property stopped. The Bishop died in 1632; his cousin had died the previous year. Many of these epidemics of sadism ceased only when the instigator died a natural death.

The prince-bishops of Würzburg and Bamberg were brutal sadists. Other notable witch hunters have been callous rogues. England's most infamous figure, Matthew Hopkins, 'the witch-finder general', claimed to have 'the Devil's list of all the witches in seventeenth-century England' when, in fact, he had only read two books on demonology. Like Senator Joe McCarthy, he set up a committee, and was soon travelling from end to end of England to examine witches, charging large sums of money for his services. He was an unsuccessful lawyer who became a highly successful prosecutor for fourteen months. He declared that the sign of a witch is that she has a familiar – a demon in the form of an animal – and the deposition against his first victim, Elizabeth Clarke, of Manningtree, Essex, included his sworn statement that he had seen four imps in the form of a dog, a polecat, a greyhound and a black demon with her. (His assistants also swore to having seen them.) His methods of extorting confessions were less horrible than those of the German witch-finders, but equally effective: he threw trussed-up women into duckponds to see if they sank, forced victims to sit cross-legged on a low stool until they confessed. He also made them walk continuously until their feet blistered. This form of torture demanded relays of 'walkers'. A seventy-year-old parson, John Lowes, of Bury St. Edmunds, was kept awake for several nights, and run backwards and forwards across the room at top speed, until he confessed to all the accusations. He retracted the confession later, but was hanged all the same.

The Civil War was still raging, and the tension found outlet in these witch trials. When a dozen people had been condemned and hanged everyone had an illusory feeling that everything would be better from now on. There were mass trials, and in 1645 nineteen people were condemned and hanged at Chelmsford. Four of the thirty-two accused had already died in prison, and several others went back there for a long time. At Bury St. Edmunds, eighteen were hanged. Hopkins was responsible for sixty-eight executions in Suffolk alone during 1645. But by the following year, moderation had begun to assert itself. A Huntingdon clergyman, John Gaule, preached against him when he heard that Hopkins intended to begin a witch hunt there; Hopkins blustered and threatened, but his authority collapsed as quickly as it had been established; he retired to his home in Manningtree and died of tuberculosis later in the same year. He had been responsible for some hundreds of deaths in fourteen months. The repeal of the witchcraft act in 1736 – so that the punishment ceased to be death – put an end to the witchcraft craze in England, although witches continued to be 'swum' for fifty years or more after it was repealed.

To read straight through a large number of accounts of witch trials, as I did before writing this chapter, is to begin to feel slightly insane. The accounts of tortures lead one to wonder whether human beings are ultimately redeemable; for every saint, the human race has apparently produced a hundred murderers capable of the last degree of viciousness. And the sheer absurdities to which so many of the accused confessed add a discordant note of farce to the tragedy. Yet oddly enough, the final impression is one of pity – a pity that embraces the accusers and accused. The human mind was never intended for narrowness, and when it is trapped, it becomes trivial and vicious. The real tragedy of Suffolk in 1645 is not that Matthew Hopkins hanged a hundred or so innocent people, but that human beings in general were so demoralised and devitalised that they could accept it. Village communities had become stagnant pools that bred pestilence.

This is difficult for us to understand in the age of big cities and mass communication; we cannot imagine that kind of stagnation, in which the human mind had no escape from itself except through malicious gossip about the neighbours. Towards the end of the eighteenth century, all this began to change. The dividing line between that world of the past and our own world was an event that occurred in the year 1740: the publication of a novel called *Pamela*. The statement sounds absurd; but consider it more closely. Before Richardson wrote *Pamela*, the chief form of 'escapist' entertainment that issued from the printers was the pamphlet, usually with a title like *A True Narration of the Horrible Crime Committed at York by So and So*. The novels of Defoe, issued a quarter of a century before Richardson began to write, are enlarged pamphlets containing 'true narrations'; *Pamela* is a novel told in letters, a description of a virtuous girl's resistance to her would-be seducer, and it is very long. Its reader could enter the world of another person's life, and stay there for days on end.

If we imagine Jane Austen, or the Brontë sisters, being brought up in a country vicarage in the year 1700, we can immediately grasp the import of what has happened. No doubt Jane Austen would still have read Homer and Dante and Shakespeare, and become a literate and articulate young lady; but it would not have been the same; the classics are bound to be a little remote. But Richardson's *Pamela* and *Clarissa*, Rousseau's *Julie* (or *The New Héloise*), Goethe's *Werther*, were entirely different; this was rich food for the emotions as well as the intellect. The human mind was like a bird when the cage has been left open. Novels poured from the presses; Byron's *Corsair*, Scott's *Lady of the Lake*, were Romantic novels in verse. The plays of Shakespeare and Dryden and Sheridan could only be seen in the big cities; but these small pocket-sized volumes could penetrate to the remotest corner of the remotest county. It is true, of course, that most people could not read; but that is a minor point. Anyone with enough intelligence to want to read could learn to do so – the children of farm labourers as well as vicars.

The creating of 'other worlds' became a major industry in the nineteenth century; novelists like Balzac, Hugo, Dickens, Trollope, set out to create an actual world as rich and complex as the real world. We take this for granted; we are used to having a choice of 'alternative worlds', from Tolstoy and Flaubert to the latest soap opera on television. And we know that there were literary masterpieces long before Richardson: Chaucer, Malory, Montaigne, Cervantes, Rabelais, Boccaccio. We forget that there were so few of them, and that they were known only to scholars. Life in the fifteenth century was dull and repetitive for everybody, from the lord of the manor and the local priest to the ploughman and the shepherd. There were probably as many imaginative and sensitive people as there are today – at least in proportion to the population – but they had no alternative to letting themselves grow as dull as their surroundings. The only touch of the bizarre or unusual that entered their lives was when a pedlar offered a pamphlet containing the confessions of witches, or when the vicar warned them to avoid an old crone who could turn herself into a hare.

For five centuries or more, the human spirit was starved of an essential vitamin, a vitamin that the Church of the Middle Ages had been able to supply, although in smaller quantities. Man not only possesses a capacity for 'otherness', for turning away from his own narrowness to the greater world that surrounds him; he possesses a raging appetite for it. I see the witchcraft craze as a direct consequence of this vitamin starvation. When the broad current of Romantic culture began to satisfy the appetite, witchcraft suddenly became a thing of the remote past.

This conclusion is reinforced by one of the most remarkable novels ever written on the subject of magic and witchcraft, Valery Briussov's *Fiery Angel*, which Prokoviev turned into his most powerful opera. Briussov was of the Russian symbolist school in the early years of this century; and although he remained in favour after the Revolution, his early work was frowned upon. Prokoviev's opera *The Fiery Angel* is still unknown in Russia.

The novel tells the story of a soldier, Rupprecht, who returns from South America in the 1530s, at the time when Agrippa and Paracelsus were famous throughout Germany. In a small tavern where he stays overnight, he hears a woman moaning and crying. In the next room he finds a young girl named Renata, who calls him by his name before she collapses in convulsions on the floor, screaming that she is possessed by devils. Rupprecht finally calms her and makes her lie down. She then insists on telling him her story: how, at the age of eight, a golden-haired angel, flaming as if with sunshine, came to her nursery and played with her. His name was Madiël. For years they played together, and he told her that she was destined to be a saint, and encouraged her to undertake harsh ascetic exercises. Renata was willing enough to be a saint, but she also wanted to be the bride of Madiël. And one night, after she had made a determined effort to seduce him, he left her. Some time later, he appeared to her in a dream and told her to expect to see him again, in human form, in two months. And in exactly two months a young nobleman called Count Heinrich visited her family. She seduced him, and they eloped to Heinrich's castle on the Danube. But after two years' happiness, he left without explanation, and had not been back since. Renata had been searching for him ever since, tormented by demons.

Rupprecht spends the night lying beside her on the bed, in perfect chastity, and the next morning takes her away with him. By this time, of course, he is in love with her. But when he tries to get her into bed, she has hysterics and tells him that she must save herself for Count Heinrich. And Rupprecht is by now so enslaved that he agrees to help in the search. The novel turns into a powerful clinical picture of Rupprecht's masochistic relation with Renata.

She persuades him to rub himself with a witches' ointment and visit a sabbath. Briussov's description of the sabbath is authentic, and should be read by anyone who wants to understand what witches were supposed to do on these occasions. The ointment makes him dizzy, and he lies down. Then he finds himself flying through the air on a goat. Half an hour later, they land in a valley between two hills. He is immediately surrounded by frenzied naked women. They carry him to the foot of a wooden throne, on which the Devil is seated:

> The Seated One was enormous in stature, and made like a human being down to the waist, like a hairy he-goat below; his legs ended in hoofs, but his hands were like human hands, so was his face human, red, sunburnt like an Apache, with large round eyes and a medium beard. He had the appearance of being not more than forty years old, and there was in his expression something sad and rousing compassion; but this feeling disappeared as soon as one's glance rose above his high forehead to see, emerging distinctly from his curly black hair, three horns; the two smaller ones behind and the larger one in front; and round the horns was placed a crown, apparently of silver, that emitted a soft glow like the light of the moon.
>
> The naked witches placed me before the throne and exclaimed: 'Master Leonard, he is new!'
>
> Then sounded a voice, hoarse and devoid of inflection as though he who spoke was not accustomed to pronouncing words, but strong and masterful, which addressed me saying: 'Welcome my son …'

Rupprecht has to denounce God, Jesus and the Virgin, then kiss the Devil's hand and his rump. The hand, he notices, has all its digits of equal length, including the thumb, and crooked like a vulture.

There follows a dance among huge toads, snakes and wolves, and then a meal, with coarse food and poor wine, at the end of which

Rupprecht is drawn into the wood by a young witch and seduced. He wakes up and finds himself on the floor of his room with a sensation like a hangover. But he has not learned the whereabouts of Count Heinrich.

The detail of the coarse food and poor wine seems curious; why should the Devil give his servants cheap food, when he is, after all, 'the prince of this world'? On the other hand, if the sabbaths really took place as described, the witches themselves would have to provide the food, which would be of poor quality. The Devil remains seated, and sounds human enough, apart from his enormous stature; could he be a human being, wearing trousers made of goat-skin and hoofs on his feet? Parts of Briussov's novel are taken from the actual trial of Sister Maria Renata von Mossau, who was tortured, beheaded and burned in 1749 near Würzburg. Her confession contains the usual lurid sexual details – more than usual, if anything – so Briussov was justified in placing so much emphasis on the sexual aspects of the case.

The fine seventh chapter of the novel contains an account of Rupprecht's visit to Bonn to see Cornelius Agrippa. There can be no doubt about the authenticity of the material here, and it is interesting to note that Agrippa dismisses magic as childish nonsense, and insists that philosophy and mystical contemplation are of greater importance. By the time he published his *Occult Philosophy*, he regarded it as a juvenile work.

Back in Cologne, Renata finally allows Rupprecht to possess her; but it is a highly unpleasant night in which she is feverish and insatiable, and obviously thinking about someone else all the time. Briussov wallows in his hero's masochism.

After this, Renata persuades Rupprecht to challenge Count Heinrich to a duel – he has finally appeared in Cologne. Rupprecht agrees, much against his will, and begins to realise that Renata is not the innocent maiden she makes out. She had seduced Count

Heinrich, who was a Rosicrucian, and dedicated to chastity, and then persuaded him to practise black magic. He now hates her. No sooner has Rupprecht forced Heinrich to agree to a duel than Renata changes her mind, and makes Rupprecht promise not to harm him. The consequence, inevitably, is that Rupprecht is badly wounded, and Renata has to nurse him back to health. After this, she seems cured of her obsession with Heinrich, and gives herself to Rupprecht. Then she decides she has to be a saint, leaves him again, and goes to a nunnery.

Several chapters of the novel are devoted to an encounter between Rupprecht and Dr. Faustus (with Mephistopheles, of course). And at last, Rupprecht finds the convent where Renata has taken refuge. The demons have entered her again, and all the nuns are having convulsions. She is arrested by the Archbishop of Trier, and subjected to torture. Eventually she dies in Rupprecht's arms before she can be brought to the stake. Prokoviev makes the scene of the possessed nuns the most hair-raising in the opera.

What makes this novel so remarkable is that Briussov has set out to try to understand what really took place during the 'witch craze'. Renata is a hysteric, driven by sexual craving; but she also knew Rupprecht's name as soon as she saw him. She possesses certain occult powers. But Count Heinrich is certainly not Madiël, the fiery angel, and the whole search is futile. The book is about people who are sucked into the whirlpool of their own fantasies, and whose fantasies take on a strange reality because of the subconscious forces that have been set in motion. For a writer of the pre-Freudian era (the book was published in 1907), it is a remarkably convincing *tour de force* of abnormal psychology. Being a poet, Briussov had an inkling of the strange truth about witches: that the powers of the human mind are far greater than we understand, and that they can be released by *symbols*. Is it an accident that 'Master Leonard' wears a crown that emits a *moony* glow – the moon, the White Goddess, symbol of the powers that lie below the everyday personality?

There is a story by the Japanese writer Akutagawa that states clearly the point I have been making throughout this book; it is called *The Dragon*. A priest wants to take revenge on a certain monastery; the monks are always making fun of his red nose. So by a pond near the monas¬tery he sets up a board with the sign: 'On March the third, a dragon shall ascend from this pond.' It has the expected effect. The news spreads, and on the third of March, there are vast crowds waiting at the side of the pond. The monks are deeply embarrassed; they are aware that when the dragon fails to materialise, they will somehow get the blame. As the day drags on, the crowds stretch for miles around, and the priest begins to regret his joke. Gradually he becomes affected by the atmosphere of intense expectancy, and finds himself staring eagerly at the calm surface of the pond. Then, quite suddenly, clouds appear in the sky; there is a tremendous storm; and in the midst of the thunder and lightning, the smoky shape of a dragon flashes out of the pond, and ascends to the sky. Everyone sees it.

Later, when the priest confesses that it was he who set up the notice board, no one believes him.

The most important statement in this story concerns the eager, tense expectancy of the crowd, which affects even the priest who painted the notice board. He knows there is no dragon; yet the telepathic pressure of thousands of believers finally compels his own instincts into tune with it. There is no self-division. And the psychic pressure is like the rhythmic tramp of feet that cracked the walls of Jericho. First, the clouds form out of the clear sky. Then the storm, the visible symbol of the release of tension; something is about to happen. To call the dragon a mass hallucination would be to miss the whole point. It is a mass *projection*, a spontaneous manifestation of the forces of the subconscious. Like all magic.

The power of mass telepathy to 'make things happen' is known to most primitive people. The late Negley Farson told me on several occasions how he had seen a Liberian witch doctor conjure rain out of a clear sky.

My neighbour Martin Delany, whose own curious powers of divination I have described in the appendix to my *Rasputin*, described an equally strange occurrence. The local Nigerian witch doctor assured his company that torrential rain, which had lasted for weeks, would stop for two hours during a party given for the staff. The rain stopped immediately before the party was due to start, and started again immediately after the party ended.

In the same appendix I have recounted at length the curious story of the band-saw that belonged to the same company. A hen had flown into the band-saw, and the Negro workers declared that this was because the god of iron had to be propitiated. Mr. Delany refused to have this ceremony performed because it involved decapitating a puppy dog. Two days later, another hen flew into the band-saw. Not long after, it was necessary to make some slight adjustment to the saw; although the electricity was switched off at the mains, the saw began revolving and cut the manager's hand badly. Engineers spent hours checking the saw and the mains, and agreed that it was completely impossible that it could have 'switched itself on'. Finally, the saw blade 'peeled' one day as it was cutting a log, and a twisted ball of metal struck the operator, killing him. Mr Delany finally agreed to the sacrifice of the puppy, after which the accidents ceased.

If we dismiss the idea of coincidence, there seem to be two possible explanations. Either the witch doctor himself was able to cause the accidents by some form of psychokinesis, 'the evil eye', or the fear exerted by the mass of workers caused them. Mr. Delany ruled out the witch doctor, who was apparently a kindly old gentleman. The second hypothesis certainly fits in better with what we have been saying. Most people have experienced some thing of the sort on a smaller scale: a tense, nervous feeling that something is going to go wrong, followed by a minor catastrophe.

Probably the best way to come to an understanding of the witches of Europe is to study eye-witness accounts of modern African witchcraft. Harry B. Wright's *Witness to Witchcraft* offers some curious examples. He describes the 'thunder dance' in Abomey, West Africa, as an example of 'the strange rapport that seemed to exist between the primitive practices of these people and the forces of Nature itself ...' A tall native danced with intricate contortions, swishing a long dancing stick in the air. 'The day had been bright and clear when the dance started, but suddenly I looked up and the heavens were overcast.' The prince, however, told Wright: 'It will not rain, because we will not permit the rain without the rain dance.' And it didn't. Again, it is notable that Wright felt himself participating in the frenzy caused by the dance. When the dance came to an end, the sky cleared again.

Wright also describes a 'leopard dance' that is perhaps less difficult to explain. A tall, beautiful native girl danced by the light of fires, and Wright's African companion asserted that he could see leopards. Wright could only see shadows around her. The natives appeared to be following the invisible leopards with their eyes. And then, at the height of the ceremony, three full-grown leopards stalked out of the jungle, across the clearing, and went into the jungle on the other side; one of them had a chicken in its mouth. 'If I had been put under a trance through some process of mass hypnosis, it was a good one, because I felt otherwise quite sane and normal.' But there is no need to think in terms of hypnosis. Animals are telepathic; under the circumstances, nothing is more likely than that a family of real leopards should look in to see whether the 'mental leopards' were really invading their territory, or whether it was just the natives playing games again. (The chief explained to Wright that they summoned the thunder 'for their own amusement'.)

This suggests at least a partial explanation for two myths that have persisted since the earliest times: the vampire and the werewolf. Montague Summers unearthed so many of them that he was able to devote two large volumes to the vampire alone.

In the post-Freudian period the sexual basis of vampirism and lycanthropy has been recognised. Male sexual desire is generally far stronger than the woman's desire. Nymphomaniacs are rare among women; but almost every healthy male is – in imagination at least – a satyr. The mini-skirt is a tacit recognition of this; that a quite impersonal appetite is aroused in the male by glimpses of a woman's sexual regions. It is difficult to imagine a society in which the men wear short tunics and try to give girls glimpses of their sexual members; not many women would *want* to see them; it would be a sexual depressant rather than a stimulant. Woman, on the other hand, realises that a man may be caught more easily by a glimpse up her dress than by a more subtle parade of her charms. (I was amused by an account of a journalist friend of how he became interested in his wife; they were both in amateur theatricals, and she was climbing a ladder when her tights split, revealing transparent panties; 'I decided there was more to her than met the eye,' said my friend. They have now been happily married for many years.)

This violent, impersonal sexual appetite of the male becomes dangerous if subjected to frustration, and may develop an element of cruelty. Robert Musil's portrait of the sex murderer Moosbrugger in *The Man Without Qualities* emphasises the frustration of the journeyman carpenter who 'sleeps rough' and wanders from village to village, never having the opportunity to satisfy the appetite: 'Something that one craves for, just as naturally as one craves for bread or water, is only there to be looked at. After a time one's desire for it becomes unnatural. It walks past, the skirts swaying round its ankles. It climbs over a stile, becoming visible right up to the knees ...' I have pointed out in my *Casebook of Murder* (1969) how often vagrants like Moosbrugger become sexual killers. The fierceness of the desire may turn to resentment against women. The Birmingham Y.W.C.A. murderer, Patrick Byrne, said that he killed to 'get my own back on women for causing tension through sex'. The German murderer Pommerenke committed his first sex murder in a park after seeing a film called *The Ten Commandments* and convincing himself that women were all evil. (In that case, why rape them as well as killing them?) At the time of writing (1970), John Collins is on trial in Ann Arbor, accused of the murder of Karen Beineman; she was not only raped and strangled, but tortured with some pointed object and with acid.

Psychologists argue that all men have a 'social personality', an obligation to behave in a balanced and friendly manner, and that this may cover a depth of murderous frustration. This applies particularly in young men. (Most sex crimes are committed by men under twenty-five, often under twenty.) Walking down a street crowded with girls on their way to the office, they feel like starving men surrounded by food that does not belong to them. In a woman like Isobel Gowdie, this kind of 'split personality' leads to witchcraft; in a man, it may lead to a form of lycanthropy, in which his 'beast' personality takes over and commits rape. This is the view put forward by the Jungian psychologist Robert Eisler in his classic study *Man into Wolf* (1949). He advances the interesting view that man was once a peaceful, herbivorous ape, living on roots and berries. But man is also an imitative creature, and in his battle against wild animals, a life-and-death struggle, he began to deliberately acquire the ferocity and bloodlust of the wild animal. A modern manifestation of this is the sneaking, fear-tinged admiration that many people have for criminals, particularly violent ones. They feel that violent people need 'taking account of', and that the most effective way of taking account is to generate a certain sympathy.

This view would certainly explain the leopard dance witnessed by Harry Wright, and the cults of leopards and other wild animals in Africa. William Seabrook tells the story of a quiet little native clerk who donned a panther skin with iron claws and killed a girl. The clerk was totally convinced that he *became* a panther periodically, and he told Seabrook that he much preferred a panther's life to his own. The natives of Africa naturally fear the panther and the leopard – far more than the lion or tiger, which rarely become man-killers – and from the most distant times, the response to this fear, on the part of the bolder spirits, was an attempt to achieve some kind of empathy with the killers. The response of primitive man to the cave bear no doubt illustrates the same thing.

In medieval Europe, wolves were the commonest and most dangerous beasts of prey, and the sexual obsessions that drove Isobel Gowdie caused sexually frustrated peasants to identify with wolves. But the most curious question is how far their obsession caused actual physical changes. William Seabrook has a remarkable description of how a Russian emigrée woman meditated on hexagram 49 from the *I Ching* whose meaning is associated with an animal's fur, and with moulting. She imagined herself to be a wolf in the snow, then began to make baying noises, and slaver at the mouth. When one of the witnesses attempted to wake her up, she leapt at his throat and tried to bite it. In the case of Gilles Garnier, executed as a werewolf in 1574, he seems to have carried out the attacks on children either in the shape of a man or a wolf. The charge, drawn up at Dole, alleged that he had seized a twelve-year-old girl and killed her in a vineyard with his hands and teeth, then dragged her along the ground – with his teeth – into the wood at La Serre, where he ate most of her. He so enjoyed it that he took some home for his wife. (This does not indicate that she was also a *loup-garou*; three hundred years later, in the same area, a peasant named Martin Dumollard made a habit of murdering girls that he lured into lonely places, and taking their clothes to his wife. He would say, 'I've murdered another girl,' and then go off with a spade. She seems to have regarded these activities as a sign of mild eccentricity.) He killed a twelve-year-old boy in a wood, and was about to eat the flesh ('although it was a Friday') when he was interrupted by some men. They testified that he was in human form, and Garnier agreed. But he insisted that he was in the shape of a wolf when he strangled a ten-year-old boy and tore off the leg with his fangs; he does not explain how a wolf could strangle anybody. He also attacked another ten-year-old girl – again wearing his wolf-shape – but was forced to flee when interrupted; she died of her wounds. On this occasion, the peasants who interrupted Garnier saw him as a wolf, but nevertheless thought they recognised Garnier's face. He was sentenced to be burned alive.

It is by no means unusual for sex killers to eat part of the body of the victim. Albert Fish cooked and ate parts of a ten-year-old girl, Grace Budd, at Greenburgh, New York, in 1928. Ed Gein, the Wisconsin murderer, ate parts of the women he killed, and also made waistcoats from their skin. (This also brings to mind the fertility rites of the Aztecs, described by Ornella Volta in her book on vampirism, in which the priest first sacrificed a virgin, then skinned her and dressed in her skin to perform the ritual dance.) So Garnier's strange appetite for human flesh need not be taken as evidence that he really became a wolf. But it is impossible to doubt that he entered a trancelike state in which he felt himself to be a wolf, like Seabrook's Russian emigrée. And is it not conceivable that *some* physical transformation did take place, a physical expression of the instinctive forces that erupted from his subconscious? In the Lon Chaney film *The Wolf Man*, Chaney becomes a kind of upright beast, closer to an ape than a wolf. The descriptions of the peasants in the case of Garnier make it seem that this is what they also saw.

The most celebrated European werewolf trial occurred near Cologne fifteen years after Garnier's execution, and is altogether more closely connected with orthodox cases of witchcraft. Peter Stube, or Stumpf, confessed that he had been sexually intimate with a succubus, a demon in female form, for twenty-eight years, and that the demon had given him a magic belt, whereby he could transform himself into a wolf, an enormous, powerful creature. Over the twenty-eight years, Stube committed many murders – the details closely resemble those in the Garnier case – and also made an attempt on the lives of two of his daughters-in-law (which sounds remarkably like sexual jealousy). The sentence passed on Stube was particularly cruel: to have his flesh pulled off with red-hot pincers, and his bones broken with blows of a hatchet, before being decapitated. The fact that Stube was tortured in order to force the confession raises the possibility that the whole thing may have been imagination. The 'magic belt', which he claimed to have hidden in a valley, was not found. The case caused excitement all over Europe.

Montague Summers tells a great many tales of werewolves, in his credulous way, but few of them add anything to what we have already said. On the contrary, it becomes quite clear that most of them must be dismissed as inventions and old wives' tales. There is one element common to most of them: someone attacked by a werewolf manages to cut off its paw (or put out its eye, or wound it in the throat); later, a man or woman is found without a hand and confesses to being the werewolf. Olaus Magnus, a medieval chronicler, tells the story of a slave who wanted to convince his mistress that werewolves existed, and came out of the cellar in the form of a wolf; attacked by her dogs, he lost an eye. The next day, the slave was found to have lost his eye. Both Montague Summers and Sir James Frazer (in *The Golden Bough*) tell the story of a huntsman of Auvergne who cut off the paw of a wolf that attacked him; recounting the story to a friend, he discovered that the paw had changed into a woman's hand, with a ring on the finger, which the friend recognised as belonging to his wife. The wife, nursing a wrist from which the hand had been amputated, confessed to being a werewolf, and was executed. Frazer then goes on to tell stories of Chinese were-tigers, were-cats and even were-crocodiles, making it clear that each part of the world has its own variation on the theme. Common to many of these stories is the notion that transformation occurs only at the time of the full moon (the White Goddess again), and that if the hands or feet of the were-creature are amputated, its power is permanently lost. In some accounts, there seems to be a certain confusion as to whether the were-creature (wolf, cat, hare) is a demon or simply a witch.

Werewolves have failed to survive the age of witchcraft, and it is interesting to speculate why this should be so. The answer may be that urban civilisation has no room for this kind of abnormality. The victims of werewolves were generally children, and men like Garnier and Stube may well have felt the need to escape the torments of conscience by convincing themselves that they were victims of a terrible destiny. The modern child rapist is usually so feeble-minded and demoralised that the need does not arise. This may also explain why tales of vampires have retained their hold on the human imagination. It is a rationalisation of a more general and powerful emotion. In every large modern city the police are familiar with the activities of a sexual pervert called the piqueur; this is a man who takes a sharp pointed instrument, an ice-pick or awl, and stabs women in crowds. The woman feels a sudden sharp pain in the thigh or buttock; by the time she has looked around, the man has gone. In most cases the wound is painful but not dangerous; occasionally, when the piqueur has an obsession with breasts, the instrument may penetrate the heart and cause death. To speak of 'sadistic aggression', as the medical textbooks do, is to leave the phenomenon unexplained. All that has happened is that a man or youth with a strong *romantic* fixation on women lacks the necessary courage or indifference to approach them, until the desire becomes a torment. His daydreams of making love to women lack conviction, because he feels he would be rejected. But daydreams of sadistic attacks can be altogether more satisfying because he *can* imagine himself raping a girl. When he drives his ice-pick into the buttocks of a pretty girl in a crowd, he feels that he is taking revenge on her for rejecting him.

This clearly explains the psychology of vampirism. It is a frustrated sexuality turned to aggression. Add to this the fear of the dead and of supernatural entities, and the story takes on a power that fascinates the human imagination. But this is not to assert that vampirism is merely a superstition or a delusion. Examples of it are so well authenticated that it would be absurd to try to maintain a strictly rationalist position. We are again in the realm of the borderland of the mind where strange forces can erupt from the subconscious and take on apparently material shape. Montague Summers cites a case from *The Proceedings of the National Laboratory of Psychical Research*, 1927, in which a young Rumanian peasant girl, Eleonore Zugun, showed 'devil's bites' on her hands and arms. The investigator describes how she was about to take a sip from a cup of tea when she cried out. Marks of teeth appeared on the back of her hand and developed into bruises. A few minutes later she was bitten on the forearm, under her sleeve, and again the teeth marks were deep. Was it a 'ghost', or Eleonore's own subconscious mind, somehow out of control? The question is futile, since we have no idea of what forces *could* exist. No one has ever descended into the subconscious and traced all its corridors. Why should we assert that it was Eleonore Zugun's subconscious mind? If Jung is right and there is a collective subconscious. then it might have been somebody else's mind. Readers of Thigpen and Cleckley's *Three Faces of Eve* will understand this point without difficulty. The book describes how a quiet, well-behaved married woman is completely taken over by 'another self', a noisy, sexy, empty-headed female who loves a good time. This sounds less baffling than it actually is; we all know cases of people who seem to become completely different when drunk. But as one reads the book, it becomes more and more obvious that the 'two faces of Eve' were really two completely different people; it is literally a case of possession, and in the fifteenth century would have been treated with exorcism and perhaps torture. Since Eve finally managed to achieve an integrated personality that united her 'two faces', we can just about accept that 'Eve White' and 'Eve Black' were only two aspects of her personality. But the mind cannot *grasp* it; we can only accept it intellectually. One suddenly becomes clearly aware of the limitations of consciousness, and correspondingly less ready to advance pat explanations for what happened to Eleonore Zugun.

Less celebrated than the Eve case, but in many ways even more baffling, is the story of 'Sally Beauchamp' that disturbed the world of American psychology in the late 1890s. In 1898 a girl named Christine L. Beauchamp approached Dr. Morton Prince of Tufts Medical School; she was suffering from nervous exhaustion. When normal treatment failed, Dr. Prince tried hypnosis. And one day, quite unexpectedly, a new personality emerged under the treatment – a cheerful, brash, noisy girl, who explained she was Sally Beauchamp. Sally was insistent that she was *not* Christine, although she admitted they had the same body. As in the Eve case, this second personality knew all about the first, while the first – Christine – was ignorant of Sally's existence. Sally was bouncingly healthy, and was contemptuous of Christine for being such a weakling. One day, Christine decided to go to Europe for a holiday, but was so exhausted that she went into hospital to regather her strength. Dr. Prince called to find how she was, and was told she was full of energy. He went to see her, and discovered that Sally had taken over. Sally didn't want to lose a holiday in Europe, and was determined to sit in Christine's body until they got on the boat! Dr. Prince managed to persuade Sally that this was immoral, and eventually Christine became strong enough to take the holiday.

In the beginning, Sally always had her eyes closed (because Christine was under hypnosis). Finally, she succeeded in getting them open; and then Christine's life became altogether more complicated. Sally would take over for hours, and Christine would wake up, wondering what she had done during her 'amnesia'.

At this point, a *third* personality appeared – as distinct as Sally and Christine – rather schoolmistressy and sharp. (Sally called her the idiot.) This new personality, who apparently had no name, knew about Sally, and the two loathed one another. Sally learned to read her mind. The three women strove for possession of the body – although it is not entirely accurate to say that Christine strove; she simply got pushed around. Her confusion must have been enormous. One day she decided to get a job in New York. Sally took over and got off the train at New Haven. Sally got a job as a waitress in a dining room. Christine found the job exhausting. The schoolmistress hated it because it was menial. One day, the schoolmistress quit the job and took her wages. She pawned Christine's watch, and went to Boston. Then Sally took over and rented a room rather than return to Christine's flat. When Christine came back, she was baffled to find herself in a strange room in Boston instead of in a hotel dining room in New Haven.

Dr. Prince discovered that Sally and the schoolmistress seemed to have memories of different parts of Christine's life, and the schoolmistress apparently came into existence for the first time as the result of a shock when a man-friend climbed in through her window and tried to kiss Christine. It was all very confusing. Eventually, by hypnotising the schoolmistress, Prince managed to get her integrated with Christine. But Sally had to be bullied and persuaded to go away;

she yelled: 'No, I won't be dead! I have as much right to live as she has …' But she was persuaded eventually. The psychologist William McDougal decided that Sally was not a part of Christine's hidden self, but a completely separate spirit or psychic entity. One is inclined to agree with him.

The closest thing I have seen to a rational phenomenological explanation of this problem occurs, strangely enough, in a work of science fiction called *Forbidden Planet*, by W. J. Stuart, in which a scientific expedition to a distant planet tries to determine why all previous expeditions have been destroyed. The only man who seems to be able to live safely on the planet is an old scientist named Morbius, and he is able to tell them that the other expeditions have been destroyed by a kind of invisible, and apparently indestructible, monster.

Morbius is studying the remains of an earlier civilisation on the planet – beings who had apparently achieved the power to amplify their thoughts, their power of 'intentionality', so that mental images could be projected as an external reality. And at the end of the novel, Morbius realises what has destroyed the previous expeditions. Without even suspecting it, he has also been amplifying the intentional forces of his subconscious mind, his subconscious desire to be left alone on the planet; and this is the 'invisible monster' that has been destroying the previous expeditions.

The book should be read by every student of phenomenological psychology; it may have been intended as fiction, but it probably comes closer to the truth about the human psyche than Freud or Jung.

Now, if this hypothesis is correct, it may explain not only the mystery of vampires, werewolves and poltergeists – which we shall consider in the next chapter – but all so-called 'occult phenomena'. The subconscious mind is not simply a kind of deep-seat repository of sunken memories and atavistic desires, but of forces that can, under certain circumstances, manifest themselves in the physical world with a force that goes beyond anything the conscious mind could command. We are all familiar with certain moments when our conscious personality seems to become more real, more solid and authoritative, and we experience a peculiar sensation of power. Imagine this kind of strength and authority carried through to the far greater forces of the subconscious, and we begin to get a shadowy outline of a theory of the occult that avoids both extremes of scepticism and credulity.

It is because of the lack of such a general theory that most books on vampirism have been so unsatisfactory. Summers mixes stories of the wildest improbability with accounts that have a ring of authenticity. Ornella Volta, one of the most recent historians of the vampire, adopts a medical and anthropological approach, but she fails to establish the connection between sexual criminals like Jack the Ripper and Sergeant Bertrand and the Dracula myths.* She appears to be arguing that strange epidemics of vampirism, such as the one that occurred in Central Europe between 1730 and 1735, are outbreaks of sex crime or necrophilia, when in fact this explanation fails to apply to 99 per cent of the cases cited by Summers, in which the vampires are dead bodies, animated either by demons or by the spirits of their former tenants.

A typical vampire story, recounted in Augustian Calmet's *History of Apparitions* (1746) and repeated in every book on vampires since, is as follows.

In the 1720s, the Austrian empire was enjoying a period of peace, after years of sporadic war against the Turks, and there was a deliberate build-up of troops in the southwest. A young soldier (whose name is given by one authority as Joachim Hubner) was billeted in the village of Haidam, on the Austro-Hungarian frontier.

---

* Her facts are often wildly inaccurate. She states, for example, that Jack the Ripper committed nine murders between 1887 and 1889: in fact, he committed five murders in 1888, then stopped. She asserts that John George Haigh, 'the acid-bath murderer', drank the blood of his victims through a straw. Haigh *claimed* to have drunk blood from a cup, but this was only an attempt to get himself certified insane.

One evening at supper, as he sat drinking wine with his host and the fifteen-year-old son of the house, the door opened, and an old man came in. He sat down at the table, and everyone looked terrified. The old man leaned forward, touched the farmer on the shoulder, then went out.

The next morning the farmer was found dead in his bed. The boy told Hubner that the old man was his grandfather – who had been dead ten years.

Hubner naturally told the story to other soldiers in the regiment; eventually, it came to the ears of the colonel, who decided to have it investigated, since it was spreading alarm among the men. The Count de Cadreras, commander of the Alexandetti Infantry, was instructed to take sworn depositions in the village. Cadreras set up his headquarters in the church, and took sworn depositions from every member of the dead farmer's household. The evidence was so convincing that Cadreras ordered the grave of the old man to be dug up. The body was found to be completely fresh, as if it had only just been buried. On the orders of Cadreras, the head was severed from the trunk.

The commission had been told of other similar cases of one man who had returned three times during the past thirty years, and who had tried to suck the blood of members of his own family. The graves of all these other 'vampires' were opened; all were found to be as fresh as the first one. The villagers asserted that one vampire was so dangerous that they were not contented until the count had the body burned.

The Emperor Charles VI heard about these events, and sent a second commission to investigate. They verified the story of the original commission. In 1730 Cadreras dictated the story to an official at the University of Friborg, and Calmet must have seen this deposition during the next five years, since he states that the events took place 'about fifteen years ago'. Montague Summers claims that the manuscript is still extant.

The story sounds circumstantial enough, although this is, of course, no guarantee of its truth. I cannot find a village called Haidam on the map or in encyclopedias, but this proves nothing, since villages change their names if the frontier moves. Whether true or not – and Summers cites it as one of the best-documented of all vampire cases – it has all the typical features of the vampire story: the walking dead, who can only be destroyed by burning or decapitation (or sometimes by a stake driven through the heart), the attacks on living people that are said to result in the victim also becoming a vampire after his death.

Ornella Volta points out that the body of St. Theresa of Avila remained undecayed in the tomb for a considerable time after her death. Miss Volta mentions 178 years, but J. M. Cohen, in his introduction to her autobiography, contents himself with the remark: 'These mysterious levitations [she floated in the air during prayers] were matched after her death by the mysterious incorruptibility of her body.' Mr. Cohen suggests that this phenomenon of incorruptibility, which seems to occur after the death of so many saints, 'can only be accounted for by some actual change in the physical structure that takes place at the same time as spiritual transformation.' The same may be true of vampires.

The vampire epidemic of 1730–1735 seems to have started at the village of Meduegna, near Belgrade, through a young soldier named Arnold Paole, who returned from active service in Greece in 1727. He told the girl to whom he was betrothed that he had been attacked at night by a vampire in Greece (another country famous for vampire legends), but had located its grave and destroyed it – which should have removed the curse. However, he died, and then was seen around the village after dark. Ten weeks later, after several people claimed to have Seen him, or dreamed about him and felt strangely weak the morning after, his body was disinterred by two army surgeons and the sexton and his assistants. The body still had blood on its mouth. It was covered with garlic, which is supposed to be a protection against vampires, and a stake had been driven through the heart.

Five years later, says Summers, there was an epidemic of vampirism at Meduegna, and this time several distinguished doctors investigated; the medical report was signed on January 7, 1732, by Johannes Flickinger, Isaac Seidel, Johann Baumgartner and the lieutenant colonel and sub-lieutenant from Belgrade. They testified to examining fourteen corpses, all listed and described, including a girl of ten. Only two of the fourteen – mother and baby – were found in a normal state of decomposition, all the others being 'unmistakably in the vampire condition'. It is not recorded what was done, but presumably the corpses were burned or impaled.

Henry Moore, in the seventeenth-century *Antidote Against Atheism*, tells a story of a man with the delightful name of Johannes Cuntius, of Pentach in Silesia, whose corpse was scratched by a black cat as it lay in the deathbed; subsequently, he began to reappear and drink blood. When the body was disinterred, it was found to be 'in a vampire condition', and apparently resisted furiously when it was cut up.

Augustus Hare, the diarist, recounts a vampire story in *The Story of My Life*; it was told to him by a Captain Fisher, and may be taken as typical of the vampire tales of the nineteenth century.

The house called Croglin Grange in Cumberland was let to two brothers and their sister. It stood alone on a hillside. The house was only one storey high, which is perhaps why the Fisher family decided to let it, and find a larger place.

The winter passed peacefully for the tenants, whose name is given in one account as Cranswell. One night in June the moon was so bright that the sister decided to open the outer shutters, although she kept the window itself closed. Sitting in bed looking across the lawn, she was puzzled to see two yellow lights moving among the trees. Soon she realised that they belonged to a man, who proceeded across the lawn towards her window. She rushed for the door, which was close to the window, and saw 'a hideous brown face with flaming eyes' looking at her; at the same moment, she saw that the creature was unpicking the lead of the window frame. She was so terrified that she stood there as it reached in through the window, opened the catch and climbed over the sill. The creature seized her by the hair and bit at her throat; at this moment she found her voice and screamed and her brothers rushed into the room, having broken open the locked door. One brother saw the intruder fleeing over the lawn, but it seemed to disappear in the region of the nearby churchyard.

They took her to Switzerland, and eventually all three returned to Croglin Grange, apparently convinced that the creature had been an escaped lunatic. The winter passed quietly with no more alarms. And then, in the following March, she was awakened one night by the sound of scratching on the window, and saw the brown face looking in. This time she screamed immediately. Her brothers, instead of rushing into her room, went out of the front door, and fired at the figure as it made away across the lawn. It stumbled, then ran on. They both pursued it to the churchyard and saw it enter a tomb. The following day the brothers went to the tomb, accompanied by the servants from Croglin Grange. The coffins were scattered wildly and the bones were lying all over the floor; the only undisturbed coffin was the one that contained the vampire, who had the pistol wound on his leg. They burnt the body.

The story sounds unlikely enough; even Hare does not state that he believes it. But it could well have been based on fact. The same scattering of the coffins occurred in a case that is much better authenticated, the 'unquiet tomb' of the Elliott family on the island of Barbados. The vault, which stands above Oistin's Bay above the cemetery of Christ Church, is hewn partly out of solid rock. In 1807 the body of a Mrs. Thomasina Goddard was interred there. A year later, a child, Mary Chase, was interred, and in 1812 two more members of the Chase family. It was on the occasion of this fourth interment that the child's coffin was found standing on end and the one containing Mrs. Goddard had been thrown across the vault. The third coffin – of Dorcas Chase – was undisturbed. On the next opening of the tomb, in 1816, it was Mrs. Goddard's coffin that was undisturbed; the others were scattered around. After the same thing had happened a third time, Lord Combermere, the governor of the island, conducted an investigation and found the coffins scattered; this was on July 17, 1819. The floor was covered with fine sand, and the marble slab that served as a door cemented into place. On April 18 of the following year, the governor, accompanied by his military secretary, Major the Hon. J. Finch, the local rector, the Rev. Thomas Orderson, the Hon. Nathan Lucas and two more whites, opened the tomb (with the aid of a party of Negroes). With immense difficulty, the slab was moved. This time there could be no doubt that a human intruder was not responsible for the chaos inside. Only Mrs. Goddard's disintegrating coffin was undisturbed. Three witnesses – Combermere, Orderson and Lucas – wrote accounts testifying to what had been discovered, and these can be found quoted in many books: Schomburg's *History of Barbados*, Combermere's memoirs, Sir J. E. Alexander's *Transatlantic Sketches* and half a dozen other books; an account by Andrew Lang appeared in the *Folk Lore Journal* in 1907. The mystery is still unsolved; neither does it clarify it to know that three of the six coffins in the vault were those of people who met violent deaths – two were suicides, and a third was murdered by his slaves.

The unquiet spirit that disturbed the Elliott tomb was not a vampire, but its activities could have given rise to legends of a vampire; so it is conceivable that an apparently preposterous story like that of the Croglin Grange vampire could be based upon fact.

Summers points out that ghosts *have* been known to make their presence felt physically. The old Darlington and Stockton station was as famous for ghosts in its day as Borley rectory later became. One night the night watchman, James Durham, was struck by a man who had walked into the porter's cellar; when he struck back, his hand passed through the stranger. But the stranger's black retriever dog seemed real enough when it sank its teeth into Durham's calf. The man called off the dog with a lick of his tongue, and they vanished into the coal cellar, from which there was no exit. Naturally, they were not there when Durham looked a moment later. The ghost seems to have been a man who committed suicide on the premises; W. T. Stead printed Durham's attested account in his *Real Ghost Stories*.

It must be admitted that Summers offers no convincing evidence, of the kind that would satisfy the Society for Psychical Research, throughout his two large volumes. And this is undoubtedly because his curiosity about such things was avid but superficial; he had no insight into what lay behind them.

The case is quite different with Dion Fortune, one of the greatest of modern occultists, whose book *Psychic Self Defense* (1930) is a classic of its kind. She connects vampirism directly with negative psychic forces, the 'evil eye'. In this connection, I have already mentioned her account of the school principal who launched a 'psychic attack' on her.* As reported in the first chapter of her book, the attack hardly sounds 'psychic'; Dion Fortune went to announce that she was leaving the school – ignoring the warning of a colleague who told her that if she confronted the principal, she would never leave. The woman's method of attack was to assert that Miss Firth (Dion Fortune's real name) was incompetent and had no self-confidence. She repeated this assertion over and over again for four hours. 'I entered [the room] a

* See Part One, Chapter 1.

strong and healthy girl. I left it a mental and physical wreck, and was ill for three years.' She remained drained of vitality for a long time. Whether or not the principal really employed 'psychic' methods – I am inclined to doubt it* – her attack had the result of turning Miss Firth's interests to the field of psychology, then of occultism.

Dion Fortune's short chapter on vampirism is probably the most sensible account that exists of the subject. She begins by remarking on cases that she encountered as a psychiatrist, when one marital partner seemed to drain the other of energy, or when a parent seems to feed on the energy of a child. (She claims that most Oedipus complexes are of this nature.) 'Knowing what we do of telepathy and the magnetic aura, it appears to me not unreasonable to suppose that, in some way we do not as yet fully understand, the negative partner of such a rapport is "shorting" on to the positive partner. There is a leakage of vitality going on, and the dominant partner is more or less consciously lapping it up, if not actually sucking it out.' She goes on to quote Commander Baring-Gould, the author of *Oddities*, who claims that certain of the Berberlangs of the Philippines practise vampirism by liberating the 'astral body' from the physical body, and performing their vampirism – a draining of vitality, not of blood – as ghosts, so to speak. She then describes a case of which she had personal knowledge. The French windows of a certain house would blow open in the course of the evening, and locking them seemed to have no effect. A young homosexual who lived in the house was under psychiatric treatment, but seemed continually drained of vitality. One evening an adept in occultism was present when the local dogs began

---

* Although this type of suggestion involves the same basic principle as hypnotism: to take advantage of the self-division of most people by turning one half against the other. In Appendix A of *Beyond the Outsider* I describe the case of the novelist Margaret Lane, who was plunged into a two-year depression by reading John Hersey's account of the bombing of Hiroshima when she was recovering from a difficult childbirth. The mind develops a negative reflex, like a nervous dog that flinches every time someone moves.

to bark and the windows opened. He told them that something had come in. 'When they turned off the lights they were able to see a dull glow in a corner of the room; ... when they put their hands into the glow, [they] felt a tingling sensation such as is experienced when the hands are put into electrically charged water.' The occultist despatched the spirit by 'absorbing' it through sympathy – of which more will be said in a moment. The young homosexual then admitted that he thought he knew the source of the trouble. It was a cousin, also homosexual, who had been caught on the battlefields of France practising necrophilia on dead soldiers, and sent back to England for psychiatric treatment. The young boy had often been sent to sit with his cousin, and sexual relations developed. (On one occasion he bit the boy on the neck, drawing blood.) It was after the two separated that the phenomena began, and the boy had nightmares of being attacked by a ghost, which left him drained of energy.

The occultist, says Dion Fortune, was of the opinion that the necrophile cousin was not the primary vampire in the case. Her theory is that some of the soldiers on the Western front were of Eastern European origin – especially Hungarians – and that some of these knew certain traditional 'tricks' of occultism, the most important being how to avoid the 'second death', the disintegration of the astral body after the death of the physical body. They 'maintained themselves in the etheric double by vampirising the wounded. Now, vampirism is contagious; the person who is vampirised, being depleted of vitality, is a psychic vacuum, himself absorbing from anyone he comes across in order to refill his depleted sources of vitality. He soon learns by experience the tricks of a vampire without realising their significance, and before he knows where he is, he is a full-blown vampire himself.'

However, the occultist did not believe that the vampire was the necrophile cousin. He was of the opinion that the astral body of some deceased Magyar soldier had attached itself to the necrophile, and had then transferred to his young cousin after the neck-biting episode.

To the sceptic, all this is bound to sound absurd; but it has a ring of its own kind of logic about it, and certainly explains vampirism in a way that Summers fails to do.

Dion Fortune's explanation of werewolves also involves the astral body, or etheric double. She explains that powerful minds can create thought forms that actually possess a life of their own, and become 'elementals'; she goes on to describe how she once did the same thing, involuntarily, herself. She was lying on a bed thinking highly unpleasant and negative thoughts about a friend who had done her an injury. In a semi-dozing state, 'there came to my mind the thought of casting off all restraint and going berserk. The ancient Nordic myths rose before me, and I thought of Fenris, the Wolf-horror of the North. Immediately I felt a curious drawing-out sensation from my solar plexus, and there materialised beside me on the bed a large wolf … I could distinctly feel its back pressing against me as it lay beside me … I knew nothing of the art of making elementals at that time, but had accidentally stumbled upon the right method – the brooding highly charged with emotion, the invocation of the appropriate natural force, and the condition between sleeping and waking in which the etheric double readily extrudes.'

Although scared stiff, she managed not to panic, and ordered the creature off the bed. It seemed to change into a dog, and went out through the corner of the room. That night, someone else in the house reported dreams of wolves, and of seeing the eyes of a wild animal shining in the darkness. She decided to seek the advice of her teacher – almost certainly Crowley – who told her that she had to 'absorb' the creature she had made. But since it had been created out of the desire to settle accounts with a particular person, she had to begin by forgetting her longing for revenge. And, as if by coincidence, the ideal opportunity for revenge presented itself at that exact time. 'I had enough sense to see that I was at the dividing of the ways, and if I were not careful would take the first step on the Left-hand path.' She decided to forgive the offender, and to re-absorb the wolf, which she describes:

> It came in through the northern corner of the room again (subsequently I learnt that the north was considered among the ancients as the evil quarter), and presented itself on the hearthrug in quite a mild and domesticated mood. I obtained an excellent materialisation in the half-light, and could have sworn that a big Alsatian was standing there looking at me. It was tangible, even to the dog-like odour.
>
> From it to me stretched a shadowy line of ectoplasm; one end was attached to my solar plexus, and the other disappeared in the shaggy fur of its belly ... I began by an effort of will and imagination to draw the life out of it along this silver cord, as if sucking lemonade up a straw. The wolf-form began to fade, the cord thickened and grew more substantial. A violent emotional upheaval started in myself; I felt the most furious impulses to go berserk and rend and tear anything and anybody that came to hand, like the Malay running amok ... The wolf-form now faded into a shapeless grey mist. This too absorbed along the silver cord. The tension relaxed and I found myself bathed in perspiration.
>
> It is a curious point that, during the brief twenty-four hours of the thing's life, the opportunity for an effectual vengeance presented itself.

Unlike her master, Crowley, Dion Fortune never gives the impression of being an exhibitionist, avid to create effects. The extraordinary material in her books, and the sober, factual manner in which it is presented, make her almost unique among writers on occultism. Even a sceptic has to admit that she writes as if she knows what she is talking about, and without the overblown, romantic language of most occultists. And what she says here about the temptation of the 'Left-hand path' explains a great deal about the lives of the magicians. In the Kabbalah, the world of magic – Yesod, the moon – is on a lower level than the world of intellect and imagination, Hod, or the vital, creative forces of nature, Netshah. Certain people posses natural 'magical' faculties, but unless these are subservient to intellect and imagination, they will tend to be used in the service of negative emotion – malice, envy and so on. The result is character degeneration. Most people possess magical faculties. Most people are, fortunately, unaware of it.

It is interesting to observe that the vampire bat seems to have been named after the legendary vampire, rather than vice versa. Until recent years, little was known about the creature. When it was finally studied by zoologists, it was discovered that the bat is not a blood *sucker*, but that it laps blood as a cat laps milk. Unlike Dracula and his confrères, the vampire bat does not leave two tiny punctures; it slashes an incision in the skin of the victim with its incisors, then its tongue flickers in and out with great rapidity, drinking the blood as it runs. The cut usually continues to bleed after the bat has finished drinking. The only attribute of the vampire bat that sounds at all supernatural is its ability to make the incision without causing pain, or waking a sleeper. Men who have been attacked by vampires – in tropical countries – wake up to find that they have bled on to the bedsheets. Scientific observers have noted that animals stand quite still while the bat makes the incision, apparently quite unalarmed by the attack. No one has tried to explain why this is so.

It will be interesting to observe whether the legends of vampires change their character as the facts about the vampire bat become better known.

A story printed in the *Daily Express* in August 1970 reveals that the vampire legend is still alive.

Armed with a wooden stake and a crucifix, Allan Farrow prowled among the tombstones of a graveyard. He was hunting the 'vampire' of Highgate Cemetery. And 24-year-old Farrow told a court yesterday; 'My intention was to search out the supernatural being and destroy it by plunging the stake in its heart.' Farrow pleaded guilty at Clerkenwell, London, to entering St. Michael's churchyard, Highgate Cemetery, for unlawful purposes ... He was remanded in custody for reports.

Last night, Mr. Sean Manchester, leader of the British Occult Witchcraft and Lycanthropy Society, said: 'I am convinced that a vampire exists in Highgate Cemetery. Local residents and passers-by have reported a ghost-like figure of massive proportions near the north gate.

Until the year 1953, it was generally assumed that magic in England came to an end with the dissolution of the Order of the Golden Dawn in the mid-thirties. (A Crowley disciple named Frances Israel Regardie published a full account of the Golden Dawn rites in four huge volumes between 1937 and 1940, and the few remaining members of the society decided it was hardly worth going on.) But in 1953 a book called *Witchcraft Today* by Gerald Gardner created an immediate stir. Gardner expounded the well-known Margaret Murray theory that witchcraft is a survival of pagan cults, after which he went on to reveal that witchcraft is as common in England today as it was in the fifteenth century. Modern witches, said Gardner, worship a Horned God and a Moon Goddess. Readers of *Witchcraft Today* observed a certain gusto in the accounts of torture and flogging, and may have concluded that Gardner's brand of witchcraft had strong sexual overtones. Francis King, in *Ritual Magic in England*, says frankly that 'Gardner was a sado-masochist with both a taste for flagellation and marked voyeuristic tendancies.'

Gardner, who died in 1964 at the age of eighty, seems to have been a distinctly flamboyant character in the Crowley tradition – that is to say, something of an exhibitionist. The son of a highly eccentric timber merchant (who used to remove all his clothes and sit on them whenever it rained), Gardner apparently developed his taste for voyeurism and being spanked during boyhood travels in the Middle East with a buxom Irish nurse. He lived in the East until 1936, when he returned to England and became a student and practitioner of magic. He joined a witch coven in 1946, according to his own account. As a result of his book *Witchcraft Today*, a number of 'Gardner covens' sprang up in England. Their purpose, according to Gardner, was to practise white witchcraft – curing the sick, performing ceremonies to assure good crops, etc. – but there was a heavy sexual emphasis. In *Man, Myth and Magic*, a journalist and photographer named Serge Kordeiv described his own involvement with a witch coven that sounds distinctly Gardner-esque. On arriving in a large Victorian house, he and his wife found themselves in a cloakroom whose pegs seemed to contain complete sets of clothes, including underwear. The ceremony, in front of an altar with six black candles, had strongly melodramatic touches, with oaths signed in blood and the sacrifice of a black cock. The 'Master', a naked man shining with red-coloured oil, placed his hands on their genitals. On another occasion a girl was ravished on the altar by the Master, as a punishment for betraying confidences. Kordeiv claims that his luck changed abruptly for the better while he was a member of the coven, and suddenly for the worse when he broke with it.*

Gerald Gardner's rites also included ritual scourging and sexual intercourse between the High Priest and Priestess. He insisted that witchcraft (or 'wicca') was a healthy cult, and should be regarded as a religion. Whether he is right remains a matter of controversy; some

---

* *Man, Myth and Magic*, Issues 30 and 31.

investigators feel that there may be a certain amount of invention in his two books, and Francis King states that he forged a 'witch's rulebook' called *Book of the Shadows*. In his will, Gardner left a witchcraft museum in Castletown, Isle of Man, to Mrs. Monique Wilson, another well-known contemporary witch, known in witch circles as Lady Olwen; Mrs. Wilson now runs the museum, together with her husband, and weekly coven meetings are held in Gardner's old cottage. She asserts that a sex rite known as 'the sacred marriage' is performed only once every five years, and insists that English 'wicca' is basically the worship of the Mother Goddess, the Earth.

Francis King states that there has been a recent revival of interest in the Golden Dawn and its rituals. Regardie's four-volume work is now almost unobtainable; and when it can be obtained, is likely to cost as much as £80; but a book on the 'inner teachings' of the Golden Dawn has recently been issued in England.* The new converts, according to King, are young red-brick-university graduates, and the leaders of the two leading groups both claim to be the reincarnation of Aleister Crowley. An order flourishing in Wolverhampton and the Midlands calls itself the Cubic Stone, and seems to be more closely related to Crowley than to the Golden Dawn. A long quotation from *The Monolith* (the order's magazine) given by King seems to indicate that its magical invocations have been remarkably successful; on various days the room was permeated by a blue glow, a rose-coloured glow and a golden glow; voices were heard, presences felt, and blasts of cold air swept through the 'temple'. In King's opinion, the members of the Order of the Cubic Stone are to be regarded as serious and painstaking students of the occult, pursuing the 'Enochian' method.

It would probably be safe to say that there are now more witches in England and America than at any time since the Reformation.

---

* *The Golden Dawn, Its Inner Teachings*, by R. G. Torrens (Neville Spearman, 1969).

The best known among English practitioners are Patricia Crowther (who runs covens in Sheffield and Manchester), Eleanor Bone (who runs covens in Tooting and Cumberland), Monique Wilson and Alex Sanders. Sanders, born in 1926, claims the title King of the Witches, and has reintroduced into modern witchcraft some of the flamboyance associated with Crowley and Gardner. He was initiated into a coven by his grandmother at the age of seven, and introduced to Crowley three years later. He explained to Frank Smyth, the author of *Modern Witchcraft*, that he had deliberately used black magic to achieve money and sexual success. 'It worked all right,' he explained. But he then made the discovery that it all had to be paid for: several members of his family died of cancer, and his girlfriend committed suicide – after which, he set about purifying himself by magical ceremonies. Since 1967 he has held meetings at a flat in Notting Hill, London, and achieved considerable notoriety via newspapers and television. Like Monique Wilson, he insists that sexual rites are kept to a minimum. But, as with the majority of modern covens, most of the rites are performed naked.

Madeleine Montalban, who also knew Crowley, describes herself as a magician rather than a witch; she runs a correspondence course in magic from London, teaches levitation ('even my young pupils can levitate one another, but it is a perfectly useless exercise'), and bottles demons, which occasionally explode the bottle. For her, magic is a strictly practical and rather cheerful affair. 'Magic should make life easier. That's what it's all about,' she told a reporter from *Man, Myth and Magic*.

To summarise: modern witchcraft seems to be far more varied than its earlier counterpart. Some witch covens are undoubtedly an excuse for sexual orgies, and have a large element of showmanship. Others are distinctly puritanical, and treat witchcraft as a pantheistic religion. Some are conducted in a spirit of research, with the aim of finding out how many of the traditional rites actually produce results, either objectively or subjectively. Perhaps these latter deserve to be taken the most seriously. For reasons we do not understand, certain rites *do* produce results – at least, when performed by the right person. This must mean that there are certain laws underlying the phenomena. In earlier centuries there was no curiosity about these laws, because the Devil and his cohorts were supposed to be at the back of them. By the time the age of scientific analysis arrived. witchcraft had vanished. And now, when faith in science has been eroded, magic is seeing a revival. The timing, at least, is excellent.

TWO
THE REALM OF SPIRITS

I have mentioned already that the strange and ambiguous history of spiritualism began on March 31, 1848, when Mrs. Fox asked neighbours to come and witness the rapping noises that resounded through her house when her daughters, aged twelve and fifteen, were present. From then on, spiritualism spread like a flood over the world. It seems as if the 'spirits' who had remained more or less mute for centuries had suddenly decided that it was time for the human race to take an important step forward. Tales of ghosts are obviously as old as the human race itself, but this was different in that the ghosts suddenly seemed anxious to *communicate*. Or was it simply that human beings began to try to communicate with the dead? It is certain that effort and desire are important. In 1822 a thirty-year-old Scots minister named Edward Irving began to preach in the Caledonian church in Hatton Garden, London, filling his sermons with thrilling imagery about the second coming of Christ and producing violent transports of religious emotion among his hearers. In 1830, he instituted a series of services in which prayer was offered up for some 'miracle' to attest the imminence of the Second Coming, and after eighteen months, members of his congregation suddenly began to 'speak with tongues' – in languages other than their own – and to show powers of healing. His colleague Robert Baxter sometimes spoke sentences in French, Latin, Spanish and Italian – none of them languages with which he was familiar – as well as in languages that he could not identify. But it was not long before 'the spirits' began to manifest that curious ambiguity that seems to be universally characteristic of spiritualism. That is to say, while the manifestations are often plainly 'genuine' in the sense that they have not been deliberately engineered, they always seem to fall short of being finally convincing. They provide 'phenomena' for those who want to believe, and raise doubts for those who want to doubt. The voices told Baxter, and Irving's congregation, that he would go to the Chancellor's Court and there be inspired to testify, and that for his testimony he would be cast into prison. He went to the court and stood there for three hours, but the spirit failed to descend, so he went home disgruntled. On another occasion the voices informed him that he had been chosen to be a new Isaiah and that at the end of forty days miraculous powers would descend upon him, and that he must then separate from his wife and family. But at the end of forty days, nothing happened. The 'voices' periodically announced important new doctrines for the salvation of the Irvingites, and then contradicted themselves later. It is not surprising that Irving and Baxter finally decided that they had become the sport of evil spirits. The scandals created by these extraordinary events finally led to Irving being dismissed, only two years after the 'voices' had begun; he died less than a year later in Scotland of tuberculosis.

Dostoevsky once said that God had denied man certainty because it would remove his freedom; there would be no virtue making the right choice if you knew for certain that it was the right one. Anyone who reads a history of spiritualism may well feel that the spirits have adopted the same principle: that too much evidence of 'another world' would condition mankind to a lazy mode of thought and behaviour. The philosopher C. D. Broad remarked to me in an interview on this subject: 'If these facts of psychical research are true, then clearly they are of immense importance – *they literally alter everything.*' And the alteration would not necessarily be for the better. In fact, it would certainly be for the worse if we take into account the basic peculiarity of human nature: the *need* for uncertainty and crisis to keep us on our toes. One day it may be that we shall learn to keep the *will alert* as automatically as we now breathe, and if that happens, we shall be supermen living on a continual level of 'peak experience'. But until we achieve this new degree of self-determination, life had better remain as bewildering and paradoxical as possible.

This condition is certainly satisfied by the history of spiritualism. The Fox family – mother, father, son and three daughters – all produced rapping sounds (which Madame Blavatsky said were the easiest phenomena to get). Within a very short time, dozens of people in New York State discovered that they also had mediumistic powers and could produce rappings. A relative of the Fox family later denounced them, asserting that Margaretta Fox had explained to her how she made the rapping sounds by cracking her joints. There may be an element of truth in this; but how does it account for raps coming from other parts of the room? The journalist Horace Greeley observed the Fox family for several weeks, and pointed out that every precaution was taken to avoid trickery: they were taken unexpectedly to strange houses and asked to produce their rappings; they were stripped and searched by committees of ladies; their rooms were searched repeatedly.

When they appeared in Buffalo, New York, two brothers named Davenport – Ira and William – decided to try it. Their results were even more spectacular than the Fox family's. When they went into a trance, musical instruments were taken up by invisible hands and played. In Ohio a farmer named Jonathan Koons became interested in spiritualism, only four years after the Fox sisters had started the craze. He put himself into a trance in the dark, and spirits began to speak through him. One of them informed him that all his eight children were gifted mediums, and ordered him to build a special séance room next to his house. Koons accordingly built a log room, sixteen feet by twelve, next to his farmhouse, and placed in it assorted musical instruments, bells suspended from the ceiling, plates of copper cut into the shapes of birds and various tables and chairs.

Neighbours were often invited to the séances, which began by putting out the lights; after which, Mr. Koons played hymns on his fiddle. Soon the musical instruments would be taken up, and a noisy concert would commence. The sceptical explanation is that the Koons family played the instruments in the dark but the music was just as noisy when there were only two of them present. Paper covered with phosphorus would float around the room over the heads of the audience, and the tambourine would fly around, producing a powerful breeze. Hands were sometimes seen holding the paper, but no arms. The 'spirits' identified themselves as 165 'pre-Adamite men', and one of their 'descendants', John King, explained that he was actually the pirate Sir Henry Morgan. John King manifested himself to many mediums besides the Koons, and his daughter Katie also became something of a favourite in American spiritualist circles.

By 1860 the Foxes were producing veiled, ghostly figures, and a Dr. Livermore held conversations with the visible spirit of his dead wife that left him totally convinced. The two Eddy brothers, at whose house Colonel Olcott met Madame Blavatsky, also produced 'materialisations', The brothers would be tied to chairs in a cabinet, whose curtains were drawn. After a while, spirits would appear and sometimes walk around the room. When the lights were finally switched on, the brothers were found in their former positions, with the seals intact.

But opportunities for fraud were obviously considerable. The Davenport brothers always declined to state whether they were genuine mediums. or whether their 'performances', which often took place in theatres, were simply 'magical' performances like those of Houdini or the Maskelyne brothers. When a member of the audience at Liverpool used a special 'Tom Fool's knot' to tie them, so that they were unable to free themselves, no 'manifestations' took place, and the audience mobbed them. In 1874 two mediums named Showers

– a mother and daughter – gave a séance at the house of a 'believer' named Sergeant Cox. When a tall spirit appeared in the aperture of the curtains, Sergeant Cox's daughter tried to open them further, and the 'spirit' resisted; the spirit's headdress fell off and revealed the head of Miss Showers, while the audience was able to see clearly that the couch, on which the medium was supposed to be stretched, was empty. Sergeant Cox chose to take the charitable view that the medium had been impersonating a spirit in her trancelike state.

A young medium named Florence Cook often 'materialised' Katie King. One of the great scandals of the early spiritualist movement occurred on December 9, 1873, when a séance was held at her house. A Mr. Volckman, feeling resentful that he had only been admitted to the séance after pleading with the medium for nine months and presenting her with jewellery, decided to make a grab for the spirit that floated around the room. It seemed quite solid, and struggled. Indignant spiritualists forced Volckman to release the spirit; the lights went out completely, and when they came on again, there was no spirit present. Mrs. Cook was found tied up in the cabinet, the seals intact. Presumably, then, the spirit was not Mrs. Cook herself; it could, perhaps, have been an accomplice – like Eliza White, who confessed to being the spirit of Katie King manifested through Nelson and Jennie Holmes.

But no matter how much deliberate fraud took place, there can be no doubt that many of the manifestations were genuine. Dr. Franz Hartmann, a famous occult student in the last years of the nineteenth century, describes a séance held by Mrs. N. D. Miller, of Denver, when thirty or forty shapes materialised from the cabinet, men, women and children, and walked around the room. Some of them were local people who had died, and were clearly recognised by people present.

It is a pity that so many mediums have resorted to fraud, but not, after all, surprising. Mediumship seems to be like poetic inspiration; it depends on the energy of the medium and on her state of mind. No poet could produce good poetry on demand. It would take an extremely high level of moral conviction for a medium to reject every opportunity to convince her 'sitters', especially if she knows that they want to be convinced. And mediums do not necessarily possess this sterling quality. On the contrary, unusual powers of receptivity often seem to be accompanied by weakness of character.

This can be seen clearly in the case of Daniel Dunglas Home (pronounced Hume), perhaps the most remarkable and convincing medium who has so far appeared. He was born in the village of Currie, near Edinburgh, Scotland, on March 20, 1833. His mother was a Highlander who came of a long line of 'seers' – she always foretold the deaths of friends and relations. Daniel began to have 'visions' at the age of four, 'seeing' things that were happening in other places. Nothing much seems to be known about his father. and from Home's reference to Currie as the place 'where my adored mother suffered so greatly', we may infer that he was illegitimate. He was brought up by his aunt. He states that his father was a natural son of the Earl of Home, so it seems possible that his mother was seduced by an aristocratic rake, then deserted. This would also explain why, at the age of nine, Daniel travelled to America with his mother's sister, a Mrs. Cook, and her husband. His mother also moved there at some point, together with a husband and seven children; it is not clear why Home lived with his aunt rather than his own family.

He was a delicate child, subject to fainting spells; he suffered from tuberculosis from an early age. He was definitely 'artistic', playing the piano well and singing in a clear soprano voice. His memory was excellent, and he could recite whole poems and sermons.

When he was thirteen he had a vision of a friend named Edwin, who appeared to be standing at the foot of his bed; Edwin made three circles in the air, which Home believed to mean that

Edwin had died three days earlier. When this later proved to be correct, the Cooks were impressed, but not entirely happy. Four years later, after the death of his mother, they became definitely unhappy when tables began sliding around the room of their own accord and raps sounded from all parts of the room at breakfast. Mrs. Cook accused her nephew of bringing the Devil to her house, and threw a chair at him. The Baptist minister asked Daniel to kneel beside him and pray, and the knocks accompanied their prayers like a music teacher beating time. After more violent movements of the furniture, his aunt requested him to find another home.

He could hardly have chosen a better moment to go into the world. His own original 'rappings' occurred in 1846, two years before the Fox sisters started the fashion; so when he left home in 1851 the world was full of people who were eager to offer him shelter and test his powers.

These soon proved to be staggering. A committee from Harvard, including the poet William Cullen Bryant, testified that the table they had been sitting around, in broad daylight, had not only moved enough to push them backwards, but had actually floated several inches off the ground. The floor vibrated as if cannons were being fired, and the table rose up on two legs like a horse rearing. Meanwhile, Home kept urging those present to hold tightly on to his arms and legs. There could be no doubt whatever that this was genuine.

What is finally convincing about Home is the sheer volume of the evidence. He continued to perform feats like this for the remainder of his life, and hundreds of witnesses – perhaps thousands – vouched for the phenomena. Home's powers were so strong that he never asked for the lights to be lowered. He would allow himself to be tied if necessary; but often as not, he sat in full view of everyone, in a chair apart from the main table so there could be no doubt that he could not make the table tilt or float.

He never bothered about 'atmosphere'; the circle was told to chatter away about anything they liked. The manifestations began with a vibration of the table which might extend to the whole room. If his powers were strong, anything might then happen. Bells would be rung, tambourines shaken, hands appear out of the air to wave handkerchiefs, huge articles of furniture moved as if they were weightless. Grand pianos would float across the room, and chairs jump on top of them. Music played; water splashed; birds sang; ducks squawked; spirit voices spoke. The spirits usually ended the display by saying, 'Good night. God bless you.' A visiting clergyman, S. B. Brittan, was shocked and startled when Home went suddenly into a trance and began to utter wild and broken sentences in a woman's voice. Before going into the trance Home had identified the visitor as Hannah Brittan – Brittan was certain that no one knew of her existence; she had been a religious maniac who died insane, pursued by visions of eternal punishment.

Home's manifestations can only be described as spectacular, as if the 'spirits' were determined to convert the world by sheer weight of evidence. On one occasion, as a heavy table shook and vibrated, the crashing sound of waves filled the room, together with the creaking of a ship's timbers. The 'spirit' spelled out its name with the use of an alphabet, and was immediately recognised by someone present as a friend who had drowned in a gale in the Gulf of Mexico. The laws of nature were suspended by the spirits. When a table tilted, the objects on it seemed to be glued to its surface; a burning candle not only continued to burn, but the flame burnt at an angle, as if still upright.

There were always plenty of people to test Home, for he had great charm, and impressed people with his culture and sensitivity. From the beginning his success was enormous. The highest in society took him up, and rich families offered to adopt him. He was naïve, adaptable and talkative; he enjoyed playing with the children because he obviously identified more closely with them than with the adults. People who did not like him called him weak, boastful, vulgar and unreliable; and he was certainly all these things. His photographs reveal his character: the pale face that bears a distinct resemblance to Poe, the 'arty' hair-do, the expensive and vulgar dressing gowns, the mournful or soulful expression. In fairness to Home, it should also be said that as he grew older, his character became stronger, he became more self-sufficient. But he was always gentle, rather effeminate (although not, apparently, homosexual), easily pleased or upset and highly dependent on other people. There was nothing of the lone 'outsider' about him. He was a snob; he liked to wear expensive jewellery and to stay in rich houses. At the same time, he was completely 'uncommercial'. He wanted to be accepted as an equal by the aristocrats and celebrities among whom he moved, so he became mortally offended if anyone tried to offer him money.

As to the manifestations themselves, he insisted that he knew no more about them than any of his audience. There was no 'secret'. Things simply happened when he was in the room; all he had to do was to relax and put himself into the mood. While still in America, he also began to give exhibitions of his most convincing manifestation: levitation. On August 8, 1852, sitting in a circle and holding the hands of his neighbours, Home floated up until his head touched the high ceiling – the neighbours had naturally let go. Home said it felt as if someone had put a belt around him under the arms and drawn him up. But on other occasions he seemed unaware of what had happened; one of his hosts pointed out one evening that he was hovering two inches above the cushion of the armchair, and Home seemed surprised.

As a spirit medium – that is, in communication with the dead – he was neither better nor worse than other mediums. He was often surprisingly accurate, but then, this is one of the normal characteristics of all mediums. The Fox sisters were seldom wrong when it came to giving the precise age of a member of the audience by means of raps. On other occasions, Home's messages were obscure or so personal that they could not be verified by a third person.

In 1855, when he was twenty-two, he decided to visit Europe. Although he had no immediate prospects outside America, some instinct seems to have told him that interesting things awaited him. He was not mistaken. In London he went to stay at Cox's Hotel, in Jermyn Street, and the owner, William Cox, took Home under his wing. London hostesses were soon queueing up to invite him to their homes. There were plenty of sceptics. Lord Lytton, an ardent student of magic and occultism, agreed that Home's powers were astonishing, but believed that the phenomena were somehow due to Home himself rather than to spirits. Sir David Brewster and Lord Brougham, a Voltairean rationalist, saw a bell flying about the room when Home was sitting at the table; Brewster agreed that he could not explain how it was done, but he declined to believe that spirits had anything to do with it. The table itself hovered several inches off the floor, and Brewster crawled under it to verify that no one was touching it; but his Scots common sense was revolted at the idea of admitting the existence of spirits.

The movement of tables was often so spectacular that people could sit on them, or hang on to the edge as they tilted, suspended in the air. This form of sport became popular at Home's séances.

It is also necessary to record that many so-called rationalists behaved in a thoroughly irrational manner when it came to finding out whether Home was genuine or not. Charles Dickens referred to him as 'that scoundrel Home', but declined to attend any of his séances. Browning became almost hysterical if Home's name was even mentioned, and once threatened to throw him out of the house. (He referred to him as 'that dungball'.) Dingwall's opinion is that Browning had heard gossip that Home was a homosexual, and that this struck the sturdily normal and moral Victorian as nauseating. Dickens apparently hinted at Home's influence over young men in an article. There is no evidence whatever that Home was a practising homosexual, although his mannerisms certainly struck many as effeminate. Browning himself had been ardently attached to his own mother, to such an extent that his poetic identity was permanently eroded;* his reaction to homosexuality may have been based on a recognition of it in himself. At all events, Browning continued to be flagrantly unfair to Home. Although he knew that most of Home's manifestations were genuine, he portrayed him as Mr. Sludge, the fake medium, thereby spreading the impression that Home had been exposed. In fact, Home is one of the few mediums who were never seriously accused of fraud. He passed all 'tests' triumphantly.

Mrs. Browning, on the other hand, was totally convinced of Home's powers, and would certainly have cultivated his acquaintance if it had not been for her husband's violent opposition. It seems just conceivable that Browning's dislike was based on ordinary sexual jealousy. He was certainly enraged by an episode that took place at a séance in Ealing, at the home of John Snaith Rymer, when, at Home's request, a perfectly visible and detached spirit hand took up a garland of flowers that lay on the table and placed it on the poetess's brow. Beautiful music came from the air. Mrs. Browning spoke to the medium with tenderness mingled with respect, and her husband sat there fuming and damning all spirits. Home, with his usual lack of tact, later remarked that Browning

---

* Browning's biographer, Betty Miller, points out that the Browning household was a 'matriarchal society', Browning's mother was a Sunday School teacher and a woman of inflexible morality. In his teens, Browning was bowled over by the poetry and personality of Shelley. But it was impossible to model himself upon his idol without alienating his mother. He chose his mother, thus violating his intellectual integrity. This, Mrs. Miller argues, is why he preferred to write 'dramatic monologues', using other people as a mask, rather than speaking with his own voice.

had deliberately placed himself in the path of the garland so that it would settle on *his* brow.

Home travelled on to Italy, where the English community awaited his coming with intense expectation. In Florence his powers were stimulated by the scenery and adoration; a grand piano rose into the air while the Countess Orsini was playing on it, and remained floating throughout the piece. Tables danced, chandeliers gyrated, spirit hands serenaded the visitors on concertinas or shook hands with the sitters, who observed that they felt warm and human. Nathaniel Hawthorne recorded that all these 'soberly attested incredibilities' were so numerous that he forgot most of them, and was amused that his reaction to real-life ghosts was boredom: 'they are absolutely proved to be sober facts … yet I cannot force my mind to take any interest in them'. Hawthorne expressed with great clarity what most balanced minds feel about ghosts. There certainly were quite genuine apparitions in Florence; in a convent rented by the famous sculptor Hiram Powers, the ghosts of twenty-seven monks disturbed a séance, behaving with a rowdiness reminiscent of poltergeists and tearing Mrs. Powers's skirt. In a haunted bedroom in another villa, Home conversed with a ghost that spoke Italian (which had to be translated), which identified itself as a murderer who had been haunting the house for several hundreds of years, and materialised a hand with skinny yellow fingers. While the spirit was present the room became so icy cold that they had to huddle round the fire. It was apparently impossible to do anything for the rest of the murderer's soul, but he promised to stop disturbing the present tenants.

It was in Florence that a few dark clouds appeared on the horizon of his unbroken success. Home had travelled to Florence with the son of Rymer, his Ealing host; but success and lionisation swept Home off his feet, and he was 'kidnapped by a strong-minded society lady of title, an Englishwoman living apart from her husband', according to Conan Doyle in *Wanderings of a Spiritualist*. 'For weeks he lived at her villa, though the state of his health would suggest that it was rather as a patient than as a lover.' English and American society was scandalised. Doyle said that he saw letters written by Home to Rymer at this time that revealed a certain callousness and lack of gratitude. Elizabeth Barrett Browning remarked in a letter that part of the trouble was that Home 'gave sign of a vulgar yankee nature, weak in the wrong ways', and that he 'succeeded in making himself universally disagreeable'. But Home also failed to realise that he was now in the land of Popery, and that what was now called a 'spirit medium' had been called a witch only a century earlier and tortured by the Inquisition. It was less than sixty years before that Cagliostro had died in the dungeons of San Leo. The Italian Minister of the Interior took him aside and warned him that he had better keep away from lighted windows at night in case someone tried the effect of a silver bullet on the sorcerer. Not long after this, he was attacked on his way home to the hotel and slightly wounded. Gossip about him exaggerated his weaknesses to the rank of calculated outrages. When he was invited to travel to Naples and Rome with a Count Branicki and his mother, he seized the opportunity to leave the unfriendly city of Michelangelo. And then, the final blow: on February 10, 1856, the spirits told him that he was about to lose his powers for the space of a year, because his recent conduct made him an unworthy vessel.

Chastised and humiliated, he accompanied the Branickis to Naples. But the gods had not deserted him entirely; people still came to see him, even though he made no secret of his loss of power. The brother of the King of Naples presented him with a ruby ring. But a confidential letter from an old friend warned him that he had better not venture to Rome, because the authorities had decided that he was an undesirable. Home reacted in a manner that was consistent with his highly conciliatory nature; he went to Rome, and became a Roman Catholic.

He was immediately given an audience by the Pope, who showed himself friendly, and recommended a confessor in Paris, which was the next capital on Home's itinerary.

His confessor there, a Father Ravignan, assured Home that he need have no fear of a return visit from the spirits, provided he remained a good son of the Church. But he was, of course, missing the point. Why should Home want to banish his spirits? They were the source of his celebrity and income. Everyone knew the date when his powers were due to return, and on the morning of February 11, the Emperor sent a marquis as emissary to find out whether Home's powers had returned. Home assured him they had – on the stroke of midnight. Immediately after the marquis came Father Ravignan, who was greeted by loud rapping noises from the spirits. He told Home that even if he couldn't prevent the manifestations he could at least 'close his mind to them'. Home said he would try. But as the priest raised his hand in a parting benediction, the raps started up again with the equivalent of a ghostly raspberry.

Home's career now entered a new phase of celebrity. He was summoned to the Tuileries by Napoleon III. He was dismayed to find the room crowded, and explained that a séance was not a theatrical performance and that the spirits would not allow more than eight people to be present. The Empress Eugénie was not used to being thwarted, and she stalked out. However, Napoleon III decided the request was reasonable; he was a magical amateur himself, and was curious. He asked for the room to be cleared. Then Home gave of his best. The table floated, and the raps proved their supernormal origin by answering a question he put mentally. He sent for the Empress Eugénie; she marched in coldly. But within minutes, a hand gripped hers under the table, and she recognised it by a characteristic defect as her father's hand. Her coldness vanished; Home had made perhaps his most important conquest. At the next séance, the spirits went through most of their repertoire: a child's hand formed in space and held the Empress's hand; a concertina, held at one end by Napoleon, played melodies; handkerchiefs floated around; bells chimed; the table floated on command. At the next séance, Napoleon Bonaparte himself deigned to appear – at least, his hand did, and signed his name. The Empress was allowed to kiss the spirit hand, which then vanished.

Home was the social discovery of the season; aristocrats queued up to call on him and take him out for drives. His relationship with the Emperor and his wife became considerably more intimate than that of Rasputin with the Russian royal family half a century later; Home dined at the Tuileries as often as he felt inclined. His success must have inspired wild hopes in the breasts of other contemporary magicians, such as Eliphaz Levi and the Abbé Boullan; but none of them possessed Home's incredible luck.

There were plenty of enemies, and Home was constantly aware of their hostility, and of preposterous stories of his own sinister powers. He returned to America for a few months to allow things to cool down, and to collect his sister Christine, whom the Empress had agreed to take under her wing. Back in Paris, he continued to dine with princes and even kings. But the social round was beginning to tell on his powers, and when he gave a séance for the imperial family at Biarritz, all he could do was make a table float in the air and armchairs canter around the room like circus elephants.

In January 1858, one year after the return of his powers, Home went to give séances for Queen Sophia at the Hague, and after a cold and rainy itinerary around the northern parts of Europe, decided that he would return to Italy to throw off the series of colds and coughs he had picked up. In Rome he was invited to spend an evening with a Russian count, Gregory Koucheleff-Besborodka, and was introduced to his beautiful seventeen-year-old sister-in-law, Alexandrina de Kroll, known as Sacha. The moment Home set eyes on her, his second sight operated and he recognised her as his future wife. She also told him jokingly that he would be married before the end of the year, because it was a Russian superstition that any man who sat between two sisters was destined for matrimony. It was a pity that the spirits did not also warn Home that his tuberculosis was catching (this was not recognised in those days); she was dead after three years of marriage.

But the three years were a delightful time for Home. He travelled with Dumas to St. Petersburg, where Sacha's relatives organised a spectacular wedding feast; Dumas was best man, and wrote an account of the Russian trip. Home was kindly received by the Tsar himself, Alexander II, who was to liberate the serfs three years later and be assassinated in 1881. After their marriage in August 1858, the Homes became frequent guests of the Tsar at Tsarskoe Selo. Home's wife was an heiress, so his financial troubles were now over – at least, for a long time. A pleasant winter, during which Home became the darling of St. Petersburg society, was followed by an equally pleasant spring and summer, during which Home's son was born. He was christened Gregory, and called Grisha. In August the Homes set out for England, stopping in Paris and Switzerland. In London they established themselves at Cox's Hotel, and London society, which flocked to meet them, agreed that the 'Yankee' was in every way improved by his alliance with the gentle and charming Russian girl.

Home attended a lecture on Cagliostro, and was startled when the spirit of the Grand Copt strolled into the lecture hall and sat beside him. Later, when he and Sacha got into bed, Cagliostro put in another appearance, sat down on the bed and chattered amiably to the young couple. Sacha must have found it all very odd.

In 1862 Home's luck took a turn for the worse again. Sacha died in July. Although it must have been some consolation for Home to be able to keep in touch with her, her death was a blow; he had been devoted to her. It also meant that his income ceased, for her relatives contested her will, and the legal wrangling was to continue for some years. He wrote an autobiography, *Incidents in My Life*, to make money, but its royalties could scarcely keep him in the style to which he had become accustomed. He stayed with various friends, then decided to return to Rome. But after a few days there, he was summoned to the police station, informed that he was a sorcerer (an accusation which the spirits helpfully confirmed with loud raps) and told he had to leave Rome within three days. He went to Naples, then on to Nice. His supporters hoped to turn his ejection into an international scandal, but his royal patrons seemed bored by the whole affair; Napoleon III was noncommittal, and the King of Bavaria, who had shown Home much cordiality, feigned deafness. Londoners proved altogether more interested; there were questions asked in Parliament and articles in newspapers, and Home had the satisfaction of seeing the Protestant press firmly behind him. Another visit to St. Petersburg, where he was again warmly received, did much to soothe his wounded feelings. But the run of bad luck was not yet over. In 1866 he made the acquaintance of a rich widow, Mrs. Jane Lyon. She was an effusive and vulgar old lady of seventy-five, who was immensely impressed by the photographs of royalty that adorned the walls of Home's modest lodging. When he told her that the rooms were provided by a society calling itself the Spiritual Athenaeum, of which he was the resident secretary, she gave him a generous cheque for the society. This surprised him, for '[he] thought she might be a kind-hearted housekeeper, but it never crossed [his] mind that she could be rich'. Soon she talked of adopting him, and presented him with a cheque for £24,000. Home settled annuities on various relatives and bought a cottage for the aunt who had brought him up in America – apparently having forgiven her for throwing him out on the world. He changed his name to Home-Lyon, and Mrs. Lyon continued to present him with large cheques. She later claimed that

Home himself had relayed instructions through her late husband concerning the various sums and items of property she made over to him.

The whole Lyon episode seems to illustrate that Home lacked the common sense of self-preservation. He should have asked himself at a very early stage whether he could actually stand being the 'son' of the vulgar old lady with the northern accent. As it was, he had to learn the hard way. Her manners began to distress him; she was either being effusively affectionate – in front of his aristocratic friends – or working herself up into a state of resentment about his coolness towards her. He had a nervous breakdown, and went to get himself cured at Malvern, where his friend Dr. Manby Gully – famous for his part in the Charles Bravo murder case (which still lay in the future) – had set up a clinic for hydropathic cures. When he returned to London, he found that Mrs. Lyon had found herself another medium – a woman this time. In June 1867, Mrs. Lyon set out to recover her 'presents' legally. And although Home was in the right, it was inevitable that he should get the worst of it. He was hissed as he entered the courtroom; the public had already decided he was a charlatan who had conned a silly old lady out of £60,000. Home's case was that the old lady had tried to seduce him after he became her adopted son; she alleged that he had obtained the money under false pretences. If Home had been anything but a spirit medium, Mrs. Lyon's frequently exposed lies would have won him the case. As it was, the judge remarked in his summing up that if everyone who gave money to a religious body was allowed to change his mind, chaos would result. He ordered Mrs. Lyon to pay her own costs and Home's. But, because he held spiritualism to be a delusion, he ordered that Home should give Mrs. Lyon her money back. It was an appallingly unfair verdict, for it was not the judge's business to decide the case upon his own opinion of spiritualism. It was also a blow for the spiritualist movement, since Home never managed to shake off the imputation that he had faked the spirit messages from Mr. Lyon. Worst of all, from Home's point of view, it left him financially worse off than ever, since he had spent so much of the money which he now had to repay. He decided to follow Dickens's example and do a reading tour of England. The result was an enormous success; Home proved to be a natural actor. And also a natural comedian. His readings of dialect stories had the audience convulsed.

In 1870 a young acquaintance of his Malvern days, Lord Adare, published a book describing his experiences with Home, and it is still one of the best portraits of Home that exist. Adare was not a spiritualist – just a normal, healthy young man whose chief interests were hunting, shooting and fishing. He had no previous interest in spiritualism, and later on, came to look back on it as an adolescent phase. It is this lack of partisanship that makes his account so impressive. With three aristocratic cousins, and various other friends who occasionally lent a hand, he observed Home's powers closely over several months. In Adare's rooms, in the presence of Dr. Gully and a Captain Smith, Sacha materialised beside Home as he stood illuminated by the dim light from the window. She seemed quite solid. On another occasion, the American actress Ada Mencken, recently deceased, appeared in the rooms, and then took over Home's body and had a long and friendly conversation with Adare. It is interesting to observe that there were occasions when Home could see her and Adare could not, and others when Adare could see her and Home could not. Probably this has something to do with the position of the spirit in the room; other writers on ghosts have recorded that the ghost vanishes if it comes too close, and reappears when it has reached a certain distance from the observer.

Adare and his three friends witnessed so many wonders that the sheer quantity overwhelms the imagination. Fireballs wandered over the room and through solid objects; spirits appeared as dim shapes, and sometimes as walking clouds; draughts howled through the room when all doors and windows were closed; doors opened and closed; flowers fell from the ceiling; spirit hands appeared; furniture moved around as though it was weightless. Home himself floated around like a balloon. He floated out of one window head first – it was only open a foot – and returned through another window. He also added two more astounding effects to his repertoire. He would elongate, standing against a wall, while one man held his feet, another his waist, and another watched his face. Home's height would then increase from five feet ten to six feet six inches, both heights being marked on the wall. And he began to handle fire. He would cross to the firegrate, and stir the red-hot coal with his fingers, then kneel down and bathe his face in the coals as though they were water. His hair was not even singed. He would carry a burning coal to the circle – it was so hot that no one else could endure it closer than six inches, unless Home deliberately transferred his immunity to them. Lady Gomm took a red-hot coal and felt it to be slightly warm. She put it down on a sheet of paper and it instantly burst into flames. Home sometimes declined to allow people to hold the coal, on the grounds that their faith was not strong enough.

When Home went to stay at Adare Manor, the home of Adare's father, Lord Dunraven, he quickly spotted a ghost in the abbey, and strolled over to have a conversation with it, after which he and the ghost, quite visible to his companions, walked back through the moonlight. Then the ghost vanished, and Home floated through the air and over a low wall.

Adare's book was privately printed, but caused so much commotion that it was withdrawn. (It was reprinted by the Society for Psychical Research in 1914.) Adare remained a friend of Home's, but lost interest in spiritualism on the grounds that although the phenomena were obviously genuine, they didn't get anywhere or prove anything.

In the Franco-Prussian War of 1870, during which Home's former patron Napoleon III was made a prisoner, Home became a correspondent for the *San Francisco Chronicle* and covered the war from the Prussian headquarters at Versailles. He then paid another visit to Russia, where he met his second wife, Julie de Gloumeline; she heard a voice above her head telling her that this was to be her husband, so made no objection when Home proposed marriage.

Back in London in March 1871, he agreed to be 'investigated' by a brilliant young physicist, William (later Sir William) Crookes. British scientists who heard of the investigation smiled; they had no doubt that Crookes would finally demolish Home's reputation. To everyone's astonishment and dismay, Crookes's report, which appeared in the *Quarterly Journal of Science* in July 1871, was entirely favourable. Crookes admitted that his rational mind told him that the things he had seen were impossible. In spite of that, he had to admit that he was totally convinced by Home's amazing repertoire of levitation, fire handling, elongating, causing to float and so on.

Scientists were furious at the report; they assumed that Crookes had been deceived or gone mad. Charles Darwin voiced the general feeling when he said that he could not disbelieve in Crookes's statements, or believe in his results. (Crookes also reported favourably on Florence Cook, the medium who materialised 'Katie King'; a recent critic has conjectured that she and Crookes were lovers.) For a while, it looked as though Crookes had simply ruined his own career as a scientist; but he was slowly taken back into favour, particularly when pressure of work forced him to stop taking an active part in spiritualist affairs.

In the following year, 1872, Home decided to retire. He had another fourteen years to live, and they were pleasant and peaceful years, spent partly in Russia, partly on the Riviera. The lawsuit over his first wife's estate was decided in Home's favour. His retirement, like his debut, was perfectly timed. It will be remembered that this was the period when Madame Blavatsky was finding that interest in spiritualism had declined severely. Home had always taken care not to associate himself with the spiritualist movement. He was a loner – naturally, since his success placed him on a different plane from all other mediums – and his comments on other mediums were not calculated to make him popular. Now he became simply a 'private gentleman' who occasionally gave séances for the amusement of his friends or hosts. His powers continued undiminished. The reason, one might speculate, is that he was slowly wasting away with consumption, and he was always at his best when the 'material' side of his nature was suppressed. The publisher Vizetelly describes an afternoon spent in a café during the Franco-Prussian War. Home was sipping sugared water, and explained that he was fasting because 'the spirits will not move me unless I do this. To bring them to me, I have to contend with the material part of my nature'. It will be remembered that Home was consumptive from birth. His mother possessed mediumistic powers, and Home's son, Gregory, also inherited some of his father's gift. It seems possible that the unique level of mediumship in Home's case may be due to this combination of inherited 'faculties' and extreme physical delicacy.

He died in 1886, at the age of fifty-three, and has remained a subject of controversy ever since. It is difficult to see why. He was one of the most uncontroversial mediums who ever lived. If the vast number of reports of his 'manifestations' does not constitute unshakable scientific evidence, then that term is completely meaningless.

Powers so well attested and so extraordinary again raise the question: What does it all mean?

It must be frankly admitted that the chief difficulty in answering that question is that we lack a starting point. When Benjamin Franklin made a kite conduct lightning, he already had some idea of the nature of electricity. When scientists learned to split the atom, they had a fair idea of its structure. It is this kind of 'minimum working hypothesis' that we lack in considering 'occult phenomena'. My own grandmother was a convinced spiritualist, and she felt that it solved all the basic problems. Spirits live in heaven, then they enter bodies, and when they die, they finally go back to heaven. But this is simply another version of the infinite regression that arises when we ask, 'Where does space end?' or 'Who created God?' The Hindus believed that the world is supported on the back of an elephant, which is supported on the back of a tortoise … and so on.

What is left out of account by the spiritualist view is the mystery of the internal universe of the mind. Dreams often reveal to us that we are multi-layered beings. Ninety-nine per cent of my dreams may be straightforward enough, as unproblematic as daydreams. But there are always the few dreams that strike me as *utterly strange*, as though I have accidentally tuned in to a foreign radio station. Jung records this feeling in the chapter called 'Confrontation with the Unconscious' in his *Memories, Dreams, Reflections*. Various dreams seemed so strange and symbolic in content that they seemed to be trying to *tell* him something. After describing a dream in which the corpses in a row of tombs kept on stirring as he looked at them, he remarks, 'Of course, I had originally held to Freud's view that vestiges of old experiences exist in the unconscious. But dreams like this, and my actual experiences of the unconscious, taught me that such contents are not dead, outmoded forms, but belong to our living being.' The distinction is important, for Freud's 'archaic vestiges' are like dead leaves at the bottom of a pond.

What Jung then goes on to describe is so startling that only his serious reputation keeps the reader from doubting the whole thing. In the autumn of 1913 he began to experience a sense of oppression, and finally, on a journey: 'I was suddenly seized with an overpowering vision: I saw a monstrous flood covering all the northern and low-lying lands between the North Sea and the Alps. When it came up to Switzerland I saw that the mountains grew higher and higher to protect our country. I realised that a frightful catastrophe was in progress. I saw the mighty yellow waves, the floating rubble of civilisation, and the drowned bodies of uncounted thousands. Then the whole sea turned to blood. The vision lasted about one hour. I was perplexed and nauseated, and ashamed of my weakness.' The vision recurred two weeks later, with a voice that said: 'Look at it well; it is wholly real …' In the spring and summer of 1914 he had dreams of an arctic cold wave freezing the world. On the third occasion when the dream recurred, it ended on a note of optimism: he saw a tree with grapes, which he plucked and handed out to the crowd.

He suspected that he was slipping into neurosis until the outbreak of war revealed that the dreams had been prophetic.

A mental upheaval now began. He remarks, 'One thunderstorm followed another. My enduring these storms was a question of brute strength. Others have been shattered by them – Nietzsche and Hölderlin … But there was a demonic strength in me.' As the mental disturbances became more violent he tried to turn the emotions into images that could be grasped by the conscious mind. Then occurred a 'dream' that came while he was sitting, fully conscious, at his desk:

I was … thinking over my fears. Then I let myself drop. Suddenly it was as though the ground literally gave way beneath my feet, and I plunged down into dark depths … But then, abruptly, at not too great a depth, I landed on my feet in a soft, sticky mess. I felt great relief, although I was apparently in complete darkness. After a while my eyes grew accustomed to the gloom, which was rather like deep twilight. Before me was the entrance to a dark cave, in which stood a dwarf with a leathery skin, as if he were mummified. I squeezed past him through the narrow entrance and waded knee deep through icy water to the other end of the cave where, on a projecting rock, I saw a glowing red crystal. I grasped the stone, lifted it, and discovered a hollow underneath. At first I could make out nothing, but then I saw that there was running water. In it a corpse floated by, a youth with blond hair and a wound in the head. He was followed by a gigantic black scarab and then by a red, newborn sun, rising up out of the depths of the water. Dazzled by the light, I wanted to replace the stone upon the opening, but then a fluid welled out. It was blood ...

This might be called 'controlled hallucination'; it seems, from the context, that what Jung did was to allow his subconscious mind to well up, and allow himself to be carried along, still conscious, by its images. He recognised the dream as a hero and solar myth, a drama of death and renewal, but was puzzled by the ending – the blood – unaware that it foretold the war which started the following year (this took place in December 1913).

Other dreams and visions followed; he acknowledges that they were fantasies of extraordinary clarity. In a dream he shot the hero Siegfried with a rifle – an indication that he knew who the enemy would be. And then, 'in order to seize hold of the fantasies, I frequently imagined a steep descent. I even made several attempts to get to the very bottom. The first time I reached, as it were, a depth of about a thousand feet; the next time I found myself on the edge of a cosmic abyss. It was like a voyage to the moon, or a descent into empty space. First came the image of a crater, and I had a feeling that I was in the land of the dead. The atmosphere was that of the other world. Near the steep slope of a rock I caught sight of two figures, an old man with a white beard, and a beautiful young girl. I summoned up my courage and approached them as though they were real people, and listened attentively to what they told me. The old man explained that he was Elijah, and that gave me a shock. But the girl staggered me even more, for she called herself Salome! She was blind … But Elijah assured me that he and Salome had belonged together from all eternity …'

I cite this at length, not because of Jung's interpretation of the symbolism of these figures (Elijah – intelligence! Salome – the erotic element; a black snake – the hero) but to point out the startling extent to which Jung had learned to make a daylight descent into the subconscious. What is surprising is the extent to which he could converse with these figures of his imagination. He underlines this point in speaking of another symbol of intelligence, whom he came to call Philemon: 'Philemon and other figures of my fantasies brought home to me the crucial insight that *there are things in the psyche which I do not produce, but which produce themselves and have their own life* [my italics]. Philemon represented a force which was not myself. In my fantasies I held conversations with him, and he said things which I had not consciously thought. For I observed clearly that it was he who spoke, not I. He said I treated thoughts as if I generated them myself, but in his view thoughts were like animals in a forest …' Aldous Huxley put forward a similar view about the 'antipodes of the mind' in *Heaven and Hell*. A Hindu later told Jung that his own guru had been Shankaracharya, a commentator on the Vedas who died centuries ago.

Later still, Jung came to recognise a kind of separate feminine entity in his subconscious – the 'anima' that we have already encountered in Part Two, Chapter 2. (In a woman, the corresponding figure is male.) He remarks, 'For decades I always turned to the anima when I felt my emotional behaviour was disturbed, and that something had been constellated in the unconscious. I would then ask the anima: "Now, what are you up to? What do you see? …" After some resistance, she regularly produced an image. As soon as the image was there, the sense of unrest or oppression vanished. The whole energy of these emotions was transformed into interest in and curiosity about the image.'

There were also external manifestations. Philemon first appeared in a dream about a blue sky covered with clods of earth; he appeared as an old man with a bull's horns and the wings of a kingfisher. Jung painted this image, and while he was engaged in painting, was startled to find a dead kingfisher in his garden – startled because the birds are rare in the Zurich area. In 1916, when he felt full of inner tensions, his eldest daughter saw a white figure passing through the room. The blanket was snatched twice from the bed of his second daughter. On a quiet Sunday afternoon, when the front door stood wide open upon an empty square, the front doorbell began to ring violently, although there was no one there. 'The whole house was filled as if there was a crowd present, crammed full of spirits.' And Jung thought he heard them crying out: 'We have come back from Jerusalem where we found not what we sought.' Jung made this the first sentence of a book, *Seven Sermons to the Dead*. He records that as soon as he began to write, the atmosphere quietened down.

It is interesting to note that Jung had experience of certain 'phenomena' even in the presence of the arch-sceptic Freud, and that they presaged the break in his relation with Freud. He describes how, in 1909, he and Freud argued about psychical phenomena, and Freud's shallow positivism annoyed Jung. He writes:

While Freud was going on this way, I had a curious sensation. It was as if my diaphragm were made of iron and were becoming red-hot, a glowing vault. And at that moment there was such a loud report in the bookcase, which stood right next to us, that we both started up in alarm, fearing that the thing was going to topple over on us. I said to Freud: 'There, that is an example of a so-called catalytic exteriorisation phenomenon.'

'Oh come,' he exclaimed, 'that is sheer bosh.'

'It is not.' I replied. 'You are mistaken, Herr Professor. And to prove my point, I now predict that in a moment there will be another loud report!' Sure enough, no sooner had I said the words than the same detonation went off in the bookcase.

To this day I do not know what gave me this certainty. But I knew beyond all doubt that the report would come again ...

He adds: 'I never afterwards discussed the incident with him.' A fascinating example of the scientist's ability to close his mind to anything that will not fit into his pattern of generalisations. Or perhaps Freud suspected, rightly, that Jung's subconscious hostility lay behind the explosions.

These considerations begin to shed a new light on the whole question of the occult. A 'spiritualist' who accepts that there is an after-life, a spirit world, a realm in which everything will be explained, is only scratching the surface. He still accepts himself as a kind of unity, a Leibnitzian monad, an ultimate unit. Jung emphasises that our sense of 'individuality' (meaning literally something which is indivisible) may be an illusion. We have to grasp that one of the basic principles of our psychic life is a kind of 'as if ...' I am working for an exam and I concentrate on my book *as if* it were the most important thing in the world. It isn't and I know it isn't. The more I can concentrate, while still knowing it isn't, the healthier I am. If I begin to forget that I am only playing an 'as if' game, if I begin to believe that this is really a matter of life and death, I become overtense and neurotic and my whole psychic balance is disturbed. But then, what I call my personality, my individuality, is actually a series of 'as if' acts of concentration. If I am suffering from a fever, my personality feels diffused, disintegrated, and I am also unpleasantly aware of the independence of my mental imagines, for they run around wildly like a crowd of people, ignoring me as

I stand in the corner. If I am in an intensely healthy and happy state, I experience this sense of 'otherness' welling up from my subconscious in an altogether delightful sense, as a kind of coolness and strength.

But this has an even more general importance. Supposing I am standing on a cliff top, watching the sea wash around rocks. If I am in a low, depressed state, the sight produces a kind of tension and foreboding, perhaps accompanied by some image of danger, like the octopus in the cave of *Toilers of the Sea*. It all seems *alien*, indifferent to me, and that is why it frightens me. If I am in a state of happiness and optimism, it no longer seems alien. The forces of 'otherness' bubbling up from my subconscious, and the 'otherness' out there, are somehow related. I have a feeling that even if I was down there, swimming among them, I would be in no danger.

These ideas do not 'explain' the powers of a medium like Home; but they begin to shed a kind of light. Observe that when Jung's mind was in a turmoil, the subconscious manifested itself in visions, and even in 'poltergeist' activities like the ringing of the doorbell and pulling the sheets off a bed. As soon as he began to write creatively, the manifestations ceased. Home was an 'artistic' personality, but not, in the ordinary sense, creative. Unlike Jung, he was a superficial man; he never questioned the 'spirits'; he never did any serious thinking. He remained a socialite, rushing around Europe, dining with royalty. What would he have discovered if he had been a 'mental traveller' like Jung? Jung's anima rang the doorbell; Home's moved pianos.

This is not to suggest that all the manifestations were simply Home's subconscious forces, acting in the manner of the 'monster' in *Forbidden Planet*. The question of the reality of 'spirits', of life after death, must be considered further. But these considerations certainly suggest that Lytton was right when he spoke to Home of '*your* powers'. Home never completed the alchemical process of reconciling the conscious and the subconscious; in fact, he hardly even began it. Was it Home's spirits who told him that he was about to lose his powers for a year? Or was it the anima, the weight of his own self-disgust? Geologists understand that there are certain terrains where rainfall sinks deep underground and joins subterranean rivers, and others where it almost immediately bubbles out in the form of a spring. Psychologically speaking, Home resembled this latter terrain. The subconscious forces bubbled out easily.

Once this is understood, the question of life after death is also seen in a different light. We have an image of the body dying, and of the 'spirit' rising out of it like a cloud and flying off to some 'other place'. If Jung is correct, then it seems altogether likely that what occurs is more like a descent into the inner world of the collective mind.

This view would certainly explain one of the most disturbing things about spirit communications – their frequent triviality. In the world of the 'noösphere' – of human intelligence – triviality is something that has to be avoided by a deliberate effort, like beating off flies. If the 'spirit world' is not 'another place' but only 'another part of the mind', then the same law would presumably apply.

Let us consider a recent and fairly well-authenticated case of communication with the dead, the one recounted by Bishop James Pike in his book *The Other Side*.

The story Bishop Pike tells is briefly this. In the mid-sixties, his son Jim (aged twenty) had been experimenting with psychedelic drugs in San Francisco. These produced some 'bad trips'. In February 1966 Jim Pike locked himself in a New York hotel room and shot himself with a rifle. Various friends had a powerful sense of 'something wrong' at about the time he killed himself. After his son's death, poltergeist phenomena began to occur in Bishop Pike's apartment, which he was sharing with his chaplain, David Baar, and his secretary, Maren Bergrud. First of all, books and letters would be arranged at an angle to one another in places where they would be seen. Then part of the bangs on Mrs. Bergrud's forehead was burnt off during the night. (The son, Jim, had never liked her bangs.) The missing hair had vanished. The next day, still more of the bangs had disappeared. The following day, she woke up in pain, with two of her fingernails injured, as if a needle had been driven under them. (One of them later came off.) Mrs. Bergrud entered Bishop Pike's bedroom late one night for a book, and he sat up in bed, asleep, and delivered a discourse on the importance of selfishness, of only caring about 'Number One'. Gradually, it dawned on them that Jim might be trying to 'communicate'. They finally visited a medium, Mrs. Ena Twigg, in Acton, London, and there discovered that it was, in fact, Jim Pike who had been doing his best to communicate. There were so many personal references, and references to matters that could not be known to the medium, that it seems reasonable to infer either that she was reading Bishop Pike's mind, or that Jim Pike was really present. Halfway through the séance, the theologian Paul Tillich, a friend of Pike's, interrupted to thank him for a dedication to a book. Tillich commented on Jim Pike: 'The boy was a visionary born out of due time. He found a society distressing in which sensitivity is classed as weakness.' It seems that Jim Pike was not, at this stage, much changed from the person he had been when alive. His first words were: 'I failed the test, I can't face you, can't face life. I'm confused. Very sudden passing … God, I didn't know what I was doing. *But when I got here I found I wasn't such a failure as I thought* [my italics]. My nervous system failed.' That is to say, the suicide arose from the premature defeat we have been discussing, the conscious mind 'opting out'. Later on he remarked, 'I thought there was a way out; I wanted out. I've found there is no way out. I wish I'd stayed to work out my problems in more familiar surroundings.'

There were later séances with other mediums in America, but little of importance was added. The spirit of Jim Pike apparently had precognition, as all spirits have, according to those who know; he was able to tell his father that he would be meeting a certain old friend soon, and that he would shortly be in Virginia. (Bishop Pike was convinced this was a mistake, until his plane landed at Dulles airfield and he remembered that this is on the Virginia side of Washington.) But it must be admitted that the rest of the book is anticlimactic; the reader comes up against the usual frustration: that the spirits so seldom say anything important. Perhaps this is because they recognise the human inability to learn from them. Mrs. Bergrud later committed suicide.

Bishop Pike's story does not end there. In August 1969 he and his newly married wife, Diane, went on a trip to the Middle East, and became lost in the Israeli wilderness. When he was too exhausted to walk further, his wife went off to try to find help. She found her way back to civilisation, but was unable to lead the rescuers back to the cave where she had left her husband; he was later found dead. On September 4, three days before his body was located, he 'communicated' with Ena Twigg, the London medium through whom he had first contacted his son. He gave details of what had happened and described where the body was to be found. Diane Pike later wrote, in an article: 'In that session there were sufficient references that corresponded to the circumstances of our ordeal and that expressed concerns that I knew to be uppermost in Jim's mind at the time of the mishap to enable me to affirm that Jim communicated through Mrs. Twigg.'*

The same article contains the interesting comment: 'Because she believes everyone is potentially mediumistic, she favours aiming at direct communication through meditation.'

* *Psychic News*, November 7, 1970.

It was Professor G. Wilson Knight who revived my own interest in the subject of spiritualism; consequently it was natural that I should ask him to explain how he came to be convinced of human survival of death. The accounts he has sent me of communications from his mother, his brother, W. F. Jackson Knight, and John Cowper Powys are circumstantial and impressive. I found his descriptions of communications from Jackson Knight particularly convincing. I had met JK (as he was generally known) several times between 1960 and his death in 1964. He was the sort of person it would be hard to forget – very much a 'personality', bubbling with a genial nervous energy. Wilson Knight describes his manner accurately: '... in excited talk and repetition, in fun, in exaggerated protestations of gratitude and praise; and still more in subtle turns of half-comic thought impossible to define.' This brings back to me my first meeting with JK: the warm, nervous, jerky handclasp, the rather high, precise voice saying enthusiastically, 'Oh my! How *very* kind of you to come! How very flattering for me too! Well! I really didn't imagine ...' and so on, until I thought he was pulling my leg. But he wasn't; it was his natural manner. So that when I read in Wilson Knight's manuscript the following transcription – taken down for him by Miss K. Neal in shorthand (at an Exeter circle in March 1965, four months after JK's death)* – I could instantly hear JK's voice saying the words:

How wonderful, here I am talking to you and supposed to be dead, how very exciting! I have been once or twice but wasn't able to get through.

Fifi [a spirit guide] has been so good in helping me, telling me what to do, but I'm not very good at it, never mind, I shall learn. But it is all so true, so very true, I hardly believed it would be so, but it is so. Lovely!

First going off I was so excited to make myself felt just to

---

* JK spoke directly through the medium of Dorothy Perkins.

let you know I was there. Sorry I cannot make Dick [Wilson Knight] feel me more, but there, never mind, I shall in time. I shall learn. How wonderful, how exciting!

I have been and tried, it is rather difficult, more difficult than what I anticipated, but nevertheless under Fifi's directions I shall be able to get on better ...

Give Dick my love, tell him I like the arrangements.

Sorry I was not able to finish several things that I had in mind, but he is a good chap, he will get them done I know. He is wonderful – much better than I was at organising. I had rather an untidy mind, he has a very tidy mind ...

A very very wonderful experience for me to be able to come and talk in this room! – where I used to come and talk to others. Now I am talking to you.

For anyone who knew him, this could be no one else than JK – the self-deprecating humour, the tendency to expostulation.

Wilson Knight was himself present at a séance a month later when JK was the first to speak through the medium, Dorothy Perkins. He writes:

He started talking to me volubly. 'Thank you *so* much!' was repeated emphatically. Then breaking off suddenly and most characteristically: 'Oh, I'm so sorry, I should be greeting everybody ...' Then to me: 'Fifi has given me permission to speak first. How very kind of her. It really is a wonderful experience.'

Asked what his life was like now he replied with words recalling those of T. S. Eliot's spirit seer in *Little Gidding*, 'between two worlds become much like each other'. 'Not a lot different except that things are more beautiful than perhaps they were. Flowers, trees, animal life. Very lovely. And there's no pain, no ugliness.' He added: 'If I wish, I can see the dark places. I'm not quite ready yet. I would be interested. The "hell" of people's own making.' [Swedenborg had also described this aspect of the spirit world in some detail.] And later: 'All that we were told is absolutely true … It's so important that everybody should know. It would make people so much happier – *and* more careful.' He said that it was not easy to influence people. 'When you see what has to be done to get through to earth, all the mechanism …'

I must admit that I find the flavour of JK's remarks more convincing than any purely 'factual' evidence, which Wilson Knight is also able to offer in abundance. In 1965 a message from JK was relayed through Vera Broom of Dawlish at the Exeter church; he wanted Wilson Knight to give something he greatly valued to his godson, Peter Fletcher, but had difficulty getting his meaning across. Wilson Knight goes on: 'Picture language was used. The medium saw a top drawer with a key, and was told that there was in it a small object in a leather case. Thinking of medals, I asked if it was military. "In a way" came the answer. There was no such drawer in our house, but there was, on the top of a *narrow* cupboard, a small *case* with a key, about the width of the cupboard. This might have looked like a top drawer. It contained a few unimportant objects, but with them was a small leather case, and in it a longish pin with thistle decorations, made to imitate a dirk or dagger.' Wilson Knight occasionally engages in spirit-writing which purports to come from either his mother or his brother. On November 14, 1965, he used it to enquire about the pin, and was told: 'It was a military symbol meaning the regiment's persisting life, and it was given to me by the Colonel of my regiment in 1918.' Wilson Knight adds: 'I do not regard my spirit-writing as authoritative on matters of factual detail, though in other things I have found it valuable. But I regard the main message as wholly convincing. JK's friends and godsons meant very much to him – he loved giving them presents – and his army and

O.T.C. experiences were probably the greatest passion of his life. Whatever the story of this pin may have been, my brother's anxious injunction bore every sign of his personality.' It was forwarded as requested.

'I now offer an example that does not concern myself,' Wilson Knight writes.

For this I rely on a detailed report made for me by Professor Bonamy Dobrée of Leeds University. On 7 June 1952 I invited some of the university staff to accompany me to a demonstration by a famous visiting medium, Mr. Gordon Higginson. There was a large audience, perhaps a thousand. One, whom I shall call 'Mr. A.', was told, correctly, his Leeds house-number and road-name, and was asked if the name of his neighbour was 'B'. 'B', being new to the neighbourhood, 'A' was not sure. Two Christian names were given, 'C' for the Mr. B, and 'D-E', two female names, presumably for his wife. Of these names 'A' knew nothing. 'D-E' was said to have had a conversation that morning, and there was a message for her.

After the meeting 'A' made enquiries next door. The surname and both Christian names were correct. A number that had been given turned out to be the number of a house which 'B' had recently left, and where he still kept his car. Both Mr. and Mrs. B however at first denied any 'conversation' by 'D-E', as she had been alone all the morning; but soon after they returned to say that there *had* indeed been a conversation over the *telephone*, and 'B' said: 'Please tell us what the message was, because the conversation was about something important; indeed, about the most important thing we have ever done in our lives.' Unfortunately 'A' had been so shattered by the identifications that he could not recall the message.

'A' was, as it happened, a laboratory assistant at the

University, though not of our party. He must have seen Professor Dobrée there, because he visited him in a state of considerable disturbance to tell him what had happened. I then asked Professor Dobrée to make out for me an exact transcript, from which I have drawn in this account, of all that he remembered of Gordon Higginson's rapid-fire questions and the subsequent ratifications …

Such accounts as these may not be spectacular – concerning, as they do, mainly small details – but when taken together they constitute an overwhelming argument for human survival of bodily death. Wilson Knight remarks: 'No theories of the "unconscious mind" can explain such messages,' and this is surely true. In the above case, the Society for Psychical Research would have obtained signed statements from everybody involved, and regarded the case as proven; and it is hard to see how the most hostile sceptic could fault this procedure, short of suggesting mass collusion between the medium, the laboratory assistant, the next-door neighbours and Professors Dobrée and Wilson Knight. But then, cases like this one turn up with such frequency in the records of the S.P.R. that it is surely more logical to accept the phenomena as genuine. Whether or not we are prepared to attach any great importance to it, the case for 'survival' must be regarded as conclusively proven. I shall leave a discussion of its ultimate importance to the final pages of this book.

On this topic, Wilson Knight himself concedes: 'Having had enough evidence to convince me that helping powers are near, I am not nowadays over-anxious for "messages". My main interest is probably in trance addresses by a Spirit personality speaking through a medium in trance. The best of these bear external impress of their authority: in use and harmonisation of vocal tone, physical poise, gesture and syntax, they rival and perhaps surpass our leading exponents of church or stage.'

After the death of his mother, Caroline, in 1950, JK received messages from her via a South African medium, Margaret Lloyd. (JK was in London when Caroline Knight 'came through'; he reports: 'I had nursed her during her last weeks, and now she was transmitting messages in detailed and intimate terms about her death and much else that concerned her family.' One of the African messages had mentioned a silver cup with a history, which JK thought he could identify. Before he was executed, Charles I took his last communion from the hands of Archbishop Juxon, and two gold or silver cups were used. There was a tradition in Wilson Knight's family that these cups had passed to certain ancestors in Jamaica, and Caroline Knight was said to have been christened from one of them. Wilson Knight engaged a researcher, R. S. Forman, to see if he could find any reference to the cups in family documents. But no mention of them could be found in various wills; it began to look as if the cups were a myth. But Caroline Knight continued to insist, through mediums, that they really existed. In April 1951, Wilson Knight attended a service at which Mrs. Nella Taylor was the medium; she singled him out, and told him that she could see a figure with a red hood, an Oxford hood, holding out a roll of parchment towards him. He assumed this to be a will. A few days later he received an excited letter from his researcher. A will *had* been found that proved the existence of the cups 'which formerly belonged to Archbishop Juxon'; they had been left to an ancestor of the Knights, Samuel Jackson – who, oddly enough, had been at Oxford. The figure with the red hood had appeared when news of the will was leaving Jamaica for London.

'Perhaps the most striking of all my experiences,' writes Wilson Knight, 'came when I thought I was being advised, through Mrs. Gwen Jones at the Exeter church, not to go to Cape Town in 1952 for a visiting lectureship. This I could not understand. But the confusion was my own fault. The message only referred to "going abroad" and

I had forgotten that I was also dallying with the offer to take up a permanent appointment in Drama at the University of California. Still anxious, I attended a circle in Exeter. With some difficulty and a sense of great strain and urgency, my mother herself "controlled" the medium, Dorothy Perkins – she had only once done this before – saying very slowly: "I want you to go to South Africa. *Not* to America. Get the house settled first." All was then clear. My brother and I were buying a house, and it would have been most unwise to take up the California appointment. What was so convincing was the sense of urgency on an important family issue, causing my mother to labour hard to put things right.'

Wilson Knight knew John Cowper Powys well. In a preface to the 1960 edition of *Wolf Solent*, Powys wrote: 'Whatever death may mean, and none of us really know, I have come to the conclusion for myself that when I die it is the complete and absolute end of me ...' He died on June 17, 1963, aged ninety. One month later, Miss Frances Horsfield, a medium of Bideford, Devon, addressed Wilson Knight during a demonstration in the Exeter church. A man was standing by him: 'He has rather gaunt features, with high cheek bones and unruly hair. He *is* a personality. I find it difficult to get close to him. He is nearly controlling me [i.e. speaking through her] but I do not want that. He was himself an occultist, and knew as much as anyone about the continuity of life ... He wrote, didn't he?' Wilson Knight said yes. Miss Horsfield then asked, 'Can I go to Wales?' confirming his suspicion that it was Powys. The medium went on: 'He is so close to you. It's a wonder you can't sense him yourself ... His power is so strong that you may well see him yourself some time ... He has a lovely smile, and a wide, gleaming mouth. He is thanking you for what you did for him, and in return he wants to help you ...' Afterwards, the medium added that Powys had a 'beaklike nose'. She had not herself read any of Powys's books, but she repeated that his power was greater than any she had experienced.

When Wilson Knight told her that Powys had often discussed life after death in his books, but had become sceptical towards the end, she commented, 'Anyway, he knows all about it now.'

Later Jackson Knight received a message from Powys via the same medium, which he sent to Wilson Knight on a postcard. 'Powys wants to give you some evidential cross-reference. Miss Horsfield gets the word "sensualism" for you to explain.' Readers of Powys will know that sensuality is a key word in all his work (one of his best philosophical books is called *In Defense of Sensuality*). The word carries mystical overtones. Wilson Knight adds: 'In some letters to me of January or February 1957 Powys had emphasised the importance of masturbation as a way to the mastery of dangerous impulse; and he had urged me to act as "a kind of missionary" in this cause. When I last saw him in 1963, he was weak and hardly spoke at all, but instead used an emphatic sign language of knotted hands, which I took to hold a sexual reference; perhaps it was a final injunction to me to hand on the masturbatory doctrine. It is probable that Powys's second message through Miss Horsfield had a more than "evidential" purpose, and was intended to remind me about the doctrine.'*

It must be frankly acknowledged that the objection that many intelligent people feel towards spiritualism is less a doubt about the validity of its evidence than about the way it seems to simplify the universe. The worst thing about human life is the way that human beings remain stuck in the 'triviality of everydayness', the way they accept the limitations of their narrow consciousness. Plato points out that the philosopher and the poet spend their lives trying to escape the limitations of the body, aware that consciousness *can* take in wider vistas – William James's 'distant horizons of fact' – but not sure how to wriggle out of the trap in

---

* See Wilson Knight's study of Powys, *The Saturnian Quest*, 1964; also his *Neglected Powers*, 1971.

which we all seem to be caught. Poets, philosophers and saints are centrally concerned with escaping this trap (which Christians call original sin). Perhaps the sceptic's central objection to spiritualism could be expressed like this: that after Dante's *Comedy*, the visions of St. John of the Cross and William Blake, Beethoven's Ninth Symphony, the paintings of Van Gogh, there is something anticlimactic about the 'messages' that come through at spiritualist meetings. But it would be a mistake to make too much of this point. After all, messages from the dead to the living are bound to be concerned mainly with everyday affairs. (We might also bear in mind that the young couple in Bonamy Dobrée's script said that the message concerned 'the most important' action of their lives.) And 'spirit teachings', whether in Swedenborg, Stainton Moses or a modern exponent like Maurice Barbanell, bear a stamp of healthy-minded authenticity. If the *evidence* was unassailable, a universal acceptance of life after death could only have a beneficial effect on our civilisation.

We might, at this point, take note of an odd fact recorded by Wilson Knight in an article written in 1960: 'Physical mediums are now more scarce than in the past; the great ones of the last century are looked back on as classics; and it may well be that other kinds of phenomena will grow rare,'* It *is* a matter for regret that now when we have elaborate apparatus for testing the claims of mediums like Home and Eusapia Palladino, such powers should be dying out. This is a matter to which I must return in the concluding pages of this book.

Wilson Knight ends his article on spiritualism: 'It is not to be supposed that Spiritualism can replace our set disciplines, but rather that it is, in different ways, basic to all … Sources must be tapped from deeper levels which owe nothing to our own minds.' And this suggests at least a partial answer to the question raised in the last

---

* Leeds University periodical, *Gryphon*, March 1960.

paragraph. In a case like Home, the 'hidden powers' lay at the red end of the spectrum, and this is no doubt why many intelligent men – like Hawthorne – thought them interesting but irrelevant. The powers Gurdjieff was striving to develop lay at the violet end. Home was like an iceberg; most of his being lay in the realm of the subconscious; Gurdjieff aimed at an extension of consciousness, an attempt to develop a *strength* of the mind equivalent to an athlete's strength of body. Inevitably, he acquired 'infra-red powers' at the same time, for if the tree is to grow higher, its roots must also go deeper. Could it be that mediums are becoming scarcer because, at this point in human evolution, ultra-violet powers are more important than infra-red?

This raises another central point. Christian Science is in agreement with occult tradition in regarding the subconscious powers as a source of health. The simplest, and perhaps crudest, statement of this notion is expressed in the work of D. H. Lawrence. If man becomes too intellectual, says Lawrence, he destroys his deeper powers, breaks his contact with the realm of instinct, which is also the realm of enriched vitality. All that Lady Chatterley needs to rescue her from her devitalised existence is to return to the deep, dark realm of sex. But Lawrence's own work reveals the fallacy behind this notion. At the end of his novels the reader wants to ask: What do the characters do now? Gurdjieff would have had no trouble in pinpointing the fallacy. He is concerned with people whose centres are out of harmony – whose sexual centre tries to work with emotional energy, and so on. Lawrence would advise such 'dislocated people' to go back to nature, to their primitive origins. They do, and the instinctive and sexual centres begin to work with their own energy. What now? Now, Gurdjieff would say, the serious work can begin. But this is precisely the point where Lawrence stops.

The subconscious powers are not the source of health – not on their own. Otherwise Lawrence would not have died of tuberculosis at forty-five. And Sri Ramakrishna, who could plunge into *samadhi* a dozen times a day, would not have died of a cancer of the throat. Paracelsus knew better: that the source of health is the evolutionary drive, whose major instrument is imagination – Faculty X. Life that marks time, whether on the highest intellectual or the lowest instinctive level, is in danger of stagnation. Occult powers *on their own* are no more desirable than the power to do enormous sums in mental arithmetic. Aldous Huxley remarks, in a letter to J. B. Rhine (December 30, 1942): '... the mystics ... have been unanimous in warning aspirants to the knowledge of God to have nothing to do with the psychic powers which they are likely to develop while pursuing the path of contemplation; for such powers, and the "miracles" which they allow their owners to perform, have no more to do with divine Reality than the more familiar kinds of psycho-physical phenomena ...' And in the same letter, Huxley makes the vitally important point that all occult powers stem from the human mind itself, not from gods or demons or spirits. 'This means that any religion, if intensely enough believed in, creates the objects of its worship – gods, defunct saints, and the like. These objectifications or projections may become centres of energy reinforcing the energies of individual prayers, desires and imaginations, and thus may assist the worshipper in getting the result he desires. Thus, in ... *The Tibetan Book of the Dead* ... are to be found the most categorical statements to the effect that the tutelary deities of the worshipper and even the High Buddhas themselves are objectifications projected by human minds and ultimately unreal. The finally independent reality is the Clear Light of the Void ...' According to this view, even the Christian Scientist notion that God is the source of health is a misunderstanding; the source lies in the worshipper's own mind.

And so we reach the paradoxical conclusion that the apparitions of the dead that speak through mediums are already in the mind of the medium, and *yet* are objective realities. It would be a mistake to draw a distinction between Home's 'own' powers and the power of spirits operating through him; they are one and the same.

In 1882, ten years after Home's retirement, W. F. Barrett, F. W. H. Myers and Henry Sidgwick founded the Society for Psychical Research, and a brilliant young intellectual, Edmund Gurney, became one of its leading lights. The date should have marked a turning point in the history of occultism, since it meant that solid, sceptical Englishmen with a scientific turn of mind would now investigate a subject whose advocates had so far been cranks, or at least romantics.

The results were disappointing. Gurney committed suicide in a Brighton hotel in 1888 when he discovered that certain trusted mediums were tricksters.* And although the S.P.R. has had many eminent adherents – from Sir William Crookes, Sir Arthur Conan Doyle and Sir Oliver Lodge down to Professors C. D. Broad and Wilson Knight – it has failed to make any general impact. The Reverend Stainton Moses, a remarkable psychic who developed his powers by conscious effort, left the Society in 1886 because he felt it was too cold and scientific; for him, spiritualism was a religion. But the general public was not interested in spiritualism as a science or religion. This is as true today as it was in 1882. And the reason, almost certainly, is the one we have already discussed: that there is something oddly uninspiring about these accounts of messages from the dead, apparitions of the living and so on – like a cold Methodist Sunday School on a wet afternoon.

There is a failure, for example, to note the sexual origin of some of the phenomena. One of the most notable of the mediums after Home, Eusapia Palladino, never made any secret about her strong erotic tendencies. When W. F. Monck was exposed as a fraudulent

* See *The Strange Case of Edmund Gurney*, by Trevor Hall (London, 1964).

medium in 1876, obscene letters were found in his luggage; they were from women with whom he had been carrying on intrigues in the darkness of the séance room. Myers himself had a reputation as a would-be Don Juan, and it was undoubtedly some odd sexual obsession that made him insist on accompanying Gurney on his honeymoon to Switzerland, in spite of Mrs. Gurney's protests. Houdini, who investigated many mediums for fraud, disclosed that they often offered 'payment in kind' for his collusion; the late Negley Farson told me of an interview with Houdini during which Houdini claimed to have spent one séance with his hand inside the knickers of the medium. Trevor Hall has pointed out that Myers was a 'queer character' in other ways; there was a scandal at Cambridge about Myers's theft of twenty-five lines from someone else's poem in an effort he claimed to be his own, and a fellow student described returning unexpectedly to his room and finding Myers reading his letters.

I am not asserting that all this proves anything against spiritualism; it doesn't. Eusapia Palladino was undoubtedly a genuine medium; yet she was exposed for fraud several times; a kind of genial dishonesty seemed to be part of her character, as of Madame Blavatsky's. At her early séances, spectators were enraged when the spirits relieved them of their wallets and watches. Eusapia was often firmly tied to a chair when this happened; but her subconscious desires clearly affected the spirits. Myers's dubious character in matters of sex or other people's correspondence does not prove that he would be capable of faking the results of a séance; but it should be taken into account that his motives in forming the S.P.R. may have been highly charged and emotional rather than purely scientific. No one would suspect this in reading the carefully objective publications of these early members of the S.P.R.: Myers's *Human Personality and Its Survival of Bodily Death*, *Phantasms of the Living* (by Myers, Gurney and Podmore), *Apparitions* (by G. N. M. Tyrrell) or even C. D. Broad's *Lectures on*

Psychical Research (1962). All this has tended to present a picture of spiritualism as a harmless branch of Christianity, when, in fact, it is more closely related to the witchcraft of the Reformation or the Dionysian religion of ancient Greece. Perhaps if this was more generally recognised – by spiritualists themselves as well as by the general public – the result might be a more widespread interest in the movement, as well as a deeper understanding of the forces involved. In the case of the S.P.R., the sober public image may be explained by the following comment from Harry Price: 'The late Sir William Barrett [the founder] once wrote me that he was "treated like a child" at the Council meetings, and that "Mrs. Sidgwick always gets her own way" – which I could quite believe. The feminine element was always a factor at the S.P.R., as in most psychic societies.'

Price, who made his name as a highly sceptical investigator of psychic matters, was himself the subject of a vigorous debunking by the S.P.R. after his death. The case is worth citing as an example of the virtues and limitations of the sceptical approach to the occult.

In June 1929 a London newspaper carried an article about alleged hauntings at a rectory near Sudbury, in Essex. Harry Price, an eminent member of the S.P.R., decided to investigate. In 1940 Price published a book about Borley Rectory called *The Most Haunted House in England*, calling it 'the best-authenticated case of haunting in the annals of psychical research'. The book caused a sensation. In 1956, not long after Price's death, the S.P.R. published a book called *The Haunting of Borley Rectory*, by E. J. Dingwall, Kathleen Goldney and Trevor Hall, whose main purpose was to discredit Price. Price, amusingly enough, had made a name for himself by his investigation into fraudulent mediums. The strange legends about Borley date from long before Price heard of the place. It had been built in 1863 by a clergyman named Bull, and his son had lived there after his death; Bull junior was interested in psychical research.

When Price investigated the house in 1929, the tenant was the Rev. G. E. Smith and his wife, who left not long after. A couple named Foyster moved in; the wife, Marianne, was much younger than her husband. (She was thirty-one.) Poltergeist phenomena now began to occur in earnest. Mrs. Foyster was struck and thrown out of bed; objects flew around; a child's footsteps were heard; messages addressed to 'MF' were found scrawled on walls; bells rang; raps sounded; doors were locked, furniture overturned. Price was inclined to suspect Marianne's honesty in connection with some of these occurrences. At all events, the Foysters moved out in 1935. In 1937 Price rented the rectory and moved back with a team of investigators; but very little occurred. It was burned down in 1939. Price died in 1948.

In *The Most Haunted House in England*, Price states that on his first day there he saw a shadowy shape like the phantom nun in the garden, and his colleague (a journalist) actually saw her clearly. The window of a sealed room was smashed from the inside, and a tile and a candlestick thrown out. The various legends and stories seemed to be fairly unambiguous; the Rev. Harry Bull (the spiritualist) claimed that he had often seen ghosts, including the nun, a phantom coach and an unidentified man. His daughter, Miss Ethel Bull, confirmed in a letter to Trevor Hall in 1953 that she had been wakened to find a strange man standing beside her bed, and had felt someone sitting down on the bed on one or two occasions. She also saw the nun several years after her father's death.

Perhaps the most weighty piece of evidence against Price is a letter written by Mrs. Smith, the wife of the rector in 1929, flatly denying that they ever believed the house to be haunted; this appeared in the *Church Times*. In a longer statement in 1949, Mrs. Smith suggested that Price himself probably produced some of the phenomena – a pebble that whizzed across the room, a glass of water that turned to ink. But she admitted that even when Price was not present, odd things happened: she heard the gate open and saw the headlamps of some vehicle in the darkness outside, but there was no vehicle; her husband heard voices; doors and windows were found open. But when the authors of the later 'investigation' looked through the files of letters written by the Smiths to Price in 1929, they discovered that both the Smiths seemed to be convinced that there *were* ghosts. 'Borley is undoubtedly haunted,' said the Reverend Smith.

The technique of the S.P.R. book is to attempt to discredit as many of the 'hauntings' as can be discredited, to advance natural explanations as often as possible, including the dishonesty of Price and Marianne Foyster. But all their 'natural explanations' cannot obscure the basic facts. The house had a reputation of being haunted before Price heard of it. The Smiths believed it was haunted at the time Price investigated it in 1929. All kinds of poltergeist phenomena occurred when the Foysters were there. And Price took the trouble to rent the house and investigate it again in 1937. If he produced the phenomena in his earlier investigation, what prevented him from doing it again now, since none of his 'team' had any suspicion of him? Price devoted his life to psychical research, and witnessed many genuine phenomena – for example, those of Willy Schneider, also described by Thomas Mann in *An Experience in the Occult*. Why should he take so much trouble to build up a 'worthless legend' on a slender foundation? While a sense of drama and desire to convince often led him to exaggerate, it is a long way from this to believing that he actually fabricated phenomena. In fact, another lengthy report on the case prepared for the S.P.R. by R. J. Hastings ends by admitting that there is no evidence of fraud.

The same rather uncharitable attitude to Price is shown in another book by Dingwall and Hall, *Four Modern Ghosts*, which examines Price's account of a séance at which a little girl named Rosalie materialised. Price's story (in *Fifty Years of Psychical Research*) is that after a broadcast about Borley Rectory in 1937, a lady rang him up and invited him to a séance where Rosalie was expected to materialise. The lady's one condition was that Price should not publish the address of the house or anything by which the people could be identified. He attended the séance at a house in south London, met the mother of the dead Rosalie and various other people. Not long after the séance began, Rosalie appeared, and Price was allowed to touch her, a naked child of about six; he could also see her by means of a luminous plaque. When the séance was over, Price investigated and found that the seals on the room were all intact.

The next morning, Mrs. Kathleen Goldney (one of the authors of the 'exposure' of Borley Rectory) saw Price, and found him haggard and distraught; he told her about his experience, stuttering badly. (Price normally had a slight stutter.) Subsequently Price told the story at a gathering of the Ghost Club (which he had formed) and wrote the account in his book. Dingwall wrote Price a jeering letter about the story, suggesting that if they could have materialised a white horse, too, Rosalie could have played Lady Godiva. He was surprised, apparently, when Price failed to reply. In the article in *Four Modern Ghosts*, the authors admit that Mrs. Goldney really saw Price looking badly shaken the morning after the Rosalie experience, but go on to explain why they disbelieve the story. Price described the house in some detail while not revealing which part of London it was to be found in. In a letter he had apparently mentioned it as being in Brockley. The authors thereupon got hold of an ordnance survey map of Brockley, and ascertained that no house there fitted Price's description; at least, there was one, but the tenants had only been there for a year in 1937, and Price claimed that the Rosalie séances had been going on since 1929. However, Price himself *had* lived in Brockley as a child, and even attended a séance in the road in which the authors found their house. They inferred that Price had seen the house a number of times when he lived in Brockley and had used its description in his invented tale of Rosalie.

It is significant that Mrs. Goldney, who worked closely with Price for many years, remarked during the Borley investigation: '… though I credited Price with intellectual dishonesty, I had not imagined he would ever himself stoop to fraudulent *actions*.' Mr. Dingwall, who had also known Price since 1922, was equally convinced that Price would do anything for publicity. He said something of the sort in an essay that he was invited to contribute to Dr. P. Tabori's biography of Price; this scathing little pen portrait was so harsh that it was not printed in the book, but Dingwall prints an extract from it in *Four Modern Ghosts* which makes it quite clear that he disliked Price. So the 'unbiased' examination of the two books is based on personal dislike. This is not to say that Dingwall is deliberately unfair; but it does suggest that he sets out to play the prosecutor rather than the detached judge. He concludes his remarks on Price: '… he never, in my opinion, advanced our real knowledge of the supernormal in any way whatsoever'. Precisely the same thing can be said of Mr. Dingwall. His attacks on Price did not even advance our knowledge of the normal. For what can we conclude, having read them, and read Price's own accounts of the same events? Borley *could* have been a series of coincidences and fakes. But if we are willing to admit the existence of 'supernormal' phenomena, there is nothing very extraordinary here. The rectory was built in 1863 – whether on the site of an old monastery or not is beside the point. The Rev. Harry Bull was a medium, and he even stated his intention of returning to the rectory after his death. He contacted various 'spirits' there, and his daughter, who inherited his sensitivity, also saw spirits. The Smiths were not particularly sensitive, but they observed a few poltergeist phenomena. But Marianne Foyster provoked a whole crop of poltergeist phenomena; whether these were entirely due to her own 'psyche' or to 'spirits' is not known. When she left, the phenomena stopped, although *Man, Myth and Magic* prints a photograph allegedly showing a brick floating in the air at the time when the rectory was being demolished. There is nothing very hard to accept in all this: from the records of the S.P.R. or Sir Ernest Bennett's carefully documented *Apparitions and Haunted Houses* (1939) a hundred other similar cases could be extracted. And the same applies to the account of the materialisation of Rosalie. If it was the only case of its kind, it might be worth a great deal of sceptical investigation. But there have been many more materialisations, and there is nothing inherently improbable in the story. Unless someone can produce a book proving that Price was a pathological liar with a craving for publicity, it is necessary to suspend judgement. And this leaves us back where we started.

It should be noted that Dingwall himself is not a sceptic about psychical phenomena; on a number of occasions in *Very Peculiar People* and *Some Human Oddities* he is willing to admit that he cannot suggest any natural explanation for certain phenomena (e.g. the flying monk of Copertino), and presumably he would not have bothered to write books about such things unless they interested him.

This problem – of the ambiguity of psychic phenomena – was raised again in the year 1970 by appearance of an extraordinary record entitled 'Rosemary Brown's Music'. Rosemary Brown is a London housewife, now in her forties; she is also a medium. Sometime in the mid-sixties, she began to hold spirit-conversations with an elderly gentleman who introduced himself as a musician. In 1965 she became aware that he was the composer Liszt. Mrs. Brown could play the piano, although not particularly well, and knew a little about music. At Liszt's dictation she wrote down a few pieces in his style. Then Liszt brought other composers, including Beethoven, Chopin, Schubert, Brahms and Debussy. Mrs Brown was soon taking down music as fast as she could write. Influential people became interested, and a fund was started to allow her to devote full time to her musical activities. The BBC did a programme about her, and it was impressive. For it seemed reasonably clear that Mrs. Brown must be receiving the music from *somewhere* – it was not purely her own invention. Other 'musical mediums' who were played on the programme could have been frauds, consciously or unconsciously; improvisations 'in the manner' of Chopin or Liszt were no better than, say, Victor Borge's imitations of various composers. Mrs. Brown's work was usually more complex, and one got the impression that she found some of it quite bewildering.

The record can allow listeners to judge for themselves. On one side, Mrs. Brown plays Liszt, Grieg, Chopin and Schumann; on the other, the concert pianist Peter Katin plays pieces by Beethoven, Schubert, Debussy, Chopin and Brahms – all of them too difficult for Mrs. Brown's modest abilities as a pianist. The spirit of Sir Donald Tovey, the musicologist, dictated a typical introduction to Mrs. Brown on January 1, 1970:

> Humanity is now moving into an age of increasing emancipation from many of its past limitations. Technical achievements and medical advances confer growing freedom from various oppressions and ills. Man's greatest problem is still himself and his orientation to his fellow beings. To understand himself fully he should become aware of the fact that he does not consist merely of a temporary form which is doomed to age and die. He has an immortal soul which is housed in an immortal body and endowed with a mind that is independent of the physical brain. In communication through music and conversation, an organised group of musicians who have departed from your world are attempting to establish a precept for humanity: i.e. that physical death is a transition from one state of consciousness to another wherein one retains one's individuality. The realisation of this fact should assist man to a greater insight into his own

nature and potential super-terrestrial activities. The knowledge
that incarnation in your world is but one stage of man's eternal
life should foster policies which are more far-seeing than those
frequently adopted at present, and encourage a more balanced
outlook regarding all matters ...

This is clear enough: the musicians wish to convince humanity that
death is not the end. But does the music achieve this effect? That
is hard to say. Enos Shupp, Jr., a reviewer in *The New Records* (a
magazine issued in Philadelphia) says of the Peter Katin side: 'Some
of them could be considered practically first quality by the particular
composer; none could be considered other than very fine.' But if we
try to imagine Beethoven or Brahms agreeing to compose music in
order to convince us that they are still alive, we immediately anticipate
something *totally* convincing, something that startles the listener
with its power and audacity, as the opening bars of the Fifth
Symphony startled Beethoven's contemporaries. And there is nothing
of the sort on this record. In fact, all of it could have been composed
by any skilled musician – for example, by Peter Katin himself. But
Mrs. Brown is not a skilled musician; she does not even have a
gramophone in her house. And so the balance of probability is on her
side. The question remains: If the great composers wish to convince us
of life after death, why do they not do it by composing a masterpiece?
That would be the most overpowering evidence. If the spirits could
add one poem or symphony of genius to our present stock, it
would make more converts for spiritualism than all the publications
of the S.P.R.

Mrs. Brown is apparently taking down Beethoven's Tenth
Symphony at this moment, so perhaps the spirits have already reached
the same conclusion. In the meantime, Mrs. Brown's recorded music
will convince those who want to believe, and leave the sceptics as
incredulous as ever.

In his excellent book *Apparitions*, G. N. M. Tyrrell makes a useful distinction between ghosts and 'crisis apparitions'. He cites a typical crisis case. A woman bending over her baby turned around and saw her brother, an airman; he looked perfectly solid and normal; she assumed he had been given leave from France, where he was in the air force (this was 1917), and spent a moment putting the baby in a safe position before turning to speak to him. But he had vanished. She was still not convinced that she had seen an apparition; she called out to him, thinking he was hiding for a joke. But he was nowhere to be seen; she then began to feel sick and afraid. It was another two weeks before she learned that her brother was missing.

A ghost may also look perfectly lifelike – most real-life ghost stories concern quite solid-looking ghosts – but they usually behave in a way that indicates that they are hardly aware of the human beings present; Tyrrell speaks of their 'somnambulistic or automatic behaviour'. The theatre critic W. Macqueen Pope, in his book *Pillars of Drury Lane*, describes actually seeing one of the theatre's most famous ghosts, 'the man in grey', who, on one occasion, walked out of a wall in the upper circle, walked through the bar and disappeared through the opposite wall, completely ignoring the people present. He could be seen at a distance of several feet, but vanished at close quarters, reappearing again when he was several feet away from the onlooker. While it would not be entirely true to say that ghosts of this type always ignore people, it does seem that they are not fully conscious of their surroundings. In this sense, they bear an odd resemblance to spectres of the living. I have already pointed out that Powys did not know that he had appeared to Theodore Dreiser until Dreiser rang him up and told him. Tyrrell cites the curious and quite inconclusive case of Canon Bourne, who was out hunting with his two daughters and a coachman; the daughters decided to return home, and the father went on. As they turned to go home, both daughters and the coachman saw

Canon Bourne waving to them from the other side of the valley, signalling them to follow; he looked dirty and shaken. They hurried to the place where he had been, but found no one there. This story should end with the daughters arriving home and learning that their father had been thrown from his horse and was seriously injured. In fact, he returned home not long after they did, perfectly unharmed, and verified that he had not waved to them, and had not met with an accident. What seems to have happened is that, in some unconscious way, he had projected a figure of himself waving to them.

Tyrrell cites a similar case in which someone deliberately tried to 'appear' to two sisters who lived in a house at Kew; the experimenter (presumably a woman) sat by the fire in her room and made an intense effort of concentration, which resulted in a kind of trance, during which she was conscious but could not move. Half an hour later, she threw off the trance with an effort of will. The following day, she visited Kew and discovered that the experiment had been remarkably successful; a lady in the house (but not one of those to whom she was trying to 'appear') said that she had seen her walking along the passage at 9.30 the previous evening – the time she had started making the attempt. She had reappeared in the front bedroom at midnight, when she had taken the hand of the lady in the bed (who was awake) and stared into her eyes. The odd feature of this second appearance is that the experimenter was asleep in her own bed at the time, although she had determined to 'appear' in the front bedroom of the Kew house at midnight.

We are here quite clearly dealing with some form of telepathy, and it is tempting to assume that all crisis apparitions are the result of telepathy between people who are close together. But there are too many well-attested cases of the apparitions appearing to several people for this to be wholly acceptable. Tyrrell cites a case in which a housewife saw an unknown naval officer bending over the end of the bed; she drew her husband's attention to the man, and the husband shouted irritably, 'What on earth are you doing here, sir?' and leapt out of bed. The naval officer then walked off through the wall. The housewife wondered if the apparition portended some danger to her brother, who was in the navy, but her husband said impatiently, 'No, it was my father' – who had been dead for fourteen years. The husband was in financial difficulties, and the apparition was there to warn him not to take a certain step he was contemplating.

In his book *The Vital Message*, Conan Doyle states: 'The physical basis of all psychic belief is that the soul is a complete duplicate of the body, resembling it in the smallest particular, although constructed of some far more tenuous material. In ordinary conditions these two bodies are intermingled so that the identity of the finer one is entirely obscured. At death, however, and under certain conditions in the course of life, the two can divide and be seen separately.' This view certainly sounds naïve, and most intelligent people would no doubt dismiss it as wishful thinking. But it must be admitted that the more one reads on these matters, the more common-sensible it sounds. Naïve or not, evidence supports the view that physical death is not total extinction (as materialists believe) or even a transition to some higher mystical plane that is completely incomprehensible to human beings – a view that is tempting to the mystically inclined – but for the time being at any rate, some kind of continuation of the physical personality. The view expressed satirically by Noël Coward in *Blithe Spirit*, where the ghosts behave exactly as though they were human beings, is well supported by the evidence. Sir Ernest Bennett's *Apparitions and Haunted Houses*, one of the best-documented books on the subject, cites a case in which an old chimney sweep, Samuel Bull, died of 'sooty cancer', leaving behind a bed-ridden widow in the charge of his daughter and son-in-law. There were five children in the house, as well as a twenty-one-year-old grandson. The family were living in overcrowded and unhappy conditions in a condemned cottage, and no doubt the widow experienced considerable distress. About nine months later, the children became nervous and restless; they were unable to sleep because they said someone was outside the door. Then one evening, the ghost of the chimney sweep walked up the stairs and through the door of the room in which he had died, and in which his widow now lay. On the first occasion this happened, the grandchildren were terrified; but as it continued over two months, they began to get used to it, and took it calmly. The apparition would stand by Mrs. Bull's bed, with his hand on her forehead – she said it felt firm but cold. These visits were not brief – one lasted more than an hour – and everyone in the family saw them. The S.P.R. was notified only a short time before the family was re-housed in April 1932, when the appearances had ceased, but the signed statements and long interviews with members of the family make it unlikely that this was a plot to gain publicity. The ghost seems to have appeared because he was worried about his wife and the generally unhappy condition of the family; he usually looked sad, but on his last two appearances, seemed much more cheerful – by this time, the family expected to move to a better house.

Under the circumstances, it would obviously be of interest if 'the spirits' would take the trouble to explain exactly what *does* happen after death, and how long they are kept hanging around in an earth-bound condition. Bishop Pike's son Jim began by explaining, 'I am not in purgatory – but something like hell here,' and added that nobody blamed him. It might seem that only confused 'spirits' find themselves in Jim Pike's 'limbo', but since Bishop Pike alleges that Paul Tillich also communicated, this cannot be maintained. Swedenborg explains that in the 'after-life', spirits progress and evolve just as they do on earth, and that 'hell' must be understood as a mental condition of confused and self-tormenting spirits. This sounds immediately plausible; but Swedenborg's extraordinary comments on the inhabitants of the moon lead one to suspect his reliability as a witness of the other world. Conan Doyle's descriptions of 'the other side' makes it sound like an idealised version of this one: 'They are very busy on all forms of congenial work. The world in which they find themselves is very much like that which they have quitted, but everything keyed to a higher octave. [The word 'octave' is interesting in this connection – Gurdjieff asserts that the universe is based on a principle of octaves.] As in a higher octave the rhythm is the same, and the relation of notes to each other the same, but the total effect different, so it is here.' Children grow up, but there is no ageing apart from this, and there is 'close union between the sexes' but no physical side to love. (Jim Pike explained, 'Yes, there is sex, but it is not like it is there. It is not physical, of course, but actually there is less limitation … Here you can actually enter the whole person.')

We may consider all this absurd, but then, the whole subject of the occult is full of 'absurdities' that offend the logical mind and yet cannot be dismissed as fantasies. Our position in the world is absurd; life seems solid and real enough; but the moment we try to pursue any problem beyond a certain limit, it vanishes into a misty realm of ambiguities. We are enmeshed in dreams and illusions, and the strongest characteristic of the human race is stupidity and short-sightedness. And when we study some of these messages from the spirit world, there seems to be good reason for scepticism. G. K. Chesterton devotes several excellent pages of his *Autobiography* to spiritualism, and they have a ring of cheerful sanity that carries conviction. He agrees that in séances 'something happens which is not in the ordinary sense natural, or produced by the normal and conscious human will. Whether it is produced by some subconscious but still human force, or by some powers, good, bad or indifferent, which are external to humanity, I would not myself attempt to decide. The only thing I will say with complete confidence about that mystic and invisible power is that it tells lies' (p. 82). He then tells some hilarious stories of his own experiments with a planchette (an apparatus for 'automatic writing'). Asked what advice it would give to a very solid, dull member of Parliament of the group's acquaintance, the planchette replied promptly 'Get a divorce'. Since the wife was equally dull and respectable they asked it to elaborate, whereupon the planchette wrote at great speed and in one word. ''Orrible revelations in 'igh life.' Chesterton senior tried testing the 'spirits' by asking the name of a distant relative. and the board answered 'Manning.' The father pointed out that this was untrue. The board replied. 'Married before.' To whom? they asked, and the board replied promptly, 'Cardinal Manning.'

But when we have reached the point of agreeing with Chesterton that belief in 'mediums and moonshine' is probably a sign of feeblemindedness, we then have to recognise that the standpoint from which he is criticising them is that of orthodox Catholicism, which insists on the infallibility of the pope and the reality of the Devil, and that Chesterton's air of strong-minded sanity is not to be trusted. The only thing that emerges with any certainty from the study of spiritualism and occultism is that our normal, sane, balanced standpoint is built upon quicksand, since it is based upon a commonsense view of human consciousness that does not correspond to the facts. Perhaps the only valid criticism of spiritualism is that it would be better to learn to grasp the facts of human consciousness before we concern ourselves with the facts about the 'other world'.

And this brings us back again to the baffling subject of poltergeists, for a large number, if not all, of these are undoubtedly human in origin. The 'phantom drummer of Tedworth', one of the most celebrated of all poltergeists, was not a phantom but a living man. The 'drummer' was a vagabond named William Drury, who in March 1661 was making a nuisance of himself at the small town of Ludgershall in Wiltshire. A magistrate from nearby Tedworth, a Mr. John Mompesson, was told that the drummer was trying to blackmail local people into giving him money to stop his racket; and he had Drury arrested. Drury's 'pass', authorising him to beg in that part of the world, proved to be counterfeit, Mr. Mompesson had the drum confiscated and the beggar sent to jail. The drum was sent to Mr. Mompesson's house, and thereupon, an incredible series of poltergeist phenomena commenced. There were tremendous bangs and thumps on doors and walls. The disturbances would conclude with a tattoo beat on the drum. After a lull, the poltergeist began to terrorise the young children, beating tattoos on their bed, lifting them up into the air, shaking them and making sinister scratching noises under the bed. Mr. Mompesson had them removed to a neighbour's house for peace. The 'spirit' attacked the blacksmith with a pair of pincers, snatched a sword from a guest and wrestled for it when he tried to take it back, and grabbed a large stick from a servant woman who was trying to bar its path. The Rev. Joseph Glanvil, who investigated the case and wrote about it, heard the scratching noises around the children's bed, and was puzzled to find his horse sweating with terror when he went down to it the next morning. (The horse died shortly after.)

Mompesson attempted communication with the spirit, asking it to knock three times if Drury lay behind the disturbances; three clear knocks sounded. Although the drummer was acquitted on the charge of forging a false warrant – for lack of evidence – he was transported for stealing a pig, whereupon the disturbances ceased.

It would be pointless to ask how Drury caused the disturbances (as he admitted he did). Probably he didn't know himself. The power had something in common with Home's strange knack of making furniture float, and something in common with Powys's 'astral projection'; that much is apparent. It is also safe to say that we all possess the power – at least, potentially. It seems to be stronger, or at least, closer to the surface, in children than in adults, but it is not true, as some writers have stated, that children are always involved in poltergeist disturbances. It is impossible to doubt that they are caused by 'monsters from the subconscious'; case after case makes this clear. In *The Personality of Man*, Tyrrell describes the case of a neurotic child, a girl of fourteen, who was going through the usual tensions of puberty when odd phenomena began to occur; they were not very spectacular, but unexplainable; when she was asleep, the bed made clicking sounds, and noises occurred in other parts of the room that had no obvious cause. In *Poltergeists*, Sacheverell Sitwell describes a female child who became flushed and breathed more heavily when poltergeist disturbances occurred; but no matter how loud the bangs and raps became, she slept on. Dingwall describes a case that he personally investigated. A mother and daughter lived alone in a house in southern England while the father was absent; both were bored. The mother often went out in the evening, leaving the child alone. Then the disturbances began – plates flying about, doors banging, raps and crashes all over the house. The mother stopped going out, and the disturbances ceased. The child was not counterfeiting the disturbances – they were genuine enough – but her subconscious mind was making sure that her mother stayed home.* But beyond this, it is difficult to generalise about poltergeist phenomena. There have been cases in which a house has remained 'haunted' by a poltergeist throughout a number of tenancies, and others where the poltergeist has been active for many years. (The Willington Mill poltergeist, cited by Sitwell, displayed enormous inventiveness over twelve years, showing itself as an apparition of a monkey, a cat, a veiled woman or a heavy-footed man, and produced every conceivable kind of noise from whistles and bangs to guttural remarks and the sound of machinery.) In most cases, the

---

* *The Unknown – Is It Nearer?*, by E. J. Dingwall and John Langdon-Davies (London, 1956).

disturbances are not of long duration – perhaps a month or so. An article 'Four Months in a Haunted House' in *Harper's Magazine* (1962) describes a typical case of poltergeist activity in a house in Cape Cod: thumps, bangs, rappings on walls. Its one unusual feature is a noise that the author (who uses the pen name Harlan Jacobs) describes as 'the Grand Piano Smash', which sounded as if a grand piano had been dropped on the floor; it shook the house. They were in the garage, from which the sound had come, three seconds after the crash, and found everything undisturbed. They heard the crash on two more occasions. The fourth time it happened, it was heard only by three visitors sleeping in the bedroom normally occupied by the author's wife; *they* heard it, and described it as shaking the house; but the author and his wife, sleeping in another part of the small house, didn't hear a thing. It is this aspect of ghost phenomena that leads Tyrrell, in common with Myers and Gurney, to theorise that some of the sights and sounds may be purely mental, a kind of telepathy, and that when they are heard or seen by a number of people, it is a case of telepathic intercommunication between the witnesses.

The energies that produce these disturbances may or may not be those known to physics. In *The Night-Side of Nature* (1849), Mrs. Catherine Crowe describes the case of Angélique Cottin, a fourteen-year-old French girl, who was weaving silk at an oak frame in January 1846 when the frame began to plunge about. The other girls all retreated to the other side of the room, then returned, one by one; the frame remained still until Angélique returned, then began to jerk violently again. Her family assumed it to be a devil and tried to have her exorcised, but the priest was inclined to believe it to be a physical phenomenon. He was probably right. The disturbances became less violent if she was standing on a carpet or waxed cloth and her 'field of force' did not affect metal. But 'organic' objects – even a heavy stone trough – would rear like a frightened horse if her apron touched them.

When she was tired, the effects diminished. Wilhelm Reich, of whom I shall speak in the next chapter, would undoubtedly attribute the phenomena to 'orgone energy', a form of universal energy not known to physics, and it must be admitted that it is hard to explain the forces produced by Angélique Cottin on any other hypothesis. The disturbances went on from mid-January until April, and then gradually died away. They were widely investigated at the time. Mrs. Crowe mentions a number of other similar instances, and adds the curious statement: 'Many somnambulistic persons are capable of giving an electric shock; and I have met with one person, not somnambulistic, who informs me that he has frequently been able to do it by an effort of will.' She goes on to describe the case of Mlle. Emmerich, sister of a professor at Strasbourg, who became 'electrified' as the result of a bad shock, which made her a sleep-walker, and whose body 'became so surcharged with electricity that it was necessary for her relief to discharge it; and she sometimes imparted a complete battery of shocks to her brother and her physician, and whoever was near.' She had apparently developed some degree of the power of the electric eel, which is still a mystery to science. (The electric eel can produce as much as 600 volts; its 'bursts' of electricity are extremely rapid, like machine-gun fire, and can be sprayed out at the rate of 3,000 a second.)

It seems probable that the 'spontaneous combustion' that fascinated the Victorians so much was related to this same curious energy. Since the nature of static electricity has been understood, it has ceased to provoke the same interest. But cases continue to occur, and they cannot always be explained by static electricity – at least, not the kind normally produced by dry hair or silk clothes. Several cases are cited in a chapter of *Strange Unsolved Mysteries* by Emile Schurmacher. A nineteen-year-old girl named Maybelle Andrews was dancing in a Soho nightclub with her boyfriend, Billy Clifford, when flames suddenly burst from her back, chest and shoulders, igniting her hair. She died on the way to hospital. Her boyfriend, who was badly burned trying to put her out, explained that there were no open flames in the room – the flames seemed to come from the girl herself. The *Sheffield Independent* reports a case of a building contractor, G. A. Shepherdson, who waved a hand at some workmen as he drove past, and then turned into a human torch. The London *Daily Telegraph* reports that A. F. Smith of Birkenhead burst into flames in the cab of his lorry; but the fire was confined to the cab, and did not originate in the cushions of his seat; a coroner's jury was unable to determine the cause of the accident.

Professor Robin Beach, formerly of the Polytechnic Institute of Brooklyn, has made a study of human beings who are capable of building up enormous static charges. An Ohio manufacturer asked him to investigate inexplicable outbreaks of fire in his plant. He tested all the employees with a static electricity voltmeter, and discovered that one young woman carried a charge of 30,000 volts. Apparently this was due to a combination of circumstances: her dry skin, silky clothes, the dryness of the air in the plant and the carpets on the floors. Beach described a case of a man who was seriously injured when he unscrewed the cap of his car battery; an electrical discharge from his dry fingers exploded the hydrogen escaping from the battery and blew acid in his face. Most people, says Professor Beach, can, under certain circumstances, build up a charge of 15,000 volts, which is released when they touch any metal that is earthed. But this fails to explain how Maybelle Andrews burst into flames. If she was dancing – Schurmacher specifies the watusi – she was probably covered with a thin film of perspiration, which is not conducive to a build-up of static. Even supposing that she built up some immense charge, and brushed against an object that was earthed, there should only have been a brief flash, not an explosion of flames. And how could a man burst into flames in the cab of his lorry, when the rubber tyres insulate it from the earth?

Where do we draw the line between mental and physical powers, between the 'normal' and the psychic? When I bend my fingers, my nerves carry a message from my brain to the hand, but I have no idea of what happens in physical terms. I do not 'make' my fingers bend; there seems to be no intermediate process between wanting them to bend and bending them. Is this any less mysterious than the power of the electric eel to discharge 600 volts, or Angélique Cottin's knack of making heavy objects jump when she approached them?

Jule Eisenbud, M.D., a member of the University of Colorado Medical School in Denver, has devoted a whole book to his amazing researches into the powers of an alcoholic bellhop, Ted Serios, who can cause photographs to appear on a film by merely concentrating on the camera. Dr. Eisenbud's book also illustrates the phenomenon I spoke of in the introduction to this book: the firm desire of ordinary people to ignore anything they cannot explain, and pretend it has never happened. Dr. Eisenbud was bothered by the problem of the non-repeatableness of most 'psychic phenomena', and wrote an article in which he said he looked forward to a more satisfactory phase in the history of psychical research. Someone thereupon sent him a paper that had been printed in *Fate* describing how Serios could produce photographs by staring into the camera lens with great concentration. The report stated that tests had been carried out over a number of months by scientists and photographers. Dr. Eisenbud's first response was to wonder why the hell, in that case, this wasn't a subject of general knowledge; then he decided that the answer must be that the people involved had not conducted their experiments with the necessary care and rigour. However, he eventually agreed to see a demonstration in Chicago. Ted Serios, a small, thin man, turned up in the hotel lobby – rather to Eisenbud's surprise, since he had been warned about the psychic's alcoholism. In the hotel room, Serios took a Polaroid camera loaded with film, stared into the lens with an intense concentration that made the veins stand out on his forehead, then relaxed after twenty seconds or so. The print, when taken out of the camera, was black. He tried seven more times before a plate came out with a dim, blurry picture of a tower-like building on it, which a lady present identified as the Chicago water tower, Serios complained of headache; he had drunk a certain amount of whisky. After a rest, there were more tries, and one of these produced another blurry but unmistakable picture of a hotel front with the words 'Stevens' across it; it was a hotel that had burned down some years before.

Eisenbud was understandably excited. He writes: '... I had also tried to show [that] it was necessary to postulate that we all had latent capacities to do unconsciously essentially what Ted was doing ... in order to close in on what to my mind was the number-one problem in science, the phenomenon [of] precognition.' He adds: 'Now here it was, just as predicted, like the planet Pluto.' He proceeded to ring up people who ought to be interested, and some professors who had seen the phenomenon agreed it was probably genuine. The result was a blank; they agreed it was genuine but couldn't be bothered to investigate further. 'So a guy takes pictures with his mind. So what?' said one magazine editor. One professor explained that he had lost interest because in one of the photographs Serios had got the wrong building. (Eisenbud says that it reminds him of the joke about the talking horse that ends, 'Don't believe a word that horse says – he's a pathological liar.')

Serios's claim to be included in this chapter lies in the way he developed his thought-photography. In 1955 he was working as a bellhop in a Chicago hotel, when a fellow employee discovered that he was an exceptionally good hypnotic subject. And under hypnosis, Serios became a 'travelling clairvoyant' – a subject already discussed in an earlier chapter – and journeyed mentally to distant places. On these mental expeditions, he made the acquaintance of a spirit who claimed to be Jean Laffite, a pirate and smuggler who died in the early nineteenth century, and Laffite took Serios to spots where he claimed buried treasure was hidden. An expedition to Florida to uncover some of this treasure was a failure, and Laffite seems to have got bored with his new acquaintance, for he became more difficult to summon up, until he vanished altogether. In spite of this, Ted's powers of scrying turned up a few minor finds, and at one point a syndicate was formed to exploit it. Several hundred dollars were unearthed at one spot, but a rival syndicate had got there first. One of the problems was pinpointing the spots where the treasure was hidden, and at this point Serios's fellow employee, George Johannes, handed him an ordinary camera and told him to try that. The resulting photographs astounded Serios, who thought at first that Johannes was pulling his leg. He bought his own camera, and got the same results. Finally, ill-health forced him to give up scrying, and one psychiatrist even convinced him that the whole thing had been some sort of an illusion. Eisenbud arrived on the scene after many years of ups and downs.

Eisenbud got Serios to Denver, and began a series of tests. In the first one, Serios managed to get a recognisable shot of the clock tower of Westminster Abbey – he had seen a photograph of it in a magazine the day before. A group of professors present were sufficiently impressed to sign testimonials about what they had witnessed. Eisenbud's account of Serios does not reveal a strong personality – endless talk about himself, jejune talk about his attitude to the opposite sex, a large daily consumption of whisky. He failed to arrive for his second big demonstration, fleeing back to Chicago and making various excuses; returning later, he irritated the committee of professors prepared to bear witness by getting incoherently drunk.

Then, sensing that everybody's patience had reached a limit, he grabbed the camera, concentrated hard and produced an excellent photograph of a double-decker bus, with the remark, 'Put that in your pipe and smoke it.'

Eisenbud's book *The World of Ted Serios* (1967) contains over a hundred of these 'mental pictures', and reproductions of various pictures that he had in mind when trying. There is immense variety. Buildings (sometimes in colour), cars, people, rockets and many weird and unidentifiable shapes. The usual method of taking them was as follows: Serios would take a small plastic tube, which he called a 'gismo', and hold it over the lens of the camera, then concentrate very hard and press the trigger of the camera. Anyone who has used a Polaroid will know that such a procedure would normally produce a blur. The camera and film were produced by Dr. Eisenbud or anyone else present. Serios could produce a 'photograph' whether or not there was a lens in the camera, and whether or not he was blindfolded. He usually had a fairly clear idea of what the picture would be, and on occasion, was quite certain that it had been successful. When trying to 'get' the Chicago Hilton, he muttered, 'Missed, damn it,' and produced the Denver Hilton instead (in colour).

Almost as remarkable as Ted Serios's photography was the reaction of people approached by Eisenbud for co-operation. At a meeting where he was describing his results, one friend and colleague grunted, 'Don't believe it,' and walked out; another became insulting; a third suggested that Serios should be stripped. If Eisenbud had been asking them to attend a séance, this kind of reaction might be understandable; but he was only asking for help in a controlled scientific experiment. Why should people react in this way? The answer, surely, is that there is still a gulf between science and 'paranormal phenomena', like the gulf between science and religion; and 'normal, rational' people react to tales of the paranormal as they might react to a religious crank trying to force his way in through the front door. Besides, there *is* some justification for the remark of the editor: 'So a guy takes pictures with his mind. So what?' If we consider Serios's photographs, or Daniel Dunglas Home's levitation, in isolation, they are strange, but they have no connection with everyday life. And *if* they have no connection, then they are certainly interesting but irrelevant, and busy people are right to ignore them. Eisenbud agrees that, at present, there is no connection, but he cites the story of Faraday, who was asked by three tax inspectors why His Majesty's Government should continue to support experiments with electrical jars; Faraday replied, 'I'm not quite sure myself where all this is going ... But maybe someday it will be taxable.' If Serios can produce pictures with his mind, what is to stop anybody doing it? There are powers involved here that we probably all possess, but are unaware of. What if Serios's manifestations are the equivalent of Faraday's Leyden jars? – the beginning of the discovery of a far bigger phenomenon? After all, the Leyden jar must have struck businessmen of the nineteenth century as an odd but limited phenomenon. You could produce sparks with it, and electrocute chickens; but so what? Who could guess that the Leyden jar would lead to the electric generator?

Whether Eisenbud is correct to believe that precognition and 'mind photography' are somehow connected is a question that must be considered in the final chapter. The 'active' powers of Serios, and the 'passive' powers of mediums, seem to be diametrically opposed. It is true that Serios can sometimes 'see' photographs in a sealed envelope and reproduce them on a Polaroid plate; but according to Eisenbud's account he is wrong more often than not. On the other hand, most 'psychics' simply have the power to 'see' things that other people cannot see. And even in this field, the powers vary widely. Peter Hurkos and Gerard Croiset can sense an object's history by touching it. Tom Corbett, of whom Diana Vernon has written at length in *The Stately Ghosts of England* (1963), can sense the presence and nature of ghosts in haunted houses, but may or may not 'sense something' about the person to whom he is speaking. Corbett explained to Mrs. Vernon: 'I haven't got any power over [the ghosts], like exorcising them or telling them to go away. But if there's a ghost around I can tell you where, and sometimes what it looks like. Other people have this gift in varying degrees. Some, like me, see them, some hear them, others just sense them. Most people, of course, aren't psychic at all, so they won't ever see a ghost – even if it's standing right beside them.'

Corbett's observations about ghosts throw some interesting light on the basic problem raised in this chapter. At Longleat, the home of the Marquis of Bath, Corbett was asked to give his opinion on two alleged ghosts, one in a corridor known as Green Lady's Walk, the other – supposedly of a bishop – in the library. To begin with, Corbett was deliberately shown the wrong corridor, by way of testing him. He immediately recognised that it was the wrong corridor, and led the way to another one, which led off the first. 'Something dreadful happened here. This is your corridor, not the other one.' As it happened, the nature of the 'something dreadful' was known. The Marquis of Bath in the time of Queen Anne caught his wife *in flagrante delicto* with her young lover; a sword fight ensued that ended with the lover being run through. The lover was (according to legend) buried in the cellars, and the marquis moved out, and lived for the rest of his life at a nearby village. When the present Marquis of Bath was a young man, the story was verified when workmen installing central heating found the skeleton under the cellar flags. But the ghost, according to Corbett, is not that of the lover or the avenging marquis, but of a woman – almost certainly Lady Louisa Carteret, the lady in question. Corbett acknowledged that he could not state definitely that the ghost was Lady Louisa, but added: 'A spirit retains the identity and sex it had when it was alive. The men [the lover and the marquis] can't haunt, presumably, because they had what it takes to progress, while Louisa's grief kept her shackled here.' He also explained that ghosts have no sense of time, and that they are therefore unaware of the passing of the centuries.

When shown the library in which the ghost of Bishop Ken was supposed to appear on the anniversary of his death, Corbett asserted that it was not haunted, and that, in any case, ghosts are not observers of anniversaries. (If time stands still for them, this is logical.) However, he was able to verify the presence of a friendlier spirit in another library in the house, pointing out the exact spot where the librarian had frequently sensed its presence; he was able to add that the ghost was almost certainly the builder of Longleat, a Sir John Thynne – a wealthy Elizabethan – which explains his attachment to it.

In another corridor of the house, Corbett stopped, and rapped with his knuckles on a door. He could not explain why he did it, but the librarian explained that when she had slept in that room, there had been a knock on the door every night, at about the same time; it happened so often that she ended by ignoring it.

Corbett's verdict on the house was: 'Certainly two very strong ghosts, the one in the corridor and the one in the Red Library. Then there's another, very faint, which causes the knock on Miss Coates's door. There's a heavy malevolence in the linen cupboard caused, I think, by someone who was probably once a housekeeper – a most unpleasant woman. All the hauntings are done independently, and each ghost is unaware of the others' existence. But our intrusion wasn't welcome, I'm afraid. The Bishop of Ken doesn't haunt, by the way.'

The comment about being unwelcome seemed to be verified when Corbett, Mrs. Vernon and the photographer who had accompanied them all fell ill after the visit to Longleat.

This chapter would be incomplete without some discussion of the evidence for reincarnation, the doctrine of the rebirth of the spirit in different bodies. The Greeks called it metempsychosis, or the transmigration of souls. The belief is so widespread as to be almost universal. It can be found among the ancient Egyptians, the Hindus, the American Indians and in the folk-lore of Europe and Africa. In the Bhagavad Gita, Krishna tells Arjuna:

You and I, Arjuna, have lived many lives.
I remember them all; you do not remember.

The doctrine of reincarnation, as found among the Hindus and Buddhists, is in some ways a flat contradiction of the Christian notion that eternal bliss or eternal punishment may be the outcome of a man's activities during a single lifetime. The Hindus assert that the soul returns to earth again and again, moving higher or lower, according to the degree of perfection it achieved in its previous incarnation. A 'great chain of being' descends from the ultimate Godhead to the lowest forms of dead matter, and everything has, its place on it. Man stands midway between matter and spirit, and his problem is to move upward. Reincarnation also plays an important part in the Kabbalah.

The Society for Psychical Research has paid less attention to cases of reincarnation than to various forms of psychical phenomena; Myers devotes only one page to it in his *Human Personality and Its Survival of Bodily Death*; and although he accepts the doctrine, he also points out the objections to it. In the long run, all spirits are bound to 'progress'; so the generality of men today ought to be altogether more moral and idealistic than the men of five thousand years ago. This hardly seems to be true. In the same way, if the 'reward' for success in a previous existence is to be born at a more comfortable level, then the aristocracy ought to be on a spiritually higher level than the *polloi* – an arguable assertion.

In 1956, the subject of reincarnation became the most popular topic of the day when a businessman from Pueblo, Colorado called Morey Bernstein published his accounts of hypnotising a local housewife named Virginia Tighe. Under hypnosis, Mrs. Tighe clearly recalled her previous existence as an Irish girl named Bridey Murphy. *The Search for Bridey Murphy* topped the national best-seller list for weeks, and was almost as popular in England. Edgar Cayce had asserted the reality of reincarnation since 1923, but the Bridey Murphy case seemed more conclusive and more spectacular than any of Cayce's examples. Then the bubble burst: the house in which Mrs. Tighe had been brought up was found to resemble the one in which Bridey Murphy had lived in Cork; it was discovered that one of her childhood neighbours had actually been called Bridie Murphy, and that Mrs. Tighe had once been in love with her son. It was finally established, beyond all reasonable doubt, that most of the things that had happened to Bridey Murphy had also happened to Mrs. Tighe. The *Chicago American* published a shattering exposé of Bridey Murphy, and the craze ended as suddenly as it had begun. Professor C. J. Ducasse of Brown University published a book on the belief in life after death in which he completely exonerated Mrs. Tighe from all suspicion of fraud and defended Bernstein as a serious and dedicated student of hypnosis and reincarnation; but for most Americans, the case was closed.

This was a pity, for the serious evidence for reincarnation is as convincing, if not quite so voluminous, as that for life after death. Volume 26 of the Proceedings of the American S.P.R. is devoted to *Twenty Cases Suggestive of Reincarnation*, by Ian Stevenson, M.D. These cases, selected from more than two hundred investigated by the Society, have the usual thorough documentation. Most of them seem to follow a certain pattern. A child of between two and four years old begins describing events and people in a previous existence. The parents decide to look into it, and the details are found to be accurate. Such stories are not unfamiliar; for example, the case of Shanti Devi can be found in Frank Edwards's *Stranger than Science*. She was born in Delhi in 1926. When she was seven, she informed her parents that she had been born before, in a town called Muttra (Mathura). She described her life in some detail – how she had been married and had three children; she died when giving birth to the third. Her name, she said, had been Ludgi. Her parents assumed this was pure imagination. But in 1935, a man called at the house on business, and Shanti Devi stared with amazement, declaring that he was her husband's cousin. The man confirmed that he was from Muttra, and that he had a cousin who had lost his wife, named Ludgi, in childbirth ten years earlier. Ludgi's husband was brought to the house – without telling the girl he was expected; she recognised him instantly and threw herself into his arms. Taken to Muttra, she was able to point out various people and places correctly, and converse with relatives of the dead Ludgi in local dialect, although Shanti Devi had been taught in Hindustani. A scientific commission which investigated the case found that she was able to direct a carriage through the town even when she was blindfolded, and recognise various landmarks. She recognised her two eldest children, but not the one whose birth had cost her her life. Ian Stevenson mentions the Shanti Devi case in his book, and adds that he has discovered that Ludgi's husband often came to Delhi, and frequented a sweetmeat shop not far from Shanti Devi's home. There is no suggestion that Shanti Devi met her former husband there; Stevenson only mentions it to raise the hypothesis of some kind of telepathy – which he then rejects.

One of the most interesting points that emerge from Stevenson's book is that a large number of subjects who could recall previous lives had died a violent death in this earlier existence; this may explain the continuation of memory. A boy named Ravi Shankar, born in July 1951, later gave details of his murder in his previous existence; as a child of six, he was killed and beheaded by a relative (aided by an accomplice) who hoped to inherit the property of the child's father. Ravi Shankar actually had a scar on his neck resembling a long knife wound. A child named Jasbir claimed to be a man who had been given poisoned sweets, and had died as a result of a fall from a cart in which he had sustained a head injury. Imad Elawar, a Lebanese child born in 1958, had died of tuberculosis in his previous existence, but he had been unpleasantly shocked when a cousin had been run over by a truck, driven by an enemy, and died soon afterwards; Imad's earliest statements about his previous existence concerned this violent death. H. A. Wijeratne, born in Ceylon in 1947, had memories of the life of his paternal uncle, who had been hanged for the murder of his wife. Jimmy Svenson, a Tlingit Indian of Southeastern Alaska, began to claim (at the age of two) that he was his maternal uncle, a man named Jimmy Cisko, who had died under mysterious circumstances, probably murdered; the child had marks on his abdomen resembling gunshot wounds.

On the other hand, Swarnlata Mishra, the daughter of an inspector of schools in Madhya Pradesh, only recognised the scene of her previous life when she happened to be passing through the city of Katni on a journey with her father; she was three and a half at the time. Norman Despers, a Tlingit Indian, was taken to visit a cove thirty-five miles away, and suddenly asserted that he had once owned a smokehouse (for smoking fish) on the strait, and had later gone blind; the description fitted his grandfather. The child was three at the time of the 'recognition' scene.

Some of the cases have extremely unusual features. Jasbir Lal Jat was three and a half years old when he suddenly 'became' Sobha Ram, the man who had fallen from the cart after eating poisoned sweets. But Sobha Ram did not die until Jasbir was three and a half. One day in the spring of 1954, Jasbir apparently died of smallpox. His father went to get help to bury him, but neighbours advised him to wait until the next day. Before morning, the child began to stir. When he eventually recovered, his personality had changed completely, and he began speaking about his previous existence. Unfortunately, he had been of the Brahmin caste in this existence, and his new family were Jats; the child declined to eat with them, and his food had to be cooked by a nearby Brahmin lady. It was only when he began to suspect that his family occasionally cheated him by cooking his food themselves that he decided to abandon himself to his new caste. When the child was taken to the village of Vehedi, some twenty miles away, he showed accurate and detailed knowledge of relatives, places and events.

The closeness of the villages might give rise to the suspicion that Jasbir had visited Vehedi often enough to learn about Sobha Ram; but Stevenson points out that the two villages are accessible only by means of dirt roads, and that since they are on either side of the local market town, one to the north, one to the south, inhabitants of one would have little or no reason to visit the other. (Stevenson always goes into the question of the relative locations of the places where his subjects lived – before and after reincarnation; there are few cases where there could be the remotest possibility of the subject having visited the scene of his 'previous existence'.)

Jasbir eventually came to spend as much time with his 'previous family' as with his new one, showing great affection for his son, or rather, Sobha Ram's son. This also occurs in a number of the cases cited by Stevenson, although in others, the 'new family' may show violent jealousy about the child's previous existence; there are several cases in which the child was beaten into silence about his 'other life'. It is also interesting to note that memories of a previous existence often fade as the child grows older.

Another noteworthy feature of many of the cases in Stevenson's book is that the subject seems to be able to *choose* where he will be reborn. Maria de Oliveiro, of Rio Grande do Sul, Brazil, deliberately contracted tuberculosis and died at the age of twenty-eight. (She had had two unhappy love affairs.) She promised her friend Ida Lorenz that she would be reborn as her daughter. Ten months later, Ida gave birth to a daughter. At two and a half years of age, this child began to speak of events in the life of the dead Maria, and gave detailed evidence of her knowledge of Maria's life. (There were no fewer than 120 occasions on which she recognised previous acquaintances or made remarks that were later verified.) Emilia Lorenz, also a Brazilian, committed suicide at nineteen by swallowing cyanide; she hated being a girl and often said she would return to earth as a man. After her death, her spirit made communication at séances and declared that she intended to rejoin her family, this time as a boy. Shortly thereafter, Mrs. Lorenz produced a boy, Paulo, who soon declared himself to be Emilia, and exhibited markedly feminine traits. (Again, Stevenson offers a four-page table itemising the evidence for identifying Paulo with Emilia.) William George was a Tlingit fisherman, who told his favourite son that he intended to return to earth as *his* son, and that the evidence would be certain birthmarks, identical with his own. He died mysteriously, vanishing from his fishing boat at sea, in 1949. In May 1950, his daughter-in-law gave birth to a boy who had the predicted birthmarks. (During her labour she dreamed of her father-in law, who told her he was anxious to see his son again.) At four years of age, the boy, named after his grandfather, began to exhibit a knowledge of people and places in his grandfather's life, and to develop some of his characteristic mannerisms, including his walk. When he came in one day, and found his mother going through a box of jewellery, he stated, 'That's my watch,' and grabbed a gold watch that had, indeed, been presented to his mother by William George senior. His parents both asserted that he had never seen this watch before, or heard of it.

Altogether, *Twenty Cases Suggestive of Reincarnation* is a convincing, if bewildering, volume, carrying the stamp of authenticity throughout. The conclusions it seems to suggest may be tabulated as follows: (a) reincarnation occurs all the time, but memory of previous existences is rare; it happens most frequently when the death was violent; (b) 'spirits' seem to have a certain amount of choice about reincarnation; (c) cases in which there *is* memory of a previous existence occur most often among people who already accept the idea of reincarnation; (d) more than one spirit may occupy the same body, as in the case of Jasbir. This last conclusion recalls the remark of the psychologist McDougal about Sally Beauchamp,* that her other personalities seemed to be separate psychic entities rather than aspects of the same person.

The case of the Singhalese 'murderer' Wijeratne deserves further mention. Wijeratne was born in 1947 with a deformity of the right breast and arm. Because of his resemblance to the paternal uncle, Ratran Hami, his father remarked, 'This is my brother come back.' The family assumed that the deformities were due to some bad 'karma' from a previous existence. When the child was two and a half, his mother overheard him remarking that his arm was deformed because he had killed his wife. The child later related details of the crime, and of the arrest and execution of Ratran Hami, in a way that convinced his parents that this was not imagination. (Stevenson gives a full account of the boy's descriptions of the murder.) The crime had been due to a violent fit of temper (Wijeratne admitted that he had had an ungovernable temper in his previous existence, but that it was now improved). The girl had been married to Ratran Hami, but had continued to live with her parents until the second half of a two-part ceremony should take place. When he called for her,

* See pp. 581 et seq.

she suddenly decided not to go with him, whereupon he drew a knife and stabbed her. At the trial, Ratran Hami defended himself by saying that he had not intended to kill his wife. Her family had set upon him, and were beating him, while she held his arms; he stabbed her in freeing himself. The family claimed that he attacked her with a *kris* (Malayan dagger), and that only then had they attacked him. Wijeratne acknowledged that the family account was the true one and that his execution was justified, adding, nevertheless, that if he was faced with a similar situation again, he would do the same thing. Stevenson mentions that he has many cases in which light has been thrown on a murder in this manner.

The year 1956, the date of publication of *The Search for Bridey Murphy*, produced a number of other interesting cases of alleged reincarnation in England. Henry Blythe, a professional hypnotist of Torquay, Devon, hypnotised a thirty-two-year-old Exeter housewife named Naomi Henry, whom he had earlier cured of smoking. A tape recorder was used at some of the sessions, and a long-playing record was subsequently issued on the Oriole label. First, a number of witnesses identify themselves, and a Dr. William Minifie describes what is about to take place; Mrs. Henry is already asleep. The hypnotist takes her back in time to her childhood, then asks her about previous existences. She speaks of being an Irish girl, Mary Cohen, and gives the year as 1790. The hypnotist takes her to her wedding day, four years later, and she explains that she doesn't want to get married, that her mother has forced it upon her because she doesn't want to keep an unmarried daughter. Later she dies as a result of a broken leg, inflicted by her husband in the course of a beating. The hypnotist then takes her on, four years beyond her death, and her breath ceases. (The record sleeve asserts that her heart also stopped beating for five seconds.) Then she describes an incarnation as Clarice Hellier, a nurse born in 1880, and ends by describing her death, from a goitre, and even the number of her grave.

At the same time, the record sleeve makes it clear that the record is not intended to be a proof of incarnation – only an unusual experiment. This is perhaps as well. While the listener entertains no doubt of the sincerity of everyone involved, he is likely to find himself wondering whether the hypnotic subject is giving the answers that she knows are required, out of a desire to please the hyponotist. One can see how easily the same thing may have occurred in the case of Bridey Murphy. Unless researchers can find definite proof of the existence of Mary Cohen in Cork in 1890, or Clarice Hellier in Downham (and there are no fewer than six places of that name in England), this kind of thing must be regarded simply as an interesting experiment.

But this is not to say that deep hypnosis might not become a valuable instrument for investigating past incarnations. Arnall Bloxham, an expert on old furniture, was also, apparently, stimulated by the Bridey Murphy case to use his hypnotic powers to investigate reincarnation. The result of his first experiments was a book, *Who Was Ann Ockenden?*, written by his wife Dulcie, in which a young girl under hypnosis describes her previous existence in prehistoric times. Mr. Bloxham has gone on to make many more similar experiments, recording all on tape, and has accumulated an impressive library of recordings. A woman who claimed to be Henriette, exiled sister of Charles II, showed detailed knowledge of the Stuart period, and was able to describe in detail the court of Louis XVI and of his brother, Philippe, Duke of Orléans, to whom she was married. A man who recalled a previous existence as a naval gunner in the time of Napoleon gave so many authentic details about naval life at that time that Earl Mountbatten borrowed the tape to play to experts on naval history.* One can only say that if experiments like this are carried on for long enough, and on a sufficiently widespread scale, there are bound to be cases whose authenticity cannot be challenged. Robert Heinlein

* See *Man, Myth and Magic*, No. 33, 'Frontiers of Belief'.

predicted, in *Amazing Stories* for April 1956, that by the year 2001, reincarnation would have been demonstrated with scientific rigour, and there seems a fair possibility that he will be proved right.

Arthur Guirdham is a well-known English psychiatrist who was, until his recent retirement, senior consultant in psychiatry to the Bath clinical area. He is also a believer in reincarnation. His pamphlet *Religious Aspects of Extra-Sensory Perception* opens with the challenging sentence: 'The study of parapsychology will be the next major development in psychiatry'; he goes on to argue that certain psychological illnesses may be quite literally 'psychic' in origin, due to powers of extrasensory perception, or to dream-memories of previous incarnations. He adds, 'I have a patient whose capacity to add to the knowledge of European medieval history has been recognised by two professors of that subject.' This patient, a woman, was an exponent of Catharism, the sect we have already encountered in connection with the origins of witchcraft. 'Without ever studying it she has a detailed knowledge of its ritual and practices. She acquired some of this knowledge from dreams, others from her recurrent nightmare, and from what she calls visions, but most of it was provided by stories and notes she felt impelled to write as a schoolgirl in her early teens. It is utterly impossible that she could have had access to the detailed literature of Catharism at that age.' He cites one of the proofs that the patient's 'visions' were authentic: '[She] insisted to me that the priest with whom she was associated wore dark blue robes, and [it] is more than twenty years since she was first aware of this fact ... It is only in the last two or three years that it has been established that they sometimes wore dark blue or dark green.' He adds that it would take a full-length book to detail all the other evidence of his patient's knowledge of Catharism.

In 1970, Guirdham published this book – *The Cathars and Reincarnation* – and it is certainly one of the most remarkable and controversial documents ever printed on this subject. The author has deliberately avoided the kind of dramatic treatment that made *Bridey Murphy* a best seller, and many readers may feel he has moved too far in the opposite direction, allowing the story to become too overburdened with the details of his historical researches. But the result is one of the most convincing accounts of reincarnation that exist in English.

The story begins with a series of odd coincidences. In March 1962, Dr. Guirdham saw the patient, whom he calls Mrs. Smith, who was suffering from nightmares accompanied by screams. The dreams were always of a man who entered a room as she lay on the floor; his approach filled her with terror. Oddly enough, Dr. Guirdham had himself suffered from an almost identical nightmare until shortly before meeting Mrs. Smith.

From the beginning, the subject of the Cathars was involved in this odd chain of coincidence. Since before the war, Dr. Guirdham had been fascinated by the Pyrenees, and particularly by Montségur, where – he discovered later – a great massacre of Cathars had taken place in 1244. Eighteen months after he met Mrs. Smith, the subject of Catharism began to recur with increasing frequency. 'To this day, only a few people in England know anything about the Cathars, but it seems that it is preordained that, sooner or later, I meet all of them.' In December 1963, he spoke to Mrs. Smith about the Pyrenees, where she had spent a holiday, and mentioned the Cathars. She was startled, for she had come across the name for the first time earlier that afternoon. She had casually opened a book in the library, found a chapter on Catharism and become fascinated by the subject. (It was later the same day that Dr. Guirdham came across the name of Little Gaddesden in a book on the Pyrenees, and encountered the name of the inn he had been trying to remember all day.*) On

* See p. 60.

another occasion, Dr. Guirdham's wife read a magazine article in the hairdresser's in which the writer speculated that the order of Bonshommes at Edington in Wiltshire derived from the Cathars. (Bonshommes is the name by which the Cathars of Languedoc were known.) Dr. Guirdham wrote to the author, and discovered that it was one of his own patients, with whom he had never discussed Catharism. When he and his wife attended a cocktail party, he met an RAF officer who had climbed Montségur, and had been oppressed by a feeling of horror, the sense that the whole place was saturated in blood.

Mrs. Smith was definitely psychic. (Dr. Guirdham gives an example. She had been reading about water divining and wanted to know more about it. On impulse, she decided to go out to play cards that evening, feeling that something interesting would develop. Her partner proved to be a wart-charmer, whose uncle was a water diviner – and presumably able to satisfy her curiosity.) On her first visit to the Pyrenees, she had experienced the sense of 'I have been here before'. On a later visit, at St. Jean Pied de Port, she was able to walk around the old medieval town as if she knew it well, and knew in advance that there would be many steps to climb before she reached the old fortress. She also had a feeling of horror about Toulouse, although she had never been there, and once had a dream in which someone was trying to force her to enter a cathedral called St. Etienne. She later discovered by chance that the cathedral in Toulouse *was* called St. Etienne.

Some form of unconscious telepathy began to develop between doctor and patient (although, it should be added, Mrs. Smith's nightmares had ceased after her first meeting with Dr. Guirdham). 'On one occasion she received from me a letter containing the identical longish sentence which she herself had written to me ...' And on another, the two of them, quite independently, had written on the same day to the author of an article about Catharism – both having stumbled on the article, again quite independently, in the back number of a specialist journal.

It was more than two years after their first meeting that Mrs. Smith began to speak openly about her dreams, and the part Dr. Guirdham had played in them. And this is certainly the most remarkable and incredible part of the whole story – the part that will prove the major stumbling block to many people who cannot accept the evidence for Mrs. Smith's previous incarnation. She wrote to Dr. Guirdham:

> I think I was living just outside Toulouse, or maybe in Toulouse itself, when you first came to my house years ago in that snowstorm. We were a very poor family but you were of noble birth. I fell in love with you then, and my father said I must never meet you again – you were not of our class and, what was more important to him, you were not of our faith. We were Roman Catholics. I refused to be parted from you, and was eventually excommunicated. I went to live with you. We weren't married. You told me that if anything should happen to you, I must go to Fabrissa …

One's first thought, on reading this, is that Mrs. Smith had developed the usual patient's fixation on the doctor, and somehow convinced Dr. Guirdham that they had been lovers in the thirteenth century. In fact, this view cannot be maintained. For Dr. Guirdham threw himself into historical research to find just how much of Mrs. Smith's story would stand up to analysis. And the answer is: All of it. It must be remembered that although Mrs. Smith had been having circumstantial dreams and 'visions' since her teens, she did not connect them with the Cathars. Her first meeting with Dr. Guirdham and immediate recognition of him as 'Roger', the lover of her 'visions', was almost her first intimation that it was not all some odd trick of her subconscious (she had experienced a sense of *déjà vu* in the Pyrenees, as already recorded). When he called upon her subsequently in a snowstorm, to arrange a hospital appointment, the memory of her first meeting with Roger – also in a snowstorm – returned. The persecution of the Cathars of Toulouse had been a fairly small and localised event, and the Inquisition records still existed. Various names had recurred in Mrs. Smith's dreams – Fabrissa, Roger, Alaïs, Pierre de Mazerolles – and Professor René Nelli (one of the world's greatest authorities on the period) suggested that something might be discovered about them in the records. Mrs. Smith's dreams were full of other details about the period: the poems that Roger had recited, the layout of the hall of the castle, the ceremonies and rituals of the Cathar religion, what they ate and drank, and what kind of utensils were used at table. Dr. Guirdham's task, with the help of Professor Nelli and Jean Duvernoy (another eminent authority), was to check as much of this as possible. And as the investigation proceeded, he became more and more impressed with what he calls the 'uncanny accuracy' of Mrs. Smith's memories. She stated that when Roger was ill they gave him loaf sugar, and Dr. Guirdham found this hard to accept. But Professor's Nelli's researches revealed that sugar did exist at that time, although it was a scarce commodity (Mrs. Smith mentioned that it was kept locked up). Guirdham discovered that it was regarded as a medicine. Again, Mrs. Smith mentioned the cathedral of St. Etienne in Toulouse; Guirdham, who had been there, was convinced that this was a slip, that it was actually called St. Sernin (which is the name of a church in Toulouse). It was only when he came to revise the script of his book, and checked with a guide book, that he realised she was right again.

The story that slowly emerged was as follows. Roger-Isarn was a Cathar priest or preacher, who travelled around a great deal in the area of Toulouse. He had taken refuge in a snowstorm in the house of a Catholic family, which included the young girl whom Guirdham calls Puerilia. (Oddly enough, Mrs. Smith's dreams did not include her real name.) She fell in love with Roger, and later attended Cathar meetings at which he was present. They became lovers. When her father found out, he beat her and threw her out of the house. She went to Roger's house, and lived with him. But he travelled a great deal, and often became ill. (Dr. Guirdham feels that his symptoms point to tuberculosis.) In 1242, two inquisitors came to the area, searching out heretics. Pierre de Mazerolles, a distant relative of Roger, plotted to kill them. The inquisitors, with their entourage, stayed with one Raymond D'Alfar, who sent word to Mazerolles. The inquisitors were murdered in D'Alfar's house; the motive of the crime was to seize lists of heretics, members of respected local families, in possession of the inquisitors. Mrs. Smith dreamed of Pierre de Mazerolles coming into the room where she was asleep, gloating about the murder, and remembered Roger's horror. Catholic reaction to the crime was violent. Roger was among those arrested and interrogated. Prison wrecked his already delicate health, and he died. Puerilia was so shattered by the news that she tried to commit suicide by starvation (one of the methods favoured by Cathars, apparently). Bitter fighting between Cathars and Catholics followed – all of it, like the murder of the inquisitors by Pierre de Mazerolles, a matter of history. Cathars, including Puerilia, were held for interrogation in the cathedral of St. Etienne. Puerilia eventually died at the stake. Mrs. Smith's description of her dream is particularly harrowing: 'I didn't know when you were burnt to death you'd bleed. I thought the blood would all dry up in the terrible heat. But I was bleeding heavily. The blood was dripping and hissing in the flames. I wished I had enough blood to put the flames out. The worst part was my eyes … I tried to close my eyelids but I couldn't. They must have been burnt off …'

It is not surprising that the trauma of these experiences echoed down seven centuries. As to the 'coincidence' that Dr. Guirdham should have been Roger-Isarn d'Arborens, we can only accept it, like the other strange coincidences recorded in the book, as a concomitant of intense psychic activity. Guirdham mentions that 'in a letter … she had mentioned a quotation by some medieval scholar and asked me if I could help her locate it. I could not do so. Just previous to writing a further letter she had been to the library, picked up a book, and was confronted immediately by the quotation. This kind of thing is a commonplace with people of this type.' That is to say, it is not coincidence, in the ordinary sense of the word, but some kind of psychic radar, about whose nature we know nothing whatever.

To further complicate an extremely complex issue, it should be added that reincarnation is one of the few matters upon which there is basic disagreement among spiritualists. J. J. Morse, an editor of *Two Worlds*, wrote down 'spirit teachings' at the dictation of a spirit named Tien Sein Tie, a sixteenth-century Chinese; and Tien Sein Tie stated flatly that reincarnation is nonsense. He pointed out that if men are brought back to the world to work out a 'bad Karma', then we would have no right to alleviate misery. On the other hand, an eminent spiritualist I consulted told me that some mediums – or rather, the spirits that speak through them – accept reincarnation, while others deny it. The Continentals seem more prone to accept it than Anglo-Saxons. All 'spirit teaching' accepts that there are 'ascending levels' in the 'other world', not unlike Dante's spheres in the *Paradiso*, and that one's life on earth determines which of these levels becomes one's habitation immediately after death. (There is no hell, no punishment – although there are 'dark places'.) But spirit teaching generally has little to say on reincarnation. The medium Dorothy Perkins was kind enough to put a question on the subject to a spirit known to her circle as 'the Philosopher'; the Philosopher replied that while he does not deny reincarnation, he has never met anyone on 'the other side' who goes in for it. From which we might infer that the 'bad Karma' doctrine is untrue, and that reincarnation is a matter of choice for the individual spirit.

Let us try to summarise some of the conclusions that have been reached so far.

It is certain that human beings possess latent powers of which they are only dimly aware, and that these latent powers produce a variety of phenomena, from poltergeist activity to 'thought photography' and spontaneous combustion. These 'positive' powers are connected to, but not identical with, the power of precognition and of 'sensing' ghosts.

Apart from man's own 'latent powers', there seems to be strong evidence that 'ghosts' have an independent existence. Their chief characteristic appears to be a certain stupidity, since a tendency to hang around places they knew in life would appear to be the spirit-world's equivalent of feeble-mindedness. I have suggested elsewhere* that the state of mind of ghosts may be similar to that of someone in delirium or high fever: a disconnection of the will and inability to distinguish between reality and dreams. It must also be admitted – although for me personally, it goes against the grain to do it – that it is not improbable that the dead may be around us a great deal of the time, and that premonitions of danger, precognitions and so on, may be due to them rather than to our own psychic alarm system. This view seems so unsophisticated, so typical of primitive tribes, that I hasten to qualify it by saying that most of the 'phenomena' are explainable on either hypothesis. Tyrrell cites the case of a woman who unwrapped a packet of pound notes and went into the kitchen to throw the wrappers into the fire, her mind on other things. As she was about to throw them, she felt a hand laid on her own, pushing it down, and realised she was holding the pound notes instead of the wrapping paper. She was so convinced that someone had touched her that she shouted, 'Is anyone there?' No doubt some departed spirit could have been

* *The World of Violence*, Part I, Chapter 3.

responsible; so could her own subconscious. The notion that the dead are voyeurs is certainly not a pleasing one: besides, one feels they ought to have something better to do.

It should also be borne in mind that the mysteries of the split personality are still unexplored territory for psychology. Was Yeats's *A Vision* dictated by spirits, or by some dark side of his personality, operating through his wife's mediumship? Eisenbud has a whole chapter on this question entitled 'Who's in the Back of the Store?'; and he explains elsewhere in the book that he often asked Serios, under hypnosis, 'Who are you?' in the hope of finding some alien alter-ego (he suspected a rebellious small boy). But there are cases where the ordinary alter-ego theory seems to break down. For example, that of José Pedro de Freitas, reported by Frank Smyth in *Man, Myth and Magic* (No. 8), a Brazilian peasant who, at the age of thirty-two (in 1950), was 'taken over' by the spirit of a German surgeon who had been killed in the First World War. De Freitas operated with a kitchen knife, scissors, a scalpel and a pair of tweezers. Dr. Ladeira Marques of Rio de Janeiro described an operation as follows:

> The patient lay on an old door, and scissors, scalpel, a kitchen knife and tweezers stood nearby in an old empty can. Without the help of a speculum – an instrument for dilating the cavities of the human body for inspection – he introduced three scissors and two scalpels into the vagina – brusquely, one can even say with violence. He was holding one handle of the scissors when all of us saw the other handle start moving along, opening and closing the scissors. Although we could not see whether this was also the case with the other instruments we could all clearly hear the noise of metals rattling and the characteristic sounds of tissue being cut. After a few minutes, 'Dr. Fritz' removed the scissors, and at the sight of the blood, stopped and said: 'Let there be no blood, Lord.'

And the operation continued with no further haemorrhage at all.

The other witnesses were Dr. Ary Lex, lecturer at São Paulo University and member of the State Medical Academy; Dr. Oswaldo Conrado, director of the State Hospital in São Paulo; and Dr. Leite de Castro of Rio de Janeiro. De Freitas went on to remove the tumour from the womb of the young woman, who remained conscious, and sealed the cut by pressing the edges together. The whole operation took only a few minutes. De Freitas seemed to be able to produce a state of total relaxation in the patients, and they felt no pain. He seems to have been in some kind of trance himself during the operations, for when shown a photograph of one of them afterwards, he was sick.

Between 1950 and 1964, De Freitas performed hundreds of similar operations, always at lightning speed, always with a kind of casual carelessness and always successfully. He also showed an uncanny skill in diagnosis. In 1964, however, he was charged under Article 284 of the Brazilian code which states spirit healing to be a crime – Brazil is, of course, a rigidly Catholic country – and sentenced to sixteen months in prison. He has apparently given up his operations since then.*

Accounts like this make all attempts at speculation seem a waste of time. If it is true, then we had better acknowledge that we are little better than children, and adopt some of the observant open-mindedness that is characteristic of children.

Before leaving this subject of 'other worlds', we should consider briefly a hypothesis that has steadily gained support in the past

* This account is apparently taken from *The Moon and Two Mountains*, by Anthony Stratton-Smith. Richard Cavendish, the editor of *Man, Myth and Magic*, tells me that the Brazilian embassy in London admitted they knew of the case, but refused to confirm or deny anything. Understandably.

two decades: that we are under observation by intelligences from outer space. 'Flying saucers' have become something of a joke, understandably. Among my own small library on the subject are titles like *The Flying Saucer Menace*, *Why Are They Watching Us?*, *The Invasion from Outer Space*, and the general air of sensationalism repels serious enquiries. On the other hand, David Foster's 'intelligent universe' hypothesis suggests that wherever there is already life, it is likely to evolve to higher levels of intelligence. You do not have to be a science-fiction writer to imagine that if there are highly intelligent beings elsewhere in the universe, they would exercise caution in making themselves known to us. We know what happens when the civilised white man goes among primitive tribes, whether in Australia, Africa or America. Even when the colonisers are well-meaning, the result is always the same: the destruction of the primitive culture. If the white races were more advanced, they would make laws to prevent this kind of brutal incursion into primitive cultures. And if extra-terrestrial intelligences exist, they have no doubt already done just that.

Scientists have now begun systematic investigation into life on other planets or stars. In April 1960, the 85-foot radio telescope at Deer Creek Valley in West Virginia was directed towards various stars that may have planets, hoping to pick up radio signals that would indicate intelligent life. Although the project was abandoned after a few months, a conference of scientists was held at Green Bank, West Virginia, the following year, to discuss the topic of extra-terrestrial life. Although it was not kept secret, it was not advertised either; nobody wanted sensational reports in newspapers. (The whole project, it may be noted, was government-sponsored.) In late 1962 the Soviet Academy of Sciences published a book by an eminent astronomer, Joseph Shklovsky, discussing these problems seriously, and in 1965, not long after a Soviet conference on extra-terrestrial civilisations, a colleague of Shklovsky's reported that the star CTA 102 was emitting radio signals that suggested intelligence.

On June 17, 1908,* there occurred in central Siberia an event that must be regarded as one of the oddest unsolved mysteries of the twentieth century. What appeared to be an enormous meteor streaked northward across the sky; it could be seen for thousands of square miles. It struck close to a river called the Podkamennaya ('Stony') Tunguska (the adjective being used to distinguish it from two brothers, the Lower and Upper Tunguskas). A pillar of fire rose into the air, turning into a mushroom-shaped black cloud. The explosion was heard more than six hundred miles away. Two villages were wiped out, but the 'meteor' had fortunately crashed in a relatively uninhabited area, and most of the damage – with a twenty-mile radius – was to trees. The next day there were high, silvery clouds.

In 1908 the government had more to worry about than earthquakes (which is what they probably assumed it was). It was not until 1927 that an expedition succeeded in penetrating the almost roadless area near the source of the Podkamennaya Tunguska, where there was evidence of an immense explosion: trees blown down with their tops pointing outward from the explosion, all of them burned. *The Space Encyclopaedia* lists the explosion under meteorites, along with the Arizona meteorite, the Sikhote Alin meteorite of 1947 and various others. But the Tunguska meteor had certain very peculiar features. The evidence revealed that it exploded in mid-air – like a hydrogen bomb, as Willy Ley remarks in his history of astronomy, *Watchers of the Skies*. And there were no meteor fragments, such as were found in abundance at the Sikhote Alin site (30 tons of it). Willy Ley, unhappy about the idea of a nuclear explosion, suggests that the 'meteor' may have been made of anti-matter, which seems to be even more far-fetched.

The late Frank Edwards, after mentioning that a subsequent expedition under a Dr. Kazantsev found radioactivity in the soil,

* Russian Old Style dating; by European style this would be thirteen days later – June 30.

draws the conclusion that this was probably the explosion of a flying saucer. And there would seem to be at least a 50 per cent probability that he is right.

Much of the 'evidence' for Unidentified Flying Objects must be regarded as untrustworthy – due to a vivid imagination, self-hypnotism or the desire for publicity. As to the assertion of various writers that references to flying objects can be found in ancient manuscripts, that might also be regarded as unproven. It is true that Ezekiel's 'cloud with a brightness round about it, and fire flashing forth continually, and in the midst of the fire, as it were gleaming bronze' *sounds* as if it could be a flying saucer, but it could also be just a prophetic vision. The same applies to a 'circle of fire that was coming in the sky' mentioned in an Egyptian papyrus of the time of Thutmose III (about 1500 B.C.) and the 'two large shields, reddish in colour, in motion above the church' described in the Saxon *Annales Laurissenses* for the year A.D. 776. The American Air Force, which has been closely involved in U.F.O. investigations since 1947 (when Kenneth Arnold, an American businessman, saw six 'saucers' flying in the area of Mount Rainier, near Seattle) affirms that between 70 and 90 per cent of the 'sightings' can be explained by 'conventional effects', and responsible investigators are inclined to accept this estimate. But there remains an undismissable residue of 10 per cent or so that demands to be taken seriously. The most famous of these is the Mantell case of January 7, 1948, when the military police notified the Goodman Base of the U.S. Air Force at Fort Knox, Kentucky, of the presence of a flying object over the town. Three P.51 pursuit planes took off. They followed the disc and saw that it had a top shaped like a cone, with a red light blinking on it. Captain Thomas F. Mantell got closest to it, and reported back that it was increasing in speed and gaining height. Then his plane disintegrated in mid-air. The flying object was seen before and after the disaster by hundreds of people in Madison, Indiana, and Fort Knox and Columbus, Ohio.

But what have flying saucers to do with the occult? Carl Jung establishes one link when he speculates (in a short book on flying saucers) that the world-wide sightings of U.F.O.s may be the expression of 'a wave of hope in a reappearance of Christ', a universal longing for some apocalyptic second coming. Jung's theory, wild enough for science fiction, is that the flying objects *have* an objective existence, but as projections from the racial unconscious mind, like the monsters of *Forbidden Planet*. In that case, flying saucers might be regarded as being related to 'spectres of the living'. But this view is contradicted by some of the phenomena. For example, when I was living in Roanoke, Virginia, in 1966–1967, a motorist reported discovering a flying saucer in the middle of the road late at night. The police investigated, and the report was confirmed to the extent that a large patch of the road, at the point where the saucer had been, showed melted tar. Jung's theory cannot explain this, and many other pieces of commonplace factual evidence in the reports.

The possibility of more direct links between flying objects and the occult was drawn to my attention in 1967 by the San Francisco poet Richard Roberts. He had already spoken to me about a remarkable Dutch 'yogi' named Jack Schwarz, born in 1924 in Dordrecht, near Rotterdam – also the birthplace of Peter Hurkos – and it was after this first mention of Schwarz that he told me that the 'yogi' was worried about some very odd events that had been taking place. A woman under hypnosis had begun to speak in a metallic voice, and had informed him that he was actually from Pluto and that It, his metallic informant, was a Venusian. And this, apparently, was not the first time he had received similar messages.

It all sounded very odd, very cranky, almost certainly some kind of self-delusion. However, I asked Dick Roberts if he would be kind enough to write down for me the story of Jack Schwarz, as circumstantially as possible, and he obliged with a nine-page typescript, which I shall summarise here.

Schwarz was introduced to Dick Roberts as a 'sufi', but he denied this, saying that he was only a sufi in the sense of possessing a spiritual force that worked through him. They got along so well that Schwarz invited Roberts to stay with him for a few days in Upland, California. 'On this visit, I discovered that he slept only two hours each night and ate approximately four meals a week. At seven each morning, his day began with persons arriving every half hour until noon for massages, ostensibly to satisfy the State of California's medical licensing laws. In addition to the massage, however, what these people were receiving was psychic and spiritual counselling, and often hypnotic and healing treatments. Afternoons were given to his family and to preparations for evening lectures which he gave around the greater Los Angeles area. Returning from these, during the week that I visited him, we would talk together until 3 a.m., when he would go into meditation for an hour, and then to bed at four. At seven the front doorbell would ring for the first counselling. To quote Roberts:

> His friends impressed me with their eyes-open approach to psychical research, and with their basically good mental health, a rare thing in the era of gurus preying upon the emotionally dependent. I was also impressed with Jack's near-encyclopedic knowledge of the occult, and convinced that he was a force for the good.

> Nearly a year later I witnessed his bed of nails demonstration, which he formerly used in introducing his lectures. The nails, a dozen or so in number, protruded from a thin wooden frame. Unlike the familiar yogi's bed, they are sharp, long (4 to 6 in.) and widely separated so that the weight of the body is supported by only a few nails. Except for trunks, he is naked for the demonstration. The heaviest man in the audience is

selected and asked to stand upon his body as he reclines on the nails. On this particular evening I assisted a man who weighed nearly 250 lb. onto Jack's chest. I then saw one of the nails pierce his calf and come out some three inches on the other side. But there was no bleeding from the wound. Subsequently he got up and walked through the audience, allowing any and all to examine the deep holes in his back. A doctor was present and examined one hole with a probe, stating that the depth was about one half of an inch. At no time was there any bleeding from these punctures.

The import of his following lecture was that matter at a low rate of vibration is solid, whereas at a high rate of vibration it is subtle. Thus for physical and spiritual health one needs to raise one's vibrations. How is this accomplished? Although there are many paths to God, Jack stresses meditation techniques. By the end of his lectures the punctures had disappeared from his back.

Dick Roberts then offers a biographical summary of Schwarz. As a child and youth he could see the colours of people's 'psychic auras'.* He became a hypnotist and worked on the stage; subsequently he worked in the Dutch Resistance.

The curious intimations about other planets apparently began in 1958, when Schwarz was a welfare officer of the Dutch ship *New Holland* going through the Suez Canal to Indonesia with two thousand soldiers on board. Everyone was watching a magician who had been brought on board to entertain. 'It was on the bridge of the ship,' said Schwarz in a taped interview with Dick Roberts, 'when suddenly a tall, lanky Arab in a striped robe appeared and went down on his knees before me and kissed my feet, saying, "You

* See Phoebe Payne in the next chapter.

are my master." Then, just like that, he got up and walked out. Naturally I tried to follow him because it was poor security to allow him on the bridge, or even on the ship, unless he was connected with the entertainment. But he had disappeared. I checked with the watch at the gangway, and no one of his description had been seen coming aboard or leaving. And he was not connected with the magician – all those people had been accounted for.'

In 1959, Schwarz continues, he was living in Los Angeles with his wife. He was invited to attend a lecture on hypnosis at Whittier. As they left the lecture, a woman approached their group saying, 'A man wants to talk to you.'

He was sitting at the wheel of a green station wagon, and as we walked up Bill said: 'You want to speak to us?' 'Not you, not you, him!' said the man pointing at me. 'Get in the car.' His manner was very abrupt and he seemed a little angry, so my wife said: 'Don't do it, Jack.' But I told her to go along with Bill, because I wanted to hear what he had to say, and I told her not to worry. He wasn't very big – about five foot six – slight, with a toupée. The way you knew it was false was because the wax was sticking out from under the hair. He didn't look very dangerous …

As soon as I got into the car, he grabbed my hand. 'It's all right, I just want to be sure I have the right man. Once before I got the wrong man, but from your vibration I know you are the right man.' Then he kissed my hand. I look at him like what the heck is this? 'Once before I kissed you, but I kissed your feet. Do you remember, I told you you were my master.'

Looking at the man in the car now, I could see no connection between him and the tall Arab. But then he began to tell me details of this incident which I had told to no one else. He must have been reading my mind, because I was thinking it could not be the same man when he said: 'We can appear in any shape or form we desire. I have just come from Australia, and before that I was in Nepal where your master is. I bring you a message from him.' 'How do you get the idea I have a master?' 'Because we come from a tribe of people who crash-landed in a rocket ship on earth thousands of years ago. My code name is XB-15 and you are my master. The message from your master is that you should now begin teaching the spiritual truth that is being given to you inspirationally. You are God's vehicle to bring the truth that is meant to be. That's all I have to tell you. You can go now. I will get in touch with you again.'

The remainder of this story, to date, is odd and rather frustrating. A phone message purported to come from the Rev. Elvira Shreider, but when Schwarz phoned the only man by that name in the phone book, he denied all knowledge of the call. But two weeks later, the man with the toupée rang up to congratulate Schwarz, telling him that he had been chosen to be a member of a steering council of the New Age. He gave Schwarz eleven other names, one of which was Elvira Shreider. In 1966, after attending a lecture on flying saucers and the language of their occupants, Schwarz's meditations were constantly interrupted by four syllables that sounded like 'El, Su, Shei-la', and afterwards he felt dazed. He made enquiries with the group who were responsible for the lecture on saucer language, and was told that the syllables meant 'God's vehicle to bring to truth that is meant to be'. It was after this that the 'hypnotic messages' came. The first was through a woman patient, who suddenly began to speak in a metallic voice, informed him that he was from Pluto and that he, the voice, was from Venus and was called Linus. Linus added that Venusians were composed of a gaseous substance. The scientific detail that the hypnotised woman proceeded to give about Venusian life would have been completely beyond her normal intellectual capacity – she was amazed when the tape was played back to her.

Two months later, 'Linus' again made contact through a hypnotised patient – Schwarz does not go into detail about the message – and finally, a psychic girl in Vancouver told him, out of the blue, that she had travelled astrally to Venus the previous night and had seen him there with Linus – she mentioned the name. She added that he was instructing the Venusians because he was from a higher plane than theirs. And that, to date, is the last contact Jack Schwarz has had with his Venusian friend Linus.

I would be the first to agree that the story is one of the weirdest in this volume. With the talk about 'God's vehicle on earth' and so on, it bears all the signs of ordinary religious monomania. The kind of thing for which hundreds of people get committed to asylums every year. But there are several factors here that incline me to reject this view. I have not met Schwarz, but Dick Roberts describes him as a very solid, ordinary kind of person, quite un-guru-like. This is borne out by Schwarz's own comments on all this: 'By this time I was beginning to get upset by the whole thing. I was happy with my wife and children and I was not interested in steering the spaceship, or even going along for a short ride. I was very happy to stay on earth as ordinary Jack Schwarz.'

This rings true. So does the inconclusiveness of the whole weird story. Schwarz has not tried to set himself up as 'God's vehicle' or to teach spiritual truth inspirationally; he has remained 'ordinary' Jack Schwarz, a highly gifted psychic with remarkable talents as a fakir. Neither of these faculties necessarily indicates great spiritual advancement; in India, fakirs – men able to perform remarkable feats of physical self-control – are regarded as being on a lower level than the God-obsessed yogis.

The probability is that Jack Schwarz is genuine, that he believes every word of his story as it appears above. There remains, of course, the equally plausible hypothesis that the events are an example of Jung's 'psychic projection' – that is, the active interference of the subconscious mind in everyday life. We all know how unexpected and alien dreams can be. Could this not be an example of the subconscious manifesting itself physically, as, for example, when Jung produced explosions to disconcert Freud? This hypothesis strikes me as altogether more likely, certainly in the case of the metallic voice speaking from hypnotised patients. But it does not cover 'XB-15' in the car, or the Arab on the ship.

Let us, for a moment, make the assumption that the whole story is literally true. It is staggering, but no more strange than many things we have discussed in this volume. In fact, it suggests some tentative unifying principles. If we can accept reincarnation, then there is nothing surprising in the idea of Jack Schwarz being the reincarnation of a traveller from Pluto. The idea that he is 'teaching' on Venus when his earthly body is asleep in bed may sound strange, until we reflect that in 90 per cent of cases of astral projection, the 'projector' has no idea that he has left his body, as in the case of Powys or Yeats, already cited.

Schwarz's theory of vibration sounds very close to David Foster's. Explaining this theory to me in a letter, David Foster wrote, using capital letters to emphasise his point: 'The universe is a total construction of waves and vibrations whose inner content is "meaning", and man is a micro-system of the same vibratory nature floating at some depth in the universal and meaningful wave system. The universal wave system is qualitative or value-structured (this is quantum theory) according to its vibration rate spectrum (faster frequencies have more information capacity).' He goes on to remark that the dualism of mind and matter is a false one, since all is mind and meaning, and we assume that 'body is matter' simply because its frequencies are too fast for our minds to understand and analyse. In fact, the human body understands the meanings in nature *directly*, by harmonic resonance. 'And how on earth could the human body control its fantastic chemical complexities unless it was all mind ...

But the human mind is a vibratory system that operates so slowly that it is capable of analysis, and thus of synthesis, and so can partake in your "step by step" thinking operations.' He goes on to say that the mind is a radio set that can 'tune in' to thousands of different vibrations in the ether. We only have to think of Powys or Wordsworth to see what he means. In poetic experience, the mind becomes oddly negative, 'open', tuning in to vibrations that it normally 'cuts out' for the purposes of getting on with everyday life.

Obviously, the most incredible part of Jack Schwarz's story, because the least substantiated, is the talk about Venus, Pluto and so on. This is not, *a priori*, more incredible than Arthur Guirdham's story of the Cathars and reincarnation or the various cases already discussed; but the evidence there is strong, and there is no evidence whatever for Jack Schwarz's assertion (or Linus's) that life forms on Venus are gaseous – although space probes indicate that the surface of Venus is too hot to support life, and that the upper atmosphere is filled with vapours. (On the day I am writing this, a Soviet space probe is due to make a soft landing on Venus; but I doubt whether it will do anything to confirm or contradict Linus's assertion.) As to the statement that Jack Schwarz originated on Pluto, the outermost of the planets, there is nothing to contradict this in our knowledge of the solar system; millions of years ago, Pluto must have been as warm as the earth is now, and undoubtedly could support life. If this life managed to evolve to a high level without destroying itself, it may have learned the secret of staying alive on a planet that is now around minus 230 degrees centigrade – only 43 degrees above absolute zero. Its density is the highest in the solar system – about 50 grams per cubic centimetre, which almost certainly means that any beings who lived on it would have had denser bodies than human beings. If David Foster is correct about his 'vibrational system', this would also imply a higher level of powers than most humans possess; but all this, of course, is mere guesswork.

If other planets, and their inhabitants, *were* involved in the 'chain of reincarnation', it would certainly simplify some awkward problems – for example, how the present population of the earth could be so many times greater than it ever has been in previous centuries. (Did the souls in the next world have to form a queue, waiting for a body?) No doubt space travel will eventually provide an answer; meanwhile, we can at least regard it as an entertaining speculation.

THREE
GLIMPSES

All physicists understand that when you are dealing with unobservable phenomena, such as what goes on inside an atom, the first necessity is to formulate a theory that fits the available known facts. Without a theory, facts are merely baffling pieces of a jigsaw puzzle, lying disconnected in the box. In the present chapter, I shall try to suggest a general theory that might impose some order on the bewildering mass of occult phenomena already examined. The essence of this theory can be stated in a few sentences. For various reasons, 'ordinary consciousness' is hopelessly sub-normal and inefficient. There is something wrong with it, rather as if a whole batch of cars were sent out of a factory with some tiny but essential component missing. Various religious, ascetic and mystical disciplines have attempted a cure for this deficiency, which Christians call original sin, but the greatest stride forward was taken in the final years of the nineteenth century, when Edmund Husserl began to work out the discipline called phenomenology, a form of analytical psychology based upon the recognition of the *intentionality* of all our mental acts. This discipline – which even now is only partly understood – is slowly leading to an understanding of the precise mechanisms involved, and therefore of the part that is missing. The basic position of this book is that if the machine could be made to work *normally*, man would acquire, or learn to use, various powers and faculties that at present are 'occult' (latent, hidden) and would discover that they are perfectly natural after all.

All occultism has recognised the existence of a vital force that has never been identified by orthodox science. Mesmer called it 'animal magnetism', and Mary Baker Eddy believed that it was the secret of health.

In 1845, there appeared in Germany a bulky work whose lengthy title can be abbreviated: *Physico-Physiological Researches on the Dynamics of Magnetism, etc., in Relation to the Vital Force.* It was by a respected chemist and physicist, Baron Karl Von Reichenbach, and it caused a sensation. It was the kind of book that today would become an immediate best seller. He stated on an early page:

Through the kindness of a surgeon practising in Vienna, I was introduced in March 1844 to one of his patients, the daughter of the tax collector, Novotny, No. 471 Landstrasse, a young woman of 25 years of age, who had suffered for eight years from increasing pains in the head, and from these fallen into cataleptic attacks … In her, all the exalted intensity of the senses had appeared, so that she could not bear sun or candlelight.

I allowed the father of the girl to make the first preparatory experiment … I directed him to hold before the patient, in the middle of the night, the largest existing magnet, a nine-fold horseshoe capable of supporting about ninety pounds of iron … This was done, and the following morning I was informed that the girl had really perceived a *distinct continuous luminosity* as long as the magnet was kept open … The fiery appearance was about equal in size at each pole … Close upon the steel from which it streamed, it appeared to form a fiery vapour, and this was surrounded by a kind of glory of rays …

He found four more neurasthenic girls, and they all saw the same light; some of them saw it as a kind of Aurora Borealis, radiating a brilliant reddish-yellow light from the South Pole and bluish-green from the North. Suggestion hardly seemed to account for it; for example, he made an assistant go into the next room and uncover a huge magnet directly behind the girl's bed; she became uncomfortable and declared there was a magnet around somewhere. He tried blindfolding her; she knew when the magnet was uncovered (i.e. when the armature was no longer joining its two poles). When Miss Novotny was out cold, in a cataleptic condition, and a horse-shoe magnet was brought near her hand, the hand stuck to it as if the flesh had been a piece of metal. But as Miss Novotny's health improved – no doubt because of all the attention she was getting – she lost her ability to see the 'aurora' around magnets.

Reichenbach was no crank. When he heard that certain 'sick sensitives' had been able to magnetise needles by holding them, he carefully tested this, and found it to be untrue.

He tried magnetising other substances; crystals were an obvious choice. These affected his patients in the same way. He then tried the effect of unmagnetised crystals, and to his surprise, these also worked. He bought a huge crystal, and drew it gently down the patient's arm; she felt a pleasant sensation like a cool breeze. Drawn upward, it produced a warmth that was not entirely pleasant. He tried it on a fellow experimental scientist, and to his surprise, this completely healthy man unmistakably felt the action of the crystal. The obvious inference was that magnets and crystals both conduct electromagnetic force; but this quickly proved incorrect. So what *was* the force they both seemed to possess? Reichenbach decided to call it 'odic force' or odyle. And as he went on to try more and more substances – zinc, sulphur, alum, salt, copper – he found that all seemed to have some degree of odic force, although the colours were often quite distinctive. His experiments with the 'odic force' of precious and semi-precious stones seemed to confirm the occult and alchemical tradition about their nature, although this aspect did not interest Reichenbach in the least, for there was nothing of the occultist about him.

Human beings possess odic force in an unusual degree, he

discovered; it can be seen as a kind of light streaming from the finger ends. And not only by 'sick sensitives'; Reichenbach discovered that about a third of all people seem to be more or less sensitive to the odic force.

By the time his book appeared in English in 1851, the activities of the Fox sisters and the youthful Daniel Dunglas Home were exciting the world. It seemed perfectly natural to attribute the activities of the 'spirits' – or whatever they were – to odic force. The more sceptical were inclined to believe that it was the medium's own odic force that made the tables move. As to how the odic force could be transmitted across rooms, or even across oceans, the spiritualists were inclined to accept the suggestion that there is some kind of 'psychic ether' that carries the 'waves' – a hypothesis that has been revived in our own time by Professor C. D. Broad.

Experimenters in other countries tried Reichenbach's experiments and obtained the same results; for example, Dr. John Ashburner, the English translator of Reichenbach, packs the book with his lengthy notes on his own experiments, sometimes agreeing and sometimes disagreeing with Reichenbach. It is not surprising that all this Germanic thoroughness impressed everybody. But even from the beginning, there were critics who declared that Reichenbach's book was a tissue of absurdities and fallacies. And in England, James Braid, the man who investigated hypnotism, found a simpler explanation for the odic phenomena: hypnotic suggestion. That, he said, was why the patients had to be sick and sensitive. The people who had hailed Reichenbach's book as the most important contribution to science since Newton's *Principia* began to mute their enthusiasm and express misgivings. And in 1859 the great Darwin controversy swept across the world, and odic force was looked back upon as a passing fad, and its discoverer as a misguided crank. Any scientist whose work could be quoted by spiritualists must be a crank.

And yet … Although Reichenbach's *Researches in Magnetism* has been long forgotten, and the few libraries who possess a copy usually classify it under electricity, it remains an unforgettable and convincing book. Could it be that he was right after all? The Hindus believe in a force called *kundalini*, which the yogis attempt to control; it ascends the spine, and moves from 'centre' to 'centre' in the body. Temple painting in India, Ceylon and Japan often show 'auras' emanating from the body, and the colour schemes are strangely reminiscent of Reichenbach. Paracelsus states: 'The vital force is not enclosed in man, but radiates round him like a luminous sphere … In these semi-natural rays, the imagination of man may produce healthy or morbid effects.'

In *Man's Latent Powers* (1938), Phoebe Payne describes the 'psychic aura' of living things:

I remember well that as a tiny child my absorbing interest in flowers was due not only to their beauty, but to the curiosity of 'watching their wheels go round' in the form of their different emanations, some of which showed as a fuzz of luminous mist, while others radiated in a shower of minute sparks or 'prickles', and I soon learned to associate a 'nice smell' with a flower from which there rose a column of silvery smoke. In the same way, my delight in playing with any kind of animal was partly caused by the fun of experimenting with different effects produced by tickling or clutching at the responsive 'something' with which it was surrounded. Throughout my early years I was unaware that not everyone experienced such contacts.

That this sensitivity to the 'odic force' is fundamentally of the same nature as the powers of psychics like Hurkos or Croiset is clear from the remark:

As time went on, adaptation to my personal environment only became more difficult, an uncompromising affair in which I suffered defeat most of the time, chiefly because the behaviour of the ordinary world differed so much from the slow tranquillity on the one hand, or the swift creations constantly blossoming into beauty on the other, of what was to me the more real side of life. Added to this was the constant misery of being acutely aware of people's thoughts, and still more of their emotions, as something objective which they themselves usually did not seem to recognise.

In the year 1939 an eminent Freudian psychologist, Wilhelm Reich, startled and enraged his colleagues by announcing that he had discovered a new form of energy unknown to physics: the vital energy which regulates the health of living creatures. The case of Wilhelm Reich is so strange that it is worth considering at some length; it recalls Reichenbach in many ways.

Reich was born in 1897, and by the mid-1920s he occupied an influential position in the psycho-analytic movement in Vienna. He was a member of the Communist party until expelled in 1933 for expressing the view that fascism is the outcome of sexual repression rather than economic forces.

One of his most interesting concepts was that of 'character armour', the tortoise-like shell which neurotics create to cover up inner weakness and anxiety, and which may even express itself in the form of muscular rigidity or paralysis. Reich saw the psychiatrist's task as the breaking down of his armour.

But clearly, there is something negative about this concept. Anyone's character can be interpreted as defensive armour, whether he is extrovert or introvert, destructive or creative. And if one becomes too obsessed by Reich's notion, one is likely to end by seeing everybody as sick. Reich *had* a concept of a healthy personality: someone who has learned to express sexual impulses with complete freedom. But he was perceptive enough to see that this was also negative. (It is, in fact, merely a restatement of D. H. Lawrence's position.) The orgasm cannot really be the ultimate goal of the human race. His mind groped for some more positive concept. And in 1939, in Norway, he believed he had found it: orgone energy. 'Orgone is a visible, measurable and applicable energy of a cosmic nature,' says Reich in a footnote to *Character Analysis* (p. 304).

'Modern natural philosophy, in order to explain the world, has been obliged to recognise an imponderable, universal agent, [and] has even proved its presence ... On this main principle of cosmogony, Zoroaster is in agreement with Heraclitus, Pythagoras with Saint Paul, the Kabbalists with Paracelsus. Cybele-Maïa reigns everywhere, the mighty soul of the world, the vibrating and plastic substance which the breath of the creative spirit uses at will ... The fluid becomes transformed, it rarefies or densifies according to the souls it clothes or the world it envelops.'

This is not a quotation from Reich, but from Edouard Schuré's *Great Initiates*, and he is speaking about the 'astral light'. Reich rediscovered the 'astral light' and called it orgone energy. This is a blue energy which permeates the whole universe, and which forms a field around living beings – Reichenbach's odyle, Phoebe Payne's 'aura'. The reason that the physical contact between child and mother relieves anxiety, for example, is that their orgone fields unite like two drops of water.

In the sexual orgasm, orgone energy becomes concentrated in the genitals; it is the tingling feeling experienced in sexual excitement. Living matter is made up of 'bions', which are tiny cells pulsating with orgone energy.

How did Reich come to make this astonishing discovery? It is important to understand that he saw it as a strictly logical development of his Freudian psychology. Neurosis is caused by 'sexual stasis', stagnating 'sexual fluid', and the orgasm discharges the sex energies and eliminates the neurosis. Reich found himself inclined to belief in some specific biological energy, distinct from physical energies; the biologist Kammerer had postulated a similar energy; it is Shaw's 'life force'. But this biological energy *is* physical, not somehow 'spiritual'. Sometime around 1933, Reich believed that he had detected the basic unit of living matter, the bion, under the microscope. If living matter is made to swell up, with potassium hydroxide, for example, these bions become clearly visible. If particles of carbon are dropped into a filtered solution of bouillon and potassium chloride, says Reich, the blue bions soon begin to appear, and the heavy carbon particles change their nature and become living matter. When bions degenerate, the result is what Reich calls T-bacilli, which cause cancer.

It was after years of performing experiments to create bions, which Reich claims are quite clearly visible under the microscope, that he stumbled on orgone energy. He had been examining a sea-sand culture under the microscope daily, and his eye developed conjuctivitis. He concluded that this sea-sand culture gave off some powerful form of radiation. Tests for radioactivity were negative, yet he discovered that the sea-sand culture could cause flesh to become swollen and painful. People in a room with many such cultures became headachey and tired. He observed that in the dark the cultures seemed to give off a grey-blue light. Objects could become charged with this blue energy, and would then influence an electroscope. He finally concluded that this new, unknown energy comes from the sun, and that organic substances have the power to absorb this energy and retain it.

He constructed a box to prevent the energy escaping. It had to have metal walls – because organic matter absorbs orgone energy – and layers of organic matter outside, which would absorb any energy that managed to get through the metal. He observed bluish light around the dishes of the culture in this box. And then, to his amazement, he observed the same blue light in the box *when the cultures had been removed.*

On a holiday in Maine in 1940, Reich observed that stars on the eastern horizon seem to twinkle more than those on the western horizon; he reasoned that if twinkling is due to the diffusion of light in the atmosphere, it should be the same everywhere. Then he observed that there seemed to be blue patches between the stars that flickered and gave off flashes of light. Then the answer came to him. Orgone energy permeates everything, and it causes the flickering of the stars. His 'box' had been picking up this energy in its outer, organic layer and sending the energy in through the metal walls, where it became trapped, like heat in a greenhouse. This was the origin of Reich's 'orgone box', which one of his disciples has described as the greatest discovery ever made in medical science. The orgone box is an energy accumulator, says Reich, and if sick people sit inside one, they can quickly be recharged. If they sit too long, the result is headache and a feeling of sickness, like getting sun-stroke.

Reich was totally convinced of the importance of his discovery, but his fellow scientists and doctors would not have it at any price. They said that his photographs of 'bions' were simply bacteria that had got in from the air. Reich said that if you stare at the blue sky, you see waves passing rhythmically across it; the scientists said that the 'waves' were simply the fatigue of the eye muscles. As to Reich's belief that the twinkling of stars, the blueness of the sky, the rippling waves above a hot road, the darkness of a thunder-cloud, are all due to orgone energy, they simply pointed out that there are less fanciful explanations for each of these phenomena.

The last years of Reich's life were tragic. He was convinced of the vital importance of his discoveries, and his Foundation in Maine set out to make them known. He made many converts, but the medical profession reacted as it has reacted to all innovators since Paracelsus. In 1956, Reich was sent to prison for two years and fined £10,000, having been accused by the Food and Drug Administration of selling harmful quack remedies. He died of a heart attack after eight months in prison.

Only careful and unprejudiced examination of his claims by

scientists can decide whether Reich was totally deluded during the last twenty-five years of his life, or whether he had really stumbled on an important discovery. All that can be said at the moment is that there is still no sign that any scientist is prepared to make such an examination; his claims have been dismissed out of hand. It will be seen that these claims by no means conflict with the theories advanced in this book – for example, with Dr. David Foster's notion that cosmic rays may carry information codes. According to Reich, 'cosmic rays' are fundamentally orgone energy, and nothing is more likely than that they possess inherent organising powers over matter. Reich points out that we feel emotional energies to be of a different nature from electrical energies, and again he is obviously right. In fact, if we may state the minimum working hypothesis that has emerged in the course of this book, it is this: that there are energies concerned with vital processes that have not yet been identified in the laboratory. Reich argues that cancers develop in organs of the body that have 'played a dominant role in the muscular armour that repressed sexual excitation'. There is still a tendency among research workers to consider cancer a virus disease, but it is equally certain that it bears a curious relation to a drop in vitality; for example, American research revealed that students who had succumbed to severe nervous depression as a result of overwork showed an unusually high incidence of cancer. The view of George Bernard Shaw, expressed in *Back to Methuselah*, is closer to Reich's; Shaw believes that the universe is permeated with 'life energy', and that some matter is a good conductor and some is a bad conductor. If I sustain a bad bruise, the 'conductivity' of the flesh may be damaged, so that it conducts a lower life-current, which may enable it to develop on its own as a separate entity. Reich would say that the bruised flesh shows a degeneration in its bion structure.

And this raises another interesting question. Most bruises do not turn into cancers. What is the law involved here? The process seems to bear some resemblance to the process involved in mental illness. That is, a person sinks into a condition of vague defeat and depression, but it makes no real difference to his everyday activities, and his mental states vary from day to day. Then one day, some unpleasant event or momentary fear plunges him to a lower level, and *he stays there*, as if he had fallen down a steep step or over a cliff. And a tremendous, long-term effort is needed to raise him back to his old level. It is as if human evolution is not an uphill *slope*, but something like a steep flight of steps. As Shaw points out in the *Methuselah* preface, evolution does not progress steadily, but by sudden leaps. If you are learning to ride a bicycle, you fall off fifty times, and then find yourself suddenly riding it the fifty-first time. As if each time you tried to ride it, you accumulated a little more skill which *did not show immediately* but went into a 'reserve supply', until you are ready to go 'up the next step' on the stairway. The significance of this must be discussed later in the chapter, but one point can be made immediately. If we can tumble down the evolutionary stairway through boredom and defeat-proneness, we can also clamber up to new levels by a gentle, cumulative effort; no frenzied leap is required. And evidence indicates unmistakably that these higher levels are the levels upon which man's 'latent powers' cease to be latent.

Reich's comments about sexual excitement raise a point of vital importance in this discussion. Sexual excitement occurs in two parts: a mental part, where the imagination is important; and a physical part, where the body takes over and explodes into physical climax. We take this for granted; but it is almost unique in the realm of human experience. If I am moved by a piece of music, or by the smells of a spring morning, my 'imaginative' excitement increases, then it recedes, without any physical counterpart. This imaginative part is 'intentional': that is, a sudden noise can break my concentration and ruin the whole thing. The teenager who experiences an orgasm for the first time recognises the astonishing nature of the occurrence. It is almost as strange as if he sprouted wings and flew. What had before been largely an 'intentional', mental excitation has burst into the realm of the physical. And this in itself seems amazing; for after all, the body catches colds, get hungry, feels fatigue, without asking my mind's permission.

Human beings suffer from this mistaken notion that the body and mind run on parallel tracks, without really influencing one another. But most people who experience early sexual development do so because they are intensely preoccupied with the subject, and this preoccupation 'adds up', like efforts to ride a bicycle, until one day the 'leap' occurs – in this case, the power of experiencing a physical climax.

Which raises the interesting question: what other powers could we develop if we made a determined effort?

Consider a curious case cited by C. D. Broad, from the *Occult Review* for 1929. A Mr. Oliver Fox describes how he developed a capacity for – apparently – leaving his body.

In 1902, Fox had a dream, during the course of which it struck him suddenly that he must be dreaming. He went on dreaming; but the knowledge that this was only a dream produced a feeling of great clarity, and the scenery of the dream became unusually vivid and beautiful. He tried to develop this knack of 'self-awareness' in dreams; it happened infrequently, but when it did, he always experienced the same feeling of clarity and beauty.

He also discovered that once he was 'in control' of the dream, he could float through brick walls, levitate and so on. What was happening was, in fact, the reverse of a nightmare, where your legs refuse to run. He gradually became fairly expert at inducing these dreams, but observed that if he tried to prolong them, he experienced a pain in his head. He assumed this to be in the pineal gland, the unused 'eye' in the centre of the brain, which occult tradition declares to be the doorway to 'other' states of being. If he ignored the pain and continued the dream, the result was a feeling of 'bilocation', as if he had left his body and was floating above it, although still aware of his body.

Eventually he discovered that if he tried determinedly he could overcome the pain. When this happened, there was a kind of 'click' in his head – which he identified with the opening of the pineal 'door' – and he then felt himself to be wholly located in the scenery of his dream, which, as before, would appear far more beautiful than normal. These dreams were followed by a return to his body, and another dream to the effect that he was back in bed and waking up. (Broad points out that another observer, the Dutch physicist van Eeden, also had false awakening dreams after 'lucid dreams' similar to Fox's.)

Fox then attempted to induce these states while awake, lying on a bed and putting himself into a trance. He would feel his body becoming numb, and the room would seem to take on a golden colour. He had then to use his imagination, and picture himself hurtling towards the 'pineal doorway'. If he was successful, he felt himself passing out of his body, and the golden colour increased; he would experience a sense of great clarity and beauty, just as in his dreams. Sometimes he was unsuccessful, and would then experience a depressing sense of his 'astral body' fading and the golden colour dying away. Once he had passed the 'pineal doorway', he would be able to float over scenery which was sometimes familiar, sometimes not, and see people at their ordinary occupations – although they did not seem to see him. Sometimes they seemed to sense his presence, and were frightened.

Van Eeden (also cited in Broad's *Lectures in Psychical Research*) actually held conversations during his 'lucid dreams' with people he knew to be dead, and had a strong sense of their reality, although they seemed to be deliberately hesitant and vague in answering his questions about life after death.

These stories immediately bring to mind (a) Swedenborg's conversations with the dead, and (b) John Cowper Powys's 'apparition' to Theodore Dreiser. Raynor C. Johnson remarks in *Nurslings of Immortality*: 'It is not, I think, generally known that apparitions have been created deliberately and experimentally. The well-attested cases of this are not numerous, but there are a number of records which show that the concentrated efforts of the will-to-appear to another person have led to the latter perceiving an apparition ...' (p. 101). I have already cited the case from Tyrrell's *Apparitions* in which a woman appeared to friends in Kew by an effort of will; it is also observable that she passed into a kind of trance, similar to Fox's, in which her body slowly became numb.

In *Man's Latent Powers*, Phoebe Payne describes man's 'etheric body' as follows:

This body of subtle physical material acts as the vehicle for the circulation of human vitality, and is an infinitely delicate bridge between the psychic worlds and the physical brain consciousness ... It is the special qualities of this body ... which constitute the main difference between the psychic and the non-psychic person. The etheric counterpart interpenetrates the whole of the physical anatomy, corresponding to it cell for cell, and also extends beyond it to a distance of four to six inches according to the nature and health of the individual. This outlying portion is called the *health aura*. It is visible to ordinary sight under favourable conditions of lighting ... Many people can catch a glimpse of it in a half light by bringing the fingertips of the two hands near together and slowly drawing them apart, when a nebulous emanation can be sensed or seen flowing from one hand to the other ... This duplicate subtle body appears often as a fine filmy mesh completely surrounding the ordinary physical body, mainly grey in colour. To trained clairvoyant sight it is an intricate structure of delicate hues.

The mention of fingertips certainly leads one to suspect that the etheric body and 'odic force' are somehow connected. And another paragraph suggests that the 'etheric body' functions on 'orgone energy': 'In addition to being the bridge that connects man's subjective experience with the brain and nervous system, the etheric body has the very important function of transmitting vitality from the surrounding atmosphere into the dense physical vehicle and of eliminating used etheric matter.'

Eisenbud treats the etheric body as a serious hypothesis in his book on Ted Serios. For the images that Serios imprinted on the photographic plate could not always be explained as photographs he had seen and memorised; two exceptionally clear shots of Russian Vostok space rockets, apparently in space, could not be traced at all in the literature on the subject, and a shot of Westminster Abbey was taken from an angle that would require an actual cameraman to hover well off the ground. Serios began, of course, as a 'travelling clairvoyant', and in the absence of more down-to-earth explanations, Eisenbud is willing to consider the hypothesis that this is how Serios obtained some of the images he fixed on the Polaroid plate. He goes on to make the interesting assertion that about 25 per cent of people have experienced 'out-of-the-body' experiences in which the body seems to be seen from a higher point in space. (While researching this present chapter, I mentioned the subject to a neighbour, Mrs. Kay Lunnis, who described a similar experience that occurred when she was seriously ill. At the crisis point of the illness, she had the sensation of seeing her body recede away – below – and then gradually come closer, until she re-entered it.) Eisenbud says: 'A significant aspect of these experiences is the unanimity of agreement among those who report them – a unanimity all the more striking in that the great majority of the subjects had never heard of the phenomenon before having experienced it – as to the complete qualitative difference between the experience of being out of the body and state of dreaming or reverie.' He goes on to cite at length an experience sent to the S.P.R. by an armoured car officer who was blown up by a German anti-tank gun in 1944 and hurled through the air covered with burning phosphorus:

> ... the next experience was definitely unusual. I was conscious of being two persons – one, lying on the ground in a field ... my clothes, etc., on fire, and waving my limbs about wildly, at the same time uttering moans and gibbering with fear – I was quite conscious of both making these sounds, and at the same time hearing them as though coming from another person. The other 'me' was floating up in the air, about twenty feet from the ground, from which position I could see not only my other self on the ground, but also the hedge, and the road, and the car which was surrounded by smoke, and burning fiercely. I remember quite distinctly telling myself: 'It's no use gibbering like that – roll over and over to put the flames out.' This my ground body eventually did, rolling over into a ditch under the hedge where there was a slight amount of water. The flames went out, and at this stage I suddenly became one person again.

A parallel example of travelling clairvoyance is cited by Sir Oliver Lodge in his article on 'Psychic Science' (in *The Outline of Science*); it is from Sir Alexander Ogston's book *Reminiscences of Three Campaigns*. He describes feeling separated from his body during an attack of typhoid:

> In my wanderings there was a strange consciousness that I could see through the walls of the building, though I was aware they were there, and that everything was transparent to my senses. I saw plainly, for instance, a poor R.A.M.C. surgeon,

of whose existence I had not known, and who was in quite another part of the hospital, grow very ill and scream and die; I saw them cover his corpse and carry him softly out on shoeless feet, quietly and surreptitiously, lest we should know that he had died, and the next night – I thought – take him away to the cemetery. Afterwards, when I told these happenings to the sisters, they informed me that this had happened just as I had fancied.

A case cited by Thurston Hopkins* raises a further speculation. A Miss Helen Brookes described her experiences of 'astral projection' (which she calls 'exteriorisation') in dreams. Hovering over some sleeping children, she observed a 'misty vapour emanating from the tops of their heads … On peering closer, I was able to see what they were doing astrally. For reflected in the vapour were the activities of their astral bodies.' Miss Brookes speculates that ordinary dreaming is actually the activity of the astral body – a view also held by many primitive people, who believe that a person must be waked cautiously, to allow the spirit to return to the body. Miss Brookes's account brings to mind Ouspensky's description of seeing 'sleeping people' with their dreams hovering around their faces. He also commented that it was almost possible to read their minds.

Now all this is conceivable; we may or may not feel disposed to accept it, but it does not in any way *conflict* with our knowledge of the workings of the world. In the same way, if Dante could have looked into the twentieth century, he would have thought radio and television very strange, but their existence would not have contradicted everything he already knew about the universe. There is no scientific evidence for or against the astral body (although there *is* plenty of evidence for travelling clairvoyance, which seems to point to it).

* *Ghost Stories*, 1955.

On the other hand, experience of precognition *does* contradict what we know, or think we know, about time. By 'time', we mean process, something happening. If you could imagine a completely empty universe, with nothing whatever in it, it would also have no time. Time is something that is measured by things happening to physical entities – by a spring unwinding inside a clock, by my body slowly becoming older. As far as we know, it is irreversible. If I am listening to a record, and I want to hear something over again, I can put the stylus back on to earlier grooves. But there is no time machine to carry me back to yesterday, and the very idea is an absurdity. Because if I could go back to yesterday, or even ten seconds ago, I would meet another 'me', ten seconds younger. I could, in theory, collect millions of duplicates of myself and bring them all back to the present. No, the trouble lies in our use of language and ideas. I have elsewhere used the following illustration. Suppose people were born on moving trains, and stayed on them all their lives. They might invent a word to express the sensation of objects flowing past the windows of the train – a word like 'lyme', for example. And if the train stopped, they would say that 'lyme' had been arrested; and if the train reversed, they might say that 'lyme' is going backwards. But if someone wrote a book about travelling backwards or forwards in 'lyme' it would obviously be the result of sloppy thinking; 'lyme' does not exist in itself – it is made up of several things: landscape, a train and myself observing the flow of the landscape past the window. The same goes for time. It does not exist. Only a process exists.

In that case, how the devil can I possibly dream of the future? Common sense tells me that anything can happen. Imagine a swarm of bees, humming around above a flower garden. No calculating machine in the world could predict the position of a particular bee twenty seconds from now, because it depends upon the movements of thousands of other bees, all flying at random.

If precognition is possible, it would indicate that this view is false.

But even the dottiest occultist would hesitate to assert that there is no such thing as chance. Gurdjieff asserted that most people's lives are *all* chance.

But consider the following experience of J. B. Priestley's, mentioned in his *Man and Time*:

The ... dream belongs to the middle 1920s. I found myself sitting in the front row of a balcony or gallery in some colossal vague theatre that I never took in properly. On what I assumed to be the stage, equally vast and without any definite proscenium arch, was a brilliantly coloured and fantastic spectacle, quite motionless, quite unlike anything I had ever seen before. It was an unusually impressive dream, which haunted me for weeks afterwards.

Then in the early 1930s I paid my first visit to the Grand Canyon, arriving in the early morning when there was a thick mist and nothing to be seen. I sat for some time close to the railing on the South Rim, in front of the hotel there, waiting for the mist to thin out and lift. Suddenly it did, and then I saw, as if I were sitting in the front row of a balcony, that brilliantly coloured and fantastic spectacle, quite motionless, that I had seen in my dream theatre. My recognition of it was immediate and complete. My dream of years before had shown me a preview of my first sight of the Grand Canyon.

Priestley mentioned that he became fascinated with the Grand Canyon, and later visited it many times; it was this intense interest, he believes, that made him dream about the Grand Canyon in advance. He cites a similar case of 'intuition' of the future that makes the same point; it involves two people he knows well. A doctor noticed that he experienced a curious excitement on receiving duplicated official reports that came from the department headed by a Mrs. B. This excitement intensified as he received more of them, although they were in no way personal reports. A year later he met her, fell in love with her and married her. Mrs. B. experienced no similar excitement with regard to the doctor; on the contrary, she did not particularly like him on first acquaintance.

For the most part, the cases quoted by Priestley – and there are hundreds – all involve a happening of some importance. A mother dreams that she has left her one-year-old child by a stream while she goes to get soap to wash clothes; when she returns, he is face down in the water and dead; later in the summer, on a camping holiday, she suddenly recognises the scenery when she is, in fact, about to leave the child alone on the edge of the water as she goes to get the soap. Sensibly, she picks up the child and takes him with her, so there is no way of knowing whether the dream was truly premonitory. But the chances are in its favour.

He cites other cases, less dramatic, but perhaps more important. A woman who had had a strong intuition of some impending disaster, so that she began to cry during the service at St. Martin-in-the-Fields, realised it was connected with her nineteen-year-old son as soon as she saw him, on returning home. Three weeks later, he became ill and died. What happened during his illness is equally curious. He told his mother, 'A dog is going to bark from a long way off.' A few seconds later, the dog began to bark. He said, 'Something is going to be dropped in the kitchen and the middle door will slam.' Seconds later, an aunt dropped something in the kitchen and the door slammed. The illness had apparently caused his brain to work just ahead of time. Priestley also cites a case in which Sir Stephen King-Hall had a sudden clear premonition that a man would fall overboard in a moment. He decided to act on the hunch and gave orders about mustering the boat crew. As the commodore was asking him what the devil he thought he was doing, there was a cry of 'Man overboard' from a ship behind them in the convoy, and then, immediately after, from another ship; their boat was in the water within seconds and both men were pulled aboard. Here it may have been the fact that it was a double emergency that somehow triggered the intuition.

Inevitably, Priestley devotes a great deal of space to the time theories of J. W. Dunne, theories that caused a great deal of excitement in the 1930s and inspired three of Mr. Priestley's own plays. In *An Experiment with Time*, Dunne describes how he was puzzled by the accuracy of some of his dreams. He dreamed his watch had stopped at half past four, and when he looked at it, the watch had stopped at half past four; the next morning, checking with a clock, he realised it had stopped only minutes before he woke up and found it had stopped. In a posthumous book, *Intrusions*, he mentions that a great crowd was yelling 'Look ... Look' at him as the dream ended. A subsequent attempt to 'see' the time by closing his eyes and dozing was equally successful. Later, he dreamed of a volcanic eruption, and then saw in a newspaper that there *had* been such an eruption in Martinique. The newspaper account mentioned that forty thousand people might be killed; in his dream, Dunne had been convinced that four thousand had been killed. But the newspaper later proved to be quite wrong about the number. It was this that led Dunne to assume that what he had dreamed about was not the eruption itself, but seeing the newspaper headline, with its mistaken figure. (He had obviously misread forty thousand as four thousand.) He then began to experiment, keeping a pencil and paper by his bedside, and writing down unusual dreams on waking. The result convinced him that he often dreamed of things that would happen in the future.

Dunne was an intelligent man, an aeronautical engineer with an amateur interest in physics and mathematics; so he tried to construct a theory that would fit in with Einstein's 'relativistic' notions of time. The result convinced many people at the time, but has steadily lost ground since then. Roughly, what he says is this. If time is something that flows or marches on, then there must be another kind of time by which we measure its speed, so to speak. And there must surely be yet another kind of time by which we measure the speed of this Time Two. However, this puzzling assertion is not really important to his central thesis, which is that human beings also have several levels. There is the 'me' who lives and suffers my life. There is another 'me' who is conscious of this first 'me', and which becomes apparent when I speak of 'my-self', Probably, Dunne says, there is also an infinite series of 'me's'. It is this second, detached 'me' who exists in Time Two, and who is able to look backwards and forwards in time.

To explain this strange assertion, Dunne makes another assumption. Suppose everything that happens to me during my life is laid out in a series of pictures, like a technicolour film starting with my birth and ending with my death. If I go through life dully and passively, like a cow, it would have a singularly monotonous quality. In fact, I 'pay attention' to some things and ignore others. So there is one 'me' who drifts through life merely 'seeing', and another 'me' who directs *attention* at some things I 'see' and not at others. Dunne calls this second observer 'mind'. Normally 'mind' has a narrow choice of what to look at – the events of my life. But when I am asleep, it no longer has anything to focus on; and then, says Dunne, it may occupy its time glancing at the past or future.

He decides finally that there is a Universal Mind, of which individual minds are small aspects. And at this point, we may leave him, for he has obviously taken the leap into a kind of mysticism that has no relevance to the present discussion.

Priestley takes Dunne as his starting point, and has some penetrating suggestions. He rejects Dunne's notion about an infinite number of 'selves', pointing out that all we need is three. There is the 'me' who merely observes blankly, the 'me' who exists as I stare out of the window of a train, half asleep, merely recording passing scenery. If I pull myself together and begin to reflect on what I am seeing – if, for example, I am passing through scenery that interests me and I stare with great intensity, looking for something – then a second 'me' comes into existence, the 'me' who judges and discriminates. And then there is a third 'me' who often observes the other two. For if I am able to observe the second 'me', there must be a third 'me' to do so. Priestley gives a good example of the three 'me's'. On an aeroplane journey, 'Self 1' observed unpleasant sounds in the aircraft and felt himself hurled out of his seat; 'Self 2', jerked into existence by the accident, observed that something was wrong (i.e., judged the situation instead of observing it passively); 'Self 3' thought coolly that he would shortly know what it was like to be fried alive.

As to time itself, Priestley suggests that there seems to be three varieties. There is the ordinary time that passes as I go about my ordinary tasks; there is the 'time' I become aware of in moments of stillness and contemplation – for example, what Arnold Toynbee experienced in the moment when he became aware of all history; and there is a kind of time that I seem to be able to control in moments of great intensity, the time I experience when I am intensely creative. Of the second kind he writes:

> ... I remember coming to a halt outside a fine large fish shop. As I stared at the scales and the fins and the round eyes, looking indignant even in death, I lost myself and all sense of passing time in a vision of fishiness itself, of all the shores and seas of the world, of the mysterious depths and wonder of oceanic life. This vision was not in any way related to myself. My ego was lost in it. And real poets, I suppose, must be always enjoying such selfless and timeless visions. They came to me only rarely: it might be from the sight of something, like those fishes gleaming on the marble, or after I had heard somebody merely say 'France' or 'Italy', or from simply reading the words 'eighteenth century'; but they brought me at once a

725

feeling of immense variety, richness and wonder of life on this earth. (p. 289)

As to Time Three, he goes on to speak of the tremendous speed with which he wrote four of his most successful, and difficult, plays, and comments that looking back on the experience, 'I felt like a man watching himself run at a headlong pace across a mine field.' He is inclined to believe that the unconscious mind has its own kind of time, and that this is what is involved in this kind of headlong creativity.

What Priestley now suggests is close to the time theories expressed by Ouspensky in *A New Model of the Universe* and Ouspensky's follower, J. G. Bennett, in *The Dramatic Universe*: that time *has three dimensions*, like space. He cites the case of the wife of General Toutschkoff, who dreamed three times that her husband had been killed at a place called Borodino. They looked up Borodino on a map but could not find it (it is only a tiny village). But Napoleon invaded Russia; the Battle of Borodino took place, and she was informed of her husband's death under the precise circumstances of her dream. This certainly suggests that time is predetermined, like a gramophone record. But what of the case of the mother who decided not to leave her child by the stream? Priestley cites several similar cases in which a warning in a dream enabled someone to avoid disaster. This suggests a second kind of time 'connected in some way with the power to connect or disconnect potential and actual' (to quote Bennett).

Priestley's theory, then, is that Time One is the ordinary passing time of everyday living – 'living and partly living', as Eliot says. Time Two is 'contemplative time', which sometimes becomes apparent to us in dreams. Time Three is the time in which changes can be made. Blake seems to have been describing this when he wrote:

Each man is in his Spectre's power,
Until the arrival of that hour,
When his Humanity awake
And cast his own Spectre into the lake.

We might say, following Gurdjieff, that man is usually in a sleeping state. In moments of contemplation, such as Toynbee experienced near Mistra, he wakes up – or Faculty X wakes up. But a further awakening is still possible, in which he lives and acts with real freedom, in which he can really 'do' things.

Priestley's final view is that we are faced with a future 'already shaped but still pliable', and that even when the body dies, we somehow continue to exist in Times Two and Three. Ouspensky is inclined to accept Nietzsche's eternal recurrence – the notion that we relive our lives over and over again; but he also believes that slight changes are possible, that some people have 'an inner ascending line' that slowly raises them to a higher level. (He distinguishes two other types: those for whom success becomes increasingly easy, and those who have an inbuilt degenerative principle that causes them to 'sink' from life to life.) That this view of Ouspensky's was no casual speculation is proved by his novel *The Strange Life of Ivan Osokin*, in which the hero, disappointed in love, asks the magician to allow him to go back in time so he can avoid making the same mistakes. But, as in Barrie's *Dear Brutus*, he repeats the same mistakes all over again, and comes back to the same point, the meeting with the magician. But this time, he realises what has happened, and asks the magician if things cannot be somehow altered. The magician, obviously Gurdjieff, smiles and says, 'Ah, that is the question you should have asked earlier ...' In other words, things can be changed if man can learn to *be*. He must cultivate the tiny grain of freedom he possesses.

Ouspensky's vision may seem unnecessarily gloomy. And if, in fact, we really possess some of the powers suggested in this chapter, then it is almost certainly true. He suggests that a man is chained to his body, and his destiny, like a galley slave. But if that is so, how is travelling clairvoyance possible? Moreover, Priestley describes a number of dreams in which the dreamer appears to have dreamed *someone else's life*. For example, he himself had an extraordinarily convincing dream in which he seemed to be some kind of spy in a foreign city who was shot by security police as he tried to steal some naval secret; Priestley says he thinks the balance of probability is that he somehow relived the last moments of a real man.

The poet Ronald Duncan, in reply to my question as to whether he had had any 'occult' experiences, sent me a story entitled *Flame of the Forest*,* in which he had fictionally embodied his own experience of having 'lived before'. He comments, 'As a child I found that I was worried by images which would flash into my mind without any apparent cause. For example, when I was going to tie my shoelace on the way to school, I would, as I bent down, always visualise a street scene in a city where I had never been … I became interested in race memory as a possible explanation, for I constantly had the experience of remembering something which I had not myself experienced.'

The story is told by a Hindu (Duncan spent many years in India as a disciple of Gandhi), who declares that he was born in England as Abercrombie Martyn, and tells how he had been completely dominated by his father, who seemed to want to relive his own life vicariously through his son. Experiences of a certain ford on a certain river kept flashing into his mind, particularly when he bent down to pick things up. He went to India and wandered around as a kind of tramp. One day he found himself by the ford at the river, in a kind of daydream. Suddenly a woman spoke to him – his wife – and he was no longer an Englishman named Abercrombie Martyn but a Hindu

* *Argosy*, March 1968.

named Jitendra Narayan, who had gone to fetch water in a jar, and fallen into a daydream by the river.

Duncan is here trying to catch the essence of certain moments when one's feeling of certainty and identity dissolves, revealing not a world of confusion or insanity but strangely logical vistas. In the preface to his epic poem *Man*, he describes how, sitting in his London flat, he was possessed for several days by memories that belonged to the past of the human race; a sense of *déjà vu* not simply about himself but about his remote ancestors. He explains that he had daubed the bare walls with colour to relieve the monotony; glancing up from his writing later, he realised that he had, without realising it, drawn a bison, matchstick men and prehistoric animals. This happened before he saw similar drawings reproduced from the caves of Lascaux. Duncan also experienced 'a sense of smell so acute as to be intolerable … while it lasted, I found I could smell every odour in the adjoining flats'. (The experience brings to mind Louis Singer's parallel experience described in Part One, Chapter 3.) It struck him: 'I was not 47; some parts of me were possibly 20,000 years old.' He later came to see the experience as a proof of Jung's 'racial memory'.

Equally odd, and (as far as I know) unique in kind, is an experience recounted by Robert Graves in an autobiographical fragment called *The Abominable Mr. Gunn.** He describes how, one summer evening, sitting on a roller behind the school cricket pavilion, he suddenly 'knew everything': 'I remember letting my mind range rapidly over all its familiar subjects of knowledge; only to find that this was no foolish fancy. I did know everything. To be plain: though conscious of having come less than a third of the way along the path of formal education, and being weak in mathematics, shaky in Greek grammar, and hazy about English, I nevertheless held the key of truth in my hand, and could use it to open the lock of any door.

* *Collected Stories*, p. 90.

729

Mine was no religious or philosophical theory, but a simple method of looking sideways at disorderly facts to make perfect sense of them.' The 'vision' was still there the next morning, although attempts to set it down on paper raised problems of self-expression that undermined it, and it faded the following evening.

What Graves means by 'knowing everything' becomes clearer in another episode he recounts: how a boy in the class called F. F. Smilley was suddenly able to do a very difficult mathematical problem instantaneously (it was to find the square root of the sum of two long decimals, divided by the sum of two complicated vulgar fractions). The boy wrote the answer on a sheet of paper, only to be told by the master that it could not be accepted unless he went back and did the 'working out'. Smilley apparently continued to show this same curious ability for the remainder of the term when, owing to the closure of the school, Graves lost sight of him.

Now, the ability to do enormous sums is fairly common: mathematical prodigies reappear in every age, and they are, as often as not, uneducated young men who otherwise show no particular ability. The boy Zerah Colborn, asked if 4,294,967,297 was a prime number or not, replied after a moment: 'No, it can be divided by 641.' (The best brief account of these prodigies can be found in W. W. Rouse Ball's *Mathematical Recreations*.) How feats like this are performed by the brain is not known – the prodigies themselves cannot explain the process – but Priestley's hypothesis about time immediately suggests that what we are dealing with here is one of those lightning creative processes that occur in Time Three. What solves problems is what the philosopher Bernard Lonergan calls 'insight' (in his important book of that name). That is, you suddenly seem to be lifted above the ground, as if you could take a bird's-eye view of a maze, and *see* the way out instead of ploddingly working it out on the ground by some formula. Lonergan cites Archimedes' cry of 'Eureka' on suddenly grasping the law of floating bodies, as a typical example of insight, and we can see that the essence of such a 'flash' is that it distinctly has the quality of a *key*, just as Graves says. It answers dozens of questions all at one go, and the excitement of this realisation makes the mind see further vistas of questions that it can answer – and so on, with a feeling like ripples expanding across a pool.

If I am asked to work out a mathematical problem, I approach it through analogy with other problems, and then begin to calculate step by step, as if I was climbing a flight of stairs. But if real 'insight' comes – which it seldom does, since I am a poor mathematician – the whole thing is speeded up, and it seems possible to reach the top of the stairs in two quick bounds.

It sounds, then, as if this is what happened to Graves. He states clearly that it was not some religious or philosophical *idea*, but a 'key'. (I have discussed the experience with him, and he was not able to elaborate on the account as already quoted.) Insight always has the effect of 'connecting up' disconnected ideas, like those children's games where you connect a series of numbered dots and the result is suddenly a rabbit or a gnome on a toadstool: a result you could not possibly have inferred by studying the dots. Now, I think there can be no doubt that 'insight', whether it utilises Time Three or not, is a 'normal' faculty of the human brain that we have not yet got around to developing. The process of 'insight' is described lucidly in an essay by William James called 'A Suggestion about Mysticism'. His suggestion, 'stated very briefly, is that states of mystical intuition may be only very sudden and great extensions of the ordinary "field of consciousness"'. He says of such a glimpse, 'It will be of unification, for the present coalesces in it with ranges of the remote quite out of its reach under ordinary circumstances; and the sense of *relation* will be greatly enhanced' (i.e. the sense of having a key to other experiences). He mentions three experiences in which he experienced such a glimpse, and says:

What happened each time was that I seemed all at once to be reminded of a past experience; and this reminiscence, ere I could conceive or name it distinctly, developed into something further that belonged with it, this in turn into something further still, and so on, until the process faded out, leaving me amazed at the sudden vision of increasing ranges of distant fact of which I could give no articulate account. The mode of consciousness *was perceptual, not conceptual* [my italics] – the field expanding so fast that there seemed no time for conception or identification to get in its work. There was a strongly exciting sense that my knowledge of past (or present?) reality was enlarging pulse by pulse, but so rapidly that my intellectual processes could not keep up the pace. The *content* was thus entirely lost to retrospection – it sank into the limbo into which dreams vanish as we gradually awake. The feeling – I won't call it belief – that I had had a sudden *opening*, had seen through a window, as it were, distant realities that incomprehensibly belonged with my own life, was so acute that I cannot shake it off today.

This is exceptionally clear. James had momentarily 'wakened up', in Gurdjieff's sense, and consciousness ceased to drag itself like a wet fly over a table-top and launched itself into the dimension of pure 'insight'.

James goes on to recount a story of dream experience that is baffling and difficult to grasp. He says that when he woke up in the morning, the dream he had just been having and some earlier dream seemed to somehow telescope together: '… the apparent mingling of two dreams was something very queer that I had never before experienced'. The following night, the confusion increased when he awakened from a deep, heavy sleep to find that three dreams now seemed to be somehow telescoping together.

They were distinct dreams, each with its own atmosphere – one of London, one about trying on a coat, one about soldiers. There was a sensation of 'belonging to three different dream systems at once'. 'I began to feel curiously confused and *scared*, and tried to wake myself up wider, but I seemed already wide awake. Presently, cold shivers of dread ran over me: *am I getting into other people's dreams?* Is this a "telepathic" experience? Or an invasion of double (or treble) personality?' The description of misery and confusion that follows – of losing all sense of an anchor, anything to cling on to – is very moving. Then it came to him that he always slept very deeply from midnight until about 2 a.m., and that possibly the three dreams that were 'telescoping' were dreams that belonged to his deep sleep on previous nights. This explanation restored his sense of balance. He concludes by saying, 'To this day I feel that those extra dreams were dreamed in reality, but when, where and by whom I cannot guess.' This helps to uncover the source of his panic: the feeling that somebody else's dreams had somehow got into his head, and that our normal sense of security and 'reality' is an error. But then, when one wakes from a deep sleep, it is to immediately experience what Priestley calls Self 1, the everyday self that drifts through Time One. What James's 'everyday self' seems to have glimpsed is the bewildering vistas of other 'dimensions' of time. This negative experience seems to confirm Priestley's notion of time, particularly when we bear in mind that James called it 'the most intensely peculiar experience of my whole life'. Clearly, it seemed to hold significances that he was not able to express on paper.

It can, I think, be seen that James's experience of 'expanding horizons of fact' is nothing less than a sudden total awakening of Faculty X, which is, as I have said, a sense of the objective reality of other times and places, instead of the usual subjective worm's-eye view in which we are trapped all our lives. It is like standing on a mountaintop and seeing far more than you are able to see from the valley. In fact, Priestley's image of the mist rising on the Grand Canyon expresses it admirably. It can be understood why Graves felt he 'knew everything' while this glimpse lasted. Equally interesting is the fact that, although James believes that such experiences are bound to be momentary, Graves's lasted for about twenty-four hours. This is of immense importance. For the experience that suddenly happened to Graves was a kind of mental counterpart of Home's ability to float in the air. And it lasted. If it could last for a day, there is no reason why it should not last all the time.

It is necessary to try to gain further insight into the nature of this 'glimpse'. It is quite clearly what the mystics have always talked about. And the mystics have asserted that it is 'ineffable', that it cannot be talked about or analysed. In this book we have gone a long way towards analysing it, and perhaps may go further still.

Warner Allen, in his interesting book *The Timeless Moment*, describes how he experienced the fundamental mystical 'glimpse':

When the writer was on the threshold of fifty, it occurred to him as it must have occurred to many another ordinary journalist, no less hostile to the apparent sloppiness of fashionable mysticism than he was, that he had lived for nearly half a century without discerning in life any pattern of rational purpose. His views on the matter might have been roughly summed up in a vague notion that the universe was shrouded in impenetrable darkness by the powers of Life and Death, for fear life should lose its savour as a brave adventure, if the mystery of death and suffering was solved, and uncertainty was exchanged for the assurance of future beatitude. A curiously vivid dream shook his faith in this tentative explanation of human ignorance … This quest of truth led through paths of unforeseen darkness and danger, but within a year … an answer came.

It flashed up lightning-wise during a performance of Beethoven's Seventh Symphony at the Queen's Hall, in that triumphant fast movement when 'the morning stars sang together and all the sons of God shouted for joy'. The swiftly flowing continuity of the music was not interrupted, so that what Mr. T. S. Eliot calls 'the intersection of the timeless moment' [with time] must have slipped into the interval between two demi-semiquavers, When, long after, I analysed the happening in the cold light of retrospect, it seemed to fall into three parts: first, the mysterious event itself, which occurred in an infinitesimal fraction of a split second; this I learned afterwards from Santa Teresa to call the Union with God; then Illumination, a *wordless* stream of complex feelings in which the experience of Union combined with the rhythmic emotion of the music like a sunbeam striking with iridescence the spray above a waterfall – a stream that was continually swollen by tributaries of associated Experience; lastly, Enlightenment, the recollection in tranquillity of the whole complex of Experience, as it were, embalmed in thought-forms and words.

That this is the experience William James is talking about becomes almost certain when we consider James's preliminary remark that his own experiences were extremely brief: 'In one instance I was engaged in conversation, but I doubt whether the interlocutor noticed my abstraction.' Allen's second phase – the wordless stream of complex feelings that was 'swollen by tributaries of associated Experience' – makes it clear that this is that outward expansion of associations described by James. In short, the pleasure and excitement of the music energised Warner Allen's mind until suddenly, like a spark flying upward, it achieved 'insight', the bird's-eye view.

This is the mystical experience that Chesterton described as a feeling of 'absurd good news', the joy that burst on Faust as he heard the Easter bells, the overwhelming feeling of insight that often accompanies the sexual orgasm.

Charlotte Brontë describes a similar glimpse in *Shirley*, a sudden ecstatic 'vision of life as she wishes it. No – not as she wishes it; she has not time to wish: the swift glory spreads out, sweeping and kindling its splendour faster than Thought can effect his combinations, faster than Aspiration can utter her longings.' Here, the language is so similar to James's that one could almost believe he was unconsciously quoting it.

In *A Drug Taker's Notes*, R. H. Ward describes his own experiences with lysergic acid, but then concludes that they were not genuine 'mystical' experiences. By way of contrast, he quotes a mystical experience of a friend of his:

Last night as I was walking home from the station I had one of those strange experiences of 'rising up within oneself', of 'coming inwardly alive' ... A minute or so after I had left the station, I was attacked ... by indigestion ... I thought to myself, though I suppose not in so many words, 'I could separate myself from this pain; it belongs only to my body and is real only to the physical not-self. There is no need for the self to feel it.' Even as I thought this the pain disappeared; that is, it was in some way left behind because I, or the self, had gone somewhere where it was not; and the sensation of 'rising up within' began. (... I have the impression that movement encouraged this sensation ...)

First there is the indescribable sensation in the spine, as of *something mounting up*, a sensation which is partly pleasure and partly awe, a physical sensation and yet one which, if it makes sense to say so, is beginning to be not physical. This was accompanied by an extraordinary feeling of *bodily lightness*, of well-being and effortlessness, as if one's limbs had no weight and one's flesh had been suddenly transmuted into some rarer substance. But it was also, somehow, a feeling of living more in the upper part of one's body than the lower, a certain peculiar awareness of one's head as ... the most important and intelligent of one's members. There was also a realisation that one's facial expression was changing; the eyes were wider open than usual; the lips were involuntarily smiling. Everything was becoming 'more', everything was *going up on to another level ...*

I found that I could think in a new way. Or rather, it would be more accurate to say that I could think-and-feel in a new way, for it was hard to distinguish between thought and feeling ... *This was like becoming possessed of a new faculty.* [My italics.]

He describes the feeling of delight associated with ordinary objects, and this has much in common with Aldous Huxley's description of his sensation of the 'is-ness' of things under mescalin. However, the experience certainly seems to have involved an awareness of those 'other dimensions of time'. For example, he explains that the thought of death not only ceased to be something to fear, but that death seemed positively to become 'Dear, beauteous death ...' He adds that he felt as though he could easily give up his own life because 'it was self-evident that we live in other ways than corporeally'. Significantly, it was important to avoid negative emotions – distrust, fear, contempt – because they immediately began to 'bring him down'. And even more significant, he felt that if his present state of mind could somehow be conveyed to a friend dying of cancer, she would be cured, because 'like any other ugliness or evil, [cancer] could not exist as such in the presence of God'. At the same time, he felt that it did not matter that this physical organism of hers died.

This experience calls for many comments. Although he says that he 'separated himself' from the pain of indigestion, it is clear that the indigestion vanished; it was a negative thing, and the 'upward leap of the mind' dismissed it, This method of achieving a higher state of mind – deliberately reminding yourself that 'you' are quite different from your body – is familiar to mystics; for example, the modern Hindu saint Sri Ramana Maharshi experienced his first 'ecstasy' as a result of thinking about the death of his body, then suddenly grasping, *as a fact*, that 'he' was a 'deathless self' quite distinct from the body.* Certainly, the sensation of something 'mounting up' in the spine corresponds to the Hindu description of the rise of *kundalini*. The reference to the flesh feeling as if it had been 'transmuted into a rarer substance' seems to confirm what Jung says of alchemy as a symbol of higher states of mind. The feeling that cancer could be cured by this state of mind certainly echoes the belief of Christian Science which, as we have seen, receives abundant confirmation in occult tradition.

Another example will reinforce the point I am making here. In *Arrow in the Blue*, Arthur Koestler describes two experiences in which he achieved this sudden 'transcendence'. In the first, he was reading a pamphlet about atrocities in Palestine, and feeling himself 'choke and seethe with impotent anger'. He admits that he suffers from 'chronic indignation' as others do from chronic indigestion. While still in this state, he picked up a book by Hermann Weyl on Einstein, and read the comment that relativity had led the human imagination 'across the peaks and glaciers never before explored by any human being'. And then: 'I saw Einstein's world-shaking formula – Energy equals Mass multiplied by the square of the velocity of light – hovering in a kind of rarefied haze over the glaciers, and this image carried a sensation of infinite tranquillity and peace. The martyred infants and castrated pioneers of the Holy Land shrank to microscopic insignificance ... The fate of these unfortunates had to be viewed with the same serene, detached,

* See *Ramana Maharshi*, by Arthur Osborne (London, Rider, 1954), p. 18.

meditative eye as that of stars bursting into novae, of sunspots erupting, of rocks decaying into swamps, and primeval forests being transformed into coal. This change in perspective was accompanied by an equally pronounced physiological change. The sensation of choking with indignation was succeeded by the relaxed quietude and self-dissolving stillness of the "oceanic feeling".' This is a phrase used by Freud in his *Civilisation and Its Discontents*, and Freud tries to explain it away in terms of father-fixations, etc.

The second experience makes the point even more clearly. Koestler was in a Spanish jail during the Civil War, sentenced to death, and he began scratching mathematical formulae on the wall to pass the time. He went on to work out Euclid's classic proof that there is no 'largest prime number'. As he did so, he experienced a deep satisfaction, due to the sudden thought that Euclid was establishing a truth about infinity using finite means.

The significance of this swept over me like a wave. The wave had originated in an articulate verbal insight; but this evaporated at once, leaving in its wake only a wordless essence, a fragrance of eternity, a quiver of the arrow in the blue. I must have stood there for some minutes, entranced with a wordless awareness that 'this is perfect – perfect'; until I noticed some slight mental discomfort nagging at the back of my mind – some trivial circumstance that marred the perfection of the moment. Then I remembered the nature of that irrelevant annoyance: I was, of course, in prison, and might be shot. But this was immediately answered by a feeling whose verbal translation would be: 'So what? is that all? have you nothing more serious to worry about?' – an answer so spontaneous, fresh and amused as if the intruding annoyance had been the loss of a collar stud. Then I was floating on my back in a river of peace, under bridges of silence …

This makes it quite clear that the experience we are now discussing is Priestley's second level of time, Time Two, which he experienced looking at the fish.

But is it necessary to postulate these different 'times'? Surely, all we need postulate is different levels of the personality. Let us say, for the sake of convenience, that human beings have two 'poles', a personal and an impersonal pole. The personal pole is evident if I am suddenly in danger. Let us say that I nearly have a street accident, and instantly feel 'contingent'. For a brief moment, the only thing I care about is self-preservation. Most people are excessively personal – they brood too much on their ills and their worries and resentments. When this happens, the vision becomes narrow. I have elsewhere suggested a convenient term for this narrowness: mono-consciousness. If I am sitting in a stuffy room, bored and dull, I am stuck in one single reality – the reality that surrounds me. If rain patters on the window, the sudden delight I experience is due to being suddenly reminded of the existence of another reality 'out there'. This is duo-consciousness, and it is what happens to Faust when he hears the Easter bells: the delighted feeling – yes, *something else exists*. We are normally trapped in this stuffy room of subjectivity, but when duo-consciousness comes, it is as if I can breathe deeply. I then realise the immensely important fact that my soul can suffocate just as easily as my body; it can die for lack of a kind of oxygen. It is exactly like the relief of the sexual orgasm, as described by D. H. Lawrence, for example. And it is accompanied by an odd sensation of invulnerability, an insight to the effect: 'I need never suffocate again now I know this …' and as if I had obtained a magic talisman capable of forever protecting me from suffocation. It is a sudden knowledge of my own strength.

The various experiences described above sound as if they are 'visitations', sudden 'descents of the dove' that human beings can do nothing to control. Shelley addresses the 'spirit of beauty' and asks:

Why dost thou pass away and leave our state,
This dim, vast vale of tears, vacant and desolate?

And that is, indeed, the most fundamental problem of human existence. Why does it? Why do our certainties, our ecstasies and intensities, evaporate so easily; leaving us with a feeling like a hangover?

Husserlian psychology teaches that the correct approach is to examine the problem with the practical eye of a garage mechanic wondering why a car is not 'pulling'.

And at this point, I must make an attempt to present my own analysis of the *totality* of man, and try to pull the themes of this book into some sort of unity.

My most basic insight is this: that *there is something wrong with human beings.* When you have a bad cold, you have a continual sense of oppression; you don't seem to be able to draw a really deep breath; you feel as if you are suffocating. And you are certainly aware that this state is not normal. But all human beings are suffering permanently from a kind of spiritual head cold, and they are not aware of it. Sometimes, when they are unusually worried or tired, the sense of suffocation becomes so oppressive that it turns into panic, and this can be the beginning of severe mental illness.

And then there are the occasional moments when the head clears; a kind of bubble seems to burst at the back of the nose, and you can suddenly breathe *and* see and hear with a new freshness. Something inside us wakes up, and is delighted by the world it finds itself in. The universe is seen to be infinitely interesting and complex.

In all these moments of intensity, 'newness', we are aware of a sense of inner *contraction*, as if one's consciousness were a fist that had become clenched.

And this is the vital clue. We know that our bodies are made up of a swarm of electrons, buzzing around like bees, held together by inner forces of attraction. But the same is true of the 'astral body', or whatever you choose to call the living, thinking, feeling 'me'; it is also a swarm of particles, like bees. But it differs from the physical body in one important respect. Your physical body always has the same size and shape, more or less. But this 'mental body' can expand into a vague, diffuse cloud, or contract until it seems to be a glowing ball of intensity. It was A. E. Housman who pointed out that the test of true poetry is that it makes the hair prickle. It also causes this 'mental body' to *contract*. The skin seems to become tighter. Sartre describes it in his novel *Nausea*: 'I felt my body harden and the nausea vanish; suddenly it was almost unbearable to become so hard, so brilliant.' He also says, 'I feel my body at rest like a precision machine.' These images capture the feeling of 'contraction': hardness, almost as if the skin had changed into chrome-plated steel.

The same thing happens in the sexual orgasm: a feeling of inner contraction. It is the first step towards what Shaw calls 'the seventh degree of concentration'. This is what Proust experienced when he tasted the madeleine dipped in tea and suddenly ceased to feel 'mediocre, accidental, mortal'.

The feeling was not an illusion. He had accidentally stumbled upon a perfectly normal power of the human soul: Faculty X. We are *not* 'mediocre, accidental, mortal', even though most of the time we feel we are.

I have pointed out that there is an impressive mass of evidence for the existence of the astral body. But for present purposes, it makes no difference whether it really exists, or whether it is regarded as a figure of speech. To verify the reality of the 'inner contraction', you only have to take the trouble to observe yourself next time you experience sudden intense delight.

Once this is recognised, the analysis may be carried further. It will be seen that a certain degree of 'contraction' produces the sense of poetry, Shelley's spirit of beauty, the 'peak experience'. A further contraction produces a sense of 'being', *of being able to act,* that Priestley calls the third dimension of time. This is the state of insight, when all the faculties seem to be speeded up. It explains why men become racing drivers and mountain climbers, or go into the desert like T. E. Lawrence: because they want to face an emergency that forces them to 'contract' to this new level of control.

At a certain point of concentration, a chain reaction begins to develop. Readers who have studied atomic physics will know that this is the principle of the atom bomb. Uranium 235 is an isotope that disintegrates continually because of its radioactivity. In small masses, the disintegration proceeds slowly. But if more than a certain 'critical mass' is brought together, the distintegration suddenly accelerates wildly, because the 'bullets' of energy thrown out by the atoms score direct hits on the nuclei of other atoms, causing them to disintegrate; and the exploding atoms shoot out still more bullets, which strike still more nuclei. The result is an atomic explosion. In an atomic bomb, two small masses of Uranium 235 are suddenly hurled together, creating a critical mass, which explodes.

There is an analogous principle in concentration. At a certain point, one's mental being – the 'swarm of bees' – seems to reach a certain critical mass, and a chain reaction develops. Something of the sort seems to have happened to Robert Graves as he sat on the garden roller.

And at this point, an interesting phenomenon occurs. States of sudden intense happiness often seem to disintegrate as if from their own inner pressure. In the same way, if two small masses of Uranium 235 are brought together to form a critical mass, the result will not be a massive explosion, because the reaction that ensues will blow them apart again, scattering the uranium before it can explode. In an atomic bomb, they have to be held together. This explains why mystical intensity – such as was experienced by Warner Allen in Queen's Hall 'between two notes of a symphony' – is usually so brief. It causes its own disintegration. But why, if the mystic *wants* to keep it so badly?

The answer is of fundamental importance. Because the 'muscles' that could hold it are flabby and undeveloped. We only make use of these muscles *involuntarily*, when suddenly stirred by beauty or by a sense of crisis. And this in itself is preposterous – as if you only used the muscles in your leg when someone tapped you on the knee, causing a reflex action.

We possess the muscles for compressing consciousness and producing states of intensity, but we use them so seldom that we are hardly aware of their existence.

My simile of the atom bomb can be carried further. An atom bomb can be used as the detonator of a hydrogen bomb; the fusion of hydrogen – which is what produces the sun's heat – requires temperatures and pressures as intense as those in the heart of the sun. These can be produced momentarily if an atom bomb, which works on 'fission' (disintegration), is exploded inside a mass of compressed hydrogen, which then *fuses* into the more complex helium atom, producing an explosion a thousand times more powerful than the atomic bomb. Human consciousness is theoretically capable of this kind of power. Man is literally a god: a god suffering from laziness, amnesia and nightmares.

The Catholics call this 'fault' of human consciousness Original Sin; Heidegger calls it 'forgetfulness of existence'. But it is important to understand that it is not a basic flaw. As odd as it may sound, we suffer from the 'spiritual head cold' because we want to. A man who wants to think locks himself into a quiet room, and perhaps closes all the windows. This has its advantages and disadvantages; it allows him to concentrate, but it cuts out the fresh air and the sound of the birds. When I have to concentrate – for example, when I am writing these pages – I lock myself into an inner room, and close all the windows. If I now decide to go for a walk, I cannot simply open all these windows again. It takes time to 'unwind', to relax.

This is why most human beings spend their lives in a highly

uncomfortable state of 'generalised hypertension' without knowing what to do about it.

When we are worried, there seem to be two possible courses. One is to *do* something about it, to look for a way out. The other is to go on feeling worried, to accept it passively as we accept a bad cold or a toothache.

There is a third course, but most of us are unaware of it. When a man wants something badly, or wants to avoid something badly, he makes an immense effort of concentration, an inner convulsion. The mental body 'contracts', and the result is a new sense of power, control and *freedom*. Graham Greene's 'whiskey-priest', on the point of being shot by a firing squad, realises that 'it would have been so easy to be a saint'. Why? Because the threat of immediate extinction causes the inner convulsion, a greater effort of will than he has made in years, perhaps in the whole of his life. And he realises, with a shock, that if he had made this same effort of will earlier, he need not have wasted his life.

Man possesses the power to contract his 'astral body' by an act of will. He is not aware that he possesses this power. The proof of his ignorance is his capacity for boredom. Boredom is the expansion of the 'astral body', in which the swarm of bees becomes a vague, diffuse cloud. In this state, we experience a kind of 'nausea', and the sense of meaning vanishes. Life 'fails'; the inner energies drop. The next stage in human evolution will be the deliberate development of this 'muscle' of the will, and a corresponding development of the sense of meaning.

It can be seen that, according to this scheme of evolution, Priestley's three orders of time become unnecessary. Time One is the way I experience time when I am passive and unfocused. Time Two is the way I experience it when my mind becomes self-governing, which is what happens when it focuses on *meaning*. Time Three is the way I experience time when the creative chain reaction begins, when I experience a sense of total control of my mental processes and unwavering perception of meaning.

There are some interesting points to observe about these three time experiences. The most tiring of the three is Time One, a passive living-in-the-present. If I feel exhausted, the best way to recover is to find something that deeply interests me and concentrate on it. If I am exhausted *and* bored, the curious result is that I continue to run down still further, like a car whose ignition has been left switched on. This principle has been used in the brainwashing of spies. The spy is placed in a completely black and silent room, and as soon as he becomes acutely bored, his will relaxes, his sense of meaning ebbs away, a feeling of misery and panic begins to build up, and his vital forces disintegrate. He begins to feel increasingly 'mediocre, accidental, mortal'. In this state, he is easy prey for an interrogator.

On the other hand, if I am bored and tired, and then something happens that arouses my deepest interest, I ignore the fatigue; I concentrate; and my vital batteries begin to recharge at a fast rate.

The Time Three experience is the most interesting because it involves the most total control. If I am deeply involved in the contemplation of something else – like Toynbee at Mistra, or Priestley outside the fish shop – I am still basically passive, my mind turned outward: this is Time Two. But in times of intense mental activity and concentration, I am aware of being in charge of a chain reaction. That is, the more deeply I concentrate, the more I focus meaning; and the more I focus meaning, the more intensely I concentrate.

I have myself experienced the sense of 'power over time' on two occasions. On the first of these, I was working in a hospital in a job that bored me. Weeks of inactivity and minor irritations had reduced me to a passive state where I felt almost incapable of concentration. At this time I was deeply interested in Nijinsky (who had died recently), particularly in his attempt to create a new kind of choreography with tense, heiratic movements. When I was alone I used to practise ballet exercises; and if there was suitable music on the radio I would experiment with these 'Nijinsky movements'. One evening, the 'Liebestod' from *Tristan* came on; its unexpectedness produced a shock of pleasure and concentration. I made an effort to retain this concentration; it seemed as difficult as balancing on one toe, but the movement helped. As my attention began to waver, the climax of the 'Liebestod' induced a new effort of concentration, and quite suddenly, for a space of a second or two, I had a sense of *absolute and total* control over time, as if I could order it to stand still. The past ceased to be something that receded from me, like the scenery going past a train; it felt as if I could relive it as easily as I could put on a gramophone record for a second time. The metabolic processes of the body seemed to be as much within my control as the muscles in my arms and legs.

The second occasion was related to the first in that I was again listening to *Tristan* in the gods at Covent Garden. The sheer length of the opera ends by inducing a sense of freedom, for the unwonted concentration leads to 'second wind'. It was in this second wind that I decided to try to re-create the sensation of timelessness; accordingly, I again began to make an all-out effort of concentration in the last ten minutes. This time there was no need for physical movement to reinforce the effort; after a few moments there was again the sensation of floating, or being suspended, and again the feeling that I could arrest the time-processes of the body.

This should make clear why I am inclined to reject the notion of a three-dimensional time. Is not Priestley making the same mistake as Dunne in treating time as though it were a real entity, like the sea, when in fact it is a process, like a wave in the sea? And as a process, it is a function of what I have, for convenience, agreed to call 'the astral body', to distinguish the living, conscious 'me' from the physical shell that will eventually die.

What happened in these two cases should be fairly clear. Instead of allowing the aesthetic experience to operate upon passive sensibilities, I made an effort to accelerate the process by concentration. This may seem the wrong attitude: for surely doesn't music, like poetry, require a wide-open attitude, Keats's 'negative capability'? But phenomenologists know that this is an error. All perception is an intentional act, even if we are not consciously aware of it. If you relax too much, as in watching television, you begin to feel bored and depressed. I convulsed the muscle of concentration in an all-out effort, and the result was a glimpse of the kind of control over the body that *will* be possible at the next stage of human evolution.

This, incidentally, can be done at any time, without preparation (although it is a good idea to try it early in the day, when you are feeling fresh). By way of checking this, I just broke off my writing and looked at a coloured picture in a *Country Life* volume on England. It showed a half-ruined monastery against a background of Yorkshire hills. To my ordinary, 'un-boosted' perception, it was just a picture that produced little or no response. I half closed my eyes and concentrated hard, as if preparing for some enormous effort; there was an instant shock of response to the picture, a sense of brooding meaning, as if the hills and the sky were *saying* something. It remained when I relaxed again.

This enables me to state my belief about human evolution very clearly. Certain of our functions are automatic – breathing, digesting, responding to crisis; this means that I may sink into a completely will-less state, and they will continue unaffected. Other functions *ought* to be automatic, but they aren't yet. For example, a girl is often surprised at the intensity of her love for her first baby; her everyday personality may have given her no reason to expect that she would respond so deeply to motherhood. This *is* an example of our sense of meaning becoming automatic, being taken care of by our instincts. Unfortunately we do not have the same built-in response to spring mornings and the thousands of other natural phenomena to which we *occasionally* react with delight. A man who has just been released from prison may have a 'peak experience' when he looks at the sunset, but most of the city dwellers take it for granted; or worse still, they look at it, say, 'Yes, it *is* beautiful.' and don't feel a thing.

We have a deeply ingrained habit of passivity which is more dangerous than cigarette smoking or drugs. Why 'dangerous'? Because it produces an inner condition of boredom and stagnation that makes us long for crisis, for excitement, and which explains, for example, the steady rise in the crime rate, and the increasingly violent and motiveless nature of crimes. If poisons accumulate in my bloodstream, my body has an automatic method of getting rid of them: I develop boils, which burst and release the poisons. But if I allow myself to sink into a state of inner stagnation, I have no automatic defence system against it; I have to seek out some challenge or excitement to restore the vital balance. The sex criminal who goes out looking for a girl to rape is seeking a remedy for his sickness, like a sick dog chewing grass. At this point in evolution, when the earth is overcrowded, man needs to develop an automatic system for dealing with these poisons that arise from stagnation, from the endless triviality of civilised life. He must develop the 'mental muscle' I have spoken of: Faculty X. This is less difficult than it sounds; anything can become a habit if *we really want it to*. We must first recognise the necessity.

What is the relation of Faculty X to other 'occult' faculties – powers of mediumship, for example? I can best illustrate the difference with an example.

During the First World War, the playwright Harley Granville-Barker deserted his first wife, the actress Lillah McCarthy, for an American heiress named Helen Huntingdon. The new Mrs. Barker hated her husband's former theatrical contacts and made him give up the theatre. In 1925, Bernard Shaw was asked to second a vote of thanks to Barker at a public meeting. He took the opportunity to say that Barker's retirement from the theatre was a public scandal, and went on to urge him to come back. Suddenly Shaw experienced a violent pain in his back, 'as if my spine had been converted into a bar of rusty iron which grated on the base of my skull'. He could not even bend down to enter a taxi, and had to walk home. One month later, to the very hour, he decided that he must force himself to go for a walk, and the pain vanished as suddenly as it had come. It was later that he told this story to Lady Colefax, who had been sitting next to Helen Granville-Barker at the meeting. Lady Colefax told him that while he was speaking, Mrs. Barker was leaning forward in her seat staring at his back, 'every muscle in her body rigid with hate'.

It seems likely, then, that Helen Huntingdon was a witch, whether consciously or unconsciously; she possessed some of the powers of the 'evil eye' that John Cowper Powys found so disconcerting in himself. This hypothesis might seem to be further confirmed by her extraordinary influence over her husband. Barker was undoubtedly one of the greatest men of the theatre in the first decade of this century; he was also a major playwright. He and his first wife had always been happy together and there was no sign of a break before he met the American heiress. In 1914, Barker was thirty-seven. Helen Huntingdon was fifty. Whether she 'bewitched' him in the true sense of the word (bearing in mind Graves's remark that young men sometimes use 'magical' powers to seduce girls), or whether he simply fell in love with her in the normal way, she certainly retained an iron hold over him to the end of his life.

Lillah McCarthy described how she went to Shaw, numb with misery:

I was shivering. Shaw sat very still. The fire brought me warmth … How long we sat there I do not know, but presently I found myself walking with dragging steps with Shaw beside me … up and down Adelphi Terrace. The weight upon me grew a little lighter and released the tears which would never come before … he let me cry. Presently I heard a voice in which all the gentleness and tenderness of the world was speaking. It said: 'Look up, dear, look up to the heavens. There is more in life than this. There is much more.'*

It might seem a quibble to say that Shaw also used a form of witchcraft to comfort her. But he certainly used the authentic magical method: to allow his intuitions to operate; to avoid the obvious, rational way of comforting her with words and arguments, but to allow a telepathic link to grow up between them. A lesser man might have felt constrained to hold out false hopes. Shaw somehow lanced the emotional boil, then tried to restore her sense of *objectivity*. 'There is more in life than this. There is much more.' This is the 'secret in the poet's heart' of the last lines of *Candida*, as Eugene walks out into 'Tristan's only night'.

And here, I think the distinction becomes very clear. Helen Huntingdon seems to have possessed 'magical' powers, but she used them in the service of narrow personal ends. Shaw used them in the service of Faculty X, the expansion of the human faculties beyond the merely personal. This is ultimately the only correct use of the occult powers. Most of the examples described in this book – from calling porpoises to raising the shade of Apollonius of Tyana – are the misuse of such powers.

But I must repeat that it is incorrect to use the term 'occult powers' as if they were different *in kind* from our normal faculties. They are simply another part of the spectrum; they are 'occult' only in the sense that human beings have half-forgotten them in the process of developing the rational powers. But the next stage of evolution, the development of a still higher range of rational powers, will involve the redevelopment of these faculties.

* Quoted in *Harley Granville-Barker*, by C. B. Purdom (London, Rockliff, 1955), p. 175.

This point has been interestingly confirmed by researches into the 'pineal eye', the organ in the brain that the Hindus declare to be the seat of the 'occult powers'. (And even the thoroughly rational Descartes identified it as the point where man's soul and his body interact.) The pineal organ was assumed to be a vestigial eye, 'the third eye', although no one could quite decide what use an eye would be in the middle of the brain. In the present century, scientists began to recognise an odd connection between the 'pineal eye' and sexuality. Otto Huebner, a German doctor, discovered that a young boy with over-developed genitals had a tumour of the pineal organ. An American, Virginia Fiske, found that if rats were constantly exposed to light, their pineal organs decreased in size while their sexual organs increased. It was finally established that the pineal organ is a gland, not a vestigial eye, and that it produces a hormone that was labelled melotonin. And a great deal more research established that melotonin is produced by the action of a certain enzyme upon a chemical called serotonin.

And here the real mystery begins – one that has only been partially solved at the time of writing. This chemical serotonin seems to have a great deal to do with evolution of species. The primates, men and apes, have more serotonin than any other species, far more. It seems to be manufactured in the pineal eye, and one of its functions is to inhibit sexual development and to increase intelligence. This seems to explain why most intelligent human beings seem to be late developers, sexually, and why early developers are seldom, if ever, remarkable for intelligence.

One of the fascinating sidelights on this discovery is that the bó-tree, the tree under which the Buddha is said to have achieved enlightenment, produces figs (called *ficus religiosus* in honour of Gautama) with an exceptionally high serotonin content. Which leads to the interesting speculation that the Buddha's diet was the ideal one on which to achieve rational enlightenment on the human condition.

In 1948 the 'mind-changing' properties of LSD 25 were discovered accidentally, when a Swiss chemist named Hofmann working with ergot (a fungus found in rye plants) began to suffer from hallucinations; it was discovered that this was caused by a component of the ergot that was later named LSD 25, and whose properties were closely allied to those of mescalin, a chemical derived from the Mexican plant peyotl. Both mescalin and LSD may produce intensified consciousness, a feeling of oneness with the universe, beautiful patterns of colours and lights, new vividness of perception. They do this, apparently, by somehow 'blocking' man's rational faculty. I have said that we close our mental doors and windows in order to think clearly. These chemicals open them, and leave them propped open. The exact way in which they did this was not known; but it now seems fairly certain that the LSD molecule produces its effect by destroying the serotonin molecule.

A team of scientists in the Fairfield Hills Hospital in Newtown, Connecticut, made the interesting discovery that schizophrenic patients had exceptionally low serotonin levels in the brain, and for a while it was hoped that medicine had at last discovered a cure for schizophrenia – serotonin. But no one has discovered, so far, how to convey the serotonin to the place where it matters: the pineal gland. I would also speculate that this notion that schizophrenia is due to serotonin deficiency may be putting the cart before the horse. Schizophrenia is a state of low vitality in which our subconscious 'robot' takes over most of the vital functions, which means that the 'I' walks around in a kind of dream, alienated from existence. It may well be that the serotonin deficiency is the result of this drop in vitality and stagnation of the will.

I have described elsewhere* my own experience with mescalin. It made rational thought difficult, and seemed to flood me with

---

* See *Beyond the Outsider*, Appendix I.

tides of emotion and intuitive insight. (For example, I had a strong intuition that the area where I live – in Cornwall – had been connected with witchcraft in the past; I have not been able to verify this.) There was certainly a strong sense of universal benevolence; but, as far as I was concerned, this did not compensate for the loss of the ability to 'focus' with my mind, the feeling that the 'muscles' of concentration had been paralysed. It was clear to me that mescalin produced its effects by switching off the brain's normal 'filtering' mechanisms, allowing the senses to become flooded with the richness of the physical world; in doing this, it immobilised Faculty X. The 'illuminations' produced by mescalin were the reverse of the mental intensity that sometimes develops in me when I am working well. In fact, the mescalin experience was the reverse of 'intensity'; it was a lowering of the mental pressure, a diffusion of the beam of concentration. I find that when I am in a state of intense insight, this 'beam of concentration' narrows until it has a laser-like intensity, and there is a 'feedback' relation between the concentration and the perception of meaning. Mescalin destroyed all possibility of feedback; it simply opened the senses and let everything in.

All this would suggest, then, that serotonin is a chemical that is connected with concentration and with Faculty X. It also explains precisely why 'occult powers', such as mediumship, telepathy, E.S.P., are in some ways the opposite of Faculty X. They are certainly related to the state of 'receptivity' produced by mescalin or LSD; and Faculty X is related to the state of concentration that depends on serotonin. I do not write 'produced by serotonin', because I believe that our serotonin production may depend on the amount of concentration we habitually engage in. John N. Bleibtreu writes in his biochemical study *The Parable of the Beast*: 'So far … all that we really know is that minute quantities of serotonin affect mental states, alter perceptions, and that new dimensions of conventional reality accompany changes in the level of serotonin in the brain,' and he adds that serotonin is crucial to rational thought. This would seem to support my guess that concentration is accompanied by a rise in the serotonin levels of the brain and increased activity of the pineal gland, and that serotonin is the Faculty X chemical.

But observe the corollary to this. *If* serotonin production depends on *the amount of concentration we habitually engage in,* then it can be increased by an increased habit of concentration. (Conversely, the chief danger of psychedelic drugs, and probably of marihuana, is that their habitual use would cause a drop in the brain's serotonin production.) It seems that the next step in human evolution depends simply upon acquiring habits of mental intensity to replace our usual habit of passivity. The antelope can run like the wind, the salmon smell its home river from three thousand miles away, the electric eel deliver a shock of six hundred volts, the dolphin swim with the speed of an express train, the robin navigate by picking up vibrations from the Milky Way. In each case, a faculty we all possess has been developed into a super-faculty *by effort.* The faculty that distinguishes all the primates, man in particular, from these creatures is the ability to *focus meaning,* to learn. The most impressive thing about man is his ability to master such a variety of skills, and to master them to such an incredible degree. Acrobats turn somersaults on high wires; Houdini escapes from an iron safe full of water; William Rowan Hamilton knows Latin, Greek and Hebrew at the age of five; Zerah Colborn multiplies enormous figures in his head within seconds; athletes continually establish new world records. A century ago the Matterhorn was regarded as unclimbable; now mountaineers stroll up it for a Sunday excursion. There seems to be nothing that man cannot do *if he sets his mind to it.* Once he has a clear idea of what he wants to do, he seems to be unconquerable. His problem has never been will-power, but imagination: to know what he ought to turn his will towards.

And this constitutes the greatest cause for optimism at this point in history – Nostradamus and Edgar Cayce notwithstanding. Evolution proceeds in leaps, and man has now reached the interesting point where he is prepared to understand it consciously, and move forward with a full understanding of what he is doing. Our trouble in the past has been poor communication between intelligence and instinct, which has meant that the intelligent people lacked power and vitality, while the instinctive people lacked vision and long-distance purpose. Intelligence and instinct can be united by the development of Faculty X. Once man understands this, nothing can hold him back.

And now I come to the most important point in this book: the attempt at a general theory. Let us, for the moment, forget the evidence for telepathy, precognition, reincarnation and life after death, and stick to logic and facts revealed by science.

The vitalist theory of evolution, for which I have argued in this book, affirms that spirit and matter are antagonists. There is a war going on, and we are in the front line.

Our universe is apparently expanding. Astronomers have calculated that if it has always expanded at its present rate, then it must have started about ten billion years ago – ten thousand million years. Our sun is about six billion years old (and is expected to last about another six billion). This earth we inhabit is probably around five billion years old. For the first billion years of its existence, it remained a roaring furnace, sweeping around the sun and slowly cooling. And, at some point, the force of life managed to establish a foothold in the realm of atoms. T. E. Hulme, a disciple of Bergson, described life as 'the gradual insertion of more and more freedom into matter', and went on: 'In the amoeba, then, you might say that impulse has manufactured a small leak, through which free activity could be inserted into the world, and the process of evolution has been the gradual enlargement of this leak.'

Life began by moulding atoms into the molecules known as amino-acids, and then used these to create living cells. The modern Darwinian school of biology would have us believe that this 'complexification' was an accident – which is like asking us to believe that a pile of rusty car parts in a scrap yard might be blown together into a new Rolls-Royce.

For another billion years or so, these minute living cells floated in the warm seas, birthless and deathless. No change took place. It was not until a mere half billion years ago that true evolution began. Life somehow managed to overcome its most basic problem – forgetfulness. Evolution cannot proceed without the accumulation of knowledge, and a single amoeba cannot accumulate much knowledge. It was not until the life-force invented the trick of coding knowledge into the reproductory processes that new advances became possible. The Pre-Cambrian creatures shed old cells and grew new ones in the same way that my body replaces all its old cells every eight years. With the invention of death and reproduction, *they shed old bodies and grew new ones.* Variety replaced monotony as the basic law of existence.

Life invented death. There is no escaping this extraordinary fact, although a more conservative view might be that life simply learned to make use of death for its own purposes. The implications are the same. Life is not at the mercy of death. It is in control of death. Half a billion years ago, it learned the secret of reincarnation.

The aim of all this manoeuvring was to establish a firmer bridgehead in the universe of matter. Individual creatures tend to stagnate when they have discovered a comfortable ritual of habit. A young creature fights and struggles and learns; an old creature vegetates. Death was invented to replace the vegetables with fighters and learners, to get the old soldiers out of the front line and replace them with shock troops.

The next major step in this war – or process of colonisation – was the invention of consciousness: that is to say, of a group of faculties set apart from the instinctive drives. And their purpose? To observe and record and keep files. Consciousness might be described as the life-force's secret police organisation. And, like the secret police in any totalitarian state, it is the servant of the government – a powerful and formidable servant, but a servant nevertheless. Consciousness was a late evolutionary development because it was a long time before life could afford the energy for such an experiment. The instincts pay attention only to what deeply concerns them. The job of consciousness is to pay attention to everything, to keep watch on the surface movements of the world of matter. Most of the information it accumulates in this way is repetitive and useless, but occasionally its non-stop vigilance pays off, and a few random observations coalesce to form a new piece of knowledge.

Consciousness has one immense disadvantage: it divides life against itself. When life was confined to the instinctive levels, its drives were simple: its aim was to increase its foothold in the realm of matter. Consciousness is concerned with superficial problems. The secret police know nothing about the ultimate aims of the government, about its economic and foreign policies. This does not matter so long as the government retains a firm control. But the success of consciousness has been so spectacular that it has become a kind of government department in itself. And this is dangerous. The danger has been immeasurably increased in the past few centuries. The invention of writing gave immense impetus to human evolution, and changed man's vision of himself. There is no evidence that Isaac Newton was more intelligent than Moses or Confucius, but he had subtler methods of storing and utilising his knowledge. As a result of three centuries of Newtonian science, man has become king of his earthly castle. He no longer takes life and death for granted, as his ancestors did. He looks out on the universe with the eye of a master. But consciousness is *not* the master; it is the servant. It lacks the power and drive of the instinctive life forces. Left to itself, it tends to become passive and bewildered, alienated from the world of instinct and the world of matter. It is a master who has lost all feeling of mastery.

Human evolution has advanced too fast; its processes have become too complicated for its own good. But they can be simplified. Consciousness can be turned inward, to the understanding of the vital processes and the evolutionary drives.

The chief enemy of life is not death, but forgetfulness, stupidity. We lose direction too easily. This is the great penalty that life paid for descending into matter: a kind of partial amnesia.

But it is the next step in the argument that is the crucial one. The universe is full of all kinds of energies. Matter is energy – the most resistant and uncompromising kind of energy. And if life has succeeded in achieving some degree of conquest of matter, is it absurd to suppose that it has not succeeded with more malleable forms of energy?

We are back to David Foster's notion of an intelligent universe, but now it is unnecessary to ask, Who does the coding? We know the answer. The force of life itself, which has been conducting its campaign for colonisation for more than a billion years.

All this arises logically from the recognition that life is not an 'emanation' of matter but an opposed force. Shaw's Lilith says, 'I brought life into the whirlpool of force, and compelled my enemy, Matter, to obey a living soul. But in enslaving Life's enemy, I made him Life's master ...' And earlier in the same act of *Back to Methuselah*, he expresses the intuition that life may exist on higher energy levels: 'In the hard-pressed heart of the earth, where the inconceivable heat of the sun still glows, the stone lives in fierce atomic convulsion, as we live in our slower way. When it is cast to the surface it dies like a deep sea fish ...' Alfred North Whitehead, another vitalist philosopher, also expressed this notion that life permeates the universe as water might fill a sponge.

The great unsolved mystery is that of individuality. If life is somehow a unity, how is it that each of its units feels so separate and unique? Chesterton expressed it in the magnificent last chapter of *The Man Who Was Thursday*: 'Why does each thing on the earth war against each other thing? Why does each small thing in the world have to fight against the world itself? Why does a fly have to fight the whole universe?' Not only why, but *how*? Perhaps there are creatures in the world, as Sir Alister Hardy suggests, who possess a 'communal consciousness'. Perhaps there are gnats, hovering in a cloud, who are as aware of one another's existence as of their own. But we cannot even conceive of this. A crowd of pot-smokers practising 'togetherness' are deceiving themselves, as a child might deceive herself that her doll was alive. Human individuality is so absolute that we can no more imagine ourselves without it than we can imagine one and one making three.

The 'how' is unanswerable; we can only assume that the force of life began its conquest of matter by somehow splitting itself into units, each of which felt 'separate' from the rest of the universe. Chesterton answers the 'why': 'So that each thing that obeys the law may have the glory and isolation of the anarchist. So that each man fighting for order may be as brave and good a man as the dynamiter.' Which means simply that without individuality, life would not build up the same desperate force. The man of the crowd is a weakling; people who need people are the stupidest people in the world. And so the basic paradox of human nature seems to be inherent in the force of life itself: without challenge or crisis, it takes things easy, and collapses into mediocrity. So far, all life on earth has had to be driven forward, as slaves once had to be whipped into battle. It has never possessed positive purpose – only the negative one of staying alive and avoiding pain. 'Evil is physical pain,' said

Leonardo, going to the heart of the matter. The old theological question 'Why evil?' is answered by the recognition that without evil, there would be universal mediocrity, terminating in death. It is only at this point in the earth's history that this has ceased to be wholly true. With the development of art, science, philosophy, man has acquired the possibility of a *positive purpose, a purpose towards which he can drive forward, instead of being driven from behind.* (It is true that religion has always been an expression of this purpose; but religion was content with paradox: the assertion that 'the world' must somehow be denied by 'the spirit', without trying to understand why this should be necessary.) *If* positive purpose could be established as the human driving force, it would be a turning point in evolution, for it is many times stronger than the negative purpose of avoiding pain. A man can do things out of love or enthusiasm that would be impossible out of fear. His chief problem at the moment is to escape the narrowness of everyday triviality and grasp the nature of his goal; this, in turn, will require the development of what Blake called 'imagination', but which it would be more accurate to call Faculty X.

Our universe seems to be based on the principle of individuality, in which each unit of life is a kind of oasis. We have only to concede that individuality transcends the physical body – that is, to recognise that, like death, it is a *tool* of life, not an accidental consequence – to see that logic is in favour of some form of 'life after death', as well as of reincarnation. The whole purpose of life's campaign against matter is to establish continuity, to overcome 'forgetfulness'; this is the purpose behind instinct and racial memory and the DNA code. These are all forms of survival of bodily death; if other forms did not exist, it would be, to say the least, an extraordinary waste of opportunity.

Nathaniel Hawthorne felt that Home's feats of mediumship and levitation were interesting but irrelevant. Why? Because he was an artist, and the artist loves the physical world. Like Camus watching the great birds in the sky at Djemileh, he wants to feel the weight of his life squarely on his own shoulders, and the talk of an after-life seems a false promise. The artist sees clearly that the 'solution' to the curious pointlessness of most human existence is not *another* life, but the occasional moments of ecstatic intensity and control when this universe seems infinitely interesting and the idea of eternal life, in this universe, entirely delightful. This is an idea that can be found in Russian mysticism – in Fedorov, Dostoevsky, Rozanov – that eternal life means life *on this earth*, not in another world. The Jehovah's Witnesses, oddly enough, hold a similar doctrine: that after the Day of Judgement, the earth will turn into Paradise. All this explains why the poet is distrustful of the after-life; he is less inclined than most human beings to devalue this one.

The theory I have propounded resolves the contradiction. The poet is right to be mistrustful about 'other worlds' as a solution to the problems of this one. If my reasoning is correct, then the 'other world' is not intended to be a solution. We are in the front line; the general is back at headquarters; the 'other worlds' that exist between us and the headquarters are support units and supply depots, not a higher level of existence. There is probably more freedom on these levels, the possibility of broader vision, wider consciousness – but of less actual achievement. The possibility of achievement lies back here, where we are. We see the 'answer' to the riddle of physical existence in all moments of great intensity. 'God is fire in the head,' said Nijinsky; when the brain blazes like a bonfire, we no longer need to ask why we are alive. The aim is total control. With this control established, life would become a unity; there would no longer be a distinction between 'other worlds' and this one. And is this not suggested by the sudden birth of spiritualism in the nineteenth century? The nineteenth century was the Age of Romanticism; for the first time in history, man stopped thinking of himself as an animal or a slave, and saw himself as a potential god. All of the cries of revolt against 'God' – Sade, Byron's *Manfred*, Schiller's *Robbers*, Goethe's *Faust*, Hoffmann's mad geniuses – are expressions of this new spirit. Is this why the 'spirits' decided to make a planned and consistent effort at 'communication'? It was the right moment. Man was beginning to understand himself.

I do not regard myself as an 'occultist' because I am more interested in the mechanisms of everyday consciousness. In the past, man's chief characteristic has been his 'defeat-proneness'; even the giants of the nineteenth century were inclined to believe that insanity is a valid refuge from the 'triviality of everydayness'. But the answer lies in understanding the mechanisms. Once they are understood, they can be altered to admit more reality. The operation requires concentration and precision, the virtues of a skilled watchmaker.

We return to the assertion of the opening chapter: man's future lies in the cultivation of Faculty X.

BIBLIOGRAPHY

General books on Magic and Occultism

AHMED, ROLLO. *The Black Art*. Jarrold, London, 1968.

BESSY, MAURICE. *A Pictorial History of Magic and the Supernatural.* Spring Books, London, 1963.

CAVENDISH, RICHARD. *The Black Arts*. Routledge & Kegan Paul, 1967.

BARRETT FRANCIS. *The Magus*. University Books Inc., 1967.

BUDGE, E. A. W. *Egyptian Magic*. Kegan Paul, 1899.

BUTLER, E. M. *Fortunes of Faust*. Cambridge University Press, 1952.

The Myth of the Magus. Macmillan, London, 1968.

Ritual Magic. Cambridge University Press, 1949; Noonday Press, N.Y., 1959.

CROWLEY, ALEISTER. *Magick in Theory and Practice*. Castle, N.Y.

DE GIVRY, EMILE GRILLOT. *Pictorial Anthology of Witchcraft, Magic and Alchemy*. University Books Inc., 1958.

GARDINER, GERALD B. *Witchcraft Today*. Jarrolds, London, 1968.

HILL, DOUGLAS, AND WILLIAMS, PAT. *The Supernatural*. Aldus, 1965.

IDRIES SHAH, SAYED. *The Secret Lore of Magic*. Muller, 1965.

KING, FRANCIS. *Ritual Magic in England*. Spearman, London, 1970.

LEVI, ELIPHAS. *History of Magic*. Rider, 1957.

Transcendental Magic. Rider. 1958.

PAUWELS, LOUIS, AND BERGIER, JACQUES. *The Morning of the Magicians*. Stein & Day, N.Y., 1963 (in England, *The Dawn of Magic*).

ROBBINS, R. H. *Encyclopedia of Witchcraft and Demonology*. Peter Nevill, 1959.

SELIGMANN, K. *The History of Magic*. Pantheon Books Inc., N.Y., 1948.

SINGER, CHARLES. *From Magic to Science*. Constable / Dover
  Books, 1958.

SPENCE, LEWIS. *Encyclopaedia of Occultism*. Routledge, 1920;
  University Books Inc., N.Y., 1960.

SUMMERS, MONTAGUE. *The Geography of Witchcraft*. University
  Books Inc., N.Y., 1958.
  History of Witchcraft. University Books Inc., N.Y., 1956.

THOMPSON, C. J. S. *Mysteries and Secrets of Magic*. Bodley Head,
  London, 1927.

WAITE, ARTHUR E. *The Book of Ceremonial Magic*. University Books
  Inc., N.Y., 1961.

WEDECK, HARRY E. *A Treasury of Witchcraft*. Philosophical Library
  Inc., 1961.

Myth and Ancient Man

DANIEL, GLYN. *The Megalith Builders of Western Europe*. Pelican,
  London, 1963.

ELIADE, MIRCEA. *Cosmos and History*. Harper & Row, N.Y., 1959.
  Myths, Dreams and Mysteries. Harvill Press, 1960.

FRAZIER, SIR J. G. *The Golden Bough, a Study in Magic and Religion*.
  Macmillan & Co., London, 1957.

FREUND, PHILIP. *Myths of Creation*. W. H. Allen, London, 1964.

GRAVES, ROBERT. *The Crane Bag*. Cassell, London, 1969.
  The White Goddess. Faber & Faber, London, 1959.

HAYS, H. R. *In the Beginning: Early Man and His Gods*. Putnam,
  N.Y., 1963.

LISSNER, IVAR. *Man, God and Magic*. Cape, London, 1961.

MALINOWSKI, BRONISLAW. *Magic, Science and Religion*. Doubleday
  Anchor Books, 1948.

MORLEY, RECINOS, GOETZ (tr.). *Popuh Vuh.* Hodge & Co.,
London, 1951.

SMITH, HOMER W. *Man and His Gods.* Grosset's Universal
Library, N.Y., 1957.

WESTON, JESSIE L. *From Ritual to Romance.* Cambridge University
Press and Doubleday Anchor Books, 1957.

Mysticism

ALLEN, WARNER. *The Happy Issue.* Faber & Faber, London, 1948.
The Timeless Moment. Faber & Faber, London.

BRINTON, HOWARD. *The Mystic Will.* Allen & Unwin Ltd., 1931.

BUCKE, RICHARD M. *Cosmic Consciousness.* University Books, N.Y.,
1961.

HIRST, DESIREE. *Hidden Riches: Traditional Symbolism from
the Renaissance to Blake.* Eyre & Spottiswoode, London,
1964.

HUXLEY, ALDOUS. *The Perennial Philosophy.* Chatto & Windus,
London, 1946.

JAMES, JOSEPH. *The Way of Mysticism.* Cape, London, 1950.

LASKI, MARGHANITA. *Ecstasy: A Study of some Secular and Religious
Experiences.* Cresset Press, London, 1961.

STACE, WALTER T. *The Teachings of the Mystics.* Mentor Books, N.Y.,
1960.

SWEDENBORG, EMANUEL. *The Theological Writings of Em. Swedenborg.*
Swedenborg Society, London, 1901.

VON HUGEL, FR. *The Mystical Element of Religion*, 2 vols. Dent,
London, 1908.

YOGANANDA, PARAMHANSA. *Autobiography of a Yogi.* Rider, London.
1963.

Witchcraft, see also *General books on Magic and Occultism*

HOLE, CHRISTINA. *A Mirror of Witchcraft.* Pedigree Books, 1957.

HUGHES, PENNETHORNE. *Witchcraft.* Pelican Books, 1967.

LETHBRIDGE, T. C. *Witches: Investigating an Ancient Religion.*
Routledge & Kegan Paul, London, 1962.

MURRAY, MARGARET. *The God of the Witches.* Doubleday Anchor
Books, N.Y., 1960.

PARRINDER, GEOFFREY. *Witchcraft.* Pelican Books, 1958.

RHODES, H. T. F. *The Satanic Mass.* Jarrolds, 1968.

SEABROOK, WILLIAM. *Witchcraft, Its Power in the World Today.*
Sphere Books, 1970.

SETH, RONALD. *In the Name of the Devil: Great Witchcraft Cases.*
Arrow Books, London, 1970.

SMYTH, FRANK. *Modern Witchcraft.* 'Man, Myth and Magic' original,
Macdonald Unit, 1970.

TINDALL, GILLIAN. *A Handbook on Witches.* Panther Books, 1967.

TREVOR ROPER, HUGH R. *The European Witch-craze of the 16th and
17th Centuries.* Pelican Books, 1969.

WILLIAMS, CHARLES. *Witchcraft.* Meridian Books Inc., N.Y., 1960.

WRIGHT, HARRY B. *Witness to Witchcraft.* Souvenir Press, London,
1957.

Psychical Research – Neglected Powers

BARBANELL, MAURICE. *He Walks in Two Worlds.* Flagship Books,
N.Y., 1964.

EISENBUD, JULE. *The World of Ted Serios.* Morrow, 1967.

FODOR, NANDOR. *Between Two Worlds.* Prentice-Hall, 1964.
The Haunted Mind. Helix Press, N.Y., 1963.

HEYWOOD, ROSALIND. *The Sixth Sense.* Pan Books, London, 1966.

HOUSE, BRANT. *Strange Powers of Unusual People.* Ace Books Inc., N.Y., 1963.

HURKOS, PETER. *Psychic: The Story of Peter Hurkos.* Barker, London, 1962.

INGALESE, RICHARD. *The History and Power of Mind.* Occult Book Concern, N.Y., 1905.

LANGLEY, NOEL. *Edgar Cayce on Reincarnation.* Paperback Library, 1967.

LYTTLETON, EDITH. *Our Superconscious Mind.* Philip Allan, London, 1931.

MAPLE, ERIC. *The Realm of Ghosts.* Pan Books, 1967.

MILLARD, JOSEPH. *Edgar Cayce, Mystery Man of Miracles.* Fawcett Gold Medal Books, N.Y., 1967.

MONTGOMERY, RUTH. *A Gift of Prophecy: The Phenomenal Jeane Dixon.* Bantam Books, N.Y., 1966.

NICHOLS, BEVERLEY. *Powers that Be: Authenticated Cases of Man and the Supernatural.* Popular Library, N.Y., 1966.

OSBORN, ARTHUR W. *The Future Is Now: The Significance of Precognition.* University Books Inc., N.Y., 1961.

POLLACK, JACK HARRISON. *Croiset the Clairvoyant.* Doubleday, N.Y., 1964.

RHINE, J. B. *The Reach of the Mind.* Pelican Books. London, 1954.

STEARN, JESSE. *Edgar Cayce – the Sleeping Prophet.* Doubleday, N.Y., 1967.

STONE, W. CLEMENT, AND BROWNING, NORMA. *The Other Side of the Mind.* Paperback Library Inc., N.Y., 1967.

THOULESS, ROBERT H. *Experimental Psychical Research.* Pelican Books, London, 1963.

TYRRELL, G. N. M. *The Personality of Man.* Pelican Books, 1948.

WEST, D. J. *Psychical Research Today.* Pelican Books, London, 1962.

WILSON KNIGHT, G. *Neglected Powers: Essays on 19th and 20th Century Literature.* Routledge & Kegan Paul, 1971.

Spiritualism and Life after Death

BENNETT, SIR ERNEST. *Apparitions and Haunted Houses.* Faber & Faber, London, 1939.

BROAD, C. D. *Lectures on Psychical Research.* Routledge & Kegan Paul, London, 1962.

CERMINARA, GINA. *Many Mansions.* Spearman, London, 1967.

CONAN DOYLE, SIR ARTHUR. *The Vital Message.* Hodder & Stoughton, London, 1919.
The Wanderings of a Spiritualist. Hodder & Stoughton, London, 1921.

DREARDEN, HAROLD. *Devilish but True: the Doctor Looks at Spiritualism.* Hutchinson, London, 1936.

DINGWALL, ERIC J., AND HALL, TREVOR H. *Four Modern Ghosts.* Duckworth, London, 1958.

EAGLESFIELD, FRANCIS. *Silent Union, a Record of Unwilled Communication.* Stuart and Watkins, London, 1966.

EDWARDS, HARRY. *Spirit Healing.* Herbert Jenkins, 1963.

FLAMMARION, CAMILLE. *Death and Its Mystery.* Fisher Unwin, 1923.

FLEW, ANTHONY. *A New Approach to Psychical Research.* Watts, 1963.

GUIRDHAM, ARTHUR. *The Nature of Healing.* Allen and Unwin, 1964.

HALIFAX, VISCOUNT. *Lord Halifax's Ghost Book.* Bles, London, 1936.

HALL, TREVOR H. *The Strange Case of Edmund Gurney.* Duckworth, London, 1964.

JACKSON KNIGHT, W. F. *Elysion. Ancient Greek and Roman Beliefs Concerning Life after Death.* Rider, 1970.

JOHNSON, RAYNER C. *The Imprisoned Splendour, an Approach to Reality ...* Hodder & Stoughton, London, 1965.

LODGE, SIR OLIVER. *The Survival of Man.* Methuen, London, 1911.

MOSES, REV. W. STANTON. *Spirit Teachings.* Spiritualist Press, 1962.

MYERS, F. W. H. *Human Personality and Its Survival of Bodily Death.* University Books Inc., 1961.

NORMAN, DIANA. *The Stately Ghosts of England.* Muller, London, 1963.

PIKE, BISHOP JAMES A. *The Other Side.* W. H. Allen, London, 1969.

PODMORE, FRANK. *Modern Spiritualism.* Methuen, London, 1902.

PRICE, HARRY. *The Most Haunted House in England.* 1940.

    Fifty Years of Psychical Research. Longmans, 1939.

RAUDIVE, KONSTANTIN. *Breakthrough, an Amazing Experiment in Electronic Communication with the Dead.* Colin Smythe, 1971.

SITWELL, SACHEVERELL. *Poltergeists.* Faber & Faber, London, 1940.

SMITH, ALISON J. *Immortality, the Scientific Evidence.* Signet Books, N.Y., 1954.

SOCIETY FOR THE PSYCHICAL RESEARCH PROCEEDINGS. *The Haunting of Borley Rectory. A Critical Survey of the Evidence.* London, 1956.

TURNER, GORDON. *An Outline of Spiritual Healing.* Parrish, London, 1963.

TYRRELL, G. N. M. *Science and Psychical Phenomena.* University Books Inc., N.Y., 1961.

UNDERWOOD, PETER. *Gazeteer of British Ghosts.* Souvenir Press, London, 1971.

Miscellaneous

BAILEY, ALICE A. *A Treatise on Cosmic Fire.* Lucis Co., N.Y., 1930.

BELLAMY, H. S. *A Life History of Our Earth*. Faber, London, 1951.
Moon, Myths and Man. Faber, London.

BESANT, ANNIE. *The Ancient Wisdom: An Outline of Theosophical Teachings*. Theosophical Publishing Soc., London, 1910.

BLAVATSKY, H. P. *The Secret Doctrine*. Theosophy Co., Los Angeles, 1947.

CHURCHWARD, JAMES. *The Children of Mu*. Paperback. Library, N.Y., 1968.
The Lost Continent of Mu. Crown Publishers, 1961.

COLLIN, RODNEY. *The Theory of Celestial Influence*. Stuart & Watkin, London, 1971.

CROSS, COLIN. *Who Was Jesus?* Hodder & Stoughton, 1970.

DONNELLY, IGNATIUS. *Atlantis: The Antediluvian World*. Sampson Low, 1884.

EDGAR, MORTON. *The Great Pyramid: its Symbolism, Science and Prophecy*. Bone & Hulley, Glasgow, 1924.

FORTUNE, DION. *The Mystical Qabalah*. Benn, 1970.

FULLER, JEAN OVERTON. *The Magical Dilemma of Victor Neuberg*. W. H. Allen, London, 1965.

GALANOPOULOS, A. G. AND BACON, EDWARD. *Atlantis: The Truth Behind the Legend*. Nelson, London, 1965.

GARNIER, J. *The Great Pyramid*. Banks, London, 1905.

GUIGNEBERT, CHARLES. *The Jewish World at the Time of Jesus*. University Books, N.Y., 1959.

HOWE, ERIC. *Urania's Children: The Strange World of the Astrologers*. Kimber, London, 1967.

I Ching: The Book of Changes, Foreword by C. G. Jung, 2 vols. Routledge & Regan Paul, London, 1951.

INGALESE, RICHARD. *Cosmogony and Evolution*. Watkins Press, N.Y., 1907.

JESSUP, M. K. *Unidentified Flying Objects*. Arco, London, 1955.

KRAMER, SAMUEL N. *Mythologies of the Ancient World*. Doubleday, N.Y., 1961.

LEADBEATER, C. W. *The Hidden Side of Things*. Theosophical Publishing House, Madras, 1923.

LEGGE, FRANCIS. *Forerunners and Rivals of Christianity*. University Books, N.Y., 1964.

MACNEICE, LOUIS. *Astrology*. Aldus Books, London, 1964.

MATHERS, MACGREGOR S. L. *The Kabbalah Unveiled*. Routledge & Kegan Paul, London, 1951.

MEAD, G. R. S. *Fragments of a Faith Forgotten*. University Books, N.Y., 1960.

MICHEL, AIME. *The Truth about Flying Saucers*. Transworld Publ., London, 1958.

PAPINI, GIOVANNI. *The Devil, Notes for a Future Diabology*. Eyre & Spottiswoode, London, 1955.

SAURET, DENIS. *Atlantis and the Giants*. Faber & Faber, 1957.

SEPHARIAL. *Cosmic Symbolism*. Rider, London, 1912.

SINNETT, A. P. *Esoteric Buddhism*. Theosophical Publ. Soc., Madras, 1898.

SPENCE, LEWIS. *The Mysteries of Britain*. Rider, London, 1905.

    The Problem of Atlantis. Rider, London, 1925.

WAITE, ARTHUR E. *The Brotherhood of the Rosy Cross*. University Books, N.Y., 1924.

    The Holy Grail. University Books, N.Y., 1961.

    The Holy Kabbalah. University Books, N.Y, 1929.

    The Pictorial Key to the Tarot. University Books, N.Y., 1959.

ANALYTICAL TABLE

latent power to reach beyond the present to other realities. Arnold Toynbee's experience at Mistra.

2 *The Dark Side of the Moon*
Five per cent of people possess occult powers. The dominant 5 per cent in biology. Cure of physical ailments by deep hypnosis. Dr. Stephen Black's experiments. Robert Graves and the genesis of *The White Goddess*. The tree alphabet. The dark side of the mind: man's 'lunar powers'. The problem of generalised hypertension. Yeats's experience in a London teashop. Ouspensky on the truth of occult vision. Arthur Grimble's description of the porpoise callers of the Gilbert Islands. E. H. Visiak's 'cramp'. Poetry and its use of symbols. The Egyptian *Book of the Dead*. The Tibetan *Bardo Thodol*. The Chinese Book of Changes, the *I Ching*. The formation of the hexagrams. Jung on the *I Ching*. His theory of synchronicity. The meaning of Taoism and Zen. Chuang Tzu's story of the carpenter. The *I Ching* as a book of wisdom.

3 *The Poet as Occultist*
Are poets 'super-psychic'? Louis Singer's researches into paranormal phenomena. Influences séances by telepathy. A group mind? Strindberg and black magic. 'Travelling clairvoyance.' A. L. Rowse's telepathy. Grimble's *Pattern of Islands*: the place of the dead. Irene Muza's precognition of tragedy: 'my end will be terrible'. W. B. Yeats's theory of symbols. Yeats and the Kabbalah. Yeats on racial memory. Power of our response to symbols. *A Vision*. The Tarot pack – its derivation and use. The mystery of the Hanged Man.

PART TWO: A HISTORY OF MAGIC

1 *The Evolution of Man*
Goethe and Schiller at Jena. The weaknesses of scientific determinism.

H. G. Wells's account of evolution. Science and teleology. An alternative account of evolution. The flattid bug. Are the genes influenced by telepathy? The *Ammonophilas* wasp. Sir Alister Hardy and the *Microstomum* worm. The place of man. Why is human consciousness so narrow? Ramon Medina, the Mexican shaman; his detection of a murder. J. B. Rhine's PK tests. PK affected by boredom and repetition. Mystical experiences – when man completes 'his partial mind'. Lawrence and the Arabs. L. H. Myers: *The Near and the Far*. 'The promise of the horizon.' Consciousness needs a 'weight'. 'The vibration of seriousness.' Faust and the Easter bells. T. S. Eliot and *Ash Wednesday*. Graham Greene's whisky-priest. Contemplative Objectivity and the Peak Experience. Peak experiences and drugs. The use of sex: tantric yoga. Keilner and the Order of Oriental Templars. Aleister Crowley joins the order. Consciousness as a spectrum. The powers of the subconscious and the powers of the superconscious mind.

2 *The Magic of Primitive Man*

Ivar Lissner's theory that primitive man was monotheistic. The magical use of cave art. A mother's precognition of disaster. The shamans of Siberia. Maslow's marine. Initiation of shamans. Why did primitive man stop making statuettes? The dawn of magic. How man became a city-dweller in 4000 B.C. The rise of man's sexual obsession. The concubine of the Emperor Wu. *The Epic of Gilgamesh*. Incest taboos. Lévi-Strauss's theory. Poltergeist phenomena and sexual excitement. Robert Graves on seduction. *The Miraculous Mandarin*. Appearance of Cro-Magnon man. Sorcery. Did the Flood change mankind's history? Evidence in the *Gilgamesh* epic. George Smith's discovery of the missing tablets. Hoerbiger and the world-ice theory. The capture of our present moon. Denis Saurat and the primitives of Malekula. The legend of Atlantis. Lewis Spence. The latest hypothesis: Santorin and Crete. Why Plato multiplied his figures by ten. Velikovsky and *Worlds in Collision*. Edgar Cayce on Atlantis. Jung's theory of symbols. The anima. Egyptian magic. Superstitious credulity, ancient and modern. Use of wax figures. Egyptian religion and magic. The bear cult of the Ainus. Gibbon on Roman superstition.

3 Adepts and initiates

The 'curtain of everydayness'. Human beings are like blinkered horses. The magical powers of Hitler. Colonel Olcott's development of healing powers. Cornish wart-charming; Fred Martin of Bodmin Moor. Gilbert Murray's telepathic powers, as reported by Aldous Huxley. The need for 'positive consciousness'. The Magi described by Herodotus. Jacob Boehme's mystical illumination. The cruelty of ancient man. The Mysteries of ancient Greece. The Essenes. Demeter and Persephone. Orphism and the worship of Dionysus. Pythagoras. His number system. The murder of Polycrates. Pythagoras in Egypt; in Crotona. Numbers. The philosophy of Pythagoras. Apollonius of Tyana: his magical powers. The divining of treasure.

4 The World of the Kabbalists

The birth of Gnosticism. World rejection. Was the universe created by a demon? The Manichees. The Mystical Kabbalah. Its ten powers or Sephiroth. The sacred tree and its triangles. Correspondences. Simon Magus. His resemblance to Daniel Dunglas Home. The magician Cyprian sells his soul to the Devil. St. Augustine. *Accidia* – the disease of life-failure. St. Paul invents Christianity. Civilisation neurosis. The disaster of Christian domination. The legend of Theophilus. The Emperor Constantine. Julian the Apostate: his unsuccessful attempt to reestablish paganism. Christianity versus magic. The flying monk – Joseph of Copertino. Thomas Mann's *Experience in the Occult*. Johann Jetzer and his visions. The Abbé Vachère and the bleeding picture. Gaufridi and the possessed nuns. Urbain Grandier and the nuns of Loudun. Probable sexual nature of the disturbances. The methods of ritual magic. Benvenuto Cellini: the invocation in the

Colosseum. The nature of mysticism. Dionysius the Areopagite. Albertus Magnus. Sympathetic magic. Astrology – Kepler's accurate predictions. Cornelius Aggripa. The siege of the Black Fort. Agrippa's *On Occult Philosophy*. His downfall and death. Legends of Agrippa. Paracelsus. Success at Basel, then disaster. Split personality. Paracelsus's theory of imagination. Alchemy. Helvetius and the stranger. James Price, the gold maker. Alexander Seton, the Scottish alchemist. His imprisonment and escape. Jung on Alchemy. Karl Ernst Krafft, 'Hitler's astrologer'. The career of Nostradamus. His prophecies. The end of the world in 1997? The French Revolution foretold.

5 Adepts and Impostors

The nadir of magic. Reginald Scot's *Discovery of Witchcraft*. King James's *Demonologie*. Dr. John Dee. His life and travels. His use of 'scryers'. His death. The age of scepticism. Emanuel Swedenborg. His visions and powers of second sight. His hysteria. Anton Mesmer and animal magnetism. His success and downfall. Puységur discovers hypnotism. Casanova – lover and magician. His natural occult faculty. Cagliostro, the Grand Copt. His early life. Success in Strasbourg. The Diamond Necklace affair. Freemasonry – the key to Cagliostro's character. The science of numerology. Cazotte's prophecy of the Revolution. The Count of Saint-Germain, the Man of Mystery. The mystery explained.

6 The Nineteenth Century – Magic and Romanticism

Saint-Martin, the 'unknown philosopher'. His study of ritual magic. His mystical doctrines. His optimism – man is basically a god. Husserl. E. T. A. Hoffmann and magic. *The Golden Pot*. The Outsider as a key figure of the nineteenth century. Balzac's mysticism in *Louis Lambert*. Eliphaz Levi and the magical revival. Levi conjures up the shade of Apollonius of Tyana. Francis Barrett's *The Magus*. Fiji fire walkers. The beginnings of Spiritualism. The Fox sisters and their rappings. Madame Blavatsky and the Theosophical Society. Colonel Olcott. The trip to India. Success. The S.P.R. investigates H.P.B. Her downfall. *The Secret Doctrine*. French occultism. Eugène Vintras and the pretender Naundorf. The Abbé Boullan. The magical battle between Boullan and Guaita. Huysmans and *Là Bas*. Satanism. Yeats and Mathers. The Order of the Golden Dawn.

7 *The Beast Himself*
Crowley's childhood. His sexual obsession. The Laird of Boleskin. Crowley and Paracelsus. Crowley's explanation of magic. The quarrel with Yeats. Marriage. The Kanchenjunga disaster. Seabrook on Crowley. The Abbey of Theleme. Disaster. Crowley's death. The robot in the subconscious mind.

8 *Two Russian Mages*
The Russian character and occultism. Gregory Rasputin. The Rasputin legend. His thaumaturgic powers. Phineas Quimby and healing. Success at Court. His enemies – Illiodor and Hermogen. The coincidence of Sarajevo and Pokrovskoe assassination attempts. The murder of Rasputin. His prophecy of the downfall of the Russian monarchy. George Gurdjieff and the Institute for the Harmonious Development of Man. Childhood and origins of interest in occultism. Travels. David Lindsay's *Haunted Woman*, and its relation to Gurdjieff's basic ideas. William Seabrook's description of Gurdjieff in New York. Fritz Peters's *Boyhood with Gurdjieff*. The 'word'. Ouspensky's occult experiences with Gurdjieff. The Fourth Way. William James and habit neurosis. Professor M. Welford's experiments in telepathic control of subjects. J. G. Bennett and Subud. The *latihan*. Subud as Gurdjieff's successor.

Analytical Table

PART THREE: MAN'S LATENT POWERS

1 Witchcraft and Lycanthropy
The female as evil. Blake's *Europe*. Isobel Gowdie and the Auldearne witches. The murder of Charles Walton. The origin of European witchcraft – the rise of Catharism. The heresy hunters. Albigenses and Waldenses. Jehane de Brigue. The case of John Stewart. The spread of the witch craze. The Black Death. Franz Buirmann, the torturer. Margaret Murray's theory of witchcraft as a pagan survival. Goethe's *Honest Attorney*. Exorcism of nuns. The martyrdom of Dietrich Flade. Matthew Hopkins, the witch-finder general. Why the witchcraft craze died out. The rise of the novel. New freedom of imagination. Valery Briussov's *Fiery Angel*: its description of a witches' sabbath. Akutagawa's story *The Dragon*: the power of expectation. Nigerian witch doctors – Martin Delaney's story of the band-saw. The rain makers of Abomey. Leopard dance. Vampirism and lycanthropy – their sexual basis. Martin Dumollard. Garnier and Stube. *The Golden Bough* on werewolves. Eleonore Zugun and the 'devil's bites'. The case of Sally Beauchamp. *Forbidden Planet*: monsters from the subconscious. The vampires of Haidam. Arnold Paole. Johannes Cuntius. Augustus Hare's story of the Croglin Hall vampire. Dion Fortune's theory of vampirism. The vampire bat. The witchcraft revival: Gerald Gardner. Modern witch cults.

2 The Realm of Spirits
The ambiguous nature of spirit manifestations. The Fox family. Jonathan Koons. The Davenport brothers. Spirit frauds. Volckman and Mrs. Cook. The career of Daniel Dunglas Home. His reception in England. Browning and Home. Home's loss of powers. Home becomes a Catholic. The Empress Eugénie. Cagliostro talks to Home. Mrs. Lyons. Lord Adare's testimony. Sir William Crookes. His death. Dreams. Jung's 'confrontation with the unconscious'.

Controlled hallucination. Philemon. Freud and Jung – the 'psychical explosions'. Bishop Pike's account of his son's suicide, and subsequent 'communications'. Bishop Pike's death in the desert. Wilson Knight on spiritualism. 'Messages' from Jackson Knight. The Juxon cups. 'Return' of John Cowper Powys. Christian Science and the occult powers. Aldous Huxley and J. B. Rhine. The Society for Psychical Research is founded. Eusapia Palladino. The debunking of Harry Price. Borley Rectory – 'the most haunted house in England'. The case of Rosalie. The music of Rosemary Brown. Drury Lane ghosts. Spectres of the living. The apparition of Samuel Bull. G. K. Chesterton on the spirit world. Poltergeists. The phantom drummer of Tedworth. 'Four months in a haunted house.' Angélique Cottin. Spontaneous combustion. The strange powers of Ted Serios. 'Mental photography.' His travelling clairvoyance. Tom Corbett, the 'ghost hunter'. The question of reincarnation. *Twenty-Six Cases Suggestive of Reincarnation*. Arthur Guirdham and Mrs. Smith. The strange case of José de Freitos. Flying Saucers and communications from outer space. The Tunguska explosion. The story of Jack Schwarz.

3 *Glimpses*

The 'vital force' and animal magnetism. Reichenbach and the 'odic force'. Phoebe Payne and man's psychic 'aura'. The case of Wilhelm Reich. The psychology of cancer. Sexual excitement. Oliver Fox and the projection of the astral body. Officer blown up in a tank. Examples of 'exteriorisation'. Miss Brooks and dreaming. The problem of precognition. J. B. Priestley's *Man and Time*. Dreams of the future. J. W. Dunne and serial time. Priestley's three-dimensional time. Ouspensky's *Ivan Osokin* and Eternal Recurrence. Ronald Duncan's experience of *déjà vu* and of racial memory. Robert Graves's experience of 'knowing everything'. Mathematical prodigies. William James's 'suggestion about mysticism'. James's mystical experiences – 'distant horizons of fact'. Warner Allen's 'timeless moment'. Other experiences of mystical consciousness. Koestler's 'arrow in the blue'. The romantic longing. Something *basically* wrong with human consciousness. 'Contraction of the astral body.' The Seventh Degree of Concentration. The chain reaction. The evolution of man in the immediate future. My own 'time experiences'. The dangerous habit of passive consciousness. Harley Granville-Barker's wife 'bewitches' Shaw. Shaw's power of 'sympathy'. The pineal eye. The discovery of serotonin, the Faculty X hormone. LSD 25. My own psychedelic experience. The age of the universe. Development of life on earth. Life invents death. The invention of consciousness. The disadvantages of consciousness. The unsolved mystery of individuality. The need for challenge and crisis. A theory of 'the other world'. Conclusions.

INDEX

Index

Index

Index

Index

Index

Index

Index

Index

Index

Index

Woodman, Dr. William, 454
Woolley, Leonard, 199–200
Wordsworth, William, 56, 66, 408, 419,
    538, 701
Wright, Harry B., 573, 576
Wu, Emperor, 192
Würm, 204
Wyatt, Sir Thomas, 350
Wynne, Justiniana, 375, 378

Xenophanes, 37

Yeats, W. B., 129, 130–36, 137, 141,
    147, 169, 187, 217, 220, 403, 428,
    438, 439, 441, 453, 454, 455, 464,
    689, 600
Yogananda, Paramhansa, 441
Yussupov, Prince Felix, 502

Zandt, Herr, 561
Zen, principle of, 108 *et seq.*
Zola, Emile, 447, 458
Zoroaster (Zoroastrianism), 224, 239,
    241, 243, 258, 709
Zugun, Eleonore, 197, 580, 581
Zwinger, Jacob, 320

WATKINS

Sharing Wisdom Since
1893

The story of Watkins began in 1893, when scholar of esotericism John Watkins founded our bookshop, inspired by the lament of his friend and teacher Madame Blavatsky that there was nowhere in London to buy books on mysticism, occultism or metaphysics. That moment marked the birth of Watkins, soon to become the publisher of many of the leading lights of spiritual literature, including Carl Jung, Rudolf Steiner, Alice Bailey and Chögyam Trungpa.

Today, the passion at Watkins Publishing for vigorous questioning is still resolute. Our stimulating and groundbreaking list ranges from ancient traditions and complementary medicine to the latest ideas about personal development, holistic wellbeing and consciousness exploration. We remain at the cutting edge, committed to publishing books that change lives.

DISCOVER MORE AT:

www.watkinspublishing.com

Read our blog

Watch and listen to
our authors in action

Sign up to
our mailing list

We celebrate conscious, passionate, wise and happy living.

Be part of that community by visiting

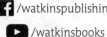 /watkinspublishing   @watkinswisdom

/watkinsbooks   @watkinswisdom